The Tourism System

An Introductory Text

Third Edition

Robert Christie Mill
School of Hotel, Restaurant, and Tourism Management
University of Denver

Alastair M. Morrison
Department of Restaurant, Hotel, Institutional,
and Tourism Management
Purdue University

KENDALL/HUNT PUBLISHING COMPANY
4050 Westmark Drive   Dubuque, Iowa 52002

This book was previously published by: Prentice-Hall, Inc.

Copyright © 1998 by Kendall/Hunt Publishing Company.

ISBN 0-7872-3327-7

Library of Congress Catalog Card Number: 97-76576

Printed in the United States of America
10 9 8 7 6 5 4 3 2 1

To
Patty Mill
Calum and Jessie Morrison

Contents

Acknowledgments

There are several people who helped the two authors in their early studies on the subject of tourism. In particular, we would like to acknowledge our lecturers and advisors at The Scottish Hotel School who gave us our first taste of tourism as an academic field of study. These included **David Pattison, Joyce Lloyd, Kit Jenkins,** and **Roger Carter.** At Michigan State University, **Robert McIntosh** influenced us with his knowledge and dedication to tourism, and to his students. We both greatly admire Dr. McIntosh's pioneering work in publishing the first edition of *Tourism: Principles, Practices, Philosophies* in 1971.

As we have progressed in our careers in tourism, many people and places have further shaped our knowledge and appreciation of different viewpoints on tourism. In particular, we would like to mention **Don Anderson** of the University of Calgary, **Joseph O'Leary** and **Jim Russell** of Purdue University, and **Philip Pearce** and **Gianna Moscardo** of James Cook University. We would also like to acknowledge the assistance of **Jonathon Day** of The Queensland Tourist & Travel Corporation and **Teresa McKee** of the Brown County Convention & Visitors Bureau for their help in supplying photographic materials.

Several people have reviewed the two previous editions of *The Tourism System*. We have greatly appreciated their viewpoints and acted upon many of their suggested improvements. These include **Brian King** of Victoria University of Technology, **Don Getz** of the University of Calgary, **Chris Cooper** of Bournemouth University, and **Jonathan Goodrich** of Florida International University.

The assistance of many fine graduate students has helped both of us steal the time to write various parts of this book. In particular, we would like to acknowledge the help of **Heidi Sung, Xinran You,** and **Liping Cai.**

Finally, but certainly not the least, we want to thank our families. They have had to endure long hours of writing at home in Highlands Ranch and West Lafayette. To Patty, Allison, Stephen and Jessica we say the greatest thanks in making this new edition a reality.

> "A tourist is someone who travels to see something different, and then complains when things are not the same."

Tourism: An Overview of the Tourism System

What is Tourism?

In writing this book we set out to do two things: Describe how tourism works and indicate how people can use this knowledge to make tourism work for them, their destination areas or businesses. Our first challenge was to put a label on the phenomenon about which we wanted to write.

Tourism is a difficult phenomenon to describe. The authors have trouble in thinking of tourism as an industry. Wells (1989) defines an industry as a "number of firms that produce similar goods and services and therefore are in competition with one another." In no sense of the word does this describe a *tourism industry*. While there is intense competition in tourism, many businesses and other types of tourism organizations offer complementary rather than competing products and services. An airline, hotel, restaurant, travel agency, and at-

traction do not compete with each other. They complement each other and combine to offer visitors a satisfying vacation or a business trip.

However, the idea of a tourism industry gives some unity to the idea of tourism. It enhances the image, credibility, and political acceptance of tourism. Tourism's *image is ambiguous* to many scholars and certainly to the "person on the street." For example, scholarly arguments are common as to whether the label should be "tourism" or "hospitality." Most ordinary people are astonished to find out that it is possible for a person to pursue a career in "tourism." While many attempts have been made to define tourism in the past 30 years, there is no single definition that is universally accepted. There is a link between travel, tourism, recreation, and leisure, yet the link is fuzzy. All tourism involves travel, yet not

all travel is tourism. All vacation travel involves recreation, yet not all tourism is recreation. All tourism occurs during leisure time, but not all leisure time is spent on tourism activities. Defining tourism as an industry helps people to get a clearer picture of what tourism is all about. With a clearer image comes a better understanding.

The idea of a tourism industry gives those involved a feeling of *greater credibility and respectability*. It builds a sense of belonging and camaraderie. It allows comparisons with other industries such as agriculture and manufacturing. It establishes tourism's standing in the "pecking order" of economic activities. This is certainly useful and builds a greater public awareness of the broad scope and impacts of tourism.

The idea of a tourism industry is *politically attractive*. One of

1

tourism's strengths is that its benefits are felt by many businesses, organizations and people. Visitor spending finds its way into many pockets and purses. At first glance, this might seem an ideal way to get political support for the planning, development, management, and marketing of tourism. However, this apparent strength has been a huge challenge for those interested in tourism. As tourism touches so many businesses and people in varying amounts, its overall impacts are difficult to measure. There is no single Standard Industrial Classification code called "tourism" (although the proposed *satellite tourism accounts* should remedy this problem). Additionally, many people whose lives or businesses are touched by tourism are mainly engaged in other activities. The storekeeper sells to visitors and local people. The museum serves visitors and residents. While they may know that tourism affects them, it is often difficult to evaluate how much it does. From a political standpoint, the idea of a tightly defined tourism industry allows organizations to demonstrate the impact and importance of tourism. This results in more effective lobbying with governments which brings greater political support and assistance for tourism.

Yet, tourism is not an industry. Tourism is *an activity*. It is an activity that takes place when, in international terms, people cross borders for leisure or business and stay at least 24 hours, but less than one year. Tourism also occurs within each country, as people travel certain distances from their home environments for pleasure or business trips. The study of tourism is the study of this activity or phenomenon and its effects. The business of tourism is the business of encouraging this type of activity and taking care of people while they are engaged in tourism.

The World Tourism Organiza-tion (WTO), Madrid, Spain, is the only multinational tourism organization that is officially recognized by the United Nations. WTO's definition of tourism is the most widely accepted around the world. At the International Conference on Travel and Tourism Statistics convened by WTO in Ottawa in 1991, tourism was defined as "*the activities of a person outside his or her usual environment for less than a specified period of time and whose main purpose of travel is other than exercise of an activity remunerated from the place visited*" (Chadwick, 1994). WTO identifies the following branches of tourism:

- **Inbound international tourism**: Visits to a country by nonresidents of that country.
- **Outbound international tourism**: Visits by the residents of a country to other countries.
- **Internal tourism**: Visits by residents of a country within their own country.

- **Domestic tourism**: Internal tourism + inbound international tourism.
- **National tourism**: Internal tourism + outbound international tourism.

A variety of other definitions have been offered for tourism. Although tourism is not an industry, tourism does incorporate a variety of different types of tourism businesses and other organizations. These can be divided into sectors and include (Leiper, 1990; Middleton, 1988; Morrison, 1996):

- **Accommodations, food service, and retailing sector**: Restaurants and food services of various types, hotels, resorts, guest houses, bed & breakfasts, farmhouses, apartments, villas, flats, condominiums and time-sharing, vacation villages, conference center resorts, marinas, ecolodges and other specialist accommodations, shops of various types including duty free.

The Billabong Sanctuary in Townsville, North Queensland, is an example of the attractions and events sector of tourism. Photo from *Top Shots* CD Rom. Courtesy of Queensland Tourist and Travel Corporation.

- **Association sector**: International, regional, national, and state trade and travel associations.

- **Attractions and events sector**: Theme parks, museums, national parks, wildlife parks, gardens, heritage sites, festivals and events.

- **Convention and exhibition sector**: Convention and exhibition centers, congress centers, auditoriums.

- **Destination marketing sector**: National tourist offices, state, provincial and territorial tourist offices, regional travel or tourism organizations, convention and visitors bureaus, local tourist authorities, tourism associations.

- **Miscellaneous sector**: Recreational facility operators, providers of travelers checks and insurance, tourism educators, travel writers, publishers of travel guides and books, and other businesses that serve travelers' needs.

- **Regulatory and coordinating sector**: Government agencies and non-governmental organizations that regulate and coordinate different aspects of tourism, e.g., World Tourism Organization and International Civil Aviation Organization.

- **Transportation carrier sector**: Airlines, shipping lines, ferry services, railways, bus and motor coach operators, car rental operators.

- **Travel trade intermediary sector**: Tour operators and wholesalers, retail travel agents, convention/meeting planners, corporate travel departments, incentive travel planners, and consolidators.

Why Use a Systems Approach for the Study of Tourism?

Many people talk about the subject of this book as "the tourism industry." You have already heard that there are at least three good reasons for talking about tourism as an industry. However, the authors choose to characterize tourism as a *system*, rather than as an industry. This is done for several reasons. The first is to emphasize the *interdependency* in tourism; that it consists of several interrelated parts working together to achieve common purposes, which we call *the tourism system*. The tourism system is like a spider's web—touch one part and reverberations are felt throughout the system.

The tourism system approach is based upon *general systems theory*. The father of general systems theory was a biologist, Ludwig von Bertalanffy. He defined a system as "a set of elements standing in interrelation among themselves and with the environments." Von Bertalanffy (1973) also suggested that general systems theory was "a way of seeing things which were previously overlooked or bypassed."

The authors are not the first to talk about a *tourism system*. Two of the pioneers of this concept were Clare Gunn of Texas A&M University and Neil Leiper of Southern Cross University in Australia. Gunn (1994) describes the *functioning tourism system*, consisting of the supply side of attractions, services, promotion, information, and transportation, and states that:

"No matter how it is labeled or described, tourism is not only made up of hotels, airlines, or the so-called tourist industry but rather a system of major components linked together in an intimate and interdependent relationship."

Leiper (1990) believes that a *tourism system* consists of five elements: a human element (tourist), three geographical regions (traveler-generating region, transit route, and tourist destination region), and an industrial element (the travel and tourism industry). Although Leiper acknowledges the term "industry" in his system, he firmly supports the need to more holistically view tourism as a system rather than as an industry:

"Unfortunately, many persons closely involved with the business of tourism hold as dogma that tourism is an industry. The dogma has been reiterated in academic literature. The origins of this belief are understandable, but that does not mitigate the flawed thinking."

Clearly, it is very easy to use a "laundry list" approach to describe tourism; describing one by one the businesses that obviously are part of tourism such as airlines, hotels and resorts. However, this approach fails to include local communities, and other businesses and organizations affected by tourism, that may or may not see themselves as part of the so-called "tourism industry." For example, many people working for hotels and restaurants do not feel they are in tourism. Their business begins with customers walking in the front door. They fail to examine the question "Why are they walking in our front door?" This *myopic* view has meant that many organizations have ended up being reactive to changes that have occurred outside their front doors, rather than being proactive and anticipating future changes in tourism. For a student beginning to study tourism, it is important to get "the bigger picture" right away. *The Tourism System Model* framework of this book provides a more comprehensive view of tourism; it captures "the big picture."

Tourism is definitely not the reason for the existence of the San Marco Basilica in Venice, but many visitors go there. Photo by Corel.

A second reason for using the systems approach is because of the **open system** nature of tourism. The tourism system is not a rigid form; rather it is dynamic and constantly changing. New concepts and phenomena are always arriving in tourism. Adventure travel, branding, destination management, ecotourism, global distribution systems, strategic alliances, sustainable tourism development, and tourism satellite accounting are just eight of many examples. Tourism is greatly affected by external influences such as politics, demographics, technology, war, terrorism, and crime. For example, changes are sweeping through tourism as a result of the World Wide Web, and after many years of political uncertainty, South Africa and Vietnam are emerging as very popular tourism destinations. The Gulf War had a very negative effect on tourism in many parts of the world. The seedy "sex tourism" trade of Southeast Asia is increasingly receiving stronger international criticism as an unacceptable form of social behavior and as a promoter of child prosti-

tution and drugs. The sustainable tourism movement is changing traditional ways of thinking about tourism by demanding that more of the responsibility for tourism should be in the hands of local communities. The following quote underlines the susceptibility of tourism to outside influences:

"Sri Lanka will launch a global public relations campaign next month to attract investors and tourists by playing down a 13-year old war with separatist Tamil rebels. A Tourist Board official said the government selected New York-based Manning Selvage and Lee to run the $2.5 million (U.S.) campaign to improve the Indian Ocean island's image abroad." (Globe & Mail, 1997)

As each year passes, tourism is becoming more and more complex to describe. Therefore, a third reason for the system is the **complexity and variety** in all aspects of tourism. For example, there are hundreds of specialized tours and packages available for travelers to-

day; you can select from a menu that ranges from archaeology to zoology. There is an enormous variety of approaches to each type of tourism business and organization. For example, travel trade intermediaries seldom play just one role today; a travel agent may also be a tour wholesaler. "Laundry list" approaches to tourism fail to reflect the enormous complexity present in tourism as it enters the twenty-first century. Above all, you will learn that it is difficult to put each part of tourism into its own neat pigeonhole. It just does not work that way any more.

Competition in today's tourism is both fierce and intense. Huge multinational tourism companies are vying for business on a global scale. Destination areas are competing with others with marketing budgets unprecedented in size. The systems approach better displays the great level of **competitiveness** present in tourism today. Grasping the full implications of the tourism system has led many previously competitive organizations and destination areas to acknowledge the similarity of their goals and form **partnerships**.

Tourism involves an interaction of many organizations and people, whose goals and interests are sometimes not compatible. The fifth reason for using the systems approach is to acknowledge a level of **friction and disharmony** in tourism in the late 1990s. As tourism enters the twenty-first century, a monumental struggle is looming over how tourism services will be distributed. Lured by the economics, convenience and speed of new technologies like the World Wide Web, many suppliers and transportation carriers may **bypass** the traditional channels of distribution, especially retail travel agencies. Airline companies are forsaking the restrictions of government agencies by teaming up with foreign airlines to form **global stra-**

tegic airline alliances. The government stranglehold on tourism marketing in many destination areas is being challenged, as private-sector businesses, associations, and non-profits are demanding a greater say. Local residents are questioning the "development at all costs" paradigm as they see precious local environments and ecosystems being threatened.

The spider moves when its web shakes and another insect is trapped. Likewise a change in one part of the tourism system often causes a change in another part of the system. Therefore, the final reason for using the systems approach was because of the need for *responsiveness* in a specific system part to changes in another system part. Tourism is dynamic and ever-changing. The linkages in the system represent the feedback mechanism between pairs of system parts that allow changes to be assimilated. Expanding the spider's web metaphor just one more time might provide a good example of the feedback-response mechanism. An intelligent spider may recognize that the larger the web, the more insects that are caught. Feedback from travelers through research studies has shown that more visitors are tending to favor multi-destination over single-destination trips. Tourism destination areas are responding by joining together in multi-destination partnerships and new *regional destination brands* to better accommodate this change in demand. By grasping "the bigger picture," former marketing foes are becoming friends, with each partner having the potential to get a larger share of the visitor market.

The Parts of the Tourism System

The Tourism System Model described in this book consists of four

The Olympic Stadium in Montreal, Quebec, Canada served a huge number of travelers for the event. Photo by Corel.

parts—*Demand, Travel, Destination, and Marketing*. The authors started this book with Demand out of choice, but it could easily have begun with either *Travel, Destination, or Marketing*.

Part 1: Demand—The Factors Influencing the Market

Part 1 of the book is devoted to demand or the factors which influence people in making travel decisions. A consumer behavior approach is used to describe the travel decision-making process. People decide to travel if they have learned that travel satisfies their *needs*, if they *perceive* that future travel trips will satisfy needs, and if they are able to travel based upon their *external constraints* including money, time, and other family and work commitments. Travelers buying decision processes are described. Insights are shared on how tourism marketers can influence demand.

**1.
Demand:
The Factors Influencing
the Market**

A consumer behavior approach to market demand emphasizing the internal and external influences on travelers including needs, motivation, and perception; the alternatives to travel; the marketing by tourism organizations; and the process by which travelers make buying decisions

---

Link 1: The Travel Purchase
The linkage between Parts 1 and 2 (*Demand and Travel*) is called the *travel purchase*. It is characterized by an arrow pointing in both directions, clockwise and counterclockwise. This means that each of the two parts (*Demand and Travel*) may influence the other part. For example, new segments in the market may emerge based

upon the special interests or characteristics of groups of people (**Demand**). These people may decide to take advantage of exploring these special interests or mixing with people of similar characteristics while traveling (**Travel**). A new travel mode may be introduced or become more popular (**Travel**). An example would be multi-mode systems, e.g., where traveler's cars are placed on railway cars and then transported to their destinations. This new travel mode may be favorably perceived by travelers (**Demand**).

Part 2: Travel—The Characteristics of Travel

When the decision has been made to book a travel trip, a set of decisions are taken on who to travel with; and where, when, and how to get to the destination. Trends in the business and pleasure/personal *travel market segments* are identified. *Flows* of travelers among destinations are described. *Modes of transportation* are discussed along with their trends and future prospects.

**2.
Travel:
The Characteristics of
Travel**

A description and analysis of
major travel segments, travel
flows, and modes of
transportation used

Link 2: The Shape of Travel
The linkage between Parts 2 and 3 (**Travel and Destination**) is called *the shape of travel*. It is the combination of who is traveling (travel market segments), and where, when, and how they are traveling. Again, a change in either **Travel** or **Destination** may cause a response in the other part of the system. If

the airlines decide to introduce "super jumbo jets" with 500-plus passenger capacities (**Travel**), countries may have to reconfigure their airports and ground handling arrangements (**Destination**). If a destination decides to build a modern cruise ship terminal (**Destination**), this may attract a new flow of visitors in the cruise market segment (**Travel**).

Part 3: Destination—Planning, Developing, and Controlling Tourism

Every destination area that chooses to encourage tourism must be prepared to handle the inflows of visitors, and to deal with the challenge that tourism has the potential of generating both positive and negative impacts. A *destination mix* is assembled consisting of attractions and events, facilities, infrastructure, transportation, and hospitality resources. *Tourism policies* and *tourism plans* are developed. The many different *tourism organizations* involved in these processes are described. A *legislative and regulatory framework* is required to ensure that the tourism policy and plan are implemented properly, and that impacts are controlled. The process of *tourism development* and the analysis of individual tourism project development opportunities is explained.

**3.
Destination:
Planning, Developing and
Controlling Tourism**

An identification of the
procedures that destination
areas follow to set policies,
plan, control, develop, and
cater to tourism, with an
emphasis on sustainable
tourism development

Link 3: The Tourism Product
The linkage between Parts 3 and 4 (**Destination and Marketing**) is called *the tourism product*. Again, a change in the destination may cause a change in marketing, and vice versa. For example, the staging of a mega-event (**Destination**) may result in a major shift in the marketing of the destination area (**Marketing**), as is the case for the Sydney Olympics in 2000. If one of the travel trade intermediaries, such as a tour operator, begins to send larger groups (**Marketing**), this may require a change in the size of accommodations and other facilities and services (**Destination**).

Part 4: Marketing—Strategy, Planning, Promotion, and Distribution

Now in the fourth part of the system destination areas must reach people in the market and encourage them to travel by using marketing principles and techniques. The uniqueness of tourism marketing is explained. The processes of *market segmentation* and *positioning*, and the application of the *product life cycle*, are described. A step-by-step procedure for marketing is introduced. Marketing success depends to a large extent on effective communications through *promotion*, and through the selection of the right *distribution channels* (travel trade intermediaries). The different types of *destination marketing organizations* and travel trade intermediaries are reviewed. The trend toward greater *electronic distribution* of travel is highlighted.

**4.
Marketing:
Strategy, Planning,
Promotion, and
Distribution**

An examination of the process by which destination areas and tourism businesses market services and facilities to potential customers with an emphasis on the effective use of promotion and distribution channels

Link 4: The Promotion of Travel
The link between Parts 4 and 1 (*Marketing and Demand*) is called the *promotion of travel*.

A change in the marketing approach may cause a change in the market. For example, if a cruise line introduces a two-for-one promotion for first-time cruisers (*Marketing*), this may convince more people to reserve their first-ever cruise with that company (*Demand*). Often it is the other way around, there is a shift in demand, and marketing is changed accordingly. When people started to take shorter vacations (*Demand*), tourism destinations and suppliers began to offer short-break and weekend getaway packages (*Marketing*).

The Tourism System Model is a simple model. The actual situation in tourism is much more complex. There are sub-systems within

the overall system. For example, Gunn's (1994) supply-side *functioning tourism system* might be considered as a sub-system for *Destination* (Part 3). The *hospitality and travel marketing system* developed by Morrison (1996) displays a possible sub-system for *Marketing* (Part 4).

The Tourism System Model

The four system Parts and four Links combine in *The Tourism System Model* shown below. The model is displayed in this way to emphasize the interactions and interdependency among the four

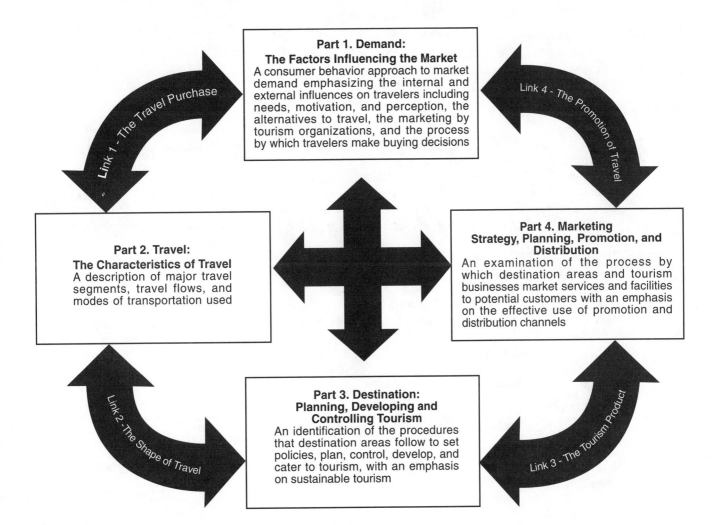

Figure 1.1 The Tourism Model.

parts of the system. The four-way arrow in the middle of the model indicates that interactions happen between other pairs of the system Parts (***Demand*** and ***Destination***, ***Travel*** and ***Marketing***).

The Tourism System goes beyond a mere description of tourism and its basic principles. Principles, concepts, and theories from disciplines such as psychology, economics, planning, and marketing that influence tourism are incorporated into the book. Students will realize that tourism is a multidisciplinary field in which many contributions are valued and made. In examining the parts of ***The Tourism System Model*** and their linkages, those involved in tourism can see where they fit, who is affected by their actions, and how they are affected by the actions of other system participants.

Terminology

In this book, ***travel*** refers to the act of moving outside of one's usual environment for business or pleasure, but not for commuting or traveling to or from school. ***Tourism*** is the term given to the activity that occurs when people travel. This encompasses everything from the planning of the trip, the travel to the destination area, the stay itself, the return, and the reminiscences about it afterward. It includes the activities the traveler undertakes as part of the trip, the purchases made, and the interactions that occur between host and guest in the destination area. In sum, it is all of the activities and impacts that occur when a visitor travels.

The term ***recreation*** overlaps in many ways with tourism. Recreation is what happens during an individual's leisure time. Leisure time is the time people have discretion over. During leisure time people can do what they want. The activities that people engage in during leisure time are known as recreation. Some say that to be recreation, the activity should be constructive or pleasurable. This might involve either aspect to recreation. A game of tennis or golf two miles from home after work would constitute recreation. If one were to drive 100 miles to a resort for the weekend, the game of tennis would be part of tourism and the golfer would be on a ***trip***. A tourism trip does not have to include an overnight stay in the destination area. To avoid the sometimes negative connotations associated with the word "tourist," the term ***visitor*** has been used throughout this book.

References

Bertalanffy, L.V. (1973). *General systems theory: Foundations, development, applications.* New York: G. Braziller.

Chadwick, R.A. (1994). Concepts, definitions, and measures used in travel and tourism research. In J.R.B. Ritchie, & C.R. Goeldner *Travel, tourism, and hospitality research: A handbook for managers and researchers,* (2nd ed.) New York: John Wiley & Sons, Inc., 65–80.

Gunn, C.A. (1994). *Tourism planning: Basics, concepts, cases* (3rd ed.). Washington, DC: Taylor & Francis.

Holloway, C. (1994). *The business of tourism.* Plymouth, England: Pitman.

Leiper, N. (1990). *Tourism systems: An interdisciplinary perspective.* Palmerston North, New Zealand: Massey University.

Middleton, V.T.C. (1988). *Marketing in travel and tourism.* Oxford, England: Butterworth-Heinemann.

Morrison, A.M. (1996). *Hospitality and travel marketing* (2nd ed.). Albany, New York: Delmar Publishers.

Sri Lanka: Polishing its image. (1997, May 28). *Globe & Mail.*

Wells, A.T. (1989). *Air transportation: A management perspective* (2nd ed.). Belmont, California: Wadsworth Publishing Company.

> "Travel leads to understanding. It increases the chances for peace, and, therefore, it increases the chances of a better life for all."
>
> *President Bill Clinton*

Tourism: Yesterday, Today, and Tomorrow

Yesterday: The Historical Development of Tourism

> *"Boil it, peel it, cook it, or forget it."*
>
> *Standard traveler's adage*

For tourism to occur, there must be people who have the ability (both in terms of time and money), the mobility, and the motivation to travel. While the era of mass tourism is a relatively recent one, an individual's propensity and ability to travel has been advanced by numerous developments throughout time.

In pre-industrial times much of the motivation for travel was to develop trade. As empires grew, the conditions necessary for travel began to develop. Ancient Egyptians traveled for both business and pleasure. Travel was necessary between the central government and the territories. To accommodate travelers on official business, hospitality centers were built along major routes and in the cities. The ancient Egyptians also traveled for pleasure. Public festivals were held several times a year. Travel was also for curiosity—people visited the great tombs and temples of the pharaohs.

Assyria comprised the area now known as Iraq. As the empire expanded from the Mediterranean in the west to the Persian Gulf in the east, mobility was made easier to facilitate moving the military. Roads were improved, markers were established to indicate distances, and posts and wells were developed for safety and nourishment. Even today the influence of military construction aids pleasure travel. The U.S. Interstate highway system was developed initially to facilitate transportation in the event of a national emergency.

While previous civilizations had set the stage for the development of travel, the Greeks and, later, the Romans brought it all together. In Greek times water was the most important means of moving commercial goods. This combined with the fact that cities grew up along the coast to ensure that travel was primarily by sea. Travel for official business was less important as Greece was divided into independent city-states. Pleasure travel existed in three areas: For religious festivals, for sporting events (most notably the Olympic Games), and to visit cities, especially Athens.

Travel was advanced by two important developments. First, a system of currency exchange was developed. Previously, travelers paid their way by carrying various goods and selling them at their

9

The temples of ancient Egypt were among the first travel attractions. Photo by Corel.

destinations. The money of Greek city-states was now accepted as international currency, eliminating the need to travel with a cargo of goods. Second, the Greek language spread throughout the Mediterranean area, making it easier to communicate as one traveled.

Travel flourished in Roman times for five reasons: The control of the large empire stimulated trade and led to the growth of a large middle class with the money to travel; Roman coins were all the traveler had to carry to finance the trip; the means of transportation—roads and waterways—were excellent; communication was relatively easy, as Greek and Latin were the principal languages; and the legal system provided protection from foreign courts, thereby ensuring the safety of the traveler.

The sporting games started by the Greeks were copied in the gladiators' fights to the death. Sightseeing was also popular, particularly to Greece, which had become a part of greater Rome and was the place to see. Touring was also popular to Egypt, site of the Sphinx and the pyramids, and to Asia

Minor, scene of the Trojan War. Aristotle visited Asia Minor before establishing his school for students. A final development was that of second homes and vacations associated with them. Villas spread south to Naples, near the sea, the mountains, or mineral spas.

As the Roman Empire collapsed in the fifth century, roads fell into disuse and barbarians made it unsafe to travel. Whereas a Roman courier could travel up to 100 miles a day, the average daily rate of journey during the Middle Ages was 20 miles. It was not until the twelfth century that the roads became secure again. This was due to the large numbers of travelers going on pilgrimages. Pilgrims traveled to pay homage to a particular site or as an atonement for sin. In other cases, pilgrims journeyed to fulfill a promise made when they were sick.

The next important factor in the history of travel was the Renaissance. As society moved from a rural to an urban base, wealth grew, and more people had the money to travel. Pilgrimages were still important, though journeys to Jerusalem declined due to the growth of

Protestantism in Europe. The impetus to travel to learn was aided by the arrival of Renaissance works from Italy. Stable monarchies helped ensure travelers' safety.

The beginning of the sixteenth century saw a new age of curiosity and exploration, which culminated in the popularity of the **Grand Tour**. The Grand Tour was initially a sixteenth-century Elizabethan concept, brought about by the need to develop a class of professional statesmen and ambassadors. Young men traveled with ambassadors over Europe to complete their education. The practice continued to develop in the seventeenth and eighteenth centuries until it became fashionable. No gentleman's education was complete until he had spent from one to three years traveling around Europe with a tutor.

The Grand Tour began in France, where the young man studied French, dancing, fencing, riding, and drawing. Before Paris could corrupt the morals or ruin the finances, the student headed for Italy to study sculpture, music appreciation, and art. The return was by way of Germany, Switzerland, and the Low Countries (Holland, Belgium, and Luxembourg). The Grand Tour reached its peak of popularity in the 1750s and 1760s but was brought to a sudden end by the French Revolution and the Napoleonic Wars.

In the late eighteenth century and early nineteenth century, two major factors affected the development of tourism. Increased industrialization accounted for both of them. First, the industrial revolution accelerated the movement from rural to urban areas. This produced a large number of people in a relatively small area. The desire or motivation to escape, even for a brief period, was there. Associated with this was the development of steam engines in the form of trains and steamships. This allowed the means or mobility to escape. Because of the proximity of the coast to the major urban areas, it was only natural that train lines extended in these directions. However, the vast majority of visitors to the seaside were day-trippers. It was well into the second half of the eighteenth century before the working classes in Britain had regular holidays and sufficient income to use their leisure time to travel.

The development of spas was largely due to the members of the medical professions. During the seventeenth century, they began to recommend the medicinal properties of mineral waters. The idea originated, however, with the Greeks. Spas on the continent of Europe were developed two to three hundred years before their growth in England. Development occurred because of three factors: The approval of the medical profession, court patronage, and local entrepreneurship to take advantage of the first two.

Patronage by court helped establish spas as the place to be. Today we talk about *"mass follows class"*—the idea that the masses are influenced in their choices of vacation spots by people they consider influential. Today film stars seem to have taken over the role of influencer.

The number of people who could afford to "take the waters" was rather small. By the end of the seventeenth century the influence of the medical profession had declined, and spas were more for entertainment instead of health. Their popularity continued, however, into the nineteenth century. It is possible today to drink form the mineral waters at Bath in England. Hot Springs in Arkansas and Glenwood Springs in Colorado still attract many visitors. Additionally, many Eastern European towns proclaim the beneficial effects of mud packs and hydrotherapy.

The medical profession, the British court, and Napoleon all helped popularize the seaside resort. The original motive for sea bathing was for reasons of health. Dr. Richard Russell argued that sea water was effective against such things as cirrhosis, dropsy, gout, gonorrhea, and scurvy and insisted that people drink a pint of it. It is worthy to note that the good Dr. Russell was a physician in Brighton, a resort close to London and on the water. Brighton's fame was assured after the patronage of the Prince Regent, who later became George IV. Similarly, Southend and Cowes are associated with Princess Charlotte and Queen Victoria respectively.

The growth of the seaside resort was stimulated by the French Revolution and the Napoleonic Wars. As stated earlier both put an end to the Grand Tour; those who would have taken the Grand Tour could not travel to the Continent. The now fashionable seaside resorts were the alternative. Toward the end of the nineteenth century, the seaside resorts in Europe became the palaces for the working classes due to the introduction of paid holidays and better wages.

The term *holiday* comes from holy days—days for religious observances. Ancient Rome featured public holidays for great feasting. As Europe became Christian, certain saints' days and religious festivals became holy days when people fasted and prayed and refrained from work. After the Industrial Revolution, the religious holidays gradually became secularized, and the week's holiday emerged. The vacation was negotiated between employer and workers and was again due to the economic and social changes brought about by the Industrial Revolution. It made sense to take the holidays during the warmer summer months. For the employer, it was advantageous to close the entire factory down for one week rather than face the problems of operating with small groups of people absent over a longer period of time. Still today certain weeks are associated with the general holidays of specific cities or towns.

Prior to World War I, the principal mode of domestic transportation was the railway. This meant that development was concentrated at particular points. Regional development occurred with particular resorts growing to serve specific urban areas. Mass production of the

The waters of Hot Springs, Arkansas still attract many visitors. Photo Credit: Paul Johnson—Combs & Co.

automobile, as will be seen later, allowed the dispersion of destination developments.

Tourism in the U.S. developed for the same reasons as in Europe. At first, travel was limited by the need for transportation. The first development of note was that of resorts. With the encouragement of physicians, resorts like Saratoga in New York became fashionable by the early 1800s. The ocean also became attractive for health reasons initially, although amusements soon sprang up as well.

The development of the railway opened up the country to travelers. By the 1870s, the completion of the Erie Railroad spurred the development of Niagara Falls as a honeymoon paradise. The vast river network of the country's interior allowed the development of steamboat excursions, particularly gambling and amusement trips, between New Orleans and St. Louis.

The Industrial Revolution produced a class of wealthy people who had the time to travel. Touring became popular. Many took the Grand Tour while, for most in the South, an American-style grand tour to the North took a comparable amount of time and money. Three attractions were paramount: Northern cities, historical sites (of the American Revolution and the Civil War), and resorts.

By the late 1800s, the West was attracting not only Easterners but also Europeans who came to see the natural beauty and hunt buffalo. Foreign travelers were also fascinated by travel for religious reasons; many wanted to visit the places where the various religious sects had sprung up.

In the U.S., the late nineteenth and early twentieth centuries were characterized as days of high society. The population was rural and centered in the Northeast and Midwest. Many of the 50 million people lived in large families with a strong puritanical work ethic and a belief in self-denial. A 64-hour workweek with Sundays off was the norm. Much of the working classes' leisure time was centered around the church. For the wealthy, travel was by railroad and ship to luxury hotel resorts and large second homes. Only the wealthy few were able to travel overseas. By the end of the 1800s, the 12-hour workday had been reduced to 10 hours. **Vacations** were beginning to be recognized. While travel had been for the few, now it began to come within the reach of more people.

Between the World Wars, today's consumer society and an era of mass recreation emerged. The 130 million people in the U.S. spread increasingly to the West Coast and a rural-urban population emerged. Families were smaller, a 50-hour workweek was common, and more workers were given paid vacations. The development of the automobile allowed the freedom to travel and led to the emergence of the motel. Attractions and facilities became more dispersed as people were not restricted in their movements by the use of public transportation. More middle-class people purchased second homes and saw leisure time as something that was a privilege to enjoy. In Europe, legislation was passed giving paid vacations.

Mass tourism as we know it today is a post-World War II phenomenon. Women who had to work during the war felt more independent; men and women who traveled overseas to fight wanted to return as visitors; travel overseas was encouraged as part of the U.S. attempt to aid war-torn European economies. The introduction of the passenger jet reduced travel time from the U.S. to Europe from five sailing days or 24 flying hours to eight hours; and surplus propeller airplanes were made available to charter operators to transport travelers, not troops, as airlines rushed to purchase new jet aircraft.

The sixties marked the **democratization of travel**. In the U.S., the growth of the population—the **baby boomers**—together with the 40-hour workweek that increased numbers of three-day weekends and higher levels of disposable income, enabled large numbers of people with the time and money to indulge themselves. Travel was a right. A **hedonistic attitude** (pleasure for the sake of pleasure) increasingly overtook the self-denial of the work ethic.

Temporarily stunned by the **energy crises** of the seventies and the Gulf War in the early 1990s, tourism continued to grow. The late seventies and eighties saw the development of single-parent families and low-income families, together with an increased accent on individual awareness and self-improvement. For many, the indulgence was replaced by a concern for physical fitness.

Tourism Today: At a Crossroads

> "The tourism industry is still fixated on promoting tourism as an activity of the industrial age, rather than the post industrial society. The future of the tourism industry lies in its ability to develop tourism as being part of an overall lifestyle that complements, rather than contradicts, the rest of people's lives."
>
> J.S.P. Hobson and
> U.C. Dietrich, (1994)

Tourism at present is greater in size and scope than it has ever been. The World Travel & Tourism Council claims that tourism is already "the worlds biggest industry" and destined to become even bigger (WTTC, 1997). There are more travelers than ever before. The World Tourism Organization states that there were nearly 593 million tourist arrivals in the world (WTO, 1997). There are more tourism textbooks and academic tourism journals than in any point in previous history. The amount of information available to us on travel and tourism destination areas is mind boggling as the digital era moves into high gear.

But tourism at the end of the 1990s is at a crossroads. The winds of change are blowing strong and the shape of tourism will be much different in the future. Some of these forces include the increased concern with the world's environment, the shifts in economic power among the peoples of different continents, the globalization of tourism, the deregulation and removal of barriers to travel and tourism, the increasing sophistication and expectations of travelers, the creation of new tourism partnerships, commission "capping," and the impacts of new technologies (Bloch, Pigneur, & Steiner, 1996; Pollock, 1993).

The sustainable development movement has gained a strong foothold in tourism. The evidence of the negative effects of tourism has never been greater. The Internet and the World Wide Web are in the early stages of revolutionizing how travel information is distributed and how trips are booked. Global partnerships of airlines are an early indicator of how the global business of tourism might be played in the future. There are a cornucopia of travel market segments and travel offerings, as the market has continued to fragment.

Tourism Tomorrow: Virtually a Reality

"The tourism industry is in crisis—a crisis of change and uncertainty; a crisis brought on by the rapidly changing nature of the tourism industry itself. In the year 2000, tourism will look nothing like it used to be. The industry is in metamorphosis— it is undergoing rapid and radical change. New technology, more experienced customers, global economic restructuring and environmental limits to growth are only some of the challenges facing the industry. Creative gales of destruction and more stormy weather lie ahead. The era of sunny weather management is over."

A. Poon, (1993)

What will tourism be like in the twenty-first century? There is only one thing that is certain; it will be very different. The relative power of different origin markets for international tourism is shifting more toward the Asia-Pacific, and people are still awaiting the travel boom from China, the world's most populated country. Technology has had a huge impact on tourism in the 1990s, and will almost certainly revolutionize tourism in the next decade.

The World Tourism Organization has noted the following trends and expects these to continue into the future (Jones, 1996):

- **Old travel patterns to new travel patterns**. The old east-west flows of travelers are shifting to north-south flows. In Asia, for example, this means movement away from Hawaii and toward Australia and the Pacific Islands. A second shift is away from long trips in favor of short breaks.

- **Established destinations to emerging destinations**. The principal new destinations include Indochina, Eastern Europe, North Africa, and Latin America. In addition, countries such as Korea, Taiwan, Hong Kong, and Singapore are emerging as new generating markets.

- **Old products to new products**. New leisure products will move away from environmentally- and culturally-sensitive areas and use new technology to create artificial environments close to origin markets. Artificial ski hills and simulation and virtual reality experiences are two examples.

- **Fragmented tourism to economic development tool**. Government will acknowledge the economic importance of tourism and encourage increased cooperation between the public and private sectors.

- **Developer control to community control**. As host communities become increasingly sophisticated, developers will have to demonstrate economic, social, and environmental benefits before development can occur.

- **Financial illusion to financial reality**. Increased emphasis will be placed on: first, improving the performance of existing assets and, second, acquiring strategic undervalued assets before considering major new investments.

- **Mass markets to specialty markets**. Targeted communications to specialty markets will increase.

- **Passive consumers to involved consumers**. As more travelers become increasingly sophisticated, they will want new experiences, interaction with the community, and knowledge about the destination.

- **Mass marketing to direct customer communication**. As marketers harness the new technology, they will turn to tailored and targeted marketing to individuals through the management of sophisticated database management systems.

Many of these themes of change are picked up again in *The Tourism System* as you progress through the book. Above all, you will see that the future of tourism is exciting. The World Tourism Organization predicts that international tourism arrivals in the world will top one billion by 2010 and reach 1.6 billion by 2020 (WTO, 1996 and 1997). Tourism's future holds great challenges for many professionals and superb career prospects for the tourism students of today. It is hard to grasp that the Grand Tour of Europe can now almost be taken on your personal computer through the World Wide Web. The great train journeys of yesteryear are being reinvented in luxurious rail tours. We may be close to seeing the launch of the first 5000-passenger cruise ship. Who would have thought that this would happen 15 years ago? While the routes may be similar, the journeys of the future will be different from those of the past. Bon voyage!

References

Bloch, M., Pigneur, Y., & Steiner, T. (1996). The IT-enabled extended enterprises: Applications in the tourism industry (http://haas.berkley.edu/~citm/travel-proj/enter96.htm)

Hobson, J.S.P., & Dietrich, U.C. (1994). Tourism, health and quality of life: Challenging the responsibility of using the traditional tenets of sun, sea, sand and sex in tourism marketing. *Journal of Travel & Tourism Marketing*, 3 (4), 21–38.

Jones, C. (1996). *The future ain't what it used to be.* Paper presented at the World Tourism Organization Affiliate Member Seminar "Tourism Prospects for the World and for the Americas in the Next Decade," Mexico City, Mexico.

Pollock, A. (1993). *Information technology and the emergence of a new tourism* (PATA Occasional Paper Series No. 9). San Francisco: Pacific Asia Travel Association.

Poon, A. (1993). *Tourism, technology and competitive strategies.* England: C.A.B. International.

World Tourism Organization. (1996). International arrivals to top 1 billion by 2010. Madrid: World Tourism Organization.

World Tourism Organization. (1997). Tourist arrivals to reach 1.6 billion by 2020. Madrid: World Tourism Organization.

World Tourism Organization. (1997). Tourism industry sets new records. Madrid: World Tourism Organization.

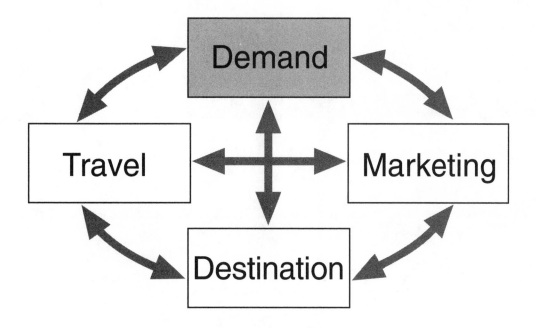

Part I

Demand

The Factors Influencing the Market

The marketing done by a destination area attempts to influence demand. However, travelers are influenced by many other internal and external factors. Part 1 of **The Tourism System** examines these internal and external factors including needs, wants, and motives, perceptions and images, information sources, socioeconomic and family characteristics. It also looks at how people make travel decisions and how they select travel destinations.

Part 4

4. Marketing:
Strategy, Planning,
Promotion, and Distribution

Link 4

The Promotion of Travel

Part I

1. Demand
The Factors Influencing
the Market

> "What we do during our working hours determines what we have;
>
> what we do in our leisure hours determines what we are."
>
> *George Eastman*

I

The External Environment for Tourism

···Forces Shaping Tourism ·····························

Purpose

Having examined the external environment of specific types of tourists, students will be able to suggest appropriate types of vacations for them.

Learning Objectives

Having read this chapter, you should be able to explain the effects of the following factors on travel decisions:

1. Cultural background
2. Time
3. Socio-economic background
4. Psychographic background

Overview

Models of behavior have suggested that behavior choices are determined by the types of psychological factors—motivation, perception, learning and attitudes—examined in chapters two through four. However, these factors are, in turn, determined by such things as personality, society and culture, and other such forces external to the individual (see figure 1.1).

This chapter examines these forces. The culture of which we are a part serves as a barometer of general trends within a country, and it exerts social pressure to conform to the broad cultural values presented by the majority of individuals making up that culture. The amount and type of time available also helps determine if, when, and where we can vacation. Marketers have long segmented the travel market along the socioeconomic criteria of age, income, sex, and education. It is therefore appropriate to determine whether tourism demand differs on these criteria. The characteristic patterns of demand at various stages in the family life cycle are examined, with particular reference to the effect of children on the family's demand, the demand pattern of the empty nester, and the various barriers to leisure enjoyment at different life-cycle stages. Finally, the role of psychographics in shaping demand is explored. From a marketing viewpoint the segmentation of a target market by lifestyle provides a better picture of the characteristics, likes, and dislikes of the potential visitor.

Whether or not to take a vacation, and the type of holiday chosen, is influenced by a number of factors external to the individual. In this chapter the effect of these variables is examined. Although these factors are explored separately, it should be noted that their effect is often a compound one.

The Effects of Culture on Travel

> "'There is a way of travelling cheaply in France' he said. 'One simply gets on a train, sits down, in a first-class compartment, and falls asleep. There is a law in France that no first-class passenger asleep may be awakened by a conductor. They may awaken you in second or third class, but never in first'."
>
> *Ludwig Bemelmans*

Individuals choose a vacation to satisfy their individual needs and wants (see chapter 2). The way in which these wants are satisfied, however, is heavily influenced by forces external to the individual. As individuals, we are part of larger social groups by which we are influenced. These groups themselves are part of and influenced by the surrounding culture. *Culture* can be defined as a "set of beliefs, values, attitudes, habits, and forms of behavior that are shared by a society and are transmitted from generation to generation" (Bennett & Kassasjin, 1982). A knowledge of the culture of a country or subculture within that country is important to an understanding of how individuals within that country or subculture will behave.

Culture and Society

A culture's overall values determine which goals and behavior gain social approval or disapproval. To the extent that people are concerned about how others think of them, they will be influenced to behave in ways acceptable to society. For these people, society's values determine, in part, what kinds of vacations and what types of behavior on those vacations are acceptable. For example, Thailand has long been the recipient of sex tourism. Packages promoted to the Japanese and European markets have included "hostesses" as part of the package. Changing attitudes toward women and sex, together with the fear of AIDS, have resulted in protests against both tourism operators and the visitors themselves. The World Tourism Organization has, in fact, taken a very strong position against such tourism.

This family is learning about animals during their visit to the Gondwana rainforest sanctuary, South Bank Parklands, Brisbane. Photo from *Top Shots* CD Rom. Courtesy of Queensland Tourist and Travel Corporation.

In the U.S. many people have developed more positive attitudes toward the environment. This change in attitude has been examined in light of its potential for influencing vacation choice. There are those, for example, who have shown that attitudes toward the environment may be a better predictor of what a person does on vacation than is demographic information. In one study (Jurowski & Walker, 1995) it was shown that people who believed that there are limits to growth and that the balance of nature is easily upset are less likely to participate in such vigorous outdoor activities as bicycling and snow skiing. The same study showed that people interested in relationship building are opposed to such things as hunting, fishing, and horseback riding.

Some people prefer lots of physical activity on vacation. Photo by Corel.

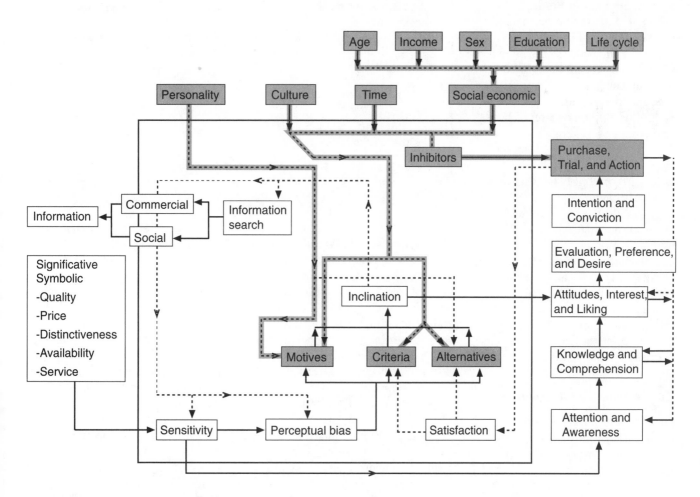

Figure 1.1 The Impact of External Factors on Vacation Purchases.

The many social institutions of a society are also reflective of its culture. In the U.S., for example, the ideas of individual initiative and equal opportunity for all influence the way in which the educational system is organized. The result is a system of mass education with a somewhat liberal child-rearing philosophy. Education is seen as an investment in personal development and success. If vacations are seen as something that will advance a child's progress in society, they will be more attractive to the parents.

Culture affects the social backdrop in the established conventions and practices of society. Society adopts various practices relative to such things as which foods can be eaten, how to entertain, and which gifts are or are not appropriate. It is acceptable, for example, for horse meat to be eaten in France but not the U.S. On the other hand, in most countries of the world corn is shucked and is considered a food suitable only for animals. While the established dinner hour in the U.S. is between 6 and 8 p.m., in Spain it is 10 p.m. or later. When attracting or servicing visitors from a culture different from our own, it is necessary to know the established practices to avoid inadvertent behavior.

Last, culture's effect on society is felt in the language people use with one another. It is important to consider not only words, but also gestures, expressions, and other body movements. In Western culture a smile is a warm signal to further a relationship, but in Asian culture it may be used to cover embarrassment and shame.

Culture and Social Groups

Social groups have roles or standards of behavior peculiar to each group. These group norms differ from one culture to another. Groups can be classified either as **primary** (family or friends) or

---

> ## Quick Trip 1.1
> # Is There a Vacation Role?
>
> There was a time when mention of a Briton abroad conjured up an ageless image of inexpensive good taste and even elegance. Today's image is of thousands of Britons shambling scruffily about the Rivieras, Costas and even the capitals, without a shred of regard for the people in whose towns and cities they are temporary guests. In Venice, just because the temperature was at a sweltering 88F, scores of British tourists stripped off . . . with people in bathing trunks (even underpants) and bikinis. It is not unusual nowadays to see British couples holidaying abroad publicly groping at each other, apparently oblivious to the considerable discomfort their behavior imposes on those around them.
>
> Of course, many of our international fellow travelers are no better than we are. Germans on holiday can be incredibly selfish and are frequently rude.
>
> The argumentative French take their clothes off and make public exhibitions of themselves at the drop of a chapeau. Scandinavians tend to be proper and well-dressed until they reach the nearest bar, after which they can frequently be found falling down in the street.
>
> Today the boundaries of good taste are under constant pressure, its walls are buckling and the ill-mannered hordes are swarming though wherever there is a beach.
>
> ### Question:
>
> 1. Do people behave differently when on vacation?
>
> 2. Why?
>
> 3. Is there a "vacation role"?
>
> Source: Shame of the Englishman Abroad, G. Levy, *Daily Mail*, (July 12, 1991).

---

secondary (unions, fraternities, church, and so on). An individual will belong to more than one group, and consequently, he or she will adopt a role for each social group. These roles may overlap. The surrounding culture will help define for each group the appropriate objects people use to show their membership in the group as well as the relevant status symbols.

Is there a distinct vacation role? One of the attractive features of taking a vacation is that it allows the freedom to be someone other than who we are in everyday life. Traveling to places where we are not known, meeting people who do not know us, allows us to choose how we will behave.

The social role that an individual takes is learned through socialization—the process of social learning by which cultural role expectations are handed down from one generation to another. The link between participation in recreational activities as a child and subsequent participation as an adult has been repeatedly demonstrated. If we also accept that travel is a learned experience, the importance of encouraging travel participation at an early age can be demonstrated. The norms of behavior for a group change by virtue of both internal and external sources. Within a group there are those people (innovators) who are more willing than others to try new things. Usually these group members are better educated, have high incomes, and are more achievement-oriented than others. The innovators also tend to be **opinion leaders** and, as such, highly sought after by marketers. A common saying in explaining destination development is "mass follows class." This phrase suggests that a destination first attracts a relatively small number of high-status individuals whose actions are eventually copied by a larger number of less-innovative others.

Cultural patterns also change by virtue of external forces. As a result of contact with other environments, previous attitudes and behaviors may change. A visit to a foreign country may result in a change in attitude toward the people of that country as well as stimulation of a desire for a cuisine from the destination visited. A vacation in Germany might improve the chance of purchasing a German car upon one's return home.

It can readily be seen that in order to understand a consumer fully, it is necessary to understand the surrounding culture of that consumer. A knowledge of how the culture affects the individual, the social groups to which that individual belongs, and society as a whole will better enable the marketer to sell a travel product. Insight will be gained as to what to say, to whom to say it, and how the message should be phrased. As hosts, we will be better able to understand why visitors act the way they do and be in a better position to anticipate and satisfy their needs and wants.

Analyzing a Culture

When marketing internationally, there are four possible strategies to overcome cultural barriers: adapt, do not adapt, pattern globalization, and changing the culture. In the first instance—adapt—the entire marketing mix is changed to fit the market better. In the second case a single message is given to all markets. Third, pattern globalization occurs when an overall image is adapted slightly at the local level while still following the overall plan. The message is the same but delivered differently. The final option is—change the culture being marketed to—expensive, time consuming, and ethically questionable. From a marketing viewpoint, the most desirable course of action is to adapt the marketing mix to the culture.

The cultures of different countries can vary greatly. In order to successfully attract people from a particular country, it is necessary to be aware of these cultural differences.

Table 1.1 illustrates some of the major differences between the culture of East Asian countries and that of the U.S. A marketing effort aimed at people from these cultures would have to take these differences into account in order to be successful. For example, education is important to people from both cultures. However, East Asians look at education as an investment to help the family; in the U.S., it is viewed as an investment in oneself. Thus, while the educational advantages of travel can be marketed to both groups, the approach taken would differ. Messages in East Asia would stress the educational impact on the family and the prestige involved for the family, while the individual benefits would be the focus to U.S. audiences.

In addition, in light of the above findings relative to the influence of personal values on activity preferences, we could speculate that, because of their attitudes toward conserving resources, East Asians are less likely to prefer vigorous outdoor activities.

One model for analyzing cultures has been suggested by Hofstede (1985). He has analyzed certain work-related values of over 50 countries. He found that the

Table 1.1   A Comparison of Cultural Differences

EAST ASIAN COUNTRIES	UNITED STATES OF AMERICA
Equity is more important than wealth.	Wealth is more important than equity.
Saving and conserving resources is highly valued.	Consumption is highly valued; awareness for conservation is growing.
Group is the most important part of society and is emphasized for motivation.	Individual is the most important part of society and is emphasized for motivation.
Cohesive and strong families and ties often extend to distant relatives.	Nuclear and mobile family. Fluid society that de-emphasizes strong, social ties.
Highly disciplined and motivated workforce/societies.	Decline in the protestant work ethic and hierarchy.
Education is an investment in the prestige and economic well being of the family.	Education is an investment in personal development/success.
Protocol, rank, and status are important.	Informality and competence is important.
Public service is a moral responsibility.	Distrust of big government and bureaucracy.

Source: Harris, P.R. and Moran, R.T., *Managing Cultural Differences*, Second Edition (Houston, Gulf Publishing Company, 1987), 388.

value patterns dominant in these countries varied along four main dimensions:

1. Individualism vs. collectivism
2. Masculinity vs. femininity
3. Large or small power distance
4. Strong or weak uncertainty avoidance

On the first scale—individualism vs. collectivism—the issue is the closeness of the relationship between one person and other persons. At the individualistic end of the scale, individuals look after their own self-interests and those of their immediate families. At the other end of the scale, the ties between individuals are very tight. People are supposed to look after the interests of their in-group and have no other opinions and beliefs other than those of their in-group. Wealthy countries are on the individualistic side while poorer countries are on the collectivist side. We might speculate that people from countries that score high on individualism would have different motives and behaviors than those from countries with high-collectivist scores. High individualists might be more inclined to travel independently than in groups and to be more motivated by the desire to improve themselves, for example.

The second dimension is masculinity vs. femininity—the division of roles between the sexes in society. The point is the extent to which societies try to minimize or maximize the social sex role division. Masculine societies make a sharp division between what men and women should do. In these cases, men always take more assertive and dominant roles, while women take more service-oriented and caring roles. In masculine societies more importance is given to such things as showing off, achieving something visible, and making money. In feminine societies more

importance is placed on such things as people relationships over money, the quality of life, and preservation of the environment. Masculine countries are Japan, Germany, Austria and Switzerland, some Latin countries, and most Anglo countries. On the feminine side are the Nordic countries. Placement on this scale would have implications for appropriate marketing appeals. We would expect major decisions, such as for a vacation, to be made by the male in societies that score high on that scale, for example.

The third dimension is power distance—how society deals with the fact that people are unequal. Some societies let inequalities grow over time into inequalities in power and wealth, while others try to play down inequalities as much as possible. Asian, African, and Latin American countries have large power index scores (indicating inequalities), while France, Belgium, Spain, and Italy score rather high. The Nordic and Anglo countries score low on this scale. We might expect messages of a more humanitarian and egalitarian type to appeal to cultures low on this scale.

The last dimension is uncertainty avoidance—how societies deal with the fact that time runs only one way. We all have to live with the uncertainty of the future. Some societies teach their people to accept and live with this uncertainty. People will take personal risks rather lightly, will not work so hard, and will be relatively tolerant of behaviors and opinions different from their own. These are weak uncertainty avoidance societies. Others try to control the future through such things as formal and informal rules to protect themselves from the uncertainties of human behavior. In societies like this, the word of experts is relied upon much more heavily than in weak uncertainty avoidance societies. Latin countries score high, while Asian and African countries, with the exception of Japan and Korea,

score medium to low. Germany, Austria, and Switzerland score high, while the Nordic and Anglo countries score low. It might be expected that, in high-scoring countries, the role of opinion leaders (as experts) would be stronger.

Eight specific clusters have been developed and are contained in figure 1.2. While realizing the dangers of stereotyping, the profiles presented here are a useful first step in determining the types of vacation behavior expected from people in these countries. It also suggests that countries in separate segments have cultures sufficiently different to warrant different marketing approaches.

Louden and Britta (1979) have developed a checklist of factors to be considered in analyzing a culture. The analysis would be particularly appropriate before developing a marketing approach to people from different cultures.

- Determine relevant motivations in the culture: Which needs do people seek to fulfill? In a comparison of travel motivations for vacations in the U.S., for example, Germans were particularly interested in status, while, to the Japanese, people were of prime importance (Shields, 1986).

- Determine characteristic behavior patterns: How often are vacations purchased? In Great Britain the annual vacation in the summer is paramount, while those who can afford it take an additional, off-season break. In the U.S., on the other hand, there is movement away from the long vacation once a year to several shorter breaks taken more often during the year.

- Determine what broad cultural values are relevant to this product: Are vacations, leisure, and recreation thought of in positive terms? In Great Britain, the annual break is seen as very impor-

1. More Developed Latin

▶ High power-distance
▶ High uncertainty-avoidance
▶ High individualism
▶ Medium masculinity

    ARGENTINA
    BRAZIL

2. Less Developed Latin

▶ High power-distance
▶ High uncertainty-avoidance
▶ Low individualism
▶ Whole range on masculinity

    COLOMBIA
    MEXICO
    VENEZUELA
    CHILE
    PERU

3. More Developed Asian

▶ Medium power-distance
▶ High uncertainty-avoidance
▶ Medium individualism
▶ High masculinity

    JAPAN

4. Less Developed Asian

▶ High power-distance
▶ Low uncertainty-avoidance
▶ Low individualism
▶ Medium masculinity

    PAKISTAN
    TAIWAN
    THAILAND
    HONG KONG
    INDIA
    PHILIPPINES
    SINGAPORE

5. Near Eastern

▶ High power-distance
▶ High uncertainty-avoidance
▶ Low individualism
▶ Medium masculinity

    GREECE
    IRAN
    TURKEY

6. Germanic

▶ Low power-distance
▶ High uncertainty-avoidance
▶ Medium individualism
▶ High masculinity

    AUSTRIA
    GERMANY
    SWITZERLAND

7. Anglo

▶ Low power-distance
▶ Low to medium uncertainty-avoidance
▶ High individualism
▶ High masculinity

    AUSTRALIA
    CANADA
    GREAT BRITAIN
    NEW ZEALAND
    USA

8. Nordic

▶ Low power-distance
▶ Low to medium uncertainty-avoidance
▶ Medium individualism
▶ Low masculinity

    DENMARK
    FINLAND
    NORWAY
    SWEDEN

Figure 1.2 Country Clusters and Their Characteristics.

Source: Hofstede, G., (1985)

tant, something to save for and look forward to all year.

● Determine characteristic forms of decision making: Who makes the vacation purchase decision? When is it made? What information sources and criteria are used in making the decision? As noted above, we would expect the vacation decision to be male dominated in both Japan and

Germany. The planning time varies by market segment. Japanese travelers interested in vacationing in Colorado begin planning their trip an average of eleven weeks ahead of time; the British begin twenty-five weeks ahead; and the Germans begin the process thirty-one weeks ahead.

● Evaluate promotion methods appropriate to the culture: What kinds of promotional techniques, words, and pictures are acceptable or not acceptable to people of this culture? In Great Britain, for example, the humor is more subtle than in the U.S. Advertisements use the double meaning to get the point across in a clever way. Such an approach would probably fail in the U.S. where the punch line has to be very direct to gain attention.

● Determine appropriate institutions for this product in the minds of consumers: Do people tend to purchase vacations directly from suppliers, or are retail travel agents used? What alternatives, acceptable to the consumer, are available for distributing the product? Germans, for example, are more inclined to use retail travel agents than other Europeans when planning vacations to the U.S.

The U.S. Culture

Many argue that because of the size and diversity of the U.S., it is not possible to talk about a national culture. Indeed a number of groups in the U.S. have managed to maintain elements of their own geographic, religious and ethnic identities. In addition, any attempt to describe a U.S. culture is fraught with potential charges of promoting stereotypes. Some degree of generalization is possible and desirable, however, if we are to better understand the impact of culture on vacation behavior.

The U.S. places a relatively high value on the following (Ferraro, 1990):

1. Individualism—The U.S. dominant culture places a great deal of emphasis on a high level of achievement motivation, which distinguishes it greatly from certain subcultures and cultures of other countries.

Quick Trip 1.2
Serving Different Cultures

United Kingdom

The reputation of the British amongst foreigners is that they are very formal, however, in reality they are far more approachable and accessible than their reputation would suggest. The use of last names is important at introductions, but thereafter it is very acceptable to use first names.

The decrease in formality within the British culture has not necessarily broken down some of the barriers of reserve. The traditional British understatement tends to give the impression of coolness or indifference. In our industry we should certainly be aware of British politeness which can hide a true meaning and therefore guest interaction can leave you with a vague interpretation of the guest's real meaning. In general, the British have an aversion to seriousness. Humor is expected at all levels of business dealings and on all occasions.

Germany

Germans are very competitive and ambitious. They hate failure of any nature and show no sympathy for it. They place a great deal of importance on individual success and outward trappings . . . The car you drive and where you take your holidays are very important factors.

They are very highly organized people and have a strong distaste for non-conformism . . . the Germans like to know what they are buying in advance. They study itineraries and schedules with a great deal of depth. So much so that it becomes totally unacceptable to change itineraries or to alter a planned excursion at the last minute.

The very formal public behavior displayed by the Germans is in sharp contrast to the informality and warmth of private life and the genuine friendships that ensue. Germans are probably the most punctual people. Their humor is reserved for the private life. . . .

Germans are individuals. They certainly enjoy traveling alone as opposed to being in groups.

Japan

The Japanese culture has many unique features and is made up of many layers old and new; foreign and native. Among the reasons for this multi-layered quality of Japanese culture is the curiosity the Japanese people have for other cultures and the historic process of assimilation as the Japanese have welcomed foreign cultural elements over the centuries without discarding indigenous customs and traditions. Traditionally, primary importance has been placed on the group rather than on the individual and this heritage accounts for much of Japanese society's uniformity. Their pursuit of work is not based so much on the profit motivation as the value of working.

Questions:

1. If this observer's view of these cultures is correct, what impact does culture have on vacation behavior of the British, the Germans, and the Japanese?

2. How would this be the same as and different from the vacation behavior of Americans, given their cultural background as noted in the text?

Source: "Serving Different Cultures" D. Roberts, Chateau Whistler Resort, Proceedings of the 24th annual conference of The Travel and Tourism Research Association. (1993) 375–379.

2. A precise reckoning of time—Time is important to many because it is equated with money. Many things are organized and run by the clock.

3. A future orientation—There is an overall feeling of optimism on the part of many in the U.S. The general feeling is that the future can and will be better than the past.

4. Work and achievement—Hard work and hard play are valued. This stems from the Puritan ethic that idleness is evil. People place great value on the number of possessions they have and the necessity to be progressive both materially and educationally.

5. Control over the natural environment—Corporations and individuals continuously devise new technology and ideas that will be of benefit to the economic goals and to the goals of people striving to become knowledgeable and well educated.

6. Youthfulness—Many people turn to youth activities and procedures for renewed inspiration.

7. Informality—People are less concerned with the one "right" way of doing things. First names are used upon first meetings.

8. Competition—Achieving goals and becoming individualistic through intense competition.

9. Relative equality of the sexes—Compared to many other cultures, women are given the same opportunities as are men.

Within this general pattern, however, there are constant movements. Donald Hinman of NDL/ The Lifestyle Selector identifies the following likely changes in lifestyle in the year 2000 (see quick trip 1.3):

1. The arts will gradually replace sports as society's primary leisure activity

2. The 1990s: Decade of Women in Leadership

3. Religious revival

4. Triumph of the individual

The United Way of America's Strategic Institute has gone beyond lifestyle to identify what they call "Nine Forces Reshaping America" (1990).

1. The maturation of America. They see a maturing and increasing sophistication of taste related to the maturing of the baby boomers and the graying of America. This will result in a population that is "More realistic, more responsible and more tolerant of diversity."

2. The mosaic society. Mass society will give way to customized products and services for each of the parts of the mosaic.

3. Redefinition of individual and societal roles. The boundaries defining the roles of public and private sectors will become blurred as the private-sector takes over many of the traditional functions of government. At the same time business will become increasingly involved in social issues.

4. The information-based economy. Advances in computers will change the way we do business and "do" leisure.

5. Globalization. There will be increasing foreign ownership of U.S. companies and a *relative* decline in the economic power of the U.S. Consumers will have more global tastes and ideas.

6. Personal and environmental health. Quality of life issues regarding both individuals and society will become more important.

7. Economic restructuring. Newly industrializing countries will compete with older, more established economies. Middle management will continue to suffer job cuts and small companies will continue to grow in number.

8. Family and home redefined. Many of the functions handled by families—such as meal preparation and child care—will be

The maturation of the population will influence the future of tourism. Photo by Corel.

offered as services while other services previously available only outside the home—shopping and movies, for example—will be brought into the household.

9. Rebirth of social activism. Increased concern on the part of many about such social issues as the environment, racial tensions, and homelessness will produce more citizen activists less likely to be intolerant of what they perceive as "anti-society" behavior on the part of business.

The Effect of Time on Travel

> "Time has become a currency which we 'spend' instead of 'pass'."
>
> *Edward Thompson*

Time, or rather the availability of time, acts as a major inhibiting factor to travel. The amount of available time and the form in which it is available is, in fact, a major shaper of the destinations that can be visited, the modes of travel that can be used, and the activities that can be engaged in at the destination or en route. The desire to travel and the financial ability to travel are insufficient if one does not have the time to travel. All three factors must be present for travel and tourism to take place.

Our time can be spent in one of three ways (see figure 1.3).

Spending Time

Time is spent in many **maintenance activities**—activities that involve a certain degree of obligation and that are necessary to sustain and maintain life. Included in this definition are such activities as eating, sleeping, maintaining the house, and caring for the lawn.

Quick Trip 1.3
Changing Lifestyles and Their Impact on Tourism

According to some the following trends form the background against which tourism will develop:

1. The arts will gradually replace sports as society's primary leisure activity.

   Reasons/Implications:
   - More affluent society.
   - More educated, professional workforce.
   - More women in workforce.
   - Sophistication and willingness to pay.
   - Greater access to arts through the urban society, cable television, and videotape.

2. The 1990s: Decade of Women in Leadership.

   Implications:
   - Day care.
   - Elder care.
   - Creative leave policies.
   - Work sharing.
   - Work from home.

3. Religious revival.

   Implications:
   - When buffeted by change, the need for spiritual belief intensifies.
   - The year 2000: The Apocalyptic Millennium?
   - Growth of religious "products."
   - Religion replaces communism.

4. Triumph of the Individual.

   Implications:
   - Society rewards individuals rather than organizations.
   - Less need for cities.
   - Need for the information highway.
   - Information is sought rather than bought.
   - In-home selling rather than in-store selling.

Question:

1. What changes will we see in tourism if, in fact, these changes do occur?

Source: "The Changing Customer: Lifestyles in the Year 2000" D. P. Hinman, Vice President, NDL/The Lifestyle Selector. Proceedings of the Travel and Tourism Research Association Annual Conference. (1994) 354–361.

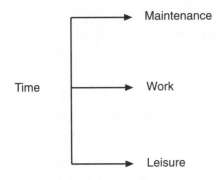

Figure 1.3 Time Divisions.

Time can also be spent at work. For many this involves a degree of obligation greater than the time spent in maintenance activities. **Leisure** can be defined, although some people may feel it is a rather simplified definition, as the time remaining after work and maintenance activities have been completed. By its very definition leisure implies that the individual has a level of discretion over how to spend time that is not present in the other two categories. Leisure is often contrasted with the economic activity of work, and is connected with pleasure and a feeling of freedom with a minimum of obligation. Leisure is also seen as inner-directed rather than other-directed. It is the time for one's self. Although leisure time offers opportunities for creativity and personal growth, the accent must

be on freedom of choice. Traditionally, researchers have talked about leisure as time spent in productive pursuits. Yet this imposes a value system upon the individual's discretionary time. **Productive** is a term defined by the researcher. The crucial point is that leisure-time activities are those that are undertaken freely by individuals within their discretionary time.

By seeing time broken down into these three categories, it is easy to demonstrate a relationship between all three. Because time is absolute—there are twenty-four hours in a day, seven days in a week, fifty-two weeks in a year—any change in one of the three parts will automatically affect the others. As the workweek declines, more time is freed for maintenance and/or leisure activities. This is important because in the study of tourism, we are concerned with the use of leisure time, and a recognition that leisure time is bound to the other two concepts helps us to be concerned with changes in those concepts as they might affect leisure time.

How is time actually spent? In a typical week most time is spent on maintenance activities. This is true for both females and males. The significant difference between the sexes is that females spend more time on housework, necessary

home maintenance, lawn care, and playing with or helping the children, than do males.

Schor (1991) suggests that in the last twenty years the amount of time Americans have spent on their jobs has risen steadily. According to her research the average American has only sixteen and a half hours of leisure a week. The decline in the workweek ended abruptly in the late 1940s and since then, according to Schor, paid time off has actually been shrinking. This is a result of the economic squeeze faced by many companies in the 1980s. Cost-cutting often reduced vacation time. Fearful of losing their jobs, many employees spent less time away from the workplace. Schor's figures indicate that, comparing 1969 and 1987, the average employed person was spending 163 more hours on the job a year.

In addition, many companies restructured their labor markets by firing long-term employees and hiring temporary workers. Because vacation time is based on the length of employment, the result was less time off with pay for many people. A third factor is the growth of the service sector where length of employment tends to be less than in the manufacturing industries.

Americans themselves seem to agree that they are working harder.

Often families spend vacation time camping in scenic areas. Photo from *Top Shots* CD Rom. Courtesy of Queensland Tourist and Travel Corporation.

An NBC/*Wall Street Journal* survey in 1996 found that 59 percent of those questioned described themselves as busy, while 19 percent said life had become busy to the point of discomfort (*Denver Post*). According to the Bureau of Labor Statistics, among men between the ages of twenty-five and fifty-four, the percentage of those working more than forty-one hours a week rose from 36 percent in 1976 to 43 percent in 1993. For the same years, among full-time working women of the same age, the share of those working more than forty-one hours rose from 13 percent to 22 percent.

We might expect that the above distribution would change relative to changes in the family life cycle. This relationship is demonstrated in figure 1.4. In the young and single phase, people are characterized by great physical capacity, disposable time, and few demands on their income. In the family phase, discretionary income and time decrease, and the physical capacity of the family is limited by that of its weakest member. The third phase is characterized by an excess of discretionary time and a decrease in physical capacity.

We can speculate on the impact this might have on vacation behavior. Young singles would have the time, money, and ability to participate in physically demanding activities. Family activities would be geared to those allowed by the youngest child. Older people would be likely markets during the off-season as well as for last-minute bargains.

Historical Development of Leisure Time

The distribution of time between the three categories mentioned has changed over the years. In 1791 Philadelphia carpenters went on strike for the *ten* hour day. In 1850 the average workweek was close to seventy hours; by 1900 it had declined to about sixty hours; today it is approximately forty. The reasons for the long workweek in the nineteenth century have been traced to the Industrial Revolution. Prior to the Industrial Revolution in Great Britain, most people were connected with the farm. Hours of work and leisure time were dictated by the farming seasons. People worked long hours when the harvest had to be brought in, but in winter, because of the lesser number of daylight hours, hours of work were less. The Industrial Revolution brought a movement of a rural population, which had work hours conditioned by nature to an increasingly urban population, which had work hours determined by employers who sought to have output on a continuous basis year round. In addition, many of the leisure-time pursuits of the working class were rough and violent. In order to control their workers better, owners adopted various strategies. Wages were kept low so that saving money was difficult, and in order to live, people had to continue working rather than take time off. In addition, the Sabbath was strictly enforced. As a complement to this, the idea of work was made the most important part of life. The idea of spending time at work was praised almost to the point of sanctification, but the idea of spending time at leisure was derided. Religious movements developed this thought into an ethic—the Protestant ethic. Leisure time was first given to celebrate various religious festivals. These holy days were the forerunner of our **holidays**, as the idea of associating a break from work with religion has gradually diminished. The average number of weekdays enjoyed as paid vacation time varies from country to country. In Austria, Denmark and Sweden the workers have thirty paid weekdays of vacation, not counting public holidays. Most European countries give their workers from eighteen to twenty-five paid weekdays off. In contrast, workers in Canada, Japan, and the U.S. have a measly ten. U.S. manufacturing employees work the equivalent of two months more than those in many European countries.

Although, according to many, the workweek has decreased, other factors have prevented more people from seeing an increase in their leisure time. As affluence has increased the incidence of material possessions, much of the reduced work time has manifested itself in increased maintenance time to take care of the new possessions, such as the car and the house. In addi-

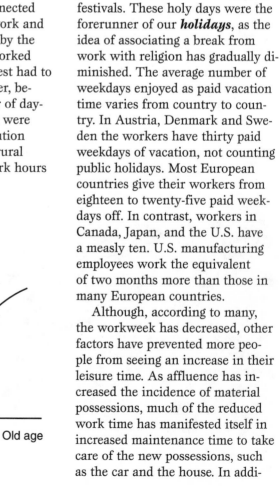

Figure 1.4   Time Phases in the Family Life Cycle.

tion, as cities have grown as a result of the country becoming more urbanized, commuting time to work has increased. A related factor is that, for many, the stress of big-city living means that more time is required before individuals are mentally ready for leisure pursuits. A third factor is that, as the economy moves from primary and manufacturing industries to a service economy, the distinction between work and non-work becomes increasingly blurred. It is easier for the steel worker to punch out at the end of a shift and forget about work problems than it is for the manager of a business.

The time we spend at work is used to gather resources beyond what is needed for survival. This acquisitiveness is the result of cultural training. Anthropologists have found that most hunter-gatherer groups, who live day to day on the resources they can kill or forage and stash very little away for the future, generally work only three to five hours daily. In our "advanced" society the extra time spent working is to purchase products, and services, including vacations, deemed necessary to our well-being.

Attempts have been made to show a relationship between the type of work and the type of leisure activities engaged in. Leisure has been seen as a compensation for work in that leisure activity is different from work activity. A passive job, for example, may result in active leisure-time activities. A second view is that the development of certain skills and lifestyles learned at work will spill over into a demand for similar kinds of leisure-time activities. The problem, of course, is that any leisure-time behavior can be explained by reference to whichever theory is more appropriate to one's purpose. The link between type of work and leisure activities has not been demonstrated. In fact, several studies have demonstrated that there are

Ad © 1996 by KeyCorp. Reprinted by permission. Photo © by Tony Stone Images.

no significant differences in leisure activity between workers who are doing what they consider boring jobs and those who are doing more interesting and enjoyable jobs. It does seem clear, however, that the place of leisure in a person's life is becoming more important relative to that of work.

More important than the absolute amount of leisure time available, however, is the way in which it is spent. An individual who finishes dinner at 7 p.m. and plans to go to bed at midnight has five hours of leisure time. The amount of time available limits what activities can be done and where they can be pursued. Leisure time may be thought of as being divided into three categories (see figure 1.5).

Leisure occurs on weekdays, weekends, and on vacations. The importance of this distinction can be illustrated by means of an example. If the workweek were to be

reduced by 20 percent, the opportunities for tourism activities would be affected by the way in which the reduction was taken: the workday could be shortened to six-and-a-half hours from eight; the workweek could be shortened from five to four days; one week's paid vacation could be granted in each of three quarters of the year, with one month's vacation in the fourth quarter, and with six months' vacation every five years. All three alternatives represent a cut of 20 percent in the workweek, yet the form in which it is taken affects the opportunities to participate in various activities and to visit various destinations.

It is clear that, although the absolute amount of leisure time may have increased little over the past several decades, the form in which it is being taken is changing. Although most of the gains in leisure in the past century have been taken in the form of a shorter workweek, since 1950 added leisure time has increasingly been taken in blocks of extended periods away from work. Yet the vast majority of full-time U.S. workers still are engaged in a five-day workweek.

The concepts of work, leisure, and money are intertwined as far as tourism is concerned. Individuals need both leisure and money to travel. Usually this money is earned by working. Thus, it is necessary to work in order to earn money to engage in leisure-time

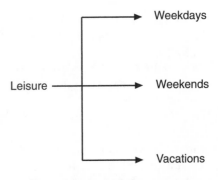

Figure 1.5   Leisure Time Divisions.

Many people today put greater value on having time to spend on leisure activities. Photo from *Top Shots* CD Rom. Courtesy of Queensland Tourist and Travel Corporation.

pursuits. The more one works, the more money is earned (and, therefore, available for leisure activities), but the less time one has to spend and enjoy it. Consumers can thus be thought of as having both a time budget and a money budget, and some make rational decisions in allocating one over the other. The auto worker who takes Friday off to lengthen the weekend for a fishing trip chooses time over money. The college professor who chooses not to teach during the summer, but to travel cross-country also chooses time over money. This idea has been expressed as the principle of *resource value inversion*. As consumers' incomes rise, time becomes increasingly precious to them compared to money. Money, after all, can be saved; time cannot. Combined with this is a perception on the part of many that "time is money." To what extent are people increasingly unwilling to put off gratification? Are people choosing more time over more money? Several generalizations can be made. First, although Americans desire both more income and free time, it

appears that three units of income are preferred for every unit of free time. Second, this preference gap seems to be closing as free time is gradually increasing in importance relative to more income. In times of economic slowdown, this statement does not hold true. Third, the income-free time choice is made within the context of other factors and values associated with an individual's perception of the quality of life. Fourth, the choice between income and free time may be affected by the way in which the free-time options are offered. Some

options were demonstrated above with the example of the 20 percent workweek reduction. It appears that most workers prefer free time in the form of extended time away from work.

There is some indication that increasing number of Japanese would rather have more free time than pay if given the choice. About 57 percent of those polled in a 1990 survey (*Wall Street Journal*) said they would prefer more leisure time to a pay raise, compared with about 53 percent in a 1989 poll. Twenty-two percent said they would take a higher salary at the expense of leisure time, the lowest since the government initiated the poll in 1975.

Much has been made of the effect of a four-day workweek on pleasure travel. People representing a nationwide sample were asked to indicate what activities would be undertaken if every week included a three-day weekend. The activities chosen by more than half of either male or female respondents are indicated in table 1.2.

The major response given indicated that a significant proportion of both male and female respondents would take weekend trips. However, studies of workers engaged in a four-day, forty-hour workweek have indicated that, because of fatigue from the workweek, most people tended to be more favorably inclined to home-centered relaxation. Another study compared the leisure partici-

Table 1.2   Activities Respondents Would Engage in with a Three-Day Weekend Every Week

ACTIVITY	FEMALES %	MALES %
Take weekend trips, visit places I've always wanted to see	70	63
Socialize, visit friends	56	45
Spend time with family, play with children	53	50
Drive around, go sightseeing	52	48
Spend time on outdoor hobbies	45	52

Source: D. K. Hawes. Time budgets and consumer-time behavior, in *Advances in Consumer Research*, vol. 4, 228.

pation of four-day-a-week and five-day-a-week workers. It found that both sets of workers devoted approximately equal amounts of time to participation in leisure activities. The only difference was that those who worked only four days a week pursued, on average, a greater number of different activities than the five-day-a-week worker. It may be that the extra day offers an opportunity to experiment with new activities, spending less time on each of more activities. This is rather interesting because, if this can be generalized, an extra day of non-work actually places more time pressure on different leisure activities.

Socioeconomic Variables and Their Effect on Tourism Demand

"I was disappointed in Niagara— most people must be disappointed in Niagara. Every American bride is taken there, and the sight of the stupendous waterfall must be one of the earliest, if not the keenest, disappointments in American married life."

Oscar Wilde

Age

The relationship between tourism and age has two components: the amount of leisure time available relative to age and the type and extent of activities undertaken at various age levels. The amount of leisure time available changes curvilinearly, with the younger and older age groups having proportionately more leisure time.

Yet the amount of available time is, by itself, insufficient to explain age as a factor in tourism behavior. It is safe to conclude that the rates of participation in the overwhelming majority of leisure activities declines with age. There is a greater

---

Quick Trip 1.4

Travel Requires Both Time and Money

Fifty-year-old Bill Cecil is in the top 1.2 percent of U.S. wage earners: He earned $101,000 in 1995. Mr. Cecil did so by working eighty-four hours a week at his job as a millwright, transporting heavy machinery and fixing minor machinery problems in Chrysler Corporation's Trenton plant. He gets up at 5 a.m. every day, clocks in by 6 a.m. and works until 6 p.m. with no more than sixty minutes off for lunch and breaks. He usually falls asleep in front of the TV before 10 p.m. While the forty-plus hours of overtime a week cost him his "freedom and time with family" and was a major factor in the breakup of his first marriage, Mr. Cecil is happy with his choice. It brings him a well-furnished home and money to travel, eat out often, send his children to college, and play golf.

Nor is he alone. The Bureau of Labor Statistics estimates that 28,000 of the nation's 11 million precision, production, and craft workers make over $100,000 a year.

Much of Mr. Cecil's motivation comes from a deep-seated insecurity, one felt by many autoworkers. The industry tends to experience drastic swings ranging from layoffs to round-the-clock overtime. Remarried in 1992, he and his wife, Dawn, 33, and her thirteen-year-old son, Roger, live in the suburbs in a house they bought for $88,000 two years previously. Much of his paycheck goes into the house on such things as a large-screen television, recliners, and furniture. Mrs. Cecil also works overtime—sometimes as many as seventy hours a week—allowing her husband to cut back his workweek to 55 to 60 hours.

The money also allows him to indulge in his favorite pastime: golf. He recently purchased a set of $2,200 Taylor Made golf clubs and has been known to work a twelve-hour shift beginning at 3 a.m. so he can play a late-afternoon round of golf.

A great deal of the money goes to his children. Stepson Roger is the recipient of a Super Nintendo and a Soloflex exercise machine while the three children from his first marriage—all in their twenties—have had help in financing their college education as well as trips back home and a time-share in Puerto Vallarta, Mexico.

Questions:

1. What is the link between free time and money as far as tourism is concerned?

2. What kind of choices has Bill Cecil made in this regard? Is this part of a growing trend in this country?

3. Is the above a typically American picture, or is it representative of how people from other countries behave?

4. What does this story tell us about the competition for tourism—both in terms of how people spend their time and money?

Source: A. Luccetti. An auto worker earns more than $100,000 but at a personal cost. *Wall Street Journal*, 135, 23. (August 1, 1996) A1, A5.

decline for active recreational activities than for the more passive forms of recreation. Preferred activities among the elderly are the more passive ones such as visiting friends and relatives, sightseeing, fishing, and playing golf. Yet for many retirees, although the number of activities participated in may drop upon retirement, the amount of time spent on each remaining one in terms of participation often increases.

There appear to be several differences between patterns of travel based on age. Older people tend to represent a smaller share of tourists in proportion to their numbers than do younger people. This may also be influenced by other socio-economic factors, such as income. Although younger people tend to select more adventurous destinations than do older people, older tourists tend to travel to farther destinations. The older tourists tend to dominate ship travel, spend less than middle-age tourists but more than younger tourists, and, while preferring to travel in the summer (in common with younger travelers), tend to travel more in the spring than do younger tourists. In one study older people considered restfulness and the historical aspects of a vacation site more important while younger people emphasized adventure and physical activities. Single people stressed physical activities, meeting new

people, and having fun. Married people, on the other hand, put more emphasis on restful and physically refreshing destinations (Kaynak, Kara, Kucukemiroglu, & Dalgic, 1995).

In analyzing the impact of age on travel and tourism, the generational influence must be considered. The ***generational influence*** is the common set of values and attitudes shared by those who came of age during a particular decade. There are seven generational groups now living in U.S. society. The groups and their implications for travel and tourism in the year 2000 are shown in table 1.3.

An analysis of this information would suggest that the shared attitudes experienced in the formative years continue to have an influence on buying patterns even as the group matures and ages. For example, it might be expected that spending patterns of the Depression Babies are forever influenced by the fact that they went through the Depression at an early age. In fact, this group still today uses credit cards less often than do other segments.

The generational influence may impact future demand in the following ways (U.S. Travel Data Center, 1988)

1. Baby Busters, who were raised in the less socially interactive environment of the 1980s, may

prefer to travel independently in the future. However, the convenience of buying a package will appeal to their need for expediency in the arrangement of their leisure time. Several factors have influenced their experiences (Dunn, 1993):

- Many are the children of divorce
- Many were the latchkey children of working mothers
- They are the first group widely exposed to computers
- They entered the dating scene in the age of AIDS
- They are entering the workforce at a time of layoffs and downsizing

By some estimates, this group has the wanderlust, but for travel on the cheap. The newly opened countries in Eastern Europe may appeal, as will unspoiled places with outstanding natural amenities. They are interested in fitness and diet. Affinity groups are popular. For many, cooking (which they were forced to learn to survive) is seen as a hobby and a way to entertain.

2. Late Baby Boomers will be time-constrained working parents looking to create worthwhile family experiences. Their general familiarity and sophistication with travel will cause them to demand a high level of service.

Table 1.3   The Seven Generational Groups

GROUP	BORN	FORMATIVE YEARS	DOMINANT DECADE	AGE IN 2000	% IN 2000
Baby Boomlet	1977–88	1989–2000	1990s	12–23	17%
Baby Bust	1965–76	1977–1988	1980s	24–35	17%
Late Baby Boom	1955–64	1967–1976	1970s	36–45	21%
Early Baby Boom	1946–54	1958–1966	1960s	46–54	18%
World War II Babies	1935–45	1947–1957	1950s	55–65	11%
Depression Babies	1924–34	1936–1946	1940s	66–76	8%
World War I Babies	1923 & earlier	1935 & earlier	1930s & earlier	77 +	8%

Source: *Highlights of Discover America 2000* (Washington, D.C., Travel Industry Association of America, 1988), 2–3.

3. Early Baby Boomers will be reaching the peak of their earning potential. Many will have sent their children to college and acquired long-term assets. One segment may be early semi-retirees. Because of the social environment in which they were raised, the less traditional vacation destinations could be very attractive to this group.

4. Many World War II Babies may find themselves encouraged to take early retirement to make way for the arrival of Early Baby Boomers into managerial ranks. Their upbringing could have them looking for opportunities for social interaction and learning as part of their travel experiences.

5. Depression Babies offer a challenge. They have life experiences very different from young Americans. They are intent upon hunting for bargains; they do not like to buy on credit; and they have strong family and community ties. Yet many will have time, money, and health to travel.

6. World War I Babies represent people for whom travel is not seen as an integral part of life.

In summary, leisure time decreases with age until children leave the nest; then the amount of leisure time increases. This increase continues with retirement. Though participation in physical activities declines with age (together with a corresponding rise in participation in the gentler forms of recreation), interest levels in activities previously participated in remain high. Opportunities may exist for tapping these interests by developing non-participatory means of expressing that interest. A skier, for example, may be unable to ski for reasons of age, but may be interested in other related activities such as watching skiers or sharing experiences.

A relaxing trip to an exotic beach is one way to spend your disposable income. Photo by Corel.

Income

Income is obviously an important inhibiting factor in shaping the demand for travel. Not only does travel itself entail a certain cost, but the traveler must pay for services rendered at the destination as well as have money to engage in various activities during the trip. In addition, expenditures may be required in the form of specialized equipment to engage in various recreational activities while at the destination or en route. It is difficult, however, to determine the relative importance of income per se, because this variable is interrelated with other socioeconomic variables. Generally speaking, higher income is associated with higher education, with certain jobs, and with certain age groups. Total family income has risen steadily as more wives have entered the labor force. The fact that family income has risen will have an effect upon tourism demand. Yet the fact that more families have two spouses in the labor force will also affect the shape of tourism demand. Different types of vacations and recreational activities may be demanded because of the time pressures involved in having two working spouses. The difficulty arises in determining the effect of these two interrelated variables on the demand for new tourism and recreation products.

It is important to see that the income spent on travel is spent at the expense of something else (see figure 1.6). Travel expenditures are in competition with other expenditures, some of which are discretionary.

An individual's **personal disposable income** is the amount of income left after paying taxes. After various necessary personal outlays to maintain basic living needs have been spent, an individual has discretion to do with the remainder whatever is desired. A mink coat may be purchased, money may be saved, or a trip taken to Hawaii. It is important to look at income in this way to realize that the trip to Hawaii is in competition not only with a trip to the Bahamas, but also with various other recreational activities and other uses of that discretionary income. As the level of personal income increases, so does the amount of **discretionary income**.

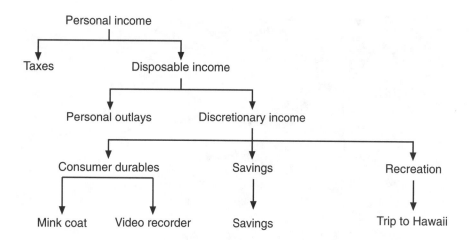

Figure 1.6   Personal Income Distribution.

Many studies have attempted to determine the percentage of income spent on recreation as a whole. It appears that at the lower levels of income and education approximately 2 percent of income is spent on recreation. As income increases the proportion spent on recreation increases to between 5 and 6 percent for all education levels. The highest recreation expenditures, 7 percent, are reported by respondents who are heads of households, under forty years of age, and without children. Other studies have indicated a positive correlation between income and recreation expenditures. In fact, it appears that increases in income result in a proportionately greater increase in recreation expenditures. As might be expected, higher-income tourists stay longer and spend more per day than do those with lower incomes. The type of recreational activities participated in differs based upon income. Higher-income people tend to participate in activities such as reading, bridge, fencing, squash, and chess; and middle-income people tend to engage in bowling, golf, and dancing. Lower-income families are identified with television viewing, dominoes, and bingo. The implication of these activities is clear to companies who wish to put together travel packages with specific activi-

ties involved aimed at particular market segments. A package, for example, aimed at a high-income segment of the market might be built around a recreational activity in which that segment tends to participate.

In addition to the relationship between income and recreation expenditure, some work has been done on the amount of participation in recreation and income. It has been shown that participation in most recreational activities in-

creases as income increases up to a certain point, but declines slightly at incomes higher than this.

The only significant demographic difference between U.S. domestic and foreign travelers is that of income. A greater percentage of foreign travelers had higher incomes.

Sex

There are more similarities than differences between the sexes in terms of leisure participation rates. Overall, participation rates in leisure activities do not differ between men and women, although many women engage in slightly fewer activities than do men. As might be expected, non-working women have slightly higher participation rates than do employed women, except for such things as going out to dinner and either taking part in active sports or watching sports. There is a clear difference between the sexes in terms of preferred activities. Women are more involved in cultural activities, and men lead in outdoor recreation and playing and watching sports.

Golfing is a prime leisure activity. Courtesy of Brown County Convention & Visitors Bureau, Nashville, Indiana.

One study (Williams & Lattey, 1994) indicates that the traditional responsibilities of females relating to domestic work and child care have led to them viewing leisure activities in a way that are task-oriented rather than time-oriented; social rather than physical; relational as opposed to self-interested. The study specifically dealt with skiing and found that women placed more emphasis on the emotional and social benefits of skiing than on the physical benefits. Women, it was found, are more likely than men to ski if friends and/or family are involved. The activity is viewed as recreational rather than competitive.

Education

The strong correlation between education as it relates to income has been well-established. Independent of income, however, the level of education that an individual has tends to influence the type of leisure and travel pursuits chosen. The amount of education obtained will most likely determine the nature of both work and leisure-time activities. By widening one's horizons of interest and enjoyment, education influences the type of activities undertaken. Education itself can serve as the primary reason for travel.

Researchers have found that participation in outdoor recreation tends to increase as the amount of education increases. There is also some evidence to suggest that the more educated prefer those activities that require the development of interpretive and expressive skills. Such activities include attending plays, concerts, and art museums, playing tennis and golf, skiing, reading books, attending adult education classes, and undergoing a wilderness experience.

In summary, it appears that the more education people have the broader their horizons and the more options they can consider.

Quick Trip 1.5
A Golden Opportunity

According to *Modern Maturity* men and women over age 50 take more trips than those under 50. On the way, they spent more than $30 billion on vacations in 1994. To appeal to this segment of the market Choice Hotels have created a Senior Room for its Rodeway and Econo Lodge brands.

The room includes features that seniors are used to having in their own homes and that make life easier for them. These include such things as brighter lighting, large-button telephones and TV remotes, and lever handles on doors and faucets. Representatives from the American Association of Retired Persons helped Choice with the design. According to the architects the bathroom is the most important consideration when designing a room. Grab bars should be placed in tubs at an appropriate height, lighting should be balanced, levers make faucet handles easier to turn, and there should be no sharp edges on the furnishings.

Rodeway increased its proportion of senior rooms from 10 percent to 25 percent, citing increased demand for the concept. At a cost of $500 per room for the conversion, the company gets a return on its investment in two to three months.

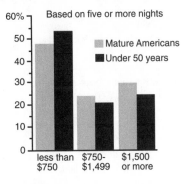

Mature Americans spend more money on their trips.

Source: AARP

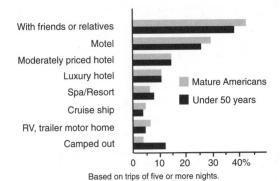

Where mature Americans stay on vacation.

Source: AARP

Question:

1. Changing demographics indicate an increase in the number of older Americans. What changes will this mean for businesses in travel and tourism?

Source: Golden Opportunity by J. Miller. *Hotel and Motel Management.* (April 1, 1996) 45–46.

The more-educated travelers also tend to be more sophisticated in their tastes. They may not, however, be bigger spenders. A study of visitors to Hawaii found that visitors with less education spent more per day while on vacation in Hawaii. The authors suggested that the less-educated visitor may equate having fun with spending money.

Life Cycle Stages

"In America there are two classes of travel—first class and with children."

Robert Benchley

Families evolve through a certain life cycle. The characteristics of the family at the various stages of its life cycle offer certain opportunities or exert various pressures that affect purchase behavior.

The traditional divisions of the *family life cycle* are shown in table 1.4 together with the purchase patterns common to each. It has been suggested, however, that this traditional life cycle has become outdated because of changing demographics such as the growing number of "*dinks*" (double income, no kids) and an increase in single parent families. One study of German vacationers looked at the life-long pattern of respondents and found that destination choices are dependent upon the stage in the family life cycle (Oppermann, 1995). The categories used are detailed in table 1.5.

While the author of the above study cautions against generalization, it is useful to examine the findings as a guide to travel behavior. In stage I young travelers (15–25) are still taking vacations with their parents. Vacations occur predominantly in summer and winter, reflecting school breaks. The activities undertaken—sunbathing and skiing—are linked to the seasons

during which the holidays are taken. Stage II consists of young singles/couples, 15–25 years old taking independent holidays from their parents. This group has the most average seasonal and travel party size distribution of any of the groups. Sunbathing and skiing are the preferred activities. The length of trip at this stage is longer, indicating

they have a great deal of available time to go on longer holidays.

As people get older—stage III consists of singles/couples aged 26–40—culture sightseeing takes on greater importance while beach tourism is not as important. As income increases, trains give way to planes as the preferred transportation mode. (Bear in mind the study

Table 1.4   A Traditional Family Life Cycle

STAGE IN LIFE CYCLE	BUYING OR BEHAVIOR PATTERN
Bachelor stage: Young, single people not living at home.	Few financial burdens. Fashion leaders. Recreation oriented. Buy basic kitchen equipment, basic furniture, cars, equipment for the mating game, vacations.
Newly married couples: Young, no children.	Better off financially than they will be in near future. Highest purchase rate and highest average purchase of durables. Buy cars, refrigerators, stoves, sensible and durable furniture, vacations.
Full nest I: Youngest child under six.	Home purchasing at peak. Liquid assets low. Dissatisfied with financial position and amount of money saved. Interested in new products. Buy washers, dryers, baby food, chest rubs and cough medicine, vitamins, dolls, sleds, skates.
Full nest II: Youngest child six or over.	Financial position better. Some wives work. Less influenced by advertising. Buy larger-size packages, multiple-unit deals. Buy many foods, cleaning materials, bicycles, music lessons, pianos.
Full nest III: Older couples with dependent children.	Financial position still better. More wives work. Some children get jobs. Hard to influence with advertising. High average purchase of durables. Buy new, more tasteful furniture, auto travel, non-necessary appliances, boats, dental services, magazines.
Empty nest I: Older couples, no children living with them, head in labor force.	Home ownership at peak. Most satisfied with financial position and money saved. Interested in travel, recreation, self-education. Make gifts and contributions. Not interested in new products. Buy vacations, luxuries, home improvements.
Empty nest II: Older married couples, no children living at home, head retired.	Drastic cut in income. Keep home. Buy medical care products that improve health, sleep, and digestion.
Solitary survivor, in labor force.	Income still good, but likely to sell home.
Solitary survivor, retired.	Same medical and product needs as other retired group. Drastic cut in income. Special need for attention, affection and security.

Source: W. D. Wells and G. Gubar. Life cycle concept in marketing research. *Journal of Marketing Research*, November 1986, pp. 355–363, in J. P. Peter and J. C. Olson. *Consumer Behavior: Marketing Strategy Perspectives* (Homewood, Illinois; Irwin), 459.

Table 1.5   The Family Life Cycle Stages

STAGE	AGE	CHILDREN	WORKING STATUS	FAMILY STATUS
I	15–25	—	Dependent on parents	Taking holidays with parents
II	15–25	—	Yes	Single/couple
III	26–40	—	Yes	Single/couple
IV	41–62	—	Yes	Single/couple
V	(*)	Yes	Yes	Preschool kids
VI	<40	Yes	Yes	School-age kids
VII	41–62	Yes	Yes	School-age kids
VIII	(**)	Yes	Yes	Children take independent holidays
IX	63+ (***)	—	Retired	Single/couple

(*)   Varying age; category depends on age of children.

(**)   Varying age; category depends on time when children take independent holidays.

(***) In Germany the usual age for retirement is between 63 and 65. The determining variable for this category is working status.

Source: M. Oppermann. Family life cycle and cohort effects: A study of travel patterns of German residents. *Journal of Travel & Tourism Marketing,* Vol. 4(1), 1995, 23–44.

was conducted in Germany where the train system is much better than in the U.S.) Off-season travel is common, as are short trips of four to seven nights. In stage IV, singles/couples 41–63 years old, cultural tourism becomes even more important and beach vacations even less so than before. This category has the highest incidence of travel to overseas destinations. Coach (bus) travel is also high, possibly indicating participation in organized tours. Off-season travel is prevalent with an emphasis on late winter/early spring and fall. These months represent times when the weather in Germany is unpleasant. This, plus the time and money available to the respondents, accounts for the travel to areas with a better climate at these times of the year.

In stage V the presence of preschool children is felt. As the children are not dependent on school holidays the family tends to avoid the main season. Apartments are used more frequently than with other segments. As the children get older, camping and apartments, because of cost savings, are used as an alternative to hotels. Financial considerations impact the way vacationers travel and where they stay

and eat. Seasonal trips are taken, reflecting the timing dependence on the school calendar. In stage VII parents are over 40 and traveling with school-age children. Timing is still school-calendar dependent. Sunbathing and skiing becomes less important as parents get older and camping loses its appeal. Seeking to balance increased comfort with the costs incurred, apartments continue to be more important than hotels.

In stage VIII children, who may still be living at home, take holidays independent of the parent(s). No longer dependent on the school timetable, off-season travel takes on more importance. Finally, as people retire (stage IX) they travel more within Central Europe and return to vacationing by coach. Cultural sightseeing is the preferred activity—sunbathing is out—and hotels are the preferred type of accommodation.

Other studies have examined the impact of marriage on vacation behavior. They indicate that single people take part in a much wider variety of activities outside the home than do married people. Married life brings about certain changes in leisure habits. Activities that were previously done alone

with friends are participated in less for reasons intrinsic to the activity itself and more for reasons related to the role of being a spouse.

Presence of Children

The narrowing of the types of activities participated in is intensified by the presence of children. When a married couple has children, there is a shift from activities engaged in primarily for intrinsic satisfaction to activities that are role-related, such as family activities. Before children came on the scene, the spouse was the chief leisure companion. This companionship is diluted by the presence of children. The presence of children seems to be crucial. Travel is curtailed; more leisure is spent at home; and few new leisure interests are acquired. In at least one case, that of camping, the onset of parenthood has varied effects. Although the addition of young children in a camping family may produce a curtailment of camping activities, the shift to the empty-nest stage produces either an increase or a decrease in the activity. For those couples who enjoy camping, the situation of children leaving the nest may actually increase their participa-

Family vacations often include activities such as biking. Photo Credit: Robert Holmes.

tion. For others who saw camping primarily as a family activity, the departure of children from the home may result in less camping.

Most research indicates that family vacation decisions are joint between husband and wife. However, at least one study suggests that, when there are children in the home, the wife exerts more influence over the decision-making process and is more likely to seek information on the possible destination choices than when the couple is childless (Fodness, 1992).

Basic attitudes and behavior patterns of family life established in the early years of the family life cycle affect the future activities of both husbands and wives throughout the marriage (Nickerson, Salcone & Aaker, 1995). Activities undertaken in the early stages of the lifespan tend to be repeated throughout life. In addition, the types of vacations taken with parents as a child and during early adulthood serve as a model for future vacations.

For the young child, leisure pursuits are restricted by the dictates of parents and the limitations of money. As children enter school,

leisure activities outside the home increase. As children grow older, their leisure habits and attitudes are more heavily influenced by their peers. Because of the high rate of social interaction among young people, leisure fads are easily spread. There is also at this stage an attempt to duplicate the behavior and attitudes of older age groups. Particularly important in this respect are college students, who tend to be leaders, often being the first to try new products and services.

Empty Nesters

As children leave the home, more time and money tend to be available for leisure. Some studies indicate that, in the U.S., travel patterns change significantly after age 60. Up until that time, auto travel is the favored mode of transportation. After that point, travel by bus, plane, or boat is preferred. This can be explained by an increase in available time and money and, perhaps, a reduction in physical abilities.

The empty nesters left behind have been the subject of a focus

group study conducted by Plog Research (undated). A focus group consists of a small group of people, usually ten to twelve, getting together for a two-hour discussion. The groups are made up of individuals who have already been screened through questionnaires and interviews to arrive at a group that has members similar to one another in background. The discussion is led by a psychologist who attempts to develop a picture of the needs, interests, and personal psychologies of the group. The findings of the study are revealing. The typical empty nester doesn't think of extended trips by air, especially to foreign destinations. Their thinking is geared to the kinds of trips taken with their children; trips which have typically involved travel by car and visits to friends and relatives. There appears to be a strong desire for travel experiences as a means of self-actualization. Several barriers present themselves. The surface barriers of lack of time and money are true up to a point. For couples who work, scheduling may be a problem, and there is a reluctance toward using all of one's vacation time at once. Financially, although more discretionary income may be available, many empty nesters feel uncomfortable in spending their money on an intangible, such as travel. In addition, they tend to believe that the cost of a trip is more expensive than it really is, estimating the cost at twice the actual one. More than anything, however, they express fear as a barrier to traveling. They are afraid of not knowing how to act in a new environment, of being taken advantage of. In a more subtle way, they feel that travel may be a way for them to learn how to be a couple again. Combined with this, however, is the fear that they may discover that they really do not like each other.

It is necessary to understand the particular inhibiting factors felt by each of these market segments at each stage of the family life cycle in order to be able to offer a product or service that will overcome the barriers and induce purchase behavior. For the empty nesters, for example, a tour would be very appropriate. A package tour relieves the participants of making decisions they may feel inadequate to make. The regular tour may have a negative connotation for them, however. Empty nesters usually want to spend more time in fewer places than many tours offer. Popular kinds of destinations are those that help the empty nesters find their roots. This appeals to the need to give some meaning to their lives. The tour also helps alleviate some of the fears of being a couple again with no children around. The fact that there are other people around means that the empty nesters do not have to rely totally upon each other for companionship and support during the trip.

Barriers to Leisure Enjoyment

The barriers to leisure enjoyment have been the subject of study by Witt & Goodale (1981). They iden-tified the relationship between various barriers to the enjoyment of leisure and stages in the family life cycle. Understanding these barriers is a crucial step toward knowing what to say, do, and offer to lower those barriers. It was found that the different patterns of change developed over the family life cycle relative to the barriers under discussion. Figure 1.7 illustrates the fact that various barriers (see table 1.6) showed an approximately U-shaped pattern, with the barriers having the least effect when the youngest child was between six and eighteen years of age.

These barriers refer to difficulties in knowing which activities to get involved with and with whom to share participation. This suggests that as children reach school age, parents have more knowledge of what is available and how to utilize those opportunities. It may also be, as mentioned earlier, that their leisure activities are more closely defined for them by the expectation of their role as parents of school-age children. The time when the youngest child leaves home appears to be a critical passage relative to

Table 1.6 Barriers Exhibiting a U-Shaped Pattern

Not being sure what activities to be involved in
Not knowing what's going on or what's available
Not being sure how to use available resources
Difficulty in planning and making decisions
Not having anyone to do things with
Not being at ease in social situations
Difficulty in carrying out plans

these barriers, a point made in the earlier discussion of the empty nesters.

A second group of barriers exhibit an inverted U-shaped pattern when expressed over the life cycle of the family (see figure 1.8). During the child-rearing period, family obligations increase significantly for women and, to a similar but lesser degree, for men. This fact and the fact that neither parent feels there is enough free time represent the barriers felt; they increase until children leave the home, and then their effect drops off sharply.

The effect of various barriers has been found to increase as the family goes through various life cycle stages (see figure 1.9). The expectations of family and friends increase for women, but for men they are more constant and less of a limitation over the family life cycle. The feelings of daily stress increase for both sexes as time goes on, while often the feeling of not doing anything stays somewhat constant during the child-rearing stage and increases dramatically when children leave the home. Two other barriers have been analyzed for males only. It has been found that there is an increased effect by males who don't feel fit enough or don't have the physical skills for certain activities. This is reflected

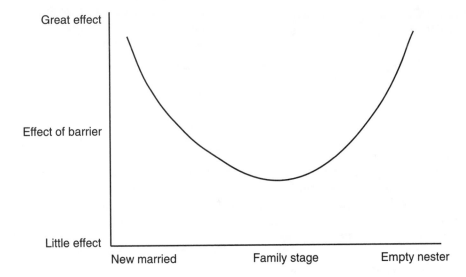

Figure 1.7 Barriers to Leisure Enjoyment at Different Family Stages (U-Shaped Pattern).

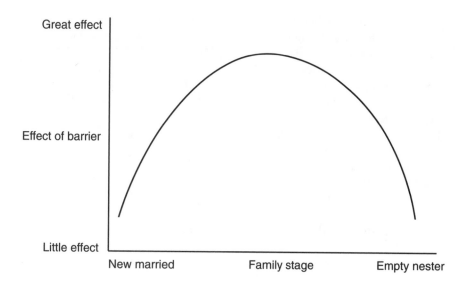

Figure 1.8   Barriers to Leisure Enjoyment at Different Family Stages (Inverted U-Shaped Pattern).

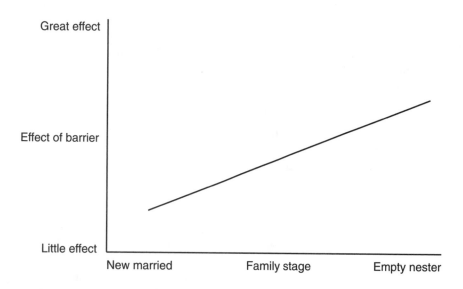

Figure 1.9   Barriers to Leisure Enjoyment at Different Family Stages (U-Shaped Pattern).

in the effect of a falling off in physical skills and fitness levels with age.

Certain points are worthy of note. First, it appears that stages in the family life cycle can help explain and help predict leisure-time behavior. Care must be taken, however, in the use of correlation or regression techniques for projecting or forecasting leisure activities because of the nonlinear pat-

tern of many of these barriers. Second, it is noted that the family life cycle stage can only explain leisure behavior very partially. Third, it is determined that noting which barriers are predominant at various life cycle stages will enable products, packages, and messages to be targeted to reflect an understanding of these barriers and potential objections of the many market segments.

Personality

> "I have found out that there ain't no surer way to find out whether you like people or hate them than to travel with them."
>
> *Mark Twain*

It has been suggested that most people view their vacation as an extension of their personality. Howard and Sheth (1969) have postulated that the effect of personality is felt on two areas—nonspecific motives and the alternatives considered for purchase. They have proposed that the more authoritarian a person is, for example, the fewer alternatives that will have to be considered in arriving at a purchase decision. The relationship between personality and nonspecific motives has been explored by various researchers in an attempt to understand existing behavior better and predict future behavior with greater accuracy.

The personality of an individual can be described as "the summation of the characteristics that make the person what he or she is and (that) distinguish each individual from every other individual" (Walters, 1978). It is logical that there is a link between the type of person one is and the type of purchases one makes: A conservative person will tend to make conservative purchases.

Personality Traits

Personality can be thought of as consisting of a variety of traits. Individuals who participate in recreational and tourist activities can be typed in terms of their personality traits in an attempt to determine whether such participants exhibit markedly different personality traits than do non-participants. The purpose of such analysis is to determine whether or not personality can be used as a variable for segmenting the market. If it is found

Quick Trip 1.6
Family Travelers

According to Dennis Marzella, senior vice president of research and strategic marketing for Yesawich, Pepperdine & Brown, the increase in family travel is, in part, explained by the fact that most people see the family as the main source of "all or most of the happiness found in life." This also goes along with research indicating renewed interest in values such as simplifying one's life and spending money on experiences rather than things.

The number of two-parent, married-couple homes with children increased by 700,000 from 1990 to1995. Thirty percent of adults take at least one vacation with children a year. The influence of children in the planning of a vacation is seen by the number of adults—more than half—who say that children are influential in the selection of a destination and who agree that they are willing to take their children out of school to take a family vacation.

Much of the motivation may be as a result of guilt from not spending enough time with the family.

Question:

1. According to Peter Yesawich, "The biggest challenge to travel marketers is the persistent decline in message credibility, including advertising . . . as it becomes easier to reach people, it also becomes more difficult to influence them." Bearing in mind the high ethical standards that are particularly important when marketing toward children, how do travel marketers approach the family segment?

Source: Research Shows Increase in Family Travel. *Hotel and Motel Management.* (May 6, 1996) 40.

---

that certain personality traits are dominant in winter vacations, marketers will know better the kind of tourist to appeal to and will gain valuable information as to what to say to appeal to this potential vacationer. To date, the research evidence is inconclusive as to whether or not personality is a significant variable in explaining purchase behavior. Although several studies indicate a strong relationship between personality and consumer behavior, and a few indicate no relationship, the great majority indicate that any existing correlation is weak.

The relationship between personality and participation in recreational activities is also of interest. As we have seen, recreational activities can serve as a major reason or motivation for vacation travel. If a relationship between certain activities and certain personality traits can be established, an appropriate marketing strategy can be developed.

Personality Types

Often a person is described as having a certain type of personality. Personality types consist of characteristics that, when taken together, form a certain kind of person. One way of typing people is to the extent that they are perceived as being *introverted* or *extroverted*. Introverts look into themselves and troverts tend to be shy and reserved. Extroverts are other-oriented, looking outside the self, and tending to be objective rather than subjective in outlook. Participants in vigorous physical activity in general tend to be extroverts. In fact, outdoor recreational activities in general are not participated in by introverted personality types.

Psychographics and Lifestyle

The application of studies of personality to the business world has been hampered because the terminology of personality has come from clinical sources. Psychographics has developed as a way of describing consumer behavior in terms of a distinctive way of living in order to determine whether or not people with distinctive lifestyles have distinctive travel behaviors. Psychographics is the development of psychological profiles of consumers and psychologically based measures of distinctive modes of living or lifestyles.

Stanley Plog developed a model in the 1970s that is designed to explain the types of destinations chosen by people based upon their psychographic characteristics. According to the model, travelers can be described based upon their place on an allocentric/psychocentric continuum. Allocentrics prefer traveling independently to destinations that have few tourists while psychocentrics prefer to vacation with tour groups and travel to well-developed tourist regions. Allocentrics tend to be slightly wealthier, more adventurous, extroverted and self-confident, travel more, spend more time away from home, and traveled more as a child (Plog, 1991). Plog estimates that 4 percent of the U.S. population are pure allocentric while 2½ percent are pure psychocentric. The remainder of the population exists along the continuum as ***near-allocentrics***, ***mid-centrics***, and near ***psychocentrics***. The personality characteristics used to describe these individuals are represented by three dominant personality traits: territory boundedness, generalized anxieties, and a sense of powerlessness (Griffith & Albanese, 1996). To this, Plog has added an energy dimension that ranges from high energy to low energy or lethargy (see figure 1.10). Psychocentrics tend to be described as being territory bound, experiencing general anxieties, a sense of powerlessness and low energy. The opposite extreme would be true for allocentrics. The theories underlying Plog's model suggest that, while specific destination choices will vary over time, the general types of destinations chosen will remain relatively stable. Personality traits tend to be learned as children and remain consistent as the individual matures.

While some researchers have been unable to replicate Plog's findings, others have found support for the concept within a student population and among visitors and non-visitors to museums (Salcone &

Nickerson, 1995). Travel agents might use this concept to suggest better alternative destinations for their clients. Instead of immediately asking for destination preferences, they could ask about previous vacation behavior and examine issues relating to the client's likely place on the allocentric-psychocentric scale. As a result they would be in a position to suggest better alternatives to their clients.

The most widely recognized use of this segmentation method is the **VALS *system***. VALS stands for Values And Life Styles and is a copyrighted, syndicated lifestyle study conducted by SRI International (formerly the Stanford Research Institute). It divided Americans into nine lifestyles or types, which are grouped in four categories based on their self-images, aspirations, values and beliefs, and the products they use. It is possible for people to move from one category to another as they grow and mature.

Survivors and Sustainers make up the Need-Driven category. Survivors are struggling to survive.

They seek to satisfy basic and immediate needs. Sustainers are struggling, but they are hopeful. They are the least satisfied with their financial status and the most anxious to get ahead economically.

The Outer-Directed Groups are middle America. They are very concerned about how they appeal to others, and their lives are influenced by others' perceptions of them. The largest group is the Belongers. They are uncomplicated, conservative, conventional, and lead comfortable lives. They are highly conforming and extremely patriotic. They are older, heavily female, have little college education, and are slightly below average income.

While Belongers are satisfied, Emulators are trying to make it and become the second largest group. Its members are successful, happy, hardworking, self-reliant, and wealthy. There are proportionately more men who are well-educated with careers in managerial or professional occupations.

Approximately 20 percent of the population are what are called Inner-Directed. The basic rewards of life for them are internal and emotional rather than external and materialistic. The I-Am-Me's are young, typically single, and confused. They are fiercely independent. The Experientials are the most inner-directed of any group. They actively seek direct experience, personal involvement, and a sense of inner growth. They are young, well-educated, artistic, and attracted to the exotic, the strange, and the natural. The Societally Conscious group is made up of individuals who are self-assured and well-off. They stress conservation, simplicity, and environmental concerns.

The Integrated Group makes up the Combined Outer- and Inner-Directed Category. This small group has it all together. They are self-assured, self-actualized, self-expres-

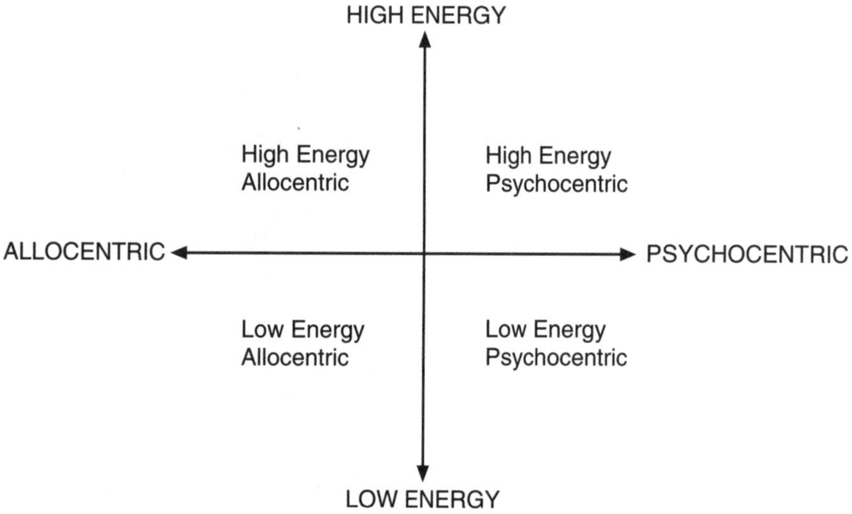

HIGH ENERGY

High Energy Allocentric   High Energy Psychocentric

ALLOCENTRIC ←→ **PSYCHOCENTRIC**

Low Energy Allocentric   Low Energy Psychocentric

LOW ENERGY

Figure 1.10   Allocentrism/Psychocentrism and Energy Dimensions.

Source: N.P. Nickerson & G.D. Ellis, Traveler types and activation theory: A comparison of two models, *Journal of Travel Research*, Vol. 29, No. 3. (Winter 1991) 26.

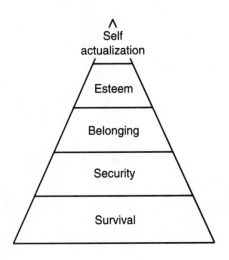
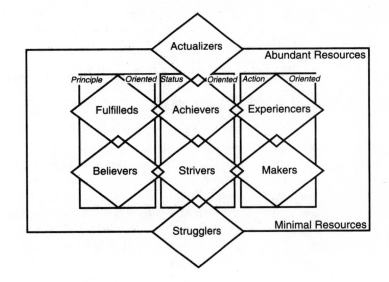

Figure 1.11   Comparison of Maslow and VALS Schemes. © 1995 SRI International. All rights reserved. Unauthorized reproduction prohibited.

sive, and have a global perspective on issues.

There is a similarity between the VALS typology and **Maslow's hierarchy of needs** outlined in chapter 2. This similarity is illustrated in figure 1.11. The Survivors correspond to Maslow's survival needs, while security needs are most important for the Sustainers. Belongers are principally concerned with belonging or love, while the Achievers and Emulators

focus on the need for esteem. Self-Actualization is the focus for those who are Integrated, in addition to part of the Societally Conscious group.

Specific implications for travel and tourism are illustrated in table 1.7. The most important segments for tourism are Achievers, Societally Conscious, and to a lesser extent, Experientials. Achievers travel frequently for both business and pleasure. They prefer luxury hotels

and like to stay at resorts when on vacation. Of all the groups, Achievers are most likely to indulge themselves when on vacation. They tend to prefer independent travel, but they will take tours if it is the most convenient way to see the country. They enjoy traveling with their families and are most likely to travel with their spouses on a vacation trip. While on vacation they like to unwind and do not feel compelled to do anything.

Table 1.7   Travel Habits by Lifestyle

	SURVIVORS	SUSTAINERS	BELONGERS	EMULATORS	ACHIEVERS	I-AM-ME	EXPE-RIENTIALS	SOCIETALLY CONSCIOUS
Pleasure Travel								
Travel by air	—	—					+	+
Stay at hotels/motels	—	—			+			+
Use rental car	—				+			+
Use travel agent	—	—			+			+
Travel abroad					+	+	+	
Business Travel								
Travel by air	—	—	—		+			+
Stays at hotels/motels	—	—		—	+		+	+
Use rental car					+			+
Use travel agent					+			+

Note: A plus sign (+) indicates that people in a given group participate in the activity more than ten percentage points above the average of all the VALS groups; a minus (–) indicates participation ten or more percentage points under average.

Source: Compiled by Shih based on Mitchell, *The Nine American Lifestyles*. Reprinted with permission of Macmillan Publishing Co.

Quick Trip 1.7
Do People Undergo a Personality Change on Vacation?

According to Mary Jane Rolfs, she spends her vacation each year with a "slim, handsome man, dashingly dressed, debonair, witty, extravagant, worldly, impulsive and multi-lingual." Ricardo, for that is the name she gives him, is unlike her husband, Daniel, who suffers from chronic indigestion, is totally predictable and is reluctant to try anything new. Yet, they are one and the same person. The difference in Daniel's demeanor and behavior begins to show itself when the time comes to plan the annual vacation.

While Daniel is very practical about getting walking shoes broken in weeks before the trip, Ricardo hates to make hotel reservations in advance because "that might stifle a sudden impulse to leap off the train in some picturesque walled town in Spain."

The metamorphosis is completed at the airport as Daniel realizes that he has forgotten the raincoat bought especially for the trip. Suddenly, Ricardo takes over, "I'll pick one up in Paris." While Daniel would remind his spouse that they do not have unlimited funds, Ricardo, overcharged for two bottles of wine in a nightclub, responds, "It was worth it to hear authentic fado." They eat things and go places Daniel wouldn't think of. They eat "roasted sparrows, drink ouzo, taste eels and stare at the riches in palaces and museums." While at home they argue constantly about silly things, on the road they do not quarrel about anything for, if they did, "we would have no one to talk to. We are alone, the two of us, without friends or enemies or influence. We can neither escape from each other nor do without each other."

At the airport as they are set to return, Daniel slowly come back. ". . . maybe we better hang on to it (the last traveler's check). We might just have to pay duty on some of this stuff—you don't really want to buy anything do you? . . . I'll be awfully glad to eat some fried chicken the way you make it . . . I suppose the batteries in the cars are dead. I'll take care of that first thing tomorrow."

As Rolfs says, "Ricardo is fun to travel with but you wouldn't want to live with him."

Questions:

1. What does this article tell us about the personality and travel?

2. Do people live more in the two weeks they spend on vacation than in the other fifty weeks of the year?

3. What implications does this have for those developing tourism?

Source: M.J. Rolfs. The man I travel with is not at all like my husband. *New York Times.* (October 13, 1974) 8 XX.

Travel is very important for the Societally Conscious. They travel a great deal and look forward to it. They would rather spend their time and money on travel than on almost anything else. They take longer trips than any other group and get a great deal of pleasure from planning the trip. Having done extensive research and received personal recommendations from friends, and ideas from travel articles, they are the best prepared upon arrival at the destination and may, therefore, be the most difficult to please. They tend to distrust both advertising and travel agents. They prefer off-the-beaten-track vacation spots and, once there, are self-reliant, adventurous, and price conscious. The Societally Conscious are comfortable traveling alone. They explore, try new and unusual foods, like to experience the culture, and value the educational aspects of travel. They tend to avoid guided tours, chain hotels, and other tourists.

Differences can be expected when specific destinations are considered. The visitors to Pennsylvania, for example, consist largely of Achievers, Belongers, and Societally Conscious.

These three same types accounted for the bulk of travelers to Hong Kong. Each segment of the market, however, had travel patterns different enough to justify separate marketing action plans. The existing marketing program, based on the upscale traveler was on-target for the Achievers but needed adaptation for the Belongers and the Societally Conscious. This latter group was not as well represented as it should have been. The problem was that this group perceived Hong Kong as a tour destination where independent travel was not as readily available as they would prefer. This finding led to changes in the way the message was communicated to this group.

The Belongers who travel to Hong Kong are mainly wives or widows of Achievers. Belongers prefer to travel domestically, most likely with their spouses or friends. On vacation, they are structured and cautious. They need to feel assured. They often select all-inclusive tours, staying in chain hotels. They are the least likely to indulge themselves when on vacation. To appeal to this group, the advertising message was changed to emphasize the fact that Hong Kong is more suited to their tastes than European cities. English is spoken, it is easy to get around, and the water is drinkable. Savings on shopping would probably be a good idea, as well.

Segmenting the market in this way also has implications for where to advertise. Achievers, for example, are not big TV watchers but are interested in magazine and newspaper reading.

It has been shown that lifestyles vary according to different socioeconomic variables. Although it is beneficial to segment a market on the basis of lifestyle dimensions for marketing purposes, it is necessary to identify the socioeconomic characteristics of these segments in order to reach the target markets effectively.

Summary

The vacation choices that people make are influenced by, and often constrained by, various factors external to them. The culture of which they are a part and the significant events that helped shape their values all act to determine, in part, when, where, and how they will vacation. The time available also determines if and where people will travel. Developments in paid vacations, as well as advances in technology, have enabled people to take a vacation and have influenced how far they can go with the amount of free time they have.

Demographic and psychographic factors also shape the vacation decision. Early attempts to explain vacation behavior using demographics alone have been found to be incomplete. A full understanding of travel purchases comes from a consideration of both.

Certain attractions, like zoos and theme parks, are more popular with families in the earlier life-cycle stages: The zoo in Budapest, Hungary. Photo from *Budapest in 101 Photos; Multimedia CD for the IBM PC* (Selester, Hungary, 1996). Printed with permission.

Exercise

The Sunshine Seekers: German Travelers to Florida, the Caribbean, and Mexico

Data were collected in a study funded jointly by the (then) U.S. Travel and Tourism Administration and Tourism Canada of Germans who had taken overseas vacations in the previous three years to Florida, the Caribbean, or Mexico. Three market segments were identified based on activities undertaken while on vacation: Relaxed Vacationers (22.3 percent), Community Visitors (42 percent), and Enthusiasts (34.5 percent).

Based upon the profiles in tables 1 through 4, what would you recommend to tourism authorities in Florida, the Caribbean, and Mexico seeking to attract this market?

Table 1   Summary of Characteristics of Activity Cluster Segments

ACTIVITY CLUSTERS	SOCIODEMOGRAPHIC	TRAVEL CHARACTERISTICS
Relaxed Visitors	Age: 45–54 (21%) Income: 32% make between 39,000–52,000 DM a year Junior high educated: 43% Female: 39% Married: 56% Professional/technical worker: 21%	57% stayed between 17–29 days on trip 46% traveled with one companion 54% took a package vacation 43% were on a resort trip
Community Visitors	Age: 45–54 (32%) Income: 25% make between 39,000–52,000 DM a year Junior high educated: 32% Female: 52% Married: 47% Professional/technical worker: 40%	46% stayed between 17–29 days on trip 42% were in parties of two 66% took a package vacation 62% were on a resort trip
Enthusiasts	Age: 45–54 (43%) Income: 40% make between 39,000–52,000 DM a year Junior high educated: 41% Female: 56% Married: 76% Professional/technical worker: 39%	56% stayed between 17–29 days on trip 54% were in parties of two 63% took a package vacation 44% were on a resort trip

Table 2 Selected Activity Participation Rates for Cluster Segments

	CLUSTER SEGMENTS		
ACTIVITY	RELAXED VISITORS (%)	ENTHUSIASTS (%)	COMMUNITY VISITORS (%)
Attending festivals/events	14	49	42
Getting to know inhabitants	46	97	64
Restaurants/dining out	43	88	88
Short guided excursions	21	54	58
Golfing/tennis	4	10	18
Sampling local foods	25	76	82
Shopping	46	93	76
Sightseeing in cities	21	93	80
Sunbathing/beach	46	83	66
Swimming	57	85	82
Taking pictures	54	88	84
Tour countryside	21	80	74
Visiting wilderness areas	11	59	12
Visiting amusement/theme parks	25	63	14
Visiting casinos/gambling	0	27	2
Visiting national parks/forests	18	46	0
Visiting entertaining places	4	32	42
Visiting seaside	25	90	48
Visiting historic places	14	78	34
Visiting commemorative places	7	63	24
Visiting archaeological places	14	51	24
Visiting scenic landmarks	36	98	54
Participating in water sports	7	32	32
Taking a day cruise	11	27	16

Reprinted by permission of the Travel and Tourism Research Association.

Table 3 Average Ranking of Selected Benefits Sought by Segments

	CLUSTER SEGMENTS		
BENEFIT	RELAXED VISITORS	ENTHUSIASTS	COMMUNITY VISITORS
Getting away from the demands of home	2.6	2.9	3.1
Seeing as much as possible	2.9	3.2*	2.8
Experiencing new and different lifestyles	3.2	3.3	3.3
Trying new foods	2.8	3.0	2.9
Traveling through places that are important in history	2.9	3.2*	2.7
Finding thrills and excitement	2.8	3.0	3.1
Traveling to places where I feel safe and secure	2.6	2.6	2.9
Having fun, being entertained	2.8	2.9	3.1
Getting a change from a busy job	3.0	3.1	3.2
Learning new things, increasing one's knowledge	3.2	3.2	3.1
Doing nothing at all	3.0	2.4*	3.0
Being free to act the way I feel	3.0	33.2	3.3
Escaping from the ordinary	2.8	3.2*	3.0
Indulging in luxury	2.7	2.3	2.6
Feeling at home away from home	2.8	2.6	2.8
Being daring and adventuresome	3.0	3.0	3.0

Note: Rating scale: 4 = strongly agree, 3 = agree somewhat, 2 = disagree somewhat, 1 = strongly agree

*Significantly different from other segments when rating this item. Significance level at p = 0.05.

Reprinted by permission of the Travel and Tourism Research Association.

Table 4   Average Rating of Travel Philosophy by Segments

| | CLUSTER SEGMENTS | | |
TRAVEL PHILOSOPHY	RELAXED VISITORS	ENTHUSIASTS	COMMUNITY VISITORS
Have things arranged before trip	3.2	3.0	3.0
Choose places already been to	2.1	1.8	1.9
Don't like to stay put at the destination	2.1*	3.0*	2.5*
Like different places on each vacation	2.8	3.0	2.9
Choose places friends have been to	2.6	2.3	2.5
Important that people speak my language	2.4*	2.0	2.0
Use travel agent to decide place	3.0	2.9	3.0
Prefer guided tour on vacation	2.7	2.7	2.8
Like to travel from place to place on vacation	2.4	2.9*	2.4
Usually travel on all-inclusive vacation	2.8	2.5	2.4
Value for vacation money is important	3.0	3.2	3.4*
Don't have a lot of money to spend	2.9	2.6	2.6
Don't have to travel to enjoy vacation	2.6*	2.2	2.3
Safety is important when choosing overseas vacation destination	3.1	3.1	3.3

Note: Rating scale: 4 = strongly agree, 3 = agree somewhat, 2 = disagree somewhat, 1 = strongly agree

*Significantly different from other segments when rating this item. Significance level at p = 0.05.

Source: "The Sunshine Seekers: German Travelers to Florida, the Caribbean, and Mexico," proceedings of the 25th Annual Conference of the Travel and Tourism Research Association, 1994, 106–115.

Reprinted by permission of the Travel and Tourism Research Association.

References

Bennett, P.D., & Kassasjian, H. J. (1982). *Consumer behavior*. Englewood Cliffs, NJ: Prentice-Hall, Inc., 123.

(September 8, 1996). *Denver Post*, 8G.

Dunn, W. (1993). *1994 outlook for generation X/baby busters*. Proceedings of the 1994 Outlook for Travel and Tourism. Washington, DC: Travel Industry Association of America, 83–86.

Ferraro, G.P. (1990). *The cultural dimension of international business*. Englewood Cliffs, NJ: Prentice-Hall, Inc., 94.

Fodness, D. (1992). The impact of family life cycle on the vacation decision-making process. *Journal of Travel Research*, 31 (2), 8–13.

Griffith, D.A., & Albanese, P.J. (1996). An examination of Plog's psychographic travel model within a student population. *Journal of Travel Research*, 34 (4), 47–51.

Hofstede, G. (1985). *The cultural perspective*. People and Organizations Interacting, Edited by Art Brakel. New York: John Wiley & Sons, Inc.

(Undated). *Increasing your sales to new and existing markets*. Plog Research, Inc.

Jurowski, C., & Walker, G. (1995). *Personal values and environmental attitudes effect on pleasure trip preferences*. Proceedings of the 26th annual conference of the Travel and Tourism Research Association, 193–199.

Kaynak, E., Kara, A., Kucukemiroglu, O., & Dalgic, T. (1995). *Salient attributes lead to travel preferences: Irish travelers*. Proceedings of the 26th Annual Conference of the Travel and Tourism Research Association, 246–253.

Louden, D.L., & Britta, A.J.D. (1979). *Consumer behavior: Concepts and applications*. New York: McGraw-Hill Book Co., 135–139.

Nickerson, N.P., Salcone, M.L., & Aaker, S.R. (1995). Life-span travel patterns. *Proceedings of the 26th Annual Conference of the Travel and Tourism Research Association*, 4 (1), 406–411.

(July–August 1990). *Nine forces reshaping America*. The Futurist, 9–16.

Oppermann, M. (1995). Family life cycle and cohort effects: A study of travel patterns of German residents. *Journal of Travel & Tourism Marketing*, 4 (1), 23–44.

Plog, S.C. (1991). *Leisure travel market: Making it a growth market . . . again!* New York: John Wiley & Sons, Inc.

Salcone, M.L., & Nickerson, N.P. (1995). *Psychographic differences in visitors and non-visitors: A case of El Ranco de las Golondrinas.* Proceedings of 26th Annual Conference of the Travel and Tourism Research Association, 203–206.

Schor, J.B. (1991). *The overworked American: The unexpected decline of leisure.* New York: Basic Books.

Shields, H. (1986). *Cross-cultural differences among international travelers: A market segment probe.* Paper presented at the 17th annual conference of the Travel and Tourism Research Association.

(1988). *Highlights of Discover America 2000.* U.S. Travel Data Center. Washington, DC: Travel Industry Association of America, 5–6.

(October 3, 1990). *Wall Street Journal.*

Walters, C.G. (1978). *Consumer behavior: Theory and practice.* Homewood, IL: Richard D. Irwin, Inc., 296.

Williams, P.W., & Lattey, C. (Fall 1994). Skiing constraints for women. *Journal of Travel Research*, 33 (2), 21–25.

Witt, P.A., & Goodale, T.L. (1981). The relationship between barriers to leisure enjoyment and family stages. *Leisure Sciences.* 4 (1), 29–49.

Additional Reading

"The Cultural Process," Geert Hofstede, in *People and Organizations Interacting,* Aat Brakel, ed., John Wiley & Sons, Inc., New York, NY, 1985.

Leisure Policies in Europe, P. Bramham, I.P. Henry, H. Mommass, and H. van der Poel, eds., University of Arizona Press, 1230 North Park Avenue, Tucson, AZ 85719, 1993.

Managing Cultural Differences Philip R. Harris and Robert T. Moran, Gulf Publishing Company, 1985.

Sociology of Leisure Joffre Dumzedier, Elsevier Scientific Publishing Company, 1974.

World Class Service Germaine W. Shames and W. Gerald Glover, Intercultural Press, Inc., Yarmouth, Maine, 1989.

"Travel is motivated by "going away from" rather than "going towards" something or somebody. To shake off the everyday situation is much more important than the interest in visiting new places and people . . . travelers' motives and behavior are markedly self-oriented: Now I decide what is on and it should be good for me."

Jost Krippendorf, The Holiday Makers

2

Why Do People Take Vacations?

···Needs, Wants, and Motivation ························

Purpose

Based upon an understanding of what motivates people to travel, students will be able to suggest vacation products and communications that will appeal to tourist needs and wants.

Learning Objectives

Having read this chapter, you should be able to:

1. Realize that the key to understanding why people travel is to view travel as a satisfier of needs and wants.

2. Explain, and give appropriate examples of, the role of travel marketers in motivating people to take vacations.

3. Suggest strategies to combat people's given reasons for not taking vacations.

4. Describe how past vacation experiences influence future vacation decisions.

Overview

The reasons people give for taking vacations are insufficient to explain their travel motivations. In order to market to potential visitors and to serve them at their destinations, it is essential to understand the underlying needs that visitors wish to satisfy when considering a vacation. Vacation behavior is, in fact, determined by such things as motivation, perception, learning, and attitudes—factors that are themselves influenced by personality, culture, and society.

This chapter explores tourism as a satisfier of needs and wants. The relationship between lists in travel literature showing reasons for pleasure travel and Maslow's hierarchy of needs is developed.

Some people hypothesize that people travel if they have learned that travel for a particular reason will help satisfy various needs and wants considered important to them, and if they perceive that, then their needs and wants will be satisfied within the constraints of such things as time, money, and social pressure.

Taking a "surfing vacation" might be a way to not only spend time surfing, but also a way to spend time with friends. Photo from *Top Shots* CD Rom. Courtesy of Queensland Tourist and Travel Corporation.

Importance of Motivation

> "Often I go to some distant region of the world to be reminded of who I really am. There is no mystery about why this should be so. Stripped of your ordinary surroundings, your friends, your daily routines . . . you are forced into direct experience. Such direct experience inevitably makes you aware of who it is that is having the experience. That is not always comfortable, but it is always invigorating."
>
> Michael Crichton, 1988

Why do people take vacations? To date, studies of motivations have concentrated on developing lists of the reasons why people travel. A variety of studies report that people travel, for example, to view scenery, learn about other cultures, or visit friends and relatives. One study of North American ecotourists, for example, notes the following "motivations" for experienced ecotourism travelers: scenery/nature; new experiences/places; wildlife viewing; wilderness; uncrowded (Wright, 1996). This approach to understanding motivation is insufficient for two reasons. First, the visitors themselves may be unaware of the true reasons behind their travel behavior. Individuals are often unaware of the real reasons for doing certain things. A person leaving for a tennis vacation may see the trip as simply a reason to play tennis. When questioned, however, the traveler may reveal that a concern for his or her health prompted the trip. Secondly, a person may not wish to divulge the real reason or motivation behind the trip. For instance, much of the literature mentions "status" as a motivator, yet many travelers will not feel comfortable admitting that a major reason for taking a vacation is that they will be able to impress their friends upon their return home. A third reason that such lists are insufficient for explaining consumer motivations is that they concentrate on selling the product, the stated reason for the trip, rather than on satisfying the needs of the market. But the development of such lists is a necessary first step toward establishing a classification system that will enable us to understand and ultimately predict the visitor's decision-making process.

Dann (1977) noted two stages in a travel decision: *push factors* and *pull factors*. Push factors are internal to the individual, install a *desire* for travel, and are aimed at satisfying various psychological needs. Pull factors are external to the individual, stress benefits of particular destinations, and determine where, when, and how that person vacations. Thus push factors must be present before pull factors can be effective.

Crompton (1979) identified seven push motives and two pull factors. The push factors were only identified after an in-depth inter-

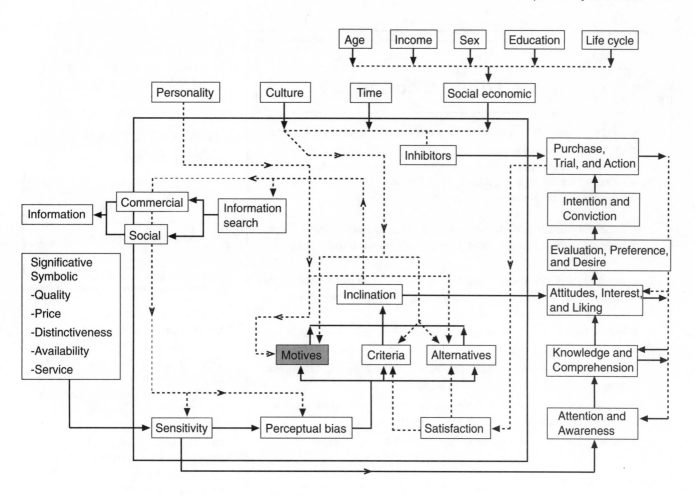

view. (This gives further support to the argument that visitors may be unaware of what motivates them.) They are escape from a mundane environment; exploration and evaluation of self; relaxation; prestige; regression; enhancement of kinship relationships; and facilitation of social interaction. The pull factors are novelty and education.

A study of German tourists (Jamrozy, 1992) examined the importance of various push and pull factors. Five market segments were identified: lone travelers, couples, families, friends, and an organized tour group. It was found that most of the variations between market segments occurred within the push factors that motivated the tourists as distinct from the pull factors that explained the attributes they were looking for. For example, the escape factor is very important for those traveling alone, couples, and friends and less so for tour groups. This latter segment is also less motivated by family and friends togetherness than were couples. Prestige is most important to people traveling as friends. Another study of German tourists found that the ordering and importance of both push and pull factors varies across destinations (Turnbull & Uysal, 1995). For Caribbean vacations, warm weather, beaches, and a relaxed atmosphere are important while the visitor to Latin America is more interested in culture.

There is some indication that the relative importance of push and pull factors varies by culture. In one study (Yuan & McDonald, 1990) a comparison was made of tourists from four countries: the United Kingdom, Japan, France, and Germany. It was found that both the motivation to travel (push factors) and the specific destination chosen (pull factors) were a product of the culture tourists were from. While the rankings between the motivation factors are similar—novelty and escape are ranked one and two for all four segments—the level of importance attached to the factors varies somewhat (see table 2.1). Tourists from France and the United Kingdom give it more importance than do those from Japan and Germany. This suggests that the stress placed on this factor should vary depending upon the country being marketed to. The pull factors are indicated in table 2.2. While the rankings for tourists from the United Kingdom and Japan are the same, several differences are evident in looking at responses of people from the other countries. For example, those from

Quick Trip 2.1
The More Things Change . . .

In 1980 *Psychology Today* conducted a survey of its readers' vacation behavior. While it is not suggested that the readers of this magazine are representative of the U.S. population as a whole, it is interesting to compare the motivation for taking a vacation then and now.

The survey identified six vacation needs:

● Relieving the tension: 37 percent said relaxation, time off for rest, recharging tired batteries, and getting renewed were the most popular motives.

● Intellectual enrichment: 18 percent emphasized learning, seeking intellectual or spiritual enrichment, investigating places they have never seen, or discovering their roots.

● Family togetherness: 13 percent took vacations to be with family, get to know their kids better, or visit friends and relatives.

● Exotic adventure: 12 percent sought excitement, exotic adventure, danger, new friends, and sexual escapades.

● Self-discovery: 11 percent preferred being alone and used vacations to solve personal problems or just enjoy themselves.

● Escape: 8 percent wanted to escape routine and get a tan.

Questions:

1. To what extent do you think this list is representative of the U.S. population when it was taken? What do you think the differences are?

2. To what extent is this list representative of the U.S. population today? Of your generation?

Source: "Vacations: Expectations, Satisfactions, Frustrations, Fantasies," C. Rubenstein *Psychology Today.* (May 1980) 62–76.

Germany place less importance on culture and history while respondents from France find ease of travel to be of less importance.

Travel as a Need/ Want Satisfier

"Seventy-two hours seems to be the maximum time people can stay together without friction developing."

Dr. Joyce Brothers, quoted in The New York Times

The key to understanding tourist motivation is to see vacation travel as a satisfier of needs and wants. Tourists do not take vacations just to relax and have fun, experience another culture, or educate themselves and their children. They take vacations in the hope and belief that these vacations will satisfy, either wholly or partially, various needs and wants. This view of tourist motivations is critical. It is the difference between seeing a destination as a collection of palm trees and hotel rooms for the tourist and seeing it as a means for satisfying what is important to tourists. It is the difference between those travel agents who see themselves as sellers of airline seats and those who view themselves as dealers in dreams.

Table 2.1   Means and Ranks of Push Factors

PUSH FACTORS	UNITED KINGDOM		JAPAN		FRANCE		GERMANY	
	MEAN	RANK	MEAN	RANK	MEAN	RANK	MEAN	RANK
Escape	2.24	(*)2	2.3	2	1.94	2	2.01	2
Novelty	1.72	1	1.93	1	1.69	1	1.89	1
Prestige	2.48	4	2.8	3	2.55	3	2.43	3
Enhancement of kinship relationships	2.46	3	3.05	4	2.69	4	2.87	5
Relaxation/hobbies	2.83	5	3.13	5	2.76	5	2.67	4

(*) Means based on a four-point Likert scale labeled 1 = very important, 2 = somewhat important, 3 = not very important, 4 = not at all important.

Source: Yuan & McDonald (1990).

Table 2.2   Means and Ranks of Pull Factors

PULL FACTORS	UNITED KINGDOM		JAPAN		FRANCE		GERMANY	
	MEAN	RANK	MEAN	RANK	MEAN	RANK	MEAN	RANK
Budget	1.78	(*)1	1.79	1	1.83	1	1.90	1
Culture and history	2.10	3	2.09	3	1.94	2	2.23	4
Wilderness	2.18	4	2.27	4	1.95	3	2.19	3
Ease of travel	1.85	2	1.84	2	2.01	4	2.01	2
Cosmopolitan environment	2.66	5	2.62	5	2.79	5	2.79	6
Facilities	2.87	6	2.69	6	2.81	6	2.66	5
Hunting	3.71	7	3.53	7	3.35	7	3.42	7

(*) Means based on a four-point Likert scale labeled 1 = very important, 2 = somewhat important, 3 = not very important, 4 = not at all important.

Source: Yuan & McDonald (1990).

A Model of Buyer Behavior

Several researchers have suggested that tourism managers do not make sufficient use of buyer behavior models to assist them in understanding how and why people make vacation purchase decisions. The advantage of such a model is that it helps managers approach the task of influencing vacation behavior in a systematic, focused manner. One useful model is that outlined in figure 2.1. The model suggests that stimuli internal to the individual relating to needs and wants is the beginning of the process. Based on external stimuli the potential traveler is aware (or not) of possible destinations. Destination possibilities are then evaluated as to their viability. Travel to that destination is likely if the traveler likes the destination and develops a preference for it. As a result of the trip the traveler learns whether or not that experience did, indeed, satisfy the needs and wants previously identified.

Needs, Wants, and Motives

*"We used to fly airplanes;
Now we fly people."*

Jan Lapidoth, SAS

A description of the process begins with a consideration of the needs of an individual. When an individual takes a trip, buys a cruise, or rents a cabin, the action is done in hopes of satisfying some **need** of which he or she may only be partially aware. We could provide a better service if we could identify which need or

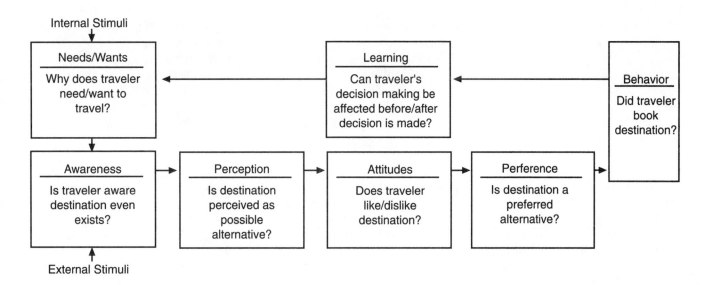

Figure 2.1   Buyer Behavior Model.

Source: K.G. Baker, G.C. Hozier, Jr., and R.D. Rogers, "Marketing Research Theory and Methodology and the Tourism Industry: A Nontechnical Discussion," *Journal of Travel Research*, Vol. 32, No. 3. (Winter 1994) 5.

Quick Trip 2.2
"I Want To Be Alone . . ."

"You get to a point where the last thing you want to see on vacation is other people," sighs a New York investment banker as she sits on the terraced pool patio at the $430 a night Amankila resort on the island of Bali. A growing number of resorts are appealing to this need for privacy. While low on opulence, the resorts feature such personal features as individual villas, private plunge pools and a small number of rooms.

Says the company's founder Adrian Zecha, "We wanted something more personalized, more exclusive. There's nothing pretentious." Waiters leave fruit and champagne at a villa minutes after a guest checks in; gardeners stop trimming bushes as guests appear "allowing nature to be the only distraction."

While other companies have followed the lead of Amanresorts, which operates ten properties in Southeast Asia, some question whether or not a property can make money on the operation. Robert Hutchinson, group director of marketing at Shangri-La Hotels & Resorts, argues that "Amanresorts is not a hotel business; it's a real-estate business which makes money by selling the land around it." Zecha maintains that each resort by itself makes money.

For many people it seems that the formula works. According to Bill Pollock of Cardiff, Wales, "It's rather like buying a Rolls-Royce rather than a Ford. A Rolls-Royce won't take you much farther, but that's not why you buy the car."

Questions:

1. What needs and wants are being satisfied by these vacationers?

2. What kinds of things would induce them to buy such a vacation?

3. What kind of message would appeal to them?

Source: Brady, D. Asian Resorts: Privacy for the Wealthy, *Wall Street Journal.* (May 31, 1996).

---

needs the individual is attempting to satisfy.

A business is not interested so much in a person's needs as in how that person seeks to satisfy those needs. The difference between a need and a **want** is one of awareness. It is the task of the people in marketing to transform needs into wants by making the individual aware of his or her need deficiencies.

A person needs affection, but wants to visit friends and relatives; needs esteem from others, but wants a Mediterranean cruise. In these and other situations people can be made aware through advertisements, for example, that the purchase of an airline ticket to visit parents will result in feelings of love and affection for them, thereby helping satisfy that need.

Although a person may want satisfaction for a need or needs, no action will be taken until that person is motivated.

Motivation occurs when an individual wants to satisfy a need. A motive implies action; an individual is moved to do something. Motivation theories indicate that an individual constantly strives to achieve a state of stability—a *homeostasis*. An individual's homeostasis is disrupted when she or he is made aware of a need deficiency. This awareness creates wants. For the individual to be motivated to satisfy a need, an *objective* must be present. The individual must be aware of a product or service and must perceive the purchase of that product or service as having a positive effect on satisfying the need of which she or he is now

aware. Then, and only then, will the individual be motivated to buy. Again, it is the goal of marketing to suggest objectives—cruises, flights, or vacations—to satisfy needs, an awareness of which has already been created. (This process is outlined in figure 2.2.) For example, several years ago an adver-

Figure 2.2   Needs, Wants, and Motives.

tisement ran in the Scottish papers showing two little girls with one saying. "Guess what? Next month Grandma and Grandpa are visiting us—from Scotland." The advertisement was promoting flights from Scotland to Canada. It managed to say (between the lines), "We know you love your grandchildren (a need). By showing you this picture we have made you aware of that (a want). By visiting them (an objective) you will satisfy that need for love." In such a way grandparents are motivated to fly to Canada.

Behavior is influenced by a number of things, with motives being only one. We cannot even specify that an individual is motivated at any one time by only one motive. It is important, as we discuss needs and motives individually, to bear in mind that behavior results from the interaction of various motives, one of which may be dominant at any one time as well as interacting with various other socioeconomic and psychographic factors.

Motives may be *specific* or *general*. A general motive would be the end objective, and a specific motive would a means to reach that end objective. For example, a person may be motivated to take a spa vacation. This, however, may be no more than an indicator or a more general motive, that of good health. Viewed in this way, it can be seen that good health can be achieved by means other than taking a vacation. We are in competition not only with the next destination, but also with other activities for the consumers' time and money. Although a vacation represents a break from routine for many, that same feeling can also be obtained from decorating the house or laying out a garden. The marketing task is to convince an individual that the purchase of whatever we are selling is the best, if not the only, way of satisfying that need. To the extent that we are successful in accomplishing this, an individual will be motivated to buy.

Maslow's need theory and travel motivations. A study of the travel literature indicates that travel motivations can fit into Maslow's hierarchy of needs model. Maslow proposed the following listing of needs arranged in a hierarchy:

1. Survival—hunger, thirst, rest, activity
2. Safety—security, freedom from fear and anxiety
3. Belonging and love—affection, giving and receiving love
4. Esteem—self-esteem and esteem from others
5. Self-actualization—personal self-fulfillment

This hierarchy suggests that lower-level needs demand more immediate attention and satisfaction before a person turns to the satisfaction of higher-level needs. It might be better to think of the hierarchy as a series of nested triangles (see figure 2.3). This representation emphasizes the fact that higher-level needs encompass all lower-level needs. It also illustrates the relative value size of each need better.

It should be noted that Maslow's model has been criticized on the grounds that the original work was part of a clinical experiment rather than as the foundation for a theory of motivation. Maslow himself expressed some concerns about his own findings. Be that as it may, the fact is that it does seem to explain **why** people vacation. For example, Fakeye and Crompton (1992) identified the following motives for visitors to the Rio Grande Valley of Texas:

Factor 1   Escape from personal, physical, and social problems

---

Quick Trip 2. 3
The Dream Vacation?

The makers of FunSeeker Binoculars recently asked 62 men and 143 women which of the following public figures they would most like to spend a day at the beach with:

● MEN RANK 5 FEMALE PUBLIC FIGURES

Sharon Stone:	53%
Rosanne:	10%
Sophia Loren:	8%
Susan Sarandon:	8%
Hillary Clinton:	0%

● WOMEN RANK 5 MALE PUBLIC FIGURES

Robert Redford:	26%
Jerry Seinfeld:	23%
John F. Kennedy, Jr.:	21%
Denzel Washington:	10%
Bill Clinton:	8%

Source: *Travel Weekly.* (August 12, 1996) 17.

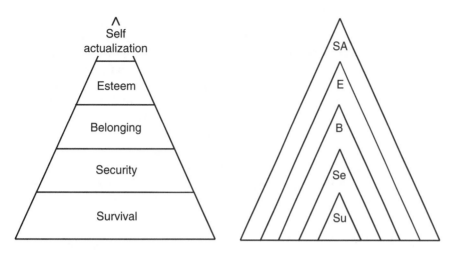

Figure 2.3   Maslow's Hierarchy of Needs.

Source: Arnold Mitchell, "Social change: Implications of Trends in Values and Lifestyles," VALS Report No. 3, January 1979.

Factor 2   Social contacts

Factor 3   Physical self, and intellectual enrichment

Factor 4   Family togetherness and curiosity

Factor 5   Temperature, exploration, and security

These factors seem to mirror Maslow's original list.

Although Maslow's first need listed is **physical**, the other four are **psychological**. To this original list two intellectual words were added:

To know and understand—acquiring knowledge

Aesthetics—appreciation of beauty

The relationship between the physical, psychological, and **intellectual** needs is unclear. It is thought that the intellectual needs exist independently of the others.

The relationship between needs, motives, and references from the tourism literature is shown in table 2.3. Those who say they travel to escape or to relieve tension can be seen as seeking to satisfy the basic survival or physiological need. Such motivation may be for physical or mental relaxation. Vacationers often return from a trip physically exhausted but mentally refreshed. Although there seems to be a difference between those people who take an active vacation and those who opt for a passive vacation, both are motivated by a need for tension reduction.

Passive vacationers are seen as achieving tension relief by giving in or submitting to the surrounding environment. From this submission comes the very relief of tension that will result in their returning refreshed and renewed. The overworked factory worker may relax by lying on a beach for two weeks. The active vacationer achieves tension reduction through physical activity. The activity can also be seen as being related to achievement and mastery of the environment and, as such, being related to the need for self-esteem. Some people who have jobs that are not physically demanding compensate by engaging in physical activity when on vacation. This illustrates the point made earlier that, at any one time, one may be motivated to satisfy more than one need.

Traveling for reasons of health can be interpreted as a way of attempting to satisfy one's safety needs. By taking care of the body and/or mind, we are protecting ourselves and helping ensure our

After a vacation of parasailing, people may come home physically exhausted, yet mentally refreshed. Photo from *Top Shots* CD Rom. Courtesy of Queensland Tourist and Travel Corporation.

Table 2.3   Maslow's Needs and Motivations Listed in Travel Literature

NEED	MOTIVE	TOURISM LITERATURE REFERENCE
Physiological	Relaxation	Escape Relaxation Relief of tension Sunlust Physical Mental relaxation of tension
Safety	Security	Health Recreation Keeping oneself active and healthy for the future
Belonging	Love	Family togetherness Enhancement of kinship relationships Companionship Facilitation of social interaction Maintenance of personal ties Interpersonal relations Roots Ethnic Show one's affection for family members Maintain social contacts
Esteem	Achievement	Convince oneself of one's achievements Status Show one's importance to others Prestige Social recognition Ego-enhancement Professional/business Status and prestige
Self-actualization	Be true to one's self	Exploration and evaluation of nature Self-discovery Satisfaction of inner desires
To know and understand	Knowledge	Cultural Education Wanderlust Interest in foreign areas
Aesthetics	Appreciation of beauty	Environmental Scenery

People who have physically demanding jobs often want to just lie on a beach to relax. Photo by Corel.

own longevity. Visits to spas can be seen in this light. Several references specifically link recreation and health, implying a relationship between the two. Some researchers have suggested that travel marketers have a particular responsibility when it comes to selling health as a motivation to travel. They cite Kotler's definition of societal marketing which "holds that the organization's task is to determine the needs, wants and interests of target markets and to deliver the desired satisfactions more effectively and efficiently than competitors in a way that preserves or enhances the consumer's and society's well-being" (1984). Given increased awareness of the relationship between sunbathing and skin cancer; of the impact of tourism development on the environment; and of the spread of AIDS, can and should tourism managers continue to promote the traditional tenets of Sun, Sand, Sea, and Sex?

Hobson & Dietrich (1994) suggest that the challenge is to "create a new image representing health, wealth, and leisure along with different activities which do not promote excessive sun exposure and its inherent dangers to the health of the individual . . . to bring attention to tourists an awareness of the health issues that are faced when traveling . . . showing destination areas that environmental damage which leads to health hazards will result in long-term business failure." They go on to suggest that promoting legal, supervised brothels might limit the health risk to both tourist and provider.

The need for belonging and love relates to the desire for affection, for both giving and receiving love. The organized tour is often mentioned as a method of encouraging and satisfying this need for companionship and social interaction.

This motivation is frequently referred to as the VFR market: visit friends and relatives. Part of this is the ethnic roots market—the desire to visit the homeland or previous

Quick Trip 2.4
Do We Really Travel to Improve Our Health?

The three most pressing problems that British holiday makers have are sunburn, excessive drinking, and unprotected sex. A survey published in *Doctor*, the weekly newspaper for general practitioners in Great Britain, found that 94 percent of doctors thought the British were irresponsible in their attitude toward sunburn. Three-quarters said alcohol abuse was the next most common problem on holiday, while 45 percent indicated unprotected sex.

Despite these opinions there is a firm belief in a holiday as a cure for health problems. Eighty-three percent of the doctors surveyed believed that patients who took regular holidays had fewer stress-related problems. An even larger percentage—95 percent—said they recommended holidays to their patients as an alternative to medication for certain conditions such as exhaustion, depression, anxiety, insomnia, and lethargy.

However, most doctors were unable to totally leave the job themselves when they went on vacation. Almost two-thirds reported that, when on holiday, they had been asked by cabin crew or holiday staff to look after a traveler who had taken ill.

Questions:

The World Health Organization defines health as a state of complete physical, mental and social well-being. (Constitution, 1964)

1. If people vacation for reasons of health, how do you explain their behavior while on holiday?

2. What needs and wants are being satisfied?

3. Can people be motivated to take "healthy vacations?" If so, how?

4. To what extent, if any, do tourism professionals have a responsibility to promote healthy vacations and stop advertising unhealthy holiday practices?

Source: Fletcher, D. (July 11, 1991). *British 'risk their health on holiday.* The Daily Telegraph.

residence of oneself or one's ancestors. This segment of the market tends to fall into two groups. First, there are those who were born somewhere else and desire to return to their own homeland. Second, there are those in later generations who wish to experience the land of their ancestors. For the people in the first segment of the market, the desire is to see people and things and to relive experiences as they are remembered. This desire to recapture previous experiences means that these tourists are willing to adjust to the conditions of the destination visited. They are there, after all, to enjoy again what they remembered from their past. Inconveniences of the homeland can be tolerated. At the same time, however, people in this market segment may have little economic impact on the destination because of the tendency to stay with friends and relatives. Later generations will have the slightly different desire to experience vicariously the land of one's ancestors; however, because the personal experience of one's roots is missing and has been replaced by standards of living learned in one's country of birth, it is these accustomed standards of living that are taken on the journey for one's roots. Therefore, living standards are expected to be comparable to those experienced at home. At the same time, however, this segment of the market tends to have a greater impact on the economy if lodging and meals are taken in hotels instead of with family.

Maslow's concept of the need for esteem breaks down into two components: that of *self-esteem* and that of esteem from others. The idea of self-esteem is embodied in such ideas as the need to exhibit strength, achievement, mastery, competence, and independence. This might explain why people take whitewater rafting trips. Esteem from others is explained by such concepts as reputation, prestige, status, and recognition. Travel can certainly boost one's ego, both at the destination and upon one's return. It may be that as people grow older, their status in society declines. Travel is one way to enhance that status.

Self-actualization can, in fact, be considered the end or goal of leisure. Leisure is the state of being free from the urgent demands of lower-level needs. Vacations offer an opportunity to reevaluate and discover more about the self, to act out one's self-image as a way of modifying or correcting it.

The need to know and understand can be viewed in light of the desire for knowledge. Many people travel to learn of others' cultures. It is also true that contact with people of another culture offers an opportunity to discover one's own culture. This same concept has also

A whitewater rafting trip, such as this one on the Tully River, gives a person a chance to exhibit strength and endurance. Photo from *Top Shots* CD Rom. Courtesy of Queensland Tourist and Travel Corporation.

yourself, explore, and grow. The message would continue by pointing out the benefits to be gained and finally suggest that the wilderness and history of the Yukon is the place to do this.

The traveler, then, is better understood and better appealed to if he or she is recognized as a person consuming products and services. Seeing the traveler in this manner will result in a change of attitude on the part of the observer and enable the marketer to provide a better product or service to the traveler. A second, more tangible benefit to be gained from this approach relates to the idea of prepotency. If one accepts Maslow's idea of **prepotency**—that lower-level needs should be satisfied to some extent before the satisfaction

been expressed as a motivation for education, wanderlust, and interest in foreign parts. The need for aesthetics is seen in those who travel for environmental reasons—to view the scenery.

In the words of one researcher, "Any product or service can be broken down into what it is, what it does, and what people get from it" (Cameron, 1992). A product-driven approach is to talk about the attributes, then the benefits, and finally the values. In a consumer-driven approach you start with the values and lead up through the benefits to the attributes (see figure 2.4). Using the Yukon as an example (figure 2.5), the product-driven approach would begin by stressing the attributes of the Yukon: wilderness and history. Messages would then point out the benefits to be gained from these attributes: get away, learn and reconnect with nature. Finally, the values to be gained would be mentioned: discover yourself and explore and grow.

The better consumer-driven approach would lead with the values, suggesting the need to discover

---

Quick Trip 2.5
The Family Vacation

When kids were asked "What vacation activities send parents up the wall?" they said:

Fighting with brothers/sisters	5%
Asking "Are we there yet?"	30%
Singing songs	4%
Telling silly jokes	4%
Always wanting a bathroom stop	3%
Getting carsick	3%

Kid's Ultimate Vacations

Coast-to-coast theme park tour	25%
Trip under the ocean	21%
African safari	18%
Trip into space	17%
Mountain climbing in Alaska	14%

Question:

1. What do these surveys tell us about the family vacation segment?

Source: *Travel Weekly* (August 12, 1996, 17, & August 15, 1996, 19). Sea World/Busch Gardens' survey conducted at the theme parks, of 433 kids ages 8–12.

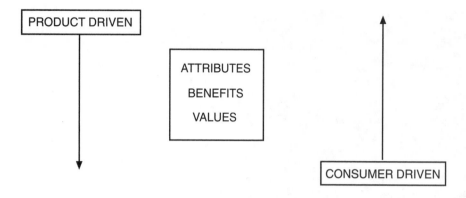

Figure 2.4   Product-Driven vs. Consumer-Driven Approaches.

Source: Bruce Cameron, "Creative Destinations: Marketing and Packaging: Who Wants What and Why? An Overview of the Canadian Pleasure Market Study," Proceedings of the 21st Annual Conference of the Travel and Tourism Research Association, 1992, 160.

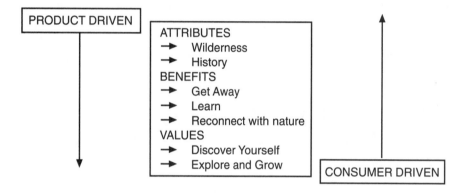

Figure 2.5   Product-Driven vs. Consumer-Driven Approaches: The Yukon Example.

Source: Bruce Cameron, "Creative Destinations: Marketing and Packaging: Who Wants What and Why? An Overview of the Canadian Pleasure Market Study," Proceedings of the 21st Annual Conference of the Travel and Tourism Research Association, 1992, 161.

(sense of mastery, learning, exploration, and relaxation) or interpersonal (involving social interaction). The model is illustrated in figure 2.6. The unequal length of the lines indicates the fact that the desire to escape from personal or impersonal environments is greater than the desire to seek personal or impersonal rewards. This has practical implications for tourism businesses. It would suggest that promoting the need to escape, and getaway vacations, would be particularly effective in triggering the need to travel. It also suggests that the destination is less important than the need to escape. This makes it more difficult to sell the differentiating qualities of a particular destination.

Why Travel?

> "What gives value to travel is fear. It is the fact that, at a certain moment, when we are so far from our own home country . . . we are seized by a vague fear, and the instinctive desire to go back to the protection of the old habits. This is the most obvious benefit of travel. . . . This is why we should not say that we travel for pleasure. There is no pleasure in traveling, and I look upon it as an occasion for spiritual testing. . . . Travel, which is like a greater and graver science, brings us back to ourselves."
>
> Albert Camus, (1963)

of higher-level needs becomes a concern—we would expect that products and services, including vacations, which are targeted toward the satisfaction of lower-level needs, would be regarded as more of a necessity than a luxury and would, as such, be more resilient to external pressures of time and money.

A number of authors, in fact, have demonstrated that the need to escape (related to the physiological need) is the strongest travel mo-

tivation. People see vacations as a way of escaping from everyday life rather than as a way of seeking pleasure. It has been suggested that the two motivational factors simultaneously influence the leisure behavior of individuals. Leisure activities are sought because they allow individuals to escape from personal or interpersonal problems. At the same time people are seeking psychological rewards from participating in leisure activities. These rewards can be personal

We have said that an individual's needs—for safety, for belonging, and so on—can be satisfied by setting different objectives or by taking certain actions. What determines how an individual will seek to satisfy a need? It is proposed that an individual is motivated to satisfy a particular need in a particular way (by taking a vacation, for example) based upon three factors. First, the vacation will be taken if the individual *perceives* that

A vacation, for many, means an escape from "real life." Photo by Corel.

in order to satisfy a need must be taken within the limitations of the individual's external environment. She may perceive that a cruise will satisfy her need, she may have learned that a cruise will satisfy her need, but if she does not have sufficient time or money or there are strong social or cultural factors that inhibit this option, she may not be able to take the cruise. The effect of the external environment on the individual's decision-making process was considered in chapter 1.

Tourist's Learning Process

An individual will purchase a specific vacation package or trip if he has learned that the purchase will help satisfy an important need. This process is illustrated in Figure 2.7. The tourist weighs various alternatives against a list of criteria important to him to determine which alternatives are most likely to satisfy a particular motive. The inclination that results will have an effect upon the "fit" between motives and alternatives—how well a chosen alternative will meet the motivation. Travelers have a low upper limit on the number of destinations that they perceive they may visit within a specified time period. Most travelers have identified seven or fewer destinations that they list as alternatives. The number of alternatives will vary relative to the characteristics of the travelers. Travelers who have previously visited foreign destinations have a larger number of destinations likely to be visited. Whether or not a destination will be included as an alternative depends in great part upon whether or not a destination has previously satisfied the individual. The level of satisfaction is a function of one's expectations of a situation and one's perception of the actual situation. If the level of expectation is higher than the actual experience, the individual will be dissatisfied. For an individual to be satisfied with a

the vacation will satisfy a need important to her. If she feels that taking a cruise will result in her returning relaxed and refreshed, and if it is important to her that she do something to relax and refresh herself, then she is more likely to take that cruise. (Perception and image is covered in chapter 3.) Second, a

particular action will be taken if the individual has *learned* that action will satisfy that need. If she has taken a cruise that has resulted in her returning home refreshed, she will be more inclined to take it again. (See the buyer behavior model in figure 2.1.) Third, the decision as to what action to take

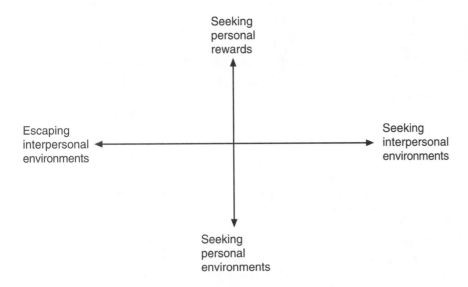

Figure 2.6 The Escaping and Seeking Dimensions of Leisure Motivation.

Adapted from: S.E. Iso-Ahola, "Social Psychological Foundations of Leisure and Resultant Implications for Leisure Counseling," *Leisure Counseling: Concepts and Applications*, E.T. Dowd, ed. (Springfield, IL: Charles C. Thomas, 1984), 111.

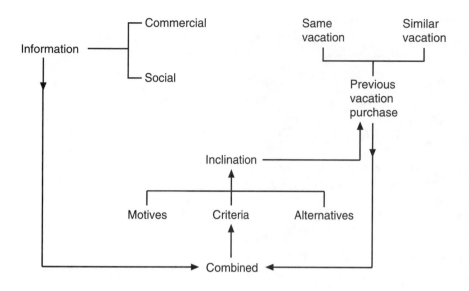

Figure 2.7 Tourist's Learning Process.

Adapted from: J.A. Howard and J.N. Sheth, *The Theory of Buyer Behavior* (New York, John Wiley & Sons, Inc., 1969).

product, service, or situation, the level of actual experience must be equal to or greater than the level of expectation. Tourists can attempt to reduce the psychological risk involved in a purchase by expecting less from the vacation. This, however, is not a popular strategy, especially in travel.

We would expect that as the amount of satisfaction increases, the number of alternatives considered next time decreases. The more an individual is pleased with a vacation choice, the higher that choice will be placed on the list of alternatives, and the fewer will be the other alternatives considered. This places great importance on the level of service given the vacationer to ensure a quality experience and a level of satisfaction that will bring the traveler back. The one exception to this might be the vacation with a high need to know and understand. If this is very important, it may not matter how satisfied he or she is with, for example, a trip to Paris. Having visited that spot, the individual, making the most of limited resources of time and money, may never return to that city.

Serving as a bridge between the motives of an individual and the perceived alternatives are the criteria used for making a decision among those alternatives. A choice is made that the individual believes will produce maximum satisfaction of a need or needs. The criteria used to distinguish between alternatives are learned. These criteria are developed as a result of past experience and from information taken in from either the commercial (business) or social (friends and relatives) environment. The effect of information on learning will be considered in chapter 3 when we look at the process of perception and image formation.

Learning, based on past experience, can come from having experienced the same thing that is being contemplated or from having experienced something similar. If you stayed in a particular town on vacation and were very satisfied, you learn that visiting that particular town is liable to satisfy you again. Those factors that accounted for your satisfaction—good weather, friendly service—are the criteria by which you determine where to take your next vacation.

On the other hand, by staying at one property of a chain and having a poor experience, you may infer that you would have a similarly poor experience at all properties of that chain and behave accordingly (which, by the way, may not be an accurate representation of what would have happened at another property in the chain). This is known as the psychology of simplification. To make the decision-making process easier, the potential tourist generalizes from what he or she perceives to be similar situations. The more experiences a traveler has, the more firmly established her decision criteria and the easier it is for her to generalize.

The individual moves from what is termed an extensive problem-solving process through a limited problem-solving process to a routine problem-solving process. In the process known as extensive problem-solving, the tourist has little in the way of information or experiences from which to make a decision. The need and, consequently, the search for information is high, and a few decision criteria have been established. We may know what criteria are important to us, but we may be unaware of whether or not they can be satisfied by the various alternatives available. Additionally, as we experience certain destinations or vacations, we may find that the criteria that were important to us previously have become less significant.

Thus, our decision criteria are developed or modified (that is, learned) in great part by our actual experiences. As we become more confident in our decision criteria, decision-making is easier for us. Our experiences, and the resultant generalization from them, are weighed more heavily than any information received. This is due, in part, to the fact that, as our decision criteria are strengthened, our need for information is weakened. Additionally, we have a tendency to filter incoming information so that it will support and re-inforce our decisions. This is explored further in chapter 3. This progression leads to a routine problem-solving process whereby little or no information is sought and the decision is made rather quickly in reference to the decision criteria that have been established.

Consistency vs. Complexity

The movement described above—from extensive problem solving to routine problem solving—suggests that people seek to maintain consistency in their lives. Indeed, many psychologists adhere to this philosophy. Their idea is that inconsistency leads to psychological tension, which we constantly seek to avoid. Other psychologists argue the opposite. They feel that individuals find change and uncertainty extremely satisfying. This is referred to as the need for complexity.

The aforementioned two concepts are balanced by Mayo and Jarvis in *The Psychology of Leisure Travel* (1981). It is their feeling that individuals vary in the amount of psychological tension they can handle. Too much repetition or consistency can result in boredom for an individual, creating a corresponding amount of psychological tension greater than the optimum for him. He will attempt to introduce some complexity in his life, thereby reducing the tension to an optimum level. Should this level be exceeded by an overly complex situation, the tension level will be greater than the optimum for him. This explains why someone, who for years has driven to a particular vacation spot, will change either the destination or the method of reaching that spot.

Similarly, too much complexity can result in more tension than an individual can handle. She will introduce consistency into the experience to reduce the tension level. An American tourist in Europe may find the different language and culture (complexity) needs to be balanced by staying in a hotel chain with which she is familiar (consistency). This model may also help explain a person's choice of vacation. The individual who experiences a great deal of consistency in everyday life may compensate by seeking vacations that offer variety. People who have less stimulation in their lives than they desire prefer more novelty and stimulation on their ideal vacation.

This goes back to the studies mentioned earlier that noted novelty as a major push factor influencing travel. What is meant by novelty? It has been proposed that the dimensions of novelty are (Lee & Crompton, 1992):

1. Change from routine
2. Escape
3. Thrill

Quick Trip 2.6
The Trip is Ruined if . . .

According to a survey of U.S. travelers conducted by Plog Research these factors can spoil a vacation.*

	PERCENT INDICATING ITEM IS VERY IMPORTANT
Hotel is dirty/run-down	77
Dirty everywhere	72
Locals try to rip you off	58
Rainy, cold, etc.	46
Poverty evident	43
Very expensive	40
Airline flights often late/canceled	40
Too many tourist traps	36
Unfriendly natives	35
Visa requirements are difficult	26
Long lines at customs and immigration	24
Too much commercial development	24
Few speak English	21
Destination lacks many home comforts	20
Food not as good as expected	19
Too many souvenir shops/fast food	15
Poor or no sports facilities	11
Too much like other places visited	9

*The percentage of respondents who gave an item a score of nine or ten on a scale of one through ten, with ten indicating it "could spoil a trip."

Questions:

1. Relate the factors listed above to needs and wants. What needs and wants are not being satisfied that might lead to a spoiled trip?

2. What, if anything, can the owner of a tourist business do to help reduce these barriers to a perfect vacation?

Source: *Travel Weekly.* (December 15, 1994) 23.

4. Adventure

5. Surprise

6. Boredom alleviation

It is felt that a tourist has a certain predisposition to either seek or avoid arousal. Depending upon the extent to which novelty is sought, the perceived attributes of a destination will be evaluated against this need for novelty in addition to the strength of other motives and, within the kinds of external constraints noted in chapter 1, a vacation destination will be chosen. Questionnaires have been developed that would allow managers to determine the extent to which novelty is important to a potential tourist. Depending upon the results destinations offering the elements of novelty noted above could be matched with that potential tourist.

Summary

People are motivated to satisfy needs that may be innate or learned. Part of marketing's task is to make people aware of their needs and present them with an objective, the purchase or attainment of which will help satisfy that need. Vacations or trips are ways of satisfying various needs. There are, however, ways other than taking vacations to satisfy those same needs. An individual will purchase a vacation to satisfy a need or needs if he perceives that the vacation will satisfy needs considered important, or if he has learned that a vacation will satisfy those needs under the constraints of external factors such as time, money, and social pressure.

An individual learns of the alternative ways of satisfying her needs from personal experience, from the same or similar experiences, and from information gained from the commercial or social environment. The alternatives considered are linked to the person's motives by a

---

Quick Trip 2.7
Attracting the British Tourist

A survey of people in Great Britain sought to identify what people interested in vacationing in the U.S. look for in choosing where and how to holiday.

The following three segments were identified. A plus deviation from the overall statement mean indicates that people in that particular segment were more inclined to agree with the statement. The greater the plus number, the greater the agreement. For example, in Segment 1 "Being daring and adventuresome" gets a rating of +0.7. People in this segment were much more inclined to agree with this statement than respondents on average. The reverse is also true. The greater the negative deviation from the statement mean, the greater the level of disagreement with the statement. For this segment there was much less importance given to "Being together as a family."

Market Segments

	DEVIATION FROM OVERALL STATEMENT MEAN
Segment 1	
Being daring and adventuresome	+0.7
Finding thrills and excitement	+0.4
Being physically active	+0.4
Participating in sports	+0.4
Roughing it	+0.3
Experiencing new and different lifestyles	+0.2
Learning new things, increasing knowledge	+0.2
Rediscovering self	+0.2
Trying new foods	+0.2
Reliving past good times	−0.2
Indulging in luxury	−0.2
Doing nothing at all	−0.2
Meeting people with similar interests	−0.3
Visiting places family came from	−0.3
Visiting friends and relatives	−0.5
Feeling at home away from home	−0.5
Travel to places that feel safe and secure	−0.6
Being together as a family	−0.7
Segment 2	
Visiting friends and relatives	+0.8
Visiting places family came from	+0.6
Feeling at home away from home	+0.5
Being together as a family	+0.4
Meeting people with similar interests	+0.4
Travel to places that feel safe and secure	+0.4
Reliving past good times	+0.3
Talking about trip after return home	+0.3
Watching sports events	+0.3
Finding thrills and excitement	−0.3
Trying new foods	−0.3
Being daring and adventuresome	−0.3
Getting a change from a busy job	−0.5
Getting away from demands of home	−0.5

(continued on the following page)

Market Segments *(continued)*

	DEVIATION FROM OVERALL STATEMENT MEAN
Segment 3	
Getting away from demands of home	+0.5
Doing nothing at all	+0.4
Getting a change from a busy job	+0.3
Indulging in luxury	+0.3
Travel to places that feel safe and secure	−0.3
Roughing it	−0.3
Participating in sports	−0.3
Going places friends haven't been	−0.3
Watching sports events	−0.3
Visiting friends and relatives	−0.3
Visiting places family came from	−0.3
Being daring and adventuresome	−0.4
Being physically active	−0.5

Questions:

1. What underlying need(s) are people seeking to satisfy?

2. Place an appropriate label or name on the segments that best describe the potential vacationers.

3. Knowing the underlying need(s) that people are seeking to satisfy, what are the implications for

   a. the type of tourism product that will be most effective; i.e., what attractions will attract and what facilities should be offered?

   b. the price that should be charged?

   c. the type of promotion that would be effective?

   d. how it should be sold—directly or as a package?

4. Design an appropriate advertisement.

Source: Joint USTTA/Tourism Canada research project.

---

set of decision criteria—guidelines used by the individual to select among alternatives. These guidelines are also learned from the sources described. If an individual has learned that a particular purchase results in satisfaction, strong decision criteria favoring that purchase will have been built up as the number of alternatives considered will have been reduced. There is a great likelihood that a specific motive under the conditions described above will result in a tendency to purchase a particular product, service, or experience.

References

Cameron, B. (1992). *Creative destinations: Marketing & packaging: Who wants what—and why? An overview of the Canadian pleasure travel market*. Proceedings of the 23rd Annual Conference of the Travel and Tourism Research Association, 160.

Crompton, J. (1979). Motivations for pleasure travel. *Annals of Tourism Research*, 6, 408–424.

Dann, G. (1977). Anomie, ego-enhancement and tourism. *Annals of Tourism Research*, 4, 184–194.

Fakeye, P.C., & Crompton, J.L. (1992). Importance of socialization to repeat visitation. *Annals of Tourism Research*, 19, 364–367.

Hobson, J.S.P., & Dietrich U.C. (1994). Tourism, health and quality of life: Challenging the responsibility of using the traditional tenets of sun, sea, sand, and sex in tourism marketing. *Journal of Travel & Tourism Marketing*, 3 (4), 28, 30.

Jamrozy, U. (1992). *Travel behavior variations of overseas German visitors: Motivations, preferences, and activities*. Proceedings of the 23rd annual conference of the Travel and Tourism Research Association, 226–229.

Kotler, P. (1984). *Marketing management*. Englewood Cliffs, NJ: Prentice-Hall, Inc., 30.

Lee, T., & Crompton, J. (1992). Measuring novelty seeking in tourism. *Annals of Tourism Research*, 19, 732–751.

Mayo, E.J., & Jarvis, L.P. (1981). *The psychology of leisure travel*. Boston: C.B.I. Publishing Company, Inc., 172.

Turnbull, D.R., & Uysal, M. (1995). An exploratory study of German visitors to the Caribbean: Push and pull motivations. *Journal of Travel & Tourism Marketing*, 4 (2), 85–92.

Wright, P.A. (1996). North American ecotourism markets: Motivations, preferences, and destinations. *Journal of Travel Research*, 35 (1), 3–10.

Yuan, S., & McDonald, C. (1990). Motivational determinates of international pleasure time. *Journal of Travel Research*, 29 (1), 43.

Additional Reading

Choice and Demand in Tourism, Peter Johnson and Barry Thomas, eds., Mansell Publishing Ltd., Villiers House, 41–47 Strand, London WC2N 5JE, U.K., 1992.

Economic Psychology of Travel and Tourism, John C. Crotts and W. Fred van Raaij, eds., The Haworth Press, 10 Alice Street, Binghamton, NY 13904-1580, 1995.

Leisure Travel: Making it a Growth Market . . . Again, Stanley C. Plog, John Wiley & Sons, Inc., New York, 1991.

The Seasons of Business: A Marketer's Guide to Consumer Behavior, Judith Waldrop and Marcia Mogelonsky, American Demographics Books, 127 West State Street, Ithaca, NY 14850, 1992.

The Theory of Buyer Behavior, John A. Howard and J.N. Sheth, John Wiley & Sons, Inc., New York, NY, 1969.

The Whole is More: Living the Travel Experience, Heide Gondek, Vantage Press, Inc., 516 West 34th Street, New York, NY 10001, 1993.

"Come to Western Australia. Relax in a state of Excitement."

Tourist slogan for the state, quoted by
Minister of Tourism for Western Australia

3

Selecting a Travel Destination

···The Importance of Image ·····················

Purpose

Based upon an understanding of the traveler's search for vacation information, students will be able to suggest specific strategies to influence where, how, with whom, when, and for how long people vacation.

Learning Objectives

Having read this chapter, you should be able to:

1. Explain the importance of perception on travel decisions and the interpretation of travel information.

2. Describe how opinion leaders form a link between the social and commercial environments.

3. Describe how a person's self-image influences his or her choices of travel destinations and services.

4. Explain how to use the factors that influence people's sensitivity to information to increase the chances of a message being noticed.

5. Explain the process through which a person forms an image of a travel destination or service.

Overview

A travel destination is chosen in part based upon our perception of its ability to satisfy our felt needs. This chapter examines the process by which we search for and receive information about potential destinations and how our perception of that information influences the travel decision.

Information is received from both the commercial and social environments. The factors that influence where the information is sought from and how much is taken in are examined. The process by which the information taken is distorted by our perceptual biases is explored. Implications for the marketer seeking to develop a specific image for a destination or to change an unsatisfactory image are pointed out.

The Search for Information

"Tahiti was put on the map by Gauguin, Fiji by Qantas and PanAm."

George Mikes, Boomerang— Australia Rediscovered, (1968)

Once individuals are motivated to travel they embark on an information search to compare alternative destinations. Information will come from two major sources: the ***commercial environment*** and the ***social environment***. The commercial environment refers to information coming from companies, destinations, countries, or tourist businesses. These businesses and organizations have a vested interest in persuading the tourist to buy and profit by such a purchase. The so-

cial environment, characterized by friends, relatives, and reference groups, presumably would have nothing materially to gain from the tourist's decision to buy. As such, it is presumed that their information or advice is more objective and worthy of trust. Although friends, relatives, and those in our reference groups may not benefit financially from the decision to buy a particular vacation, they may have their egos stroked if their advice is accepted and a decision is made based on their input.

It is likely that people will spend a longer time on an external search for a tourism purchase. There are several reasons for this. The greater the amount of risk is a purchase, the greater the search. Buying a vacation involves a great deal of risk involving both time and money. For many people the annual vacation is

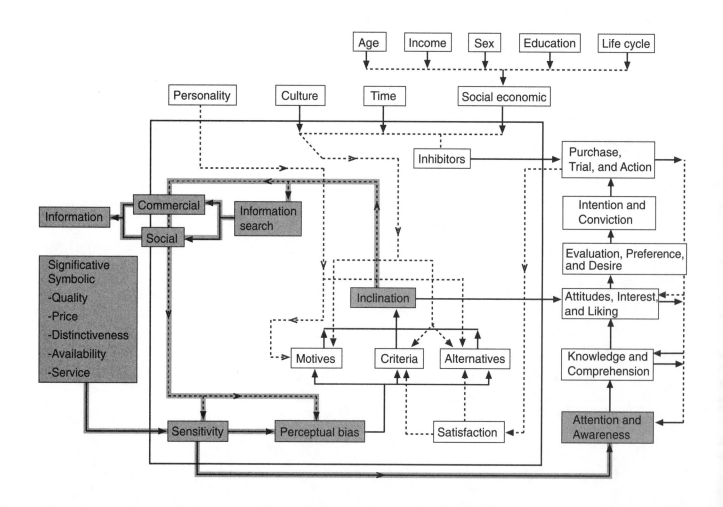

their only chance to get away. If they select a poor vacation, they may have to wait another year for the next opportunity. The vacation is also an expensive proposition—hence the risk. Second, because the purchase of a vacation involves buying an intangible that cannot be seen or touched ahead of time, there is heavy reliance on secondary and tertiary sources of information. It is, thus, likely that the search process will be longer than that for many other consumer products. There is a tendency for many vacationers to select a different vacation destination each time they holiday. This would support the need for a greater information search.

Information Sources

What sources of information are sought when planning a vacation? Much evidence suggests that the social environment—the influence of friends and family—is instrumental in selecting a travel destination. It seems that the commercial environment performs an informing function—it lets people know what is available. The social environment performs an evaluating function; the potential traveler uses it as a means of evaluating the alternatives.

Knowing how people search for information can enable marketers to segment the market based on search behavior and develop specific strategies to appeal to and reach each segment. For this to happen there must be a sufficiently large number of people who engage in a certain form of search behavior to make the effort of marketing to them worthwhile. It would also be important to know whether different segments of the market use different types and numbers of information sources. The relative importance of these sources must be known in addition to the length of time taken in the planning process. This latter piece of information is

necessary to ensure that information is available at the time when the potential travelers want it. If July vacationers plan their vacations six months in advance, the destinations should target their messages to reach that market in January. Advertising to them beforehand will have little impact because they are not thinking about the vacation. Advertising to them afterward will be too late because they will already have decided where they will vacation.

In general, longer searches using a greater number of sources of information are undertaken by vacationers who want a well-planned trip, seek excitement from their vacation, and are planning longer trips over greater distances.

The role of the retail travel agent in this process has been documented in a series of reports by Louis Harris & Associates since 1971. These reports indicate that, over the past twenty-five years, between 30 and 40 percent of those who visit travel agencies have only a general idea of where they want to go and thus rely, to some extent, on the agent's advice in selecting a destination. There is an increased tendency to use travel agents as the distance being traveled increases and as the tourist uses air transportation. Table 3.1 indicates the sources Americans use to help

make travel selections. Travel agents and friends and relatives are used to almost the same extent and much more than any other source for leisure travelers. Travel agents are used most often among the various sources by business travelers. Other research (Rao, Thomas, & Javalgi, 1992) dealing with the trip-planning behavior of the U.S. outbound pleasure travel market has supported the use of print over broadcast media, but has indicated that friends and relatives are much more important and travel agents much less so than the information in this table. Other studies have indicated that people have more confidence in recommendations of friends than in any other source. Travel agent recommendations rate second while advertising information is really not trusted.

Table 3.2 shows the services most used to book both airline and hotel reservations. Travel agents are overwhelmingly used by both leisure and business travelers to book airline reservations. However, both segments use an airline or hotel chain predominantly to make hotel reservations.

Because the role of a retail travel agent increases in importance as the use of air transportation and the distance traveled increases, it might be better to view the important sources of information for

Table 3.1   What Americans use to help make travel decisions

	BUSINESS TRIPS	LEISURE TRIPS
Travel Agents	29%	60%
Airline Reservation Centers	12%	23%
Hotel Reservation Centers	10%	31%
Friends/Relatives	10%	57%
Hotel Brochures	8%	31%
Airline Timetables/Brochures	8%	14%
Auto Club Books/Brochures	6%	33%
Newspaper Travel Sections	5%	35%
Magazine Articles/Ads	5%	32%

Source: Plog Research Inc. (August 1, 1994). American Traveler Survey of 13,500 consumers with household incomes of more than $20,000, *Tour & Travel News*, 1.

Table 3.2 Services used most to book

SERVICES USED MOST TO BOOK	AIRLINE RESERVATIONS		HOTEL RESERVATIONS	
	FOR BUSINESS	FOR PLEASURE	FOR BUSINESS	FOR PLEASURE
Travel Agent	52%	64%	30%	36%
Airline/Hotel Chain	19%	34%	42%	62%
Corporate Travel Dept.	29%	1%	27%	1%
Personal Computer	0.4%	1%	1%	1%

Source: Plog Research Inc. (August 1, 1994). American Traveler Survey of 13,500 consumers with household incomes of more than $20,000. *Tour & Travel News*, 1.

the auto traveler separately from those used by the air traveler.

Travel to the U.S.

Many informative reports have been issued by the (former) U.S. Travel and Tourism Administration. Table 3.3 summarizes information relative to sources used by travelers from four countries—Japan, United Kingdom, Germany, and France—in planning a trip to the U.S. The primary sources used in planning the trip were travel agents, brochures and pamphlets, and friends and family. In three of the four countries, travel agents were the number-one source. In Japan, brochures and pamphlets were used slightly more often than were travel agents. In Japan, also, books and library sources were used by more people than friends or relatives. It is also evident that travelers of different countries have different ways and priorities for obtaining information for travel purposes. The Japanese, as noted, make much more use of books and the library than do travelers in any of the European countries listed. Germans, on the other hand, make much more use of tour operators. Thus, while the importance of retail travel agents and personal sources can be noted, the travel marketer must be aware of the fact that information to different travelers in different countries must be communicated through different

channels to reach the intended audience.

Automobile Travel

A number of studies have been completed on the tourist's use of travel information sources when traveling by automobile. These studies indicate the importance of information from the social environment. Information from family or friends and from personal knowledge is regarded as more significant than that from commercial sources. The non-media preferred commercial sources are billboards and signs. It appears that as motorist travelers become more familiar with the location of establishments in a geographic area, they rely more on previous experience than on physical appearance and on credit-card directories rather than on commercial billboards.

A link between the social and commercial environment is suggested by a consideration of the role of opinion leaders. ***Travel Opinion Leaders (TOL)*** are defined as such based on how often they serve as sources of travel information. People are more inclined to be regarded as TOLs the more and the longer trips they take (Oh & Lee, 1995). There is evidence to indicate that the flow of communication is a two-step flow process. The tendency is for influence to flow from the mass media to opinion leaders who are receptive to the idea presented and from these opinion leaders to the general public. Opinion leaders act as channels of information. They tend to be demographically indistinguishable except for higher income or occupational levels, tend to read more media about related consumer issues, are more knowledgeable about new product developments, and participate more often in related consumer activities. Studies of TOLs found that they are active seekers of information but do not seek either personal or media sources of information as being significantly important sources for them. TOLs are more likely to rely on travel brochures and guides, highway welcome/information centers and convention and visitor bureaus than most people. It appears that TOLs may be better able to determine the credibility of various source materials and are not as easily swayed by the advice of friends and relatives as are the general population. Others, after all, look to them for advice—they do not look so much to others.

Table 3.3 Sources used to plan a trip to the United States

SOURCES	JAPAN	U.K.	GERMANY	FRANCE
Travel Agent	50%	59%	70%	48%
Brochures/Pamphlets	55%	44%	51%	37%
Friends/Family	26%	39%	44%	25%
Airline	5%	6%	13%	8%
Tour Operator	19%	12%	28%	7%
Read Articles	16%	19%	15%	15%
Books/Library	40%	19%	17%	12%

<table>
<tr><td colspan="2">Quick Trip 3.1</td></tr>
</table>

The Search for Information

Research findings indicate the following information sources used by destination-naïve visitors to Alaska:

SOURCE USED	RELATIVE FREQUENCY
Travel agent	69%
Tour brochures/guide books	37
Friends or relatives at origin	24
Alaska Division of Tourism	17
Convention and visitors bureaus	3
Chambers of Commerce	3
Airlines	3

Three search strategies were identified. They are using (1) a travel agent as the sole source of information—44 percent of the market, (2) a travel agent and one or more other sources—25 percent of the market, and (3) one or more sources other than a travel agent—31 percent of the market.

The characteristics of the three segments were as follows:

INFORMATION SEARCH STRATEGY

	TRAVEL AGENT ONLY	TRAVEL AGENT AND OTHER	SOURCES OTHER THAN TRAVEL AGENT
Travel party characteristic			
Group size	2.26	2.36	2.3
Percent male	36	39	46
Average age	45	41	42
Lodging type			
Hotel/motel	59%	62%	40%
Campground	2%	9%	44%
Ship/ferry	72%	71%	45%
Leisure activity			
Visiting national parks	54%	81%	56%
Cultural learning	30%	54%	37%
Visiting museums	43%	60%	48%
Camping/hiking	3%	13%	35%
Sport fishing	5%	6%	25%
On-Site behavior			
Took an organized tour	78%	69%	28%
Total expenditures	$4325	$4908	$2734
Souvenir expenditures	$206	$218	$198
Length of stay	8.3 days	10.7 days	13.4 days

Question:

1. What implications does this research have for people marketing the state of Alaska?

Source: Snepenger, D., Meged, K., Snelling, M., & Worrall, K. (Summer 1990). Information Search Strategies by Destination-Naïve Tourists. *Journal of Travel Research*, 29, (1), 13–16.

Sensitivity to Information

> "Modern tourist guides have helped raise tourist expectations. And they have provided the natives—from Kaiser Wilhelm down to the villagers of Chichacestenango—with a detailed and itemized list of what is expected of them and when. These are the up-to-date scripts for actors on the tourists' stage."
>
> Daniel J. Boorstin, The Image

Thus far we have considered the sources to which potential tourists turn to determine vacation patterns. The personal sources—those from the social environment—have been shown to exert considerable pressure compared with those from the commercial environment. All information from both the commercial and social environments reaches us if we are sensitive to the incoming information. Our sensitivity to receiving incoming information is first a function of how inclined we are to that information. If, for example, we feel strongly inclined toward taking a vacation, we will readily be open to information regarding vacations. If we have a strong preference for a Bahamas vacation, any information about the Bahamas—about travel packages, the weather, the political situation—is liable to receive attention. On the other hand, if we have definitely decided against a European vacation, our preference to go to Europe will be low, as will our sensitivity to information about Europe. Consequently, we will probably ignore any information that would affect those taking a European vacation. Our sensitivity to information is also a function of the ambiguity of the message. If the information received is familiar to us already, it may be too simple and straightforward and thus be ignored. On the other hand, if the information presented—an advertisement, a travelogue, a personal opinion—is too complicated for us to absorb, the high level of ambiguity may lead us to put up a shield to "defend" ourselves, and the information will not get our attention. This process may be thought of as controlling the quantity of information received. In order to gain tourists' attentions, the information presented should be aimed at their capacity to absorb it. Its chances of being taken in will be enhanced if the tourists have a preference for the destination or package being mentioned.

Getting the Message Noticed

If the decision to travel to a particular destination is linked to our perception of that destination, then an examination of the perception process may help us understand if and how we can change an individual's perception of a destination in order to increase the likelihood of that individual's visiting the destination. Any information from either the social or commercial environment is molded into an image through our perceptual processes.

A large, eye-catching sign will attract visitors' attention. Photo Credit: Robert Holmes.

The resultant image is less a function of the promotional message of a destination than of our individual perception of that message. There are many factors that affect consumer sensitivity and perception. Although these elements are working at the same time and although the effect of one often contradicts the effect of another, they are discussed individually.

The first of these factors can be referred to as technical ones. *Technical factors* refer to the object, product, or service as it actually exists. The various elements of a particular product or service, such as price, quality, service, availability, and distinctiveness, can be communicated through the product or service itself. These inputs are termed significative stimuli. The elements may also be communicated in a symbolic way through the use of words and/or pictures. There are several factors that are termed technical. *Size* is an important consideration. To many, size is equated with quality. The larger the company, airplane, or hotel, the better the service is perceived to be. Generally speaking,

larger advertisements will receive greater attention. A travel company might use a big advertisement or emphasize the size of its operation to gain more attention and give the impression of quality to the reader. *Color* also attracts more attention than black-and-white. Color advertisements are 50 percent more effective than are black and white ones. The *intensity* of a stimulus also affects the perception of it. The greater the intensity, the more the attention. Intensity can refer to the brightness of colors, the use of certain "strong" words, or the importance of a present or past purchase or experience. Stressing the importance of a decision to buy will increase the attention given a message. It can also refer to repeating the stimulus, thereby intensifying the message. The more a message is seen, the greater the chance that it will attract attention. *Moving objects* attract more attention than stationary objects. This accounts for much of the success of advertising on television. Point-of-purchase displays with moving parts—in a travel agency, for example—can also be used to good effect. The *position* of a piece of information can affect whether or not the information will attract attention. In a brochure rack, pamphlets at shoulder height will attract the most attention. When placing advertisements in a newspaper, it is important to consider that the upper part of the page attracts more attention. *Contrast* is another element that affects the attention given a stimulus. By varying the thought, color, size, pattern, or intensity of a stimulus, enough discontinuity may be created between what is expected and what is actually perceived to attract attention. If competing messages are bright, colorful, and somewhat gaudy, a very simple, dignified message may be noticed because of the contrast. The final technical factor is that of *isolation*. Advertisers are fond of putting a border called "**white space**," around their messages to isolate them from other messages on a page. As noted earlier, these elements interact often in contradictory ways. The greatest impact comes when several factors combine to give a more significant effect. This is illustrated in figure 3.1.

The task is to communicate these elements: using these means: to gain:

Quality Price Distinctiveness Availability Service	Size Color Intensity Movement Position Contrast Isolation	Attention

Figure 3.1 Getting Attention.

The Process of Perception

"The Commandant was a tired, bowed, little man, old . . . He sweated, and his blue veined hand shook as he wrote the visas—he obviously had the fever—and, as he courteously handed them back, he said: '. . . M'sieu et Madame . . . French Equatorial is the most under-paid, under-staffed . . . . and has the most abominable climate . . . of any territory in Africa. We welcome you'."

Negley Farson,
Behind God's Back, (1940)

The information-receiving process, described above, controls the quantity of information taken in. The quantity of information received, however, is distorted by how that information is perceived. Two people presented with the same travel advertisement may perceive it differently. One person may view the advertisement positively, the other negatively. Feedback from our motives, the alternatives considered, and the decision criteria used will affect our image of information received. Various studies have shown, in fact, that visiting a destination or staying at a particular lodging chain causes a positive change in the image of that destination or chain. If we are strongly motivated to seek a historical, cultural vacation, one which could readily be satisfied by a trip to the province of Quebec, and if it is important (decision criteria) that we avoid crowds, then an advertisement showing throngs of people at an art festival in Quebec will be perceived negatively. Similarly, an advertisement that stresses the magnificent scenery of the province will not be perceived positively because that image runs counter to that which motivates us.

Although information from both the commercial and social environments is distorted, information received from personal sources is less subject to **perceptual bias**. This is because information from the social environment is regarded more favorably by the individual receiving the information. It should be remembered, however, that before a friend or relative gives us information, he or she has already distorted it to meet his or her value system. A recommendation of a wonderful place to visit, stay, or eat will only be given in those terms if it has met with what our friend determines is a wonderful place to visit, stay, or eat. This, of course, depends upon whether or not our friend perceives that his or her experience satisfied unmet needs. There is also liable to be less distortion when information is actively sought. When the tourist is unsure of which vacation will result in a more satisfying experience—when preference for any particular vacation is low—there will be less bias in the way information is perceived. In addition, there will be greater reliance upon the social environment for information if the tourist is unsure of the satisfactions from various alternatives and if the purchase is important. To the extent that we are influenced by the social group of which we are a part, our motives will be influenced by the (subjectively weighted) information from our social environment. Similarly, the social environment will affect the alternatives a buyer considers, particularly where experience is lacking. Also, infor-

Quick Trip 3.2
Getting Your Attention

Activity:

Scan the travel pages of your local newspaper or the advertisements in a travel magazine. Which advertisements do *you* notice? What makes them stand out? Do any of them use the principles identified in the text to help gain attention? To what extent are they successful?

mation received will be fed into the buyer's decisions criteria and will influence those criteria in the direction in which the information is perceived. A tourist, for example, may look for the lowest priced hotel. If information is received that suggests that paying a little more will actually be a better value, and if the tourist perceives this to be true, the decisions criterion of "lowest cost" may change.

A link has been established between perception and behavior. We behave—buy, travel, stay at home, and so on—based in part upon our perception of information received. But how do we perceive products, for example, tourist destinations or services?

Perceptual Bias

> " 'I've never travelled,'. . . Dona Consolation blandly confessed, . . . 'but I dare say, dear, that you can't judge Egypt by Aida.' "
>
> *Ronald Firbank*

In chapter 2 it was suggested that, in part, a travel purchase is made based on the extent that an individual perceives that the purchase will satisfy his or her needs. The key word is "perceive," for we buy based not so much upon what information is actually presented to us, but on how we *perceive* that information. Thus, the image that an individual has of a destination plays an important role in determining whether or not a travel purchase will be made.

It will be recalled that, prior to the search for information, available alternatives are matched with motives considered important to the individual through learned purchase criteria. The result is an initial inclination—positive or negative—toward a particular product or destination (see figure 3.2). The strength of our preference has an effect on how new alternatives are

perceived and even if any new alternatives are considered. For example, if an individual is well-traveled and consequently knows which destinations please and which do not, a strong set of decisions criteria will have been developed: There must be a sunny climate; the culture must be significantly different from my own; and so on. This, in turn, leads to a strong inclination toward certain destinations. The results are:

1. The tourist is less inclined to seek out information about new places.

2. The tourist is less sensitive to any information about vacation spots; the preferred destination is protected by a reluctance to allow in any information about other destinations.

3. Because a strong preference for a particular destination has been developed, any information about that destination is filtered to emphasize the positives while any negatives are rationalized or downplayed. The reverse is also

true. In a study of perceptions regarding first-class and coach airline seating, those who preferred first-class perceived a lesser difference in ticket price but a greater difference in the positive aspects of choosing first-class, such as more luggage allowance, better meal selection, and so on (Makens & Marquardt, 1977).

The difference between reality and perception can be illustrated as follows:

● **Reality**   Some airlines have introduced **ticketless travel**, a reservation and ticketing system without issuing an actual paper ticket. Its benefits are that it saves costs by not needing to print and issue paper tickets. These cost savings are then transferred to the traveler in the form of a lesser charge in the actual fare price. The traveler goes to the gate, is issued a boarding number and proceeds on the airplane. It saves time in boarding.

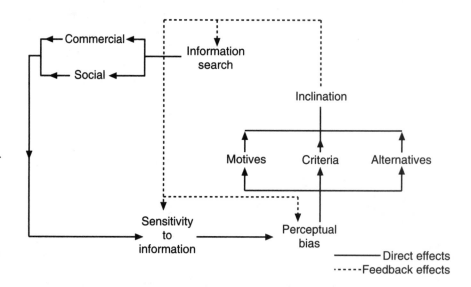

Figure 3.2   Information Sources and Perceptual Biases.

Adapted from: J.A. Howard and J.N. Sheth, *The Theory of Buyer Behavior* (New York, John Wiley & Sons, Inc., 1969).

● **Perception** Ticketless travel is mainly offered by low-frills/cost-efficient airlines that usually operate from secondary airports which are inconvenient to get to and from. Without a formal reservation and paper ticket-in-hand, I am not guaranteed that I will have a seat that I am comfortable with.

Perception is reality for most people. Irrespective of the reality of the situation people will buy, or not; travel, or not, based upon their perception of the situation. Perception, then, is the same thing as image. An image is "the set of meanings by which an object is known and through which people describe, remember and relate to it" (Chon, 1990). For an individual who has not visited a destination previously, the travel decision must be made on the perceived image of that destination. After a visit occurs, personal experience modifies that image. However, that first visit is made on the basis of whether or not the destination—or, at least, my image of the destination—is likely to meet needs and wants that are important to me. In fact perceptions are the most important factor in several important decisions made by tourists: the choice of a destination, what is purchased while on vacation, and the decision to return. Further research on the price and quality of Canadian tourism products compared to those of other countries indicated the following (Stevens, 1992):

● Price and quality perceptions are closely linked

● Value is more important than price

● Other factors are more important than price when choosing a destination

● Residents of a country are more critical of their own country's tourism products

---

┌───┐

Quick Trip 3.3
What's in a Name?

Alan Fredericks, vice president and editor-in-chief of *Travel Weekly,* suggests that travel agencies might benefit by calling themselves what they do. Looking through the roster of ASTA (American Society of Travel Agents) members, he notes that many agencies are named after their owners. While recognizing the personal gratification that results from naming a business after oneself, he suggests that it does little to let people know what the agency *does*. In the roster there are many "All About Travels," "All Around Travels" and a myriad of others with "All" in the name. Similarly, there are Gulliver Travels, Crossroads Travel, and others with travel-related words such as Atlas, Compass, and so on. He suggests that businesses that specialize in cruises should have that word in their title but asks why there are so few agencies with the word "tour" in the business name. Tongue in cheek, he wonders if the toy people would allow an agency to use "Tours R Us."

Questions:

1. Do you think the toy store "Toys R Us" would allow such a use of a name?

2. Check the local phone book for the names of travel agencies. How well or how poorly does the name reflect what the agency does? How does the name help or hurt in selling travel services?

Source: Fredericks, A. (October 17, 1996). What's in a name? editorial. *Travel Weekly*, 28.

└───┘

● The perception of price is reality to a visitor

● Visitors distinguish between the overall price of the trip and the price of individual goods and services

● Price becomes more important as visitors decide what to do or buy on the trip

● Canadians are more price-sensitive and more influenced by price than travelers in the U.S., United Kingdom, France, Germany and Japan

● More affluent travelers are less price-sensitive and more quality conscious

● Potential travelers are more price-sensitive in addition to having higher quality expectations

● Quality services are the key to repeat visitation as well as attracting potential tourists

It is important to consider the factors that influence image formation. According to Gunn (1972) an image evolves at two levels. An *organic image* is formed as a result of general exposure to newspaper reports, magazine articles, television reports, and other specifically non-tourist information. Thus, even the individual who has never visited a particular country nor even sought out information on that country will have some kind of image, probably incomplete, of that country. At this point, as mentioned earlier, other pieces of the image picture will be added that the individual perceives *should* be there to match the pieces already known in order to make a complete picture. The second level is that of an *induced image*. This refers to an image brought about by tourist-directed information, such as advertisements and travel posters. The organic image tends to develop first and, as such, may be regarded as a stronger influence than the induced one in overall image formation. There is little that can be done to influence the formation of an organic image. Filmmakers may be persuaded to shoot a movie such as *Braveheart* which, although not a travel film, influences people in their image of Scotland. In general, however, little can be done. Marketers do seek, obviously, to induce an image through the production of films, posters, and advertisements. If the organic image is set in an individual's mind, an induced image may be disregarded in favor of the previously held organic image.

The influence of image is suggested in figure 3.3. The organic image is already present to some extent before an individual is motivated to travel. It is based upon the kinds of information suggested

above. Being motivated to travel, the individual undertakes an active search for information on the destinations being considered. This will result in an induced image of the destinations. The organic image, being stronger, will modify as additional information taken in as part of the induced image. Once the destination is selected and the trip taken, the actual personal experiences at the destination have an impact upon the evaluation of future vacation plans.

It is proposed that a destination image has two main components: those that are *attribute-based* and those that are *holistic*. Each of these components contain *functional* (or more tangible) and *psychological* (or more abstract) characteristics; that images of destinations also range from those based on common functional and psychological characteristics to those based on more distinctive or unique features (Echtner & Ritchie, 1993). This is illustrated in figure 3.4. On the attribute-holistic continuum, a destination is perceived both in terms of information regarding specific features, such as

climate and the friendliness of the people, and an overall sense of the place, such as the general feeling or atmosphere of the destination.

On the functional-psychological component there are characteristics that are directly measurable (low prices) and those that are less tangible (generally safe). Functional and psychological characteristics may be individual attributes or overall impressions. Finally, on the common-unique continuum, both functional and psychological characteristics as well as individual attributes and holistic impressions may be common or consist of unique features. It is argued that, only by considering all of the dimensions noted above can the complete image of a destination be developed. This is importance because, as the authors of the study indicate, "if a destination is found difficult to categorize or is not easily differentiated from other similar destinations, then its likelihood of being considered in the travel decision process is reduced" (Echtner & Ritchie, 1993).

An image *can* change over time. Research has indicated that, although, consumers have stable perceptions about frequently bought products, their image of an infrequently bought product changes over time. Although an image can change over time, can that image *be* changed over time? There is some literature that suggests that an image cannot be changed, but it appears that the task, though difficult, costly, and time-consuming, is not impossible.

Image-Shaping Forces

Technical factors are concerned with getting information through to the potential traveler. However, the information and impressions that do get through are distorted by a number of forces into an image. First there is a tendency on our part to *stabilize our perception* even after the original basis

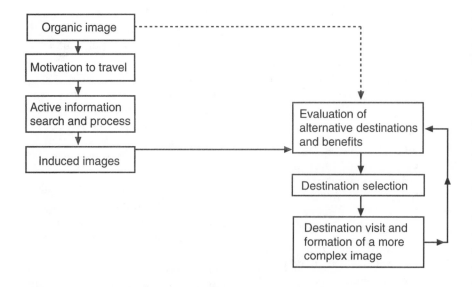

Figure 3.3 A Model of a Tourist's Image Formation Process.

Source: P.C. Fakeye and J.R. Crompton, "Image Differences Between Prospective, First-time and Repeat Visitors to the Lower Rio Grande Valley," *Journal of Travel Research*, Vol. 30, No. 2. (Fall 1991) 11.

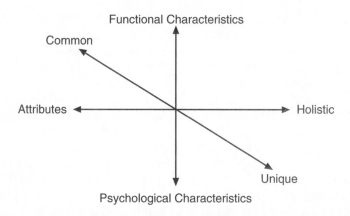

Figure 3.4   The Components of Destination Image.

Source: Echtner, C.M., & Ritchie, J.R.B. (Spring 1993). The Measurement of Destination Image, *Journal of Travel Research*, 31, (4), 4.

for the perception has changed. A traveler may continue to stay at an old favorite hotel where the level of service has declined because the perception remains in the past. An image, whether positive or negative, may continue long after the factors causing that original image have been changed. This illustrates the difficulty involved in changing an image. Linked with this very closely is that, second, as a creature of habit, a traveler will perceive in a certain **habitual way** until forced to think differently. Stress here is placed on the need for marketers to break through the traveler's "habit barrier" by means of various stimuli mentioned above.

A third shaping force relates to the extent to which individuals have a tendency to be **confident** or **cautious**. The confident individual takes in a complex situation more quickly, can more readily see positive elements in a situation, and can assimilate more detail. Decisions are made faster by confident persons, although those who are cautious make slower decisions and hence their perceptions tend to be more accurate. This factor points to the need to communicate different messages to different segments of an intended market. This, of course, will work only if marketers are able to determine that the

more-confident traveler reads different newspapers or magazines or watches different television programs than the more cautious traveler. The amount of information that can be perceived is limited by the fact that we have a **limited span of attention**. This refers to the number of stimuli that can be taken in at the same time. Experiments have shown this number to be approximately eight. This infers that messages should not consist of too many elements for fear that an important element may be missed

or that the message may be disregarded because it is too confusing. The tendency to react to a given stimuli in a certain way is referred to as an **individual's mental set**. This suggests a learned response. It may be possible, for example, to suggest in a campaign, "Whenever you think of hotels, think of Hilton." If the campaign has the desired effect, an individual will think of Hilton (the response) whenever she or he thinks of hotels (the stimulus). Parts of this mental set are the **expectations** we bring to a situation.

People tend to perceive what they expect to perceive. There is a tendency to round out a particular image in our minds by adding pieces that we do not have *based upon what we expect to be there*. For example, a highway traveler may see a sign for a motel that advertises an indoor pool. The traveler may expect that if a motel has an indoor pool, it will also have a certain high quality of service in other facilities. This is known as bringing closure to a situation. Another part of our state of readiness is the degree of **familiarity** we have with incoming stimuli. To the extent that we are familiar with

The presence of a pool at a facility gives the impression that the place has other high-quality features. Photo from *Top Shots* CD Rom. Courtesy of Queensland Tourist and Travel Corporation.

Guests who have a good experience with a hotel chain will likely stay with that chain in different cities. Photo Credit: Westin Hotels.

the stimulus we will have some idea of how to respond to it. This effect of past experience manifests itself in several ways. First, if we have visited Germany, then information about Germany will be perceived by us, in part, based upon our experience there. If we experienced negatives, we will perceive new information about Germany negatively because it evokes memories of a negative experience. The reverse is also true. In addition, if we perceive new information to be *similar* to an experience with which we are familiar, we will tend to act upon that new information in a way similar to our behavior in our previous experience. For example, assume we perceive Austria and Germany to be similar as vacation destinations, yet we have visited only Germany and were pleased with the experience. Information received about Austria will be perceived positively in light of our German experience. This, of course, can work to encourage or discourage purchase behavior. If we know positive feelings exist for a product or service, we may wish to stress the connection when advertising a new product from the same company. A major selling point in a chain operation is the uniformity of quality standards. The message is that if you stayed at one Holiday Inn and were pleased, you will be pleased when you stay at another Holiday Inn. This can also work in reverse. An unpleasant experience at one chain operation will be generalized into a perception about the entire chain. There are times when an advertiser will have to work hard against this tendency. Some tourists will have a tendency to perceive all "sun 'n fun" destinations as being similar. The task for any one such destination is to show that it is different from the others. A further complicated factor is that stimuli in close proximity to each other tend to be perceived as being similar. Despite the fact that islands in the Caribbean have unique identities because of different historical and cultural influences, the fact that they are relatively close together means they will be perceived as being similar. Again, the marketing task is to differentiate one from another. Another related part of this perceptual process relates to *context*. A stimulus will be perceived relative to the context in which it is viewed. A resort will be judged, in part, by the perceptions of the media in which the resort is advertised. Advertising in a magazine viewed as exclusive will bring a certain perception of exclusivity to the resort.

How consumers perceive a situation is also affected by various *social and cultural factors*. A Mediterranean cruise, for example, will be perceived differently by individuals from different social classes. Males and females will perceive the same advertisement differently. It is also clear that the relative merits of attractions at a particular destination are perceived differently by those from different cultures. The difference in perception necessitates different marketing themes for those different market segments. Even within the same country, a destination will be perceived in different terms by those in different social or cultural groups.

A certain cultural bias is present in the minds of those who feel that, in general, Latin American airlines are unsafe. In contrast many European and Asian carriers have a super-brand image. To counteract this Aeromexico recently had a one-word headline in a full page ad: Privatization. The intended message was that, because the private sector was now running the airline, it is safer and the employees are friendlier.

Perception of Distance

The subject of distance in general and perceptions of it in particular, are very important in relation to the study of tourism. Perception of distance influences three crucial tourism decisions: whether to go or stay, where to go, and which route to take (Walmsley & Jenkins, 1992). Perception of distance (and

People often like to travel to a destination that is completely different than their home environment. Photo Credit: Robert Holmes.

also price) are barriers to Hawaii vacations.

Much of tourist travel revolves around differences. People may travel to a different climate, from snow to sun; to see different scenery, from plains to mountains; or to experience a different culture, from modern to traditional. By its very nature, then, tourist travel to experience differences implies covering some distance. The distance to be traveled may act as a barrier, depending upon how it is perceived.

The perception of a particular distance is not a constant. For example the homeward-bound journey seems shorter than the outward-bound journey along the same route; short distances tend to be over-estimated to a greater degree than long distances. The perception of a particular distance seems to vary relative to various socioeconomic factors as well as to the activity to be undertaken. It appears that travelers in higher levels of occupation and income are inclined to travel farther. This may, of course, be partially explained by the fact that they can afford to travel farther. However, those who favored active vacations over inactive vacations are inclined to travel long distances. Some researchers feel that occupation is the key, while others link personality variables to the propensity to travel. Others have shown that distance tends to be overestimated relative to reality (Walmsley & Jenkins, 1992).

Although all of the answers are not known, it does seem that distance can be viewed either positively or negatively in terms of its effect on travel. Certainly the greater the distance the greater the financial cost. As such, distance is a limiting factor. It may also be that great distances represent a psychological barrier because of the tediousness involved in traveling in or the fear of being far from home. At the same time, a destination may increase in attractiveness because of the distance that must be

traveled to get there. It has been demonstrated that, for some tourists, beyond a certain distance the friction of distance becomes reversed—the farther they go, the farther they want to go. Especially on unplanned trips there may be a tendency to view closer-to-home destinations and attractions as stepping stones to stopping points farther away than as competition for the farther destination.

How We Perceive

It is generally felt that we perceive products and services as consisting

Skiing is just one of the benefits bought in a ski vacation package. Photo Credit: Boulder CVB/Anne Krause.

of a bundle of benefits or attributes. A vacation package consists of a variety of parts—for example, in a ski vacation, excellent snow conditions, few lift lines, apres-ski entertainment, saunas, continental cuisine, and so on. A significant association between overall preference for a particular brand and preference based on the attributes of that brand has been demonstrated in the choice of an airline, destination, and tourist attraction. Thus, we buy a bundle of benefits. The decision to purchase the over-

all brand or package will be based upon two factors. First, the skier, for example, must believe that the attributes of the package will help satisfy his or her felt needs. Second, the satisfaction of those felt needs must be important to the skier. The former contributes more to determining an individual's attitude toward a product or service. The implication is that, if we wish to sell a particular vacation, we should sell that vacation as consisting of a number of benefits that will contribute toward the satisfaction of the buyer's needs. As we saw earlier, an individual may be

seeking to satisfy several needs at the same time. Our package, therefore, should contain many elements that will aim at satisfying different needs. The provision of American-type meals and English-speaking guides may satisfy primary physiological and safety needs during a trip to Europe, while the inclusion of side trips to certain "name" resorts may help in satisfying the need for status.

Consumers have a tendency to buy things that have attributes consistent with their own perceived image. An individual's total image is made up of several parts. First, the **real self** is the objective person—what the individual is deep down. In reality, few of us know ourselves this well. Yet this true self governs our purchase and travel behavior, even if we are unaware of what it is that moves us in a particular way. Second, there is the **ideal self**. The ideal self is what we would like to be. This aspect of the individual is easier to discover for two reasons that are important to marketers: consumers are more willing to discuss what they aspire to than what they believe *really* motivates them, and by simple observation of purchase behavior much can be learned about what a consumer is striving for. Last, the **self-image**, is how consumers make purchases that will maintain or improve their self-image, as they perceive it. According to Walters (1978), consumers attempt to preserve the self-image in several ways. They

- buy products consistent with self-image;
- avoid products inconsistent with the self-image;
- trade up to products that relate favorably to group norms of behavior;
- avoid products that show a radical departure from accepted group norms.

These three aspects of the self—the real, ideal, and self-image—are totally concerned with the individual. There are two other aspects of the self concerned with external facts. The apparent self—in essence a combination of the real self, ideal self, and self-image—represents how the consumer is seen by outsiders. The impressions that outsiders have of an individual will determine whether or not any commonality of interests or desires is perceived and whether or not any friendships, will develop. This af-

fects purchases because we tend to copy the purchases of those we admire. Thus, the picture of myself that I give to others—made up of my real and ideal selves and my self-image—will tell others if they and I seem to be the same type of person. If we are, buying patterns for a vacation, for example, may influence others to purchase that type of vacation. The **reference-group self** is how we believe others see us. What is believed, however, is more important than what is real, for behavior is predicted on what we *believe* others want us to do. The important influence of reference groups will be explored further in chapter 4. This self, then, is a combination of all of these aspects.

Benefit Segmentation

> *"For myself, being alone, and not in very good health, I had some heavy moments; but I have no hesitation in saying that, with a friend, a good boat well fitted up, books, guns, plenty of time and a cook like Michel, a voyage on the Nile would exceed any travelling within my experience. The perfect freedom from all restraint, and from the conventional trammels of civilized society, form an episode in a man's life that is vastly agreeable and exciting. Think of not shaving for two months, of washing your shirts in the Nile, and wearing them without being ironed."*
>
> John Lloyd Stephens, Incidents of Travel in Egypt, etc., (1837)

So far, the link between purchase of a product, attitudes toward that product, and perceptions of that product has been stressed. We have said that individuals perceive products and services in terms of bundles of benefits or attributes. Their likelihood of buying a product is determined by the

extent to which they perceive the product to contain sufficient benefits to satisfy their felt needs and also the extent that the satisfaction of those felt needs is important to them. Also, customers buy products that are consistent with their existing self-image or that they feel will allow them to improve their self-image. This is done within the boundaries of what kinds of purchases are sanctioned by their own reference groups. To make an effective marketing application of this process, it would be possible to divide up the tourist potential into segments and develop different vacation alternatives for the different segments based upon the various benefit bundles being sought by each segment. "Market segmentation is a technique used to divide a heterogeneous market into homogeneous sub-groups or market segments" (Davis & Sternquist, 1987). For example, in the skiing market people look for different things from the skiing experience. To some, the quality of the slopes is of prime importance; to others, the apres-ski entertainment is paramount. Each segment looks for different attributes. To the first segment a campaign stressing the quality of the slopes and the short lift lines would work. This campaign would not particularly interest the entertainment skiers. A brochure showing people sipping hot buttered rum around a blazing fire would be more effective.

It has been found that benefit-based market segmentation is a viable means of determining vacation market segments (Loker & Perdue, 1990). The benefits people seek are better determinants of behavior than are other approaches, and have been shown to predict behavior better than personality and lifestyle, usage, and demographic and geographic measures. These latter describe behavior without explaining it.

It has been demonstrated, for example, that the benefits sought from a specific destination vary by season and for different segments of the market. In the first study (Calantone & Jonar, 1984) visitors to Massachusetts were segmented by benefits sought and, further, by season of the year. Spring visitors were looking for a combination of such things as good road conditions, sporting activities, and historical and cultural attractions. The summer group was also interested in sporting activities and historical and cultural attractions. In addition, however, two new segments appeared—one group looking for a clean and scenic environment at a low cost, and the other a clean environment with a good climate and quality accommodations. The major benefit sought by fall tourists was a clean and inexpensive vacation with a large number of attractions that were cultural and historical. Winter travelers were concerned about climate and relaxation, the extent of commercialization, and the quality of shopping.

The second study (Woodside & Jacobs, 1985) looked at the benefits sought by visitors to Hawaii. It was found that Canadians saw rest and relaxation as the main benefit of a vacation to Hawaii; mainland Americans sought cultural experiences, and Japanese visitors reported family togetherness as the major benefit from the trip. A study of the Taiwan outbound pleasure travel market used benefit segmentation to describe the market (Lin & Ralston, 1995). Four distinct segments were found: Adventure Seekers (1 percent of the market); Escapers (11 percent); Non-differentiators (62 percent who primarily are interested in the social aspects of the vacation); and Knowledge Seekers (17 percent).

These findings have implications for product and promotional strategy. Different travel products would be developed for different segments of the market and advertising messages would differ by market segment and by season.

There has been some question as to the individuality of specific destinations in providing unique benefit bundles. Does each destination contain those elements that will satisfy particular felt needs? It has been suggested that socio-psychological motives are unrelated to destination attributes. The emphasis may shift from the destination itself to its function as a medium through which socio-psychological needs can be satisfied. If the "escaping from" motive is more important than the "seeking" motive (as suggested in chapter 2), then destinations are, to a certain extent, interchangeable. Earlier we saw that a large percentage of tourists who use travel agents enter with only a general idea of where they wish to visit. This suggests the difficulty from a marketing viewpoint of establishing a destination as the unique place offering various unique benefits to satisfy particular needs.

Marketing Implications

> *"In a triumph of marketing over reality, readers of* Travel & Leisure *magazine selected a hotel that isn't even built yet as one of their favorites in a reader's survey. . . . It's a mystery to us, but nonetheless we're pleased,' says a spokesman for Hyatt International.' "*
>
> Wall Street Journal *(11/27/96)*

Image research does not tell us which of the destination attributes are important to potential visitors. Nor does it indicate which are unique and do a good job of differentiating a destination from its competition in terms of the ability to meet the needs and wants of the guest. The concept of *positioning*

Quick Trip 3.4

I Am Not Making This Up . . .

According to Dave Barry ("I am not making this up") the following Wisconsin communities use the following slogans:

- Babcock—"Where the Last Passenger Pigeon Was Killed"
- Cumberland—"Rutabaga Capital"
- Ellsworth—"Cheese Curd Capital of Wisconsin"
- Hurley—"Where Highway 51 Ends and the Fun Begins"
- Kewaskum—"Gateway to the Kettle Moraine"
- Mercer—"Loon Capital of the World"
- Sauk Prairie—"Cow Chip Throwing Capital"

Questions:

1. How effective are these slogans in giving you an image of the destination?

2. What is that image?

3. To what extent does this induce you to visit the destination?

Source: The 1994 Dave Barry calendar, June 2.

takes care of these deficiencies. Positioning is "the process of establishing and maintaining a distinctive place for a destination in the minds of potential visitors within target markets." The stages involved in developing a positioning strategy for a destination are as follows (Crompton, Fakeye, & Lue, 1992):

1. Identify the competition.
2. What are the strengths and weaknesses of the destination as perceived by the target market?
3. What benefits are being sought by the target market?
4. What are the strengths and weaknesses of the competition as perceived by the target market?
5. How do potential visitors perceive the destination relative to the competition?

6. Select the best position for the destination.

This has very real marketing implications. Effective marketing strategies can be determined only after determining the extent to which potential visitors perceive that our destination contains those attributes that they consider important. This involves a three-step process:

1. What do you, the potential visitor, consider important?
2. Do you *perceive* that we have this?
3. Do we *actually* have this?

In a survey of potential tourists (see table 3.4), individuals were asked what attributes they considered very important in planning a foreign trip and the extent to which they perceived that Britain did the

best job of satisfying these same attributes. By comparing these responses, various strategies are suggested. The model for this process is contained in figure 3.5.

The first consideration is "what does the market consider important or unimportant?" Potential visitors are particularly interested in physical safety, scenic beauty, historical attractions, climate, and hospitality. Because it is important to the market, it is important to us. The people in this segment of the market are not particularly interested in gambling, the country's political position, good nightlife, or American-style comforts. These latter elements should be ignored by us. To include them in any marketing effort would overload the consumer and may result in the potential visitors "protecting" themselves by ignoring the entire message.

We now know what is important to visitors. Will they be satisfied with our destination if they visit us? The answer depends upon a comparison of their image of the destination compared to our knowledge of what actually exists relating to the attributes they consider important. Several outcomes are possible. First, the visitors' perception or image may be negative when we know that it should be positive. For example, climate is important (ranked 4), but Britain rates poorly (ranked 8). There are, however, times of the year when the British climate is reasonably good. In this case, the image must be changed before visitors will feel positive. A campaign may stress the amount of sunshine or lack of rain in certain months. Some destinations in the Bahamas offer rain insurance. If you get more than a certain amount of rain during your vacation, your hotel room is free.

What if the image is negative and the actual condition is negative also? Britain's climate is rated poorly, and there certainly are some very wet months there. The solution is to change the product. If we

Table 3.4 Comparison of important attributes and perceptions of Britain*

	A RANK	B RANK
A. Safety from physical harm	1	5
B. Real scenic beauty	2	6
C. Seeing things of historical interest	3	2
D. Good weather and climate	4	18
E. Having people make you feel welcome	5	7
F. Getting really good food	6	16
G. Cost of trip fits regular income without special savings	7	11
H. Famous cities	8	3
I. Visit more than one country easily	9	8
J. Easy language communication	10	1
K. Being sympathetic to people and their achievements	11	12
L. Famous art museums	12	4
M. Finding everything different from the United States	13	17
N. Good beaches, swimming, water sports	14	21
O. Shopping for things you'd like to buy	15	9
P. Religious pilgrimage, seeing shrines	16	19
Q. Being familiar with country and area	17	14
R. American-style comfort, convenience	18	10
S. Good nightlife	19	13
T. Sympathy with political position of country's and area's government	20	15
U. Being able to gamble at casinos	21	20

*Based on 1513 people interviewed at 200 locations throughout the U.S.

A. Attributes considered very important when planning a foreign trip

B. Attributes that travelers perceive Britain as doing the best job of satisfying

Source: M. Perry, "Comparison of Tourist Destination Image as Perceived by Travelers and Travel Agents," in New Perspectives and Policies Proceedings of the International Tourism Conference, Turkey, 1978.

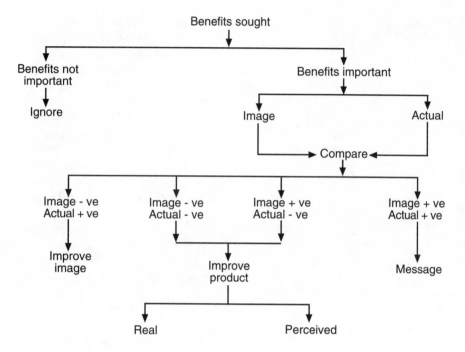

Figure 3.5 Perception—Marketing Implications.

score low on a factor important to the market, we have to get our own house in order before we can attract visitors. This may mean a real or perceived change. For example, to attract tourists during those wet months it may be necessary to develop more indoor facilities where activities can take place irrespective of the weather. The product change may, on the other hand, be perceptual. There is a segment of skiers who place high priority on short lift lines. If a ski area is perceived as having long lift lines, it will be necessary to change the product if, in fact, the lines are long. How can a lift line be shortened? A real change would be to open up more hill capacity. This, however, is expensive. A perceived change would be to make the wait *appear* shorter. Some Michigan ski areas provide entertainers or musicians to provide a diversion for those in line to make the time spent in line seem short.

The same strategy is appropriate if the image is positive but the actual situation is negative. In such a situation we may attract visitors because they think they will be made

to feel welcome. If we know that our employees do not have enough training to give this expected level of service, dissatisfaction will result unless the product (employee hospitality) is changed.

Tourists compare their initial expectations with their actual experience (or, actually, their *perception* of the actual experience). It has been found that (Chon, 1992):

- When the expectation of the destination is negative but the perceptions are positive, the tourist is most satisfied

- When the expectation is positive and the perception is positive, the satisfaction is moderate

- When the expectation is negative and the perceptions are negative, satisfaction is lower than either of the above scenarios

- When the expectation is positive but perceptions are negative, the tourist is least satisfied

Going back to the British example, what if the image is positive and the actual is positive? This be-

comes the thrust of our message. In this example, we would see Britain on a combination of history and hospitality.

This process can be displayed visually in a perceptual map. A perceptual map shows the collective perceptions of a segment of the market for a particular destination of factors considered important to them. A perceptual map of Great Britain is shown in figure 3.6. The importance of vacation attributes has been placed on the horizontal axis and the perception of Britain for these same attributes has been placed on the vertical axis.

Crosshairs dividing the map into four quadrants have been placed near the midpoint of the importance and perception scales. There are twenty-one factors in all. Half of them are above the horizontal cross bar and half are below. Similarly, half are to the left of the vertical cross and half are to the right of it.

Items in Quadrant I consist of those attributes that are important to this segment of the market and on which Britain is perceived as doing a good job of providing. These items must survive a *reality check*. Do we really do a good job of providing these? Britain is perceived as a safe, scenic country with great historical interest. The people are seen as being friendly; it is affordable; it allows the opportunity to see great cities and to visit more than one country easily; and there is no language barrier. To what extent is this really true? If this image is, in fact, a true representation of the way it is, this would be the focus of the advertising message. A positive image on items considered important to the market will bring people in, but once they get to their destination and find that what exists is less than what they imagined, they will be disappointed.

Quadrant II contains items that are important to the potential travelers but on which Britain has a poor image. There are problems

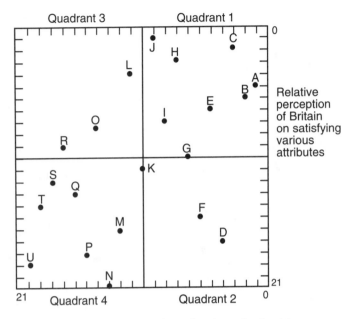

Relative perception of Britain on satisfying various attributes

Relative importance of attributes when planning a foreign trip

Figure 3.6   A Perceptual Map of Britain.

with the weather and the food. These problems must be examined to determine the extent to which they are real or imagined, and either the image or the product must be changed.

In Quadrant III there are items that are not important to the tourist, but items on which Britain has a good image. Quadrant IV contains items that are not important to the tourist and on which Britain has a poor image. Because Quadrants III and IV contain items not important to the tourist, they should not be mentioned in an advertising campaign for fear of overloading the viewer with information they do not consider important to them.

Through the use of perceptual mapping, destinations can determine how or if they should change their tourism product and advertising.

Summary

Once people are motivated to go on vacation they begin an information search to compare various alternatives. They seek and receive information from friends and relatives, travel opinion leaders as well as from the commercial environment. The latter has less credibility. Incoming information goes through a two-step process before it has an impact. The first step controls the quantity of information that is received; the second controls the quality of information taken in. It is possible to structure messages such that they have a greater chance of being noticed and giving off the intended message.

Because people perceive a destination as consisting of a bundle of benefits, benefit segmentation is a viable way of segmenting a market. By comparing what is important to the tourist with the perception the tourist has of a particular vacation spot, a perceptual map can be developed to aid in marketing.

Quick Trip 3.5
The Slave Route

The World Tourism Organization's (WTO) project to promote cultural tourism to African countries with links to the historic slave trade unveiled its new project logo. The Slave Route logo, according to WTO, "emphasizes the influence that Africa has had on popular music and aims to provide an upbeat holiday image for the project without minimizing the tragic realities of African history."

Questions:

1. To what extent does the logo fulfill the mission set down for it?

2. Will this logo help, hurt or have no impact on the development of cultural tourism to Africa?

3. Could you have developed a better logo for this purpose? Do so.

Logo reprinted with permission of the World Tourism Organization.

References

Calantone, R.J., & Johar, J.S. (1984). Seasonal segmentation of the tourism market using a benefit segmentation framework. *Journal of Travel Research*, 23 (2), 14–24.

Chon, K. (1990). The role of destination image in tourism: A review and discussion. *The Tourist Review*, (2), 2–9.

Crompton, J.L., Fakeye, P.C., & Lue, C. (1992). Positioning: The example of the Lower Valley in the winter long stay destination market. *Journal of Travel Research*, 31 (2), 20–26.

Davis, B.D., & Sternquist, B. (1987). Appealing to the elusive tourist: An attribute cluster strategy. *Journal of Travel Research*. 25, (4), 26.

Echtner, C.M., & Ritchie, J.R.B. (1993). The measurement of destination image. *Journal of Travel Research*, 31, (4), 3–13.

Gunn, C.A. (1972). *Vacationscape: Designing tourist regions*. Austin, TX: University of Texas, 110–113.

Harris, Louis & Associates (biennial since 1971). *The character and volume of the U.S. travel agency market*.

Lin, Y., & Ralston, L. (1995). *Benefit segmentation of the Taiwan outbound pleasure travel market: An exploratory study*. Proceedings of the 26th Annual Conference of the Travel and Tourism Research Association, 211–217.

Loker, L.E., & Perdue, R.R. (1990). A benefit-based segmentation of a nonresident summer travel market. *Journal of Travel Research*, 31 (1), 30–35.

Makens, J.C., & Marquardt, R.A. (1977). Consumer perceptions regarding first class and coach airline seating. *Journal of Travel Research*, 16 (1), 19–22.

Miller, J.E. (1995). *Perceptual mapping*. A travel research seminar presented at the Annual Conference of the Travel and Tourism Research Association.

Oh, I., & Lee, J. (1995). *Modification of travel information communication flow*. Poster Presentation at the 26th Annual Conference of the Travel and Tourism Research Association.

Rao, S.R., Thomas, E.G., & Javalgi, R.G. (1992). Activity preferences and trip-planning behavior of the U.S. outbound pleasure travel market. *Journal of Travel Research*, 30 (3), 3–12.

Stevens, B.F., (1992). Price value perceptions of travelers. *Journal of Travel Research*, 31 (2), 44–48.

Walmsley, D.J., & Jenkins, J.M. (1992). Cognitive distance: A neglected issue in travel behavior. *Journal of Travel Research*, 31 (1), 24–29.

Walters, C.G. (1978). *Consumer behavior: Theory and practice*. Homewood, IL: Richard D. Irwin, Inc., 182–186.

Woodside, A.G., & Jacobs, L.W. (1985). Step two in benefit segmentation: Learning the benefits realized by major travel markets. *Journal of Travel Research*, 24 (1), 7–13.

Additional Readings

"An Investigation of Consumer Perceptions of, and Preferences for, Selected Tourism Destinations: A Multidimensional Scaling Approach," Jonathan Goodrich, Ph.D. dissertation, State University of New York at Buffalo, 1977.

Psychology of Leisure Travel, Edward J. Mayo and Lance P. Jarvis, C.B.I. Publishing Company, Inc., Boston, MA, 1981.

"The Relevance of Life Style and Demographic Information to Designing Package Travel Tours," James Abbey, Ph.D. dissertation, Utah State University, 1978.

"A System's Model of the Tourist's Destination Selection Process with particular Reference to the Roles of Image and Perceived Constraint," John Crompton, Ph.D. dissertation, Texas A&M University, 1977.

> "Today's travelers have a common set of expectations. Meet those expectations and the client is happy. No complaints. Fail to meet those expectations, you may lose a client."
>
> *The Institute of Certified Travel Agents*

4

Travel Purchase

···The Traveler's Buying Process ·······

Purpose

Having learned about how people make travel decisions and destination choices, students will be able to suggest appropriate communications strategies.

Learning Objectives

Having read this chapter, you should be able to:

1. Describe the buying-process stages that people go through when making travel decisions.

2. Explain the effectiveness of different communication strategies at each stage of the buying process.

3. Identify which promotional techniques work best at each stage of the buying process.

4. Describe some of the models that have been suggested to explain how travelers choose destination areas.

5. Describe the series of sub-decisions that make up how a vacation decision is actually made.

6. Explain the influence of family life-cycle stages on vacation sub-decisions.

Overview

When travelers become aware of a need to travel, they go through a series of stages before committing to a purchase decision. The characteristics of each of these steps is examined. The communications strategy of the marketer depends upon where the target market is in the buying process. Appropriate strategies for each stage in the buying process are outlined.

A number of alternative destination choice process models are described. It is suggested that perceived travel activities and benefits play a key role in the choice of destination areas. It is also pointed out that people's travel decisions and decision-making processes change as they gain more travel experience.

The decision to take a travel trip involves a series of sub-decisions—where to go, when to go, how long to stay, how to travel, and so on. The order in which these sub-decisions are made and the influence of various family members on the sub-decisions is examined.

nation than about Tibet. To sell Tibet would require a rather lengthy educational process. Making a travel decision involves "selecting and committing oneself to a course of action that involves a series of steps or events" (Milman, 1993).

Attention and Awareness

When making a travel purchase, a consumer moves through several stages. The wise marketing manager realizes that different communication strategies are appropriate for different stages of the buying process. Figure 4.1 illustrates the various stages as defined by several authors. When deciding whether or not to visit a previously unknown destination area, an individual may at first be unaware of its potential as a travel destination. The destination area has to be brought to the awareness or attention of the potential traveler. A prime function in communicating to the consumer is to gain attention. Mass media advertising can be very influential at this point. A slogan or a jingle aimed at arousing curiosity can be

successful in gaining the viewer's attention. This is the first step in the buying process.

Research has shown that people who are familiar with central Florida were more interested in and likely to revisit it compared to those who were only aware of the destination (Milman & Pizam, 1995). As people move from the awareness stage to the familiarity stage, their interest and likelihood to visit increases. However, the same study found that moving from non-awareness to awareness does not necessarily increase the likelihood of visiting the destination area. This is not surprising. Once aware of a particular destination area, individuals, perhaps based on scanty information, might decide that visiting it will not satisfy needs and wants important to them. They "drop out" of the buying process. However, it might call into question the large amounts of money spent on making people aware of destination areas of which they were previously unaware. Targeted advertising oriented toward specific markets and travel opinion

Travel Purchase: The Traveler's Buying Process

> "Trying to escape—at least in the ways that travel brochures promise—is like trying to escape death. We know that we really can't do it, but that all the meaning we'll ever find will be in the effort."
>
> John Kritch

It is easier, less time-consuming, and less costly to sell London as a travel destination than it is to sell Tibet. Part of the reason is that more people know more about and have specific opinions or attitudes about London as a vacation desti-

It is easier to sell London as a travel destination than it is to sell Tibet. Photo by Corel.

HOWARD/SHETH	CRISSY	MCDANIEL	AIDA	IUOTO	RUSS	CUNNINGHAM
				Unawareness		
Attention	Awareness	Awareness	Attention	Awareness	Awareness	Awareness
Comprehension		Knowledge		Comprehension		
Attitudes	Interest	Liking	Interest		Interest	Interest
	Evaluation	Preference	Desire		Desire	Evaluation
		Conviction		Conviction		
Intention						
Purchase	Trial	Purchase	Action	Action	Action	Trial
	Adoption				Reaction	Adoption

Figure 4.1 The Traveler's Buying Process.

Sources: Howard, J., & Sheth, J.N. (1969); Crissy, W.J.E., Boewadt, R.J., & Laudadio, D.M. (1975); McDaniel, C., Jr. (1979); AIDA, Strong, E.K. (1925); IUOTO (undated); Russ, F.A., & Kirkpatrick, C.A. (1982); Cunningham, W.H., & Cunningham, I.C.M. (1981).

leaders (see chapter 3) might be one answer.

At this early point, there is some indication (based on one relatively small sample) that individuals make an initial judgment as to the extent to which the destination area meets their needs. If it does, it is looked at more closely. At this early stage of the process facilitators—"those beliefs about a destination's attributes which help to satisfy a potential traveler's specific motives" (Um & Crompton, 1992) —are influential. Later on in the process inhibitors—"attributes which are not congruent with his or her motives" (Um & Crompton, 1992)—become more influential.

Knowledge and Comprehension

The task in the next stage of the buying process is to make the customer *goal directed*. If the potential traveler's attention has been successfully stimulated, she or he seeks out more information on the destination area. The attempt is to become more knowledgeable about what the destination area has to offer, to comprehend what it is all about. The emphasis is on information, and the task of the communicator is to provide sufficient information to direct the potential traveler toward purchase. Advertising is again important at this stage. The choice of media is crucial. Me-

dia should be chosen that can convey a great deal of information. Brochures or the World Wide Web can do this, as can magazine and newspaper advertisements with a great deal of copy. Radio and television cannot provide the large amounts of information needed at this stage. It is important to talk about the destination area in terms of the benefits offered. It will be remembered that destination areas are perceived in terms of their benefits to the individual. To the extent that we understand a message, we are more inclined to pay attention to it.

Attitudes, Interest, and Liking

If the communication so far has been effective, the potential traveler next moves to developing a liking, interest, or attitude about the destination area. The promotional objectives at this stage are to create or reinforce existing positive attitudes or images or to correct negative attitudes or images. A positive attitude is influenced by the individual's tendency or predisposition to visit that particular destination area (see chapter 3). It is also a function of how well we have gained the traveler's attention and provided sufficient information for him to determine whether or not the benefits of the destination area match his needs and wants. Atti-

tudes are difficult to change because, as a new attitude is developed, new incoming information is often screened to conform to an old attitude. It has been demonstrated that awareness or attention must exist before an attitude can change. The interest in a particular destination area influences how much effort is put into the comprehension of a particular message.

Evaluation, Preference, and Desire

After evaluating various alternatives, the consumer develops a preference or desire for a destination area. The importance of advertising is somewhat less at this stage. The most effective types of messages are *testimonial* and *comparison advertisements*. In a testimonial advertisement, a person, usually a well-known public figure, praises what is being sold. The hope is that if the viewer or reader respects the person in the message, their opinion on the product or service being sold is respected. The same effect can be gained by "testimony" from someone who has already visited the destination area. It is crucial that the spokesperson be believable. It is also important, for maximum impact, that the person chosen to be in the advertisement have some connection with what is being sold. A good example would be James

Mitchener advertising Hawaii. Because he is the author of the best-seller entitled *Hawaii*, Mitchener is a well-respected personality with an obvious link to what is being advertised. A form of testimonial is the rating found in various guidebooks. To the extent that the rating system is respected, advertising the rating gains the respect of the readers. For example, Crystal Cruises ran an ad in *Travel Weekly*, a publication aimed at travel agents, with a quote from *Fielding's Worldwide Cruises 1995*. The quote was "Crystal Harmony offers the world's best cruise experience and sets the standard for all others in the 1990s." The hope was that the prestige of the Fielding name would act as an impartial endorsement of the cruise line.

In a comparison advertisement, one destination area or facility is mentioned in a promotional message in comparison with another. The destination areas are compared on particular attributes. For this kind of message to work, it is necessary to select, for the basis of comparison, attributes that the customer thinks are important. It is crucial that the destination area being advertised be stronger on those attributes than the competition. The tendency, however, is that visitors shift from the intensive use of travel catalogs and advertisements to sources of advice such as travel agents and automobile associations. The more educated the visitor, the more sources are used.

Another interesting concept at this point is the idea of the **decoy effect**. The hypothesis is that "the introduction of a carefully constructed 'decoy' into a choice set results in a segment of consumers shifting their choice to a higher priced targeted item" (Josiam & Hobson, 1995). This strategy is outlined in figure 4.2. The "target" is what we want the customer to buy; the "option" is what is initially offered; the "decoy" is offered as an option, but with no intent

that people actually buy it. There has been some limited research on the impact of a decoy in making a travel decision that seems to support the hypothesized contention. The implications are obvious. Offering additional choices to customers (decoys) that are within the price range of the destination area being targeted but that offer less perceived value might shift customers to the higher-priced target. In part this is because the value offered relative to the price charged for the decoy is less than that of the target. It is also because customers tend to stay away from extreme options. In the situation displayed in figure 4.2 the low price-low value "option" seems an extreme choice in comparison to the other choices.

Intention and Conviction

At this stage in the buying process, the potential travelers are convinced that the benefits of the destination area meet their needs and wants and are almost at the point

of purchase. Studies have shown that the intention to purchase precedes the actual purchase.

Purchase, Trial, and Action

If the potential traveler has reached the conviction stage of the buying process, the barrier to travel is likely to be lack of time or money. It is clear that the motivation is present. The marketing task is to identify the barrier and develop a product to breach it. If the problem is lack of money, a tour package may be successful. Lodging in smaller, cheaper hotels can be suggested. If the problem is one of time, it may be possible to offer a package that capitalizes on the time available. One of the reasons that fly-cruise packages have been developed is to respond to a market that has the money and the motivation, but not the time. Previously, when ships cruised out of New York much time was lost because two days of bad weather often had to be experienced before the ships

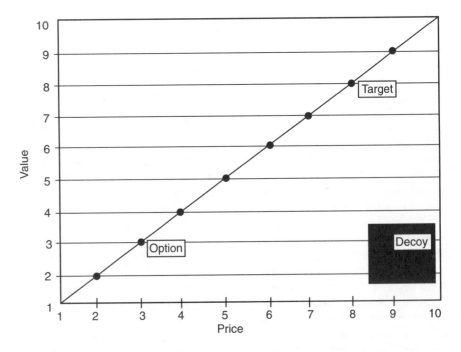

Figure 4.2   The Decoy Effect.

Source: Josiam, B.M, & Hobson, J.S.P. (1995). Consumer choice in context: The decoy effect in travel and tourism. Journal of Travel Research, 34 (1), 46.

reached sunny climates. The solution has been to fly travelers to Florida, sail out of a southern port, and give more sun for the time available.

Adoption

The final stage of the buying process is the adoption stage. At this point, the traveler has become a repeat purchaser. To achieve this end, it is necessary to provide a quality experience to the first-time traveler. However, advertising also has a role to play. The necessity for some form of communication to the purchaser results because of **cognitive dissonance**. Cognitive dissonance occurs after a choice between two or more alternatives has been made. It is a feeling of anxiety, a feeling that perhaps the choice made was not the best one. The amount of dissonance felt is influenced by the type of decision made. The anxiety is stronger if

- the rejected alternative is attractive;
- the decision is important;
- the purchaser becomes aware of negative characteristics in the alternative chosen;
- the number of rejected alternatives increases;
- the alternatives are perceived as being similar;
- the decision made goes against a strongly held belief;
- the decision is a recent one.

Because vacation travel represents an important decision, it has the potential for creating a great deal of anxiety after the purchase has been made. The potential is even greater if the traveler has chosen among a large number of attractive alternate destination areas. The key is to indicate to the traveler as soon as possible after the decision has been made that the decision has been a good one. A note to the purchaser of a package tour

Visitors may collect travel information to improve their knowledge about a special place, such as the Matterhorn in Switzerland. Photo by Corel.

or cruise may be sufficient to avoid second thoughts and cancellations. For advertisers, the key is to provide in their advertisements information that purchasers can use to justify to themselves the purchase made, as well as the messages to convince people to buy.

Buying-Communication Processes Interaction

> *"The country of the tourist pamphlet always is another country, an embarrassing abstraction of the desirable that, thank God, does not exist on this planet, where there are always ants and bad smells and empty Coca-Cola bottles to keep the grubby finger-print of reality upon the beautiful."*
>
> *Nadine Gordimer*

Visitors seek information to identify destination area options. Beyond that primary need, however, is the fact that there are three nonfunctional elements of the search (Fesenmaier, 1992). Visitors may collect travel information simply to improve their knowledge about a particular place. Second, they may collect it for aesthetic reasons—to get information (primarily pictures) about a special place. Third, the search may allow the armchair traveler to vicariously "experience" vacationing to that spot.

The role of travel information is to minimize risk through information, persuade through image creation, and justify the decision through reminders after the choice is taken. What risks does the visitor take in deciding where to go (Mansfeld, 1992)? First, visitors risk the limited amount of disposable time available to them. For many the vacation is a one-time-only annual event. Make a mistake and you wait a year for the next opportunity. Second, visitors risk the money they have saved over the year for the annual event. Third, there is the risk of choosing a vacation that does not satisfy the needs and wants discussed in chapter 2. Fourth, for those traveling for health reasons, there is the risk of putting one's health at risk. Visitors expose themselves to risk in buying vacations that they hope satisfy various needs and wants important to them. The goal for marketers "is to present the best solution to the problem at the lowest risk" (Lewis, Chambers, & Chacko, 1995).

There is an appropriate and different communications strategy for each stage in the traveler's buying process. This realization is particularly important because it helps in determining why a communications campaign failed. It is fairly easy to determine that a campaign did not work. For example, the promotion to induce travel to a particular destination area can be assumed a failure if there has been no increase in visitors to the destination area after the campaign. A more interesting question is not so much *did* the promotion fail, but *why* did it fail? Were enough people exposed to the message? Was the message memorable? Did it result in a change of attitudes? The only way that campaign managers can determine why the campaign failed is to break the process into its various stages and measure the results of each stage.

The information presented in figure 4.3 refers to this process. At the first stage in the buying process, the objective is to expose the message to a certain number of people. The number of readers or viewers **exposed** to the message serves as a measure of whether or not the campaign reached this objective. At the next level, the objective is to transfer information to those exposed to the message. To determine the effectiveness, it is possible to measure the extent to which people exposed to the message have recalled the essential parts of it.

To measure a change in attitude it is necessary to survey attitudes both before and after a campaign. A similar strategy is necessary to measure whether preferences have been developed. The extent to which a message initiates action can be measured by the percentage of those who send in a response to

BUYING PROCESS STAGES	COMMUNICATION OBJECTIVE	COMMUNICATION MEASUREMENT
Awareness, attention	Exposure	Number of readers/viewers exposed to message
Knowledge, comprehension	Transmission of information	Percentage of readers/viewers who remembered essential parts of the message
Attitudes, interest, liking	Attitude change	Attitude surveys before and after message to determine degree of change
Evaluation, preference, desire	Creation of preferences	Preference surveys before and after message to determine preferences
Intention, conviction	Initiation of action	Number of actions taken in response to a particular message
Purchase, trial, action	Purchase	Number of bookings made
Adoption	Repeat purchase	Percentage of visitors who are repeat purchasers

Figure 4.3 Interaction Between the Buying and Communication Processes.

a particular advertisement or the number who take an advertisement into a travel agent. Last, repeat purchases, signifying the adoption of a product or service, can be measured by the percentage of visitors who are repeat purchasers.

By being aware of these different stages, communication objectives, and ways to measure their accomplishment, it is possible to determine where things went wrong. For example, it may be that the promotion reached a sufficiently large number of the right kind of people, a large percentage of whom remembered the message. However, it may be that the message was not sufficiently strong to result in a change in attitude about the destination area being promoted. The promotion manager knows that the media used were on target in terms of reaching the right numbers of prospects. The program has to be strengthened to result in an attitude change. A strategy offering cheap package tours would be totally ineffective because the necessary prerequisite steps have not been taken in the minds of the readers.

Buying Process Feedback

Although each step in the buying process is a prerequisite for the next, there are also **feedback effects** or **loops**. The purchase itself has an effect on attitudes, either a positive or a negative one. Each higher stage thus tends to reinforce the lower stages. For example, study abroad has been shown to result in a change in attitude about foreigners. As international travel increases, the perception of risk associated with travel decreases. The experience is also shown to be a significant and positive predictor of travel attitudes (Sonmez & Graefe, 1995). Holding a positive attitude about a place means that the potential traveler makes more effort to understand the message being presented. Similarly, understanding the vacation attributes of a destination area means that the potential traveler is more inclined to pay attention to advertisements about that destination area.

It is easier to induce a repeat purchase if a good job has been done to satisfy the traveler the first time, than it is to get that first purchase. Satisfying the visitor reinforces each step in the buying process.

Figure 4.4 provides a summarized *tourism consumer behavior model* based upon the information in chapters 1 to 4. The travel buying-process stages are shown on the right hand side of this model. The buying-process feedback loop links the vacation purchase with alternatives (to be considered in future travel decisions) through satisfaction.

Destination Choices

> "An understanding of the modern Ulysses, whether he be a self-discovery adventurer or the most insulated package tourist, is the appropriate building block for constructing the discipline of tourism studies. Economic, sociological, geographical and economic analyses of tourists all derive from the fact that individuals are motivated to leave their homes to see the world or as Tennyson suggested to strive to seek to find."
>
> Pearce, P.L. (1988), 22

Now that the process by which travelers make purchases is known, it is useful to look at how they choose destination areas, since this choice process triggers the decisions in the next part of The Tourism System Model (Travel). There are several models that try to explain how travelers make destination choices and only a select few will be reviewed.

Moscardo, Morrison, Pearce, Lang, & O'Leary (1996) have proposed a model that integrates the theories relating to the internal and external constraints that have been discussed in chapters 1 to 4 and other chapters. They propose a simplified *destination choice model* that recognizes the contribution of four distinct bodies of research on tourism (Gilbert, 1991):

Quick Trip 4.1
The Group Tour Traveler

The average tour traveler is away for seven nights and spends just over $900 with the tour operator. Older travelers stay away longer and spend more on their tour. Travelers are interested in more active tours. One-third of travelers over 65 years of age say they prefer floating or hiking as opposed to watching from a bus. Almost 50 percent belong to travel clubs or organizations that plan tours for their members and prefer to take group tours with those travel organizations to which they belong. They feel that such organizations make them comfortable right away and create a relaxed feeling.

Three-quarters of group tour travelers are aged 65 or older. More than half are married and living with their spouses. One in five reports a disability or traveling with someone who has a disability.

The planning process begins at least six months prior to actual departure. Two-thirds of travelers say they get information about upcoming trips from the tour company or from the group of which they are a member. Convenience, value, safety, and the educational experience are the most important reasons for taking a tour. They consider the destinations the tour goes to, activities planned for the tour, and the amount important in selecting a specific tour.

Brochures and other marketing publications printed by tour operators are very important in the decision process. The most popular medium for advertising is the Sunday travel section of the local newspaper. Almost three-quarters read *Modern Maturity*. Other publications that are frequently read are *AAA Magazine*, *National Geographic Traveler*, and *Travel & Leisure*. Most group tour travelers are members of the American Association of Retired Persons (AARP).

Both price and cancellation protection are factors that strongly influence tour choice. They are willing to book a trip further in advance for a lower price. The most effective incentive for booking a tour earlier is cancellation insurance provided by the tour operator if the tour traveler cancels.

Source: National Tour Foundation's *Tour Traveler Index*. (1996).

- Travel motivation theories and research (chapters 1 and 2)
- Destination image and attraction research (chapter 3)
- Destination choice model research (chapter 3)
- Market segmentation research (chapters 3, 5, and 14)

The integrative model suggested by Moscardo et al. is shown in figure 4.5. The model suggests that the traveler's desired *activities* and *benefits* provide a link between motivation and destination choice. The components of the model follow:

- **Traveler and socio-psychological variable (A):** This variable includes the needs, wants and motives, and personalities of travelers, and the external influences such as previous travel experience, culture, age, income, education, available time, and family life-cycle stage.

- **Destination marketing variables and external inputs (B):** This includes the marketing by destination areas plus informa-

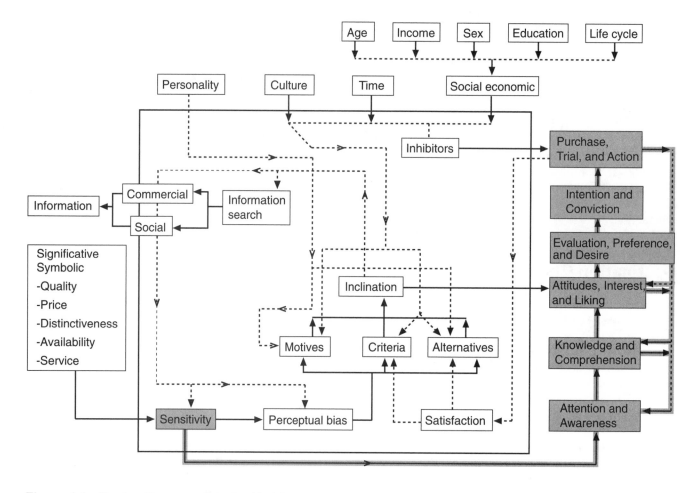

Figure 4.4   Tourism Consumer Behavior Model.

tion that travelers get through travel trade intermediaries, word of mouth, and other external sources of information.

- **Images of destination areas (C):** These are the perceptions or images of alternative destination areas. Moscardo et al. suggest that activities and benefits may be the most important attributes of these in influencing destination choice.

- **Destination choice (D):** The choice of a destination area is made on the basis of there being a match between what activities and benefits travelers prefer, and what activities and benefits they perceive that each destination area offers.

- **Destination areas (E):** The actual activities and benefits

offered and promoted by the destination areas.

By studying the model in figure 4.5 in more detail, the suggested process of destination choice can be better understood. The model shows that images of destination areas (C), in terms of which travel activities and benefits they are thought to provide, are formed through the influence of the traveler and socio-psychological variable (A) and marketing variables and external inputs (B). The destination choice (C) is made by a matching process in which travelers consider what they wish to do when they travel (activities) and what benefits they want (from A), and what they perceive each destination area offers in potential activities and benefits (C). Each desti-

nation area offers an actual set of travel activities and benefits (E), and may select to emphasize these in its destination area marketing efforts (B).

Feedback in the model occurs in several places. For example, a destination area may complete a marketing research study with travelers (B) and determine that they do not think it is a good place for snorkeling and scuba diving (C). However, the destination area has several significant reef areas, and provides excellent snorkeling and scuba diving opportunities. Therefore, marketing programs are changed to put greater emphasis on these opportunities (B) and a program is initiated to encourage more dive and snorkeling operations (E).

Moscardo et al. admit that their model is a simple one and, in fact, it may be overly simplified. However, their main argument is that activities and benefits play a key role in destination choice. This is based on a growing amount of research on the role of activities in travel market segmentation (Hsieh, O'Leary, & Morrison, 1992; Morrison, Hsieh, & O'Leary, 1994).

There are many other "grand models" of consumer behavior in tourism. One of these is the travel decision process model developed by Schmoll (1977) (see figure 4.6). Schmoll's model incorporates the following four influences on the traveler's destination choice (Gilbert, 1991):

- **Travel stimuli:** The promotions by destination areas, the influence of travel trade intermediaries, and word-of-mouth recommendations.

- **Personal and social determinants:** Needs and desires, motivations, and expectations.

- **External variables:** Confidence in travel trade intermediaries, destination area images, previous travel experience, assessment of risk, and cost and time constraints.

- **Destination or service features:** The characteristics of the destination area or travel service being considered.

Another "grand model" discussed by Gilbert (1991) is the visitor decision-making process by Mathieson and Wall (1982) (see figure 4.7). This process consists of the following five stages:

- **Felt need or travel desire:** People feel the need to travel and weigh the reasons for and against traveling.

- **Information collection and evaluation:** People collect information from travel trade intermediaries, brochures, and advertisements, and from their friends and relatives. The information is evaluated based upon costs and time availability.

- **Travel decision:** People select destination areas, modes of transportation, accommodation, and activities.

- **Travel preparations and travel experience:** People prepare for travel trips by budgeting, buying clothing and equipment. The travel trips are taken.

- **Travel satisfaction:** People evaluate their satisfaction with trips during and after the trips. This evaluation influences future travel trips.

Another tourism consumer behavior model is the one suggested by Moutinho (1987). He breaks down the decision process into the following three stages:

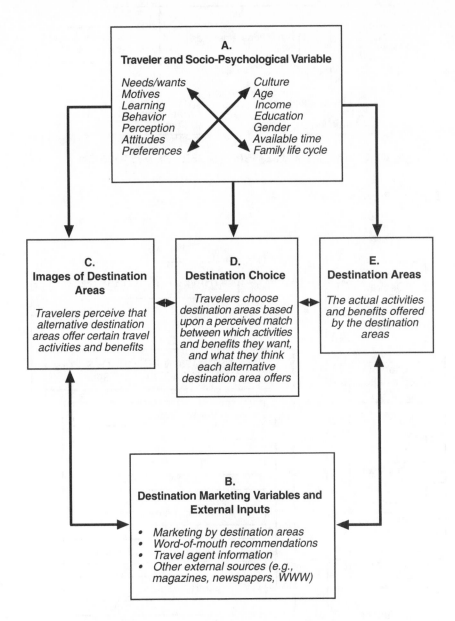

Figure 4.5 A Destination Choice Model Based on Activities and Benefits.

Adapted from Moscardo, G., Morrison, A.M., Pearce, P.L., Lang, C.-T., & O'Leary, J.T. (1996). Understanding vacation destination choice through travel motivation and activities. *Journal of Vacation Marketing*, 2 (2), 109–122.

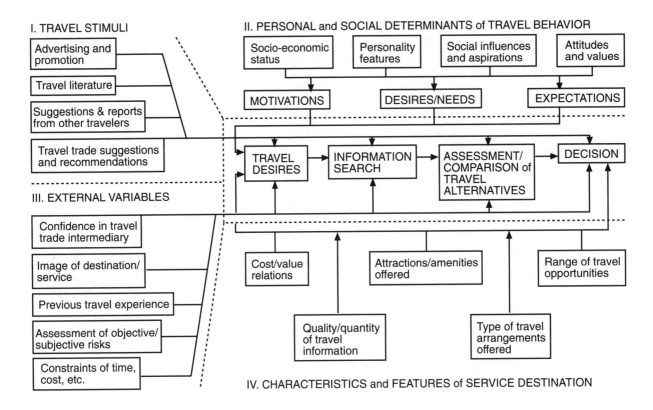

Figure 4.6   Schmoll's Model of the Travel Decision Process.

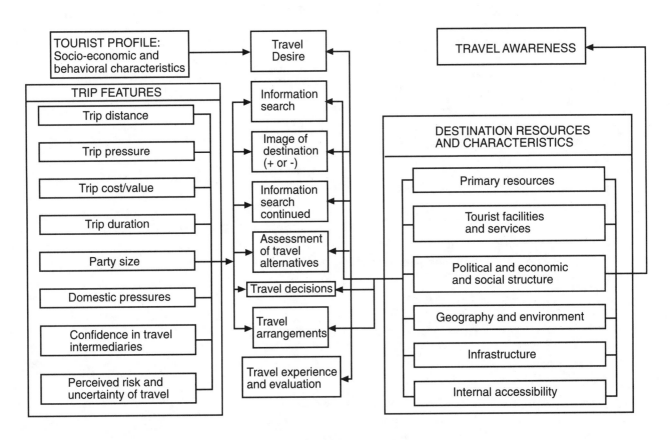

Figure 4.7   Mathieson and Wall's Tourist Decision-Making Process.

Marketing programs often emphasize opportunities that people may not realize are available, such as scuba diving off Lizard Island, Far North Queensland. Photo from *Top Shots* CD Rom. Courtesy of Queensland Tourist and Travel Corporation.

- **Pre-decision and decision:** Includes people's motivations, attitudes, financial status, family influences, preferences, and level of confidence.

- **Post purchase:** People's evaluation of travel experiences.

- **Future decision making:** People's repeat-buying behaviors that are influenced in part by the post-purchase evaluation.

Another model that is worthy of discussion here is Pearce's ***Travel Career Ladder*** (Kim, Pearce, Morrison, & O'Leary, 1996). This model, which is based on Maslow's Hierarchy of Needs theory, argues that each person has a "travel career" just as they have a "work career." The five levels of the Travel Career Ladder are (figure 4.8)

- Relaxation
- Stimulation
- Relationship
- Self-esteem and development
- Fulfillment

There are two sides of the ladder: The left side represents self-directed motivations, and the right is other-directed motivations. People start their travel careers at different levels and may change their levels during their travel careers. Some people "ascend" the ladder predominantly on the left side. Others may go through all the steps on both sides of the ladder. The main point that Pearce's career ladder emphasizes is that people's travel decisions and decision-making processes are not

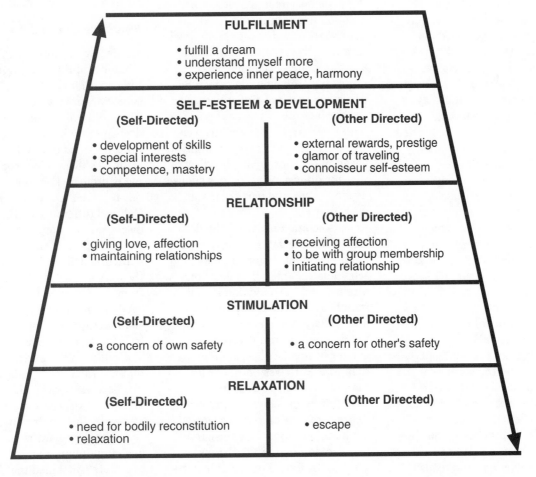

Figure 4.8 Pearce's Travel Career Ladder.

static; they change over a person's lifetime based upon their actual travel experiences. For example, the more experienced travelers become, the more they will act on higher-level needs in the ladder such as fulfillment, self-esteem, and development.

Vacation Sub-Decisions

"Worth seeing? Yes; but not worth going to see."

Samuel Johnson

Although the vacation buying process has been treated as a series of stages culminating in a buying decision, the vacation purchase is actually comprised of a series of sub-decisions. From a marketer's viewpoint, it is important to know the order in which decisions are made and who makes the particular decisions. In this way, a marketing campaign can be developed that is aimed at the decision maker.

What the order of decisions is, and who the decision maker is varies by which stage in the life cycle the family is in. At the stage in which the couple has been married for less than fourteen years, in which the couple is at most in their mid-thirties and may have young children at home, the decision to vacation tends to be a joint one. Although discretionary income is low, the first sub-decision is "where to go," followed by "whether to go." This seems to reflect a more hedonistic attitude, which indicates an expectation to take a vacation despite income restraints. Decisions are next made concerning the amount to spend, the length of time to stay, and the accommodations to be used. In the next stage, in which the couple has been married for fourteen to twenty years, has a mid-forties age median, and has children eighteen years old or more, the husband tends to

dominate the decision making slightly. This is due primarily to the vacations being designed around the husband's work schedule. At this stage, the question of whether or not to go is most important, followed by decisions on destination areas, amounts to spend, length of stay, and place to stay. When the spouses are in the mid-fifties and have been married twenty to thirty years, the process is largely wife dominated. This coincides with vacation purchases at a peak and disposable income close to a peak. The wife-dominated decision making continues until the husband is close to retirement; then he exerts a slight dominance, due perhaps to anxiety about financial matters. For couples married for over forty years, when the couple is retired, the wife once again takes over the decision making.

Other researchers have studied vacation decision making and have suggested that more joint decision making rather than individually-dominated decisions making occurs. Obviously more research is necessary to determine whether or not the decision focus changes with stages in the family life cycle.

The research to-date on family vacation decision making indicates that the dominance of either spouse depends upon the particular sub-decision to be made. External factors also come to bear on the decision. Vacation dates, for example, are probably determined by job and school dates, and hence decisions on these are husband dominated, with heavy influence by the children. There is some indication that the number of joint decisions is greater in middle-class families than in lower-class ones, but less than in the highest class ones.

A review of figure 4.9 indicates that most vacation sub-decisions are joint decisions. The husband tends to dominate in decisions regarding the length of stay, the dates

of the vacation, the amount to spend, and the route to take. Although some studies indicate that husbands tend to dominate the vacation destination area decisions, most studies indicate this to be a joint decision. These decisions are culturally based. In Mexico, for example, the decision to travel appears to be wife-dominant (Michie & Sullivan, 1990).

Kendall, Sandhu and Giles (1983) found that decisions varied by time of year and by profession. In their study, husbands had greater influence on choosing vacations in the off-peak season, while in the prime season the decision was a joint one. In comparing trips taken by medical doctors and lawyers they found that, on the decision to take a trip, the doctor husband had more influence while the wife of the lawyer had more influence on this sub-decision.

Influence of Children

Studies by Jenkins (1978) and Ritchie and Filiatrault (1980) indicate that children influence some vacation sub-decisions. The children's effect is felt on the decision of whether to go on vacation, what dates and destination areas to choose, what type of lodging is preferred, and which activities to undertake while on vacation. Cultural differences have also been discovered in a study comparing the role of children in Belgium, the United Kingdom, Italy, and France (Seaton & Tagg, 1995). Children from the United Kingdom play a smaller role in family vacation decisions than those from other countries, particularly France and Italy. The children themselves agree that the final decision is a joint one between mother and father. Where the decision was not a joint one, the children perceived it as a wife-dominant rather than husband-dominant one. The researchers concluded that involving

For many travelers, vacation times are determined by school and work schedules. Photo from *Top Shots* CD Rom. Courtesy of Queensland Tourist and Travel Corporation.

children in the vacation decision-making process improves the possibility of a child who is happy with the vacation choice, while not involving the children increases the chance that he or she will be one of the small minority who are unhappy while on holiday with the family.

A knowledge of who influences various vacation sub-decisions helps marketing managers in selling their products and services. Facilities and messages can be more clearly geared to the decision-maker in an attempt to increase the attention given the message, the comprehension, and ultimately, the final purchase behavior.

Subdecision	Standish	Jenkins	Myers	Ritchie	Omura	3M	Kendall, et al.
Whether to go							
Whether to take the children		♀					
How long to stay		♂		☿			
How much to spend	♀	♂		♂			♂
Vacation dates		♂		♂			
Vacation destinations	♀	♀	♀	♀	♀	♂	♀
Mode of transportation	☿	♀					
Route		♂	♂				
Lodging	♀	♀	♀				♂
Activities							♀

Key: ♂ male dominated decision
    ♀ joint decision

Figure 4.9 Family Vacation Decision Making.

Sources: Standish, T.C. (1978); Jenkins, R.L. (1978); Myers, P.B., & Moncrief, L.W. (1978); Ritchie, J.R.B, & Filiatrault, P. (1980); Omura, G.S., Roberts, M.L., & Talavzyk, W.W. (1979); 3M National Advertising Company (1972); Kendall, K.W., Sandhu, D.J., & Giles, G. (1983).

Summary

Before making travel bookings, people go through a buying process consisting of a series of stages. Tourism marketers can help "lead" potential visitors through this process by the kinds of messages they design. They must know at which stages people are in the process, and design messages that are appropriate for these stages.

In addition to the buying-process stages, there is also a process that people use to select destination areas for their travel. Scholars have suggested a number of different destination choice process models. The perceived activities and benefits offered by alternative destination areas may play a key role in determining destination choice.

The travel decisions and decision-making processes that people use are not static over time. First, previous experiences and satisfaction with destination areas influence future choices. In addition, people's cumulative travel experiences influence their future travel decisions. Motives for travel and destination choices are affected by people's previous "travel careers."

The decision to travel is actually composed of a series of sub-decisions, in which several people's input affects the decision. For family vacations, children have a significant influence on travel decisions.

An increasing number of people are traveling to benefit from learning about history or by taking classes at colleges and universities: The Technical University of Budapest, Buda, Hungary. Photo from *Budapest in 101 Photos; Multimedia CD for the IBM PC* (Selester, Hungary, 1996). Printed with permission.

References

Crissy, W.J.E., Boewadt, R.J., & Laudadio, D.M. (1975). *Marketing of hospitality services: Food, lodging, travel*. East Lansing, MI: The Educational Institute of the American Hotel and Motel Association.

Cunningham, W.H., & Cunnigham, I.C.M. (1981). *Marketing: A managerial approach*. Cincinnati, OH: South-Western Publishing.

Fesenmaier, D.R. (1992). Researching consumer information: Exploring the role of pre-trip information search in travel decisions. *Proceedings of the Annual Conference of the Travel and Tourism Research Association*, 23, 32–36.

Gilbert, D.C. (1991). An examination of the consumer behaviour process related to tourism. *Progress in Tourism, Recreation and Hospitality Management*, 3, 78–106.

Howard, J., & Sheth, J.N. (1969). *Theory of buyer behavior*. New York: John Wiley & Sons, Inc.

Hsieh, S., O'Leary, J.T., & Morrison, A.M. (1992). Segmenting the international travel market using activities as a segmentation base. *Tourism Management*, 13, 209–223.

IUOTO (undated). *Study and analysis of the long-term effectiveness of promotional campaigns and other tourist publicity and advertising activities*. International Union of Official Tourism Organizations.

Jenkins, R.L. (1978). Family vacation decision-making. *Journal of Travel Research*, 16 (4).

Josiam, B.M, & and Hobson, J.S.P. (1995). Consumer choice in context: The decoy effect in travel and tourism. *Journal of Travel Research*, 34 (1), 45–50.

Kendall, K.W., Sandhu, D.J., & Giles, G. (1983). Family decision making in the upscale travel market. *Proceedings of the Annual Conference of the Travel and Tourism Research Association*, 14.

Kendall, K.W., & Sandhu, D.J. (1985). What do you do when you get there?: A family decision making analysis of activity and lodging sub-decisions of vacationers. *Proceedings of the Annual Conference of the Travel and Tourism Research Association*, 16.

Kim, Y.J., Pearce, P.L., Morrison, A.M., & O'Leary, J.T. (1996). Mature vs. youth travelers: The Korean market. *Asia Pacific Journal of Tourism Research*, 1 (1), 102–112.

Lewis, R.C., Chambers, R.E., & Chacko, H.E. (1995). *Marketing leadership in hospitality: Foundations and practices* (2nd ed.). New York: Van Nostrand Reinhold.

McDaniel, C., Jr. (1979). *Marketing: An integrated approach*. New York: Harper & Row.

Mansfield, Y. (1992). From motivation to actual travel. *Annals of Tourism Research*, 19, 399–419.

Mathieson, A., & Wall, G. (1992). *Tourism: Economic, physical and social impacts*. London: Longman.

Michie, D.A. (1986). Family travel behavior and its implications for tourism management. *Tourism Management*, 7, 8–20.

Michie, D.A., & Sullivan, G.L. (1990). The role(s) of the international travel agent in the travel decision process of client families. *Journal of Travel Research*, 29 (2), 30–38.

Milman, A. (1993). Maximizing the value of focus group research: Qualitative analysis of consumers destination choice. *Journal of Travel Research*, 32 (2), 61–63.

Milman, A., & Pizam, A. (1995). The role of awareness and familiarity with a destination: The Central Florida case. *Journal of Travel Research*, 33 (3), 21–27.

Morrison, A.M., Hsieh, S., & O'Leary, J.T. (1994). Segmenting the Australian domestic travel market by holiday activity participation. *Journal of Tourism Studies*, 5 (1), 39–56.

Moscardo, G., Morrison, A.M., Pearce, P.L., Lang, C.-T., & O'Leary, J.T. (1996). Understanding destination vacation choice through travel motivation and activities. *Journal of Vacation Marketing*, 2 (2), 109–122.

Moutinho, L. (1987). Consumer behaviour in tourism. *European Journal of Marketing*, 21 (10), 1–44.

Myers, P.B., & Moncrief, L.W. (1978). Differential leisure travel decision-making between spouses. *Annals of Tourism Research*, 5, 157–165.

Nichols, C.M., & Snepenger, D.J. (1988). Family decision making and tourism behavior and attitudes. *Journal of Travel Research*, 26 (4), 2–6.

Omura, G.S., Roberts, M.L., & Talavzyk, W.W. (1979). An exploratory study of women's travel attitudes and behavior: Directions for research. *Proceedings of the Association for Consumer Research*, 7.

Pearce, P.L. (1982). *The social psychology of tourist behaviour*. Oxford, England: Pergamon.

Pearce, P.L. (1988). *The Ulysses factor: Evaluating visitors in tourist settings*. New York: Springer-Verlag.

Ritchie, J.R.B., & Filiatrault, P. (1980). Family vacation decision-making: A replication and extension. *Journal of Travel Research*, 18 (4), 3–14.

Ross, G.F. (1994). *The psychology of tourism*. Melbourne: Hospitality Press.

Russ, F.A., & Kirkpatrick, C.A. (1982). *Marketing*. Boston: Little, Brown and Company.

Schmoll, G.A. (1977). *Tourism promotion*. London: Tourism International Press.

Seaton, A.V., & Tagg, S. (1995). The family vacation in Europe: Paedonomic aspects of choices and satisfactions. *Journal of Travel & Tourism Marketing*, 4 (1), 1–21.

Sonmez, S.F., & Graefe, A.R. (1995). International vacation decisions and the threat of terrorism. *Proceedings of the Annual Conference of the Travel and Tourism Research Association*, 26, 236–245.

Standish, T.C. (1978). How the computer views the family vacation travel market. *Proceedings of the Travel Research Association Annual Conference*, 9.

Strong, E.K. (1925). *The psychology of selling.* New York: McGraw-Hill.

3M National Advertising Company. (1972). *Psychographics and the automobile traveler.* 3M.

Um, S., & Crompton, J.L. (1990). Attitude determinants in tourism destination choice. *Annals of Tourism Research,* 17, 432–448.

Um, S., & Crompton, J.L. (1991). Development of pleasure travel dimensions. *Annals of Tourism Research,* 18, 500–504.

Um, S., & Crompton, J.L. (1992). The roles of perceived inhibitors and facilitators in pleasure travel destination decisions. *Journal of Travel Research,* 30 (3), 18–25.

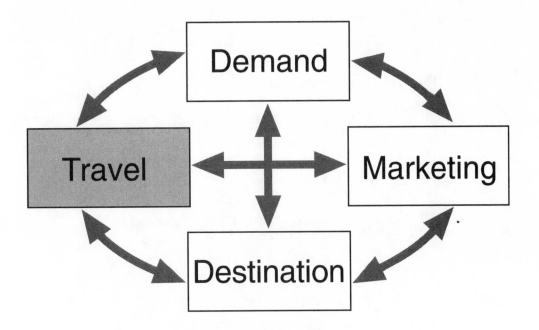

Part II

Travel

The Characteristics of Travel

The decisions that travelers make affect their travel purchases and result in certain characteristics of travel. Part 2 of **The Tourism System** examines these characteristics in terms of travel purposes and market segments, the geographic dispersion of travel flows, and modes of transportation.

Part I

1. Demand:
The Factors Influencing
the Market

Link I

The Travel Purchase

Part 2

2. Travel
The Characteristics of Travel

"Marketing is similar to shuffling and dealing a pack of cards. Many different hands are dealt and played, but only one is a winner. Cards, like customers, can be grouped in several different ways: Similar suits, similar values, similar faces, or "royals." Depending on the game, players reorganize their hands in ways that are most likely to win. They know that selecting and grouping their cards is necessary to succeed. Effective marketers recognize the same type of rule. There is, sadly, an end to this analogy. Playing and winning at cards is a gamble. Marketing should not be."

Morrison, A.M. (1996), 160

5

Purposes of Travel

···The Characteristics of Traveler Segments ·········

Purpose

Readers will be able to demonstrate their knowledge of tourists by suggesting appropriate vacations, packages, services, and messages to the major segments of the market.

Learning Objectives

Having read this chapter, you should be able to:

1. Describe the characteristics of the major segments of the travel market.

2. Suggest appropriate vacations, packages, and services to individual segments of the travel market.

3. Suggest appropriate messages to engage individual segments of the travel market.

Overview

The two major classifications of travel purpose are business travel and pleasure/personal travel. The patterns and needs of people in both segments are the topic of this chapter.

Business travel is the "bread-and-butter" market for many tourism-related businesses. Business travel is broken down into regular travel; business travel related to meetings, conventions, and congresses; and incentive travel, which is somewhat of a hybrid as the people on the trip are traveling for pleasure although the purchasers of the trip are businesses. The characteristics of those in these market segments are explored in detail.

The pleasure/personal travel market is examined from the viewpoint of traditional segments and other major growth segments, such as family travel, the senior travel market, minority travel patterns, gaming, and the cruise markets.

Introduction

". . . the explorer seeks the undiscovered, the traveler that which has been discovered by the mind working in history, the tourist that which has been discovered by entrepreneurship and prepared for him by the arts of publicity."

Paul Fussell

Chapters 1 to 4 have examined how an individual—any individual—makes a travel decision. In order to describe the larger picture of travel flows, it is necessary to describe not individuals but segments of the total travel market. Those travelers relevant to tourism are either tourists, if they are in a destination for more than a day but less than a year, or excursionists, if they arrive and depart the same day. In either case their travel may be for reasons of business or pleasure (see figure 5.1).

The Business Travel Market

"Commuter—one who spends his life
In riding to and from his wife;
A man who shaves and takes a train,
And then rides back to shave again."

E. B. White

In most developed countries, business travel is the "bread-and-butter" market for tourism for much of the year. This is certainly the case in the U.S., Canada, and the United Kingdom. Just as it is inadequate to use the "jumbo jet" approach to analyzing pleasure/personal travel markets, it is equally wrong to view the business travel market as an amorphous mass that cannot be further segmented. In fact, this first major travel market has many component segments, and the number of segments appears to grow from year to year. The business-related travel market segments can be broadly categorized as follows:

- Regular business travel
- Business travel related to meetings, conventions, and congresses
- Incentive travel

The third category of incentive is really a "hybrid" segment since it is a type of pleasure travel that has been financed for business reasons. Thus, the persons on incentive trips are pleasure travelers and the purchasers are businesses.

Regular Business Travel

Between 18 and 20 percent of all U.S. adults travel on business each year (Whitehead, 1995). This translates into anywhere from 35 to 38 million business travelers. In 1994 over 20 million business/convention trips were taken. The average round-trip distance is just over 1,000 miles. Increasingly, more trips are day trips and stays of one

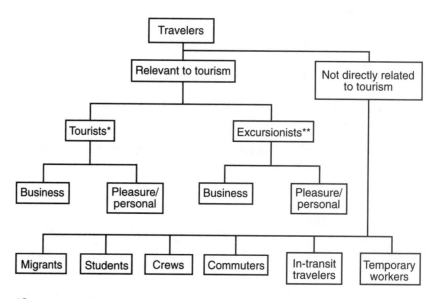

*One or more nights stay
** Arrive and depart same day

Figure 5.1   Segments of the Travel Market.

night duration. While the average number of trips taken annually is six, over half of all travelers take only one or two trips, accounting for 16 percent of all the travel. On the other hand, 15 percent of business travelers take over ten trips a year and account for 56 percent of business travel while 7 percent take over twenty trips annually.

Business travelers are more important to travel suppliers than their total numbers would indicate. They use airlines, rental cars, hotels, and travel agents to a greater extent than pleasure travelers. Business travelers, for example, account for over 40 percent of all airline trips and hotel stays, and account for almost two-thirds of rental car revenues. In selecting an airline, business travelers are primarily concerned with the convenience of the airline schedule. To a lesser extent, low or discount fares and the on-time departure record of the airline influence their choice. Reasonable rates, on the other hand, are the most important factor when choosing a car rental company. This is followed in importance by the convenience of the location and the condition of the cars. Location is the number one factor in selecting a hotel, followed by clean, comfortable rooms and room rates.

Compared to the pleasure traveler, the business traveler is more time sensitive; service quality is more important than price; and she or he is more experienced and demanding. Approximately one-third of all business travelers belong to frequent flyer programs, an average of two programs each. However, this figure increases to half when looking at air business travelers. To a majority of travelers, this is a major factor in their choice of an airline. Belonging to a frequent flyer program means that credit is collected for mileage flown on that particular airline. After a specified number of miles have been flown, the traveler can qualify for up-

grades to first class and free trips. In recent years airlines have reduced the attractiveness of their awards, making it necessary to fly greater distances in order to obtain a particular reward. There are two factors that, if enacted, will have a tremendous negative impact on travelers and the industry. First, passengers of many airlines have accumulated significant amounts of travel that, if and when these amounts show up on the company's balance sheet as a liability, will have a significant impact on the airline. Second, it is only a matter of time before the Internal Revenue Service looks at these rewards and begins to tax them. As part of the effort to reduce corporate travel costs, some companies are seeking to have the award given to the company rather than to the individual.

Almost 40 percent of air reservations are made through a travel agent and just under 30 percent are made through a company travel department. A similar percent is made directly by the travel or his/her assistant. The trend in recent years has been to substitute company-made bookings for those made by travel agents.

Interestingly enough, only 16 percent of business travelers belong to a hotel frequent stay program. Those who do are members of two programs. The more frequent the traveler, the more likely he or she is to belong. Over half of all travelers book their hotels directly. Company travel departments are used more than travel agents while one in ten travelers does not make a booking at all.

Business travel is a non-discretionary expenditure. The business traveler must travel to specific places to do business. For the pleasure tourist, taking a vacation is a discretionary purchase—one that he or she does not need to make. As a result, business travel is more stable and less price resistant than vacation travel. Business trips are taken consistently throughout

the year, while pleasure trips tend to be concentrated in the summer months.

Business travelers are likely to be more upscale than pleasure travelers. They are more likely to be men (although there is a trend toward more and more women business travelers), to be between the ages of 35 to 44 (although just over one-third are aged over 45), and to have better education, professional or managerial occupations, and higher incomes than pleasure travelers.

People traveling on business tend to get frustrated with the many demands of travel that are beyond their control. Principal among these are the time required to travel, the long waits, and the delays of arrivals and departures. They also have more personal frustrations—being away from home and families, being alone, and living out of suitcases. More and more people are taking kids with them on their business trips. In 1996, 41 million business trips included children, a 55 percent increase over 1990. In response, companies are attempting to accommodate this trend. Delta Air Lines, for example, has airport lounges for kids with computer video games; United is giving out stuffed airplane toys. In 1989 Hyatt introduced "Camp Hyatt" primarily as a baby-sitting service for vacationing parents. Today some 25 percent of the parents using the service are on business trips. When school is out in the summer the figure jumps to 50 percent. Fewer than 1 percent of companies have ever attempted to arrange travel plans to include children of employees and few, if any, have travel policies that make provisions for children.

More and more companies are concerned about the high cost of travel and are putting more time and effort into controlling their corporate travel costs (Jones, 1996). Travel remains the third-largest

More parents are taking their children with them on business trips and spend free time together. Photo from *Top Shots* CD Rom. Courtesy of Queensland Tourist and Travel Corporation.

controllable expense at U.S. corporations. Sixty percent of companies have a formal written travel policy and 30 percent have informal guidelines. In 1994 almost 20 percent of U.S. companies had no formal policy on travel. Two years later that percentage dropped to four. Almost 80 percent of companies require employees to take the "lowest logical" airfare. There is movement away from upscale accommodations and toward more moderate or economy class accommodations. More than 60 percent require employees to stay at hotels in which the company or travel agency has corporate or negotiated rates. Rental car use is also regulated. Over three-quarters of companies impose a size limit on cars rented by employees. American Express estimates that U.S. companies lose $15 billion a year to deviations from corporate policy. To combat the problem a number of companies are experimenting with systems that allow corporate travelers to make their travel plans on their personal computers, but only within the parameters of corporate policy.

Air fares take up most of the travel budget, followed by lodging and meals (see table 5.1). Business travelers tend to eat breakfast at the hotel, are split between having lunch at a fast-food or full-service restaurant and tend to eat dinner at a full-service restaurant. In an attempt to control meal costs, some companies are strengthening expense reporting procedures, enforcing more stringent receipt requirements, and increasing communication with travelers and supervisors (*Travel Weekly*, 1996). However, according to the consulting firm Runzheimer International, companies—even those serious about managing travel costs—often overlook meal expenses because many corporate cultures consider business meals a perk for travelers who have to spend many days on the road.

Companies are using more automation to manage their travel. Over 90 percent still book by telephone while 16 percent use electronic mail and an additional 11 percent book on-line. The greater the travel budget, the more companies use electronic mail.

The business executive travel market is proving to be more "segmentable" today, with many airlines and hotels making specific efforts to cater to these higher echelon persons. Airlines have been offering first-class seat service and first-class passenger lounges in airport terminals to these travelers for many years. More recent innovations include special check-in arrangements, bigger seats, and sleeper seats. Many hotel chains have begun to allocate whole floors or wings of their buildings for those business travelers seeking greater luxury in their accommodations. The rooms or suites are more spacious and contain more personal giveaways; the hotels provide their guests with complimentary drinks and express check-in, check-out service. Normally the airline and hotel companies add a surcharge to their regular prices for the extra comforts and convenience provided to executive travelers. They have achieved considerable marketing success in doing so.

Table 5.1   Business travel costs

EXPENSE CATEGORY	PERCENT OF TRAVEL COSTS (1995)
Air fare	40
Lodging	22
Meals	13
Car rentals	8
Entertainment	5
Miscellaneous	5
Personal car	4
Ground transportation	3

Source: *Travel Weekly* (September 9, 1996). Rochester, WI: Runzheimer International, 84.

Quick Trip 5.1
Appealing to the Business Traveler

According to a survey of frequent business travelers, 71 percent said they spend between one and two hours working in their hotel rooms while 16 percent indicated they spend between three and four hours working there. An additional 16 percent said they didn't work at all in their guest rooms.

When asked about their use of leisure time when traveling, 47 percent said they take advantage of the hotel fitness facilities; 41 percent said they work; 35 percent said they sightsee; 33 percent go shopping; 21 percent take advantage of cultural activities; 14 percent participate in other forms of exercise such as jogging.

The technological features that are important when selecting a hotel are in-room voice mail (68 percent), on-site business center (57 percent), in-room modem jack (52 percent), and in-room fax machine (47 percent). Other personal services regarded as important are overnight dry cleaning and pressing (90 percent), complimentary transportation to nearby business appointments (71 percent), and the availability of personal grooming services (50 percent).

Most—55 percent—stick with familiar foods when traveling. Slightly more than half prefer fine dining when selecting a restaurant, 48 percent indicated they often select casual dining while 30 percent often choose room service.

Other surveys indicate that, as business travelers get older, they increasingly want "a few creature comforts, a good night's sleep and a moment or two of privacy." In the early 1990s most business travelers were between 18 and 34 years of age—today almost 40 percent are 45 or older. At the Hyatt Regency in Chicago revenues from in-room movies has risen 20 percent in a year. Favorites are Arnold Schwarzenegger and Bruce Willis. Snack sales in minibars increased 36 percent to $62 million in 1995 from the previous year.

Most agree there's no place like home. James Chambers, 54, of Coopers & Lybrand says, "A hotel is a pretty poor substitute for home. If you're there for an extended period of time, you start to think, 'Where's my den? Where's my backyard? Where's my wife? Where's my dog?' Not necessarily in that order."

Questions:

1. Based on this information, develop a plan to attract the frequent business traveler to your hotel. Which services should be offered?

2. How much would they cost the guest?

3. Which would be incorporated into the room charge? How would they be advertised?

Sources: "Survey Shows Business Traveler Choices," *Hotel & Motel Management.* (September 18, 1995) 59.

"Business Travelers Prefer Rest to Play," *Wall Street Journal.* (November 1, 1996) B1, B39.

While we have been talking about the business traveler, there are actually several segments to this market, each with distinct characteristics. Business travelers can be divided into segments as follows:

- Frequent business traveler
- Women business traveler
- Luxury business traveler
- International business traveler
- Occupational designation

Frequent business travelers are those who take a minimum of ten trips a year. While they are just over 15 percent of all business travelers, they account for more than one-half of all the business trips taken. They tend to be upscale professionals between the ages of 35 and 44 and college graduates with high incomes. They are much less interested in rates and much more interested in frequent travel programs.

In 1970, women accounted for 1 percent of all business travelers; today they account for approximately 40 percent. This figure is estimated to increase to 50 percent by the year 2000. They tend to have less formal education and have lower incomes than men business travelers. They are also more likely to have another household member with them on the trip and to add on vacation days to the business part of the trip. As hotels sought to attract this segment of the market, several mistakes were made. Early attempts to provide "women's floors" and pink wallpaper were viewed by many women as patronizing. They were concerned about such things as security, however. This has resulted in such things as a "club floor"— open to both sexes—and accessed by a special key. More hotels are building suites so that women can hold meetings in their rooms without having a bed in view. Room service hours have been expanded as many women dislike eating alone in public. Lighting in hallways and parking lots is getting brighter.

According to the *Official Airline Guide* (Dorsey, 1996) the "typical" international business traveler is a married man over the age of 45 holding a director-level position at a company with fewer than 100 employees. This "typical" traveler takes close to twenty trips a year and states that home and family are priorities over work. This person will travel with a laptop computer but prefers watching videos and making phone calls in the air. The ideal in-flight companion is an empty seat. This person is tempted to give up a seat on an overbooked flight although an upgrade on the next flight is also of interest. Executive airline lounges are favored for the opportunity to sit in peace and quiet, use the telephone, and get a free drink.

The traveler prefers to make air arrangements by going to a travel agent, looking at a printed flight guide, and having a secretary take care of things. Airlines are chosen on the basis of convenient schedules, on-time performance, and modern planes. Frequent flyer membership also plays a role. U.S. travelers are likely to belong to five or more such programs. They belong so they can jump ahead of others on an airline's waiting list. Flight upgrades are also important. The traveler prefers to use mileage awards for personal and leisure travel rather than to save the company money on business travel.

When making hotel arrangements the preference is to contact the hotel directly, use a travel agent, or consult an independent hotel guide.

Over half of all travelers fall into the highest occupational groupings of professional/managerial with almost equal percentages found in the other classifications of lower manager/technical, sales/clerical, blue collar, and retired/unemployed. Business travel is most

Quick Trip 5.2
The Female Business Traveler

According to a survey of 2,300 business travelers from six countries, compared to males the female business traveler is younger—60 percent are under the age of 45 compared with 35 percent of male travelers. Over the age of 45 the relative percentage of female business travelers disappears, suggesting possible barriers that hold back women from senior level positions involving international travel.

Hong Kong and the U.S. have the highest proportion of female travelers, with 17 percent and 13 percent respectively. On the other hand France and Germany account for only 6 percent each in the survey results.

About half of the women are married compared with three-quarters of the men and more women than men are likely to be without children at home. However women are slightly more likely than men to say that home and family are more of a priority than work. Women are also more likely to be conscious of the status involved in being a frequent flyer program member. While men are more likely to redeem their mileage awards for business trips, women are more inclined to use them for leisure travel. Women are more likely to give up their seat for cash on an overbooked flight and are more likely to complain if there is a problem with a seat mate than are men. One in ten women report that they have been sexually harassed on a flight.

Questions:

1. Should a hotel and/or an airline market to women traveling on business differently than to men?

2. In what ways?

Source: Yet Another Way the Sexes Differ. *Travel Weekly.* (April 29, 1996) 69, 71.

prominent in the health, legal, and educational fields, with manufacturing following this group.

It is expected that the number of business travelers will not grow much, if any, but that those who do travel will, on average, take more trips. It is anticipated that there will be an increased need to have access to more information regarding available choices. This is driven by the fact that companies are increasingly looking for the best value options in travel as they seek to contain their travel costs. There is a particular interest in technology as more companies are

moving into the area of on-line or data-on-disk products. The latter is more popular at the moment as companies are concerned about the cost if all employees have on-line accessibility.

Four factors that influence the future of business travel: economic, regulatory, globalization, and automation. As a general rule, the rate of growth of the economy determines the level of business travel and the extent to which that level changes. Business travel activity tends to match the growth of the economy when overall economic performance is weak, but business travel moves ahead of the rate of growth of the economy during times of economic stability and expansion. The U.S. market follows this pattern more strongly than does the European market. The strong signs for business travel are strong trade, investment, and output growth, while the weak signs are high interest rates and unemployment levels.

Exchange rates are economic factors. The rate of exchange refers to the relative value of one's currency to other currencies. Changes in exchange rates are not felt as much in business travel as in pleasure travel. There is, however, an impact. When a substantial change in exchange rate occurs, the trade balance moves in favor of the weaker economy. When the dollar loses value against the pound, for example, U.S. goods are less expensive for the British than they were previously. The reverse is true of the cost for the traveler on either business or pleasure. It is more expensive to travel to and stay in Britain than sell the cheaper U.S. goods. This represents a psychological barrier which business travelers, however, seem able to overcome.

The second factor affecting the future of business travel is regulatory. Its impact is felt in two areas: deregulation of travel and government policy regarding the treatment of business travel expenses for tax purposes. In 1978, deregulation came to the U.S. air industry. Airlines were free to set rates based on market demand without their being subject to government approval beforehand. As a result many new airlines came into being and many went out of business. Increased competition kept fares between many major cities low. Airline deregulation is evolving much more slowly in Europe. It remains to be seen whether air fares there will be reduced significantly.

Business travel is treated as a business expense. Recent moves in the U.S. to limit the tax deductibility of business meals to 50 percent of the cost of the meal has not seemed to limit travel but has changed the way clients are entertained. For example, by bringing a speaker into a meeting, the entire cost of the meal can be deducted. Various attempts have been made to limit the tax deductibility of meetings abroad. Any attempt to do this would have an impact on the amount and type of travel undertaken.

The economies of countries are increasingly interdependent. With this globalization comes a greater need for international business travel.

Automation can work to both increase travel and limit it. The development of sophisticated computer systems makes it easier to make, confirm, and change travel reservations while controlling the cost of travel. On the other hand, innovations such as picture phones and video-conferencing can reduce the need to travel.

An increasing number of people combine business and pleasure by adding a few days of pleasure to the beginning or end of a regular business trip or attendance at a business-related convention or meeting. In fact, in 1994, 8 percent of all U.S. travelers combined their vacation trip with some business or convention attendance. Over half of these vacation person-trips were taken over a weekend or long weekend. Travel promoters at travel destinations should realize that business travelers provide a three-part opportunity. First, the business traveler visits to carry out his or her work-related activities. Second, the traveler and his or her spouse may be convinced to spend pleasure travel before or after the meeting, convention or other business-related activity. Third, she or he may be attracted to return to the destination in the future on a pleasure or business trip.

Meetings, Conventions, and Congresses

Seven out of every ten Americans belong to one or more associations (Myers, 1995). One-quarter belong to four or more. However, less than 10 percent of all business trips taken during the year are for the purpose of attending meetings and conventions. This generates $76 billion a year. Associations represent 70 percent of that total. Meetings represent 25 percent of air travel revenue and over one-third of hotel revenue, even more at business hotels. The largest associations are represented by the American Society of Association Executives (ASAE). Their members are 204 million strong and hold 12,500 membership-wide conventions each year, involving 22 million delegates. They have another 230,000 educational seminars with almost 67 million delegates.

Associations also increasingly hold trade shows. From 1990 to 1995 the percentage of associations holding such shows increased from 50 percent to almost two-thirds in 1995. The average members-only show is booked an average of three years ahead of time and consists of an average of 133 exhibitors, over 4,000 attendees, and requires 64,000 square feet of space.

The number one factor considered by associations when they look at potential venues is the quality of service at the hotel. The services considered important are, in order of importance:

1. No smoking rooms
2. Concierge
3. 24-hour room service
4. Gift shop

The second most important factor is the presence of adequate meeting facilities. When considering meeting space, association executives are concerned with light and temperature controls; variety in table size and chair types; over-

Quick Trip 5.3
The End of Business Travel?

"We need to get our people off airplanes—it's as simple as that." So says Paul Blumberg, director of product development systems for Ford's U.S.-based automotive operations. To accomplish that goal Ford has invested in a multimillion-dollar corporate infrastructure that includes hundreds of high-powered computers.

In this way Guiseppe Delena, a 43-year-old vehicle-design chief working at a Ford Motor Company studio in Turin, Italy, is able to instantly share ideas with his staff in the U.S. "Do you see this part here?" asks his image on a computer monitor in Dearborn, Michigan, as he scribbles on a graphic of a vehicle. "We should probably change it." Gary Morales, a 36-year-old design manager in Dearborn agrees that the change would make all the difference to solving the problem at hand. Through two $250,000 workstations—one in Turin, the other in Dearborn—100 percent interactive staff meetings can take place.

Prior to this technology Ford engineers tended to have a parochial mindset. Now they are expected to work with their peers worldwide to develop new and better products.

Other companies and CEOs feel it is necessary to travel in order to be at a more personal level with clients. They argue that it is important to establish a relationship that goes beyond a telephone line. They also stress the importance of business travel because they are more likely to "see things in person that you would probably miss from secondhand reports." While recognizing the amount of time spent traveling one CEO comments, "I can get a lot more done in the plane than I can in the office."

Yet another scenario is presented by the business people who continue to travel but telecommute while on the road—a style known as "hoteling." William Herndon, vice president of technology for BankAmerica Corporation's mortgage group, travels half the year. Says Herndon, "With the right technology I can do everything on the road that I used to do in the office." He has given up his office in San Francisco and instead travels with a laptop computer, wireless modem, cellular phone and personal 800 number. In the process he has turned hotels, planes and boardrooms into an ad hoc office. He insists he has been able to do two to four times more work than in his prewired days.

He sends and receives about 200 e-mail messages a day on his IBM Thinkpad laptop computer. When he's not in a location where he can reach a phone jack to plug in a modem, he uses a wireless modem and an e-mail service called RadioMail, which sends messages over cellular networks. He often substitutes his bulky laptop with a hand-held Hewlett-Packard palmtop that fits into his pocket. His personal 800 number costs $35 a month plus calls and forwards calls to whatever phone he's currently using.

There is a downside. His wife, Sally, admits that increased efficiency lets him come home from work earlier and she finds that it is much easier to reach him on the road. However, she loves when the machines are turned off, such as when they go skiing in the mountain or vacationing for two weeks in Spain. "We were out of touch completely," she sighs wistfully. In addition, the line between work and leisure blurs because the job is so portable. Herndon already works seven days a week and pushes himself to take on more work. Yet another issue is the lack of personal contact with coworkers. Life on the road can get lonely with no one to share office gossip with.

Questions:

1. What is the future of business travel?

2. Will increased technology reduce the need to travel, reshape the demand or will the need for personal contact always be as strong as ever?

3. What will be the impact on airlines, hotels, and other services used by business travelers?

Sources: Suris, O. Behind the Wheel. *Wall Street Journal.* (November 18, 1996) R14, R17.

Brokaw, L. Road Warriors. *Inc.* (March 1, 1992) 44.

Takahashi, D. Road Warrior. *Wall Street Journal.* (November 18, 1996) R27, R31.

head projectors, projector screens, and flip charts; and the availability of a variety of microphones.

One study (Oppermann, 1996) of members of the Professional Convention Management Association (PCMA) found that San Diego has the highest image score among North American cities as a convention destination. The top ten cities are:

1. San Diego
2. San Francisco
3. New Orleans
4. Orlando
5. Washington, D.C.
6. Chicago
7. Boston
8. San Antonio
9. Seattle
10. Atlanta

Over half of all conventions are held at downtown hotels, followed by resorts and conference centers. What will these planners want in the near future? They are looking for more sophisticated use of technology. They want to register online; they want to lay out their meeting room setup electronically on the hotel's blueprints; they want modem hookups and cellular phone service. In this increasingly fragmented market there is a desire for educational programs more tightly focused on particular interests. This means more small break-out sessions devoted to specialized topics. Baby Boomers want fewer weekend meetings, an opportunity to include their families, and a greater emphasis on learning. While more than half of ASAE associations offer spouse programs, only 13 percent have something directed at children. Over one-third offer pre- or post-trips in conjunction with the meeting. This is an excellent way for someone to combine business and pleasure. There

is also a demand for a greater variety of price and quality alternatives when it comes to accommodations.

Convention locations usually change from year to year as attendees do not want to return to the same spot each year. Many associations have a policy of rotating the meeting destination on a geographic basis—East one year, West the next, Midwest the third.

Attendance at corporate meetings is required. As a result the choice of destination has no effect on the number of people attending. Many corporate meetings are held at the same place year after year if the host hotel can show it can deliver quality service. The site chosen is usually close to the corporate facility. The dollar and time cost of traveling to the meeting is thereby minimized. Since the accent at a corporate meeting is on work, privacy and a lack of distractions is appreciated more than recreational facilities and sightseeing opportunities.

Incentive Travel

> "Travel is the answer to a dream —a dream of luxury, prestige, in exotic places. It is the ultimate escape from daily routine . . . and travel which is earned through effort salves not only the ego, but the conscience as well."
>
> Incentive Travel Planner

The Society of Incentive and Travel Executives defines incentive travel as "a global management tool that uses an exceptional travel experience to motivate and/or recognize participants for increased levels of performance in support of organizational goals" (Jones, 1996). One of the fastest growing segments of the business, it is expected to generate $26.4 billion in the U.S. alone by the turn of the century. The U.S. is responsible for just over half of

world demand, Europe for an additional 40 percent with Japan and Australia accounting for the rest.

As standards of living have increased, traditional incentives such as cash and merchandise have proven less effective in motivating employees to work harder or to sell more. Travel is touted as doing a better job of satisfying people's needs for achievement, recognition and rewards than cash or merchandise. Indeed the four most important attributes of company incentive travel programs are a sense of achievement, a sense of pride, reward for effort, and recognition among colleagues (Sheldon, 1995). It has been shown that, for salespeople, the most effective motivational rewards are (in order):

1. Travel incentives
2. Cash
3. Merchandise

While incentives have traditionally been targeted towards salespeople, an increasing number of programs are being developed for non-salespeople. Programs are either organized within the company sponsoring the trip or by an outside incentive travel house, of which there are over one hundred in the U.S. It is argued by many that programs are more successful when organized in-house because the organizers have a better understanding of the characteristics of the workforce and can do a better job of targeting rewards to motivate them.

A major study of Fortune 1000 companies (Sheldon, 1995) found the following:

- Forty percent use travel as an incentive
- Forty percent use cash awards
- Twenty percent use merchandise
- Over a quarter use travel as well as other incentives

- About one-third use no incentives at all

(The percentages do not total 100 percent because many companies use more than one incentive.)

- Incentive users have more dealerships and fewer distributorships, although the use of incentive travel is not dependent upon the type of industry in which the company operates.

- A corporate travel department is more likely to be present in a company that uses incentive travel. However, it is not known whether the presence of a travel department leads a company to develop incentive travel programs or whether the presence of incentive travel programs leads the company to establish a travel department.

- Cash and merchandise are more likely than travel to be used to motivate managers and non-salespeople.

- For incentive travel programs the most common criterion was for employees to reach a specified dollar amount of sales, while for cash or merchandise it was more common for employees to have to increase sales by a certain percentage.

- The most likely companies to use incentive travel are those that are in the service sector with a strong national or international presence, have a large in-house corporate travel program, and have a strong sense of corporate culture.

The people who "buy" destinations for incentive trips are influenced by:

1. *Budget*. However, incentive trip planners look for high quality rather than low prices.
2. *Time of year*. Employee participation on incentive trips tends to take place in that particular industry's slow season. The most popular months for incentive travel are February and April. Planners would look at destinations that are attractive during these months.
3. *Participant background*. The level of sophistication and previous travel experiences of the likely participants.
4. *Incentive history* of the users and the competition. Previously used destinations are less likely to produce spirited competition than are new destinations.
5. *Accessibility*.
6. *Facilities*, including hotel rooms, meeting rooms, restaurants, local transport.
7. *Activities*. Recreation and sports facilities.

The Pleasure and Personal Travel Market

"The whole object of travel is not to set foot on foreign land; it is at last to set foot on one's own country as a foreign land."

G. K. Chesterton

According to the National Travel Survey, U.S. resident person-trips rose 7 percent in 1994 over the previous year to reach 1.13 billion. This is a 48 percent increase over ten years. Domestic travel saw a 7 percent growth in 1994, outperforming international travel, which declined 1 percent due to a weak Canadian market. U.S. outbound travel increased 5 percent in 1994.

Domestic trips were shorter than the previous years, averaging 3.5 nights, way from home. On the other hand, day trips and one-night stays for business reasons were up significantly. The average round-trip distance per trip was just under 850 miles. One in five travelers visited the South Atlantic region in 1994 while the East North Central (14 percent) and Pacific (13 percent) regions were also popular. Half of all person-trips were taken over weekends, a decline of four percentage points over 1993 although the share of one-night weekend trips increased five percentage points to 17 percent of all trips.

Over half of all pleasure trips are taken to visit friends and relatives; just under a third are for sightseeing/entertainment and one in six involves outdoor recreation (Cook, 1995).

Segments of the Market

Early attempts to define the U.S. travel market used the stated motivation as the basis for the segmentation. One national probability sample divided the U.S. market into six segments using benefits/motivations. The segments are (Young, Ott, & Felgin, 1978):

- Friends and Relatives—Nonactive Visitor. Representing 29 percent of the market, these travelers look for familiar surroundings where they visit friends and relatives. They tend not to participate in any activity.

- Friends and Relatives—Active City Visitor. An additional 12 percent of the population also seek out the familiar where they visit friends and relatives. However, this group is more inclined to do such things as sightsee, shop, and engage in cultural activities.

- Family Sightseers. Six percent of the market looks for new vacation places that would entertain and enrich their children.

- Outdoor Vacationers. The 19 percent who fall into this category want clean air, rest and quiet, and beautiful scenery. Recreation facilities are important for the numerous campers who are part of this segment. Facilities for children are also important.

- Resort Vacationers. A similar percent—19—fall into this category. They are primarily interested in water sports and good weather. Popular places with a big city atmosphere are preferred.
- Foreign Vacationers. Over a quarter—26 percent—consist of people who seek destinations they have never been to before. A foreign atmosphere offering an exciting and enriching atmosphere with beautiful scenery is important. Good accommodations and service are more important than the cost.

More recently it has been suggested that segmentation on the basis of actual behavior is a better reflection of the market. It has been found that what people *say* they want is not necessarily what they actually *do*. A study, representative of the U.S. population (Shoemaker, 1994) identifies three major market segments.

1. Get Away/Family Travelers represent almost 38 percent of the total and are similar to the Friends and Relatives—Nonactive, Family Sightseers, and Outdoor Vacationers noted above. They tend to visit places which are

   - a good place for children;
   - where friends and family live;
   - scenic;
   - places they can rest and relax;
   - full of friendly residents;
   - within driving distance;
   - places where they can learn new things;
   - safe;
   - good mountain areas;
   - congestion-free.

On the other hand it is unimportant to them that the vacation destination is popular, that inclusive packages are available, or that a number of different priced accommodations are available.

2. Adventurous/Educational Travelers make up 31 percent of the market. This segment is similar to the Foreign Vacationers noted earlier. They tend to engage in cultural activities such as visiting museums, galleries, operas, and theaters. More than two-thirds visit places that

   - someone else they knew had been to;
   - offer a number of things to see and do;
   - are a famous city/place;
   - have elegant dining;
   - offer a full range of hotel accommodation.

They are less concerned with rest and relaxation, friendly locals, crime, congestion, clean air, and cost.

3. Gamblers/Fun Travelers represent just under 30 percent of the market and are linked to the Resort Vacationers in the previously mentioned study. Gamblers/Fun Travelers want a highly popular place where they can gamble, participate in recreation or sport, and enjoy a good nightlife and fine dining. They are also concerned about price, the availability of good beaches, sunbathing, and good weather. On the other hand, they are less concerned about cultural activities, being close to friends and relatives (while on vacation), and the presence of amusement parks.

TravelScope, a national survey, estimates that 9 percent of travelers gambled. In 1994 American households made 125 million visits to casinos, spending $16.5 billion.

The Family Market

Slightly less than half of all American adults take a family vacation trip (Mason, 1995). A family vaca-

Families look for destinations that will entertain and enrich children. Photo Credit: Robert Holmes.

Quick Trip 5.4
The Visiting Friends and Relatives (VFR) Market

When Gerry Soud was invited by his older brother, Kenneth, to vacation on his 28-foot trawler, he thought it was a great idea. Soud fantasized that he was going to "float to the Bahamas holding nothing heavier than a Corona." Then reality set in as he became the yacht's one-man crew, weighing anchor and doing all the chores his brother required. He longingly looked at a Carnival Cruise Line ship and dreamed about what it must be like on board. "Why didn't I just fork out $1,000 and take a real cruise?"

About 55 percent of the 475 million leisure trips taken in the U.S. are visits to friends and relatives. And when you visit someone's home you have to play by their rules.

When Chris Risse of Athens, Georgia, visited the upstate New York farm of her husband's sister, she had visions of a homey, carefree vacation. She didn't realize that she would be expected to help with the 5 a.m. milking followed by breakfast and a session baling hay. Often she was working until 8 p.m. Despite her allergies, she pitched in with this and other chores such as sweeping up cow dung.

Stay in a hotel and you can complain. How can you tell your host that the place stinks? Jon Caroulis of Philadelphia stayed with his brother, Bill, his fiancee, her two children, and a dog in a condominium in Southern California separated by a small field from a sewage-treatment plant. In addition there's an oil refinery about two miles away and they were in the flight path of planes arriving at Los Angeles International Airport. Despite his brother's hospitality Jon will stay at a hotel next time because, as he says, "I want a bed I can sleep on, and I won't have to wait my turn to use the bathroom."

Question:

1. Design a series of advertisements for a hotel company aimed at attracting the VFR market.

Source: Hellish Vacations: Staying with Friends Can be a Real Ordeal. *Wall Street Journal.* (June 25, 1996) A1, A6.

---

most popular destinations for this market segment are the ocean and historical sites. Both offer activities that are typically free or low-cost, yet still entertaining (Mason, 1993).

Within this group there are several subsegments:

- Husbands and wives without children. This represents 29 percent of the nation's households.

- Husbands and wives with children. Twenty-five percent of all households fall into this category.

- Grandparents with grandchildren. In the U.S. about 3 million children under the age of 18 live full-time with their grandparents. In households where both parents work it is becoming increasingly common for grandparents to take their grandchildren on vacation.

- Single parents with children.

Why do people take family vacations? In order of importance, the reasons are:

1. Being alone together as a family. With 70 percent of married Baby Boomer women (Baby Boomers are those born between 1946 and 1964) working outside the home, there are tremendous time pressures on getting quality family time together.

2. Getting away from the stress of home and work. As more and more people work longer and longer hours, they need breaks. Stress is a major family health problem.

3. Finding rest and relaxation. People do not want to sit around doing nothing. However the activities of interest are what is called "soft adventure."

These motivations are reflected in the top five types of family vacations. They are:

tion trip consists of two or more members of the same household traveling 100 miles or more away from home on a vacation trip. This accounts for just under three-quarters of all vacation travel in the U.S. There are major differences in travel behavior depending upon the presence of children. Over three-quarters of vacation trips with children involve an auto, RV, or truck. The family is an extremely crucial market to tourism interests. Be-

cause these parents are of the Baby Boomer generation, they make up a high percentage of the population. They feel the need to get away from job stress and spend time alone with the family. They tend to take shorter and more frequent vacations, closer to home, to maximize the use of their time. To attract this market, destinations are adding such features as baby-sitting, children's menus, and even children's dining rooms. The two

Historical sites such as the Mt. Morgan Railway Station in Queensland, Australia are popular spots to vacation with children. Photo from *Top Shots* CD Rom. Courtesy of Queensland Tourist and Travel Corporation.

1. Ocean/beach
2. Historic sites
3. City
4. Lake
5. Family reunion

About half of all family vacations are planned within one month of the trip, one-quarter planned within three months and one-fifth planned six months or more ahead of time.

Group Tours

"... two U.S. tourists in Germany ... were traveling on a public bus when one of them sneezed. A German turned around and said, sympathetically, 'Gesundheit.' The U.S. tourist commented, 'How nice that he speaks English'."

Sharon Ruhley, Intercultural Communication

In 1995 the direct impact of the group tour industry in North America was estimated to be over $10 billion. Most of the impact is in the U.S. with an impact of

$8.6 billion, the remaining $1.5 billion being spent in Canada. Slightly less than 90 percent of this is in the form of direct expenditures—hotels, meals, attractions, etc.—paid for by the tour operator or the traveler. U.S. and Canadian tour companies operate over half a million tour departures with 23 million passengers every year. Well over half are one-day trips. However, taking into account the number of people on a given tour and the tour length, 80 percent of passenger-days (one passenger taking a trip for one day) and 90 percent of the revenues are accounted for by multi-day trips. (For example, one passenger taking a six-day trip accounts for six passenger-days) (Davidson-Peterson Associates, *1995 Economic Impact Study*, 1996).

Here are some of the preferences of group tour members (Davidson-Peterson Associates, *Tour Traveler Index*, 1996):

- Those under 55 are most likely to be interested in a tour with evening entertainment (70 percent); a tour including an ocean cruise (56 percent); a heritage

tour to areas that are home to ethnic groups to learn about their culture (41 percent); and an arts/cultural tour.

- Those between 65 and 74 are less likely to be interested in a tour that includes a dinner cruise (41 percent) and one that includes an ocean cruise (34 percent).

- Gaming is very popular among tour travelers (though not those age 75 and older). While Las Vegas is the most popular destination for such trips, future gaming trips are more likely to be in their own region or one nearby.

- Nearly two-thirds are very or somewhat likely to select a tour with limited exercise included in the itinerary.

- One-half would choose a tour that offered nutritious meals and information about healthy eating.

- They are most interested in demonstrations by experts of something (e.g. cooking or arts and crafts) that could be put to daily use.

- They would rather save money than pay extra for additional meal costs.

- It is very important to them that they gain a new knowledge and understanding of the areas they visit through their travel experiences.

- The prefer a trip to several destinations than to just one.

The Gaming Market

In 1931 gaming was legalized in Nevada (Rohs, 1995). For 45 years this was the only legal location for gaming in the U.S. Nevada was joined by Atlantic City in the mid-1970s. By the mid-1990s the number of states in which there was some type of land-based, riverboat, dockside, small-stakes, video lottery machines or Indian gaming, increased from two to twenty-five.

Quick Trip 5.5
The Teen Market

Research by Hyatt Hotels shows that teenagers like to go on vacation with their families but, when at the destination, want to get away from their parents and be with other teens. Seventy-nine percent of 500 teenagers surveyed said they wanted to meet and spend time with other teens while on vacation. Romance is important with 77 percent of the boys and 57 percent of the girls hoping to find it on vacation. Nearly half say their parents drive them crazy.

Twelve percent of the teens had their own hotel room on their last vacation; 47 percent shared a room with parents, while 27 percent shared a room with a sibling. In order of importance, teens are interested in shopping, sightseeing, sports, group barbecues, and beach parties.

Based upon their research, Hyatt has identified five segments of the teen market:

1. All-Americans. This group makes up 27 percent of the market. They are conservative, wholesome, and family-oriented. They obey their parents and have a say in planning the family vacation. Likely to be girls, they enjoy nature walks, seminars, sightseeing, and cultural activities.

2. Lone Rangers. Mostly boys and representing 12 percent of the market, this segment is smart, solitary, and comes from small, high-income families. They have their own room when on vacation. They like to bike, hike, play video games, and work on a personal computer in their room.

3. The Moody Blues, 28 percent of the sample, are miserable. They get bored and depressed when on vacation, avoid organized activities, and are not interested in meeting other teens.

4. The Young and Restless, 20 percent of the group, are headstrong, lively and impulsive. They like romance, organized activities, sports, and "sneaking around." They are likely to be boys.

5. The Hot Shots, 12 percent of the group, tend to be older teenage boys who prefer beach and ski vacations, are athletic, adventurous, and independent. They often take a friend on vacation, sharing a room with that person.

Question:

1. Design a resort program aimed at teenagers. Design a brochure to attract them to the resort and its teen program.

Source: Hotel Chain's Teen Survey: The Good, the Bad and the Miserable. *Travel Weekly.* (June 1, 1992) 15.

The Aqua Caliente Festival in Palm Springs appeals to those interested in learning about different cultures. Photo Credit: Robert Holmes.

that would allow casinos to be constructed in Detroit; Arizona approved more Indian casinos in the state; Arkansas residents authorized casinos in Hot Springs, subject to local voter approval; six Louisiana parishes voted to keep legalized gambling while twenty-three others voted to approve floating casinos; Colorado voters approved expansion of gambling to Trinidad, subject to local voter approval.

Gambling is a $19 billion business with Nevada accounting for 37 percent (Las Vegas itself takes in over $4 billion in revenues). Riverboats (operating in five states) are responsible for almost 25 percent of the market. Atlantic City accounts for 19 percent while Indian gaming brings in about 18 percent. New Orleans, with revenue of $140 million, has 1 percent of the market.

It has become apparent that casino gambling is accepted as a form of entertainment. Secondly, entertainment means more than gaming. It is more than slot machines. It is

In the 1996 election voters in Ohio, influenced by strong opposition from the governor of the state and the mayor of Cincinnati, rejected a constitutional amendment to allow riverboat casinos in Cleveland, Cincinnati, Youngstown, and Lorain. However, a number of other initiatives were supported by voters. Michigan approved a plan

fake volcanoes, jousting machines, and pirate battles in Las Vegas, for example.

There are two types of casino locations:

1. Transient. Serving the day-tripper market; people travel to the site by car or bus and use little lodging or off-premises food facilities. Most Indian casinos and many riverboats fall into this category.

2. Destination casinos. The premiere example continues to be Las Vegas. Over 40 percent arrive by air while slightly less than that number drive to the destination. People stay an average of four days, 90 percent staying in hotels. On average they spend, *per day*:

   - $52 on accommodation
   - $120 on gambling
   - $75 on shopping
   - $53 on shows
   - $4 on sightseeing
   - $24 on food

The Senior Travel Market

> *"They may be 60, they seem (to act) 50 and they'd like to be marketed to as if they were 40."*
>
> *Jeff Hamblin, executive vice president for the Americas, British Tourist Authority*

The influence of seniors as a market segment in tourism will grow over the next several decades. By the year 2000 people aged 50 or more will make up 38 percent of the population and account for 75 percent of the country's wealth (van Harssel & Theobald, 1994). By the year 2030 there will be 65 million older adults in the U.S. Many older people have the time, money and desire to travel. They hold a large share of the country's discretionary income because their children are grown and they no longer have house payments. Be-

cause they are time-flexible they can fill the times of low occupancy felt by many businesses and tourist destinations.

Seniors will be increasingly important for two reasons. First, there will be more of them. Second, their lifestyles are different from those of previous generations. They are increasingly independent about how they choose to live, and enjoy, their lives. Two demographic items are of particular importance. There will be a high proportion of singles in this population and a higher proportion of women than men. The 1991 Census indicated that 11 percent of men and 17 percent of women aged 55–64 live alone; in the 65–74 year old age group, 13 percent of men and 33 percent of women live alone. Twenty-two percent of men and 51 percent of women aged 75 and older live alone.

Women also make up almost 60 percent of the aged 65 and older. This is because they live longer than men, marry men older than themselves, and more widowers remarry than do widows.

A national study of older pleasure travelers sponsored by the

American Association of Retired Persons (AARP) and American Express (van Harssel & Theobald, 1994) provides a picture of this market segment. The primary motivators include:

- Needing to change routines
- Seeing new things
- Visiting friends and relatives
- Meeting new people and experiencing new cultures
- Expanding knowledge
- Creating memories

At the same time they expressed concern about such things as:

1. The single supplement penalty. The cost of a single room is often more than half the cost of a double room. While some tour operators offer assistance in finding a roommate the process is not easy and the result not always compatible.

2. Health/mobility constraints. While 60 percent of those aged 65 or older report no activity limitations, they do consider health a problem with travel as

Casinos such as the Sheraton Breakwater Casino in Townsville, North Queensland, Australia have gained popularity. Photo from *Top Shots* CD Rom. Courtesy of Queensland Tourist and Travel Corporation.

The senior citizen traveler is often interested in visiting distant family and friends. Photo by Corel.

it prevents them from enjoying the trip or engaging in some activities.

3. The fear of falling ill. The prospect of having a doctor or nurse close by helps alleviate concern.

4. Uncertainty about political conditions. Many choose not to travel internationally when there is a question regarding the country's economic or political situation.

5. Quality and quantity of information. There was a problem in getting information about upcoming events or trips. More aggressive promotion is needed to reach this group.

6. The pace of itineraries. People indicated they needed more time to get ready when they were part of a tour. Scheduling was also a problem—packing too many things into a short period of time.

7. Language. Language is seen as a major barrier to traveling internationally. Tour guides are seen as important in helping overcome this concern.

8. Packing and unpacking. A more leisurely trip is preferred over tours that go to a new city every day.

9. Meals. Lack of variety is a problem. Most evening meals consist of chicken dinners while a greater choice at breakfast is desired.

10. Concerns related to transportation. More help is desired when getting on and off buses. Communication is really important. One participant said, "I remember hearing an announcement on the bus. I did not understand what was said. That can really throw you into a panic."

Minority Travel Patterns

Most Americans, regardless of ethnicity, share similar travel habits. Most vacation, and use cars; a typical trip includes two people, an overnight stay, and the primary activity is shopping.

The three largest minority groups in the U.S.—African-Americans, Hispanics, and Asian-Americans—account for more than 26 percent of the U.S. population (Pina, 1996). By 2020 they will make up 35 percent of the population in the U.S. African-Americans are slightly more likely than the other groups to travel on business, especially to seminars and

---

Quick Trip 5.6
The Senior Market

In 1990 there were 60 million mature adults (over 50 years of age) in the U.S., accounting for 25 percent of the population. By the year 2000 that number will increase to 74 million and reach 110 million, 37 percent of the population, by 2020. The 65+ age group will increase as a percent of the population in many countries, going from 12 percent of the population in 1985 to 16 percent in 2025 in the U.S., from 15 to 24 percent in the United Kingdom, from 10 to 19 percent in Japan, from 13 to 18 percent in France and from 10 to over 15 percent in Australia.

In the U.S., mature travelers currently have 50 percent of the discretionary income and spend 30 percent more on travel than any other group. They stay longer and travel farther and more frequently than do younger travelers. Within this segment there are several groups: the "wool rich," the "polyester rich," the "comfortable retired," the "just getting by," and the "strugglers." The polyester rich represent 80 percent of the market spending. They have no mortgage, no dependents, and a lower tax bracket. They believe in treating themselves, are eager for new experiences, and are sociable, well-educated, and lean toward group travel and upscale all-inclusives. They want reliability and will reward service with loyalty. They also remember what it feels like to deal with a human being on the phone when calling a company.

Marc Mancini offers this advice as part of a course he offers to retail travel agents in certifying them as specialists in the upscale mature market:

● Create circles of service, a group of complementary businesses that cooperate in marketing. Mature buyers like to carry trust from one business to another.

● Encourage word-of-mouth referrals. Follow up on their trip with an anniversary or birthday card.

(continued on the following page)

- Host sales parties to talk about trips and give people a chance to socialize.
- Speak at clubs and societies.
- Advertise in local newspapers. Mature travelers read. Use serif type and large print that is well-spaced.
- Prospect via your staff. Remember they have parents, grandparents, aunts, and uncles.
- Use direct mail. This market reads 92 percent of their mail.
- Prequalify suppliers, finding out who is senior-friendly.

National Tour Association operators outline the following product-related trends for the mature market:

1. Increase in demand for soft adventure tours, walking tours, and specialty tours.
2. Greater emphasis on educational tours, including historic and cultural sites.
3. Group cruises will increase in popularity.
4. There is a need to further accommodate concerns for convenience, security, and safety.
5. Incorporating a favorite activity into the tour will meet the needs of the independent traveler. Seniors want more independence and flexibility on trips.

When seniors were asked what hotel perks they would most like to receive they said:

- Special rate for buffet breakfast—70 percent
- Free newspaper—54 percent
- Free cable TV—52 percent
- Free upgrades—38 percent
- Free drinks/snacks—33 percent
- Late check-out—32 percent
- Free use of gym—26 percent
- Discounts for shops/restaurants—23 percent
- Free fruit baskets—16 percent
- Free drink with dinner—10 percent
- Free champagne upon arrival—4 percent

Question:

1. How would you design and market a tour aimed at this segment of the market?

Sources: Agents Get a Crash Course in Mature Travel Market. *Tour & Travel News.* (November 20, 1995) 18.

Adventure Products More in Demand Among Seniors. *Tour & Travel News.* (September 7, 1992) 14.

Seniors Say No to Free Champagne. *Travel Weekly.* (March 18, 1996) 61.

conventions. They are also more likely to add on vacation travel to business trips. They are more prone to taking group tours and less likely to use recreational vehicles (RVs). The most popular destinations for African-Americans are Texas, Georgia, and other southern states. Washington, D.C., and Maryland are also popular in addition to trips to the Caribbean (21). The state of Alabama published a brochure in 1993 highlighting black heritage attractions, the major reason African-Americans travel to that state. One of the biggest tourist attractions is the National Civil Rights Memorial in Montgomery. Many visitors to the site also stop in at Martin Luther King's Dexter Avenue Baptist Church (Ahmad, 1993).

Hispanics are more likely to travel with children than are other groups. They also take longer trips and are more likely to take a plane trip and stay at a hotel or motel. California, Nevada, Texas, and New Mexico are popular destinations in the U.S. while the Caribbean, Mexico, and South America are favored international destinations.

Asian-Americans use rental cars more than the average, are more likely to travel alone and are the biggest spenders of the three ethnic groups. California, Nevada, and the Far East are popular. Additional information on these market segments is contained in table 5.2.

The Cruise Market

In 1994, after twenty years of uninterrupted growth, cruise lines reported a 1 percent drop in passengers (Godsman, 1995). Only 8 percent of the U.S. population has ever taken a cruise. The growth potential appears to be excellent as cruise lines have begun to look at less traditional demographic groups. For example, the Cruise Lines International Association

Table 5.2   Profiles of ethnic travelers

CHARACTERISTICS	AFRICAN-AMERICANS	HISPANIC-AMERICANS	ASIAN-AMERICANS
Average spending per trip	$405	$559	$678
Average nights per hotel stay	3.4	3.5	3.9
Percent PC owners	28%	42%	59%
Percent AAA members	25%	23%	10%
Size of travel market (in billions)	$ 25	$ 19.5	$ 6

Source: Travel Industry Association. (August 22, 1996). Profiling Ethnic Travelers, *Travel Weekly*, 13.

(CLIA) reports that only 36 percent of people who cruise are 60 years of age or older. Those under 40 make up one in five cruisers while over a third are between 40 and 59 years old. In fact, among first-time cruisers, slightly less than half are under 40 years of age.

The CLIA identifies six market segments:

- Enthusiastic Baby Boomers. Excited about cruising, they live intense, stressful lives and want to escape and relax when on vacation. This segment accounts for 20 percent of cruisers, 15 percent of all cruising days. Forty-six percent of them are first-time cruisers.

- Restless Baby Boomers. The newest cruisers, they like to try new vacation experiences and, while they enjoy the cruise experience, cost may be an inhibiting factor. Making up one-third of all cruisers and 17 percent of all cruising days, almost 60 percent are first-timers.

- Luxury Seekers. They want to be pampered, want deluxe accommodations, and are willing and able to pay for it. Thirty percent of these cruisers are first-timers. They comprise 14 percent of the market and account for 18 percent of all cruising days.

- Consummate Shoppers. Committed to cruising they seek the best

value (though not necessarily the cheapest price). Accounting for 16 percent of the market and accounting for one-fifth of all cruising days, 20 percent of them are first-time cruisers.

- Explorers. Well-educated, well-traveled, they are interested in different and exotic destinations. Twenty percent are first-timers. They are 11 percent of the market and account for 18 percent of all cruising days.

- Ship Buffs. The most senior segment, they cruise extensively and will continue because of the pleasure and comfort it brings them. Only 6 percent of the market, this segment accounts for 11 percent of cruising days. Thirteen percent are first-timers.

Several attitudes are common to all six segments:

1. Sixty percent like to experiment with new and different things
2. In choosing a cruise over 70 percent say the destination is the most important factor, followed by cost and time of year (each 60 percent), and cruise line or ship (57 percent)

The top three benefits of cruising are the ease of visiting several destinations (91 percent), the many activities (83 percent), and the reasonable price in relation to value (83 percent).

Canadian Pleasure Market

Almost two-thirds of Canadians describe themselves as infrequent, close to home travelers; 21 percent say they are active international vacationers while 14 percent say they travel actively in North America (Cameron, 1992).

There are a number of ways to describe the various segments of the Canadian pleasure market. These are presented below. To use this information it is suggested that a four-step procedure be used:

1. Choose the relevant/most useful segmentation model
2. Determine the key segments that have a high interest in traveling to the destination
3. Examine each of these segments in terms of travel philosophy, benefits sought, products that motivate them, activities enjoyed, as well as other travel behaviors
4. Explore the reactions of key segments through focus groups consisting of the characteristics of the chosen segments

The Canadian pleasure market is made up of the following segments of the population:

- Family value makes up 17 percent of the population yet comprises only 10 percent of all travel. They are more traditional than experimental, feel uncomfortable when stared at in a crowd, do not enjoy even a small amount of danger, the unpredictable, or doing things on the spur of the moment.

- No surprises account for 15 percent of the population and 19 percent of those who travel. They share a similar approach to life to the family value segment, though are not as extreme in their actions or lack of actions.

- Active players, at 15 percent of the population, are 14 percent of all travelers. They, as distinct from the previous two segments, enjoy a small element of danger. They like to be in style and enjoy the unpredictable. Being part of a group is very important to them.

- Packaged sun and services represent 14 percent of the population in general and 12 percent of the travel population in particular. They also like to be in style but do not score high on any of the other factors mentioned.

- History and hospitality, 14 percent of the population, account for 17 percent of all travelers. They are more traditional, are the least likely segment to enjoy a small amount of danger, do not like the unpredictable and do not care to be in style.

- Culture and nature seekers make up 13 percent of both the general and travel populations. They are the most likely to be in style and experimental, do not feel that being part of a group is important and are less likely to feel

that everything is changing too fast and to pay whatever it costs to get the best quality. They are not concerned with security and enjoy the unpredictable and a small amount of danger.

- Knowledge and experience, at 12 percent of the population, comprise 15 percent of all travelers. They are experimental, do not believe things are changing too fast and are not concerned with security. They like the unpredictable and a small amount of danger.

Four travel philosophies were identified. Organized variety travelers (29 percent) like to travel throughout the country to a different place each trip. Independent variety travelers (29 percent) feel that money spent on travel is well spent, enjoy making plans, and make them as they go. Inexpensive travel is important. Familiar independent travelers (24 percent) stay places they have been before and stay put at a destination. They prefer short trips over one long trip, find making arrangements bothersome and don't feel the need to travel on vacation. Finally, the or-

ganized and familiar travelers (18 percent) feel it is worth paying for extras. They like the travel arranged before the trip begins and prefer it be done by others.

About 30 percent of travelers are described as "knowledge seekers," interested in new and different lifestyles, new foods, and foreign destinations. They also feel that history is important. One in four are breakaway travelers, looking to escape the ordinary and somewhat daring and adventuresome while slightly fewer are players. They are likely to gamble, participate in and watch sports, and like to feel at home when away. Finally, one in five are described as social, visiting family, friends and relatives.

Summary

While it is unwise to generalize, a review of the major segments of the tourism markets is key to getting the big picture of why people travel. Understanding the profiles of these segments gives an indication of how to appeal to the various markets.

References

Ahmad, I. (1993). Selling black history in Alabama. *American Demographics*, 15 (1), 49–50.

Cameron, B. (1992). *Creative destinations: Marketing and packaging: Who wants what—and why? An overview of the Canadian pleasure market study.* Proceedings of the 21st Annual Conference of the Travel and Tourism Research Association, 154–167.

Cook, S. (1995). 1996 outlook for travel and tourism: Basics for building strategies. *1996 Outlook for Travel and Tourism.* Proceedings of the 21st Annual Outlook Forum at the Travel Industry National Conference, Washington, DC: Travel Industry Association of America, 5.

Davidson-Peterson Associates (1996). *1995 economic impact study of leisure travelers & group tour takers,* National Tour Association/International Association of Convention and Visitor Bureaus.

Davidson-Peterson Associates (1996). *Tour traveler index: A profile of the group tour consumer,* National Tour Association.

Dorsey, J. (April 29, 1996). OAG creates typical traveler profile. *Travel Weekly*, 69.

Godsman, J.E. (1995). 1996 outlook for the cruise industry. *1996 Outlook for Travel and Tourism.* Proceedings of the 21st Annual Outlook Forum at the Travel Industry National Conference. Washington, DC: Travel Industry Association of America, 32, 36.

Jones, D. (December 9, 1996). SITE redefines incentive travel. *Travel Weekly*, 49.

Jones, D. (October 21, 1996). Survey: Firms tightening up on expenses. *Travel Weekly*, 55–56.

Mason, P. (1993). The changing family vacation market. *Travel Printout*, 23 (11).

Mason, P. (1995). 1996 outlook for leisure travel. *1996 Outlook for Travel and Tourism*. Proceedings of the 21st Annual Outlook Forum at the Travel Industry National Conference. Washington, DC: Travel Industry Association of America, 80–98.

(August 11, 1996). Minority travelers are a diverse force on the road. *The Seattle Times*.

Myers, E.M. (1995). 1996 outlook for meetings and conventions. *1996 Outlook for Travel and Tourism*. Proceedings of the 21st Annual Outlook Forum at the Travel Industry National Conference. Washington, DC: Travel Industry Association of America, 110–113.

Oppermann, M. (1996). *Meeting planners' decision attributes and perceptions of convention cities*. Proceedings of the 25th Annual Conference of The Travel and Tourism Research Association, 233–237.

Pina, M. (August 22, 1996). Profiling ethnic travelers. *Travel Weekly*, p. 13.

Rohs, J.J. (1995). 1996 outlook for gaming. *1996 Outlook for Travel and Tourism*. Proceedings of the 21st Annual Outlook Forum at the Travel Industry National Conference. Washington, DC: Travel Industry Association of America, 114–119.

(November 18, 1996). Runzheimer survey: Meals are often-overlooked expense. *Travel Weekly*, p. 53.

Sheldon, P.J. (1995). The demand for incentive travel: An empirical study. *Journal of Travel Research*, 33 (4), 23.

Shoemaker, S. (1994). Segmenting the U.S. travel market according to benefits realized. *Journal of Travel Research*, 32 (3), 8–21.

Van Harssel, J., & Theobold, W. (1994). The senior travel market: Distinct, diverse, demanding. *Global Tourism: The Next Decade*. Oxford, England: Butterworth-Heinemann, Ltd., 363–377.

Whitehead, L. (1995). 1996 outlook for business travel. *1996 Outlook for Travel and Tourism*. Proceedings of the 21st Annual Outlook Forum at the Travel Industry National Conference. Washington, DC: Travel Industry Association of America, 99–109.

Young, S., Ott, L., & Feigin, B. (1978). Some practical considerations in market segmentation. *Journal of Marketing Research*, 15, 405–42.

Additional Reading

The 55+ Traveler, U.S. Travel Data Center, 1100 New York Avenue, N.W., Washington, DC 20005-3934, April 1995.

The Congress Bibliography, The Main Association of Convention Professionals, Gian Carlo Fighiera, Via Natale Sandre 15, 10078 Venaria Reale, Torino, Italy, 1995.

Global Tourist Behavior, Muzaffer Uysal, ed., International Business Press, 10 Alice Street, Binghampton, NY 13904-1580, 1994.

Group Travel Report, The National Tour Foundation, 546 Main Street, P.O. Box 3071, Lexington, KY 40596-3071.

Harrah's Survey of Casino Entertainment, Harrah's Marketing Communications, 1023 Cherry Road, Memphis, TN 38117, 1996.

International Travel-Tourism Profiles, Statistics Canada, Pacific Region, 340F-757 West Hastings Street, Vancouver, BC, Canada V6C 3C9, March 1993.

Legalized Casino Gambling in Canada: An Overview, Industry, Science and Technology Canada, Ottawa, Ontario, Canada K1A 0H5, September 1990.

The Meeting Spectrum: An Advanced Guide for Meeting Professionals, Rudy R. Wright, Rockwood Enterprises, P.O. Box 370126, San Diego, CA 92137, 1988.

Special Interest Tourism, Betty Weiler and Colin Michael Hall, eds., John Wiley & Sons, Inc., 605 Third Avenue, New York, NY 10158, 1992.

Tourism to the Year 2000: Qualitative Aspects Affecting Global Growth, World Tourism Organization, Capitan Haya, 42, E-28020 Madrid, Spain, 1991.

"It seems Nepal is the really fashionable place to go at present."

"Not at all, that's passé. Ladakh is the place to go."

"I don't even know where Ladakh is!"

"Of course, that's why it's now the place to go."

Elery Hamilton-Smith, Four Kinds of Tourism

6

The Geography of Travel

Characteristics of Traveler Flows

Purpose

Applying specific models used to explain existing travel patterns, students will be able to predict future travel patterns and new travel market opportunities.

Learning Objectives

Having read this chapter, you should be able to:

1. Explain the impact of demand/origin and demand/resource factors on travel flows.

2. Indicate the magnitude of worldwide travel flows and identify the major reasons for these flows.

3. Project future major travel flows.

Overview

Tourist flows, both domestic and international, are not random. The movement of travelers when measured and explained, can be used as a basis for forecasting future tourist movements. The characteristics of traveler flows is the subject of this chapter.

International tourists are described and recent trends noted. One of the most significant trends for North America has been an increase in the number of overseas travelers to Canada and the U.S. The origins of these visitors and reasons behind this trend are explored. The unsteady growth pattern of outbound overseas travel from North America is examined and reasons for this discussed. Regional flows of tourists (between Canada, the U.S., and Mexico) far outweigh flows of overseas visitors to North America. The size and characteristics of travel flow between the countries in North America are covered in detail.

Domestic travel within North American countries is the next topic of this chapter. The major characteristics of domestic travel are examined.

A profile is given of the major European and Asian tourism countries.

Introduction

The study of tourist movements is important for several reasons. For those at a destination it is vital to know the origins of the visitors. By knowing where the market comes from, marketing plans can be drawn up to reach potential travelers. Also, by studying the geographic characteristics of existing tourists, it may be possible to identify additional untapped market areas. For example, we may note that visitors to a particular "sun

and fun" destination tend to come from cold weather cities within a 600-mile radius of the destination. Further analysis might show several large cold-weather centers of population within 600 miles where there is no marketing effort at present. These would be potential areas for expansion of the marketing effort.

From a theoretical viewpoint the study of tourist flows is also important. By analyzing existing tourist flows, general principles can be developed to explain the movements of tourists. By applying these principles to other destinations, we can forecast potential future tourist movements. This kind of information is important not only to those who market destinations, but also vital to people who plan airline routes and develop attractions for the tourist areas of the future.

Theoretical Models of Travel Flows

*"Without stirring abroad,
One can know the whole world;
Without looking out of the
    window
One can see the way of heaven.
The further one goes
The less one knows."*

Lao-Tzu (6th century B.C.)

The study of traveler flows has been called by many the geography of travel/tourism or simply **tourist geography**. As Matley (1976) notes, there is obviously an "uneven spatial distribution of international tourist activities." He attributed this to the following factors:

- The uneven distribution of tourism resources between destinations
- The wide variety of activities in which travelers participate
- Changes in season
- Weather

- International and domestic political situations
- Economic changes in countries of origin and destination
- Fluctuations in monetary exchange rates
- Increases or decreases in the prices of tourist services
- The staging of special, short duration attractions and events

A number of authors and researchers have attempted to explain past travel-flow patterns and the unevenness by developing and using theoretical models.

The hypothesis put forward by Williams and Zelinsky (1970) is that travel flows are not random but have distinctive patterns that can be explained by several identifiable factors. They suggest that these factors include:

1. **Spatial distance**. The travel time and costs involved when going between origin and destination points.

2. **Presence or absence of past or present international connectivity**. The existence of economic, military, cultural, and other ties or linkages between countries. The flow of travelers between Canada and the U.S. and between Canada and the United Kingdom are good examples of strong international connectivity.

3. **Reciprocity of travel flows**. The belief that a flow in one direction creates a counterflow in the opposite direction. Williams and Zelinsky have found that this is a poor predictor of travel flows between two countries.

4. **Attractiveness of one country for another**. The attractive features of one country can induce travel; these include such items as a favorable climate; cultural, historical, and sporting attractions; and so on. The attractiveness of Florida, Hawaii, and the

Many people visit "sun and fun" destinations to escape the cold. Photo from *Top Shots* CD Rom. Courtesy of Queensland Tourist and Travel Corporation.

Caribbean to North Americans is a good example of this, as is the climatic attractiveness of Spain and other Mediterranean countries to northern Europeans.

5. ***Known or presumed cost of a visit within the destination country.***

6. ***Influence of intervening opportunities.*** The influence of attractions and facilities between the origin and destination points that cause travelers to make intermediate stops and even to forego the journey to their original destination.

7. ***Impact of specific, nonrecurring events.*** The influence of major international events such as the Olympic Games, the World's Fair, and the World Cup of Soccer can cause temporary increases in travel between a destination and various points of origin.

8. ***The national character of the citizens of originating countries.***

9. ***The mental image of the destination country in the minds of the citizens of originating countries.***

Williams and Zelinsky developed and tested their hypothesis by examining the flows of travelers between fourteen destinations, including the U.S., Japan, the United Kingdom, France, and Netherlands, Benelux, West Germany, Scandinavia, Austria, Switzerland, Italy, Iberia, Greece, and South Africa. These authors illustrated the relationships of the flows between individual pairs of origins and destinations. They developed a model with which they calculated the actual and expected travel flows between individual pairs of origins and destinations. They then computed a relative acceptance index (an RA) by dividing the difference between the actual and expected flows by the expected flows. Williams and Zelinsky found strong interactions between several origin and destination pairs, including the U.S. and Japan, the United Kingdom and South Africa, and France and Iberia. It is probable, however, that the authors have created an artificial situation by limiting their analysis to only fourteen countries.

The simplest model of a travel flow consists of an ***origin point***, a ***destination***, and a ***transportation link***. This basic system has been adapted by introducing the two factors of the resistance of the link (a function of distance and cost) and the propensity to participate at the origin. The basic equation (Chubb, 1969) is that the flow for a link is equal to P (propensity to participate) × resistance of the link.

This gravity model is an adaptation of Newton's Law of Universal Gravity, which states that two bodies attract each other in proportion to the product of their masses and inversely by the square of their distance apart. The propensity to travel may, for example, be a measure of the population at the origin—the more people who live in the country of origin, the greater number of potential tourists to travel from that country of origin to a particular destination. The number of travelers is tempered by the time and money it takes to travel from origin to destination. This model assumes that tourist flows decrease as distance from the origin increases. This tends to be true; however, for many people, after a certain point, distance becomes an attraction rather than a deterrent. The farther a destination is, the more status might be given by traveling there. It is speculated that this might be the case where the travel is for a generic reason. For example, take the case of people traveling from Britain to Spain for beaches and sun. The fact that "everybody goes to Spain" may induce people seeking the sun to travel farther. There is more status in traveling to Greece or the Caribbean for a suntan than to Spain. (Cost factors also come into play in understanding the reasons behind such movements.)

The model also assumes a two-way flow. We have seen, however, that tourism flows tend to be one way from generating areas to destination areas. A last proviso is that the model predicts relative flows rather than absolutes. The model might, for example, predict that the flow of tourists between countries A and B would be twice that between countries A and C. It would not predict the actual number of tourists who would travel between these countries.

A model of tourist flows is shown in figure 6.1. To understand tourist flows, it is necessary to examine factors at the origin, the destination, and in-transit routes that influence these flows.

Demand and Origin Factors

The demand for tourism occurs at the origin. Demand is either effective or actual—the number of people who actually travel. **Suppressed demand** comes from the number of people at the origin who, for one reason or another, do not travel. If, however, the factors that prevented them from traveling (lack of income or time, for example) were removed, they would be inclined to travel. This is referred to as **potential demand**. **Deferred demand**, on the other hand, refers to demand that is put off because of a scarcity of supply. There may, for example, be a lack of package tours to where the tourist wants to travel. Both potential

and deferred demand can be converted into **effective demand** by, for example, an increase in income or the development of package tours to specific destinations. Last, these people who have, and will continue to have, no desire to travel exhibit a category of no demand.

Travel propensity is used as a measure of actual demand. The travel propensity of a population is the percentage of the population that actually take a trip or are tourists. The net travel propensity refers to "the percentage of the population who take at least one tourism trip in a given period of time, while gross travel propensity gives the total number of trips taken as a percentage of the population" (Boniface & Cooper, 1987). As more people take second and even third vacation trips each year, the gross travel propensity becomes more important. Dividing the gross travel propensity by the net gives the **travel frequency**—the average number of trips taken by the population.

Because of suppressed demand and no demand, the maximum net travel propensity is likely to be 70 to 80 percent. In the U.S., for example, about two-thirds of the population travel away from home

each year, while four out of five Swedish residents take a holiday of four nights or more every year. On the other hand, one in three Italians take a holiday each year. Gross travel propensity, however, can exceed 100 percent if many in the population take more than one trip a year.

The travel propensity for a given population is determined by a number of factors (Boniface & Cooper, 1987). The demand for tourism is, first, a function of the country of origin's level of economic development. As a country moves toward a developed economy, more people move from employment in the primary sector (fishing, agriculture, etc.) to employment in the secondary or manufacturing sector, and, eventually, in the tertiary or service sector. The percentage of the population that is economically active increases from 30 percent or less in developing countries to 50 percent or more for such things as recreation and tourism. Paid vacations, a healthier population, and greater educational opportunities all combine to produce a greater demand for travel and tourism.

Second, the demand for tourism is affected by the growth, development, distribution, and density of the population. Population growth is important in terms of the number of people and the relationship between births and deaths. As a society progresses, it tends to move from a stage characterized by high birth and death rates to continued high birth rates while death rates decline due to improved health care. The country still cannot afford to care for its growing population, and tourism is a luxury. As countries continue to develop, birth rates decline, and both birth and death rates stabilize at a low level. The population increasingly can afford to travel.

The distribution of the population between urban and rural areas has a significant impact upon the demand for travel and the travel

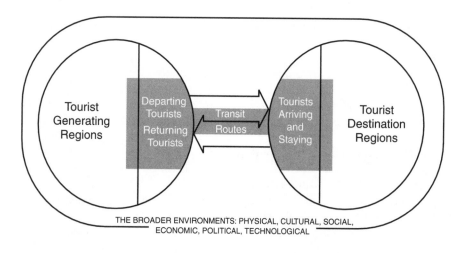

Figure 6.1   The Tourism System.

Source: N. Leiper, "The Framework of Tourism," *Annals of Tourism Research*, vol. 6, no. 1, 1979, 400.

patterns. Densely populated rural areas tend to indicate a population dependent upon agriculture with neither the time nor the money to travel. In contrast, densely populated urban areas suggest an industrialized society with the time, money, and motivation (the "escape from the urban jungle" mentality) to travel. The distribution of a population also affects travel patterns. In the U.S. two-thirds of the population is concentrated in the eastern one-third of the country. A major travel flow in the U.S. is from the populated East to the open spaces of the West.

The politics of the country of origin also affects travel patterns. Countries can, and do, act to control such things as the amount of currency that can be taken out of the country as a deterrent to people's traveling abroad. In 1966, for example, the British government imposed a 50 pound travel allowance in an attempt to curtail travel abroad. (Interestingly enough, this policy encouraged package tour operators to put together creative packages to maximize value within the travel allowance. In 1967, 18 percent more British tourists traveled to the U.S. than in the previous year). Outbound travel can also be controlled by the need for an exit visa.

Patterns of international travel are affected by patterns of domestic tourism. On a worldwide basis, domestic tourism far exceeds international tourism, although the relative percentages of domestic to international tourism vary by country.

Finally, tourism demand is a function of the demographics and lifestyles of the population. This was explored in great detail in chapter 1. It is, in part, a measure of the amount of **discretionary income** enjoyed by the population. Discretionary income is the amount of money left over when taxes have been paid and the basics of life have been provided for. The

number of employed and the types of jobs they have are important demographic considerations, also. These factors are closely related to income. Education is also important. Education broadens the mind and leaves the individual more aware of travel opportunities, while stimulating the desire to travel. The number of paid holidays affects travel demand. Greater numbers of paid holidays or entitlements encourage travel. However, the high cost of travel may mean that more of this entitlement is spent at home. We are seeing, in industrialized nations, more demands for blocks of time that could be used for short vacations. The stage in the family life cycle will influence the type of vacation chosen. The young adult has the need for independence and a fair amount of free time tempered by a lack of money. There is great demand for budget vacations using surface transportation and self-catering accommodations. Patterns change with the arrival of marriage and, even more dramatically, with the appearance of children. Marriage

may bring high income, especially with more and more dual-income families. Travel abroad may increase. As children arrive on the scene, families are constrained by more responsibility and less discretionary time and money. Vacations are role-related, with an emphasis on domestic holidays, self-catering, and visiting friends and relatives. With the advent of the empty nest and retirement, people again have the time and, importantly, the money to travel.

Finally, travel demand is a function of the **values and lifestyles** of the population. How important is travel to them? What do they like to do on vacation? An examination of the culture of the country (see chapter 1) can reveal different values regarding travel, both domestically and internationally.

Destination and Resource Factors

While factors at the origin "push" people to travel, destination characteristics "pull" them to vacation. Basically, visitors seek what they

Often married couples who have no children can afford to travel more. Photo from *Top Shots* CD Rom. Courtesy of Queensland Tourist and Travel Corporation.

cannot get at home. A number of factors help pull visitors.

Climate is a key factor. Everything from sunbathing to skiing is dependent on climatic factors. Climate is the major determinant of the length of the season for many destinations. When the snow is gone, so is the ski season.

The climates of the world are displayed in figure 6.2. The significance for tourism for each of the ten regions is shown in table 6.1. Three major factors determine the kind of weather, water temperature and physical conditions tourists encounter at a destination: water currents, wind, and mountains.

Because land surfaces heat and cool faster than large bodies of water, the oceans act as a source of heat. Both coastal areas and islands enjoy temperate conditions compared to the extremes experienced by large land masses. The Gulf Stream, which brings warmth from the ocean, brings relatively mild winters to much of western Europe.

Generally speaking, in the Northern Hemisphere oceans revolve clockwise; in the southern hemisphere they generally revolve counterclockwise. There are five major ocean currents (see figure 6.2). The Gulf Stream, mentioned above, consists of warm North Atlantic current originating in the Caribbean. It helps moderate temperatures as far north as Great Britain and Norway. The Japan current is also a warm current. It comes from the Equator past Japan and helps moderate Alaska's coastal temperatures. The Peru-Chile current consists of cold water along the Peruvian and Chilean coastline. The California current is a cold current flowing southward along the Pacific Coast of North America that causes land temperatures to be fairly constant. The Benguela is a cold Antarctic current along the southwest African Coast. Knowing this, and looking at the Pacific Ocean, we can understand why it is much colder in Los Angeles than at the southern tip of Japan even though both are at approximately the same latitude. Warm water flows from the Equator along the western shore of the Pacific up past the Philippines and Japan until it reaches the ice around the northern shores of Alaska. As a result it is cold as it continues south along the west coasts of Canada and the U.S. On the other hand the eastern shores of the U.S., benefiting from the Gulf Stream, are warmer than the Atlantic European coastal resorts. For similar reasons the waters along the east coasts of South America, Africa, and Australia are warmer than on the west coasts of these continents.

Winds generally move west to east above the Tropics in the Northern Hemisphere and below the Tropics in the Southern Hemisphere. The zone between the Tropic of Cancer (23.5 degrees north of the Equator) and the Tropic of Capricorn (23.5 degrees south of the Equator) experiences a warm climate all year long. The farther from the Equator, the shorter is the summer and the greater is the difference between day length between summer and winter.

The upper-air currents (the jet stream) are particularly strong. Be-

Table 6.1   World climatic regions and their implications for tourism

CLIMATIC REGION	SIGNIFICANCE FOR TOURISM
1. Tropical trade wind and equatorial climates	High temperatures discourage high activity. Warm year-round water temperatures encourage beach tourism.
2. Tropical wet-dry climates	Dry season suitable for sightseeing, safaris, and beach tourism. High rainy season temperatures and storms discourage tourists.
3. Dry climates	Plentiful sunshine encourages outdoor recreation most of the year. Problems with water supply, dust storms, and high summer heat.
4. Mediterranean climate	Beach tourism most of the year.
5. Warm temperature humid climate	High summer temperatures may deter active recreation. Water sports most of the year.
6. Cool temperature climate	Beach activities only in the summer. Favors strenuous outdoor recreation. All-weather indoor facilities desirable.
7. Mid-latitude continental climates	Outdoor recreation in the summer. Skiing and snow-based activities in the winter.
8. Cold marine climate	Unfavorable for recreation. Rich bird and marine animal life.
9. Subarctic and polar climates	Adventure holidays requiring much advance preparation. Canoeing and fishing in some areas in the summer.
10. Highland climates	Recreation including trekking, climbing, and naturalists. The thin air may restrict strenuous activities. Mountains in tropical countries offer relief from summer heat, while in middle latitude countries snow cover encourages winter sports.

Source: Adapted from B.G. Boniface and C.P. Cooper *The Geography of Travel and Tourism* (London, England: Heinemann Professional Publishing, 1987), 24–25.

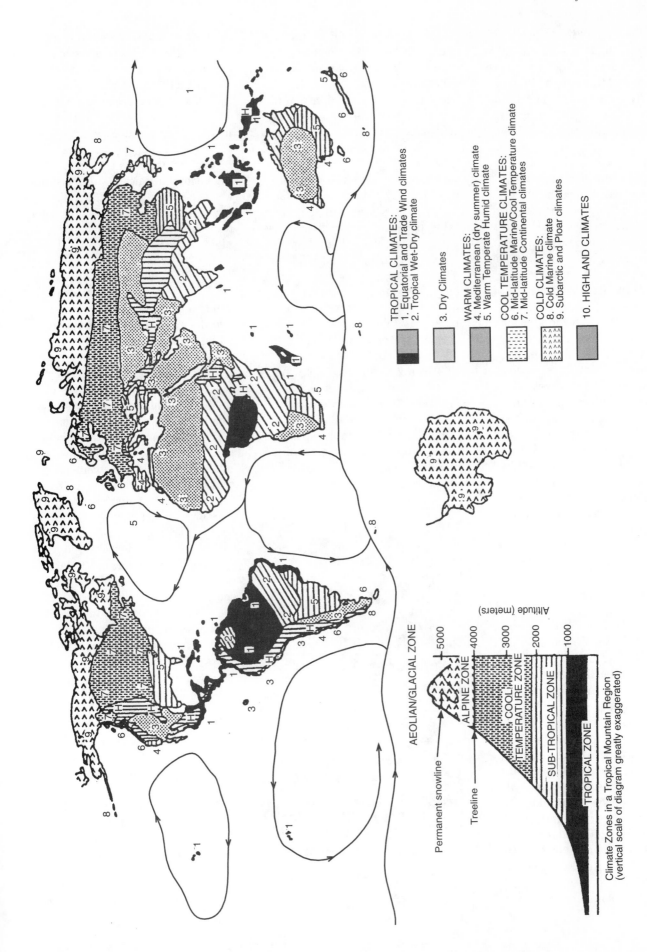

Figure 6.2 World Climates.

Source: Adapted from B.G. Boniface and C.P. Cooper *The Geography of Travel and Tourism* (London, England: Heinemann Professional Publishing, 1987), 23.

tween the Tropics the steady humid winds (trade winds) usually move east to west. The impacts are felt on flying time and on local climate. Flying against the wind (San Francisco to Tokyo) takes longer than flying with the wind (Tokyo to San Francisco).

The local climate is affected as air in the wind current picks up and drops moisture as it goes. Looking at the West Coast of North America we can see that the air is moist from the Pacific Ocean. As it blows east it brings moisture to the western coast until it reaches the third influencing element: mountains. For every 1,000 feet (305 meters) in elevation the air temperature drops 3.5 degrees F (1.5 degrees C). As the air cools, the moisture it carries drops as rain or snow. The western or windward side of the mountains are lush and green while the sheltered or leeward side of the range is dry as little moisture makes it over the mountain. Denver faces this situation in its position relative to the Rocky Mountains. In addition to the Rockies, which include the Sierra Nevada range between California and Nevada, the major mountain ranges are the north/south-running Sierra Madres, a continuation of the Rockies chain in Mexico; the Andes, a north/south continuation of the Rockies/Sierra Madres in South America; the Alps, an east/west European chain; and the Himalayas, an east/west Asian chain.

In Europe, as a result of prevailing winds and the Alps, a moist westerly wind comes from the Atlantic Ocean across Great Britain and the west coast of Europe until it hits the mountains. Because of the height of the Alps and conflicting air currents from northern Europe, the air slows and backs up onto itself. As a result there is a great deal of fog and dampness from Ireland to the Alps. In contrast, on the southern side of the

Alps little moisture makes it over the mountains. The relatively small amount of water produced by the Mediterranean has little negative impact. As a result Greece and the southern parts of Italy and the Balkans are very dry.

The combination of climate and land surface produces conditions that affect the type of tourism appropriate to the location. The land surface of the earth is either mountains, plateaus, hill lands, or plains. Approximately three-quarters of the earth is mountain or hill land. These are suitable for recreation all year long. In winter, skiing and other snow-based recreation is possible, while the clear, crisp air at other seasons allows opportunities for such things as walking, sightseeing, and photography. As noted above, mountains can provide relief from the summer heat for those in the lowlands. The lack of population adds to the attractiveness of these areas. Most of the world's population lives on the plateaus and plains. Coastal plains

Colorado's mountains influence the state's weather, and its appeal as a vacation destination. Photo Credit: Boulder CVB.

are ideal for tourism development providing, as they do, access to beach and sea. Inland waters are also attractive to tourists, allowing a variety of recreational pursuits in addition to their attractiveness as a scenic resource.

While climate and natural resources are major factors in drawing visitors to a destination, visitors are also attracted by culture, history, ethnicity, and accessibility of a destination. These factors are explored in chapter 8.

Transit Routes

While tourists may have the means and the motivation to travel, and while destinations may have features likely to attract visitors, tourists must be able to reach the places where they want to go. That is the function of the *transit route* that links origin to destination.

The vast majority of travel between origin and destination is by road. For tourists, the advantage of traveling by car is that they have the flexibility of stopping where they wish, when they wish, for as long as they wish. It also allows for the transport of sizable (depending upon the size of the car) amounts of luggage. Travel by coach is more restrictive; however, the number of destinations served by coach is significantly greater than are served by other means of transportation.

In the mid-nineteenth century rail travel opened up areas that were previously inaccessible. Some lines added special carriages, raised to allow viewing of the scenery. Trains offer a relaxing way to travel with the opportunity to get up and walk around.

Air travel ushered in the era of mass tourism. The speed and the range of the jet aircraft opened up large areas of the world to millions of people. The individual with two weeks' annual holiday can get to the destination within a few hours instead of the several days that it might have taken by road or rail.

Traveling by sea is now essentially limited to cruising and ferry crossings. The major selling point for the cruise is relaxation, luxury, and comfort.

The travel route and mode of transportation are decided upon by the visitor after evaluating the options in terms of availability, frequency, price, speed, and comfort. The various modes of transportation are covered more fully in chapter 7.

A Model of Competitiveness

It is proposed that the competitiveness of a tourism destination can be explained as follows (Ritchie & Crouch, 1993):

> TOURISM
> COMPETITIVENESS = f
> (Destination Appeal,
> Destination Management,
> Destination Organization,
> Destination Information,
> Destination Efficiency)

The appeal of a destination itself is a combination of two factors: the characteristics of a region that make it attractive to visit compared to the deterrents or barriers to travel. The determinants of destination attractiveness are outlined in table 6.2 while the deterrents to visitation of a destination are presented in table 6.3. The more the attractiveness outweighs the barriers, the greater will be the appeal.

Destination management is a measure of how effective the marketing and management efforts are to maximize the positive attributes of the destination while minimizing the negatives or barriers. From a marketing perspective managers at the destination attempt to select appropriate segments of the market and persuade people in those segments to visit the destination, in part through the development of a strong image of and believable pro-

---

Quick Trip 6.1
Identifying Market Potential

Various industries have used a category development index (CDI) and a brand development index (BDI) to identify important markets. For tourism purposes

$$CDI = \text{Visitor/Population} \times 100$$

where

Visitor = Percentage of visitors to the state
Population = Percentage of U.S. population in the market

This represents the extent to which various markets have been developed.

$$BDI = \text{Tvisit/Population} \times 100$$

where

Tvisit = Percentage of visitors to the city in the state
Population = Percentage of U.S. population in the market

For example, Atlanta, Georgia, visitors to Florida

$$CDI = \frac{\textit{Percent of Atlanta visitors to Florida}}{\text{Percent of U.S. population in Atlanta}} \times 100 = \frac{6.0}{1.7} \times 100 = 353$$

$$BDI = \frac{\textit{Percent of Atlanta visitors to Tampa}}{\text{Percent of U.S. population in Atlanta}} \times 100 = \frac{1.9}{1.7} \times 100 = 112$$

The market opportunity index is the difference between CDI and BDI. Ideally a market's CDI and BDI are both greater than 100. This would indicate that the percent of U.S. households represented by a specific market visiting a destination city within a state is equal to or greater than the percent of its visitation to the state. Once ratios are developed they are placed on a "tourism opportunity index" matrix that identifies Top Performers (High Population/High BDI), Sleeping Giants (Low Population/High BDI), Untapped Potential (High Population/Low BDI), and Low Priorities (Low Population/Low BDI).

Given the following figures:

1. Identify the CDI and BDI ratios.
2. Place the markets on an "Opportunity Matrix" for Tampa, Florida, where High Population is defined as 1 million +; Medium Population is 500,000–1 million, and Low Population is less than 500,000. High BDI is defined as greater than 120, medium BDI is 80–119, and low BDI is less than 80.
3. Identify the best potential markets for Tampa, Florida.

(continued on the following page)

1992 Tampa, Florida Visitation Report

ADI*	NUMBER OF ADI HOUSEHOLDS (1,000s)	% OF ADI HOUSE-HOLDS EXC. FLORIDA	% OF FLORIDA VISITORS	% OF TAMPA VISITORS
PLEASURE MARKET				
St. Louis	1110.9	1.3 %	1.4%	2.2%
Pittsburgh	1139.6	1.3	1.4	2.1
Cincinnati	759.0	0.88	1.0	1.5
Chicago	2999.7	3.5	3.5	4.5
Detroit	1719.0	1.99	1.7	2.4
Richmond	436.9	0.5	0.4	0.6
Louisville/Lexington	891.9	1.04	1.3	1.2
Atlanta	1456.8	1.7	6.0	1.9
Buffalo	629.4	0.73	0.7	0.8
Harrisburg	542.9	0.63	0.7	0.6
Washington, D.C.	1781.9	2.1	2.6	1.9
Raleigh-Durham	729.3	0.84	0.9	0.7
Baton Rouge	249.5	0.79	0.4	0.1
Springfield	247.7	0.29	0.3	0.1
Jackson	276.1	0.32	0.5	0.1

*This is a geographic market definition developed by the Arbitron Company that assigns each U.S. county exclusively to one television market based on dominant signal penetration.

Source: Bonn, M.A., & Brand, R.R. (Fall 1995). Identifying Market Potential: The Application of Brand Development Indexing to Pleasure Travel. *Journal of Travel Research*, 34, (2), 31–35.

Table 6.2   Determinants of destination attractiveness

NATURAL FEATURES
e.g.   General topography
       Scenery

CLIMATE
e.g.   Temperature
       Amount of sunshine, rain

CULTURE & SOCIAL CHARACTERISTICS
e.g.   Traditions
       Style of architecture
       Local foods

GENERAL INFRASTRUCTURE
e.g.   Roads
       Sewerage, water, electricity

BASIC SERVICES INFRASTRUCTURE
e.g.   Shopping
       Car maintenance

TOURISM SUPERSTRUCTURE
e.g.   Lodging
       Information

ACCESS AND TRANSPORTATION FACILITIES
e.g.   Distance and time to get there
       Frequency, ease and quality of transportation

ATTITUDES ABOUT TOURISTS
e.g.   Warmth of welcome
       Ease of communication

COST/PRICE LEVELS
e.g.   Value for money
       Exchange rates

ECONOMIC AND SOCIAL TIES
e.g.   International trade
       Common culture, language, religion

UNIQUENESS
e.g.   One-of-a-kind attractions or events

Source: Ritchie, J.R.B., & Crouch, G.I. (1993). Competitiveness in International Tourism: A Framework for Understanding and Analysis. *The Tourist Review*, 35, 53–56.

Table 6.3   Deterrents to visitation of a destination

SECURITY AND SAFETY
e.g.   Political instability
       High crime rate

HEALTH AND MEDICAL CONCERNS
e.g.   Poor sanitation
       Lack of reliable medical services

LAWS AND REGULATIONS
e.g.   Visa requirements
       Currency controls

CULTURAL DISTANCE
e.g.   Inability to communicate
       Restrictions on behavior

Source: Ritchie, J.R.B., & Crouch, G.I. (1993). Competitiveness in International Tourism: A Framework for Understanding and Analysis. *The Tourist Review*, 35, 57.

motional effort selling the destination. Packages need to be developed and alliances made with tour wholesalers and retailers.

At the same time management efforts should be aimed at making it as easy as possible for visitors to travel to and enjoy the benefits of the destinations. This includes efforts to reduce requirements for entry and measures to help ensure visitor safety.

Destination organization is a function of various internal organizational actions and the creation of ***strategic alliances*** aimed at improving the destination's attractiveness to tourists. Because tourism impacts many sectors of a destination its economic advantages are spread widely. However, as a result of this structure, the various businesses that comprise tourism tend to be small, fragmented and unfocused. Thus, it is argued, there is a need for some kind of umbrella organization—such as a National Tourism Organization or, at a more local level, a Convention & Visitors Bureau—to act as a coordinating body for both public and private tourism interests. At the same time, given the increasingly global environment, tourism concerns, even at the national level, can no longer work alone. There are economies of scale to be gained by pooling resources and working together. In Europe, for example, individual countries contribute to a joint market research effort conducted by the European Travel Commission. In recent years the U.S. and Canada have formed similar unions for the purpose of sharing research findings.

In today's increasingly sophisticated business environment, decisions need to be made on the best information available. This means internal information aimed at assisting the destination better manage the tourism product and external marketing information allowing the destination to adapt to changing market conditions. The principal components of an internal ***destination management information system*** are (Ritchie & Crouch, 1993):

- Visitor statistics detailing patterns of tourist behavior
- Performance measures that identify problems
- Economic, social, and environmental impacts
- Information to monitor and track the attitudes of local people toward tourism

At the same time, market research is necessary to focus on such things as market segmentation, the forecasting of tourist demand, visitor satisfaction ratings, the effectiveness of advertising, and the development of new products and services.

Finally, there are a series of activities that can contribute to how well tourism services are delivered to the visitor. The quality or value of the services provided should be equal to or greater than the price charged. This might involve setting standards for specific types of busi-

nesses and monitoring the extent to which these standards are reached. It might mean supporting education and training programs aimed at increasing the service abilities of employees. It might also involve educational campaigns aimed at residents, indicating the benefits to them of tourism devel-

opment. At the same time it is important for tourism businesses to be productive and profitable. Cost-benefit analyses have to be done before different services can be introduced to ensure that they can be delivered in a way that is not only satisfying to the guest but profitable to the business.

Quick Trip 6.2
Matching Clients with Destinations

Stanley Plog, a Los Angeles-based psychologist, outlines a method for matching people to destinations. Explained in his book, *Vacation Places Rated*, based on their responses to an eight-point personality quiz readers fall into one of three categories: Venturers, Dependables, or Centrics. Venturers are curious, adventurous, and hungry for new experiences. They are particularly into unique, lesser-known destinations and would accept food that others wouldn't find acceptable.

Dependables prefer well-established destinations with good reputations. They tend to revisit places and spend time when choosing a vacation spot. They travel with others (for example, as part of an escorted tour) and look for value. Centrics are open to a variety of travel experiences. They want a destination to have some commercial development but are wary of over-developed places. Within all three categories people can be "active" or "mellow."

Questions and Exercises:

1. Rate the following destinations on a scale of one through ten as to their attractiveness for each of the three categories (One being the strongest attraction).

2. How would you describe yourself using Plog's terminology?

3. Compare your responses to the numbers you gave the destinations.

	Type of Traveler		
	DEPENDABLES	CENTRICS	VENTURERS
Hawaii			
Alaska			
Colorado			
Northern California			
Maine			

(continued on the following page)

	DEPENDABLES	CENTRICS	VENTURERS
Las Vegas			
Washington state			
Vermont			
Oregon			
Arizona			
Montana			
Central Florida			
South Carolina			
Southern California			
Wyoming			
North Carolina			
Massachusetts			
Washington, DC			
New Hampshire			
South Florida			
Ireland			
U.K. countryside			
British Columbia			
Costa Rica			
Australia			
Bermuda			
New Zealand			
Switzerland			
Israel			
London, England			
Austria			
U.S. Virgin Islands			
Germany			
Rome			
France			
Cayman Islands			
Aruba			
Scandinavia			
Ontario, Canada			
Greece			

Source: Dorsey, J. Matching Clients with Destinations. *Travel Weekly*. (October 26, 1995) 100.

Travel Flows

Trends

In examining the trends in mass-market holidays over the past several decades, three items are worthy of note:

1. People have ventured farther from home
2. There has been a constant north-south movement
3. Europe has maintained its prominent role as a destination and region of origination

In 1970 the main direction of inclusive air charter flights was north-south, with traffic being centered in Spain and, to a lesser degree, Italy. Spain was linked to the eight major European markets, the most important being the United Kingdom. In fact the U.K.-Spain route was the most important in terms of volume, accounting for over one-quarter of total traffic within Europe between countries that had at least 1 percent of the market.

Movements became more complex in the 1970s as new destinations opened up. The U.K.-Spain route, while still important, saw its market share drop to 20 percent. Links between the United Kingdom and France and the United Kingdom and the Netherlands fell below 1 percent, as did those between Scandinavia and Italy. Greece not only emerged as a new destination, but as the second most important after Spain. Of its four markets—United Kingdom, France, West Germany, and Sweden—the United Kingdom was the most important. During this time major flows also developed between the United Kingdom and two new destinations: Malta and Portugal.

The north-south movement intensified as new southern destinations were developed and Norway emerged as a growing originating country. The reasons for these changing flows can be explained by developments in the countries of origin, in the destinations, and in the linkages themselves. Population growth in the countries of origin is one reason for the growth. More people with more discretionary income produced a larger potential market. Complementarity is another reason. The north-south traffic is strong because of the movement from colder, northern countries to warmer, southern areas around the Mediterranean coast. The distances involved and the fact that certain markets, in particular the United Kingdom, are insular explain the rise in importance of *inclusive tour charters*. The long coastline of Spain and the short distances involved between airport and hotel, together with the close proximity of other tourism features, lead to an ease of packaging. The availability of surplus military aircraft also helped spur the development of package tours. The Berlin airlift of 1947 and 1948 showed the advantage of having a pool of operators able to move large quantities of items on short notice. The movement of large numbers of people was seen as an appropriate use of their skills in peacetime.

Yet why did the United Kingdom develop a strong inclusive tour charter package (ITC) movement when France, for example, did not? To answer this question, it is necessary to examine the characteristics of the countries more closely. First, France has an attractive coastline of its own. Second, it is relatively close to and has overland links with other Mediterranean countries. Third, the French are very individualistic. Fourth, there have been a number of industry practices that induced the potential for ITCs. These included such things as high commissions by travel agents and restrictive practices by government authorities and parent airlines. The net result was that,

Table 6.4 International departures: Where do tourists come from?

ORIGINATING COUNTRY	TRIPS ABROAD IN MILLIONS 1994	AVERAGE ANNUAL GROWTH RATE 1985–1994
Germany	65.2	4.2%
United States	47.3	3.5%
United Kingdom	34.2	5.2%
Canada	20.9	5.2%
Italy	16.9	7.0%
France	16.7	7.4%
Japan	13.4	11.6%

Source: World Tourism Organization

in 1980, the proportion of French tourists taking an organized tour was 5 percent, while 50 percent of all British holidays abroad involved inclusive tours.

This kind of analysis shows many of the factors that must be considered in explaining and understanding the reasons for tourist flows. Only with such an understanding can future flows be predicted.

Global Travel Flows

Since World War II international tourism has grown tremendously, showing annual average growth rates in tourist arrivals of just over 7 percent from 1950 to 1990. In the nineties, however, growth has slowed to less than 6 percent a year, a reflection of a maturing market. International tourism receipts are increasing at a faster rate than arrivals. In part this reflects the influence of Asian and Pacific countries, whose tourists spend proportionately more when on vacation than do visitors from other regions (Vellas & Becherel, 1995).

Tourism is the world's largest industry and generator of jobs. To put that in perspective, if tourism were a country, it would have the third largest economy in the world, behind the U.S. and Japan.

According to World Tourism

Organization figures, there were 567 million international tourist arrivals in 1995. This number is expected to grow to 702 million by the year 2000 and 1,018 million by 2010. In 1995 they spent $37 billion, a figure expected to increase to $621 billion in the year 2000 and continue growing to $1.5 trillion by 2010. Growth is linked to the world economy in general and the state of the economies in the major industrialized countries in particular, the major generating markets for international tourism. In fact, nearly 30 percent of international departures come from the world's top seven markets (see table 6.4).

While Europe continues its domination as a tourist destination, accounting for six out of every ten international arrivals and half of all international receipts in 1995, it has lost market share over the past twenty years as other regions have experienced greater rates of growth. This trend will continue into the next century (see tables 6.5, 6.6). In part this reflects the fact that many tourism destinations, particularly in coastal Mediterranean resorts, are not being renovated. Additionally, because over 80 percent of European tourism is intraregional, arrivals and receipts are a direct reflection of the strength of European economies. Lackluster growth in the 1980s and 1990s led to poor results.

Table 6.5   Percent share of world arrivals—1975; 1995; and 2010

REGION	1975	1995	2010
Europe	69.2%	59.5%	51.6%
Americas	22.5%	19.7%	19.1%
East Asia and the Pacific	3.9%	14.7%	22.5%
Africa	2.1%	3.3%	3.6%
Middle East	1.6%	1.9%	2%
South Asia	0.7%	0.8%	1.1%

Source: World Tourism Organization

The relatively strong showing by Europe is due to the propensity of Europeans to travel and the fact that countries in Europe are smaller than in other regions of the world. A trip of 100 miles in the U.S., for example, might get an individual into another state. This would be recorded as a domestic arrival. In Europe, if that 100-mile trip meant traveling to another country, it would be classified as an international arrival. The Americas remain a distant second in both international arrivals and receipts, while also experiencing a loss of market share.

Among those regions that have been increasing their share of world arrivals since 1975, East Asia and the Pacific has made the most significant gains. It is projected that this region will pass the Americas by 2010 to follow Europe in terms of market share. The region has also seen significant increases in its share of tourist receipts. Africa has also increased its share while less dramatic increases were posted by South Asia and the Middle East.

In Europe the fastest growing subregion is Eastern Mediterranean Europe. Western Europe is experiencing the poorest growth due to saturation levels and over-valued currencies in certain destinations. The latter can be corrected while the former cannot. However, Western and Southern Europe together account for about two-thirds of European arrivals and over 70 percent of international tourism European receipts. Eastern and Central Europe benefit from Western tourist flows and long-distance travel.

The U.S., Canada, and Mexico together represent about three-quarters of total arrivals and receipts in the Americas. The U.S. alone accounts for 40 percent of all arrivals and over 60 percent of all tourism receipts in the region. Growth in the region, however, is most evident in South America. Significant increases are also projected for Latin America.

In East Asia and the Pacific the fastest growing subregion is Australasia and other Pacific Islands. Northeastern Asia, however, is the most visited subregion, ac-

counting for more than half of all arrivals in the region.

In the African region South Africa is showing most growth as a result of strong demand in both leisure and business travel. The market share in Northern Africa has been declining due to negative results from both Algeria and Morocco while East Africa is experiencing a sustained growth in arrivals from Europe. Nearly two-thirds of all international tourism receipts in Africa come from three countries: Morocco (17 percent), South Africa (23 percent), and Tunisia (22 percent) (Vellas & Becherel, 1995).

Middle East growth has been fueled by Egypt which accounts for almost half of the increase in arrivals and 80 percent of the increase in receipts for the region. Although the proportion of intra-regional traffic in the region has been declining (as long-haul travel has been increasing) it is still important. In fact, Egyptians and Saudi Arabians together account for more than 20 percent of all tourists in the Middle East. Egypt is both the largest generator and recipient of tourists. Tourism to Saudi Arabia is strictly for business or religious purposes.

While the region has great cultural wealth, attacks in the mid-nineties on tourists visiting Egypt rekindled travel concerns. The growth in South Asia is a product of strong increases to India, a sustained growth of long-haul leisure travel from Europe, the Middle East, and East Asia.

The ten leading destinations (see tables 6.7, 6.8) account for over half of all international tourist arrivals. The nineties saw a gradual diversification of tourist markets with the emergence of new destinations, primarily in East Asia and the Pacific. This phenomenon has also been seen in Central and Eastern Europe with the rise of such countries as Hungary, Poland, and the Czech Republic.

Table 6.6   Percent share of world receipts—1975 and 1995

REGION	1975	1995
Europe	63.5%	51.1%
Americas	25.1%	25.6%
East Asia and the Pacific	5.3%	18.7%
Africa	3.1%	1.9%
Middle East	2.1%	1.8%
South Asia	0.8%	1.0%

Source: World Tourism Organization

Table 6.7 World's top ten tourism destinations

RANK		COUNTRY
1990	1995	
1	1	France
3	2	Spain
2	3	United States
4	4	Italy
12	5	China
7	6	United Kingdom
5	7	Hungary
8	8	Mexico
27	9	Poland
6	10	Austria

Source: World Tourism Organization

Table 6.8 World's top ten tourism earners

RANK		COUNTRY
1990	1995	
1	1	United States
2	2	France
3	3	Italy
4	4	Spain
5	5	United Kingdom
6	6	Austria
7	7	Germany
11	8	Hong Kong
25	9	China
12	10	Singapore

Source: World Tourism Organization

spent by international tourists in the U.S. on travel-related expenses than was spent by U.S. tourists traveling internationally). The positive balance grew steadily until 1993 when it began to decline. The U.S. receives most money from visitors from Japan, followed by the United Kingdom, Canada, Mexico, and Germany. U.S. travelers spend most in the United Kingdom followed by Mexico, Canada, Japan, and Germany.

The most popular generators of visitors to the U.S. are Canada, Mexico, Japan, the United Kingdom, and Germany while the top destinations for U.S. travelers are Mexico, Canada, the United Kingdom, France, and Germany. From Europe the greatest growth will come from Germany, France, and the United Kingdom.

California, Florida, and New York are visited by over three-quarters of all the overseas (overseas excludes Mexico and Canada) visitors to the U.S., Hawaii, and Nevada round out the top five states visited. In terms of specific cities, New York, Los Angeles, Miami, San Francisco, Orlando, and Hono-

lulu all get more than 10 percent of overseas visitors. A profile of overseas visitors to the U.S. indicates the following (Department of Commerce, 1996):

- The decision to travel is made, on average, 64 days in advance (median time 41 days)
- Airline reservations are made an average of 39 days in advance (median time 22 days)
- Travel agents are, overwhelmingly, the major source of information, followed by friends and relatives, airlines and travel guides
- Two-thirds travel independently, one-third come on a package
- The most common package involves air and lodging
- One-third prebook lodging through a travel agent
- One-third travel alone, while 25 percent each travel with a spouse or with family/relatives
- The main purpose of the trip for half is a holiday, for 23 percent it is business, and for 13 percent it is to visit friends/relatives

United States

Inbound International Travel.
International visitors to the U.S. peaked in 1992 at 47.3 million and slumped to 44.3 million by 1996. In the ten years from 1986 to 1996 the share of overseas visitors increased dramatically and almost totally at the expense of market share from Canada. During the same period international departures have steadily increased in general, apart from a dip from 1990–1991 due to the Gulf War, with Canada losing market share as that of overseas destinations and Mexico increased.

The U.S. showed a positive travel trade balance for the first time in 1989 (more money was

New York is one of the most popular U.S. spots for overseas visitors. Photo by Corel.

- Visitors average seventeen nights in the U.S. (median is eight nights)

- Over three-quarters are repeat visitors

- Sixty percent visit only one state, 21 percent visit two, while 19 percent visit three or more states

- Miami, followed by New York, Los Angeles, and Honolulu are the major ports of entry

- The three most popular leisure activities while in the U.S. are shopping (84 percent), dining in restaurants (69 percent), and sightseeing in cities (64 percent). No other activity was mentioned by more than 35 percent of the respondents (multiple responses were allowed)

- On average each visitor spends $3,222 on the entire trip, $1,569 in the U.S., an average of $92 per day

- Money is spent on gifts and souvenirs (26 percent of total spending), lodging (23 percent), food and beverages (18 percent), transportation (13 percent), and entertainment (10 percent)

- The average annual household income is $76,600 (median $63,200)

> *"The American arrives in Paris with a few French phrases he has culled from a conversational guide or picked up from a friend who owns a beret."*
>
> Fred Allen

Outbound International Travel.

For many years Americans have labored under the image of being poor travelers. The "ugly American" is a phrase used to capture the idea of people unable and unwilling to adjust to foreign places. However, there is some evidence to suggest that U.S. travelers place a great deal of emphasis on cultural

understanding (Pyszka, 1990). In one study six out of ten long-haul travelers indicate that it is extremely or very important "to satisfy a curiosity about how other people live." An additional third indicate it is somewhat important. Most indicate that it is extremely or very important to interact with people from other countries. This compares with fewer than four out of ten who say that experiencing the foods and wines of other countries and just over one-quarter who say shopping are extremely or very important reasons for taking an international vacation. These responses, which indicate desires or opinions, should be compared with actual behavior outlined below. However, almost 90 percent of this nationally representative sample of people who had taken a long-haul pleasure trip indicate that "I often try to strike up conversations with local people." In addition, they give more consideration to the friendliness of the local people than to good weather, time required to reach the destination, and the amount of jet lag experienced. Further, over 90 percent indicate they would enjoy being invited into someone's home, two-thirds agreeing strongly or mostly. The next best thing for many is staying in a bed and breakfast, an activity whose primary appeal is the opportunity to meet the people of the country as well as to experience local culture.

When U.S. travelers are asked to list favorite destinations visited, just over one-third indicate an international location (*Travel Weekly* 1995). Fifteen percent list western Europe while an additional 10 percent indicate the Caribbean.

A profile of U.S. travelers to overseas destinations indicates (Department of Commerce, 1996):

- The decision to travel is made, on average, 68 days in advance (median time 44 days)

- Airline reservations are made an average of 40 days in advance (median time 25 days)

- Travel agents are, overwhelmingly, the major source of information, followed by airlines and friends and relatives

- Almost 80 percent travel independently, the remainder on a package

- Almost 30 percent prebook lodging through a travel agent

- Almost four out of ten travel alone, while 28 percent travel with a spouse and 21 percent with family/relatives

- The main purpose of the trip for 43 percent is a holiday, for 28 percent it is business, and for one out of five it is to visit friends/relatives

- Visitors average 18 nights outside the U.S. (median is 11 nights)

- Almost 90 percent are repeat visitors

- Three-quarters visit only one country, 16 percent visit two, while 10 percent visit three or more countries

- New York, followed by Miami, and Los Angeles are the major ports of re-entry into the U.S.

- The three most popular leisure activities are dining in restaurants (72 percent), shopping (70 percent), sightseeing in cities (65 percent), and visiting historical places (50 percent). No other activity was mentioned by more than 34 percent of the respondents (multiple responses were allowed)

- On average each visitor spends $2,629 on the entire trip, $1,081 outside the U.S., an average of $61 per day

- The average annual household income is $89,700 (median $76,500)

Domestic Travel.
In 1995 there were 1.173 million trips of 100 or

more miles away from home taken in the U.S. About two-thirds of these were for pleasure as distinct from business, a proportion that has remained constant for at least ten years (*Travel Weekly*, 1996).

When asked to list favorite destinations visited, almost two-thirds of U.S. travelers note regions in the U.S. (*Travel Weekly*, 1995). One third list the West while an additional 20 percent note the South.

There are significant differences in the extent to which states attract destination-oriented travel. Five clusters have been identified (Uysal, Fesenmaier, & O'Leary, 1994). The cluster with the highest level of destination-oriented travel includes California, Florida, and several Midwestern and New England states. The lowest cluster includes the western states of Montana, Utah, and Wyoming. There are also wide seasonal variations. During the winter season (January through March) California, Utah, Texas, Florida, Montana, North and South Dakota, Great Lakes and Michigan, and a large portion of New England are primary destination states. A primary destination (in this study) means that 90 percent of the people visiting these states spend between 76 percent and 100 percent of their vacation in one of these states. The Central and Mountain states are second-tier destination states in the winter while the Southeast region is made up of pass-through destinations. During the spring (April through June) and summer (July through September) seasons, Florida, California, and Michigan have the highest concentration of destination-oriented travel while Montana, Wyoming, Utah, and New Mexico have the least in the spring. In the summer these four are joined by Nebraska and North and South Dakota as the states having the least amount of destination-oriented travel. The fall tourism destination market is dominated by Florida, Texas, California, Washington,

Quick Trip 6.3
Identifying Potential Markets for the United States

The following figures are taken from the *Abstract of International Travel To and From the United States 1994* (Department of Commerce).

International Arrivals by Country of Origin, 1990–1994

COUNTRY	1990	1991	1992	1993	1994
Argentina	184,657	280,504	342,008	387,116	390,109
Australia	465,505	470,595	486,851	448,507	410,666
Austria	106,885	121,000	150,663	164,095	154,550
Bahamas	324,255	302,324	286,846	309,488	244,113
Belgium	138,134	149,099	171,146	185,836	200,510
Brazil	398,484	459,384	475,266	555,102	661,265
Canada—3	17,263,000	19,113,000	18,598,461	17,293,000	14,970,000
Chile	68,639	88,673	104,550	120,901	125,407
China—1	66,000	76,000	124,000	177,663	158,103
China/Taiwan—2	305,082	344,263	411,131	504,407	537,454
Colombia	154,998	160,755	188,808	212,688	228,407
Costa Rica	80,113	84,937	102,491	119,966	118,554
Cuba	36,871	42,379	22,338	25,384	14,903
France	716,036	770,230	795,444	844,644	863,345
Germany (West)	1,202,826	1,430,193	1,691,663	1,826,757	1,704,811
Guatemala	110,722	121,807	123,358	141,424	136,129
Hong Kong	163,457	178,381	191,237	192,691	200,828
India	110,087	109,557	105,790	102,339	107,671
Ireland	99,161	101,980	118,229	122,435	139,739
Israel	161,722	169,912	160,051	186,409	190,318
Italy	395,783	478,853	589,837	555,785	550,840
Jamaica	187,117	164,076	148,270	181,290	182,906
Japan	3,231,495	3,319,934	3,652,828	3,542,546	4,065,023
Korea, Republic of	211,260	278,182	341,311	408,213	503,757
Malaysia	42,563	42,752	47,362	49,976	57,083
Mexico	7,217,000	7,718,000	10,872,000	9,824,000	11,325,000
Netherlands	284,203	316,609	342,034	378,904	392,584
New Zealand	173,844	145,306	139,515	133,746	124,171
Norway	103,960	93,691	103,863	106,437	105,317
Panama	58,975	63,444	66,068	73,647	73,609
Peru	114,696	115,156	114,776	128,216	121,269
Philippines	93,335	103,463	117,031	115,492	107,112
Spain	242,670	291,646	343,922	309,695	295,328
Sweden	282,163	260,424	261,728	224,281	214,519
Switzerland	293,652	304,541	321,725	341,591	366,462
Taiwan	239,000	268,000	287,000	326,744	379,351
United Kingdom	2,243,792	2,495,354	2,823,983	2,999,301	2,920,975
Venezuela	264,397	310,735	372,313	444,355	424,161

Source: Tourism Industries, International Trade Administration. Summary and Analysis of International Travel to the U.S., originally released 9/13/95, trw.

Exercise:

Based on these figures, and using the principles outlined in the text to explain travel movements, identify potential untapped markets for the U.S.

California has a high level of destination-oriented travel. The Golden Gate Bridge is one of San Francisco's sights. Photo Credit: Robert Holmes.

Minnesota, Wisconsin, Michigan, and New York while southeastern and western states attract little destination-oriented travel. Other surveys (*Travel Weekly*, 1995) asking Americans to name their top choices (preference as distinct from actual behavior) for a fall vacation trip identify Florida, California, and Hawaii as the top three. In short, destination-oriented travel is very seasonal. Colorado, for example, receives a high proportion of destination-oriented travel in the fall and winter but is a pass-through state the remaining six months of the year. Different marketing approaches are appropriate for a destination-oriented or a pass-through oriented market. The pass-through market, for example, is more concerned with accessibility, is likely to stay at lower cost facilities when on the road, and might be induced to stay a few hours or perhaps a day more. The destination-oriented market will probably stay at a more upscale facility than when on the road, is more con-

cerned with the availability of a large number of attractions, and requires more space in the lodging facility.

Canada

> "When I was there I found their jokes like their roads—very long and not very good, leading to a little thin point of a spire which had been remorselessly obvious for miles without seeming to get any nearer."
>
> Samuel Butler

Inbound International Travel.

The U.S. is Canada's number one international travel market. However, over the past decade, Canada's share of the U.S. market has been decreasing. The U.S. travelers who do visit are remarkably loyal, about 90 percent being repeat visitors. It has been shown that first-time and repeat visitors are two distinct market segments and should be marketed to in different ways. When targeting new travelers the information needs to be informational. The objectives are to create awareness and develop favorable attitudes. For repeat visitors the objectives are to keep the destination (Canada) uppermost in the mind of the traveler, to get the traveler to spread positive word-of-mouth communication, to increase the number of repeat visits, and to increase the average length of stay. The American Marketing Association estimates that it costs one-fifth the amount to keep a customer than to attract a new one.

A major study of U.S. repeat visitation to Canada (Meis, Joyal, & Trites, 1994) indicates that almost one-third of the entire U.S. population has traveled to Canada at some point in their lives, just under one-quarter of the U.S. population having visited in the past five years. The importance of the Visiting Friends and Relatives (VFR) market is shown by the fact

that the more frequent U.S. visitor is more likely to come to see friends and relatives. As trip frequency increases the use of hotels/motels, motorcoach, and car rental decreases. The more frequent traveler stays longer but spends less money per trip. This is an indication of staying with friends and relatives. However, the hosts, in all likelihood, spend more money than they would ordinarily as they take guests out to eat, and attend sporting events. This uncounted multiplier effect of tourism is usually not counted when the economic impact of tourism is determined.

As trip frequency increases visitors place less reliance on commercial sources of information and promotional materials. They are more likely to use word-of-mouth, their own knowledge, and the knowledge of friends and family. Past visitation is a good predicator of future visits. This can only occur if existing travelers are satisfied with their Canadian experience.

Visitors consider the following factors the most important when selecting a leisure destination:

- safety and cleanliness
- cost of trip
- value for the money
- friendliness of the people
- beauty of the landscape and the scenery

Compared to the U.S., Canada fares poorly on "cost of trip" and "value for money." The other three items, on which Canada scores better than the U.S., are Canada's competitive advantage over the U.S. The more frequent travelers to Canada come from the border states, more specifically the northeastern states.

This profile of the repeat U.S. visitor to Canada has important marketing implications. Given the role of friends and family on trip decision making, it makes sense that Canadians themselves are well-

Quick Trip 6.4
Welcome to Vietnam!

Matt Gunderson, a 29-year-old from San Francisco, visited Vietnam last summer. He stayed in $5-a-night guestrooms, rode public buses, and ate at roadside noodle shops. His daily budget: $10. But Vietnam wants to attract upscale, free-spending tourists. In Vietnam, where the average annual income is $250, the government is attempting to position the country as a destination for luxury travelers with five-star hotels, art galleries, and trendy nightspots.

Helicopters, once owned by the army, now tour hard-to-reach limestone islands for $1,000 a day. Golf courses are opening around Hanoi and other cities. The new Omni hotel in Ho Chi Minh City features a karaoke bar, personal butlers, and suites that sell for $800 a night.

Since the United States lifted its trade embargo with Vietnam in 1994 Americans have begun to return. In 1995, 54,368 Americans went to Vietnam, a 28 percent increase over the previous year. However, according to Gillian Larkin, vice president of Abercrombie & Kent International, Inc., Vietnam "isn't just a sentimental journey on the part of the ex-serviceman." The destination is a status symbol in some circles, appealing to "highly sophisticated travelers who want to add Vietnam to their life list" of places visited. Graphic Expedition of San Francisco sent a group of naturalists from Harvard University who wished to check out the national parks. Rock singer Sting's tour of Vietnam in October 1995 prompted his manager to arrange a golf trip there. Club Med, apparently, is looking for a Vietnam "village." The French chain Accor recently spent $40 million turning a 1922 colonial hotel and golf course into a five-star resort.

Questions:

1. Based on the principles outlined in this chapter, what are the potential markets for upscale tourism to Vietnam?

2. Why?

Source: Nachman, S. (November 29, 1996). Vietnam Looks for New Travel Recruits. *The Wall Street Journal*, B6.

informed about attractions and services for visitors. A promotional campaign encouraging hosts to invite friends and family could be developed. Multi-visit incentives also could be developed.

Outbound International Travel.
The most popular international destinations for Canadians are the U.S., United Kingdom, Mexico, France, Germany, and Italy. From 1991 to 1996 the number of Canadian visitors to the U.S. dropped;

however, a slight increase is projected thereafter. In 1996 14.7 million Canadians visited the U.S., many being repeat visitors. They tended to visit New York, Michigan, Washington, D.C., Florida, and Vermont. Many of these destinations are close to the border and the most heavily populated provinces of Ontario and Quebec. The popularity of Washington, D.C., is due to it being the U.S. capital and having national museums and historic sites. Florida is a getaway des-

tination for winter breaks and is a preferred destination for older, retired travelers who prefer long stays. These travelers go to Florida because of the sunshine, good health care and the lack of problems with language. Bermuda and Mexico are also favored winter destinations. The United Kingdom and France are popular because of the historical and cultural ties with English- and French-speaking Canadians. It is expected that, in the future, there will be more west-to-east movement than north-to-south movement (*Travel & Tourism Analyst*, 1995).

Tourist Flows To and From Major Tourism Countries

Europe. Five European countries are highlighted because of their importance as originators of and/or destinations for international tourists: France, Germany, Italy, Spain, and the United Kingdom.

> *"An American woman, a tourist, a refugee from a conducted tour of the Chateaux de la Loire, she dismissed the historic safari with the words: 'Nothing but thick walls and running comment.'"*
>
> Ludwig Bemelmans

France. France is the number one destination country in the world and second to the U.S. in terms of international tourism receipts. Of late it has been losing tourists due to competition from other Mediterranean countries as a result of lower exchange rates. In addition, there have been studies indicating that the French treat visitors poorly. As one measure aimed at improving the situation the French Minister of Tourism in 1996 decided to create a five-star category for the countries' luxury properties. Other countries, most notably Spain and Italy, have been accused of drawing potential tourists away, in part because they have a five-star designation. In the minds of many tourists a four-star property in France is thought of as less quality than a five-star hotel in Spain.

While an increasing number of French people are taking vacations abroad, nine out of ten French people vacation in France for their summer holidays (Coulomb, 1995). Internationally, they travel to Spain, Italy, Germany, and the United Kingdom. The major international tourists visiting France come from other European countries, specifically Germany, the United Kingdom, Belgium, and Holland. This has resulted in a balance of payment surplus double that of the automobile industry, the next most important export indus-

try. The most popular destinations in France remain the seaside resorts.

About 60 percent of the French population take an annual holiday of four or more nights. More of them are taking second holidays with half staying with friends or relatives or using a second home, whether taking the vacation in France or abroad. There is a movement toward French travelers organizing their own vacations, preferring to book a flight only rather than a complete package. These travelers also will deal directly with tour operators. The market responds to discount holidays through last-minute bookings as operators offer special "last-minute" prices on tour packages.

> *"How many thousands and hundreds of thousands of English, with their mouths, eyes and purses wide open, have followed each other, in mournful succession, up and down the Rhine. . . ."*
>
> Sir F. B. Head

Germany. Germans are the world's most prolific international travelers. Approximately three-quarters of the population each year make at least one vacation trip lasting five days or more. The reasons are twofold: Germans have both the time and the money. In addition to having approximately six weeks paid vacation a year, the German economy has been very strong for the past decade. In addition to a primary vacation there has been a trend toward second and third trips of eight to ten days duration as well as city breaks of four to five days in length. Since the early seventies the proportion of trips abroad compared to domestic vacations has increased from 50 percent to approximately two-thirds. Almost 10 percent of the German population have vacationed in the U.S. or Canada at least once.

The largest group of travelers are those between 20 and 29 years of age. Age groups with the highest propensity to travel will continue to do so as they age. In addition, there will be a further increase of travel propensity from those currently in the 60-and-older age category (Travel Industry Association of America, undated). As in most other cases, the more education a person has, the more likely he or she will travel. As might be expected, travel propensity is also positively linked to income. Travel propensity is highest in Berlin and Hamburg although, in absolute numbers, there most travelers are from North Rhine-Westphalia.

Over 60 percent of all holidays are taken in July/August/Septem-

Most French people choose to see landmarks, such as the Notre Dame Cathedral, France—rather than traveling out of the country. Photo by Corel.

ber while an additional 20-plus percent occur in April/May/June. Twice as many holidaymakers from the former West Germany prefer staying in hotels as in bed and breakfasts or inns. Almost equally popular as staying at an inn is renting an apartment or house.

While the automobile's travel market share has remained unchanged since the seventies at about 60 percent, air transportation's market share has almost doubled. The amount of air travel has tripled in relation to travel by train. There is a trend to travel by rail for second and third holidays (Hill, 1995). There also has been an increased interest in package tourism, which now accounts for almost half of all main holiday trips. For domestic trips, over three-quarters of all Germans travel independently. However, travel agencies book more than 85 percent of all business trips as well as those to visit friends and relatives.

There is a difference in motivation between former West Germans and those from the East. Former West Germans travel primarily to relax and seek a change from their daily routine at home. Well over one-third choose pleasure trips that feature the beach, swimming, and sun. An additional 10 percent are interested in special interest and sightseeing tours. Educational tours are chosen by 6 percent while less than 5 percent are interested in sports and adventure tours (Travel Industry Association of America, undated). Those from the East are more interested in discovering new countries and cultures (Roth, 1995). For all, cleanliness and peace and quiet are very important (Klemm, 1995). Typically they choose their primary annual vacation destination by December and within the first few weeks of the year.

According to the U.S. Commerce Department's Office of Tourism Industries, 8.6 million German travelers are considering a trip to the U.S. in the next five years, and 7.9 million are likely to come. They will probably stay in midpriced or budget properties rather than with friends and family and travel for more than three weeks. The survey of German travelers who took long-haul trips in the past three years and who are planning to take a long-haul trip in the next two years found that Germans are extremely active on vacation. The most popular activities include shopping, dining, beach activities, and visiting national parks. They spend less time visiting cities and travel to more scenic areas of the U.S. The German traveler of the future is more likely to have children living at home and less disposable income. The biggest potential markets for the U.S. are small towns, ethnic culture, religious tours, and nature-oriented activities. Crime continues to be the major single barrier to German travel to the U.S.

> "A man who has not been in Italy, is always conscious of an inferiority, from his not having seen what it is expected a man should see. The grand object of travelling is to see the shores of the Mediterranean."
>
> Samuel Johnson

Italy. The major markets for Italy are Switzerland, Germany, France, and Austria. Over two-thirds of international visitors to Italy select it because of its art cities, 15 percent because of the hospitality, and less than 8 percent because of the climate. The most negative features, according to tourists, are the means of transport and infrastructure (almost half noted this), strikes, petty crime and various inefficiencies (almost 30 percent), and the lack of information on artistic and cultural opportunities (listed by over 20 percent) (Rossi & Zurlini, 1995). Geographically, there is a north-south split in visited destinations. Southern regions receive only 10 percent of all visits while the north and central regions serve as the main areas for tourists.

One-third of all Italians take an annual holiday of four days or more. Increasing numbers are taking more than one trip a year. They are expressing an interest in ecotourism or green tourism, a growth that is linked to the expansion of protected areas in Italy. There is a trend toward shorter average stays but in better hotels.

> "He, who would really see Spain, must . . . above all put all false Anglican pride in his pocket, and treat every Spaniard, from the lowest beggar upwards, as his equal."
>
> A. J. C. Hare

Spain. Over 80 percent of the visitors to Spain come from other European countries, mainly France, Portugal, Germany, and the United Kingdom. The automobile remains the favorite way to enter the country, accounting for half of all annual visitors, 60 percent in the peak summer months. Just over one-third of all international travelers came by plane. Recent promotional campaigns by the government have focused on cultural tourism, ecotourism, and leisure (Sirugue, 1995).

In the Balearics the focus is on the traditional "sun, sea, and sand." The growth experienced in the islands has led to deterioration of the environment. Tour operators, who control almost 90 percent of tourism flows, greatly influence the development of new destinations. There does seem to be an understanding that, in order to compete, the islands must place a renewed emphasis on quality that seeks to attract market segments with higher buying power, spreads the seasonal effect, and opens up new channels of distribution (Lorente & Camacho, 1995).

> "Luttrell's idea of the English climate: 'On a fine day, like looking up a chimney; on a rainy day, like looking down it.'"
>
> Thomas Moore

United Kingdom. The United Kingdom is a major generator and beneficiary of international tourism. In 1993, for the first time, there were more main holidays taken abroad than at home. In addition, there are almost as many short-breaks and off-peak second holidays as domestic main vacations. As a result, expenditure on overseas vacations is almost three times that of domestic holidays (Lorente & Camacho, 1995). Overseas, U.K. travelers visit France, followed by Spain. The U.S. has become an increasingly popular choice for vacations. Travelers to the U.S. stay twice as long as visitors to European countries.

Two factors that have a major impact on inbound tourism are weather and seasonality (Lorente & Camacho, 1995). Indeed, the perception of bad weather is a major barrier to bringing tourists into the country. The seasonal impact is felt because half the international visitors to the United Kingdom come in June, July, and August. It remains to be seen whether or not the development of all-weather facilities, the encouragement of festivals not dependent on the weather, and health concerns about the effects of the sun will have a major positive impact.

European countries comprise the major market for the United Kingdom, specifically Southern and Central Europe, although North America is of great significance.

Almost 80 percent of domestic trips of four nights or more are taken in England, almost one out of four being taken in the West Country. An equal percentage—one out of ten—domestic trips are each taken in Scotland and Wales. The decline in domestic holidays taken at the seaside has been offset by a 50 percent increase in sightseeing attractions in the United Kingdom leading to a steady increase in domestic tourism expenditures.

Tourism faces a number of challenges in the future (Baum, 1995; Holden, 1995).

- Greater propensity to travel overseas
- Limited growth from traditional European markets
- More available international destinations, creating more competition for the North American, Far Eastern, and Australian markets
- Price competitiveness problems compared to other European countries, particularly in the hotel sector
- Congested air and land transportation
- Excessive peak-season demand
- Coastal area and river water pollution
- Reduced state financial support for development and marketing

Asia. As noted earlier East Asia and the Pacific will see the greatest growth in tourist traffic over the next several years. U.S.—Pacific Rim air passenger traffic is expected to grow 8 percent annually over the next ten years. By the year 2000, 40 percent of the world's air passengers will be in the Pacific region, up from 18 percent in 1989 (*Travel Weekly*, 1996). Two Asian countries are spotlighted below: Japan because of its contribution to outbound travel and China for its success in attracting tourists as well as its long-term growth potential as an originator of tourists.

> "Japan offers as much novelty perhaps as an excursion to another planet."
>
> Isabella Bird

Japan. The number of outbound Japanese departures is three-and-a-third times the number of inbound Japanese arrivals. About three-quarters are repeat travelers. In 1996 over 15 million Japanese travelers ventured overseas, a figure projected to grow to 19.8 million tourists by 2001. This represents less than 10 percent of the population. The U.S. is the most popular destination, receiving one-third of all Japanese travelers. South Korea receives 15 percent of international travelers, followed by Hong Kong (14 percent), Singapore (10 percent), and Taiwan (9 percent). The Japanese travel market is strong for a number of reasons (Travel Industry Association of America, undated).

- Equitable distribution of wealth. More than 90 percent of the Japanese population consider themselves "middle class."
- High degree of education. Forty percent of the population enters college. Higher education develops curiosity and a hunger for knowledge which, in turn, stimulates the desire to travel.
- The strength of the yen compared to other hard currencies.
- Wages have increased steadily each year while the rate of inflation has remained low.
- Japanese feelings of insularity and high population density contribute to the desire to travel outside of the country.
- Competition within the travel industry has led to lower prices.
- More than any other nation, the Japanese media feature international travel destinations.

The Japanese take relatively short holidays with three to four nights common for nearby destinations such as Hawaii and Guam and five to ten nights for the U.S. mainland. In addition to the summer vacation period there are two traditional peak holiday periods. The so-called "Golden Week," which starts the last week of April, allows people to take a week or more off by combining three national holidays with a weekend and a "bridge" of one or two days. Second, during the year-end season, city people travel back to their rural roots. Many professionals use this opportunity to travel overseas. In fact about 10 percent of annual Japanese outbound travel is during this period of time.

It is estimated that most growth will occur in visits to Europe, followed by Oceania, North America, and Southeast Asia. In North America most growth will be experienced by Canada followed by Florida, the East Coast (New York especially), California, and Hawaii. Overall 60 percent of all overseas travel is for pleasure or sightseeing, almost 20 percent is for business, while 7 percent is honeymoon travel. Travelers to the U.S. tend to be between 20 and 30. Honeymoon couples and single women make up the largest travel segment visiting the U.S. Since single women tend to stay at home until they marry and most are employed, their living expenses are small and more can be spent on such things as travel. The major "marriage seasons" are between March and May and from September through November. The number of annual marriages will increase until the turn of the century when it will decline sharply due to changing demographics. On the other hand there will be an increase in the number of travelers in their 60s and 70s. They can be expected to take longer trips, demand high quality products and services, and be more interested in cultural experiences.

The Japanese potential as far as the U.S. is concerned comes not only from the fact that it is the number one overseas generator of tourists but that they spend a great deal of money. From 1990–1995 expenditures by Japanese visitors to the U.S. increased 30 percent and represented more spending in the country than the Canadian and Mexican markets combined (Erdmann, 1996). The size of potential activity segments to the U.S. is estimated as follows (Erdmann, 1996):

- Discount shopping—4.2 million
- Theme parks—3.8 million
- Visit friends and relatives—3.8 million
- History and culture—3 million
- Local ethnic—2.9 million
- Beach—2.5 million
- Golf—2 million

The Japanese tend to travel as part of a group. As the population ages and becomes more experienced as far as travel is concerned, they will become more independent vacationers. Packages will remain popular but will increasingly focus on air and lodging only. The family market will experience most growth while sightseeing, cruises, and gourmet vacations represent the most promising markets by purpose of travel as we enter the next century.

> "Every country expresses its destiny through its landscape; and in China, where distances are so huge and the extent of recorded history so imposing, one can see the beginning and the end of the same movement, and too much history becomes no history at all."
>
> Peter Quennell

China. In 1990 China had almost 10.5 million international arrivals. By 1995 that number grew to 23.3 million, making China the number five destination country in the world with a market share of over 4 percent. In fact, when combined with Hong Kong—which reverted back to Chinese sovereignty in 1997—it is the fourth largest receptor of international arrivals. In that same time period it increased its international tourism receipts from $2.2 million to $8.3 million, making it the number nine tourism earner worldwide. It is estimated that, between 1995 and 2005 China will experience an annual growth rate of international tourist arrivals of more than 14 percent, the largest rate of growth in East Asia and the Pacific (Qu & Zhang, 1996).

While China is not a significant contributor to worldwide outbound tourist traffic (only 1 percent of the population travels abroad) the potential for future growth is significant because of the size of the population. In addition, the average living standard of the population, especially in the coastal cities and special economic zones, has improved markedly. Spending on non-merchandise items such as housing, child and medical care, and transportation is only 12 percent of urban household living expenses (Gek, 1996). This means a greater

China's popularity as a destination spot has grown dramatically. People flock to see The Great Wall of China. Photo by Corel.

proportion of income is available for leisure and travel. Pleasure travel, which includes sightseeing and visiting friends and relatives, has overtaken business travel as the major motivation of Chinese traveling abroad. The majority of business travelers are men. Pleasure travelers tend to be younger than business travelers, one-third being under 30 years of age. They are highly educated, 70 percent having higher education and over 70 percent being in middle or top management. They average two-and-a-half times the national urban average monthly household income. The majority of pleasure travelers are married, with a higher proportion of women making up this segment.

Over half of international travelers go to Hong Kong. Japan, Singapore, Thailand, Macau, Malaysia, and Australia are also popular destinations. South East Asian countries, because of the relative proximity and ethnic ties, will continue to be favored destinations (Gek, 1996). Outside of Asia the U.S. and Germany are preferred spots; however, there is also interest in traveling to France, the United Kingdom, and Canada.

One-third of all travelers use travel agents while an additional 3 percent use package tours. While 30 percent make their own travel arrangements, they are not well prepared for their trip. Less than 20 percent of travelers have access to brochures, guidebooks, or other printed information about their trips. The most enjoyable experience for Chinese travelers is seeing new things and different cultures, beautiful scenery, sights, and the environment. They are attracted to countries that are economically and technologically advanced, civilized, and orderly with high living standards. On their travels the most unpleasant things they encounter are customs and passport control, concerns about personal safety, and language or cultural adjustments.

Quick Trip 6.5
Emerging Destinations— Tunisia?

According to the Tunisian National Tourist Office, Tunisia is "The Sunnier Side of the Mediterranean That's Never Out of Season." Tunisia's unique attraction is that it is the only place where tourists can enjoy the benefits of every Mediterranean country—and stay in one spot. From the Web page (http://www.tunisiaonline.com): "In this land of the familiar and the exotic one can watch the sunrise over the Sahara, enjoy a gourmet meal at a seaside resort and top off the evening with a midnight swim in the pool of a modern comfortable hotel. . . . Tunisia's beautiful beaches and historical treasures attract millions of tourists from all over the world. Nearly 4 million tourists visited Tunisia in 1994. . . . The capital city, Tunis, is a two-hour flight from Paris and London and a fifty-minute flight from Rome. . . . Europeans . . . continue to be the major customers and make up 59% of the total number of tourists. Increases were particularly perceptible among tourists from Germany (+19.8%), France (+8.3%) and Great Britain (+8.5%). Visitors of other nationalities also increased, particularly those from North America (the U.S. and Canada) with an increase of about 20%."

The Ministry of Tourism and Handicrafts is engaged in a number of initiatives including the following:

- Building several new hotels in the Saharan regions.
- Environmental protection is given priority in programming and planning.
- Revision of training courses in tourism.
- Increased interest is being taken in cultural and archaeological tourism.
- Additional golf courses are being developed.
- Tourism bureaus were recently opened in Montreal and Prague.
- Advertising and promotion is being strengthened.

The following figures indicate the numbers of U.S. and Canadian tourists who visit Tunisia. The government has indicated a desire to increase the number of U.S. visitors to the country.

Entries of nonresidents by nationality

COUNTRY OF ORIGIN	1994	1995
Total European	2,415,690	2,357,242
%	62.7	57.2
Total Maghreb	1,323,408	1,640,410
%	34.3	39.8
United States	11,683	11,499
Canada	12,592	13,318
Total North America	24,275	24,817
%	0.6	0.6
Grand Total	3,787,648	4,047,286
%	97.6	97.6

Source: Ministry of Tourism and Handicrafts, Government of Tunisia

(continued on the following page)

Questions:

1. What are the major barriers faced by Tunisia in its attempt to attract U.S. tourists?

2. What can be done to overcome these barriers?

3. Even with a much smaller population base more Canadians than Americans visit Tunisia. Why is this?

4. Can the Tunisian Government use its relative success in Canada to help it attract more Americans?

Summary

Travel movements occur because of the interaction between the characteristics of the origin, the destination, and the transit routes that join them. By examining existing flows of tourists both within and between countries it is possible to develop principles and models to explain traveler movements. These principles can then be used to explore the potential for movements between tourists and new destinations.

Many of the people visiting Europe are attracted by its abundant historical sites and monuments: The Fisherman's Bastion, Buda Castle Hill, Hungary. Photo from *Budapest in 101 Photos; Multimedia CD for the IBM PC* (Selester, Hungary, 1996). Printed with permission.

References

(1995). Canada outbound. *Travel & Tourism Analyst*, (5), 24–36.

Baum, T. (1995). Trends in United Kingdom tourism. *An encyclopedia of international tourism—I—Tourism trends in Western Europe*, Paris, SERDI: Francois Vellas (ed.), 233–240.

Boniface, B.G., & Cooper, C.P. (1987). *The geography of travel and tourism*, London, England: Heinemann Professional Publishing, 9.

Chubb, M. (1969). RECYS-SYMAP—Michigan's computerized approach to demand distribution prediction. *Predicting Recreation Demand*, Technical Report No. 7, Michigan State University, 23–33.

Coulomb, F. (1995). Recent trends in French tourism. *An encyclopedia of international tourism—I—Tourism trends in Western Europe*. Paris, SERDI, 72.

(December 9, 1996). U.S. travelers on the move. *Travel Weekly*, 37.

Erdmann, R. (1996). *Measuring tourism impacts: Impact of Japanese long-haul tourism.* Proceedings of the 25th Annual Conference of the Travel and Tourism Research Association, 50.

Gek, L.P. (1996). *The new Asian world travelers.* Proceedings of the 25th Annual Conference of the Travel and Tourism Research Association, 23, 24.

Hill, R., (1995). Tourism trends in Germany. *An encyclopedia of international tourism—I—Tourism trends in Western Europe*, Paris, SERDI, 82.

Holden, A. (1995). United Kingdom tourist trends. *An encyclopedia of international tourism—I—Tourism trends in Western Europe*, Paris, SERDI: Francois Vellas (ed.), 241–246.

(January 19, 1995). Our favorite destination is. *Travel Weekly*, 97.

(July 8, 1996). S.F. prepares for transpacific growth. *Travel Weekly*, 48.

Klemm, K. (1995). Trends in tourism: Germany. *An encyclopedia of international tourism—I—Tourism trends in Western Europe*, Paris, SERDI, 102.

Lorente, F.J.B., & Camacho, M.A.R. (1995). Tourism development trends in the Balearics: The challenge of sustainability. *An encyclopedia of international tourism—I—Tourism trends in Western Europe.* Paris, SERDI: Francois Vellas (ed.) 156.

Matley, I.M. (1976). *The geography of international tourism.* Washington, DC: Association of American Geographers, Resource Paper no. 76–1, 11.

(May 1996). Department of Commerce. *Abstract of international travel to and from the United States 1994*, 15–20.

(May 1996). Department of Commerce. *Abstract of international travel to and from the United States 1994*, 24–30.

Meis, S., Joyal, S., & Trites, A. (1994). *The U.S. visitor to Canada: Come again, eh!* Proceedings of the 25th Annual Conference of the Travel and Tourism Research Association, 385–401.

(October 2, 1995). Top U.S. destinations for fall. *Travel Weekly*, 31.

Pyszka, R.H. (1990). *Americans as international travelers: The search for understanding.* Proceedings of the 21st Annual Conference of the Travel and Tourism Research Association, 255–256.

Qu, H., & Zhang, H.Q. (1996). Projecting international tourist arrivals in East Asia and the Pacific to the year 2005. *Journal of Travel Research*, 35 (1), 33.

Ritchie, J.R.B., & Crouch, G.I. (1993). Competitiveness in international tourism: A framework for understanding and analysis. *The Tourist Review*, 35, 60.

Rossi, O., & Zurlini, G. (1995). Recent tourism trends in Italy. *An encyclopedia of international tourism—I—Tourism trends in Western Europe*, Paris, SERDI, 118.

Roth, P. (1995). Trends in German tourism. *An encyclopedia of international tourism—I—Tourism trends in Western Europe*, Paris, SERDI, 91–100.

Sirugue, D. (1995). Tourism trends in Spain. *An encyclopedia of international tourism—I—Tourism trends in Western Europe*, Paris, SERDI, 151.

(Undated). *Selling to Germany: Marketing the U.S. travel product.* Washington, DC: Travel Industry Association of America, 9, 12.

(Undated). *Selling to Japan: Marketing the U.S. travel product.* Washington, DC: Travel Industry Association of America, 2, 12.

Uysal, M., Fesenmaier, D.R., & O'Leary, J.T. (1994). Geographic and seasonal variation in the concentration of travel in the United States. *Journal of Travel Research*, 32, (3), 61–64.

Vellas, F., & Becherel, L. (1995). International tourism trends in the World. *An encyclopedia of international tourism—I—Tourism trends in Western Europe*, Paris, SERDI, 9.

Williams, A.V., & Zelinsky, W. (1970). On some patterns in international tourist flows. *Economic Geography*, 46, (4), 549–67.

Additional Reading

An Encyclopedia of International Tourism—I—Tourism Trends in Western Europe, Francois Vellas (ed.) (Paris, SERDI, 1995). Future editions are planned on other areas of the world.

Annual European Travel Commission Report, European Travel Commission, 2 Rue Linois, 75015 Paris, France.

Explorations: Travel Geography and Destination Study, Janice L. Landry and Anna H. Fesmire, Prentice Hall Career and Technology, Englewood Cliffs, NJ 07632, 1994.

International Tourism Reports, The Economist Intelligence Unit Ltd., 40 Duke Street, London W1A 1DW, U.K.

Tourism in China: Geographic, Political and Economic Perspectives, Alan A. Lew and Lawrence Yu, eds., Westview Press Inc., 500 Central Avenue, Boulder, CO 80301.

Tourism in Europe: Structure and Developments. W. Pompi and P. Lavery (eds.), University of Arizona Press, 1230 North Park Avenue, Tucson, AZ 95719, 1993.

Tourism Today: A Geographical Analysis, 2nd edition, Douglas Pearce, Longman Scientific and Technical, Fourth Avenue, Harlow, Essex CM19 5AA, U.K., 1995.

Travel Industry World Yearbook, The Big Picture, Somerset R. Waters, Child & Waters, Inc., P.O. Box 610, Rye, NY 10580, annual.

Travel-log Statistics Canada, Ottawa, Canada K1A 0T6.

US Travel Data Center, 2 Layfayette Centre, 1133 21st Street, N.W., Washington, D.C. 20036 has the following reports:

- Summary and Analysis of International Travel to the United States.
- Outlook for International Travel to and from the United States.
- Historical Arrivals Data Base.
- Reviews of the Market (for 25 countries).
- USTTA Office of Research Mailing List.
- In-flight Survey of International Air Travelers.

World Travel and Tourism Review: Indicators, Trends and Issues, Volume 3, 1993. J. R. Brent Ritchie and Douglas E. Hawkins, editors in chief, University of Arizona, 1230 North Park Avenue, Tucson, AZ 95719, June 1993.

Annual tourism statistics are available from:

1. The World Tourism Organization (WTO) publishes a *Yearbook of Tourism Statistics*, a comprehensive analysis of data for 150 countries. Its *Compendium of Tourism Statistics* is a pocketbook statistical guide to 180 countries.
2. The Organization for Economic Co-operation and Development (OECD) publishes *Tourism Policy and International Tourism in OECD Countries*. It covers the main generators and receivers of international tourism and includes statistics in addition to detailed sections on government policy and planning.
3. WTO's *Travel and Tourism Barometer* monitors arrivals, overnight stays and receipts for major destinations.
4. The web site for WTO is http://www.world-tourism.org/

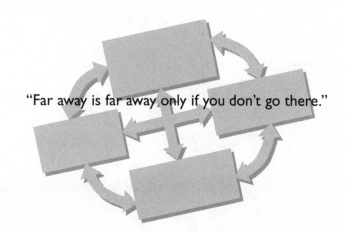

"Far away is far away only if you don't go there."

O Povo

7

Modes of Travel

···Travel Alternatives ·······································

Purpose

Through an understanding of a model of travel mode selection, students will be able to explain how tourists travel.

Learning Objectives

Having read this chapter, you should be able to:

1. Show how a knowledge of the criteria people use to select their preferred modes of transportation can be used to influence that choice.

2. Identify the reasons for the changes in passenger use of the various transportation modes.

3. Show how the characteristics of demand and supply affect the marketing of passenger transportation.

Overview

The means travelers use to reach their destinations is the subject of this chapter. A model is presented to explain the reasons people select one transportation mode over another. Marketing implications for the various modes are suggested. An in-depth treatment of each travel mode is provided. The rise and fall of travel by rail is chronicled and its competitive edge today defined. The major change through which ocean liners have gone is the shift from scheduled ocean liner service to cruise ships. The reasons and ramifications are explained. Automobile travel is the single most predominant mode in North America. The extent and advantages of automobile travel to the visitor are covered in a section that includes material on recreational vehicles and rental cars. The airplane has had a revolutionary impact on tourism. The history, scope, and significance of travel by air is an important part of this chapter. The importance of bus travel is indicated by the fact that the industry annually carries more passengers and provides service to more destinations than any other common carrier mode.

The interaction between demand and supply and its impact for transportation marketing completes this topic.

Major Transportation Modes

There can be no doubt that the development of new transportation modes, routes, and alternatives has opened up the world to tourism. People travel either in their own private mode of transportation or alternatively use a group travel mode offered by a common carrier. Figure 7.1 defines today's major travel alternatives.

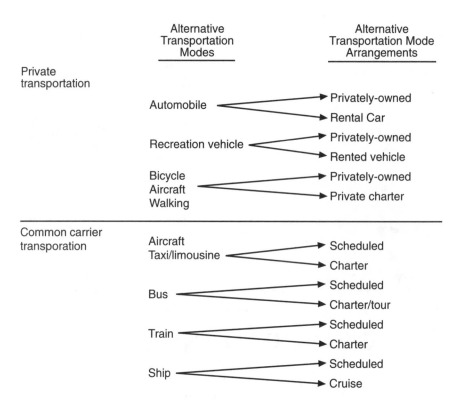

Figure 7.1   Travel Alternatives.

Transportation Mode Selection Decisions

Model

There are a variety of ways people can travel between two destinations. For example, consider a trip between New York City and Washington, D.C. In 1991 dollars, the choices were these:

- Air shuttle takes 2 hours at a cost of $167
- Amtrak Metroliner Club Car takes four hours at a cost of $134
- Bus takes five and a half hours and costs $37
- Car takes five hours and costs $42

Why do people select one transportation mode over another for business and pleasure/personal trips? Many theories have been put forward on mode selection decision processes. Most theorists, however, consistently identify availability, frequency, cost/price, speed/time, and comfort/luxury as the mode decision variables. Other factors that have been suggested are safety, convenience, ground services, terminal facilities and locations, status and prestige, and departure and arrival times. People in different segments of the travel market place varying degrees of value or utility on these criteria. For example, a business traveler is unlikely to have the same value perceptions as a pleasure traveler. Speed/time and departure/arrival times may be all-important to the business traveler, while cost/price may be the pleasure traveler's first criterion. One useful classification of selection variables and values has been put forth by Sheth (1975). He suggests that travelers choose a travel mode based upon the actual performance compared to the desired performance on five dimensions, namely the functional, aesthetic/emotional, social/organizational, situational, and curiosity utilities of the alternative modes. The ***functional utility*** of a mode is simply its likely performance for a specific purpose. Departure and arrival times, safety records, the directness of routes, and the absence of stops or transfers are examples of functional considerations. The functional utility is the *net* outcome of the positive and negative evaluations the user makes of a particular mode.

Aesthetic or ***emotional*** reasons relate to such things as fear and social concerns that affect fundamental values of the individual. Often users associate strong emotional feelings derived from early experiences with a mode of travel. Associations are also developed by early childhood socialization processes. These values often manifest themselves in terms of such things as style, interior/exterior decoration, comfort, luxury, and safety.

Social or ***organizational utilities*** refer to the stereotypes that various transportation modes have. For example, motor coach tours and cruises have been stereotyped as being a mode of transportation and vacation type for persons of retirement age. This may dissuade younger people from taking motor coach tours and cruises.

Situational utilities refer to the locational convenience of the mode and its terminal facilities to the traveler—the *total* set of activities associated with a trip. This might relate to the time in getting to and from the airport as a disincentive to fly. It is similar to the functional utilities except that the stress is on the activities that are antecedent and subsequent to the actual travel itself.

Curiosity utility concerns the traveler's tendency to try something because it is new and different. For example, flying transatlantic on the Concorde when it first came into service may have had a high curiosity value for many travelers. This feeling is usually short-lived.

The model presumes that the individual has desired expectations on these five utilities and that the discrepancy between the image or perception of the utility and the actual experience determines the extent to which that mode of travel is acceptable or not.

Certain supply-oriented and trip-purpose/traveler-profile factors influence the traveler's utility assessments. The availability of the mode—the number and convenience of flights, for example—influences the perception of functional and situational utilities. Mode design, including the variety of products or services offered to customers, affects the image of functional, curiosity, and aesthetic/emotional utilities. The way the mode is operated—on-time departures, quality of services, careful handling of the traveler's luggage—influence perceptions of functional and situational utilities. For example, advertisements for cruises that show young people onboard having a great time may dispel perceptions that cruises are just for older people. These supply-oriented factors combine to generate differential psychological utilities for different travel modes. These factors often create mass acceptance or rejection of a mode in the marketplace.

In a similar fashion, various demand-oriented factors produce differential psychological utilities for the same mode among a cross-section of users, leading to acceptance by some and rejection by others. Differences can be expected on the basis of personal demographics, lifestyle, familiarity and satisfaction of the traveler with a particular mode, and the purpose of the trip. For example, income level will influence the mode of transportation chosen. A person who values status will select a way of traveling that reflects that self-image. A person traveling from New York to London on business may choose to fly but, when traveling the same route on vacation, may choose to sail on the QEII.

Last, there is the impact of unexpected events. A death in the family requiring attendance at a funeral will influence a person to fly to the destination, even if the cost is perceived as too high or if the individual is afraid of flying.

The Concorde was a brief source of curiosity for many travelers. Photo by Corel.

Sheth's explanation of the transportation mode selection decision-making process is illustrated in figure 7.2.

Travel by Train

"The only way of catching a train I have ever discovered is to miss the train before."

G. K. Chesterton

It seems fitting to begin our review of individual transportation modes by talking about trains. They opened up the North American continent from its Atlantic to Pacific coasts, and they were the major stimulant in the nineteenth and early twentieth centuries to vacations within the U.S., Canada, and Europe. The first transcontinental route in the U.S. was completed in 1869. Britain had its first organized tour on the train in 1841 when Thomas Cook put together an excursion between Leicester and Loughborough. In 1851, 3 million English took the train to the Great Exhibition that was being staged in London. The train was also instrumental in Britain for spurring the development of many of its seaside resorts.

In the U.S. in 1929, the first year for which comprehensive train statistics are available, approximately 780.5 million paying passengers took the train. This number had fallen to about 268.9 million by 1975. In fact, the heyday of the train in most of the major developed countries lasted approximately 100 years, from the 1830s to the 1930s. In the 1920s and 1930s the automobile began to gain more popularity as a passenger transportation mode, mainly drawing away traffic from the train. Rail passenger traffic in the U.S. began to decline in the 1920s during what some persons have called the "age of abundant energy." In the late fifties the number of route miles

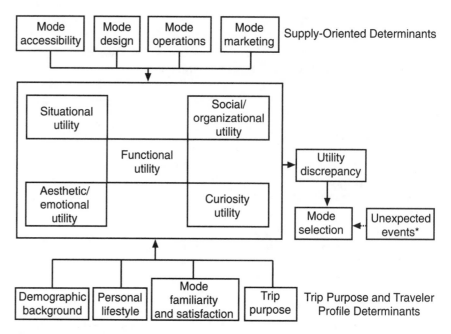

Figure 7.2   Travel Mode Selection Model.

Source: J.N. Sheth, "A Psychological Model of Travel Mode Selection," in *Advances in Consumer Research, vol. 3* (Proceedings of the Association for Consumer Research, Sixth Annual Conference, 1975), 426.

served by trains in the U.S. was surpassed by the number served by airlines. By 1963 the number of passengers carried intercity by airlines passed the number carried by trains. It was not until the mid-1970s to the early 1980s, which could be referred to as the "age of uncertain energy," that the slide in the popularity of the train as a passenger transportation mode seemed to be halted. Although the U.S. railroads had accounted for approximately 77 percent of the nation's common carrier passenger miles in 1929, this market share had slid to about 7 percent by 1970.

The demise of the railway as a passenger travel mode was so alarming that in 1958 the U.S. Interstate Commerce Commission (ICC) ordered a detailed study of the situation. The results of this study became known as the Hosmer Report, and it predicted the eventual disappearance of the train as a passenger travel mode in the U.S. The recommendations of the

Hosmer Report were never officially accepted, and it was not until 1970 that the federal government took some concrete action to improve the failing rail-passenger travel business. In October 1970, the Rail Passenger Service Act became law. The act created the National Railroad Passenger Corporation, now commonly known as Amtrak. Amtrak began its operations in May 1971, and it was intended to be a profit-making corporation. Canada's equivalent of Amtrak, Via Rail Canada, was created in 1977 in the form of a crown corporation.

Both Amtrak and Via Rail have the sole national responsibility for marketing and providing intercity passenger rail transportation. Since their inception both organizations have been successful in increasing passenger volumes that had been falling continuously beforehand. They have done so primarily by improving the equipment and services they offer, and by more effectively

Quick Trip 7.1

One If by Rail . . . Two If by Air

This is the tale of a journey between Paris and London (210 miles)—one by rail, the other by air.

By Rail

7:32 a.m.	Paris Metro express to Gare du Nord rail station: $1.35.
7:47 a.m.	Airport-style check-in for the Eurostar: $125 one way.
8:07 a.m.	Leave Paris on Eurostar, eighteen cars with almost 800 seats. By mile 18 it hits its maximum speed of 180 mph. Smooth ride, passengers stroll by, chatting and buying drinks in the café car. First-class passengers have an Anglo-French breakfast of bread, ham, cheese, yogurt, and marmalade. In second class the seats are comfortable but less cushy.
9:35 a.m.	Train shoots underground at 100 mph through the 31-mile Chunnel linking England and France.
9:58 a.m.	A signal problem in England.
10:02 a.m.	Rolling again at a top speed of 90 mph.
11:13 a.m.	Eurostar pulls into Waterloo Station, London.
11:17 a.m.	Fill out landing card, walk through customs, take taxi to Trafalgar Square: $4.80.
11:27 a.m.	Arrival at Trafalgar Square three hours and fifty-five minutes and $131 after leaving the Arc de Triomphe.

By Air

7:04 a.m.	Taxi from Arc de Triomphe to Charles de Gaulle Airport: $37.
7:26 a.m.	Arrive airport; speedy no-baggage check-in.
7:50 a.m.	Board bus to plane.
8:36 a.m.	Leave 16 minutes after scheduled departure: $270 one way.
9:01 a.m.	Served cold breakfast of croissant, ham and cheese sandwich, sweetened white cheese, citrus slices, orange juice, and coffee. Plane ride in just over one hour and noisy (prop engine).
9:36 a.m.	Landing at City Airport, six miles from London. Flying to Heathrow or Gatwick would add up to an hour to the trip.
9:48 a.m.	Walk through customs; long line for taxi; board shuttle bus for subway station: $4.80.
10:25 a.m.	Arrive at Liverpool Station after traffic delays. Walk 12 minutes to next station because platform is under repair. Take tube to Embankment station. Walk 400 yards to Trafalgar Square.
10:59 a.m.	Touch Nelson's Column three hours and fifty-five minutes and $311 after leaving Arc de Triomphe.

Question:

1. Suppose you are in charge of marketing these two routes. With reference to the material in this chapter, how would do it?

Source: Burns, C. "By Rail," Patrick McDowell, "By Air." *The Denver Post.* (November 15, 1994) 20A.

promoting the benefits of traveling by train.

Several attempts have been made to determine why travelers select the train as a transportation mode. Four factors seem to emerge consistently: cost/price, comfort, safety, and the ability to see the area through which the train is passing. Via Rail's onboard surveys of business travelers have identified user cost, convenience, travel time, and comfort as being of prime importance. A survey of Amtrak users has indicated that travelers favored the train for the following reasons:

- Safety
- Ability to look out of trains and see interesting things en route
- Ability to get up and walk around
- Arriving at the destination rested and relaxed
- Personal comfort

Negative factors often associated or perceived with rail travel are slowness in reaching the destination, relatively inflexible departure times, and a lack of quality in food service. Trains are certainly perceived as being a very safe mode of transportation and are thought to attract a significant "fear of flying" market. Recent promotions by Via Rail and Amtrak has emphasized the rest and relaxation benefits of taking the train. They have also begun to point out that the downtown-to-downtown routing of trains actually saves passengers time.

In Germany, France, and Japan, high-speed trains have been developed and are in operation. These trains travel faster than the automobile, and they actually cut down on the time that passengers would take to drive between the major cities. In France the TGV and in Japan the Shinkansen (Bullet Train) have an average speed of 186 mph, while German and Italian trains travel at speeds of 155 mph.

Amtrak plans to introduce the American Flyer between Washington, D.C., and Boston in fall 1999. The time from Boston to New York will be reduced from four to three hours as average speed increases from 100 to 135 mph. From New York to Washington travel time will be cut from three to two-and-a-half hours as average speed increases from 125 to 150 mph.

In the 1970s and 1980s British Rail became more marketing-oriented in an attempt to increase its share of the tourist market. Their policies were helped by shortages of gas and the subsequent increase in prices that had a dampening effect on travel by private automobile. Package holidays were developed with hotel companies, while other programs were aimed at the rail enthusiasts who were mainly interested in the trip itself. Originally organized as charters, these excursions were later provided on scheduled services. Longer packages, which offered travelers a short break away from home, were introduced. The high speed train—capable of speeds of 125 mph—now offers a service competitive in time from city center

to city center with that of the airlines.

Changes in the travel patterns of U.S. travelers to Europe have forced rail companies to create new products. Americans tend to take shorter trips to Europe and to go more often. They are also more adventurous. As a result Rail Europe created three new programs: the Europass, rail and drive, and the regional rail pass. The Europass covers travel to France, Germany, Italy, Spain, and Switzerland from five to fifteen days within a two-month period. The rail and drive program combines elements of rail travel and car rental while regional passes focus on one area within Europe.

In 1995 Amtrak developed a Strategic Business Plan to increase revenues and cut expenses. The goal is to eliminate the need for a federal operating subsidy by fiscal year 2002. It is assumed that a federal capital assistance program will continue. The plan is to reduce its annual operating loss to about $180 million by fiscal year 2001 and to fund that loss from other sources, including state and local contributions. While cost increases are projected at less than

Australia's train, The Ghan, provides rail transportation. Photo by Corel.

20 percent through fiscal year 2001 revenues are projected to double. Meeting this goal depends on a number of factors including continued federal capital support, large revenue increases, improvements in productivity, and increased state support. It is hoped that revenue increases will come as a result of marketing efforts and fare increases. Amtrak intends to control expenses through productivity improvements, operating efficiencies and selective restructuring of routes and services.

The West Coast Unit, which is responsible for services in California, Oregon, and Washington, and the Northeast Corridor Unit, responsible for operations between Virginia and Vermont are close to meeting their targets. However, the Intercity Unit, which provides the rest of the country's intercity rail service, is consistently overbudget.

Before leaving the subject of rail travel, the role of railways as tourist attractions should be highlighted. Short-duration train excursions through scenic surroundings have been proven to be major attractions to pleasure travelers in recent years. For example, two major excursions of this type in Canada are the Algoma Central Railway in Ontario and the Royal Hudson Steam Train in British Columbia. The Strasburg Railroad in Pennsylvania is a U.S. example of a popular train excursion of this type. The experience of riding aboard the Orient Express, made famous by mystery writer Agatha Christie, was reintroduced in 1983 after a complete restoration of the train.

Travel by Ship

> *"My experience of ships is that on them one makes an interesting discovery about the world. One finds one can do without it completely."*
>
> Malcolm Bradbury

Quick Trip 7.2
Are We There Yet?

"The Fun Starts Here!" promised a brochure for the California Zephyr, which runs from Chicago to San Francisco. "Explore the beauty, romance and exciting history of the Western frontier" in sleeping compartments that "pamper and please." That promise, together with three meals a day, movies, games, a daily hospitality hour, and on-board tour guides, was enough to convince Carrie Dolan and family to forego coach air travel for a first-class train experience. They joined the half million people a year who try the Zephyr. The trip was scheduled for 52 hours instead of the four by air at a cost for a sleeping compartment of $1,088, about the same cost as air travel.

Boarding at 3 p.m. with a variety of supplies, they see their "pamper and please" compartment. A "family sleeper" means two bunks up above, two below and a shared bathroom down the corridor. A deluxe room sleeps two and has a private bath and shower. The kids (ages three and six) seem thrilled. The first meal is a treat—prime rib and sugar snap peas eaten while watching the sun set over fields of wild sunflowers. The bunks are pulled down, those with "exceptional balance" are able to use the small communal shower, and it's time for bed. The constant rhythm of the rails is "like one of those vibrating motel beds, with an endless supply of quarters."

For a honeymoon couple the attraction is the idea of doing something different; for others, it is the sluggish pace. The views from the lounge car are spectacular. However, by day two cabin fever sets in and the day is spent waiting for happy hour—which consists of cut-rate prices on Zima malt liquor and chips and salsa. Games include a coloring contest and a competition to find the passenger with the oldest penny. The movie is one with Robert Redford and Michele Pfeiffer, but the sound goes out periodically.

On the third day a sense of excitement takes over, broken only by the announcement that the train will be two hours late. "That's nothing," says an attendant. "I've been on rides six, or eight, or twelve hours late." While some get off in Emeryville, California, others take an Amtrak shuttle bus across the bay into San Francisco. "I love it, but I'm ready for a real shower," says one passenger. "I want to stay on," pleads the three year old.

Questions:

1. What is the future of rail travel in the U.S.?

2. What is the best way to market travel by train compared to the other options available?

Source: Dolan, C. Railroading America: Are We There Yet? *The Wall Street Journal.* (October 4, 1996) B5.

Travel by ship did in fact precede travel by train, but it was not until the mid-nineteenth century that travel by ocean liner began to show its greatest prominence. Although ocean liners used to provide an important link for passengers between continents, water transport today plays two main roles in travel and tourism—ferrying and cruising.

The steamship era had its beginnings in the 1840s. Sir Samuel

Cunard pioneered the first transatlantic scheduled liner trips at that time. Just as the automobile led to the demise of the train, the introduction of intercontinental commercial airline service precipitated the rapid decline in the use of ships as a scheduled passenger transportation mode. In 1957, transatlantic ship traffic reached a new post-World War II high as some 1,036,000 passengers were transported on ocean liners. Although travel by ship remained strong for several years thereafter, the aircraft had by 1958 eclipsed it in terms of volumes of transatlantic passengers.

Transatlantic scheduled passenger ship traffic declined rapidly. Passenger departures from New York fell from approximately 500,000 in 1960 to 50,000 in 1975. So great has been the decline in scheduled liner passenger transport volumes that it has almost completely disappeared in this modern-day era.

Cruising has taken the place of scheduled liner services. Ships originally built for ocean crossings do not make the best cruise ships. Ocean liners were large and heavy—built to withstand the rigors of the Atlantic Ocean. As a result the fuel costs were great. As cruising took off, the lines built ships specifically for cruising. These ships were smaller—800 to 850 passengers and 20,000 tons—lighter, with smaller cabins, larger deck space and public areas, and a smaller ratio of staff to passengers. Fuel costs were also reduced by spending time in more ports, a move that satisfied passengers. Recent building has resulted in over-capacity in the industry. As a result, between 1983 and 1989 there were sixteen major mergers and consolidations.

About two-thirds of the passengers who cruise each year are from the U.S. The major cruise routes of the world are illustrated in figure 7.3. The cruise line industry experienced continued growth from 1980 until 1994. In that year 4.5 million passengers took a cruise of more than two days. In the following years, however, there was a softening of demand. Together with increases in capacity, the result has been declining occupancy rates (the ratio of cabins sold to cabins available). By some measures this has gone down from 90 percent in 1990 to 80 percent in 1995 (Blum, 1996). Part of the problem is that the industry has been unable to attract new cruisers. The once-high rate of 75 percent was only 40 percent in 1995. Cruise Lines International Association (CLIA) identifies two major segments as potential first-time cruisers (*Travel Weekly*,1996):

- The "want-it-alls" (11 million people or 17 percent of the total vacation market) are the most likely to cruise. With an average age of 42 and income of $53,000, they are workaholics and value

Figure 7.3   Major Cruise Routes in the World.

Source: J. Christopher, *The Business of Tourism,* 2d ed Pitman Publishers, London.

what is fashionable and trendy. They enjoy shopping, fine dining, and nightlife. They need to be convinced that cruise vacations can meet their high vacation expectations. Thirty-seven percent of this segment—some 4 million people—are considered "hot prospects" who are likely to cruise within the next two years.

- Comfortable spenders (16 million people or 25 percent of the total vacation market) are the second most likely group to buy a cruise vacation. With an average age of 44 and income of $64,000 they are physically active and enjoy nightlife, fine dining, and gambling. They are most likely to presently vacation at resorts, especially beach resorts. Thirty percent (4.8 million people) are considered likely to cruise within the next two years.

Some observers expect a few years of consolidation followed by steady growth. CLIA is projecting that, by the year 2000, there will be 7 million people taking a cruise of more than two days. This implies an annual growth of 10 percent a year. In contrast, from 1990 to 1995, demand grew by only 20 percent total. Previous forecasts have been reduced, first from 10 million to 8 then, in 1995, to 7 million.

The size of the market is limited by a number of negative perceptions about cruising. First, there is the association with ships of isolation, storms, and seasickness. While the number of outbreaks of illness has declined in recent years, ships are vulnerable because of the close quarters and the fact that there are many elderly passengers. The Center for Disease Control (CDC) runs a Vessel Sanitation Program that performs unannounced inspections of ships docked in U.S. ports and publishes sanitation ratings in a document sent to travel agents. However, the agency's mission is more advisory than regulatory. It relies on volun-

Cruise ships have gained popularity and growth is expected to continue. Photo by Corel.

tary compliance as many ships are of foreign registry and sail in international waters. The CDC also helps in designing ships' galleys and sanitation systems and trains kitchen crews in food handling and hygiene (Chase, 1996).

It does not appear that the age or passenger-carrying capacity of the ship affects its vessel sanitation score. There is a weak indication that larger cruise ships and a moderate indication that higher per diem prices produce better sanitation scores (Marti, 1995). The key seems to be that modern equipment can and has been installed on older ships to help ensure sanitary conditions. Further, higher prices might mean that more money is available for training and the production of a higher quality cuisine. The key is management.

Second, many perceive that ships are slow, cramped, and boring, with regimented activities. Cruises offer high levels of satisfaction with the industry reporting an 85 percent repeat business ratio. However, the repeat factor is not very good. Of the 19 million Americans who have cruised, there are only 2.25 million repeaters, 12 percent of the 19 million (*Tour & Travel News*, 1995).

The dominance of Americans in the cruise market has meant that strict standards have been imposed on all foreign flag carriers that operate out of U.S. ports. There are strict standards expected in the areas of hygiene, safety, and financial protection for passengers in case of the collapse of the carrier.

The most important areas for cruises from the U.S. are the Caribbean, the Mexican Riviera, and Alaska. Seventy percent of all passengers leaving the U.S. cruise in these areas. The popularity of the Caribbean has been built on warm winter weather, good sailing conditions, the ability to visit a number of varied ports in a relatively short time, and the capacity of Miami International Airport to bring in passengers.

Approximately 15 percent of the total number of cruises sail out of San Diego and Los Angeles, largely to the Mexican Riviera. Cruises to Alaska originate in San Francisco, Seattle, and Vancouver, Canada. Because of the Passenger Service Act of 1886, foreign vessels may sail from Seattle, but those passengers may not disembark in Alaska, another U.S. port. Passengers must return to Seattle via a foreign port.

Since most vessels operating out of the U.S. are foreign, this poses a problem for Seattle. A popular package to Alaska is the seven-day fly and cruise package that involves a one-way trip by ship and a fly or land return. This type of tourism must originate in neighboring Vancouver, Canada. Restrictions on the number of cruise ships into Glacier Bay have placed limits on the growth of this market.

One of the reasons for the growth of the U.S. market to the Caribbean was the deregulation of the airlines in 1978 that allowed cruise operators to offer cheap fly-cruise packages. Flights from northern cities were heavily subsidized. By flying to Florida, the time spent in warm weather was maximized. In theory, deregulation in Europe could offer the same boost to Mediterranean cruising. However, deregulation in Europe must take into account the diversity of national markets and cannot benefit from the economies of scale enjoyed in the U.S. The Mediterranean cruise industry took off in the late 1960s and early 1970s as lines expanded their fleets. The extra capacity generated additional interest from tour operators in Germany and the United Kingdom. This interest coincided with significant growth in the overseas inclusive vacation market.

While Germany and the United Kingdom make up the largest market segments for Mediterranean cruises, the development of the market differs greatly in both countries. In the United Kingdom tour operators set up their own cruise divisions, negotiating charter deals with cruise lines. The initial effect was to increase the size of the market. However, lack of expertise and experience in operating a cruise ship meant that the narrow profit margins that were a result of concentrating on volume and market share put companies at risk. Tour operators now have no operating responsibility for the cruise

and tend to feature cruises in their vacation brochures on an open-sale basis with no charter commitments. A major problem for cruise operators in the United Kingdom is the difficulty of selling a rather sophisticated travel product through retail travel agents. By some estimates less than one in ten travel agents are productive in terms of cruise sales, lacking the expertise or experience to sell cruises.

In Germany tour operators dominate the cruise booking market. In part this is because a flight must be packaged in to get the vacationer from Germany to the Mediterranean. About 75 percent of the Mediterranean cruise market travels on tour-operated chartered ships.

Incentive travel accounts for 15 percent of all cruise berths, perhaps more in the U.S. Yet, because cruise lines tend to be registered in foreign countries, they have been unable to penetrate the business or convention markets to a larger extent. Legal restrictions prevent the tax deductibility of convention-oriented expenses if they are incurred with a cruise on a non-U.S. flag vessel.

Most cruise-line marketing has been oriented to capturing market share from other lines rather than to increasing the size of the total market. In the U.S. travel agents sell about 95 percent of all sea vacations. Some lines have successfully found themselves a market niche. Premier Cruise Lines has developed a unique package by combining three days in Walt Disney World with four days of cruising. In addition to appealing to families who want a balanced vacation, the competition will find the product truly difficult to duplicate. Another niche has been developed by Windstar Sail Cruises. Aimed at the affluent active vacationers who would normally not cruise, Windstar markets cruises on a sail-cruising ship, which offers a wide variety of water sports activities and visits to

remote, small islands that traditionally ships do not visit.

Excess capacity in the industry has meant that operators are looking to larger ships to spread overheads and capitalize on economies of scale. The cruise ships being built now tend to be in the 40,000 ton range. The commercial life of a cruise ship is about twenty years, but there is increased pressure on them to make a profit by the third year of operation. This has resulted in a selling orientation on the part of the operators to fill their berths through heavy price discounting. The corresponding battle for market share has done little to expand the size of the market for cruises.

Ships are also becoming smaller with the development of a number of ships with a capacity of 150 passengers or less to cruise the more remote waters of the world.

Cruises share a kinship with other unique transportation offerings, such as traveling on the Orient Express train, in that they are more of a vacation experience than a transportation mode. The romance of cruising has been heavily promoted, and this has been helped along by a popular television program, "The Love Boat." Today cruise ships are like portable resort hotels that ply the waters of the Caribbean, Mediterranean, and other regions.

Special interest or hobby-type cruises have grown, packaging such things as the theater, gourmet dining, bridge, flower arranging, aquasports, jazz, country and western music, and many other themes and activities. This ties in closely with the trend toward more vacation travel for the purpose of learning or improving upon a leisure-time or recreation activity.

The ship remains an important passenger transportation mode in its role as a ferry service. The "floating bridge" is an essential complement to the automobile, recreational vehicle, and bus in many parts of the world, including the English Channel, the Irish Sea, the Hebridean Islands of Scotland, the North Sea, the Maritime provinces and British Columbian coast in Canada, and on the Great Lakes.

As with its "partner" in history, the train, the ship also has considerable importance in tourism as an attraction. Examples of short-duration sightseeing cruise-ship attractions are abundant in North America and elsewhere. Characteristically, these cruises are for a day and for an even shorter period of length. Viewing scenic surroundings is the major focus of many of these operations, including those featuring the Thousand Islands (New York–Ontario), the Mississippi River, Muskoka Lakes (Ontario), Niagara Falls (New York–Ontario), and many others. Other cruises combine nostalgia with scenic viewing. Steamer and riverboat cruises are examples of these. One study of a restored steamer sightseeing cruise operation indicated that its appeals were in learning about the history of steamships and the history of the surrounding area, seeing the scenic beauty of the area, watching the visible operations of steam engines, and using its dining/bar service.

Many destinations seek to develop cruising as a way of bringing economic benefits to the destination. The economic benefits of cruising to destinations can be determined only after a full consideration of the costs and benefits (Dwyer & Forsyth, 1996). Cruise ship expenditures can be divided into passenger expenses and operator expenses. The former includes such things as international air fares to the point of embarkation, internal travel, add-on expenditures such as accommodation in the port prior to departure as well as direct expenditures on excursions and shopping.

Cruise operators also make a number of expenditures. These include charges for the port and

terminal, towage payments and stevedoring charges. Goods and services must be purchased to provision the ship. If any crew members are local, their wages represent an economic impact. Usually, however, a foreign crew means that crew expenditures in port are the only economic benefit to the destination. In addition to such things as ship maintenance and the cost of maintaining a local office, various taxes will be levied.

For example, it is estimated that cruise tourism generates nearly $4 billion in direct spending each year in the Caribbean alone. This includes direct expenditure of $2.9 billion by cruise passengers, $845 million by cruise lines and $207 million by cruise line employees (Santo, 1994). It is estimated that a passenger on a seven-day cruise with 3.5 port calls spends a total of $539 at the ports during the cruise.

Travel by Automobile

> "A route differs from a road not only because it is solely intended for vehicles, but also because it is merely a line that connects one point with another. A route has no meaning in itself; its meaning derives entirely from the two points that it connects. A road is a tribute to space. Every stretch of road has meaning in itself and invites us to stop. A route is the triumphant devaluation of space, which thanks to it has been reduced to a mere obstacle to human movement and a waste of time."
>
> *Milan Kundera*

The introduction of the automobile precipitated the demise of the train in most developed countries. As mentioned earlier, the automobile as a passenger travel mode gained its momentum as far back as the

---

Quick Trip 7.3

Sex at Sea

Royal Caribbean Cruise Line in conjunction with *Cosmopolitan* magazine interviewed 2,000 passengers and found that 95 percent rated cruises as "extremely or very romantic" compared with land-based vacations. Nearly half said they had sex as many as six times a week on board compared with their usual once or twice at home. Almost eight out of ten passengers packed sexy lingerie or underwear while one in three brought body lotion or massage oils on board. In fact, almost three-quarters of the men surveyed packed special underwear and outnumbered women when it came to massage oils and body lotions.

When asked where on board ship they would like to have sex given the chance, the favored choices were: (1) a whirlpool; (2) the royal suite; (3) an elevator; (4) a lifeboat; (5) the bridge.

Question:

1. Realizing the fine line between selling on the basis of sex and the risk of offending potential customers, is there any way to effectively utilize these research findings?

Source: Sex at Sea. *Travel Weekly*. (April 8, 1996) 6.

1920s. Lundgren (1973) refers to the period after this as the automobile-based travel-system era characterized by "individual travel diffusion." He explained this point as follows:

> The private motor car siphoned off a larger portion of the potential travel market from the established mechanisms and routes toward a new tour destination concept with quite different distance dimensions. Thus, the (international) tourist dollar became diffused over wider territories (Lundgren, 1973).

The advent of the automobile, therefore, spread the benefits of tourism more widely and provided more and more people with the means to travel individually or in private, smaller groups. Nonprivate group travel had been a characteristic of the railway and steamship era that preceded the automobile. Due to the nature of the railroad's infrastructure and the limited routing possibilities by water, travel patterns were very predictable. People could only get to the destinations to which the trains and steamships would take them. Many famous resort areas, resort hotels, and city center hotels flourished at important destination and staging points for the trains and steamships. With the increased popularity of the automobile, the attractiveness of these areas and facilities began to decline, and many of them suffered significantly.

The automobile brought about a more random pattern of travel movements, opened up new destinations, and spurred the development of elaborate networks of new automobile-oriented facilities and services along highways and roads. The tourist court, motel, and the motor hotel were three of the new facility types that developed in the U.S. and Canada after World War II. In fact, the whole development pattern in North America

was fashioned directly and indirectly to accommodate the private automobile.

Traveling by automobile is now the single most predominant travel mode in North America. Most travel surveys have shown that automobile trips account for over 85 percent of the pleasure and personal and business trips taken by Canadians and 75 percent of intercity passenger miles in the U.S. The nuclear family unit traveling by private automobile has been the major source of pleasure and personal travel demand and the marketing target for a majority of tourist-oriented businesses in the U.S. and Canada. It is not difficult to see why, considering the statistics that have been discussed earlier.

Just as they have done with the trains, many experts have tried to explain why the automobile is selected over other modes of transportation. One such report found the major attractive attributes of the automobile to be as follows:

- Control of the route and the stops en route
- Control of departure times
- Ability to carry baggage and equipment easily
- Low out-of-pocket expense of traveling with three or more persons
- Freedom to use the automobile once the destination is reached

Other surveys have shown that many persons perceive the automobile to be a relatively safe mode of transportation, and others indicate that people like driving as a recreational experience.

Two other important aspects of automobile travel that remain to be discussed are recreation vehicles and car rentals, or as they are called in Britain "car hires." These two areas have developed so extensively in North America and elsewhere that they are now both significant elements of tourism.

The major U.S. car rental companies and some of their operating characteristics are noted in tables 7.1 and 7.2. Most transactions occur at airports, the exception being Enterprise, which specializes in local business. Note that several companies aim at the business traveler while others target leisure customers.

The car rental industry relies upon the auto manufacturers for their cars. As such, the strength of the auto-owning business impacts car rental companies. When manufacturers experience a strong retail demand for cars they do not need to offer incentives to car rental companies to buy large supplies of cars to keep the factories open. The result is that car rental companies keep their fleets in service longer, resulting in fleets with higher mileage caps. In addition, rental companies can experience difficulties in getting some of the more popular models. Recent changes in the rental car business have included significant shifts in car fleets toward smaller and more fuel-efficient models. Fly-drive packages offering rental cars together with flights have made significant gains in popularity as more travelers have begun to substitute air travel for travel by the private automobile.

Table 7.1   Car Rentals: Top 10 Airports

AIRPORT	LEADING COMPANY	MARKET SHARE
Los Angeles	Hertz	30 %
Orlando, FL	Alamo	26
San Francisco	Hertz	33
Miami	Alamo	27.5
Denver	Hertz	25.6
Atlanta	Hertz	29.2
Phoenix	Hertz	26.2
Boston	Hertz	29.8
Chicago (O'Hare)	Hertz	34.5
Las Vegas	Hertz	26.9

Source: Auto Rental News. *Travel Weekly.* (May 6, 1996) 43.

Table 7.2   U.S. Car Rental Companies: A Comparison (1995)

| COMPANY | U.S. CARS IN SERVICE | NUMBER OF LOCATIONS | TRANSACTIONS | | TYPE OF TRAVEL | | REVENUE PER CAR |
			AIRPORT	NON-AIRPORT	BUSINESS	LEISURE	
Enterprise	263,000	2,400	2%	98%	NA	NA	NA
Hertz	228,750	1,175	85	15	70%	30%	$ 9,923
Avis	175,000	1,128	85	15	70	30	$10,485
Alamo	150,000	121	98	2	25	75	$ 8,666
Budget	135,000	1,052	70	30	45	55	$11,111

Source: Auto Rental News. *Travel Weekly*. (May 16 & May 27, 1996) 29.

The recreation vehicle, or RV, was a further extension of Northern Americans' love affair with the automobile. The President's Commission on Americans Outdoors found that 43 percent of American adults consider driving for pleasure a main recreational pastime. RVs offer the opportunity to combine driving and camping. RVs have grown tremendously in popularity in recent years. There has been an increased interest in touring the country in rented recreational vehicles.

Since World War II, camping has grown rapidly in popularity in North America and elsewhere. The U.S. has more than 14,000 public and private parks and commercial campgrounds containing about a million campsites. Canada has been said to have 250,000 campsites and Mexico 10,000 campsites. The increasing popularity of the RV led directly to a number of new camping phenomena during the 1990s, including the franchised, condominium, and time-sharing condominium campgrounds. In a condominium campground the RV owner buys the site and pays a monthly fee for the maintenance of the common areas. In a time-share operation, the use of the site for one or more weeks each year is purchased.

Yet another phenomenon to which the RV has led is that of many European visitors to Canada and the U.S. renting these vehicles for cross-continent trips. Many companies have been formed to provide this service to overseas pleasure travelers.

Travel by Air

"I feel about airplanes the way I feel about diets. It seems to me that they are wonderful things for other people to go on."

Jean Kerr

Continuing our chronology of transportation modes, the airplane had a revolutionary impact on tourism from World War II onward. This point was already highlighted in chapter 6 where the plane's refashioning of the global travel market was mentioned.

The history of air transportation can be divided into at least three parts: pre-World War II, World War II, and post-World War II. The first period, from 1918 to 1938, was a

Camping has gained popularity as a vacation activity in recent years. Photo from *Top Shots* CD Rom. Courtesy of Queensland Tourist and Travel Corporation.

period of infancy for the scheduled airlines of North America, while the modern era can be termed the mass air-travel era. The present era has been marked by steadily improving aircraft technology and the advent of air charters and the packaged vacation, or as it has sometimes been called, the "inclusive" or "all-inclusive" vacation.

A few dates in history allow us to put the facts to be discussed later in perspective:

1918   The first scheduled domestic air service in the U.S. is on the New York–Philadelphia–Washington route.

1939   Pan American operates the first Transatlantic passenger flight using a "clipper" flying boat.

1946   BOAC (now British Airways) offers its first Transatlantic passenger service.

1946   BEA (now also a part of British Airways) offers its first passenger service to Europe.

1970   The first of the wide-bodied jets is introduced into service.

As was just pointed out, the modern era of air travel really began at the end of World War II. Between 1945 and 1960 we have seen that travelers increasingly switched from trains and ships to automobiles and airplanes. By the late 1950s the number of route miles served by airlines surpassed those served by train for the first time. By the early 1960s the number of passengers carried intercity by airlines was greater than that carried by trains. (Both numbers pale, however, compared to those route miles served and passengers carried by bus.) In the 1960s this trend continued, and airfare reductions further stimulated air travel. The 1970s was the decade of the

wide-bodied jets, and it was then that the "mass tourism" phrase was coined. By 1995 U.S. airlines were carrying over 450 million passengers domestically and generating 372 billion revenue passenger miles (a revenue passenger mile is the equivalent of carrying one passenger one mile). In addition, they carried over 46 million international passengers and generated 142 billion revenue passenger miles.

The U.S. carries 17 percent of all international air traffic, while the United Kingdom carries 10 percent. Transpacific routes are the fastest growing international routes in the world. In fact in 1995, for the first time, more passengers were carried across the Pacific than across the Atlantic. It is difficult to operate nonstop transpacific routes between Asian countries and the U.S. The 1990s will see the introduction of advanced-technology, long-range aircraft capable of flying nonstop on these routes. This will undoubtedly make transpacific travel more enticing to the pleasure traveler. For the airlines, nonstop service offers greater economic performance as more fuel is used on takeoffs and landings than when the plane achieves cruising altitude.

In 1978 the U.S. airline industry was deregulated. The National Transportation Act of 1988 accomplished the same thing in Canada. The impact of **deregulation** will be explored in more detail in chapter 11.

Air transportation can be broken down into scheduled and nonscheduled or charter operations. Scheduled services fly on defined routes and times on the basis of published timetables irrespective of passenger-load factors. Scheduled airlines may be publicly or privately owned. The amount of private vs. public ownership will vary with the political philosophy of the host country. In most countries, the public airline will be the national flag carrier and is usually the only airline designated for interna-

tional flights. In the U.S. the airlines are privately owned. U.S. carriers are designated as either major carriers, national carriers, or regional carriers. Carriers are classified as major carriers if they have annual gross revenues of over $1 billion. They include United, American, and Continental Airlines. National carriers have annual gross revenues of $75 million to $1 billion. Companies that run commuter airlines are now classified as regional air carriers. A large regional airline is one whose annual gross revenue falls between $10 and $75 million, while a small regional is one with annual gross revenues of less than $10 million.

In Canada, airlines are designated as Level I, II, III, or IV carriers, depending upon their size. There are two Level I carriers in Canada: Air Canada and Canadian Airlines.

Charter airlines fly only on routes where they can generate high passenger-load factors—typically 85 to 90 percent. Because they are not obligated to fly regardless of load factor, their revenues per flight are much higher than those of scheduled airlines. Additionally, they keep costs low by saving on marketing, offering less in the way of service both in the air and on the ground, and having lower overhead costs. In this way they can offer, in many cases, substantial fare savings over scheduled airlines. As a result, charters tend to operate to high-volume destinations. A recent trend has been the tendency for tour operators to form or take over their own charter airlines in order to ensure seat availability for their passengers. Prior to the 1960s, charters could operate only through closed groups made up of members of a club or organization whose main purpose was something other than low-cost travel. Many bogus clubs were formed, and policing became increasingly difficult. The 1970s saw a liberalization of charter restrictions. The scheduled airlines had a difficult dilemma. They did not wish to discount prices for passengers who were willing to pay the higher fares, but they wished to capture a share of the market. One answer was the **advanced purchase excursion fare (APEX)**, which required passengers to book and pay for their trip in advance.

Increased capacity brought about by deregulation has meant that scheduled airlines were forced to reduce prices to attract the traveler. The result was that charter flights lost their price competitive edge in many cases.

Charters remain popular in Europe, where deregulation is moving more slowly than in the U.S. The success of charter airlines in Europe will depend upon their ability to move with the changing demands of the market. This might mean selling seats only (instead of an air-land package), offering scheduled flights, and new, less crowded destinations. There will also be a demand for more activity holidays, winter vacations, and more flexible packages, such as multi-center and fly-drive options. Increased demands for higher-quality service will also challenge charter operators.

A major problem for airlines—particularly in North America—is the safety of air travel. While flying is still much safer than traveling by car, the high profile of one air crash puts concern into the minds of many travelers. The average age of aircraft in the U.S. is fifteen years. The age ranges from a high of 26.4 years for ValuJet to a low of 8.3 years for Southwest (*Travel Weekly*, 1996). The safety record for major airlines is slightly less than for so-called upstart airlines. The Federal Aviation Administration defines an aircraft accident as "an incident in which any person suffers death or serious injury as a result of being in or in direct contact with an aircraft." For all nine U.S. major airlines the number of

accidents per 100,000 departures is 0.300; for newer airlines the average is 0.418 (*Travel Weekly*, 1996). Many airlines train their staff in how to respond to an airline crash. They cover such things as (Carey, 1996):

- Verify the passenger list
- Staff toll-free numbers for callers worried their friends or family members might be on the plane
- Notify families of those injured or killed
- Work with government agencies on the crash investigation
- Assign trauma-response workers to assist victims' families
- Make travel arrangements for victims' families
- Protect families from the media and attorneys
- Keep the media informed about the crash
- Help with funeral arrangements

The **hub-and-spoke system** of airline routes puts increased pressure on the planes. Instead of flying from one airport to the destination, passengers gather at outlying airports and fly to hub airports where they catch connecting flights to their destinations. This means more takeoffs, which cause the body of a jetliner to expand and elongate by an inch to accommodate changes in air pressure. The supersonic Concorde jet grows by 11 inches. While aircraft design takes expansion into account, the more takeoffs and landings, the faster metal fatigue begins to set in.

New aircraft are being developed that are safer and more fuel efficient. The newest 747 (400) jet airliner can fly from New York to Tokyo entirely by computer and, if necessary, even land automatically. It offers more range, better fuel economy, and lower operating costs. Its 8,400-mile range almost doubles that of the original 747, while it consumes one-third less

fuel. One factor that makes it particularly safe is the triple and quadruple redundancy of its systems. Complete failure of any one system is a million-to-one possibility. Bigger planes are in the works. Airbus plans a new full-length, double-decker super jumbo, with one level of 300 people stacked atop another in a three-class layout, or 400 on each level on all economy flights. Boeing's version of a super jumbo, designed to seat 500 or more, involves stretching both decks of the 747. The super jumbos are too big to taxi around most airports and to park at their gates so airports would have to build structures to handle them. The airlines have their own set of demands for the super jumbos. The turnaround time of these planes—the time it takes to refuel, clean, and restock the jet and put it in the sky—must be no longer than it takes now for a 747 (about 100 minutes). The operating cost is very important to the airlines as it varies significantly by type of plane. For example, in 1995 dollars, the hourly operating cost for a 747 (400) is $6,686 compared to $1,409 for a DC-9 (30).

Concern has also been expressed over security at airports. The General Accounting Office reported the existence of security deficiencies at U.S. high-security airports. Chief among these were ineffective passenger screening and inadequate controls over personnel identification systems and over access to those parts of the airport where aircraft operate. Concern for safety has been felt in the response of travelers to terrorist threats. Concern about terrorist attacks on Americans in the mid-1980s led to dramatic reductions in travel from the U.S. to Europe, for example.

The Federal Aviation Administration (FAA) expects 673 million air travelers, flying on over 5,000 jet aircraft with 8 million domestic departures by the year 2000, rising to more than 850 million passengers, over 6,500 jet aircraft, and 9.3 million domestic departures by 2007 (FAA, 1996). According to the International Air Transport Association (IATA) the Asia/Pacific region's share of world traffic is expected to double from just over 25 percent in 1985 to more than 51 percent by 2010 (Meredith, 1983). Because airlines are limited in their ability to adjust to these new levels by increasing seat densities, much of the capacity growth will come from more flights on existing and new routes. The fear is that congestion in the skies over the region will follow the lead of Europe and will become a problem by the turn of the century. It is estimated, for example, that congestion problems in Europe are costing the airlines $5 billion each year.

In summary, the airplane has in the post-World War II era taken over as the major international and intercontinental transportation mode. It also predominates among the common carriers in domestic transportation in the U.S. and Canada. It is a particularly important mode for the business travelers who have the time factor as a major consideration. Additionally, charter flights, since their introduction, have become increasingly important as vacation travel modes, particularly in Europe.

Travel by Bus and Motorcoach

"I was disappointed in Niagara—most people must be disappointed in Niagara. Every American bride is taken there, and the sight of the stupendous waterfall must be one of the earliest, if not the keenest, disappointments in American married life."

Oscar Wilde

The third principal common-carrier mode is the bus. The term bus is used to describe intercity travel while *coach* or *motor coach* describe charter or tour travel.

Only 15 percent of person-trips on Greyhound were for pleasure travel, excluding visits to friends and relatives. This compares to 43 percent of total person-trips in the U.S. for this purpose. As can be seen, most travel by bus is of the intercity type.

In 1983 the bus industry in the U.S. was deregulated. Prior to that time an Interstate Commerce Commission-licensed bus company or tour broker had to prove need before receiving authority to operate. At that time few motor coach operators employed marketing representatives. Many had a small individual tour program, and most had a larger group tour program. The majority were still charter operators, while many operated regular group service as well. Tour brokers were generally smaller operations, many tied to a retail travel agency. The impact of deregulation can be seen in the growth of motor coach companies. In 1983 there were 1,500 motor coach companies licensed by the ICC. In 1989, that

---

Quick Trip 7.4
It's What's Inside That Counts

British Airways (BA) has recently reconfigured their first-class cabin. First class consists of twelve seats, ensuring more space and privacy. Called a "personal cabin area," it includes a fold-down visitor's seat so a companion can join you for cards, chat, or a meal. The seat converts to a six-foot-six bed. Passengers are given a big blanket duvet and a soft pillow and the choice of full meal service or a quick, light meal. The personal built-in video offers a variety of movies, TV specials, and newscasts. The round-trip first-class airfare between New York and London is $7,393.

United Airlines has several features in their business class sections. The seats have a lumbar massage device and their new design allows people to cross their legs and eat at the same time. The seat was designed with the help of back specialists and can be adjusted at the touch of a button. In addition the headrest has a seven-inch vertical range and side wings to help prevent "rolling head syndrome." Leg and foot supports can also be configured in a variety of ways.

Space has been allocated for the eventual installation of laptop computer connections.

Questions:

1. What features are important to travelers inside a plane?

2. Why would someone pay extra to fly business or first class?

3. How much more do you think it is worth?

4. How should they be marketed?

5. What percentage of seats on a plane should be coach, business, and first class?

Source: McDonald, M. United Airlines is Hoping to Rub Passengers the Right Way. *Travel Weekly.* (November 4, 1996) 119.

Fredericks, A. Just Asking. *Travel Weekly.* (November 21, 1996) 20.

figure jumped to 3,600. Tour brokers were deregulated out of existence. Many became tour operators or tour organizers.

Britain's state-owned bus industry was sold to private investors and deregulated in the mid-1980s. Instead of the initial plan of hundreds of small operators each owning a few vehicles, a few large companies have most of the business and many small operations have been driven out of business or were taken over by larger concerns. By 1996 the six largest bus groups controlled 60 percent of the market, up from just 10 percent in 1989.

In 1987 the second largest motorcoach company in the U.S., Trailways, Inc., was purchased by the nation's largest, Greyhound Lines, Inc. As the only nationwide provider of intercity bus transportation in the U.S., Greyhound Lines, Inc. operates 233 million miles of scheduled service each year, serving 2,400 destinations. It carries over 15 million passengers a year. Recovering from a rocky period in the late 1980s the company has a policy of "everyday low pricing year-round," improved the reservation system (it used to take an average of 4.4 calls to reach a sales representative), got rid of the hub-and-spoke system that required a passenger to buy tickets days in advance, and improved the availability and quality of its fleet (Robinson, 1995).

For the purposes of tourism, the potential lies with the use of coaches for touring vacations. People go on tours for reasons that are practical and emotional. The practical benefits are convenience, expertise, safety, and price (see table 7.3).

Tours are convenient in that the vacation can be spent concentrating on the experience rather than on making the arrangements. Having someone else doing the driving is important in terms of dealing with city traffic, driving in unfamil-

Table 7.3 Reasons Why Clients Choose a Motor Coach Tour

REASON	UNDER 50	50+
Make new friends	91%	72%
More convenient	91	67
Safe	83	61
Learn more	86	51
Less expensive	74	54

iar areas, and spending time reading maps rather than enjoying the scenery. Tours offer the convenience of being picked up and delivered to hotels, sights, and entertainment. Accommodation and event tickets are guaranteed, which is particularly important for high-season events or times. Last, the idea of the baggage being taken care of is appreciated. This is particularly true for single women and older people.

People who take tours feel that they can see and do more than if they were traveling alone. There is the feeling that the operator has the expertise to select the best places to see. Because of this, participants can actually see more because they do not have to spend time evaluating all of the options. Also, there is safety in numbers. This is particularly true for older or female travelers and for urban or unfamiliar destinations.

The fixed price of a tour is an important feature. The most important part, however, is not the absolute price but the fact that the costs are known beforehand. There is little or no danger of being halfway through one's vacation and running out of money because of poor budgeting. The tour is prepaid. The only other costs are some meals, sightseeing, and shopping. The most popular U.S. destinations of coach tours are listed in table 7.4. A study by the American Bus Association indicated the following average daily expenses of motorcoach riders (*Travel Weekly*, 1994):

	spend between
35%	$50 and $74
24%	$75 and $99
28%	$100 and $149
7%	$150 and $199
7%	over $200

In fact, according to the United Bus Owners of America (UBOA), each 40-seat motorcoach represents about $7,000 per day in revenue for a local community.

People also take tours for emotional reasons: companionship, an opportunity to learn, shared activities, and security. Tours offer the opportunity to meet new people and make new friends. Many see it as an opportunity to get an overview of a destination—to discover and learn. Adventure touring is important to younger travelers, while historical touring is mentioned by older tourists.

Group travel is seen as a way of participating in activities with others who have the same interests. This can include physical activity tours such as skiing or water sports, as well as theater, garden, or historic homes tours. In all of this, there is the opportunity to be further educated in a particular area.

The security angle comes from the feeling of being an insider even in an unfamiliar place. This is an

Table 7.4 Top Motor Coach Cities and States

TOP 10 CITIES	TOP 10 STATES
Branson, MO	Missouri
Myrtle Beach, SC	New York
Washington	Pennsylvania
Nashville, TN	Tennessee
New York	Florida
Orlando, FL	Colorado
Williamsburg, VA	Kentucky
Quebec City/ Montreal	Virginia
Chicago	Wyoming
Las Vegas	Alaska

Source: *Travel Weekly.* (March 21, 1996) 69.

emotional appeal compared to the physical feeling of safety, explored previously.

The negative images that people have about tours fall into four categories: perceptions of the bus, the tour experience, the group concept, and the types of people who take tours. For a number of people, tours are associated rather negatively with buses. The term **motor coach** is used by the industry to designate touring buses. Particularly in Europe most coaches are extremely comfortable with videos, attendants who serve drinks, and reclining seats. However, despite the fact that such equipment is available in the U.S. (albeit on a lesser scale), the image brought to mind is too often the school or commuter bus. The bus is seen as too slow, too confining, and too uncomfortable. It is viewed as a cheap and old-fashioned way to travel. Travelers also have a negative image of bus terminals and view this as an undesirable place to start a vacation. Additionally, some people—particularly men—dislike the idea of giving up control to the coach driver. They complain about not being able to control the lights, the fans, or where and when to stop.

For people who do not take tours, the experience itself is perceived negatively. Touring, to many, is equated with regimentation, inflexibility, and passivity. The tour is seen as a shallow, boring, and impersonal experience. There are also those who think that, rather than receiving the advantages of group power, being part of a group involves getting second-class treatment from hotels and restaurants. Yet another barrier to be overcome in selling tours is the group aspect of the tour. There is a fear of not relating well to other members of the group. To many people, a vacation involves having personal space and freedom. Being part of a group limits both. Last, many have a negative perception of

the kinds of people who take tours. People who travel as part of a group are seen by many, stereotypically, as infirm, older, inexperienced travelers. This translates into a personality profile of tour-goers as passive and lacking in self-confidence.

To rid itself of these negatives, those who package tours need to be more innovative in upgrading the image and the content of tours. Perhaps even the word *tour* needs to be changed into "adventure holiday," "expedition," "discovery trip" or "excursion." Different modes of transportation can be used in conjunction with each other: air to get the traveler there and coach to see the destination. Hub-and-spoke concepts can be used to bring people to a destination where they can relax on their own. Shorter minitrips can be packaged with more free time, and tours themed around recreational activities can be developed to appeal to the younger, more active crowd.

Contiki Holidays has identified four categories of 18- to 35-year old travelers who might be good candidates for motor coach tours (*Travel Weekly*, 1994). They are overseas students attending school in the U.S., international visitors who want to see the country, younger American travelers who want to mix with an international group, and young people who might otherwise have planned a cross-country driving trip. It notes the advantage of being able to see as much of the country as possible and traveling great distances without the problems associated with road travel, such as breakdowns, finding affordable accommodations, and getting lost.

A debate over access by motorcoaches is being heard in certain quarters. In 1993 Yosemite National Park proposed a limit on the number of commercial tours permitted to enter the park each day and indicated it would sell slots to operators in advance. The industry claims the plan is discriminatory

and unfair because it targets only motor coaches and does not get at the real cause of congestion and pollution: the private automobile.

Marketing of Passenger Transportation

> *"Travel as tourism has become like the activity of a prisoner pacing a cell much crossed and grooved by other equally mobile and 'free' captives. What was once the agent of our liberty has become a means for the revelation of our containment."*
>
> Eric J. Leed

Transportation marketing seeks to satisfy the needs and wants of the traveler by providing the right mix of services. To appreciate the difficulties involved, it is necessary to consider the characteristics of supply and demand for passenger transportation.

Characteristics of Demand

The demand for passenger transportation has a number of characteristics, all of which affect the way a company markets. First, demand is instantaneous. For carriers there is great uncertainty as to what the demand will be on a particular day at a particular time between points. While past trends are useful, they cannot be totally reliable. When demand is greater than supply, travelers are unhappy. By the time adjustments are made to supply more capacity, customers may have changed carriers or found an alternate means of transportation. The tendency, then, would be to provide more capacity than needed. Overcapacity shows up in the load factor. In a perfect match of supply and demand, the load factor would be 100 percent. Anything less indicates the measure of overcapacity. The challenge in

---

Quick Trip 7.5
Motorcoach Tours

Group travel is an experience that is shared, organized, passive, and care-free. It is defined differently by those who are repeat users and those who are non-users.

Repeat Users	*Non-Users*
"A relaxing way to travel"	"Too slow a way to travel"
"It's all planned for you"	"It's too regimented"
"You get special attention"	"The herd treatment"
"It's more fun"	"It's boring"
"Well paced"	"Hurry up and wait"
"You see the best things"	"You see things too quickly"

The appeals are both practical and emotional. From a practical view-point, someone else does all the work. It is convenient, travelers benefit from the operator's expertise and there is safety in numbers. From an emotional viewpoint, there is companionship, an opportunity to learn new things while participating in shared activities in addition to the security of feeling like an insider in an unfamiliar place.

On the other hand, some people have problems with the bus or coach, the tour experience, the group experience, and the type of people who travel in groups. The bus can be uncomfortable and lacking in glamor; the tour experience is often regimented and inflexible; there is a fear of being cooped up on a bus with a large group of people you may not like; and the image of travel participants is one of older, inexperienced travelers lacking in self-confidence.

Questions:

1. How can group travel be repositioned to overcome its image problems?

2. Which market segments have tour potential?

3. What new products can be developed to overcome customer resistance?

4. Identify suitable strategies and tactics to effectively market the products developed.

Source: The National Tour Association.

---

marketing is to create programs to fill each plane, train, ship, or bus on each trip.

Overcapacity is the result, not only of instantaneous demand, but also of the variability of demand. Demand for transportation is not the same each hour of each day of each month. It shows what is known as peaks and valleys. At certain times of the day or week or month, there is great demand; at other times the demand is light. Yet sufficient planes, boats, trains, buses, and terminal facilities have to be provided to cover peak demand. The result is that excess capital has to be invested. As a result, the costs of operation are increased. How should demand be priced? Should the peak traveler pay more than the off-peak traveler? Peak-load pricing states that those traveling at peak times should pay more for the extra capacity provided to meet peak demand. Some off-peak pricing is found in the airline industry and with passenger trains. Reduced midweek and night fares are an attempt at peak pricing.

Another characteristic of demand is that there is, in fact, more than one type or segment of demand for transportation. In its simplest terms, demand is either business demand or pleasure demand. The motivations, frequencies, and responses to price are different. The motivation for the business traveler is ***derived***—that is, the demand for travel exists because of the desire to do business in a particular territory. Demand for the pleasure travel is ***primary***—the motivation is to travel to a vacation spot. The distinction is important because derived demand tends to be affected more by factors external to the transportation industry. No matter how good the services between New York and Detroit, if business is bad in Detroit, travel demand may go down. A reduction in fares, for example, may affect primary demand but may not affect derived demand.

The business traveler travels more frequently than does the pleasure traveler. This makes the business traveler very valuable to the airline. Frequent flyer programs, which offer rewards based on miles traveled, have been targeted toward the business traveler in an attempt to capture customer loyalty. As mentioned above, derived demand may not be affected by changes in price. The company may absorb a fare increase as a cost of doing business. The business traveler may choose a more convenient, but more expensive, flight since the company and not the individual is paying for it.

In some situations people can substitute one mode of transportation for another: train for plane, bus for train, and so on. This affects the way transportation is marketed. **Elasticity** is the economic term for the sensitivity of travelers to changes in price and service. An elastic demand is sensitive to substitution; an inelastic demand is not. The extent of elasticity is dependent upon the price of the other mode of transportation and the type of demand. Pleasure travel is more price elastic than is business travel; primary demand is more price elastic than derived demand. When people choose how to travel, the decision is made on the basis of price, prestige, comfort, speed, and convenience. Amtrak could successfully compete with the plane on certain distances on the basis of these factors.

Competition also exists within one mode between carriers. Generally prices and the speed of the journey are the same or similar among competing carriers. Carriers must then market on the basis of the factors mentioned above: prestige, comfort, and convenience. Often a small change in departure time can capture a significant number of passengers. This explains much of the congestion at airports at certain times—everyone wants to offer flights at what are felt to be the most convenient times for the traveler.

Another aspect of demand is that some transportation modes offer more than one type of service. Airline passengers can fly economy, business class, or first class; trains also offer various classes of service. The different types of service are in competition with each other. Airlines, for example, have to decide the proportions of first class, business class, and economy or tourist class seats to offer on a plane. They then decide what additional services are necessary to justify the price differential—more legroom, better meals, free drinks, and the like.

Demand for transportation is also affected by the relationship between the price charged and the income level of the traveler. Pleasure travel is income elastic; that is, the demand for travel is affected by changes in the traveler's income. Economists say that demand is elastic when a reduction in price results in more demand that will result in more revenue. (Revenue equals price times number demanded.) The company gains revenue because the increased demand brought about by a drop in price makes up for the reduced price. Similarly, an inelastic demand is one where a reduction in price results in less revenue generated. More passengers may be attracted but not in sufficient numbers to offset the loss of revenue brought about by the reduction in price. Pleasure travel is discretionary—the traveler has a choice of whether or not to travel. An increase in price may mean the traveler will postpone the vacation.

Business travel is also influenced by the income of the company. Much business travel is essential; some is discretionary. Businesses may turn to **teleconferencing** as a way of reducing the travel bill if costs increase too much. Last, the demand for travel makes itself felt in a demand for nonprice items. The frequency of departures, the condition of the equipment, the service of the employees, on-time performance—the whole package—is often more important than the price. Companies have to find out what is important to the different segments of the market they are going after (the list will be different for each) and seek to provide it.

Characteristics of Supply

Just as the marketing of transportation is affected by the characteristics of demand, so is it influenced by the supply characteristics. The supply of transportation is unique in eight distinct ways. First, the transportation industry is a **capital-intensive** industry. Terminals and equipment cost a great deal of money. The costs are also **indivisible**—airlines cannot put "half a plane" in the air if the plane is only half full. Because the industry is capital-intensive and much of the capital is borrowed, many of the costs of running a transportation company are fixed; interest on the debt must be paid in full, irrespective of the number of passengers and revenue. This puts a great deal of pressure on management to |fill seats that would otherwise be empty. This may affect both the promotional and pricing decisions.

Related to this previous point is the fact that transportation costs are "**sunk**" with few alternatives. The cost of a plane is sunk in that the company has incurred the cost of it. It is up to the company to generate revenue to pay for the plane. It is not like a light that can be turned off, thereby saving money. Planes also have few alternative uses. It can fly; it might be possible to sell it as a unique type of restaurant, but essentially all the company can do with it is fly it. This puts additional pressure on the company to use the resource rather than have it lie idle. The large amounts of sunk costs also mean that there is a tendency to use old equipment rather than invest in more modern (and more expensive) equipment.

Another characteristic of supply is that, although demand is instantaneous, supply is not. There is a long time between planning for a piece of equipment and placing the order for it, between placing the order and getting it, and between putting it into service and scrapping it. Thus, while demand can shift very quickly, it takes a great deal of time to adjust supply. A company must live with its mistakes for a very long time.

Because of the high level of fixed costs, the **incremental costs** of operation are small. The incremental cost is the cost of adding one more unit. The running costs of adding another passenger car to a train, another bus to a route, or even a plane between two points is small compared to the costs of an actual piece of equipment. If a plane is scheduled to fly anyway, the cost of an additional passenger is incredibly small—an extra meal and some services. This means that, above a certain point, it makes economic sense to reduce the price charged in order to get some revenue coming in. This is the rationale behind discount fares. Airlines can predict, based on past records, how many seats on a particular flight will sell within a week before a flight. The people who book within a week before a flight are usually business people. Assume, for example, that on a particular flight 80 percent of the seats will be bought at the regular fare in the last week before the flight. This means that the airline can sell up to 20 percent of the seats at a discount for people who will book and pay for tickets more than seven days before a flight.

Another characteristic is that *supply cannot be stored* for future use. A grocery store can sell a can of dog food today, tomorrow, or the next day. Every seat on a plane or train or bus must be sold only for that trip. The sale that is lost today is lost forever. This puts additional pressure on management to sell, sell, sell.

Transportation services must be *available on a continuous basis*. The traveler expects the same level of service whether it is day or night, summer or winter, if the plane is full or almost empty. Because transportation is expected to be reliable on a continuous basis, there is little opportunity to cut costs for inferior service at odd hours. This adds to the cost of providing the service.

Last, there is the problem of *labor*. In transporting people, the company take on a great responsibility. Often the service—whether in operations or in maintenance—

is offered twenty-four hours a day. Employees must be equally alert, no matter what the time. There are strict rules about the amount of time that pilots, drivers, or operators can be on duty at any one stretch. The Federal Aviation Administration (FAA) limits pilots to thirty hours of flying in any seven-day period. Although the operating costs are small compared to the sunk costs, they can still be considerable. Airline pilots are paid well for their skills. A further complication is that there is little opportunity for the substitution of capital for labor. This is, after all, a service business.

Marketing has the task of ensuring that there is sufficient demand to utilize the supply of equipment and facilities fully. It must also ensure that there is enough of the right kind of supply to meet the demands of the passengers. Just as demand influences supply, so supply influences demand. The demand for vacations in Jamaica will influence a decision to operate flights to Jamaica; however, the existence of flights to Jamaica at the time and prices appropriate to the market will stimulate demand. Marketing brings supply and demand together.

Marketing Strategies

In marketing, the offerings of a firm are known as the four "p's": product, promotion, place, and price. In tourism it is appropriate to change the "product" to include service and to replace "place" with distribution.

Service refers to getting the ideal mix of services to satisfy existing or potential customers. This means offering transportation at the right times, in the right kinds of equipment, while giving a level of service before, during, and after the journey that will meet the needs of the customer—all while making profit.

Most carriers use a linear route structure—the equipment travels

from one point to another, turns around, and travels back. In the airline industry most fuel is used at takeoff and landing. Also, the speed of travel by plane is only appreciated on longer flights. Thus, for reasons of cost and customer benefit, jet aircraft operate in the most efficient manner when they fly on long-hauls. A piece of equipment may, however, make an intermediate stop. While this increases the time and fuel costs, it can add significant additional revenue.

The airlines also operate what is known as a hub-and-spoke concept. Airlines have identified several major cities that serve as hubs (as in hub of a wheel) for them. Smaller towns serve as the spokes of a wheel connected to these hubs. Airlines attempt to have passengers fly into their hub city on a smaller or commuter plane for connection to a larger plane for travel to their ultimate destination. Colorado Springs is a spoke city for the Denver hub, which is itself a spoke city for Chicago, which is a spoke city (on United) for London. Increasing hub development will result in more convenient service for passengers. There will be more nonstops as smaller cities become hubs and displace larger cities as connecting points.

Major air carriers have made increasing use of *code-sharing agreements* with regional airlines. Code-sharing involves the joint use by a regional carrier of a major airline's two letter designation on its air routes and usually involves a commuter traffic fleet at the major's hub. In this way, the regionals serve as feeder lines to the majors. The major benefits are (*Travel Weekly*, 1993):

- Alliances allow airlines to offer nonstop and connecting destinations that by themselves they could not support.
- They can minimize connecting times.

- Frequent flyer tie-ins can be important.
- Travelers can obtain one set of tickets and boarding passes for multi-leg travel.
- Quality control procedures among allied airlines can be merged, serving to improve service.

The concept has been taken internationally. U.S. airlines have pursued code-sharing agreements protected from anti-trust violations with international airlines in an attempt to secure gate rights at international airports. The Department of Transportation (DOT) finds that code-sharing produces substantial benefits for U.S. passengers although participating U.S. airlines do not benefit as much as their foreign partners. For example, the DOT reported that a code-sharing arrangement between British Airways and USAir resulted in an estimated annual gain to British Airways of $27.2 million and an annual benefit to USAir of only $5.6 million. The partnership has since been dissolved. DOT also indicates that Asia is the next hot spot for code-sharing alliances.

The first *frequent flyer program* was introduced by American Airlines in 1981. The idea was successful in building brand loyalty to a single airline. According to some sources, however, airlines owe participants more than 3 million round-trip domestic tickets, enough for travelers to fly 4.5 billion miles at no cost. In an attempt to minimize this cost, airlines have placed restrictions on the use of this free travel.

Service must be provided on the right kind of equipment. Equipment has two facets that must be matched: identifying the operating costs of one piece of equipment over another while offering equipment that will attract the traveler. One example is the Concorde. While this supersonic aircraft could draw passengers because of its speed and unique shape, the operating costs are so high that the potential market is relatively small.

Scheduling is a major marketing weapon for carriers. Traveling from point A to point B leaves little opportunity for differentiating one firm from another. Offering departure times most convenient for the passenger is one way to do this. Unfortunately, everyone wants to do this. The result, certainly in the airline industry, is severe congestion at the most popular times. Generally speaking, the demand for business travel peaks on Monday mornings and Friday evenings, Sunday afternoons, and early evenings.

Service can also be altered by such things as upgrading the quality of the interior of the vehicle. Research has shown that, for flights of less than two hours, the most influential factor in a choice of flight is the schedule (70 percent), followed by the airline or airplane (18 percent), and the fare (11 percent). However, for flights longer than five hours, the passengers' priorities change. Sixty-three percent rate the airline or airplane as being most important, compared to 19 percent who listed schedule, and 17 percent who listed fare as most influential. SAS used results like this to change the interior of their intercontinental planes. They had found, additionally, that on 767s people are less comfortable in the middle seats. Given the importance of the airplane in making a trip of five hours or more, they removed the middle seats from their business class cabin. Service could also be altered by providing tie-ins with other modes, such as fly/cruise or rail/drive.

The subject of promotion will be dealt with in greater detail in chapter 15. However, several points can be made. Promotion can be seen as the communications link between carrier and passenger. It is the responsibility of the carrier to communicate its message effectively. If the passenger has not understood, it is the fault of the carrier. To this end, it is important that clear promotional objectives be defined. These objectives should identify which target markets are to be reached, what tasks have to be done to reach the markets, who is to perform the task, and when they have to be completed. It is vital that the promotional theme be in synch with the marketing plan, which, in turn, must be consistent with the overall objectives of the carrier. A carrier may, for example, feel that, in order to meet its financial targets, it must emphasize quality and service. The way then, to reach the target is to stress quality and service. These concepts become the essence of the marketing campaign. As part of that plan, communicating the ideas of service and quality to the public becomes the promotional objective.

Distribution involves the mechanisms by which passengers can obtain the information they need to make a trip choice and, having made that choice, make the necessary reservations. *Direct distribution* occurs when passengers get in touch with the carriers directly. *Indirect distribution* is when the sale is made through an intermediary.

This latter has taken four forms. First is the emergence of independent companies to handle all aspects of travel. It might involve a wholesaler who arranges the specific tour, for example; it might be a retail travel agent who serves as an independent distributor for a wholesaler or carrier; it may be one of the wholesaler-retailers who package their own tours or who buy packages from other wholesalers for distribution.

A second movement has been the marketing of tourism, either regionally or nationally. Countries, provinces, and states promote travel to their particular destinations. This effort supplements the marketing plans of the carriers. In some cases the marketing effort of the carrier can dovetail with that of the destination.

A third trend has been the coordination of marketing plans by various private-sector companies. Tie-ins between airlines and hotels or bus lines and various attractions are becoming more prevalent.

Last, there is the movement toward *vertical integration*. Airlines have moved in to take control of hotels and car-rental agencies. This has been an attempt to develop a "one-stop travel shop" experience for the traveler. The strategy backfired a number of years ago for United Airlines, which formed Allegis—an amalgamation of airline, hotel, and car-rental companies. Under stockholder pressure they were forced to divest themselves of the non-airline parts of the company.

When the majority of airline passengers consisted of people traveling on business and rather wealthy tourists, the airlines felt that the demand for travel was inelastic. That is, if prices were reduced, any increase in number of passengers would not produce more revenue. Because of this and a fear that open pricing would lead to price wars that might result in bankruptcy for smaller airlines, airline pricing was closely controlled. Pricing was a reflection of operating costs. The average costs of carriers serving particular markets were calculated, and a reasonable return on investment was added to come up with the price that could be charged. With deregulation a new era has come to pricing in transportation in general and in the airline industry in particular.

Three economic concepts are important when looking at pricing alternatives. They are the ideas of differential pricing, the contribution theory, and the incremental

---

Quick Trip 7.6
How Should We Market Safety?

In light of a small number of highly publicized crashes of planes operated by low-cost airlines, the companies are coming under heavy scrutiny by both consumers and government regulators. The issue relates to whether cutting costs jeopardizes airline safety. While most low-cost airlines have had no serious accidents in the past six years, any airline crash focuses attention on the issue for everyone.

According to Jack Trout, a marketing strategist, "Cheapness never enhances quality. It detracts." He adds that travelers may think, "If they're really, really cheap, how safe can they be?" There is a problem in promoting the idea of safety. "They don't want to say they're safe because they're bringing up a subject that maybe their consumer wasn't thinking about," says Terry Trippler, editor of an airline newsletter. "You don't walk into your house and tell your wife, 'I didn't have an affair today.'"

Following the crash of a ValuJet plane in Florida the executives of Kiwi International Air Lines, another low-cost airline, met with the company's advertising agency to develop an image campaign. The new ads stress that they are very different from ValueJet in terms of experience and service. The ads spotlight the experience of Kiwi flight attendants, mechanics, and pilots. Amenities such as a beer of the month and flowers in the bathroom are also featured. While ticket prices are not spotlighted, the airline is not hiding the fact that it is a low-cost carrier.

Standard operating procedure after a crash is for all airlines to pull all advertising for at least seventy-two hours. Air South extended that self-imposed deadline for several weeks following the crash. They also allowed two television stations to film news reports aboard recent flights. At Spirit Airlines bookings fell 20 percent in the days following the crash. Reservationists were given scripts to respond to customer questions about the airlines' pilot experience and the age of their aircraft. A news team was invited to film the maintenance facility.

Other airline executives are stepping up their appearances on television and radio shows, talking positively about their own airlines while subtly putting distance between themselves and ValuJet. Others are shunning the spotlight altogether.

Questions:

1. What is the most effective way to deal with the crash of a competing airline?

2. What should be avoided?

Source: Lisser, E. Low-Fare Airlines Mute Their Bargain Message. *Wall Street Journal*. (May 22, 1996) B1–2.

---

concept. Underlying *differential pricing* is the idea that there is not one demand curve, but many. A separate demand exists for coach than exists for first class; separate demand exists for travel from Denver to New York than from New York to Denver. As such, carriers can calculate how price-sensitive demand is in one particular class or on one particular route and price accordingly. The demand for business travel, for example, is probably less sensitive to price changes than the demand for pleasure travel on that same route at that same time. A higher price can be charged where demand is inelastic.

The idea of **contribution theory** is that prices should be set at the level that contributes most to paying off costs while still allowing traffic to move. The fare charged might be low on a route where the demand is elastic and higher where demand is inelastic. In effect, segments of the market that are price inelastic are subsidizing others that are price elastic. How low should the price be? Low enough to ensure the passenger travels while contributing as much as possible to paying off fixed costs.

Tied to the ideas above is the **incremental concept**. Incremental costs are those incurred by running an additional service. The operating costs of a particular plane or train are its incremental costs. Each fare should cover its incremental costs while contributing as much as possible to fixed costs and ensuring that the traffic moves. It is up to management to analyze each route and each segment of the market to price accordingly.

Transportation Issues

Tourism destinations are dependent on transportation routes and modes. As pointed out in the previous chapter transportation, in terms of distance and cost, primarily serves as a resistance to travel between two points.

Here are two viewpoints on transportation priorities. The first of these is from a report from the U.S. General Accounting Office. In the 1992 report they outlined six major concerns (GAO, 1992)

- Invest wisely to rebuild and enhance surface transportation infrastructure. This involves developing an organizational structure that assists investment trade-offs among the various transportation modes, which are in constant competition with each other for public funds; optimizing the use of funds because needs outweigh available resources; and capitalizing on new technologies such as high-speed rail and intelligent vehicle/highway systems.

- Modernizing traffic control and enhancing airports. This means improving the process for buying costly and complex equipment in order to minimize cost overruns; consolidating air traffic control facilities without compromising safety; and applying new technologies such as satellite-guided advanced precision approaches to airports.

- Improving transportation safety. The task is to make sure that each model administration follows through on existing safety initiatives and ensure that resources are targeted to areas of the highest safety risk. For example, the odds of dying are (GAO, 1992)

    1 in 14,000 in a coast-to-coast car trip

    1 in 88,000 in a bicycle accident

    1 in 1 million in a coast-to-coast train trip

    1 in 10 million in a commercial airline accident

- Increasing airline competition and access to international markets. The U.S. position is that domestically competition is being threatened by certain aspects of the airline computer reservations systems, frequent flyer programs, and travel agent/air carrier relationships. Internationally, there is concern that

limits on the number of airlines designated to serve specific routes prevent the U.S. from entering international markets.

Even within government circles the issue is controversial. While the Department of Transportation has been working toward granting special immunity to airlines from U.S. antitrust laws, the Department of Justice questions the impact on consumers (Nomani, 1997). For example an alliance between UAL Corp.'s United Airlines and Lufthansa AG received such exemption in return for Germany's decision to open its skies to U.S. airlines. This was followed by alliances between Delta Air Lines and Swissair, Sabena World Airlines and Austrian Airlines and AMR Corp.'s American Airlines and Canadian Airlines International, Ltd. These alliances help companies jointly coordinate route schedules, fares, discounts, travel packages, frequent flyer programs, and other operational details. The Justice Department, however, fears that such arrangements may result in higher fares, particularly for business travelers, as alliances dominate certain routes.

- Strengthening Coast Guard acquisition programs and environmental protection.

- Consolidating financial management systems and revamping grant oversight.

A second view comes from a survey on American international travelers. Asked what government and policy makers should focus on, they replied (*Travel Weekly*, 1996):

- Modernize the air traffic control system (68 percent)

- Streamline immigration and customs procedures (39 percent)

- Reduce traveler taxes and user fees (31 percent)

- Relieve airport congestion (23 percent)

Quick Trip 7.7
You Want Me to Subsidize *What?*

For the first time merchants in a number of ski resort towns in Colorado are being asked to help subsidize new jet service to their areas. The picture for the 1996–1997 ski season was as follows:

SKI AREA	ASPEN/ SNOWMASS	VAIL/ BEAVER CREEK	STEAMBOAT	PURGATORY	CRESTED BUTTE & MONARCH	TELLURIDE
Number of seats for '96–'97 season	220,000	265,500	155,600	100,000	80,000	80,400
% increase over previous year	Up 10%	Up 74%	Up 35%	Up 54%	Up 9%	Up 46%
Subsidy	No revenue guarantees	Some revenue guarantees	Some revenue guarantees & subsidy	Some revenue guarantees	No revenue guarantees	Some revenue guarantees

Much of the new service to Colorado ski destinations is bypassing Denver International Airport. There is new nonstop jet service from Los Angeles, St. Louis, and Newark, N.J., although United Express flights from Denver still account for almost half of all planned ski-season flights to Colorado mountain resorts.

For years ski area operators have paid airlines to operate ski-season flights. Now they are asking small businesses in their communities to contribute to that cost. In addition to subsidies paid to the airlines for increased service, some resorts offer "revenue guarantees." Airlines figure out the cost of adding air service to a community and add a profit. At the end of the season, if the carrier has not met its target, the resort community makes up the difference.

At Vail promotion of nonstop flights from major cities brought so many passengers to the region that revenue guarantees have been phased out. For the 1996–1997 season only 11 out of 130 flights were supported by guarantees. Vail Associates had the option of dropping guarantees altogether but opted not to. According to their Senior Vice President Kent Myers, "I think it sends the wrong message to our airline partners. If I'm successful (at filling planes with passengers), I will not pay on any revenue guarantees. And we haven't paid on a guarantee in four years."

Questions:

1. Should ski-area businesses offer subsidies to airlines to operate flights into their communities?

2. Why, or why not?

3. Which businesses should pay?

4. How should an "equitable share" be determined?

Source: Leib, J. Ski Resort Skies Friendlier. *The Denver Post.* (October 13, 1996) 1H, 6H.

Summary

Developments in transportation impact where tourism is developed and the type of development that occurs. Destinations have to ensure that access to the destination is made as easy as possible for their visitors. It is necessary to know the barriers that inhibit the use of a particular transportation mode to develop programs to overcome them.

References

(August 26, 1996). Forecasts for U.S. airline growth. *Travel Weekly*, 19.

Blum, E. (December 2, 1996). Dickinson book: Lines could see 'lost profits.' *Travel Weekly*, 46.

Carey, S. (November 21, 1996). Drills help United cope with tragedy. *Wall Street Journal*, B1, B2.

Chase, M. (July 1, 1996). Avoid rough sailing on vacation cruises by cautious planning. *Wall Street Journal*, B1.

(December, 1992). *Transportation issues*. United States General Accounting Office.

Dwyer, L, & Forsyth, P. (1996). *A framework for assessing the economic significance of cruise tourism*. Proceedings of the 27th Annual Conference of the Travel and Tourism Association, 161–169.

(June 24, 1996). U.S. airlines' safety records. *Travel Weekly*, 35.

Lundgren, J.O.J. (1973). The development of the tourist travel systems. *The Tourist Review*, 1, 10.

(March 4, 1996). International traveler's priorities. *Travel Weekly*, 33.

Marti, B.E. (1995). The cruise ship sanitation program. *Journal of Travel Research*, 33 (4), 29–38.

(May 30, 1996). U.S. lines: Average age of fleets. *Travel Weekly*, 25.

Meredith, J. (1993). *The benefits and costs of air traffic growth in Asia/Pacific*, Paper no. 3, PATA Occasional Papers Series.

Nomani, A.Q. (January 3, 1997). Airline pacts antitrust question sparks controversy. *Wall Street Journal*, A10.

(October 7). CLIA survey aims to help agents identify 'likely' cruisers. *Travel Weekly*, 1, 4.

(October 13, 1994). Contiki identifies client types suitable for motorcoach tours. *Travel Weekly*, 28.

(October 13, 1994). The tourism payout. *Travel Weekly*, C8.

(October 25, 1993). U.S.-Europe air alliances: It's only the beginning. *Travel Weekly*, 61, 64.

Robinson, R. (1995). *Creating beneficial partnerships with other leading marketers, presentation*. 1995 Annual Conference of the Association of Travel Marketing Executives.

Santo, J. (November 21, 1994). Study: Cruise tourism generates $4B in Caribbean. *Tour & Travel News*, 38.

(September 25, 1995). Holland America Line president pulls no punches. *Tour & Travel News*, 25, 29.

Sheth, J.N. (1975). A psychological model of travel mode selection. *Advances in Consumer Research*, 3. Proceedings of the Association for Consumer Research, Sixth Annual Conference, 426.

(Undated). *Achieving comfortable flight, pathways systems*. Natural History Museum of Los Angeles County, Massachusetts Institute of Technology, University of California at Berkeley.

Additional Reading

Air Travel Survey, Air Transport Association, 1301 Pennsylvania Avenue, N.W., Suite 1100, Washington, DC 20004-1707, annual.

Airline Deregulation in Canada, John Christopher, National Technical Information Service, Springfield, VA 22161, March 1989.

"Airports for the Twenty-first Century," Sir John Egan, *Viewpoint*, vol. 1, no. 1, pp. 50–55, World Travel and Tourism Council, P.O. Box 6237, New York, NY 10128.

U.S. International Air Travel Statistics, Volpe National Transportation Systems Center, Center for Transportation Information, DTS-44, Kendall Square, Cambridge, MA 02142.

World Air Transport Statistics, annual statistical digest on the world's airlines—traffic, capacity, financial results and operating fleet. Available from the Publications Department, International Air Transport Association, 2000 Peel Street, Montreal, Quebec, Canada H3A 2R4: Tel. (514) 844-3210; FAX (514) 844-5286.

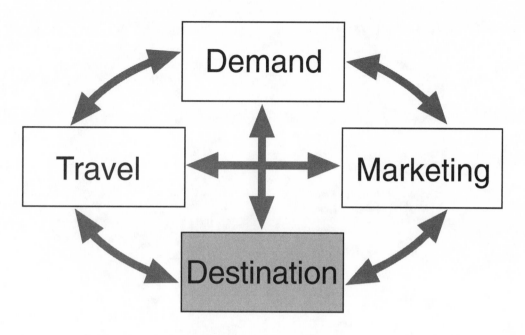

Part III

Destination

Planning, Developing, and Controlling Tourism

The characteristics of travel to a destination area contribute to shaping how the destination functions and what it provides for visitors. Part 3 of *The Tourism System* examines an area's destination mix which, in part, reflects the market segments it serves, the geographic origins of visitors, and visitors' modes of transportation. The destination must develop a tourism policy and plan, and the legislation and regulations to control tourism. It must carefully develop tourism to minimize any adverse impacts.

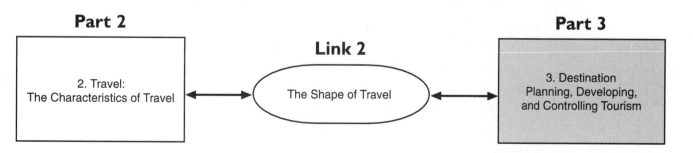

"A voyage to a destination, wherever it may be, is also a voyage within oneself; even as a cyclone carries along with it the center in which it must ultimately rest."

Lauren van der Post

8

The Destination Mix

···Attractions and Services for the Traveler ··········

Purpose

Students will be able to identify the strengths and deficiencies of a tourism destination.

Learning Objectives

Having read this chapter, you should be able to:

1. Explain the interdependencies between the five destination mix elements.

2. Identify the important elements of attractions, facilities, infrastructure, transportation, and hospitality required for a tourism destination.

Overview

At a destination there is a mix of interdependent elements. The elements are interdependent because in order to produce a satisfying vacation experience, all elements must be present. The destination is composed of:

● Attractions
● Facilities
● Infrastructure
● Transportation
● Hospitality

Attractions draw visitors to an area. Facilities serve the needs of the visitors while away from home. Infrastructure and transportation are necessary to help ensure accessibility of the destination to the visitor. Hospitality is concerned with the way in which services are delivered to the visitor.

The Sunshine Plantation, Sunshine Coast, Australia, attracts visitors each year. Photo from *Top Shots* CD Rom. Courtesy of Queensland Tourist and Travel Corporation.

Attractions

> "Pleasure is still the biggest industry. Out-of-season Cannes feels not only empty, but strangely empty, a town waiting: and you realize that this is all really the stage, beautifully equipped, of an immense theatre where the protagonists pay to act. For finally it is the other visitors the visitor comes here to see."
>
> *William Sansom*

The central aspects of tourism are attractions. Attractions, by definition, have the ability to draw people to them. Although attractions for the visitor concern the satisfactions perceived from various experiences, the task for the developer and designer is to create an environment made up in part of "attractions" that will provide an opportunity for the visitor to enjoy a visit. The addition at a site of factors other than attractions (services, transportation, hospitality) will help ensure that enjoyment.

Attractions have many characteristics. As mentioned above, they tend to draw visitors to them—they aim to serve the recreational needs of visitors. They can to a large extent be developed anywhere and act as a growth inducer, tending to be developed first in a tourist region.

Scope

The way in which attractions are characterized has implications for development and marketing. Attractions can be characterized in terms of their scope, ownership, permanency, and drawing power. A typology is suggested in figure 8.1. Destinations may be primary or secondary (sometimes called stopover or touring destinations). A *primary destination* is one that is attractive enough to be the primary motivation for tourism visits and one that is aimed at satisfying visitors for several days or longer. A *secondary* or *stopover destination* is either an interesting or necessary place to visit on the way to a primary destination, and it aims at satisfying visitors for one to two days. It may be interesting enough to attract tourists on their way somewhere else, or it may, in fact, be a required stop on the way to a final destination. Certain areas can be primary destinations for one segment of the market or stopover destinations for other segments.

Attractions at a primary destination have to have sufficient breadth of appeal to entice visitors to stay for many days. There has to be sufficient things to do and see to keep all members of the party occupied. At a stopover destination, the length of stay will be shorter and the need for a diversity of attractions is less. From a marketing viewpoint, the primary destination or attraction seeks fewer visitors staying longer periods of time, compared to the secondary destination that relies on attracting larger numbers for shorter periods of time. In terms of location, primary destinations tend to be oriented toward the location of the market (Disney World) or to the site of the resource (Aspen). Secondary destinations, although located between visitors and resources, are more reliant on their accessibility to transportation networks.

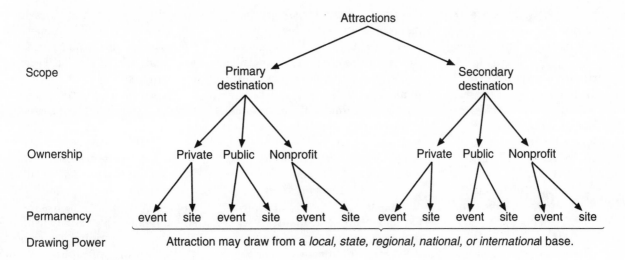

Figure 8.1   Typology of Attractions.

Ownership

The form of ownership of the attraction has great implications for tourism. Approximately 85 percent of all U.S. outdoor recreation lands are owned by the federal government. The agencies that manage this land often do not have tourism as a primary use of the land. Their outlooks will determine the degree to which tourism and recreation are encouraged.

The nonprofit sector is usually oriented to some aspect of the social good. Yet when nonprofit organizations get involved in work for the social good, such as historical preservation, their efforts can have great implications for tourism. Limited tourism may be a vehicle for getting sufficient revenue to continue the historical work. Care must be taken to ensure that the means does not become the end. The nonprofit organization involved may back out of the project and the resource may become overcommercialized and lose its original appeal.

The private sector's motivation is that of profit making. The wise manager will realize that short-run profit maximization may be detrimental to the long-run success of the attraction and the destination.

Permanency

Site attractions concern attractions of a physical nature. They are largely permanent, with their locations being fixed. *Event attractions* are rather short in duration, and their location can be changed. Site attractions are more dependent upon the resource base. Event attractions can be developed at places more convenient to the market. Because site attractions cost more to develop in terms of both time and money than do event attractions, new tourist regions can conceivably develop event attractions as a way of publicizing the area and bringing in cash to help finance more permanent site attractions.

Drawing Power

Attractions may also be defined in terms of the distance from which they are able to draw people. Attractions may be locally, state-wide, regionally, nationally, or internationally significant. The rating is inclusive in that a national attraction will draw from the state and local levels, also. If proposed and existing attractions can be objectively viewed in terms of their drawing power, appropriate strategies for the marketing of existing

attractions and a mix of future attractions can be developed. Attractions do not become attractions for the purpose of tourism until a certain amount of development has occurred to make the natural resource accessible to and attractive for visitors.

Although tourists are motivated to visit a destination to satisfy various needs and wants, they are also motivated to visit a destination because of certain characteristics. The characteristics that attract tourists are:

- Natural resources
- Climate
- Culture
- History
- Ethnicity
- Accessibility

Natural resources. The natural resources of a destination provide an excellent asset to sell to tourists. When studying the landscape or scenery of an area, it is important to note not only the natural resources but also the human imprints on the area; for this is also part of the scenery. In this respect, it is important to point out that any change in one aspect of the scenery changes the whole landscape.

For many markets, an outstanding natural resource has been, and still is, sandy beaches. In urban areas, where children do not have the opportunity to run free in safety or the chance to see the sea, an exodus occurs on weekends and holidays to spots offering such attractions. So it is that Jones Beach becomes a weekend mecca for Manhattan residents, while Manitoba advertises 100,000 lakes, together with soft warm sands and sparkling blue waters.

Two important points should be stressed when considering scenery. First, from the visitor's viewpoint, there is no cost for it. A beautiful sunset, Niagara Falls, the Grand Canyon—these cost the visitor nothing. The second point is concerned with the variety of scenery. Variety in an area can be an important selling point. In this way, Britain with a variety of views and types of countryside every few hundred yards can compete—successfully so—with such dwarfing structures as the Canadian Rockies and the Swiss Alps.

The natural beauty of The Grand Canyon—the scenery—costs nothing. Photo by Corel.

Climate. Climate is perhaps the most common marketing theme used as the basis for selling a tourism area once it has suitable visitor attractions. Although a region in some cases can be sold largely on the basis of climate, for maximum effect the area must be readily accessible to large concentrations of population. One reason for the popularity of California's coastline resorts is their proximity via automobile to millions of people. Florida, meanwhile, to attract vacationers from the northeastern and the north central states, must advertise that its sun is only an hour or so away by plane.

In addition to ready accessibility, the destination area should promise something that visitors cannot get at home. In a populous center, where most people live with enough disposable income to travel, one market segment may be attracted by warm sunshine at a time when it is cold and gloomy at home, while another segment may seek accentuated winter conditions of a ski resort. Conversely, when the population centers are sweltering with summer heat, one market segment may head for the seashore—Maine, Oregon, Florida, or even the Caribbean—for cooling breezes, while another segment wants a mountain area, whether it's New Hampshire, the Canadian Rockies, Scotland, or Switzerland.

When considering summer weather, the most comfortable living is in the populous temperate zones of the Mediterranean, which have warm, sunny, and dry climates. Tropical conditions are too hot and too wet to sell solely on this basis, so that selling of tropical climates must be amplified with a number of other attractions, which is the case of the Caribbean.

An interesting corollary of climate advertising is that those who have left home want to be kept informed about the bad conditions they have fled. In Florida and Puerto Rico, hotels post weather conditions in northern cities during the winter. In summer, it may also be cooler in Florida and Puerto Rico than it is back home because of ocean breezes.

Recreational activities are undertaken considering the combination of natural resources and climate on hand. Over the past several years we have seen a remarkable growth in recreational pursuits in general and participative recreational pursuits in particular. This has resulted in a decline in the business of many sedentary holiday areas and the upsurge of resorts offering sporting facilities. The type or recreation facilities offered is usually determined by the nature of the surrounding countryside: skiing requires mountains, water sports need water, and so on. However, we are seeing the introduction of artificial ski slopes, "dry" ski slopes, artificial lakes for boating and fishing, and artificially stocked waters and bird and hunting grounds.

The important point to remember in selling an area on its recreational facilities is to sell a variety of pursuits, not just one. This way one does not rely solely on one sport, one market, or one season for one's business.

Culture. Each country has its own unique culture—a state of manners, taste, and intellectual development. Some countries are found to be more interesting culturally and better developed than others. Culture is, for practical tourism purposes, interwoven with history. Today's way of life is tomorrow's culture.

Thus, although one can "sell" the way of life of the people of a foreign land, that way of life must be radically different from the visitor's own to induce excitement and the desire to view it.

America and the Americans have always exhibited, perhaps because of their relatively young existence, an almost insatiable appetite for historical culture. With a fusing in this country of so many races from so many different lands, these groups have jealously clung to preserving their own ethnic culture. Today, however, these cultures are not guarded quite so tightly, but are sold to the rest of the country. Williamsburg, the Pennsylvania Dutch, and Western ranch country demonstrate this feature remarkably well.

Historical resources. Historical resources may be defined by function into the following subdivisions: (1) war, (2) religion, (3) habitation, and (4) government. Past wars hold a fascination for many people. Depending on the chronological distance from the event, the emotions aroused range from morbid curiosity and excitement to sorrow and remembrance. Thus, people throng to the Tower of London and Edinburgh Castle to see the chamber of horrors and the bottleneck dungeons, excited by the thought of such distant gory deeds. The most popular World War II sites in Europe are Margraten in the Netherlands, Omaha Beach Ceremony in France on the site of the D-Day landings in Normandy in 1944, and the Luxembourg City Cemetery, where General George S. Patton, Jr. lies buried. In America, the popularity of Arlington Cemetery in Washington, D.C. attests to the national feeling of remembrance for those who died for their country.

Since the times of the earliest pilgrimages and the travelers in Chaucer's Canterbury Tales, pilgrims have made journeys to shrines, monuments, and cathedrals in the name of their Lord. Although religion can be a tremendous selling force, it can act negatively for the country. The obvious present example is in Northern Ireland, where past demonstrations against parades commemorating William of Orange's defeat of the militant Catholics have erupted into long, and sometimes bloody, battles that have served to disrupt

trade, industry, and tourism from progressing into the area.

Religion forms the basis for the Outdoor Biblical Museum in Nymegen, Holland, which is a beautiful and moving attempt to bring all faiths to a point where they can worship together. Visitors walk along narrow paths cut through a forest to arrive at a scene from the Bible. A minimum of figures and a natural landscape leave the visitor awestruck by the simplicity of it all.

From the simple house tour to the elaborate view of Buckingham Palace, human's natural curiosity to see the trappings of others' homes is a marketable item. Thousands flock to the homes of Anne Hathaway and William Shakespeare, or to the houses of George Washington and Abraham Lincoln, in an attempt to achieve some sense of rapport with the memory of these famous people. However, one need not be numbered among the dead to enjoy this admiration and visitation. The White House and Buckingham Palace are favorite tourist stops while, in Britain, many stately homes are being opened to the public, and the promise of dining with a duke and thereafter spending the night in one of the state rooms is an appealing attraction to many. After the success of the movie *Braveheart*, the Scottish Tourist Board ran a promotion centered around William Wallace.

Visitors can be encouraged to visit places where fictitious people lived. World Travel Tours advertise special Song of Norway tours and Sound of Music trips to Norway and Austria, respectively. Romania's tourism authority offers a tour to Dracula's Transylvania (now a part of Romania).

A nation's capital will always hold a fascination for those who desire to see where the decisions are made. The Houses of Parliament are as well known as the House of Representatives and the

These Civil War re-enactors give visitors a taste of historic Virginia. Photo by Corel.

Kremlin. The chance to see the country's leaders in session is an experience few visitors would miss. Even on the state and local levels, council sessions can become the focal point of an educational tour, while the City Hall "you can't fight" may also be visited.

Ethnicity. The U.S. is a cosmopolitan mixture of first-, second-, and third-generation Scots, Irish, Dutch, Germans, Russians, and so on. As such, it is easy to appeal to people's basic sentimentality to coax them "back to the homeland." The ethnic groups may be classified as first and later generations. For the first generation, no development is needed at all, because these people wish to see the area they left just as they left it.

However, first-generation travelers will generally stay with friends, and one finds that it is the later generations that will spend more money in a particular spot. This latter group of travelers, experiencing a different environment, will require some of the creature comforts afforded them at home. It should not be thought, however, that the only viable market for this kind of promotion consists of present-day U.S. citizens, though many examples of such marketing exist. One of the definite movement channels that can be readily traced is that from Ireland to New York and Boston.

In North America itself, Michigan's Tulip Festival, the Highland Games at Alma, the Beer Festival at Frankenmuth, and the weekly summer ethnic concerts in downtown Detroit show the success of a campaign on this asset.

It is possible also to spotlight movements within a country. In the U.S., it is estimated that one out of every five Americans moves each year. Nor are these movements random. States like Florida, Nevada, Arizona, and California have attracted decennial population increases in the order of 50 to 80 percent, and states like Arkansas and West Virginia have suffered population decreases in the order of 6 to 10 percent. There may well be a significant market to be reached through the sentimental pull of old friends and places.

Accessibility. The last item to consider in this section is accessibility. Though germane to every asset listed above, certain areas owe their popularity—and some their very being—to the fact that they are readily accessible to large urban areas. The development of Brighton, England, as a weekend and holiday resort despite its completely stony beach is due to its proximity to London with a potential market of 8 million people.

The accessibility of an area to a particular market should be measured in terms of time, cost, frequency, and comfort. Although attention should be paid to each factor, an area can sell on its comparative advantage in providing exceptional services in one or a combination of several of the above factors at the expense of another.

Traveling to Europe by plane,

for instance, may cost more and be less comfortable than land or sea travel, but Europe is more accessible in terms of time and frequency of service. An advertisement for a sea ferry declares, "All that divides Scotland and Ireland is two-and-a-half hours." The motorist immediately knows how long it will take him to get to Ireland, and a seemingly large and time-consuming obstacle—the Irish Sea—becomes a mere two-and-a-half hour expressway.

Part of Mexico's appeal to the U.S. market is its accessibility in terms of cost—not necessarily in terms of cost to reach the country, but in terms of what can be bought there. A two-week vacation in Mexico may be more accessible in terms of cost than fourteen days in the U.S.

Other areas have become attractions because of the difficulty in reaching them. In those few cases in which lack of accessibility increases the attractiveness, the end result (the destination) should be somewhat spectacular—a magnificent view, great food, or a wonderful culture.

Overall two patterns of attractions have emerged (Hu & Ritchie, 1993). First, some aspects have universal importance in influencing the evaluations tourists have of how attractive a destination is. Scenery, climate, and price are most critical. Second, there are certain aspects of a destination whose importance depends on the type of destination and vacation experience being provided. Culture, as an attraction, is more important to certain types of tourists than to others. Thus, a destination should emphasize its culture to those visitor segments to whom this is important rather than to all segments of the market.

Development and Design

Gunn (1972) has suggested several design principles to guide the devel-

opment of attractions. It is important to remember that the dependencies of the attraction vary. Certain types of attractions, such as ski areas and battlefields, are extremely dependent upon the resource base, but others, such as theme parks, are much less so. All attractions are, to some extent, dependent upon their relationship to the visitor's origin, upon their accessibility, and upon the number of facilities and services available. In terms of the visitor origin, the time relationship may be more important than the distance relationship. Zones of visitor origin will differ, depending upon the mode of transportation considered. A two-hour zone, for example, may include visitors 100 miles away by car and 500 miles away by plane.

As noted earlier, accessibility, although important, is more crucial to the touring destination because the time available is a major constraint.

Services and facilities tend to grow up to support the developed attraction. However, if a service center is already developed, its location may affect the development of a new attraction.

Attractions tend to be clustered for several reasons. First, there is an increased desire on the part of visitors to do more in one place. Second, clustering allows a destination a better opportunity to satisfy more people. To explore a major theme fully, a variety of different attractions may be required. A group of museums, each exploring part of an overall theme, is more effective than one. A cluster of different but related historic buildings may be necessary to explore and explain a particular time in history fully. Different rides, clustered into a theme park, are necessary to appeal to all of the senses.

The extent of clustering depends upon the type of destination involved. For the primary destination, clustering is obviously more important. This is particularly true if accessibility is dependent upon modes of transportation oriented toward mass tourism. Destinations that rely on visitors arriving by plane, boat, or train will be apt to develop more clusters of attractions than those appealing to the motorist.

Events

Events can be developed for several reasons. Events may be staged to make money; celebrate particular holidays, seasons, or historical events; provide cultural or educational experiences; or unite and give a feeling of pride to a particular community. An event may seek to combine these reasons. It is important that objectives be developed, agreed upon, and ranked, in order that subsequent conflicts over strategy can be solved by referring to the action that will help to achieve the most important objective.

An examination of special events in Illinois revealed that most events included from eight to sixteen different activities. The most common activities were parades, queen and beauty contests, carnivals with featured entertainers, lunches and dinners, musical entertainment, dancing, and children's activities.

In approximately one-third of the cases, a nonprofit corporation takes major planning responsibility. The planning of the event can take anywhere from a month to over a year. Most groups used from five to eleven committees to organize the event that involved a total of 12 to 350 people, almost all of them volunteers.

Facilities

> "The Afghan official smiled at the three Western correspondents arriving at Kabul airport and said: 'Welcome to Afghanistan. Which hotel would you like to stay in tonight before you are expelled tomorrow?'"
>
> Richard Banforth

While attractions draw visitors from their homes, facilities are necessary to serve these visitors away from home. Facilities tend to be oriented to attractions in their locations because of the need to locate close to where the market will be. They tend to support rather than induce growth and, hence, they tend to be developed at the same time as or after the attractions are developed. The relationship between attractions and other elements of a tourism destination is suggested in figure 8.2. A certain level of services is necessary for a destination to be considered by a visitor. If the level of services is lacking, that destination will not be considered. However, the mere presence of these facilities and other services, by themselves, will not bring visitors. Attractions must be present for this to occur. For example, the 1995 Yankelovich Travel Monitor identified "safety of hotel" and "safety of destination" as the two most important pleasure trip factors for U.S. visitors. If people felt a destination was not safe they would not visit. However, the fact that a destination is regarded as safe will not, in and of itself, induce travel. Attractions are necessary.

It is possible for an attraction to be a facility. A case in point would be a well-known resort hotel that not only serves to draw people to an area, but satisfies their needs as well.

Lodging. While away from home, the visitor needs to eat and sleep. Sleeping accommodations can range from hotels of an international standard and condominiums, to campgrounds and the homes of friends and relatives. Lodging accounts for between one-fifth and one-fourth of total visitor expenditures, despite the fact that almost half of U.S. visitors stay in the homes of friends and relatives when taking a trip. It is vital to the success of a tourist region that a sufficient quantity of accommodations of the right quality be provided for visitor needs.

The type of accommodation provided will be determined primarily by the characteristics of the market segment being sought. Some prefer the full-amenity type of property. In destination areas these properties will tend to have greater demands placed on them in terms of room size and services offered because guests will be staying a long time. Visitors whose prime motivation is to see friends and relatives will likely stay with them.

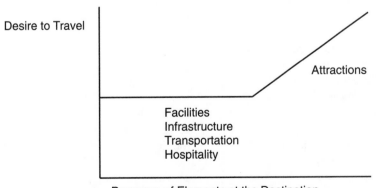

Figure 8.2 The Importance of Destination Elements.

Quick Trip 8.1
Is God a Tourist Attraction?

Every Sunday the Mount Moriah Baptist Church in Harlem is packed full of people. However, up to 80 percent of those in attendance aren't there to pray. Dressed in T-shirts, blue jeans and sneakers, most are visitors from Brazil, Germany, France, and Italy bussed in to hear the gospel music of one of Harlem's famous choirs. Most often they don't even stay around for the sermon.

The churches are increasingly using tourism to fill the pews—and the collection plates. According to the Rev. John A. Smith of Metropolitan Baptist Church, "The biggest business in the world is the church business." Not everyone agrees. Other pastors fear that services are propagating negative stereotypes of blacks while undermining the faith of others. According to the Rev. James Forbes, "When people begin to perform for spectators, that brings an erosion of authenticity. If commercialization is the key to survival, then we are in trouble." Parishioners worry that foreigners are ruining their opportunity to worship in peace. "They don't understand that this is God's house," says Marcus Morris. "It's just part of their schedule."

Black pastors point out that white churches televise their services. They point out the financial impact. People come to Harlem and spread the word that good things are happening there. Mount Moriah has sold 30,000 copies of its CD of gospel music. Tourist money has helped pay for a soup kitchen and clothing for the poor.

Questions:

1. Is it "proper" to sell church services as a tourist attraction?

2. Is there a way to balance the needs of the parishioners with those of the visitors?

3. When something becomes a tourist attraction is there a way to maintain its authenticity? How?

Source: Beals, G. & Woodward, K.L. Soul Voyeurs Invade the House of God. *Newsweek.* (June 3, 1996) 71.

The type of accommodation provided is also partly determined by what the competitors are providing. A key concept to remember in marketing is that the facilities provided should be at least equal to those provided by the competition for the same market. The type of lodging is also determined by the transportation used by visitors to the destination. In Roman times, resting places were determined when the horse, not the rider, was tired. In the U.S. in the early seventeenth century, taverns were located about fifteen miles or one day's carriage ride apart. The development of rail travel led to accommodation clusters near the stations. An increase in auto travel encouraged the roadside motel, but the growth of air travel has led to clusters of hotels and motels around airports.

Food and Beverage. More of the tourist dollar is spent on food and beverage than on any other service. It is probably no coincidence that those states highest in per capita eating place sales are also top tourist states. The type of food service provided will be related to visitor needs. Many areas have successfully developed menus indigenous to the area to promote local economy foods, while they also use the local items as a unique selling point.

Supporting Industries. Support industries refer to the facilities provided for visitors in addition to lodging, food, and beverage. These may include souvenir or duty-free shops (for goods), laundries and guides (for services), and festival areas and recreational facilities (for activities).

Support industries can either be subsistence-related by providing staple needs or requirements or pleasure-related by providing impulse or entertainment purchase opportunities.

For tourism, support industries tend to be small businesses. This fact can be both positive and negative for the destination area. It can be positive in that the encouragement of small businesses will allow for the wide distribution and sharing of the financial benefits of tourism with those in the community. On the other hand, small businesses may lack the capital and expertise required to provide a quality part of the vacation experience. Several considerations can assist in maximizing the potential of support industries. It is important that the support industries be located in places accessible to visitors. It will be necessary to observe or predict visitor movement patterns to locate facilities to serve them optimally. The number and types of facilities offered will also have to be determined relative to visitor needs. Facilities should be provided that match the quality and price level of lodging, food, and beverage operations that should themselves be provided in light of visitor expenditure levels.

If a sufficient number and mix of services is provided, the supply may actually stimulate demand or increase the length of stay of visitors by offering such a number of attractive alternatives that they will have enough things to buy and do to encourage them to stay longer. At the same time, too many facilities at one place may mean that there is insufficient sales volume to ensure a reasonable rate of return for the businesses involved.

The two primary techniques for helping ensure the effective development of support industries are:

1. Zoning and operating regulations enforced by law.
2. Ownership or control exercised through leasing of facilities to individual entrepreneurs.

The methods can, in fact, be combined with good results. People at destination areas may designate certain areas as being appropriate for tourist-support industries, and within those areas they may lay down restrictions as to theme, design, building height, and density; and they may place restrictions on signs in order to ensure the development of a destination that has attractions and facilities that meet expectations of the visitor market sought. The problem can also be effectively managed if a developer or public agency owns a large tract and establishes control through requirements in the lease agreement.

Infrastructure

> *"The usual life-saving hours are from 9:00 a.m. to 6:30 p.m. on week days. During week-ends at the more popular and bigger beaches . . . the life-saving hours are extended—from 8:00 a.m. to 7:30 p.m."*
>
> Hong Kong Tourist Association leaflet

Attractions and facilities are not accessible to visitors' use until basic

---

Quick Trip 8.2
What Travelers Do in their Hotel Rooms

Bed Sheets—59% check to make sure they're clean.

Room Service—38% order it.

Minibars—33% of the men and 19% of the women indulge.

Gideon's Bible—23% read it.

Toiletries—31% take these freebies.

Exercise—40% use fitness facilities.

Towels—4% admit to stealing them.

Left Behind—33% have left something in the room after checkout.

Quiet, please—32% have been unable to get to sleep because of noise.

Oops—7% have had a housekeeper walk in on them while undressed.

Source: *Travel Weekly*

---

infrastructure needs of the destination have been met. Infrastructure consists of all the underground and surface developmental construction of a region and comprises:

- Water systems
- Communication networks
- Health care facilities
- Power sources
- Sewage/drainage areas
- Streets, highways
- Security systems

There has been some criticism of tourism's overreliance on a fully developed infrastructure. In certain parts of the world, newly discovered tourist destinations may be able to satisfy visitor needs without developing a full infrastructure system. The lack of modern highways may, in fact, be an added attraction for some kinds of visitors. As a destination attracts more visitors, the increase in numbers may actually stimulate the development of the infrastructure. In most cases, the reverse is true. Infrastructure

development is necessary to stimulate the development of tourism. One problem faced by many communities in the U.S. is the condition of bridges. According to the American Automobile Association (AAA), of the 574,671 bridges in the United States, just under one-third are deficient. The AAA uses data from the Federal Highway Administration which defines deficient as "structurally deficient" or "functionally obsolete" (see tables 8.1 and 8.2).

The infrastructure of an area is shared by both visitors and residents. An upgrading of the elements of the infrastructure primarily for the purpose of attracting visitors will benefit the host population. The development of infrastructure is almost always a public-sector responsibility. It is one way that the public sector has created a climate suitable for tourism development.

The development of a proper infrastructure requires engineering input, but it is wise to consider the reports of engineers in light of the

Table 8.1   Bridges—The Ten Worst States

RANK	STATE	NUMBER OF BRIDGES	PERCENT DEFICIENT
1.	New York	17,308	63%
2.	Washington, D.C.	239	60
3.	Massachusetts	5,021	58
4.	Hawaii	1,070	53
5.	Rhode Island	734	49
6.	West Virginia	6,477	47
7.	Missouri	22,940	46
8.	New Jersey	6,209	46
9.	Pennsylvania	22,327	44
10.	Vermont	2,653	42

Source: *Travel Weekly*. (December 2, 1996) 57.

Table 8.2   Bridges—The Ten Best States

RANK	STATE	NUMBER OF BRIDGES	PERCENT DEFICIENT
1.	Arizona	6,147	10%
2.	New Mexico	3,475	18
3.	Nevada	1,150	18
4.	Idaho	4,002	20
5.	South Carolina	8,999	21
6.	Minnesota	12,555	21
7.	Colorado	7,688	22
8.	Wyoming	2,889	23
9.	Montana	4,808	24
10.	Florida	10,823	24

Source: *Travel Weekly*. (December 2, 1996) 57.

Infrastructure and transportation resources are crucial in the destination mix in providing access to attractions and events: The Liberty Bridge leading to Pest, Hungary. Photo from *Budapest in 101 Photos; Multimedia CD for the IBM PC* (Selester, Hungary, 1996). Printed with permission.

effects on tourism. The best placement of a coast road from an engineering perspective may not be the best route for visitor viewing.

It is necessary also that visitors receive enough communication so that their questions about travel within the state are answered. Because of federal pressure in the U.S. to restrict billboards on the highway, various alternatives have been explored. Vermont has developed a successful travel information system comprised of the following parts:

1. Local chambers of commerce are located in many Vermont communities, with manned offices or booths.

2. Vermont visitor handbooks, containing details on the facilities offered by over 600 Vermont traveler-oriented businesses, can be obtained from local chambers of commerce.

3. Official state maps, containing historic sites, museums, golf courses, campgrounds, and ski areas are offered. These maps, highway route numbers, and town destination signs will guide the visitor between towns. Once the desired town is reached . . .

4. Official business directional signs replace billboards for services available in that town and may indicate the number of miles to a hostelry or other service. These signs are located just before road junctions that require the visitor to change direction from one numbered highway to another, except at congested intersections and other important locations, and on interstate highways at rest areas, where these signs are replaced by listings on . . .

5. Travel information plazas, from which are dispensed the area . . .

6. Travelers' services guide pertaining to the section of Vermont in which the dispensing plaza is located. These guides provide

---

Quick Trip 8.3
Tourist Facilities

With the inauguration of Nelson Mandela as president of a free South Africa in 1994 the country received worldwide attention. Isolated by sanctions for many years, the country emerged as a "new" destination. Yet two years later the country is struggling with "normalcy" as the tourist boom has begun to flatten.

According to Mike Fabricius, chief director of tourism for the country, ". . . it means the country can get down to business." That means focusing on the "nuts and bolts that any destination would do." One priority is the development of a hotel-rating system that is a better representation of a hotel's qualities. Typically, ratings are done by a consultant after visiting the property with a checklist. Service and ambiance are difficult to assess on a quick visit. The new system incorporates input from customers.

Another change involves decentralizing tourism promotion, giving more power to the provinces. At the same time there is a growing recognition that tourism promotion should be led by the private sector. This is a subject of great debate. For example, tourism and environmental issues are presently combined under one ministry. According to Fabricius, "Some people say tourism is a business venture and should be treated as any consumer product. Others say that if you mess up the environment, you lose tourism."

A recent White Paper identified training, entrepreneurial opportunities and tourism's relationship with South African communities as areas crucial to tourism's development. The issues are linked together. As tribal villagers turn to cattle raising, greater pressure is put on the wildlife that attracts visitors. In addition large numbers of rural men are leaving villages to look for work in towns. With few skills, many are turning to crime. One attempt to correct this problem is the development of cultural villages. In some cases visitors are invited to visit an existing village, observe people at work and play, and buy arts and crafts. Other villages are made up of different tribes, each in its own "mini-village" specifically created for the purpose. Visitors can stay in modified versions of the village dwelling with Western-style bedrooms and bathrooms. While some debate whether or not culture can and should be "sold" operators ask different questions. "Will the cultural village contribute to keeping the family unit together? Will it keep at least some young men from resorting to more desperate acts?" Is this any different than visiting an Irish pub to hear traditional music?

Patrick Boddam-Whetham, managing director of Wilderness Safaris, points out that one lodge in a poor area employs twenty-one people who were all previously jobless. In turn, each of the employed contributes support to an average of eight relatives. Thus, he argues, the lives of more than 160 people have improved.

There are clashes between those who want to keep the traditional life and those who want to modernize it. One village near the lodge was dependent on farming. The locals want to get rid of the hippopotamuses that ate and trampled their crops. However, the hippos were a major attraction for guests of the lodge. The solution was to make villagers shareholders in the lodge. Realizing the tourism value of the hippos changed their attitude about the beasts. The negotiated effort took four years but now the villagers actually take visitors out for hippo viewings.

Questions:

1. What facilities are necessary to ensure the success of tourism?

2. How successful do you think South Africa will be in putting these elements together?

Source: McDonald, M. As Tourism Wanes, S. Africa Seeks Natural Balance. *Travel Weekly*. (September 23, 1996) 24, 26.

---

directions to businesses that are listed on each plaza where the guide's dispenser is located.

The important parts of a tourist infrastructure are the following:

- *Water*—Sufficient quantities of pure water are essential. A typical resort requires 350 to 400 gallons of water per room per day. An eighteen-hole golf course will require 600,000 to 1 million gallons of water per day, depending on the region in which it is located.

- *Power*—The important considerations are that adequate supplies of power be available to meet peak-load requirements, that continuity of service be ensured, and that, if possible, the type of power supplied be compatible with that used by the target markets of the destination.

- *Communication*—Despite the fact that many visitors may wish to get away from it all, it is necessary for most that telephone and/or telegraph service be available. The lack of telephones in hotel rooms will deter visitors from staying at a particular property because of the security aspect.

- *Sewage/drainage*—Sewer demand is often placed at 90 percent of domestic water demand. Although water-storage reservoirs and sewage treatment plants can be designed on the basis of maximum average demand, transmission lines must be designed on a basis of maximum peak demand.

- *Health care*—The type of health care facilities provided will depend on the number of visitors expected, their ages, the type of activities in which they will engage, and local geographic factors. Ski areas will tend to specialize in broken bones, for example.

- *Security*—While on vacation visitors are in an unfamiliar environment. Because of this, the need for assurances regarding their safety is important. Especially when traveling long distances and to foreign countries, the image gained of the destination may be distorted. Europeans, for example, are fed television programs that sensationalize the U.S. crime scene. This creates an image of the U.S. as a place filled with violence. In addition, the costs of medical care are so expensive that concerns about health in foreign countries may generate additional fears. Insecurities about food, water, or police protection may dissuade visitors

from visiting. It is necessary that the basic needs for security be considered and ensured to make the potential visitor feel secure prior to and during the vacation.

Transportation

> "Airline travel is hours of boredom interrupted by moments of stark terror."
>
> Al Boliska

The availability of first-class roads adds greatly to the accessibility of a region. Some areas have, in fact, refused to upgrade their road systems in order to slow down tourism development. The effect of a highway system was noted by the U.S. Department of Transportation when it estimated that the development of the U.S. Interstate system meant that the distance that could be safely driven in one day increased from 350 to 500 miles. There are certain ways to make use of the highway more interesting to visitors.

1. Provide close-range view of local scenes
2. Change the elevation

Quick Trip 8.4
Good, Clean Fun?

Every year Americans take 1.8 billion trips to beaches, rivers, and lakes. However, each year 2,000 beaches are closed due to sewage overflows, urban and agricultural runoff, and direct contamination caused by human waste.

Robert Haile of the University of Southern California found that people swimming near storm drains were 50 percent more likely to develop fevers, vomiting, respiratory infections, or earaches compared to people who stayed 400 yards away. Restricting diaper-age children to the toddler wading pool and putting kiddie pools and adult pools on separate filtration systems also help prevent the spread of disease. Here's what people can do to ensure a clean swimming spot:

1. Don't swim near storm drains.
2. Don't swim after a big rainfall (it flushes contaminants off city streets into the sea).
3. Ensure the water is checked weekly during the swimming season and reports are made public.
4. Ensure that beaches provide adequate toilets, sinks for handwashing, and diaper-changing facilities.
5. Check the annual survey of U.S. beaches conducted by the Natural Resources Defense Council at http://www.nrdc.org/

Question:

1. How safe is your local beach when compared to the above list?

Source: Chase, M. Swimmers May Find Beaches Are Not All Good, Clean Fun. *The Wall Street Journal.* (June 17, 1996) B1.

3. Develop viewpoints and overlooks

4. Independently align dual-lane highways to fit into the land contour

5. Selectively thin trees to reveal views

It is crucial to consider to what extent resident (or local) traffic is to be integrated with visitor (or regional) traffic. It may be desirable to design a dual system of higher-speed lanes flanked by roads for low-speed local traffic. Roads should be engineered for safety, taking appropriate measures designed to safeguard the highway user.

There should be a degree of co-ordination between the three modes of air, rail, and bus to facilitate passenger transfer between modes. Directional and informational signs should be easy to see and of a uniform design throughout the mode. A security system should be in place to prevent theft of luggage and/or misclaiming of checked bags at terminals. Personnel should be available to assist passengers, particularly the aged and disabled, and non-English speaking passengers. Complete information should be provided on the location, fares, schedules, and routes of local transportation services.

Hospitality Resources

> *True story: Pete arrived in La Guardia (New York) from Florida. Seeking a cab from the airport to his Bergenfield, N.J., home, he was told, "It'll cost you $120."*
>
> *"Pal, I live here," Pete told him, "I'll give you $50."*
>
> *"Thought you were a tourist," the cabby said. "Sorry, I'll take it."*

Hospitality resources refer to the general feeling of welcome that visitors receive while at a destination area. It is the way that visitor services are delivered by service providers, as well as the general feeling of warmth from the general resident population. It is a combination of a certain amount of knowledge and a positive attitude that results in specific hospitable behaviors. The way in which services are delivered is particularly important because tourism is consumed on the spot. Sales and service occur at the same time. Although excellent service cannot totally make up for a hard bed, tough steak, bumpy bus ride, or rainy weather, poor service can certainly spoil an otherwise excellent vacation experience. In the broader sense, visitors will have a much more rewarding vacation if they feel welcomed by the host population and will certainly feel awkward and unhappy if they feel resented. The best and least expensive way to reach any type of tourist market is to do such a good job of ensuring they have a great experience that they tell their friends about it when they return home. The importance of hospitality as a cause of visitor satisfaction has been noted in China where visitors have expressed dissatisfaction even though the attractions were excellent. They noted that tourist guides have poor attitudes and a lack of enthusiasm (Cai & Woods, 1993).

The former U.S. Travel and Tourism Administration (USTTA) did some research relative to visitor perception of the U.S. (Mathews, 1993). Over the years they have found that Australians, Japanese, Mexicans, and British regarded "interesting and friendly people" as a "borderline weakness" for the U.S. while Brazilians considered that factor a major weakness.

Hospitality resources can be improved by, in effect, training tourism personnel to be hospitable and encouraging positive feelings toward tourism and visitors on the part of the general public.

These two aspects will be dealt with separately.

Hospitality Training

A program of hospitality training is generally aimed at motivating service providers to be hospitable in their dealings with visitors. The assumption is that providing more hospitable service will result in a more satisfied visitor who will be inclined to return and/or spread positive reactions through word-of-mouth advertising to other potential visitors. To achieve hospitable service on the part of service providers, it may be necessary to change their present behavior. Many believe that a change in behavior is brought about by a change in attitude and an increase in the level of knowledge. The three aspects of attitude are toward self, toward others, and toward the subject matter.

Attitude toward self. If an individual's self-esteem, or attitude toward self, is low, that individual will tend to behave in such a way that the feedback from others will confirm this low opinion of himself or herself. Traditionally, tourism businesses have lacked prestige. Those who work in tourism have, by association, lacked prestige. Behavior is thus precipitated that will reinforce this feeling. The key then is to change the individual's perception of self in order to improve behaviors. If service providers can be made to believe that their work and they themselves are important, the hope is that their work and specifically their actions toward visitors will reflect this new feeling. This aspect can be put into practice by highlighting the vital part that service providers play in ensuring a positive vacation experience. If service providers can be viewed as hosts and hostesses rather than just employees, their self-image may be raised. Stress should be placed on the fact that

Quick Trip 8.5
The More Things Change . . .

A 1972 (yes, 1972) report by the U.S. Department of Transportation identified the following problems in terminal facilities and ground transportation:

- *General*—There is an almost complete lack of coordination between the three modes of air, rail, and bus. In addition, there is a noticeable lack of consistency in standards and procedures within each mode. Directional and informational signs are often difficult to see; signs are not uniform throughout the system; public-address announcements are often unintelligible.

- *Air*—Long walks are required in many terminals.

- *Rail*—Parking is inconvenient and inadequate near larger terminals; use of facilities by local transients and inadequate cleaning procedures lead to crowded, unsanitary waiting rooms and restrooms; security to prevent thefts is lacking; information and directional maps are not provided in most rail terminals; special transportation to and from rail terminals is not provided; and the urban transit and taxi service is often inadequate.

- *Bus*—Terminals are dirty and crowded due to use by unauthorized people and to inadequate cleaning procedures; boarding passes lack a system of orderly procedures resulting in crowding when passengers are boarding; inadequate protection is afforded to passengers against traffic.

The following suggestions regarding terminals and ground facilities have been made and serve as a guide to the provision of adequate services:

1. Full information about facilities, terminal location, and local transportation should be made available to all originating passengers.

2. A security system should be provided to prevent theft and misclaiming of checked baggage at terminals.

3. The information system should provide data on connecting or alternative rail and bus service, including information on fares and schedules.

4. A system of standard signs and symbols should be developed and installed in all air terminals.

5. Rapid updated arrival and departure information should be available on posted information boards, through public address announcements, and to telephone callers.

6. Personnel should always be available to assist passengers, particularly the aged, the handicapped, and non-English speaking.

7. Complete information should be provided on the location, fares, schedules, and routes of local transportation services.

8. City maps should be made available to passengers.

Question:

1. How do the air, rail, and bus terminals in your town compare to the 1972 report?

dealing with and serving people is, indeed, a most difficult task. Visitors often bring demands with them that are difficult to satisfy. Although it is relatively easy to deal with a satisfied guest, it is very challenging to deal with visitors who are dissatisfied or extra demanding. The ability to create a satisfied guest is a very demanding task. Those people who can do this have skills that should be highly regarded by themselves as well as by others.

Attitude toward others. The second aspect of attitude relates to attitude toward others. An individual's feelings toward people that she or he comes into contact with will affect, positively or negatively, behavior toward them. The task is to assist the service provider in developing positive feelings toward fellow employees and visitors that will result in positive behavior toward the visitors. This can be achieved by training the individual in the importance of teamwork and interdependence in getting the job done. Oftentimes employees are not aware of all the people and actions that are necessary to ensure a satisfied guest. It is important that employees see where they fit into the big picture of a satisfied visitor, not only to see how important their role is, but also to be aware of the interfacing roles of others.

It is obviously important to consider the employee's attitude toward visitors. The key to the development of positive attitudes toward visitors is being able to develop the ability to put oneself in the visitor's place. Role-playing can be successfully used for this purpose. If a service provider can empathize with the visitor, accept visitors as they are, understand that for them this vacation is something that they have saved for all year, and appreciate how tired they may be after a long trip, then the attitude is likely to be more positive.

Attitude toward subject matter.
The third aspect of attitude concerns attitude toward subject matter. The individual who does not believe in the work being done will display a negative attitude that will be reflected in poor service toward the guest. A positive attitude on the part of service providers toward visitors can come about only when employees are made aware of how important tourism is to their state, country, city, and property. By being aware of the amount of revenue, jobs, and taxes generated and the dispersion of the visitor dollar throughout the community, employees may become convinced of the economic and social significance of the industry of which they are a part.

Quick Trip 8.6
Trouble in Paradise

Tourism in Hawaii is experiencing only modest growth and many are saying that the state has only itself to blame. Costs are rising compared to competing places like Florida and Las Vegas. Hotel taxes and other fees have recently been raised in Hawaii while the tourism marketing budget has been cut 20 percent. Prices at a "moderately" priced hotel cost about $440 while rental cars are as high as $120 a day. These figures are almost twice as much as at places in Florida. Lorraine Conner of Crockett, Texas says the famed Aloha spirit is also missing. "If you decide not to buy, they are so rude."

Visits were also hurt by the fact that California and Japan, two major markets, suffered recessions. Upsetting to some is the so-called *Kama'aina* or local rate under which, for example, locals pay $165 a night and out-of-staters pay $410 for a seaside room in the Princeville Hotel on Kauai. Called "price-gouging" by tourists, the local rate is justified by tourism officials who say that the rate allows locals to enjoy amenities they might otherwise be unable to afford.

In addition, consultants found that half of Waikiki's 12,000 hotel rooms (which average $150 a night) were "substandard." Hotels do face a heavy tax burden. On Maui hotels pay $8 per $1,000 of valuation, compared with $6.50 for other businesses. Although the money was earmarked for tourism, it went to the counties. A five percent room tax that was enacted about five years ago was to be used to build a convention center. However, as Honolulu feuded over where to place the center, the state gave the money to the counties for general use.

The state has increased operating costs for an airline industry that is vital to its survival. For example, the landing cost for Boeing 747 increased from $409 to $1,755 while ticket prices remained very competitive and many passengers came in as non-paying frequent flyers. In 1991 the state blocked United Airlines from entering the lucrative inter-island business. United responded by cutting back on its Hawaii flights. In response that state reduced landing fees 25 percent in 1995.

Questions:

1. How important is "hospitality" to a tourism destination?

2. Is it particularly important to Hawaii?

3. If so, why?

4. What can be done to revitalize this spirit?

Source: J. Carlton, "Hawaii's Allure For Tourists Has Faded, And Some Say State Has Itself To Blame," *The Wall Street Journal.* (June 7, 1996) B1, B8.

The hope is that more hospitable behavior will come, in part, from a better self-image, more empathy with others, and a positive attitude about tourism's role in the community. To precipitate a change in attitude, it is necessary to raise the knowledge level of the individual. This may be done in group sessions or through a variety of audiovisual means.

Teaching Specific Behaviors

A second theory of behavior change is that a change in behavior affects attitudes. If people can be trained in specific desired behaviors and act them out, the positive feedback they receive will result in a positive attitude. The task is to develop specific behaviors that will be termed hospitable and instruct employees in these behaviors. If the employees act out these hospitable behaviors, the positive reactions (tips, recognition, advancement, and so on) will result in positive attitudes toward hospitality. To this end, employees can familiarize themselves with the surrounding attractions and services (to be able to give advice or directions). Some attractions will have an open house for those involved in tourism to acquaint them by means of a mini-familiarization tour. Sessions can cover both verbal and nonverbal behavior. Employees are often unaware of the negative messages their facial expressions or posture give.

By means of this joint approach—attempting to change attitudes about self, others, and tourism through increasing the level of knowledge and teaching specific hospitable behaviors—an attempt is made to raise the hospitality level of service providers.

Community Awareness Programs

Although the visitor is most directly affected by the degree of hospitality shown by service providers, the overall feeling of welcome within a community will also enhance or detract from the vacation experience. Residents of a destination area cannot be trained to act in a hospitable way toward visitors, but a community awareness program can help develop a more positive attitude toward the visitor. The objectives of such a program are two-

---

Quick Trip 8.7
Catering to Clients with Disabilities

There are almost 50 million people with disabilities. This represents 13 percent of all travelers. Seven million travelers use a wheelchair, crutches or a cane; nine million are visually impaired while 28 million have a hearing loss. Under the terms of the Americans With Disabilities Act, they have increased rights of access to travel facilities. Here are some tips for dealing with this market from Joe Regen, owner of *Able to Travel*, a division of Partnership Travel, Inc.

- Familiarize yourself with the Air Carrier Access Act which, amongst other things, allows people to take a manual wheelchair onto an aircraft on a first-come, first-served basis.
- Get to know the different facilities on each airline.
- Research ground transportation. For example, which companies have hydraulic lifts to allow wheelchair access?
- Research hotels and get testimonials. Are there, for example, roll-in showers as compared to a tub with grab bars.

Question:

1. How would a hotel, restaurant, airline or other tourism company go about making its facilities more accessible to travelers with disabilities?

Source: "Catering to Clients with Disabilities," *Travel Weekly*. (December 15, 1995) 47–48.

---

fold: to build acceptance of tourism and to build an understanding of the visitor.

An acceptance of tourism cannot be built unless the benefits of tourism are made relevant to members of the community. The benefits of tourism are many, yet many people do not realize that they are positively affected by it. To some it may mean a summer job, while to others tourism may ensure that a playhouse can survive year-round for the cultural benefit of the community. It is necessary to communicate to each part of the community messages that are important and relevant to them. An understanding of who the visitor is can assist in a greater acceptance of the visitor.

Knowing why people visit the area might result in a renewed civic pride.

There are different ways to communicate with the local community. Public meetings can be held to discuss particular problems. Some areas have successfully organized a speaker's bureau consisting of tourism community leaders who talk to community groups. Information sheets and newsletters, though infrequently used, can be distributed to the general public. Some communities have shown the effect of tourism by giving two-dollar bills in change to visitors to distribute throughout the area. In the off-season in Niagara Falls, Ontario community groups can tour many of the tourist attractions free of charge. Whatever methods are used, the objective remains to create a feeling of welcome for the visitor within the community.

Summary

To be a successful tourist destination there must be a blend of certain elements. Attractions are the first and most important of these. While attractions are needed to bring people in, they must have adequate facilities, infrastructure, and transportation alternatives to make their stay comfortable. Finally, hospitality on the part of local people will help ensure a satisfied customer who will want to return.

References

Cai, L., & Woods, R. (1993). China's tourism—service failure. *Cornell Hotel and Restaurant Administration Quarterly, 34* (4), 30–39.

Gunn, C.A. (1972). *Vacationscape: Designing tourist regions.* Austin, TX: The University of Texas.

Gunn, C.A. (1979). *Tourism planning.* New York: Crane, Rusak and Company, Inc.

Hu, Y., & Ritchie, J.R.B. (1993). Measuring destination attractiveness: A contextual approach. *Journal of Travel Research, 32* (2), 25–34.

Mathews, W. (1993). How to treat international visitors as guests. *Travel & Tourism Executive Report,* 14, 5–7.

Additional Readings

Attractions: The Heart of the Travel Product, Center for Survey and Marketing Research, University of Wisconsin—Parkside, Box 2000, Kenosha, WI 53141, February 1992.

Heritage, Tourism and Society, David T. Herbert, ed., Mansell Publishing Ltd., 125 Strand, London Wc2R 0BB, U.K., 1995.

Nature-based Tourism: An Annotated Bibliography, W. Whitlock and R.H. Becker, Regional Resources Development Institute, Clemson University, 265-B Lehotsky Hall, Clemson, SC 29634-1005, 1991.

Tourism Historic Places, Priscilla Baker, National Trust for Historic Preservation, 1785 Massachusetts Avenue, NW, Washington, DC 20036, 1995.

"The World Travel & Tourism Research Council's research shows that travel and tourism generates more than 10% of global employment and is the world's largest generator of jobs; generates more than 255 million jobs—11% of the global workforce in 1996; will sustain a 5% growth rate over the next decade—resulting in an estimated 385 million new jobs by 2006."

World Travel & Tourism Council (1997)

9

Tourism Impacts on the Economy, Society, Culture, and Environment

···The Need for Sustainable Tourism Development

Purpose

Having learned about the economic, social and cultural, and environmental impacts of tourism on destination areas, students will be able to suggest ways that the benefits of tourism can be maximized.

Learning Objectives

Having read this chapter, you should be able to:

1. Explain the three major economic impacts of tourism on destination areas and how these impacts are measured.

2. Describe the strategies to maximize the economic impact of tourism and how tourism's role in economic development can be analyzed.

3. Discuss the potentially negative social and cultural impacts of tourism on destination areas.

4. Identify the positive social and cultural impacts that may result from tourism.

5. Describe the potentially negative environmental impacts of tourism on destination areas.

6. Identify the positive environmental impacts that may result from tourism.

7. Explain the principles of sustainable tourism development.

Overview

Tourism has had significant impacts upon destination areas throughout the world. This chapter explores the potential economic, social and cultural, and environmental effects of tourism upon destinations and suggests strategies to maximize tourism's positive impacts. Tourism may be one of several alternative economic development options available to a destination area. The characteristics of tourism compared to other development possibilities are examined. Three major types of economic impacts of tourism are described. Suggestions are given to help destinations develop policies to maximize tourism's positive effects, while minimizing the negative impacts.

Although tourism brings significant economic advantages to destination areas, it can cause adverse social and cultural changes, and damage natural environments. In some ways, tourism can benefit the local environment, society, and culture. The concept of sustainable tourism development is recommended as a broad strategy for all destinations.

The Role of Tourism in Economic Development

"Notwithstanding many of the highly commendable motives for encouraging the growth of international tourism set out in the 1980 Manila Declaration, the overwhelming reason why countries proffer themselves as tourist destinations is for economic benefits."

Archer, B.H., & Fletcher, J.E. (1990), 10

The increasing fascination with tourism worldwide in the past 30 years has been motivated largely by its potential economic benefits for communities of all sizes. Many of the early books and articles about tourism emphasized the economic impact of tourism, especially in its economic development role for developing countries. In the three decades since the first English-language textbooks on tourism were published, a more balanced view of tourism's impacts has emerged. Today, it is widely recognized that tourism can have negative impacts on communities by adversely affecting the environment, society, and culture. While this chapter begins with a review of the role of tourism in economic development, this does not suggest that these economic impacts are any more important or significant than the other positive or negative impacts of tourism.

The potential economic benefits of tourism are a major attraction for many countries, states, provinces, territories, regions, counties, cities, and other communities. In particular, tourism development is seen as an attractive policy alternative to promote economic growth and diversification. This especially has been the case for developing countries where three pro-tourism arguments are identified. First, the demand for international travel continues to grow within the developed nations of Europe, North America, and the Asia-Pacific region. Second, as household incomes in the developed countries increase, the ***income elasticity of demand*** for tourism means that the demand for international travel will increase at a faster rate. Third, developing countries need ***foreign exchange earnings*** to spur their own economic development and to satisfy the rising expectations of their growing populations.

Traditionally, the developing (or so-called Third World) countries have tended to rely upon agriculture and other natural resource-based industries for economic growth. The World Bank (1979) suggests that between 50 percent and 70 percent of the people of middle- and low-income developing countries are directly dependent on agriculture. Full agricultural growth is a key to industrialization and further economic and employment growth. Recognizing that almost all developing countries have followed ***import-substitution*** (the substitution of locally produced products for those presently imported), the World Bank stresses the need to reward exports with incentives. A basic problem, however, with a reliance on agricultural development is that the developing country can easily be overly dependent on a few specific types of crops or animal products. The prices of these crops or products are unpredictable and affected by weather, disease, and outside manipulation by large buyers from the developed countries.

Another economic policy option is to promote the development of manufacturing facilities. However, the development of the manufacturing sector is not always a viable option. The potential problems with manufacturing may include:

1. The processing of raw materials is directly related to the base amount available in the area, and possible projects are likely to be few for all but the most richly endowed nations

2. For industries aimed at import substitution, the relatively small size of domestic markets restricts growth

3. Developing countries are characterized by chronic shortages of skilled labor

4. For export-oriented industries, products have to face full international competition, in terms of price and quality, as well as in marketing sophistication

One example of the problems of industrialization in a lesser-developed country is in the small West

African nation of The Gambia. Some 84 percent of its labor force is employed in agriculture, forestry, and fishing. The country has one major cash crop, groundnuts, which occupies 60 percent of its crop land. Industrialization through the development of manufacturing businesses and tourism represent the two major economic development options available to this "one-crop economy." However, according to Thompson, O'Hare, & Evans (1995), "Industrialization in The Gambia is negligible given the lack of indigenous skills, low levels of literacy, low purchasing power of the domestic market, poorly developed fuel and power resources and inadequate transport facilities." Tourism was first introduced to The Gambia in the 1960s and now contributes substantially to its economy.

Tourism faces similar problems to manufacturing in developing countries. However, many countries have the basic "raw materials" for tourism. In addition, there are usually fewer restrictions on international travel than on international trade. The distance of the destination from the market is becoming less of a problem and indeed may be an attraction to certain groups of travelers who are seeking the exotic and unexplored. When compared with primary industries such as agriculture, mining, and forestry, tourism prices are more under the control of the seller than of the buyer. The Organization for Economic Cooperation and Development (OECD) has concluded that tourism provides a major opportunity for growth in countries that are at the intermediate stage of economic development, experiencing rather fast economic growth and requiring more foreign-exchange earnings. They also caution that "there are few if any developing countries which could, or perhaps even should, rely principally on tourism for their economic salvation" (Erbes, 1973).

Tourism has particularly attracted attention in its role as an **_invisible export_**. As an invisible export, tourism differs from international trade in physical products in several ways:

1. The "consumer" collects the product from the exporting country (destination), thereby eliminating any freight costs for the exporter, except in cases in which the airline used belongs to the destination country.

2. The demand for the pleasure (vacation travel) segment of tourism is highly dependent on non-economic factors, such as local disturbances, political troubles, and changes in the popularity of countries and resort areas created mostly by media coverage. At the same time, international tourism is usually both **_price-elastic_** and **_income-elastic_**. Therefore, shifts in prices or household incomes normally result in more-than-proportional changes in pleasure travel.

3. By using specific fiscal measures, the exporting (destination) country can manipulate exchange rates so that those for visitors are higher or lower (normally the latter in order to attract a greater number of visitors) than those at other foreign trade markets. Also, visitors are permitted to buy in domestic markets at the prices prevailing for the local residents (the exceptions being the duty-free shops for visitors operated in many countries).

4. Tourism is multifaceted and directly affects several sectors of the economy (such as hotels and other forms of accommodations, shops, restaurants, local transportation firms, entertainment establishments, and handicraft producers) and indirectly affects many others (such as equipment manufacturers and utilities).

5. Tourism brings many more non-monetary benefits and costs (i.e., social, cultural, and environmental) than other export industries.

It is argued that tourism, when compared to manufacturing, is not a "smokestack" business. In other words, tourism development does not require the development of the types of factories that often pollute local environments. This position must be carefully weighed against the realization that tourism also has contributed to the environmental degradation of many parts of the world.

Economic Impacts of Tourism

> "An economic benefit is best understood as a gross increase in the wealth or income, measured in monetary terms, of people located in an area over and above the levels that would prevail in the absence of the activity under study."
>
> Frechtling, D.C. (1994), 362

Tourism has several potential economic impacts on destination areas. Generally, these impacts fall into three categories:

1. Increasing foreign exchange earnings
2. Increasing income
3. Increasing employment

Increasing Foreign Exchange Earnings

Many countries have embraced tourism as a way to increase foreign exchange earnings to produce the investment necessary to finance growth in other economic sectors. Some countries even require visitors to bring in a certain amount of foreign currency for

Quick Trip 9.1
Eighteen Reasons for Tourism Development in South Africa

In the Republic of South Africa, the government has adopted a strategy called the Reconstruction and Development Programme (RDP) to transform the country's economy. Tourism is viewed as a key tool in this economic transformation. The *White Paper on the Development and Promotion of Tourism in South Africa* released in 1996 argued that tourism was capable of "dynamizing and rejuvenating other sectors of the economy" because of 18 reasons:

1. Tourism represents a significant opportunity for South Africa.
2. Tourism is the world's largest generator of jobs.
3. Tourism can provide immediate employment.
4. Tourism is labor-intensive.
5. Tourism employs a multiplicity of skills.
6. Tourism creates entrepreneurial opportunities.
7. Tourism brings development to rural areas.
8. Well-managed tourism is kind to the environment.
9. Tourism builds cross-cultural relations and is a vital force for peace.
10. Tourism is a final good.
11. Tourism is a foreign exchange earner par excellence.
12. Tourism brings a ready market.
13. There is potential to influence visitor tastes and create export markets.
14. Tourism demand is continuous.
15. Tourism has a multiplier effect.
16. There is enormous potential for economic linkages.
17. South Africa is already a global leader in ecotourism.
18. South Africa's tourism potential has not been fully exploited.

Source: Department of Environmental Affairs and Tourism. (1996), 14–18.

each day of their stay and do not allow them to take it out of the country at the end of their vacation. However, there is a danger of overstating the foreign exchange earnings generated by tourism unless the import factor is known. The value of goods and services that must be imported to service the needs of tourism is referred to as **leakage**. The money spent leaks from the destinations economy and must be subtracted

from foreign exchange earnings to determine the true impact. In Australia, there has been considerable debate about the true economic impact of the growing number of Japanese travelers, especially to places such as Sydney, the Gold Coast, and Far North Queensland. Some have argued that, although the Japanese spend the most per capita of all international groups within Australia, many of the services they purchase are owned by

Japanese companies including package tours, hotels and resorts, duty-free shops, and attractions such as cruise operations. Stated another way, it is perceived that there is a large leakage factor to the Japanese economy for Japanese visitor expenditures in Australia.

Leakage occurs from at least six factors. The extent to which a destination can minimize leakage will determine the size of the foreign exchange earnings. Leakage occurs first from the cost of goods and services that must be purchased to satisfy the needs of visitors. If a Japanese visitor wants to eat sushi or sashimi, and if the fish and seafood have to be imported, the costs of the fish and seafood are import costs that must be deducted from earnings. Local manufacturing or handicraft industries may also import part of their raw materials to produce goods for visitors. This is a cost that needs to be subtracted from the foreign exchange earnings from souvenir sales and the sales of other locally produced products.

A second leakage occurs when importing goods and materials for infrastructure and buildings required for tourism development. The use of materials indigenous to the host destination not only reduces import costs but also adds a distinctive look to the local architecture and building interiors.

Payments to foreign *factors of production* represent a third leakage. Commissions have to be paid to overseas tour operators and travel agents. If foreign capital is invested in the country's tourism, interest payments, rent, and profits may have to be paid to those outside the country. The amount of local ownership and control is crucial in this regard. Foreign-owned chain hotels will often be staffed, stocked, and furnished by people, food, furnishings, fixtures, and equipment from the home country.

A fourth leakage is the expenditure for promotion, public relations/publicity, and similar services abroad. The cost of maintaining a national tourist office (NTO) in an origin country can be substantial and needs to be set against the foreign exchange earnings from that country.

Fifth, there are several ways that *transfer pricing* can reduce foreign exchange earnings. If visitors make purchases in the country of origin for services to be delivered at the destination, the transfer payments need not be made for the services provided. If a tourism company is multinational, payments may be recorded in the country of visitor origin rather than in the destination country, thereby reducing profits and taxes in the destination country. As mentioned earlier, this has been the case with Japanese travelers to Australia who often purchase their packages from Japanese tour operators who buy services from Japanese-owned hotels, resorts, and attractions located in Australia. Purchases by a foreign-owned hotel within the host country may be made from a foreign-owned subsidiary at inflated rates to reduce the taxable income in the destination country. The use of credit cards and traveler's checks can mean that local banks are not able to participate in the exchange. Sixth, foreign exchange earnings can be reduced when host governments exempt duties or taxes for foreign-owned companies or offer financial inducements to attract investment.

Unfortunately, for many developing countries that desperately need foreign exchange earnings, the import content of tourism is often very high, especially for small countries and island nations. Some small-island nations may have an import content in tourism of over 50 percent.

A critical issue for destination areas is to determine the net foreign exchange earnings from different types of visitors and types of tourism purchases within the desti-

nation. Visitors with high household incomes may be few and spend large amounts of money, but they may require a substantial infrastructure and facilities with high import costs. Is this better for the destination than mass-market visitors who arrive in greater numbers and spend less per capita, but who require fewer imported goods and services? The import proportion can vary significantly by type of tourism purchase. A study of tourism multipliers in Singapore showed that the multiplier was highest for the trade sector (visitor expenditures on shopping) at 1.07 and lowest for transport/communications at 0.58 (Heng & Low, 1990).

Initially, the foreign exchange cost is high as a destination begins to develop its tourism potential. Materials have to be imported and incentives given to attract investment. After this heavy initial cost period, foreign exchange costs gradually diminish for a period and then tend to increase again. This is mainly due to the *demonstration effect*. The demonstration effect occurs when local residents, exposed to goods imported for visitor use, begin to demand those goods for themselves. This automatically increases the demand for imports and is shown in figure 9.1. To what extent the cost of the demonstration

effect should be "charged" to tourism is debatable. As incomes rise and as communications through media, such as cable television and the World Wide Web, now instantly relay messages across the globe, people increasingly are exposed to many new products and services.

Increasing Income

The most popular method for estimating the income generated from tourism is by determining the income multiplier for the destination. *Income multipliers* measure the amount of local income generated per unit of visitor expenditure (Wanhill, 1994). There are two main techniques used for measuring the multiplier effect: the *ad hoc* or *simple multiplier* and *input-output analysis*.

The Ad Hoc or Simple Multiplier

Tourism generates revenues or income within the destination. The amount of income generated is difficult to determine because tourism is comprised of many different sectors of the economy. Additionally, many small businesses are involved, which leads to great problems in gathering precise data.

Visitors make an initial round of expenditures in the destination area. These expenditures may be for lodging, food, beverages, enter-

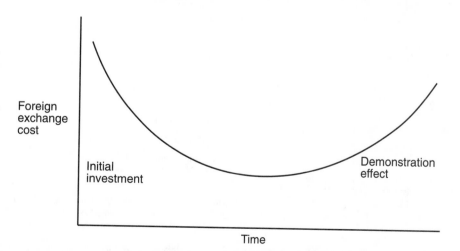

Figure 9.1 Foreign Exchange Cost Over Time.

tainment, clothing, gifts and souvenirs, personal care, medicines, cosmetics, photography, recreation, tours, sightseeing, guides, local transportation, and miscellaneous other items (see figure 9.2). These expenditures are received as income by local tour operators, handicraft sellers, hotel operators, restaurants, and other tourism businesses. In the second round of expenditures, the tourism businesses use some of the money to purchase goods, pay wages and salaries, and other expenses. The income in the next (third) round may be spent or saved. For example, employees who have received wages or salaries may spend some of that on rent or food, and may put some into their savings. The money paid for goods in the third round may be spent on the producer's raw materials such as seed, fertilizer, and imported raw materials. Any money spent on imports leaks out of the destination's economy. This process continues until the additional income generated by a new round of transactions becomes zero.

The major message that one gets from studying the multiplier effect is that it is wrong to just measure what visitors spend in the destination area. There are three levels of income that must be analyzed:

- **Direct:** The first round of spending by visitors in the destination area.
- **Indirect:** The second round of expenditures by businesses who receive the first round of visitor spending.

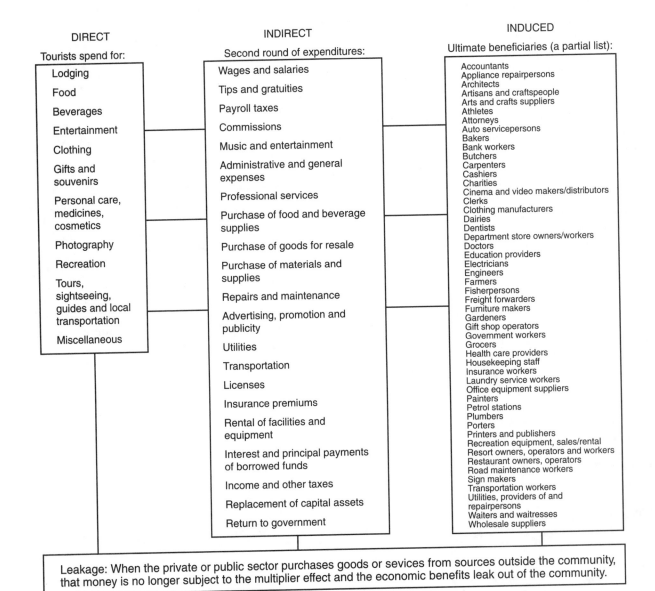

Figure 9.2   The Multiplier Effect. This Chart Demonstrates How Tourism Spending Flows through the Economy.

Source: World Tourism Organization

Quick Trip 9.2
Selected Tourism Income Multipliers

With few exceptions, the larger the area the higher the corresponding tourism multiplier value. The value of the multiplier, and therefore the economic significance of tourism to a particular destination, is determined by the level of diversification of the economy, the strength of the linkages between economic sectors, the propensity to import goods and services and the nature of the tourism product.

DESTINATION AREA	TOURIST INCOME MULTIPLIER	DESTINATION AREA	TOURIST INCOME MULTIPLIER
1. Developed Countries		**3. Larger Regions**	
Turkey	1.96	Hawaii	0.90–1.30
United Kingdom	1.73	Missouri, USA	0.88
Republic of Ireland	1.72	Walworth County, Wisconsin, USA	0.78
Egypt	1.23	Grand County, Colorado, USA	0.60
		Door County, Wisconsin, USA	0.55
2. Island Nations		Sullivan County, Pennsylvania, USA	0.44
Jamaica	1.23	South West Wyoming, USA	0.38
Dominican Republic	1.20		
Bermuda	1.17	**4. Smaller Regions or Cities**	
Cyprus	1.14	Victoria Metropolitan Area, BC, Canada	0.50
Northern Ireland	1.10	City of Carlisle, Cumbria, UK	0.40
East Caribbean	1.07	Gwynedd, North Wales, UK	0.37
Hong Kong	1.02	St. Andrews, Scotland	0.34
Mauritius	0.96	East Anglia, UK	0.34
Antigua	0.88	Greater Tayside, Scotland	0.32
Bahamas	0.79	Isle of Skye, Scotland	0.25
Fiji	0.72	City of Winchester, UK	0.19
Cayman Islands	0.65		
Iceland	0.64		
British Virgin Islands	0.58		
Solomon Islands, Melanesia	0.52		
Republic of Palau, Micronesia	0.50		
Western Samoa, Polynesia	0.39		

Sources: Archer, B., & Fletcher, J. (1990). Tourism: Its economic significance. In M. Quest (Ed.), Horwath book of tourism (pp. 10–25). London: The MacMillan Press. Vellas, F., & Becherel, L. (1995). International tourism. New York: St. Martin's Press, 232.

Source: Frechtling, D.C. (1994). Assessing the impacts of travel and tourism—measuring economic benefits. In J.R.B. Ritchie & C.R. Goeldner (Eds.), *Travel, tourism, and hospitality research* (2nd ed., pp. 359–391). New York: John Wiley & Sons, Inc.

- **Induced:** The subsequent rounds of expenditures after the second round.

The total income impact of tourism equals the sum of the direct, indirect, and induced impacts. If the multiplier is found to be 2.0 then the indirect plus the induced are equal to 1.0. If the multiplier is calculated at 1.73, then the indirect plus the induced are 73 percent of the direct. In figure 9.2, the people identified as "ultimate beneficiaries" are the ones receiving the induced income.

The size of the multiplier depends upon the extent to which the various economic sectors are linked to one another. This is a function of the diversity of activities within the destination. When tourism operators buy goods and services mainly from other local economic sectors, there is a smaller propensity to import and the multiplier ratio is higher than if the reverse was true.

The size of the destination has a great influence on the size of the income multiplier. For example, most smaller island economies have income multipliers of less than 1.0. Larger countries with developed economies, such as Turkey and the United Kingdom, have higher multipliers in the range of 1.5 to 2.0.

The simple multiplier has been criticized by some experts. It is best used in small countries with relatively small economies. The simple multiplier model does not take into account the fact that the destination country may increase export sales to other countries from which it presently imports. Although it may be necessary to import certain items to cater to visitors, once visitors return to their home countries they may want food, beverages, or other items from the destination country (e.g., wine from France, cheese from the Netherlands). Second, the model fails to account for the new investment in the destination country resulting from the additional income generated.

Input-Output Analysis   A more serious criticism of the simple multiplier model is the assumption that each type of income has the same effect. To remedy this it is necessary to break the increase in expenditures into component elements to analyze the effect of each element separately. This is done through a technique called **input-**

Visitors spend significant amounts on shopping. Photo courtesy Brown County Convention & Visitors Bureau, Nashville, Indiana.

output analysis. Input-output analysis is a method of looking at these interactions among different economic sectors and determining the effects of any possible changes. It is a means of analyzing inter-industry relationships in the production process in a destination area's economy (Frechtling, 1994). An input-output table shows how transactions flow through an economy in a given time period. A matrix is developed, the rows of which show the total value of all the sales made by each sector of the economy (or industry) to all the other sectors. The columns of the matrix show the purchases made by each sector from each of the other sectors.

There are also problems associated with input-output analysis. It is extremely difficult and expensive to get sufficient data for a detailed model, largely because visitor spending affects so many sectors of the economy. Analysis is suitable for only the short- and medium-term. Last, it is argued, input-output analysis makes too many unrealistic assumptions. It assumes that supply is elastic. Any increases in demand will require more output than can be met by purchases from the economic sectors that supplied the previous supply. It is unlikely that this will happen in the short-run because of production hindrances. Input-output analysis assumes that production functions are linear in form and that trade patterns are stable. It assumes that when production increases, purchases of imports will be made in the same proportions and from the same sources as before, negating any thought of **economies of scale**.

Additionally, input-output analysis assumes that increases in income will be spent on the same items and in the same proportions as previously. In reality, none of these assumptions are likely. Certainly, input-output analysis can show the economic impacts of different kinds of visitors, which assists in target market selection. It

can also show short-term economic effects compared with the effects of other sectors of the economy. Other tools are needed to demonstrate the best long-term policy option for investment in the various available economic sectors.

Economic Impact Models   In addition to the multiplier methods, some destination areas have developed **economic impact models** that reflect their specific needs. For example, the U.S. Travel Data Center has developed the Travel Economic Impact Model (TEIM). These models gather data on visitor expenditures and tourism employment, and then simulate the economic impacts that follow from these direct effects.

Increasing Employment

A major argument for encouraging tourism development is that it produces many jobs. Tourism creates primary or **direct employment** in such areas as lodging, restaurants, attractions, transportation, and sightseeing operations. **Indirect employment** is also created in construction, agriculture, and manufacturing. The amount of indirect or secondary employment depends upon the extent to which tourism is integrated with the rest of the local economy. The more integration and diversification that occurs, the more indirect employment generated.

Tourism is considered to be more **labor-intensive** than other industries. For this reason, it is often argued that tourism deserves special developmental support. The degree of labor intensity can be measured in terms of the cost per job created or the employment/output ratio. The employment/output ratio is the number of workers employed divided by the contribution of tourism to the national income. Although research conclusions are not unanimous, the cost per job created in tourism has been found

Quick Trip 9.3
Input-Output Analysis of Tourism in Singapore

In an input-output analysis of tourism in Singapore, Heng & Low (1990) identified six sectors (industries) of the Singaporean economy that received visitors expenditures directly from seven types of purchases: Accommodation, food and beverages, sightseeing, entertainment, shopping, local transport, and miscellaneous services. These spending levels are measured each year by the Singapore Tourist Promotion Board. The effects of these expenditures on 40 other sectors (industries) and among themselves were measured. The following table (with the six tourism-related sectors highlighted) shows that tourism has relatively strong linkages to other economic sectors of the Singaporean economy.

INDUSTRIES OR SECTORS	BACKWARD LINKAGES	RANKING	FORWARD LINKAGES	RANKING
1. Agriculture	1.784	17	1.877	10
2. Quarry	2.176	1	1.628	14
3. Food	1.619	35	1.854	11
4. Beverage and tobacco	1.881	12	1.382	23
5. Textile	1.488	41	1.121	34
6. Wearing apparel	1.653	30	1.485	18
7. Footwear	1.670	29	1.091	37
8. Leather	1.565	38	1.046	41
9. Wood	1.541	39	1.329	28
10. Furniture	1.918	9	1.231	30
11. Paper	1.684	28	1.423	21
12. Printing	1.789	16	1.847	13
13. Chemical	1.770	19	1.372	27
14. Petrol	1.082	46	2.610	8
15. Rubber products	1.093	45	1.006	46
16. Rubber	1.626	34	1.072	40
17. Plastic	1.598	36	1.496	16
18. Non-metallic	1.953	7	1.379	25
19. Cement	1.717	25	1.145	33
20. Basic metal	1.768	20	1.204	31
21. Non-ferrous	1.629	32	1.025	42
22. Fabricated metal	1.701	26	1.848	12
23. Office equipment	1.518	40	1.088	38
24. Industrial machinery	1.783	18	1.432	20
25. Electric machinery	1.637	31	1.185	32
26. Electric products	1.425	43	1.380	24
27. Transport equipment	1.863	13	1.377	26
28. Scientific equipment	1.730	23	1.008	44
29. Photographic equipment	1.690	27	1.007	45
30. Watches	1.472	42	1.017	43
31. Toys	1.626	33	1.076	39
32. Jewelry	1.314	44	1.116	35
33. Other manufacturing	1.588	37	1.097	36
34. Utility	1.791	15	2.786	6
35. Construction	1.994	8	1.412	22
36. Trade (wholesale & retail)	**2.073**	**2**	**5.950**	**1**
37. Restaurants	**1.980**	**3**	**2.841**	**5**
38. Hotels	**1.960**	**5**	**1.488**	**17**
39. Transport/Communication	**1.719**	**24**	**4.565**	**2**
40. Finance	1.894	11	2.753	7
41. Real estate	1.733	22	2.988	4
42. Professional services	1.957	6	3.070	3
43. Government services	1.747	21	1.318	29
44. Human capital services	1.969	4	1.531	15
45. Recreation/Entertainment	**1.913**	**10**	**1.485**	**19**
46. Other services	**1.823**	**14**	**2.414**	**9**

Source: Heng, T.M., & Low, L. (1990), 257.

to be no less than in other economic sectors. A major reason is because tourism is also **capital-intensive**. The heavy costs of providing necessary infrastructure and building structures drastically increase the cost of creating jobs.

In the early stages of tourism development, the cost per job created is likely to be high due to the capital costs required. Similarly, the capital/output ratio is high because of the low volume of visitors in the initial stages of tourism development. As the destination country develops and as more visitors are attracted, the capital/output ratio declines. The cost per job created is reduced due to the experience and organization of those in the destination. In addition, as tourism increases, physical development takes place in facilities that require less investment than the construction of international-level hotels and resorts. Jobs are created at a lower average cost. In the third stage of tourism development, the average cost per job created may increase due to higher land prices and increased engineering costs because of the necessity of using sites that are more difficult to develop. In addition, as tourism increases in importance, more infrastructure (roads, electrical and sewage services, etc.) may be necessary as the tourism plant becomes more spread out geographically. The increased demand for infrastructure may be caused by the larger numbers of visitors in the destination area.

The cost per job created depends upon the type of facility constructed. The cost is greater for a luxury hotel than for a smaller, more modest property. However, a luxury hotel offers more job opportunities per room and higher employment/output ratios than smaller properties. The larger properties are more inclined to use imported labor especially for managerial positions. The key to maximizing the economic and job returns is to use materials and personnel indigenous

to the destination area while maintaining standards of quality acceptable to visitors.

Several additional criticisms of tourism as an employer have been made. Tourism is a highly seasonal business in many destination areas. To ensure a balance between market demand and staff requirements, tourism businesses tend to adopt one of two strategies. Employees are either laid off during the low season, or additional employees are imported from other regions during the high season. With the first approach, tourism cannot provide a meaningful job to a resident. With the second approach, there is an increased need for housing for employees who spend most of their wages outside of the destination area. Thus jobs and income are lost to the local area.

Because tourism relies so heavily upon people for delivering a service, productivity gains are difficult to come by. The national output may be difficult to improve if tourism becomes a dominant part of the economy, particularly if the host destination lacks a strong industrial sector, where productivity gains are easier to obtain.

Economic Development Considerations and Analysis

> "However, tourism is not necessarily desirable or feasible for every place. Each community should examine whether it has adequate resources for tourism and if there are potential tourist markets that can be attracted to the community, whether it needs tourism to reach economic development objectives, whether it has sufficient labor force to support tourism without bringing in migrant workers."
>
> McIntyre, G. (1993), 7

Apart from the three major types of economic impacts, destination areas need to consider the long-term economic development consequences of tourism. Issues that need to be analyzed are the attractiveness of tourism development versus other forms of economic development and the contributions of tourism to regional economic development.

Cost/Benefit Analysis

Cost/benefit analysis is a technique used to determine which economic sector produces the most benefit in terms of foreign exchange, employment, taxes, or income generated relative to the costs of development. The factors of production are valued at their **opportunity cost**; the marginal value of their next best use. It is then possible to compare several investment options. The social cost/benefit analysis of a project determines the average annual rate at which benefits accrue to society. Critics of cost/benefit analysis argue that the results are too dependent upon the appropriateness of its assumptions. It is not possible to check actual performance against prediction.

Structural Analysis

As growth occurs, long-term economic changes can be tracked through structural analysis. Three different processes must be studied:

1. Accumulation processes (investment, government revenue, education)
2. Resource allocation processes (structure of domestic demand, production and trade)
3. Demographic and distribution processes (labor allocation, urbanization, demographic transition, income distribution)

Recently, countries have tended to become primary or industrial specialists, have balanced production and trade, or have moved through the process of import substitution. Insufficient work has been done to determine the development pattern of a country's economy as it builds its tourism sector. Early work suggests that there is a danger of developing tourism at the expense of other exports such as agriculture. For maximum economic impact, care must be taken to achieve as much integration of tourism with the national economy as possible.

Satellite National Accounting

One of the traditional problems in analyzing the true economic impacts of tourism is that it is not considered to be an industrial sector of its own in national accounting systems. The Standard Industrial Classification (SIC) systems in many countries split tourism up into other industry sectors, e.g., airlines to transportation and restaurant sales to retailing. In 1993, the United Nations Statistics Division produced a publication called the *UN System of National Accounts* that recommended the creation of a *satellite accounting system* for complex service sectors such as tourism. The World Tourism Organization and the World Travel & Tourism Council (WTTC) support the concept of analyzing tourism through a satellite account for tourism. In essence, this means adding up the impacts of tourism that have traditionally been allocated to other economic sectors.

Tourism and Regional Development

Can tourism help regional development by producing income and jobs in areas previously lacking in economic development opportunities? Many people feel that this is a key role of tourism. However, tourism normally requires a heavy investment in infrastructure. This means that the cost of developing tourism in a rural or outlying area that needs economic development may be as great as for agriculture or manufacturing.

Modifying the Host Destination's Socioeconomic Structure

Tourism development can change the economic structure of a destination area. Although such changes can easily be integrated into the economy of a developed nation, the effects in a lesser-developed country are more profound. Stresses can occur when the old and the new exist side by side. Traditional methods of farming and primitive industries contrast with modern hotels and polished entertainment for visitors. This may cause a movement away from traditional forms of employment. The fisherman turned tour-boat entrepreneur and farm girl turned waitress undergo not only a change in income but a change in status. The fisherman's catch is lost to the local people, but his own income may increase. The waitress may view her task of serving as a throwback to earlier colonial times or may look at the newfound job as a cleaner and less arduous way to earn a living. The satisfaction for locals may depend upon the range and type of jobs available and the opportunity for advancement. The problem of seasonal employment is a major concern.

As with any other economic development, tourism encourages workforce migration, with the corresponding possibility of breaking down the traditional family unit. It does appear that, even though migration occurs, family ties and responsibilities are maintained.

Tourism development can cause profound changes within a society in terms of economic power. Tourism businesses attract women and young people who gain a higher level of economic independence. Great tension can occur, particularly in traditional societies, because of this shift in the economic resources within the host destination. It is not known whether such changes result in negative effects on families.

Finally, tourism can change the value and land ownership patterns. As tourism develops, the value of potential sites increases and land speculation happens. Some destination regions take steps to prevent unhealthy land speculation. Land sold to outsiders results in a short-term profit to the local landowner. However, the land may be lost forever to agricultural production or local recreational use, and control of the land goes out of the community. Tourism may force local indigenous people off of their traditional lands. Such has been the fate of the Masai tribes of Kenya and Tanzania. According to Krotz, "Tourism is the push that is chasing the Loita Masai, just as it is pushing indigenous local peoples in many places of the world" (Krotz, 1996).

Many impacts of tourism are direct, such as the raising of land values, while others are indirect (the demonstration effect when imports increase through local resident exposure to goods imported for visitor consumption). Many of these changes would occur no matter what type of economic development took place. Whether these changes are good or bad is often a value judgment. The important point is to realize that these impacts are likely to occur, decide whether or not they are desirable for the destination area, and plan accordingly.

Maximizing Tourism's Positive Economic Impacts

> "Tourism is New Zealand's largest foreign exchange earner and an above average contributor to total export earnings compared with other overseas countries. For the past three years, tourism has surpassed meat, wool, dairy products, forestry, and manufacturing as a source of foreign exchange earnings."
>
> Lim, E. (1991), 2

If a policy is adopted to maximize the positive economic impacts of tourism, the key is to maximize the foreign exchange earnings, income, and employment within the destination area. This means tourism development and marketing to bring in more money from visitors, and organizing tourism to minimize the leakage of both money and jobs. Tourism development is discussed in chapter 13 and tourism marketing is the focus of chapters 14–16.

Encouraging Import Substitution

One of the strategies for minimizing leakage from the destination's economy is import substitution. A major economic problem, especially for lesser-developed countries, is the lack of linkages from tourism to other sectors of the economy. Foreign exchange earnings can be increased if ties can be developed between tourism and primary, manufacturing, and other service businesses. The economic feasibility of local development can be investigated in industries ranging from handicrafts to furniture. The industries showing most promise can be supported through specific subsidies, grants, or loans. Also, quotas or tariffs can be placed on the importation of goods that can be developed locally. However, this strategy may invite retaliation from other countries or regions.

Implementing Incentive Programs

The use of local architecture, design, and materials can be encouraged through incentive programs. Financial and fiscal incentives may cause an inflow of capital, both local and foreign, necessary to develop the tourism destination mix. The types of incentives for tourism development are discussed in chapter 13. Unfortunately, incentives are often given on the basis of what the competition is offering rather than on what is best for the destination area. As a result, capital-intensive activities may be encouraged when, for many destinations, the problem is a surplus of labor. Several other difficulties can arise. The easy importation of materials may make it more difficult for local industries to develop. Destination areas have found that it is difficult to phase out tax concessions. Managers may lose interest in the project or let the quality standards run down as the tax holiday comes to a close. Care must be taken to ensure that the burden of risk is borne not only by the local government, but also by local or outside investors as well. Before implementing an incentive strategy a destination should:

1. Examine the performance of other countries' incentive programs in light of their resources and development objectives.
2. Research the actual needs of investors.
3. Design codes of investment concessions related to specific development objectives, with precise requirements of the investors (such as in terms of job creation).
4. Establish targets of achievement and periodically monitor and assess the level of realization of such targets.

Dealing with Multinational Tourism Companies

As tourism has developed, the opportunity has arisen for the global expansion of large tourism companies, particularly hotels, airlines, restaurants, travel agencies, and tour operators. These multinational companies (multinationals) have been criticized for operating to benefit their own profitability at the expense of destination areas.

Most multinational tourism companies have head offices located in the developed countries. A large proportion of the world's hotels are owned or affiliated with companies headquartered in the United States, France, and the United Kingdom. There is a trend toward more hotel ownership by Japanese and Hong Kong companies, especially in the Asia-Pacific region. Problems arise for the destination countries when the multinational corporations have no financial investment in the hotels. Many overseas chain hotel and resort properties are operated without any foreign equity involvement. The chains control is exercised through management contracts or franchise agreements.

It is possible that a foreign-owned hotel can engage in policies that run counter to the national tourism plan. The chances of this happening are lessened with a direct financial involvement of the overseas company. Likewise, the criticism that a specific type of international property is out of context with the host country must be viewed in the context of the target market. If a country has correctly identified the type of visitors it is seeking, it may seek a larger "international" facility. In general, however, multinational corporation hotels usually generate lower foreign exchange receipts than do local hotels, especially the smaller locally owned and managed properties. The criticism that foreign-owned properties import too much seems to be ill-founded.

However, there has been no clear evidence that the import content would have been less if the hotel had been developed by a local developer. Hotels seem to be willing to purchase food locally if prices are competitive and supplies are assured.

Another concern among host countries has been that a foreign-owned hotel allows limited opportunity for local employees to reach positions of responsibility. International hotel chains usually employ a core of expatriate managers. Some management contracts will stipulate that within, say, three to five years the management team must be made up of locals. It appears that foreign ownership of hotels is of greatest benefit to a country in the early stages of tourism development. At this point, the destination can really benefit from the foreign know-how. Maximization of benefits comes from direct financial involvement of the multinational business in the development of local managerial and supervisory talent.

Most countries in the world still have a national airline owned by the government. Visitors generally prefer to travel by an airline of their country of origin rather than by the airline of the destination country. Because of the perceptions of quality and safety, this is particularly true for travel to a lesser-developed country. Almost every charter airline is owned and operated by companies in developed countries. Although some countries do not allow charter aircraft to use their airports, the development of mass tourism often requires the development of charter traffic.

Tour operators can wield a great deal of influence over destinations. Operators have the ability to direct large numbers of visitors to particular destinations. If a country has made a decision to develop mass tourism—and has built the infrastructure and facilities to service these visitors—it must attract suf-

ficient numbers of visitors to use and pay for the facilities. In this situation, a country can become dependent on large tour operators who have the ability to influence where people vacation. In Europe and North America, a large percentage of the charter tour market is becoming controlled by a smaller number of tour companies. The larger foreign operator dealing with the mass market is more likely to bypass local inbound tour operators and deal directly with the local hotels and attractions. If hotel supply is greater than demand, accommodation operators may be forced to promise rooms at uneconomic rates or else face a total loss of business. If destination areas become totally dependent on foreign tour operators, they risk losing control of tourism development. Also, foreign exchange revenues may suffer. Destination areas benefit more from short-haul tourism than from long-haul. In addition, by dealing with operators who specialize in smaller but more specialized markets, there is more chance that local inbound operators will be used.

To maximize foreign exchange earnings, many countries have placed restrictions on spending. Countries have limited the amount of their own currency that visitors can bring into and take out to ensure that foreign currency is used to pay bills within the destination. Visitors may be required to pay hotel bills in foreign currency. Before being allowed into the country, visitors may have to show that they have enough money for their stay, or they may even be required to enter with a specified amount of foreign currency for each day of their visit. Foreign tour operators will often barter with operators of local facilities to avoid an exchange of cash. Destination countries may require that tour operators pay in foreign currencies for services in the host country. In other cases, tour operators may issue vouchers in the country of origin for services to be

provided at the destination. Some destination countries require that these vouchers be cashed by the service provider inside the host country.

Societal and Cultural Impacts

"What the marauding army of tourists primarily leave behind is a radically changed culture. Riding in the traveler's suitcases, Western, basically American culture—sporting its other self-appointed guise as world or global popular culture—intrudes everywhere. It is both cart and horse, in advance of and as a result of, tourism. In some ways, the culture precedes the tourists in order to welcome them, to make them feel at home."

Krotz, L. (1996), 195

Tourism involves the movement of, and contact between, people in different geographical locations. In sociological terms this means (Shankland Cox Partnership, 1974):

1. Social relations between people who would not normally meet

2. The confrontation of different cultures, ethnic and religious groups, values and lifestyles, languages, and levels of prosperity

3. The behavior of people released from many of the social and economic constraints of everyday life

4. The behavior of the host population, which has to reconcile economic gain and benefits with the costs of living with strangers

The degree to which conflict occurs between hosts and guests depends upon the similarity in their standards of living, the number of visitors, and the extent to which visitors adapt to local norms.

Quick Trip 9.4
Social and Cultural Impacts of Tourism in Turkey

Turkey has experienced considerable recent growth in tourism, especially through visitors from Western Europe. A study of tourism in Turkey suggested that the sudden exposure to foreign visitors in certain regions of the country had several social-cultural impacts. According to Cooper & Ozdil (1992), "Family homes were turned into pensions, Turkish women were threatened by the behavior of foreign female tourists, agriculture and farming were given up for tourist business, and the tourists who found Turkish products cheap were exploited." These authors also found that Turkey illustrates the classic example of the social and cultural impacts of tourism:

- Commercialization of contacts with locals such as being asked for money to take photographs, overpricing and double pricing.

- Stereotyping of female tourists.

- Changing lifestyles of local people as they exploit the opportunities that tourism provides in the short term. However, their overall economic and social standing may decline in the long term if they have, for example, sold their land.

- The replacement of Turkish words by foreign words and phrases.

- Demonstration of a tourist's wealth by clothing and language, which are increasingly copied by local people. This is leading to the breakdown of traditional Turkish customs and behavior. This has also led to sexual relationships and sometimes marriage between tourists and locals. A noticeable decline in morals in some resort areas where gambling, drugs, and prostitution is evident.

- Changes in material culture. For example, poor quality Turkish carpets are produced more quickly to keep up with demand, hence quality suffers. More importantly archaeological and historic sites are picked over by tourists for souvenirs, or by local people who sell the pieces to tourists. Yacht tourism is seen as a convenient way to "smuggle" these pieces out of Turkey.

Source: Cooper, C.P., & Ozdil, I. (1992).

The social and cultural impacts of tourism are both negative and positive. Figure 9.3 identifies some of the potential negative social and cultural impacts of tourism on a destination area.

One of the most recognized group of social problems is that caused by sex tourism. There has been a history of this type of tourism especially in certain countries of Southeast Asia. This trade in the human flesh has led to other problems including the spread of AIDS and child prostitution (Chon and Singh, 1994) in countries like Thailand. So great is the problem of child prostitution that the World Tourism Organization issued a policy statement in 1995, *The Statement on the Prevention of Organized Sex Tourism*, and a global organization known as ECPAT (End Child Prostitution and Trafficking) has been established.

Tourism also produces positive social and cultural impacts on a destination. If destination areas recognize that indigenous cultures attract visitors and serve as a unique factor in distinguishing them from other destinations, attempts may be made to keep culture and traditions alive. In some cases, traditional ways and goods may be restored because willing buyers (visitors) can be found. The Aaraya women of Cuna, Panama, had to be taught to sew the traditional dress of their culture. The skill had been lost. In London, England, many theaters can survive only because of the influx of visitors. In other areas, festivals are staged for visitors by the community—these festivals help to keep its culture alive. Thus, entertaining the visitor may be the impetus for the performing of cultural activities or the production of goods, but the effect on the local community is that of preserving part of the traditional culture.

However, again there are some potentially negative sides to this. First, a process of *cultural involution* can take place. The modernization of an area and a people can be halted because of visitor demand for the old ways. Tourism in essence can encourage local people to remain artisans at the expense of industrial modernization. Second, the authenticity of culture packaged for the visitor may be questionable. Many people feel that when a cultural event is prepared for visitor consumption, its original, often spiritual, meaning is lost. In the U.S., the moving of certain historic celebrations (Columbus Day, Washington's Birthday, and so on) to Mondays to give more three-day weekends throughout the year delighted many people in tourism. The purpose of the celebrations, however, was lost. In a smaller destination, such changes in festivals, foods, and traditional ways of life have a greater impact.

Tourism's effect on architecture has largely been to the detriment of

IMPACTS	POTENTIAL NEGATIVE IMPACTS
	• Damage to family structures and subsistence food production. • Displacement of local people to make way for airports, resorts, nature reserves, historical and other attraction sites, and other tourism development projects. • Encouragement of behaviors such as begging, touting, and other harassment of visitors.
Social	• Encouragement of urbanization and emigration. • Friction and resentment between local people and visitors because of overcrowding and lack of access for residents to recreational areas and facilities. • Increase in health risks through diseases such as AIDS, malaria, hepatitis, and influenza. • Increase in drug abuse and prostitution. • Open antagonism and crimes against visitors.
Cultural and Heritage	• Commercialization of traditional welcome and hospitality customs. • Loss of cultural authenticity (e.g., vulgarization of traditional crafts, importation of foreign cultural influences). • Overcrowding and damage to archaeological and historical sites and monuments.

Figure 9.3 Potentially Negative Social and Cultural Impacts of Tourism on a Destination Area.

local styles. Part of this pressure comes from visitor demands, part from the multinational companies who seek economies of scale in construction, and part from the host countries themselves who see the building of international-level hotels and resorts as a step toward modernity. A decision to build in the local style using materials indigenous to the area gives the region a different selling point while reducing economic leakage.

Tourism appears to act as a medium for social change (because of the contact between host and guest) rather than as the cause itself. The host/guest interaction offers the opportunity for each to learn more of the other, and as such, it can contribute to a greater understanding between peoples. Each destination area must weigh the social and cultural gains (e.g., revived local arts and crafts, theater, exposure to new ideas, etc.) against the potential losses (e.g., overcrowding, a cheapening of the culture, increases in crime, etc.).

Environmental Impacts

"Evidence shows widespread ecological damage attributable specifically to tourism-related activities. Water pollution, deforestation, the drainage of wetlands and interference with fragile mountain and marine ecosystems are among the many problem areas. . . . Even in sparsely inhabited developing countries, foreign travelers have left few paths untrodden. Mount Everest has been climbed from most conceivable angles, while French students can be found crossing Mongolia's desert on camels. From the Amazon to the highlands of New Guinea, anthropological research expeditions have been succeeded by National Geographic camera teams and intrepid back-packers, leading to ground-breaking media coverage and a tentative appearance in 'alternative' travel specialist's catalogues, the first formal step on the road to tourism development."

Doggart, C., & Doggart, N. (1996), 71–72

While tourism's economic impacts have been accepted for decades, it is only recently that the potential adverse environmental effects of tourism have been widely recognized. This has come at a time when much greater attention worldwide has been given to the environment and its conservation. There are now many cases around the world where tourism has been a direct contributor to environmental degradation. Often these negative impacts occur when the level of visitor use is greater than the environment's capacity to cope with this use (known as the **carrying capacity**). The types of negative environmental impacts that may be found are shown in figure 9.4 (Doggart & Doggart; 1996; McIntyre, 1993; Mathieson & Wall, 1982; Romeril, 1989).

There is considerable and growing evidence of these types of negative effects happening in different parts of the world. Researchers in the city of Sochi on Russia's Black Sea coast found that tourism was contributing to air and noise pollution in this resort area (Lukashina, Amirkhanov, Anisimov, & Trunev, 1996). Sewage pollution is a major problem for many older Mediterranean resort areas (Romeril, 1989). The increasing popularity of trekking in Nepal's Annapurna region is leading to pollution along the trekking trails and contributing to deforestation. The development of tourism is threatening the nesting sites of loggerhead turtles in Turkey and Greece (Doggart & Doggart, 1996).

While tourism is increasingly being criticized for its adverse environmental effects, it can have positive impacts on the local ecology. For example, greater protection of specific ecosystems may result to support tourism. This may mean that other harmful economic activities, such as commercial fishing around reef systems, logging operations in forests, excessive clearing and runoffs from agriculture, may be limited or eliminated. Some of

TYPES OF ENVIRONMENTAL IMPACTS	SPECIFIC IMPACTS
Changes of land use	● Changes in traditional land uses, loss of open space, displacement of local residents, deterioration in community character.
Congestion and air pollution	● Congestion of pedestrians and vehicles with vehicle transmissions (lead and carbon dioxide) causing air pollution.
Contribution to worldwide environmental problems	● Contribution to problems such as global warming through aircraft and other transportation emissions.
Deterioration and disturbance of the natural ecology	● Damage to land and marine flora and fauna, degradation of habitats on land and in the water, disturbance of biotic communities.
Deterioration of archaeological, historical, architectural, and natural sites	● Adverse impacts on sites through littering, vandalism, desecration, and souvenir taking.
Impacts of foot traffic	● Loss of vegetation and habitats through excessive trampling, permanent changes to man-made monuments and natural features (e.g., sand dunes, rocks, coral reefs).
Pollution of beaches, lakes, rivers, and underground water	● Pollution resulting from improper sewage and solid waste disposal.
Visual clutter	● Unsightly developments consisting of poorly designed, intrusive buildings and signs.
Insufficient utility services capacity	● Lack of infrastructure capacity during peak periods for water supply, power, telecommunications, and sewage disposal.

Figure 9.4   Types of Negative Environmental Impacts.

Tourism has led to the pollution of the Taj Mahal. Photo by Corel.

the visitor expenditures to enjoy natural environments may be reinvested in research and better conservation programs. A greater emphasis on the natural environment to support tourism may result in a greater understanding among local people of environmental issues.

Sustainable Tourism Development

> "In the end, sustainable models of development will only be worked out when local communities have control over their resources and are committed to preserving them. Such a pro-environmental ethic is contradicted by the profit-seeking, growth-mentality of neo-colonial entrepreneurs operating from outside the community."
>
> Kennedy, D. (1993), 4

The key to achieving an acceptable balance between the positive and negative impacts of tourism seems to be in adopting the principles of sustainable tourism development. According to the World Commission on Environment and Development (1987), sustainable development "meets the needs of the present without compromising the ability of future generations to meet their own needs." Chapter 13 reviews this concept in detail. The three main principles of sustainable tourism development are (McIntyre, 1993):

● **Ecological sustainability** ensures that tourism development is compatible with the maintenance of essential ecological processes, biological diversity, and biological resources.

● **Social and cultural sustainability** ensures that tourism development increases people's control over their lives, is compatible with the culture and values of people affected by it, and maintains and strengthens community identity.

- **Economic sustainability** ensures that tourism development is economically efficient and that resources are managed so that they support future generations.

The objectives of sustainable tourism are to improve the quality of life of the host community, provide a high quality experience for the visitor, and maintain the quality of the environment on which both the host community and the visitor depend (McIntyre, 1993).

Summary

Tourism can have significant and beneficial economic impacts on destination areas. The three major categories of economic impacts are increasing foreign exchange earnings, increasing income, and increasing employment. A variety of techniques can be used to measure tourism impacts including multipliers, input-output analysis, and cost-benefit analysis. Tourism development has modified the socioeconomic structures of many destination areas and affected societal and cultural values. These impacts have in many cases been negative, and tourism has been widely criticized for permanently altering the societies and cultures of some destinations. Tourism has been a major contributor to environmental degradation in many parts of the world.

This highlights the inherent conflict in the tourism system between economic development and societal, cultural, and environmental values. It is vitally important for those involved in tourism policy-setting and planning to recognize and give equal consideration to both the potential positive and negative effects of tourism. The principles of sustainable development must be followed. Above all, local people must play a key role in determining the future of tourism in their communities.

Quick Trip 9.5
Agenda 21 Priorities for Environmental Actions in Tourism

The World Tourism Organization (WTO), together with the World Travel & Tourism Council (WTTC) and the Earth Council, has outlined a series of environmental priorities for tourism in *Agenda 21 for the travel and tourism industry: Towards sustainable development.* This was based on the goals of Earth Summit held in Rio de Janeiro in 1992. The following are some of the priority actions recommended in *Agenda 21:*

Government Departments, National Tourism Administrations and Trade Organizations

- Assessing the capacity of existing regulatory, economic, and voluntary structures to achieve sustainable tourism.
- Assessing the economic, social, cultural, and environmental implications of the organization's operations.
- Training, education, and public awareness.
- Planning for sustainable tourism development.
- Facilitating exchange of information, skills, and technology relating to sustainable tourism between developed and developing countries.
- Providing for the participation of all sectors of society.
- Design of new tourism products with sustainability at their core.
- Measuring progress in achieving partnerships for sustainable development.

Tourism Companies

- Waste minimization, reuse and recycling.
- Energy efficiency, conservation and management.
- Management of freshwater resources.
- Waste water management.
- Hazardous substances.
- Transport.
- Land-use management and planning.
- Involving staff, customers, and communities in environmental issues.
- Design for sustainability.
- Partnerships for sustainable development.

Source: World Travel & Tourism Council. (1997).

Tourism may lead to greater environmental appreciation. Photo from *Top Shots* CD Rom. Courtesy of Queensland Tourist and Travel Corporation.

References

Archer, B.H. (1989). Tourism and island economies: Impact analyses. In C.P. Cooper (ed.). *Progress in tourism, recreation and hospitality management* (1st ed., pp. 125–134). London: Bellhaven Press.

Archer, B.H. (1995). The impact of international tourism on the economy of Bermuda. *Journal of Travel Research*, 34 (2), 27–30.

Archer, B.H., & Fletcher, J.E. (1990). Tourism: Its economic significance. In M. Quest (ed.), *Horwath book of tourism* (pp. 10–25). London: The MacMillan Press.

Cater, E. (1993). Ecotourism in the Third World: Problems for sustainable tourism development. *Tourism Management*, 14, 85–90.

Chon, K.S., & Singh, A. (1994). Environmental challenges and influences on tourism: The case of Thailand's tourism industry. In C.P. Cooper and A. Lockwood (eds.). *Progress in tourism, recreation and hospitality management* (6th ed., pp. 81–91). Chichester, England: Wiley.

Cleverdon, R. (1979) *The economic and social impact of international tourism on developing countries* E.I.U. Special Report No. 60. London: The Economist Intelligence Unit.

Cooper, C.P., & Ozdil, I. (1992). From mass to "responsible" tourism: The Turkish experience. *Tourism Management*, 13 (6), 377–386.

Crotts, J.C. (1996). Theoretical perspectives on tourist criminal victimisation. *Journal of Tourism Studies*, 7 (1), 2–9.

Department of Environmental Affairs and Tourism. (1996). *White paper: The development and promotion of tourism in South Africa*. Pretoria: Government of South Africa.

Doggart, C., & Doggart, N. (1996). Environmental impacts of tourism in developing countries. *Travel & Tourism Analyst* (2), 71–86.

Erbes, R. (1973). *International tourism and the economy of developing countries*. Paris: Organization for Economic Cooperation and Development.

Fielding, K.A., Pearce, P.L., & Hughes, K. (1992). Climbing Ayers Rock: Relating visitor motivation, time perception and enjoyment. *Journal of Tourism Studies*, 3 (2), 49–57.

Fletcher, J.E. (1989). Input-output analysis and tourism impact studies. *Annals of Tourism Research*, 16, 514–529.

Frechtling, D.C. (1994). Assessing the impacts of travel and tourism: Introduction to travel economic impact estimation. In J.R.B. Ritchie & C.R. Goeldner (eds.), *Travel, tourism, and hospitality research* (2nd ed., pp. 359–365). New York: John Wiley and Sons, Inc.

Frechtling, D.C. (1994). Assessing the impacts of travel and tourism: Measuring economic benefits. In J.R.B. Ritchie & C.R. Goeldner (eds.), *Travel, tourism, and hospitality research* (2nd ed., pp. 384–385). New York: John Wiley and Sons, Inc.

Glasson, J., Godfrey, K., & Goodey, B. (1995). *Towards visitor impact management.* Aldershot, England: Avebury.

Heng, T.M., & Low, L. (1990). Economic impact of tourism in Singapore. *Annals of Tourism Research,* 17, 246–269.

Hughes, H.L. (1994). Tourism multiplier studies: A more judicious approach. *Tourism Management,* 15, 403–406.

Hunter, C., & Green, H. (1995). *Tourism and the environment.* A sustainable relationship? London: Routledge.

Joppe, M. (1996). Sustainable community tourism development revisited. *Tourism Management,* 17, 475–479.

Kennedy, D. (1993). Tourism and the environment—What follows? *PATA Occasional Papers Series* (5), 1–9.

Krotz, L. (1996). *Tourists: How our fastest growing industry is changing the world.* Boston: Faber and Faber.

Laws, E. (1995). *Tourist destination management: Issues, analysis and policies.* London: Routledge.

Lim, E. (1991). New Zealand tourism and the economy. Wellington: New Zealand Tourism Department.

Lukashina, N.S., Amirkhanov, M.M., Anisimov, V.I., & Trunev, A. (1996) Tourism and environmental degradation in Sochi, Russia. *Annals of Tourism Research,* 23, 654–665.

Lundberg, D.E., Stavenga, M.H., & Krishnamoorthy, M. (1995). *Tourism economics.* New York: John Wiley & Sons, Inc.

McIntyre, G. (1993). *Sustainable tourism development: Guide for local planners.* Madrid: World Tourism Organization.

Manning, E.W., and Dougherty, T.D. (1995). Sustainable tourism: Preserving the golden goose. *Cornell Hotel and Restaurant Administration Quarterly,* 36 (2), 29–42.

Mathieson, A., & Wall, G. (1982). *Tourism: Economic, physical, and social impacts.* New York: Longman Scientific and Technical.

May, V. (1991). Tourism, environment and development: Values, sustainability and stewardship. *Tourism Management,* 12, 112–118.

Pearce, P.L., Moscardo, G., & Ross, G.F. (1996). *Tourism community relationships.* Trowbridge, England: Pergamon.

Romeril, M. (1989). Tourism: The environmental dimension. In C.P. Cooper (ed.). *Progress in tourism, recreation and hospitality management* (1st ed., pp. 103–113). London: Bellhaven Press.

Shankland Cox Partnership. (1974). *Tourism supply in the Caribbean: A study for the World Bank.* Washington, D.C.: The World Bank.

Smith, V.L. (1976). (ed.). *Hosts and guests: The anthropology of tourism.* Philadelphia: The University of Pennsylvania Press.

Teo, P. (1994). Assessing socio-cultural impacts: The case of Singapore. *Tourism Management,* 15, 126–136.

Thompson, C., O'Hare, G., & Evans, K. (1995). Tourism in The Gambia: Problems and proposals. *Tourism Management,* 16, 571–581.

Vellas, F., & Becherel, L. (1995). *International tourism.* New York: St. Martin's Press.

Wanhill, S. (1994). The measurement of tourist income multipliers. *Tourism Management,* 15, 281–283.

World Bank. (1979). Development in perspective: World Bank assessment. *Tourism International Air Letter.*

World Commission on Environment and Development. (1987). *Our common future.* Oxford: Oxford University Press.

World Tourism Organization. (1996). *Agenda 21 for the travel and tourism industry: Towards sustainable development.* Madrid: World Tourism Organization.

Surfing Solutions

http://www.ecouncil.ac.cr (The Earth Council, Costa Rica)
http://www.rb.se/ecpat/ (End Child Prostitution and Trafficking, Thailand)
http://www.oecd.org/ (Organization for Economic Cooperation and Development)
http://www.unep/unep.org/ (United Nations Environment Programme)
http://www.world-tourism.org/ (World Tourism Organization)
http://www.wttc.org/ (World Travel & Tourism Council)

Acronyms

ECPAT (End Child Prostitution and Trafficking)
NTO (national tourist office)
OECD (Organization for Economic Cooperation and Development)
TEIM (Travel Economic Impact Model)
UNEP (United Nations Environmental Programme)
WTO (World Tourism Organization)
WTTC (World Travel & Tourism Council)

> "The development of long-term policies, rather than short-term fixes, is essential to guarantee that tourism growth occurs in a socially, economically, and environmentally responsible manner."
>
> *Edgell, D.L. (1993), 56*

10

Tourism Policy and Organizations

···Government Involvement in Tourism ···············

Purpose

Having learned about government involvement in tourism and tourism policy, students will be able to explain the roles of tourism organizations operating at different geographic levels throughout the world.

Learning Objectives

Having read this chapter, you should be able to:

1. Identify the reasons for government involvement and the roles of government in tourism.

2. Describe the elements of a tourism policy model and how they are used to form a tourism policy for a destination.

3. Explain the roles of global tourism organizations, including the World Tourism Organization (WTO).

4. Explain the roles of multi-country regional organizations.

5. Explain the roles of national tourism organizations.

6. Explain the roles of state, provincial, and territorial government tourism organizations.

7. Explain the roles of regional and local tourism organizations.

Overview

A tourism policy is established to guide the development of tourism in a destination area. Because of the potential importance of tourism to the destination, government involvement is desirable for establishing and implementing tourism policies. This chapter examines the governmental frameworks at different levels within which tourism policy is established and implemented. The roles played by government agencies in tourism are reviewed and a model for establishing tourism policy is given.

Tourism policy is implemented through the efforts of many tourism organizations. The number of tourism organizations involved in tourism around the world has been expanding. The roles of global, multi-country, national, state, provincial, territorial, regional, and local tourism organizations are examined.

Japanese government policy on outbound tourism has benefitted tourism in Australia. Photo from *Top Shots* CD Rom. Courtesy of Queensland Tourist and Travel Corporation.

Reasons for Government Involvement in Tourism

> "In spite of its buccaneering, commercial image, the development of tourism in the U.K. owes a great deal to the activities of the public sector. Indeed, even today, its success is often marked where it is backed by constructive public/private sector partnership."
>
> Lingard, R. (1990), 230

There are several reasons why government agencies are involved in tourism. First, there are **political reasons**. Tourism involves travel across national boundaries. Governments must get involved with policies and procedures on the entry and exit of foreign travelers and nationals. The encouragement of tourism can be used for political purposes by furthering interna-

tional relations between two countries or as a way of enhancing the national and international image of a country. For example, Japan, embarrassed by its huge international trade surplus during the 1980s, initiated the *Japan Ten Million Programme* to encourage Japanese people to take trips to foreign countries. This policy is quite different from other countries that are concerned about their international travel deficits (the differences between what their residents spend abroad and what foreigners spend in their countries on travel) and balance of payments.

Second, there are **environmental reasons** for government involvement. Tourism is based on such things as the scenery, history, and cultural heritage of a destination. One of the dangers of tourism is, in making destinations more acceptable to foreign markets, the true nature of the natural, social, and cultural environments may be permanently damaged, altered, or lost. Therefore, among other things, governments must encourage adoption of the principles of sustainable tourism development.

Third, as discussed in chapter 9, there are **economic reasons** for government involvement in tourism. Tourism generates income, creates jobs, helps in economic diversification, complements certain local industries, is an export, and provides foreign exchange earnings. To enhance these economic advantages to the destination area, government agencies must get involved.

The extent of government involvement in tourism varies from country to country. The greater the importance that the government attaches to tourism, the greater is the involvement. For example, government involvement in tourism is much greater in The Bahamas, where visitor spending represents about 40 percent of the Gross Domestic Product (Bahamas Ministry of Tourism, 1997), than in the U.S., which has a much more diverse economy. The existing conditions in a country, including the political, economic, and constitutional system, also affect the type and amount of government involvement in tourism. For example, the level of involvement in socialist countries such as China and Vietnam is greater than in countries that are predominantly free-enterprise systems.

The level of economic development is another important factor determining the level of government involvement. The greater the economic development of a country, the less the need for government involvement. The maturity and financial capabilities of the private sector are important factors. The greater the capabilities of the private sector, the less is the need for government involvement. In the U.S., politicians have argued that tourism businesses are so highly developed, sophisticated, and resourceful that there is little need for the federal government to be involved in tourism development or marketing. This philosophy was clearly demonstrated through the closure of the U.S. Travel and Tourism Administration (USTTA) in 1996.

Government Roles in Tourism

> "*The globalization of markets, the supersegmentation of demand, system economies and the creation of integrated value in tourism activities, the available technologies, the demand for environmentally and socially sustainable initiatives, in short, the challenge of achieving competitiveness through quality and efficiency, require new contents and forms in public management.*"
>
> *Fayos-Sola, F. (1996). Tourism policy: A midsummer night's dream?, 405*

Tourism Coordination

Government agencies often play a coordinating function. Coordination is necessary among the many governmental bodies concerned with different aspects of tourism.

For example, immigration may decide to relax the frontier formalities to expedite the entry of visitors into the country. This helps tourism. The agency responsible for drug enforcement may be against this proposal, for fear that it will increase the flow of drugs, as well as visitors, into the country. Some kind of coordination is necessary. Coordination is also required among government agencies at the national, state, provincial, territorial, and local levels. To be truly effective, tourism within a country must be coordinated so that all regions are working toward the same tourism goals. For the same reason, coordination is necessary among the government, the private sector, and nonprofit organizations. Many educational and cultural organizations, although they do not have tourism as a core focus, provide resources that attract visitors. The private sector is very involved in tourism. To avoid duplication of effort, it is vital that goals and strategies be coordinated. The overall responsibility for tourism needs to be assigned to a specific agency dedicated to tourism.

Tourism Policy-Setting and Tourism Planning

Government agencies are involved in developing tourism policies and plans. Among other things, these policies and plans indicate the sectors of tourism to be developed, the appropriate rates of growth, sustainable tourism development procedures, and the sources of capital needed for expansion. The key is to balance the development of supply (attractions, facilities, transportation, infrastructure, and human resources) and the promotion of demand (the number of visitors) while maintaining the principles of sustainable tourism development. Government's tourism planning role is explained in chapter 12.

Tourism Legislation and Regulation

An important role of government is as a legislator and regulator. Government legislation can affect the number of paid vacation days during the year and hence the amount of discretionary paid time available for vacations. Policies on passports

People flock to places that have beautiful and dramatic scenery, such as Death Valley, California. Photo courtesy of California Division of Tourism: Robert Holmes.

and visas also directly affect tourism. Visitors are required to have official visas when traveling to several countries. Government influence may also be felt through regulations on operating a tourism business. In some countries, tour operators, travel agents, and guides must be licensed. Businesses have safety and health regulations to abide by; they also have to meet zoning, building, and licensing requirements. The need to protect the environment and other resources that attract visitors may result in restrictions regarding the use of fragile natural resources. Visitors are no longer allowed to enter certain European monuments, and park systems often have certain areas set aside as wilderness where use is severely limited. This role is fully reviewed in chapter 11.

Tourism Infrastructure Development

Governments are expected to provide the infrastructure and transportation facilities (roads, airport

Typically, governments own and operate landmark sites. Shown here is the Lincoln Memorial. Photo by Corel.

facilities, sewage disposal, electricity, water, and other essential services) for tourism development in destination areas. These services are crucial to tourism developments and cannot be provided by private developers without government assistance.

Tourism Operations

Many governments are involved through the ownership and operation of certain attractions, facilities, and services. Typically, this involvement is limited to national and state park systems, historic and government sites, monuments, and buildings. Many countries still operate state-owned airlines, but there is a definite trend toward the privatization of national carriers. Governments own and operate chains of hotels in India, Greece, Spain, and Portugal. Government ownership and operation of hotels and resorts is not very prevalent in the developed countries. An exception to this rule is found within certain national, state, and provincial parks in the U.S. and Canada. Governments also may act as inbound tour operators such as in China.

Tourism Development Stimulation and Control

Governments stimulate tourism development in different ways. Government agencies identify tourism project development opportunities and seek developers for these projects. Financial and fiscal incentives, such as low-interest loans or non-payment of taxes for a specified period of time, are offered to induce private-sector investment in tourism. Governments must also introduce and enforce development controls to ensure that the environment is not harmed and that all other procedures and codes have been followed. This role is discussed in detail in chapter 13.

Tourism Marketing and Research

Governments sponsor research that benefits all tourism organizations and businesses. For example, research may be conducted on the characteristics of a particular foreign market. The results are made available to tourism businesses that develop plans to attract this market. Governments stimulate tourism by spending money on marketing. The marketing covers the entire country, state, province, or territory. It usually consists of travel promotion aimed at generating visitor demand. In some cases, it may also involve investment promotion aimed at encouraging capital investment for tourism attractions and facilities. The marketing role of government is highlighted in chapters 14–16.

Tourism Training and Education

Another important role played of government agencies is the provision of training and education programs for tourism. Some programs focus on training at the skill levels and this includes the many national governments that operate their own hotel and restaurant training schools, including Bahrain and Sri Lanka. Other agencies, including the CERT, The State Tourism Training Agency in Ireland, assist with the development of training programs (courses, seminars, workshops) and materials (books, manuals, guides, audio and videotapes, CD-ROMs, World Wide Web sites) for management. Some governments are concerned with the establishment of minimum standards or competencies that tourism employees must meet. In addition, several governments operate training programs for retail travel agents.

Governments' operational role is usually limited to the operation of parks: Brown County State Park, Indiana. Photo courtesy of Brown County Convention & Visitors Bureau, Nashville, Indiana.

that tourism is a form of recreation involving overnight travel or travel a certain distance away from home. In addition, both visitors and residents often share the same recreational facilities.

Tourism goals must complement broader economic, social, cultural, and environmental needs of the destination area. They must support broad national or regional interests. Against the backdrop of these national interests, tourism goals can be developed in six categories: economic, government operations, human resources development, market (demand) development, resource protection and conservation, and social and cultural. Typical tourism goals are shown in figure 10.2.

Tourism Policy Formulation

> *"It has been said that there are two things one should never watch being made, sausage and public policy. That may be good advice from an aesthetic point of view, but when it comes to tourism policy, not watching is a luxury we cannot afford."*
>
> *Richter, L.K. (1993), 179*

Whether governments like it or not, they need to become involved in tourism. To guide the government's own programs, along with the actions of private and nonprofit organizations, it is essential that a top priority becomes the establishment of a tourism policy. A statement of tourism policy provides a set of guidelines for all those directly and indirectly involved in tourism by specifying the broad goals and objectives, priorities, and actions that provide the basis for the future development of tourism. Despite this need to establish a tourism policy as a precursor for

future tourism planning and development, many government agencies have yet to develop tourism policy statements (Baum, 1994a).

The model presented in figure 10.1 illustrates the process by which a tourism policy is formulated. The many needs of a destination, such as creating employment, economic diversification, and resource protection and conservation, are identified by using research techniques. Tourism goals reflect these overall needs, but they are constrained by the existing market and resource factors. A series of strategies and programs flows from the overall policy aimed at achieving the tourism goals and satisfying needs.

Destination Area Needs and Tourism Goals

Goals for tourism have to be set before policy statements can be developed. In so doing, it is crucial that these tourism goals not be set in isolation. For example, there is a very close link between tourism and recreation. It can be argued

Constraints

Before more specific objectives can be developed for the six categories of goals, it is necessary to consider certain constraints to tourism. These constraints are external and internal to the destination area.

External constraints are those outside the direct control of the destination, while internal constraints can be influenced by the tourism policy. Because the volume of demand for travel is closely related to levels of disposable income, policy is constrained by general economic conditions in the visitor-generating countries. A stagnant economic situation suggests that a destination should plan for limited growth and a policy of improved quality rather than quantity of resources.

Policy is also constrained by the world energy situation. The price and supply of oil affect destination regions that rely upon automobile visitors. The overall effect of an increase in the price of gas or uncertainty over gasoline supplies may be a reduction in the number of auto-based visitors, a redistribution of visitors to more accessible areas, and a more center-based va-

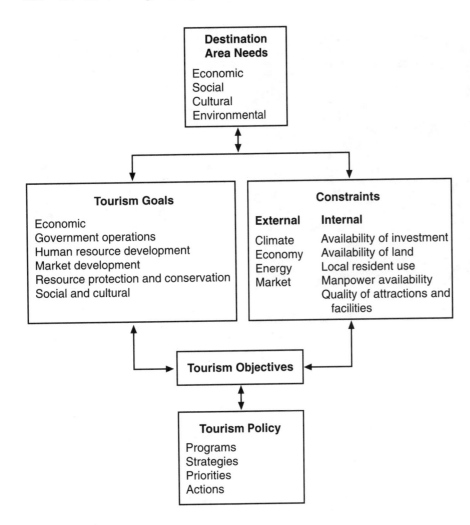

Figure 10.1 Tourism Model Policy.

Adapted from: Matthews, H.G. (1978). *International tourism: A political and social analysis.* Cambridge, Massachusetts: Schenkman Publishing Company; Scottish Tourist Board. (1975). *Planning for tourism in Scotland: Preliminary national strategy.* Edinburgh: Scottish Tourist Board; U.S. Senate. (1978). *National tourism policy study: Ascertainment phase.* Washington, DC: Committee on Commerce, Science and Transportation.

lished. The quality of attractions and available facilities limits the type of visitors that can be attracted. For example, visitors from developed countries are accustomed to private bathrooms in hotels. If these are lacking, a policy implication may be to provide financial incentives for modernization by building more rooms with private bathrooms. Facilities that have been built without private bathrooms may not be eligible for such aid.

Tourism policy cannot be separated from recreation and leisure policy. The use of attractions and facilities by local residents has to be considered as a possible constraint to tourism policy. In urban areas it may be that only a small portion of the recreational capacity will be available for visitors, particularly on weekends. However, some cultural and recreational facilities may be available to the local community only because of the support from visitor demand. The extensive theater facilities in London are a prime example. Many of these theaters rely upon visitor traffic to make them commercially viable. If this demand was not present, many theaters would be forced to close and this resource would be lost to the local population.

The availability of land and investment capital is also of concern to destination areas. In smaller countries and regions such as Singapore and the island of Tobago, difficult decisions must be made regarding appropriate land uses. In both Canada and the U.S., considerable controversy has arisen over the proposed uses of public land for parks or other wilderness or recreational uses. The scarcity of investment capital raises particular problems for many destination countries, especially the lesser-developed nations. The lack of money for investment can hold back tourism development, but the attraction of foreign capital may result in a loss of local control and leakages from the economy. This problem is

cation than a touring one. This has important policy implications for the development of facilities and the encouragement of public transportation.

The potential of various travel market segments also influences policy. For example, the best potential for increased travel to certain parts of the Caribbean is from Europe because of its increased affluence and shorter-duration air trips. This suggests that Caribbean nations develop policies encouraging more European flights to their countries.

Climatic factors constrain the types of tourism that can be developed. For example, the climate of Scotland is regarded unfavorably by many people in Britain. To a certain extent the image is not totally justified and may be remedied by promoting the seasons when the climate is conducive to holiday-making. If poor weather limits vacation activities, the implication for policy makers is to develop more wet-weather facilities.

Internal constraints influence tourism policy, but can be modified by the tourism policy that is estab-

felt not only by countries but also by local areas within a country that seek financing from domestic sources of capital. Decisions to expand, contract, build, or close are made by executives outside the community.

The availability of human resources constrains tourism policy. Tourism is a people business. The characteristics of tourism create unique employment problems. Tourism jobs are often seasonal, part-time, or low-paying. In order to deal with the public from another social class and culture, it may be necessary to learn different behaviors or different ways of serving food than those used in homes in the host country. In some cases, foreign hotel companies, before opening overseas properties, have to support the development of schools for training local employees in methods of serving their nationals.

Tourism Objectives

After considering the external and internal constraints, more specific tourism objectives are articulated. At this point, it is not unusual to find that conflicts arise between goals or within goals. For example, should casino gaming be encouraged? To do so may be consistent with tourism's economic goals, but may conflict with a country's social or cultural goals, or religious beliefs. In setting its tourism policy in 1988, the government of Trinidad and Tobago stated that it "will not permit the establishment of gambling casinos and/or any similar activities that are likely to have undesirable consequences for the society" (Trinidad & Tobago Tourism Development Authority, 1988). Although the government recognized the earning potential of casinos, the potential social costs were considered too great.

Conflicts can also arise within goals. For example, encouraging more foreigners to go to existing visitor ports of entry may help to improve the international balance of payments thus helping achieve part of an economic goal. However, this may not be compatible with another economic goal of maximizing regional economic development. Only when local residents weigh what is best for their community and what meets their needs, are such conflicts solved in the best interests of the community.

Tourism Policy

The tourism objectives, carefully formulated to complement the tourism goals, constitute the main element of the tourism policy for a destination area. Edgell (1990a) has developed a Model National Tourism Policy, which contains the following components:

- Encourage the orderly, fair, and reasonable development of tourism resources.
- Ensure the availability of public tourism training, to increase the skills and productivity of the labor tourism force and to broaden access to employment opportunities in tourism.
- Encourage the modernization and competitiveness of the accommodation sector.

FACTORS	GOALS
Economic	● To optimize the contribution of tourism to economic prosperity, full employment, regional economic development, and improved international balance of payments.
Government Operations	● To harmonize to the maximum extent possible all government activities supporting tourism; to support the needs of the general public and the public and private sectors of industries involved with tourism; to take a leadership role with all those concerned with tourism.
Human Resource Development	● To ensure that tourism has an adequate supply of professionally trained skilled and managerial staff to meet its future needs. ● To ensure that the education and training programs and materials are available to meet the needs of tourism.
Market Development	● To encourage the free and welcome entry of foreigners, while balancing this goal with the need to monitor persons and goods entering the country with laws protecting public health.
Resource Protection and Conservation	● To protect and preserve the historical and cultural foundations as a living part of community life and development, and to ensure future generations an opportunity to enjoy the rich heritage of the area. ● To ensure the compatibility of tourism policies with other broader interests in energy development and conservation, environmental protection, and judicious use of natural resources. ● To contribute to the personal growth and education of the population and encourage their appreciation of the geography, history, and ethnic diversity. ● To avoid the encouragement of activities that have the potential of undermining or denigrating the social and cultural values and resources of the area and its traditions and lifestyles. ● To make the opportunity for and the benefits of travel universally accessible to residents and visitors.

Figure 10.2 Tourism Policy Goals.

Adapted from U.S. Senate. (1977). *National tourism policy study: Ascertainment phase.*

An attraction such as a casino must not only fit an area's economic goals, but also must not conflict with social beliefs. Photo from *Top Shots* CD Rom. Courtesy of Queensland Tourist and Travel Corporation.

- Maximize the "income effects" of international tourism by encouraging, and taking, steps to reduce foreign exchange leakage.

- Ensure the availability of reliable, convenient transport services between the host country and the main tourism-generating countries and between the host country and other countries in its region.

- Expand off-season tourism and thereby increase the productivity of the accommodation sector and reduce layoffs within tourism and tourism-related enterprises.

- Facilitate the entry and exit of visitors at all ports of arrival by simplifying and expediting passenger inspection procedures.

- Encourage the development of industries that supply goods and services to hotels.

- Establish tax incentives to attract investment in tourism-related enterprises such as hotels, sightseeing services, marinas, car rental firms, and airlines.

- Identify national goals to which tourism can contribute.

- Identify tourism objectives to which other economic sectors can contribute.

- Ensure that all government departments contribute to tourism development.

- Develop a periodic tourism master plan to guide government agencies in the implementation of the national tourism policy.

- Create a better understanding among the nation's residents and civil servants of the importance of tourism to the nation's economy; and foster a spirit of hospitality and friendliness toward visitors.

- Promote tourism in a manner that fosters visitors' understanding and respect for the religious beliefs, customs, and ethnic traditions of the nation's residents.

- Monitor visitor impact on the basic human rights of the nation's residents and ensure equal access by visitors and residents to public recreational resources.

- Ensure the protection of wildlife and natural resources and the preservation of geological,

archaeological, and cultural treasures in tourism areas.

- Encourage, assist, and coordinate, where possible, the tourism activities of local and area promotional organizations.

- Ensure that the national tourism interest is fully considered by public agencies and the national government in their deliberations; and harmonize, to the maximum extent possible, all national activities in support of tourism with the needs of the general public, the political subdivisions of the nation, and tourism businesses.

Tourism Strategies and Programs

Having established the tourism policy, government officials and others involved in tourism can begin the task of developing tourism strategies, plans, programs, and perhaps also the required legislation and regulations, to achieve the policy's stated objectives. Chapter 11 considers the legislation and regulations required to support tourism and other policy areas. Chapter 12 examines how the tourism planning process results in programs and actions to support policy goals and objectives. Examples of such programs include establishing specific government financial incentives for tourism development, setting immigration rules, and developing tourism marketing programs targeting specific market segments.

Tourism Organizations

"In taking a holiday, tourists, knowingly or unconsciously, are likely to come in contact with organizations and organizational activities at each stage of their trip."

Pearce, D. (1992), 1

There is an enormous and ever-expanding group of tourism organizations around the world that either set tourism policies or try to influence them. One way of classifying these organizations is by their geographical scope. The following are the major geographical groupings of tourism organizations:

- Global organizations
- Multi-country regional organizations
- National tourism organizations
- State, provincial, and territorial tourism organizations
- Regional tourism organizations
- Local tourism organizations

Global Organizations

The first group is global in scope. Some of these organizations are primarily involved with tourism-related matters including the World Tourism Organization, International Civil Aviation Organization, and the World Travel & Tourism Council.

World Tourism Organization (WTO), Madrid, Spain   The only organization that represents governmental interests on a worldwide basis is the World Tourism Organization (WTO). The forerunners to WTO were the International Congress of Official Tourist Traffic Associations (ICOTTA) set up at The Hague (Netherlands) in 1925 and the International Union of Official Travel Organizations (IUOTO) which was established in 1947. ICOTTA and IUOTO were created to promote tourism for the economic, social, and cultural advancement of all nations. WTO, an intergovernmental organization in tourism, was approved by IUOTO members in 1970 and was officially launched in January 1975. Based in Madrid since 1976, the role of WTO is officially recognized by the General Assembly of the United Nations and represents the UN's

main instrument for the development of tourism. The mission of WTO is "to develop tourism as a significant means of fostering international peace, economic development, and international trade." WTO's six main areas of activity are (World Tourism Organization, 1997):

- **Communications and documentation:** WTO's Communications Department acts as a publishing and press contact point for the Organization. WTO's Documentation Center houses a wide range of tourism research and information sources.

- **Cooperation for development:** WTO provides advice and assistance to governments on a wide range of tourism issues including master plans and feasibility studies, investment needs and technology transfer to marketing and promotion.

- **Education and training:** WTO offers a strategic framework for the organization of tourism education and training including courses on educating educators, short-term and distance-learning courses, and a growing network of WTO Education and Training Centers.

- **Environment and planning:** WTO is working for sustainable tourism development and the translation of environmental concerns into practical measures. WTO participates in forums such as the Earth Summit in Rio de Janeiro and the Globe seminars in Canada.

- **Quality of tourism services:** Liberalization, health, and safety reflect the broad and interconnected range of issues related to improving the quality of tourism services. WTO is working toward the removal of barriers to tourism and is encouraging the liberalization of trade in tourism services.

- **Statistics and market research:** WTO collects, analyzes, and disseminates tourism data from over 180 countries and territories. WTO continuously monitors and analyzes trends around the world. A comprehensive series of publications is produced for WTO members and others involved in tourism.

A National Tourism Policy should, among other things, protect the country's wildlife and natural resources. Photo from *Top Shots* CD Rom. Courtesy of Queensland Tourist and Travel Corporation.

The WTO is also recognized as the executing agency for the United Nations Development Programme (UNDP). Each year, WTO receives funds from UNDP to carry out missions within developing countries that identify tourism development projects. About 30 of these missions are conducted each year in developing countries. If projects result from these missions, WTO implements them using funds allocated by UNDP to the developing country.

WTO helps to encourage the adoption of measures that make travel between countries easier through the reduction and simplification of frontier formalities (e.g., passport and visa requirements) and the removal of other barriers to the free movement of travelers. Collectively, this is known as the *liberalization of travel* or travel *facilitation*. WTO also plays a major role in tourism education and training including offering correspondence courses and short-term training programs throughout the world. Other types of assistance are provided to the national tourism administrations (NTAs) or national tourist offices (NTOs) of member countries including technical cooperation and the organization of international conferences, seminars, congresses, and technical meetings on various aspects of tourism. WTO works toward the preparation of draft international agreements on tourism and their eventual implementation. Three important past agreements include the *Tourism Bill of Rights and Tourist Code* (Sofia, Bulgaria, September 1985), the *Manila Declaration on World Tourism* (Manila, Philippines, September 1980), and the *Acapulco Document* (Acapulco, Mexico, August 1982).

Another important WTO function is the collection of information and issuing of publications on travel statistics and trends. It represents a "world clearing house" for all available information including statistical data on international and domestic tourism, legislation and regulation, facilities and special events. Some of its regular publications include the *Compendium of Tourism Statistics, Global Tourism Forecasts to the Year 2000 and Beyond, Tourism Market Trends, Travel and Tourism Barometer, and Yearbook of Tourism Statistics*. WTO also publishes several special books and manuals on tourism development, education and training, financing, guidelines on collecting tourism statistics, marketing, aviation, and quality. Its statistics can be accessed online via the World Wide Web at the World Tourism Organization Information Center (http://www.world-tourism.org/). Among the publications available is the *Blue Flag Manual* describing the European campaign of designating beaches as Blue Flag beaches if they meet criteria on water quality, cleanliness, and safety.

There are several groups within WTO that are responsible for its policies and programs. The WTO Secretariat consists of the Secretary General of WTO and the full-time WTO staff (about 85 people) located in Madrid. The General Assembly, held every two years, brings together all members to consider WTO's policies and programs. The General Assembly has created six Regional Commissions for Africa, Americas, Europe, Middle East, Pacific and East Asia, and South Asia who oversee the implementation of WTO programs in their respective regions. The third WTO body is the Executive Council, consisting of around 25 members. The Executive Council meets twice a year to take whatever measures are necessary to implement the decisions and recommendations of the previous General Assembly.

Although its members include many developed countries, such as France, Germany, Italy, and Japan, WTO places "particular attention on the interests of the developing countries." WTO has three membership categories: full, associate, and affiliate members. In 1997, WTO had 133 members countries and four associate members (Aruba, Macau, Madeira, and Netherlands Antilles). WTO had 300 affiliate members, which included international and regional tourism bodies, such as the Pacific Asia Travel Organization (PATA) and Caribbean Tourism Organization (CTO), and private sector tourism companies, associations, and educational institutions.

There are other United Nations' agencies that have roles which affect tourism. These include the International Labour Organization (ILO) based in Geneva, Switzerland, UN Environment Programme (UNEP), and the UN Conference on Trade and Development (UNCTAD). ILO has a Hotel and Tourism unit within its Enterprise & Cooperative Development Department that organizes training and education programs in developing countries. The World Bank (International Bank for Reconstruction and Development), International Finance Corporation, International Monetary Fund, and the Multilateral Investment Guarantee Agency are other agencies that provide assistance to tourism development on a worldwide basis.

International Civil Aviation Organization (ICAO), Montreal, Canada   The International Civil Aviation Organization (ICAO) was established in December 1944 through *The Convention on International Civil Aviation* (also known as the Chicago Convention). ICAO is made up of representatives from the governments of 183 Contracting States. The principal task of the ICAO is to promote worldwide civil aviation. The basic objective of ICAO is the development of safe, regular, efficient, and economical air transport. The main activities of ICAO are (ICAO Website, 1997):

- **CNS/ATM:** Meaning communications, navigation, surveillance, and air traffic management, ICAO has spearheaded the development of a satellite-based system.
- **Facilitation:** ICAO tries to persuade Contracting States to reduce the "red tape" associated with the entry of passengers and cargo (e.g., customs, immigration, public health, and other entry formalities).
- **Economics:** ICAO publishes comprehensive world aviation statistical data and undertakes extensive economic studies.
- **Law:** ICAO facilitates the adoption of international air law instruments and promotes their general acceptance among the Contracting States.
- **Regional planning:** ICAO helps develop regional Air Navigation Plans for air transport in seven regions of the world.
- **Standardization:** One of ICAO's chief activities, this involves the development of international standards, recommended practices, and procedures covering the technical fields of aviation (licensing of personnel, rules of the air, aeronautical engineering, aeronautical charts, units of measurements, operation of aircraft, nationality and registration marks, airworthiness, aeronautical telecommunications, air traffic services, search and rescue, accident investigation, airports, aeronautical information services, aircraft noise and engine emissions, security, and the safe transport of dangerous goods).
- **Strategic action plan:** In 1992, the ICAO Assembly approved a Strategic Action Plan for the priority activities of ICAO into the twenty-first century.

- **Technical cooperation for development:** ICAO provides technical assistance, giving special attention to promoting civil aviation in developing countries. This work has been directed toward the development of ground services, airports, air traffic control, communications, and meteorological services.

ICAO is governed by a council composed of 33 Contracting States. An assembly of all Contracting States is held once every three years. The secretariat, consisting of ICAO's full-time staff, works in its Montreal headquarters.

Two other important groups in air transportation worldwide are the International Air Transport Association (IATA) with headquarters in Montreal and the Air Transport Action Group (ATAG) based in Geneva, Switzerland. IATA is a global association of airlines with a mission "to represent and serve the airline industry" and the goal "to promote safe, reliable, and secure air services" (IATA, 1997).

ATAG's function is to press for aviation infrastructure improvements on a worldwide basis to relieve the current congestion at airports and in the skies. It actively supports the expansion and development of air traffic control capabilities, airport capacity, and surface access (ATAG, 1997). ATAG was created in 1990 and is funded by IATA, Airbus Industrie, and Boeing. It has over 80 member organizations from airlines, airports, and many other parts of tourism. ATAG produces a variety of publications including air traffic forecasts and special reports such as *The Economic Benefits of Air Transport and Air Transport and the Environment.*

World Travel & Tourism Council, London, England

The World Travel & Tourism Council (WTTC) is a private-sector,

membership organization that brings together approximately 90 chief executive officers of companies from all parts of tourism. With a head office in London, WTTC produces statistics on the economic impact of tourism worldwide and attempts to focus more attention on the substantial economic contributions of tourism. These statistics are published in its *WTTC Travel & Tourism Research Report.* WTTC also maintains *The WTTC Jobs Clock* on its World Wide Web site that provides an up-to-date tally of the number of jobs created by tourism around the world.

WTTC has other programs related to taxation, environmental issues, and human resources development. In 1993, it established the WTTC Taxation Policy Centre (WTTTPC) at Michigan State University in the U.S. The objective of WTTTPC is to conduct international fiscal policy research in travel and tourism. As part of its activities, WTTTPC produces the *WTTC Tax Barometer* which reports on car, lodging, meal, and air taxes in over 50 major cities around the world.

Green Globe and ECoNETT are two WTTC programs related to the environment. *Green Globe* is an environmental management and awareness program with the objective of providing ways for tourism businesses to improve their environmental practices. The European Community Network for Environmental Travel & Tourism (ECoNETT) was established in 1996 in conjunction with the European Commission. It is a database service on environmental travel and tourism.

The World Travel & Tourism Human Resource Center (WTTHRC) was established in 1994 in Vancouver, Canada. Its main purpose is to provide human resource information to tourism. WTTHRC provides consulting services and advice on training tools and occupational standards in tourism.

Multi-Country Regional Organizations

There are an increasing number of organizations that represent groupings of countries interested in tourism. Some of these are primarily governmental organizations and others are composed mainly of private-sector members. As the trend toward **regionalization** continues into the twenty-first century, the number of these types of organizations will grow. There are two subgroups of these organizations: organizations where tourism is just one part of a broader mandate (e.g., OECD) and organizations that specifically address tourism (e.g., PATA).

Organization for Economic Cooperation and Development, Paris, France

The Organization for Economic Cooperation and Development (OECD) was created for reasons of general economic growth and stability. It is a "unique forum permitting governments of the industrialized democracies to study and formulate the best policies possible in all economic and social spheres." The purpose of OECD is "to boost prosperity by helping to knit a web of compatible policies and practices across countries that are part of an ever more globalized world" (OECD, 1997). OECD does this by reviewing and analyzing every element that affects social policy. Its departments and directorates include: 1) Agriculture; 2) Development; 3) Economics; 4) Education, Employment and Social Policies; 5) Energy; 6) Enterprises, Financial, and Fiscal Matters; 7) Environment; 8) Science, Technology, Industry; 9) Public Management; 10) Statistics; 11) Territorial Development of Regions, Cities, and the Countryside; and 12) Trade.

Founded in 1961, OECD currently has 29 member countries, which include among others Australia, Canada, France, Germany,

---

> ### Quick Trip 10.1
> # WTTC'S Millennium Vision
>
> The World Travel & Tourism Council has developed four priorities for government and industry partnerships over the next ten years. These are identified in its Millennium Vision:
>
> 1. **Make travel and tourism a strategic economic development and employment priority:**
>   - Recognize tourism's economic contribution and include it in mainstream programs for job creation, export promotion, and investment stimulation.
>   - Establish national satellite accounts for travel and tourism.
> 2. **Move toward open and competitive markets:**
>   - Implement the *General Agreement on Trade in Services* (GATS), liberalize air transport, and deregulate telecommunications.
>   - Enhance promotion of travel and tourism and encourage product quality improvements for international competitiveness.
> 3. **Pursue sustainable development:**
>   - Establish a policy framework for sustainability based on *Agenda 21*.
>   - Encourage industry environmental initiatives such as the *Green Globe* program.
> 4. **Eliminate barriers to growth:**
>   - Expand and modernize infrastructure, particularly airports, air traffic control systems, and "FAST" border clearance (FAST is an automated entry system).
>   - Tax intelligently for growth and exports.
>   - Invest in human resource development.
>
> Source: World Travel & Tourism Council. (1997). http://www.wttc.org/

Ireland, New Zealand, United Kingdom, U.S., and the Scandinavian countries. Within OECD, a Tourism Committee was established to promote action to maximize the benefits of tourism to the economies of OECD member countries. This is accomplished by:

- Fostering international cooperation in tourism.
- Increasing understanding of the economic importance of tourism.
- Promoting the liberalization of policies toward international tourism flows.
- Providing a forum for dissemination, analysis, and benchmarking of the tourism policies

and administration of member countries against comparable economies.

OECD publishes an annual report on tourism policy, and an annual summary on tourism trends in OECD member countries. Its principal tourism publication is *Tourism Policy and International Tourism in OECD Countries*. It also develops measurements of the economic importance of tourism in OECD countries.

Organization of American States, Washington, D.C.

The Organization of American States (OAS) is a regional organization covering all of the Americas that provides a forum for dialogue on political, economic, and social issues. The Charter of OAS was signed in 1948 by the United States and 20 Latin American countries. The purposes of the OAS are (OAS Website, 1997):

- To strengthen the peace and security of the continent.

- To promote and consolidate representative democracy, with due respect for the principle of non-intervention.

- To prevent possible causes of difficulties and to ensure the pacific settlement of disputes that may arise among the member states.

- To provide for common action on the part of those states in the event of aggression.

- To seek the solution of political, judicial, and economic problems that may arise among them.

- To promote, by cooperative action, their economic, social, and cultural development.

- To achieve an effective limitation of conventional weapons.

OAS has 35 member states and has granted permanent observer status to the European Union and 37 other countries. The OAS plays an active role in tourism in the Caribbean, Central America, and South America. Its Inter-Sectoral Unit for Tourism was created in 1996 in Washington and given responsibility for matters related to tourism throughout the Americas. This Unit's two main functions are to undertake selected technical cooperation projects, especially in developing countries, and to support the Inter-American Travel Congress, a forum for formulating hemispheric tourism policy. At the time of writing, the OAS was providing technical assistance to tourism projects in Barbados, Costa Rica, Jamaica, Panama, and St. Kitts and Nevis. The Unit also supports efforts toward sustainable

tourism development, conducts research and analysis of tourism issues, and provides support to hemispheric and sub-regional conferences, workshops, and seminars.

European Union and European Commission, Brussels, Belgium
The European Union consists of 15 countries (Austria, Belgium, Denmark, Finland, France, Germany, Greece, Ireland, Italy, Luxembourg, The Netherlands, Portugal, Spain, Sweden, and the United Kingdom). Its constitutional objectives are stated in the *Treaty on European Union* of 1992.

The European Commission is one of the Institutions of the European Union. Within the European Commission several Directorate-Generals (or DGs) have been created. The one concerned with tourism is DGXXIII (or DG23), known as Enterprise Policy, Distributive Trades, Tourism & Cooperatives. A Tourism Unit is located within DG23 which has the objective of improving the quality and competitiveness of tourism within the European Economic Area. A *Community Action Plan to Assist Tourism* was created for 1993–1995 and this has been followed by the *First Multiannual Programme* (also known as PHILOXENIA).

Asia-Pacific Economic Cooperation, Singapore
Asia-Pacific Economic Cooperation (APEC) was created in 1989 and has since become a primary vehicle for promoting open trade and economic cooperation among the countries of the Asia-Pacific region. It has 18 members that include Australia, Canada, Chile, China, Japan, Mexico, New Zealand, Taiwan, U.S., and the Association of SouthEast Asia Nations (ASEAN) countries. The four objectives of APEC are to: 1) sustain the growth and the development of the region for the common good of its peoples and, in this way, to contribute to the growth and development of

the world economy; 2) enhance the positive gains, both for the region and the world economy, resulting from increasing economic interdependence, including the flow of goods, services, capital, and technology; 3) to develop and strengthen the open multilateral trading system in the interest of Asia-Pacific and all other economies; and 4) to reduce barriers to trade in goods and services among participants in a manner consistent with General Agreement on Tariffs and Trade (GATT) principles, where applicable, without detriment to other economies.

APEC created a Tourism Working Group at its seventh meeting in Japan in 1995. The Tourism Working Group brings together government tourism officials from APEC member countries to share information, exchange views, and develop areas of cooperation on tourism-related policies. It is working toward the long-term environmental and social sustainability of tourism in the region by putting a priority on the following actions:

- Developing and implementing the concepts of environmental and social sustainability in tourism development.

- Developing cooperation in the fields of information-based services related to trade in tourism.

- Enlarging the role of the business/private sector.

- Facilitating and promoting human resources development.

- Removing barriers to tourism movements and investment and liberalizing trade in services associated with tourism.

- Sharing information among APEC economies.

Multi-Country Regional Tourism Organizations
Several multi-country regional tourism organizations have been established to assist in the development and marketing

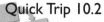

Quick Trip 10.2
European Commission's Multi-Year Program for Tourism

The European Commission has established a plan for tourism in Europe for 1997–2000. Known as *PHILOXENIA* (Greek word for hospitality), it has four objectives:

1. The improvement of knowledge in the field of tourism by developing tourism-related information, pooling tourism information from other sources and facilitating the assessment of community measures affecting tourism.

   Developing tourism-related information:
   - Consolidation of the European statistical system for tourism, improving the availability of reliable and up-to-date statistics.
   - Development of surveys, studies, and desk/field analyses, taking into account the needs of tourism.

   Pooling of tourism information from other sources:
   - Establishment of a European research and documentation network on tourism.

   Facilitating the assessment of community measures affecting tourism:
   - Establishment of a legal and financial watch allowing for a systematic assessment of community measures affecting tourism.

2. The improvement of the legislative and financial environment for tourism by reinforcing cooperation among member states, the industry, and stakeholders.

   Reinforcing cooperation with member states, the industry, and stakeholders:
   - Organization and follow-up of regular meetings with the parties concerned, to reinforce cooperation at European level and to raise awareness of community initiatives (technical/thematic meetings, roundtables, forums).

3. The increase of quality of European tourism by promoting sustainable tourism and removing obstacles to tourism development.

   Promoting sustainable tourism:
   - Support to local initiatives geared toward sound management of visitor flows and stimulation of their networking.
   - Support to the implementation of environmentally friendly management systems in tourist accommodations.
   - Organization of a *European Prize for Tourism and the Environment* (every two years).

   Removing obstacles to tourism development:
   - Identification of the principal obstacles at European level faced by various forms of tourism as well as by specific categories of tourists (such as young people, the elderly, and disabled people) and the development of appropriate resources.

4. The increase of the number of visitors from Third World countries by promoting Europe as a tourist destination.

   Promoting Europe as a tourist destination:
   - Support for multi-annual promotional campaigns in major issuing countries and/or emerging zones, with the support of participating sponsors.

Source: European Commission. (1997).

of tourism in different parts of the world. These include the Caribbean Tourism Organization (CTO), Confederacion de Organizaciones Turisticas de America Latina (COTAL), European Travel Commission (ETC), Indian Ocean Tourism Organization (IOTO), Pacific Asia Travel Association (PATA), and the Tourism Council of the South Pacific (TCSP). Although these organizations all are aimed at promoting tourism in specific geographic areas, they differ in their membership compositions and structures. For example, PATA is more of an industry association, while the TCSP is more of a grouping of national government tourism agencies.

The Pacific Asia Travel Association (PATA) was established in Hawaii in 1951 to promote Pacific-Asia's travel and tourism destinations, products, and services. It is the self-proclaimed "Voice of Pacific Asia Tourism" (PATA Website, 1997). PATA's headquarters are in San Francisco and it is a not-for-profit association. Its four main areas of activity are: 1) marketing, promotion, and sales; 2) destination promotion; 3) networking; and 4) travel marts, trade shows, and sales missions. PATA encourages travel industry education and training, quality product development, and acts as resource center for tourism research and information. PATA's members include government agencies, hotels, airlines, cruise lines, attractions, travel agencies, and tour operators. It has over 2,100 organization members and 79 PATA chapters around the world.

New regional marketing partnerships covering several different countries are on the increase. These initiatives do not necessarily involve creating permanent organizations. They include El Mundo Maya (The Mayan World) in Central America, the Jewels of the Mekong area in Southeast Asia, and the Arafura Sea tourism group.

Development Agencies and Banks

The last group of regional organizations are specialized development agencies and banks that provide funding for tourism development. These include the African Development Bank (Abidjan, Ivory Coast), Asian Development Bank (Manila, Philippines), Caribbean Development Bank (Barbados), European Investment Bank (Luxembourg), Export-Import Bank of Japan (Tokyo), Inter-American Development Bank (Washington, D.C.), Islamic Development Bank (Jeddah, Saudi Arabia), Nordic Development Fund (Helsinki, Finland), and the OPEC Fund for International Development (Vienna, Austria). Many of these banks and funds concentrate on assisting developing countries. Often the types of projects that receive assistance are large-scale infrastructure and transportation system developments. Some of the agencies have specific policies and programs for tourism. For example, the Inter-American Development Bank (IADB) funds tourism projects in its member countries that meet four objectives: 1) attracting international tourism and promoting and facilitating national tourism, with a view to improving the country's balance of payments and raising local income levels; 2) developing, primarily, areas that possess tourist attractions and are little developed economically; 3) creating new employment opportunities, particularly in areas of tourist attractions; and 4) contributing to Latin American regional integration.

National Tourism Organizations

The tourism policy of a country is developed and implemented by its national tourism administration (NTA) and/or its national tourist office (NTO) (also sometimes referred to as a national tourism organization). These are the official national bodies responsible for the development and marketing of tourism in specific countries. The national tourism organization is either one body or responsibilities are split between two organizations, the NTA and NTO. The marketing responsibilities are given to the NTO and all other responsibilities including policy-making and planning are given to the NTA (Morrison, Braunlich, Kamaruddin, & Cai, 1995). This division of tourism responsibilities is found in both Australia and New Zealand. Australia's NTO is the Australian Tourist Commission and its NTA is the Office of National Tourism located within the Department of Industry, Science, and Tourism under the Minister of Industry, Science, and Tourism. In New Zealand, the NTO is the New Zealand Tourism Board and the NTA is the Tourism Policy Group within the Ministry of Commerce.

The roles of these organizations vary according to the governmental status they are given in specific countries. First, it may be governmental and part of the civil service system as an *independent ministry*, such as the Bahamas, Israel, the Maldives, and Mexico. It may also be a named section of a shared ministerial portfolio as in Australia.

Second, the NTO may be a *governmental agency* or bureau responsible for tourism and set within a larger department. Examples here include the Sernatur (Servicio Nacional de Turismo) in Chile, the Singapore Tourist Promotion Board, and the Tourist Authority of Thailand. Generally, a governmental agency has less influence and status than the ministry form. Tourism bodies that have governmental status have the broadest range of functions of national tourism organizations.

Third, the official tourism organization may be a *quasi-public government-funded commission, board, or authority*, such as the Australian Tourist Commission, British Tourist Authority, Canadian

Tourism Commission, Hong Kong Tourist Association, Irish Tourist Board, New Zealand Tourism Board, and South Africa Tourism Board. These are sometimes referred to as **statutory bodies** or "quangos" (quasi non-governmental organizations). These organizations are governed by independent boards of directors drawn from private-sector tourism businesses and nonprofit organizations. A key advantage of the government-funded commission or board is that is has greater management flexibility in dealing with the commercial aspects of tourism marketing and promotion. A closer liaison with the private sector and other non-governmental organizations is possible with this type of arrangement. Because of the public-private partnership nature of this type of organization, there has been a trend for more countries to adopt this type of structure.

Last, the official tourism organization may be a private association indirectly supported by government funding. This approach is not found very often. A major advantage of having a governmental agency as a national tourism organization is that it has the authority within government to represent tourism and develop and implement tourism policy.

The roles of national tourism organizations (NTOs) affect both the supply and demand for all elements of the tourism destination mix. On the supply side, programs include **conducting inventories and assessments of the destination mix** prior to the development of a national tourism plan. NTOs coordinate the **national tourism planning** process. NTOs develop and operate programs to improve the quality of different elements of the destination mix. This includes protecting the environment through a national park system and other measures to encourage sustainable tourism development. Governments may establish **minimum stan-**

> ## Quick Trip 10.3
> # The Caribbean Tourism Organization
>
> The Caribbean Tourism Organization was created in January 1989 from a merger of the Caribbean Tourism Association (founded 1951) and the Caribbean Tourism Research and Development Centre (founded 1974). CTO is an international development and marketing agency with its headquarters in Barbados. CTO also has marketing offices in New York and London.
>
> CTO's objectives are to:
>
> - Create in the marketplace a greater awareness and understanding of Caribbean tourism.
> - Create a greater public awareness and understanding of tourism by host countries.
> - Design a comprehensive tourism information system.
> - Develop a capacity to assist members in defining and responding to any tourism-related need.
> - Develop the highest level of skills and professionalism in the personnel serving the Caribbean in tourism and tourism-related areas.
> - Develop the strongest possible linkage between the tourism sector and other economic sectors, for example, agriculture, manufacturing, and services of all kinds.
> - Ensure a harmonious interaction between tourism and the social and natural environment.
> - Foster close links with regional institutions and international donor agencies.
> - Give special support to those countries not able to represent themselves.
> - Increase the value and volume of tourism flows to member states.
> - Service, retain, and expand the membership of CTO.
>
> Source: Caribbean Tourism Organization. (1997).

---

dards for hotels, attractions, tour operators, and tour guides. NTOs operate **training and education programs** to increase professionalism in tourism and improve hospitality skills. A very good example of this is the *KiwiHost* program operated by the New Zealand Tourism Board. This program began in 1991 with the aim of setting a national standard for service in tourism. By 1996, 3,500 businesses had qualified as *KiwiHost* businesses and

76,000 people had received the service training (New Zealand Tourism Board, 1997). When another agency sets policy that affects tourism, the NTO may have some advisory input into that policy.

Although the government's role in economic activities in free-market economies is generally confined to **legislation and regulation**, the role of the government in socialist countries is quite different, although the differences are now becoming less obvious. In socialist countries, governments have traditionally been involved in owning and operating visitor facilities, as well as in controlling domestic travel agencies and inbound tour operators. Developing countries lacking private capital and expertise often find it necessary for the government to develop, own, and manage facilities and attractions. To further ensure the proper supply, some governments provide *financial incentives* for the development of facilities and attractions, and for human resources development to educate and train local residents for tourism.

On the demand side, NTOs are involved in *facilitation, marketing research, marketing*, and *representation* in foreign countries. The role of the NTO in facilitation tends to be an advisory one, commenting on the effect of government policies regarding visas, passports, and customs formalities on visitor demand. NTOs are primarily known for their roles in marketing, especially in attracting foreign visitors to their respective countries, and in sponsoring or generating tourism marketing research data. Some agencies, including the Australian Tourist Commission and the New Zealand Tourism Board, have no direct supply-side functions and are also not involved in the marketing of tourism to their own residents (domestic tourism). Others such as the Singapore Tourist Promotion Board have traditionally had both supply- and demand-side functions. The promotional role of national tourism organizations are reviewed in detail in chapter 15.

State, Provincial, and Territorial Tourism Organizations

Overall, the role of state, provincial, and territorial tourism organizations worldwide seems to be increasing in importance. Tourism organizations are present throughout

Service
makes the
difference

WHAT IS KIWIHOST?
KiwiHost is an internationally recognised customer service training programme that focuses on communication, customer relations and customer service. **KiwiHost** looks at our attitudes to service, the way we relate to our customers and how we can turn our relationships with customers into better business.
KiwiHost was launched in 1991 by the New Zealand Tourism Board as an initiative aimed at setting a national standard of service. By June 1997 1,755 businesses had qualified as **KiwiHost** businesses and 95,000 New Zealanders had participated in the **KiwiHost** programme. The **KiwiHost** family of programmes also includes **KiwiHost Super Service** and **KiwiHost for Managers**.

WHO IS IT FOR?
KiwiHost is for any business that has customers, and for anyone who comes into contact with customers. **KiwiHost** is for people in reception or accounts, in sales or in marketing, for people dealing with internal or external customers in any kind of business. **KiwiHost** is for people who need to understand what good customer service is all about and the part they have in giving it -because good service on every level is the key to business success.
KiwiHost is for people who know that every business is a service business.

HOW DOES IT WORK?
KiwiHost is a simple and very effective first step toward better quality service. Each of the three programmes in the **KiwiHost** family of programmes is a one day (seven hour) workshop for up to twenty people. Workshops are run regularly throughout New Zealand and are priced right for any size business.

> ### Setting the standard in
> ### New Zealand for service

KIWIHOST
KiwiHost is New Zealand's quality service training standard, covering basic communication and customer relation skills. **KiwiHost** outlines the vital role good service plays in business, and provides skills in making customer contact, effective listening and handling complaints. Successful participants receive a nationally recognised certificate and pin.

KIWIHOST SUPER SERVICE
The follow-on to **KiwiHost**, this workshop focuses on handling customers and colleagues from diverse backgrounds and different nationalities, extending customer service skills and introduces telephone techniques. **KiwiHost Super Service** outlines how to provide "knock your socks off" service to bring your customers back. **KiwiHost** is a prerequisite. Participants receive a **KiwiHost Super Service** certificate.

KIWIHOST FOR MANAGERS
KiwiHost for Managers gives managers and supervisors of staff skills to improve service quality in their workplace and business environment. Based upon the quality improvement principles of customer

CULTURAL KIWIHOST
A half day course designed to provide the skills to more confidently meet and greet people of different nationalities. It provides a much greater understanding of what different cultures see as important and participants learn the various ways to overcome communication barriers. The course looks at the many and varied service preferences from one country to another -- in language, greetings, formalitities, how people should be addressed, customs, what could cause offence, and more. **Cultural KiwiHost** brings an additional polish to service and with it, greater staff confidence and job satisfaction.

> The New Zealand Tourism Board is the national
> co-ordinator and administrator of **KiwiHost**.
> For more information, please contact:
> ## KiwiHost
> *Address:* PO Box 95, Wellington
> *Phone:* **0800 801 101** (within NZ)
> or +64 4 474 7400 (outside NZ)
> *Fax:* +64 4 499 2609

http://nz.com/infocus/KiwiHost/

Figure 10.3   KiwiHost is an excellent service training program offered by the New Zealand Tourism Board. Reprinted by permission of the New Zealand Tourism Board.

the world in the states, provinces, or territories within and associated with countries. Different types of organizational structures are found here as well. The most common organizational structures are statutory bodies and independent or semi-independent tourism ministries, departments or divisions. Examples of the first type are the English Tourist Board, Hawaii Visitors & Convention Bureau, Scottish Tourist Board, Wales Tourist Board, and the Queensland Tourist & Travel Corporation in Australia. In Hawaii, leadership is provided by the Hawaii Visitors & Convention Bureau, a private, nonprofit corporation that has a contract with the state government to handle all of Hawaii's tourism marketing and research. There is a state government tourism office known as the Hawaii Tourism Office. As was the case with the NTOs, there is a definite trend toward creating public-private partnerships and away from government-only state, provincial, and territorial tourism organizations.

There are several examples of the second organizational type in Canada. For example, the Department of Tourism, Culture, and Recreation in Newfoundland and Labrador is under the Minister of Tourism, Culture and Recreation. In Prince Edward Island, the provincial tourism organization is under the responsibility of the Minister of Economic Development and Tourism. In the U.S., the state of Tennessee represents another example of the second type of organizational structure. It has a Department of Tourist Development with an independent cabinet-level-level status. This allows for a simplification of the decision-making process because of the access that the Commissioner of Tourist Development has to the governor due to the incumbent's position as a member of the governor's cabinet. Another important plus is the advantage the commissioner has,

especially at the time of the budget, in dealing with the state legislature as a full department.

The roles of these organizations tend to parallel those of their respective NTOs but, in this case, at the state, provincial, and territorial levels. Some 49 of the 50 states in the United States, the ten Canadian provinces, and the two Canadian territories have an agency officially responsible for tourism. The six Australian states and the Northern Territory also have official tourism organizations. In Great Britain, the English Tourist Board, Scottish Tourist Board, and the Wales Tourist Board support the efforts of the British Tourist Authority by marketing their areas. A state tourism organization system is also found in India and a provincial tourism organization system is proposed for South Africa.

The primary role of state, provincial, and territorial tourism organizations is *domestic travel promotion*; promoting their destinations to their own residents and the residents of nearby states, provinces, or territories. However, these organizations are becoming more involved in international travel promotion and are spending more to attract foreign visitors. This is certainly the case with the state tourism organizations in Australia and the tourist boards in Great Britain. Additionally, these organizations are playing an increasingly important role as a cooperative partner with their NTOs.

A traditional marketing role of these organizations has been in *generating and fulfilling inquiries* through media advertising. Many of these organizations also provide travel information at *travel information* or *welcome centers* that they operate. Some of them have marketing offices in other parts of the country and overseas. They set up promotional booths at travel trade and consumer travel shows, fairs, or exhibitions. They host travel writers, retail travel

agents, and tour wholesalers visiting their state, province, or territory on *familiarization trips.*

These organizations make significant investments in *marketing research,* gathering statistics on ongoing visitor volumes and on other special tourism research studies. The level of research effort has been increasing as these organizations try to more precisely target marketing programs and to measure the effectiveness and impacts of their marketing activities.

Many state, provincial, and territorial tourism organizations play a role in *tourism development* and in the *training and education* of tourism employees. This is especially true in Australia and Canada where significant investments have been made in tourism planning and stimulating the development of new attractions and facilities, and in the improvement and expansion of existing ones. Canadian and Australian organizations have also had a well-established role in educational and training programs to upgrade management and other employee skills.

Almost all these organizations play some role in encouraging *package tour development and promotion.* In some cases, this has involved financial and or technical assistance with package or tour development. Many of these organizations have cost-sharing programs that provide grants to local groups to promote tourism to their communities.

Regional Tourism Organizations

The next level of tourism organizations found in several countries is at the regional level. Some states, provinces, and territories cover very large geographic areas. The economic and social priorities, and destination mixes are quite different from region to region. In these situations, it is very desirable for groups of communities to prepare their own policies and plans for

Quick Trip 10.4
State Tourism Organizations in the U.S.

The U.S. Travel Data Center conducts an annual *Survey of State Travel Offices* that summarizes the operations of the 50 state tourism organizations and the agencies in the District of Columbia, Puerto Rica, and the Northern Mariana Islands. Twenty-three of the state tourism organizations receive all their funding from the state governments. The other 27 get state funding plus other revenues from lodging and other tourism-dedicated taxes, membership dues, lottery funds, highway vehicle funds, motor vehicle funds, and private sources. As the following table shows, the total projected spending in fiscal year 1996–1997 by the 50 states was $433,915,836 and the average total budget was $8,678,317. Approximately 30 percent of the total budget figure was devoted to advertising.

RANK	STATE	BUDGET	RANK	STATE	BUDGET
1	Illinois	$32,756,500	26	Ohio	$6,795,225
2	Hawaii	25,319,907	27	Montana	6,791,682
3	Texas	22,990,979	28	Georgia	6,588,633
4	Pennsylvania	18,490,000	29	Kentucky	6,188,200
5	Virginia	17,436,922	30	West Virginia	5,700,000
6	Florida	17,000,000	31	New Jersey	5,445,000
7	Massachusetts	16,933,000	32	Connecticut	5,117,000
8	South Carolina	16,173,870	33	New Mexico	4,769,400
9	Louisiana	15,422,254	34	Iowa	4,356,822
10	New York	14,500,000	35	Idaho	4,146,665
11	Tennessee	13,054,200	36	Utah	4,000,000
12	Missouri	11,591,288	37	Wyoming	3,974,887
13	Mississippi	11,247,785	38	Indiana	3,805,000
14	Wisconsin	11,085,319	39	South Dakota	3,581,000
15	Michigan	11,038,900	40	Kansas	3,382,817
16	Arkansas	10,130,934	41	Vermont	3,105,467
17	Minnesota	9,010,510	42	Washington	3,057,823
18	Maryland	8,578,544	43	Oregon	2,681,850
19	North Carolina	8,577,501	44	Maine	2,495,247
20	Alaska	7,968,300	45	New Hampshire	2,325,255
21	Oklahoma	7,688,965	46	Nebraska	2,298,044
22	Arizona	7,467,000	47	Rhode Island	2,282,200
23	Alabama	7,463,677	48	North Dakota	2,127,733
24	California	7,250,000	49	Colorado	1,600,000
25	Nevada	7,199,100	50	Delaware	924,432
				Grand Total	**$433,915,836**
				Average	**$8,678,317**
				Puerto Rico	**$79,346,184**
				N. Mariana	**$11,224,600**

There has been a definite trend in the U.S. for more states to form public-private partnerships for their state tourism organizations. Alaska, Colorado, Florida, and Virginia are four of the states that have created new organizations that are not totally controlled by state government (Alaska Tourism Marketing Council, Colorado Travel and Tourism Authority, Florida Tourism Industry Marketing Corporation, and Virginia Tourism Corporation). In Canada, the Alberta Tourism Partnership Corporation (now called Travel Alberta) was created as a not-for-profit, membership tourism organization and replaced the former provincial government organization.

Source: U.S. Travel Data Center. (1997), 5.

http://www.edinburgh.org/

Figure 10.4   The Edinburgh and Lothians Tourist Board has established an excellent World Wide Web Site to support tourism in Scotland's capital and the surrounding region. Reprinted by permission of the Edinburgh and Lothians Tourist Board, Scotland.

tourism development and marketing. This may lead to the creation of a system of regional tourism organizations (RTOs).

Regional tourism organization systems are found in England, Canada, Australia, United Kingdom, and in some states within the U.S. In many cases, these systems have been initiated by state and provincial tourism organizations to increase the effectiveness of regional tourism marketing and development. Often, RTOs are created as nonprofit associations. RTOs are generally partly funded by state or provincial grants and by membership dues from private-sector tourism businesses and local tourism organizations. RTOs perform roles similar to their state, provincial, or territorial tourism organizations, especially in the area of tourism promotion.

Local Tourism Organizations

The final group of tourism organizations is found at the individual community level. Around the world, the number of communities forming these organizations is increasing rapidly. There are many different organizational formats for local tourism organizations. The tourism organization may be within the local government structure and be funded completely by local government. It may be a public-private partnership with some funding from both the local government and private-sector tourism businesses. The local tourism organization may have little or no direct local government funding, but receive its budget from user taxes, private-sector memberships, or grants from states or provinces.

States and provinces are often instrumental in the creation of local tourism organizations and in helping maintain their operations. States and provinces can assist local efforts by passing legislation enabling communities to collect taxes to support local promotional activities. In the U.S., this is usually in the form of a ***room*** or ***innkeeper's tax***, but some cities derive support from a tax on alcoholic beverages, entertainment and gaming, or tickets, or from an earmarked sales tax. States or provinces can provide matching (cost-sharing) grant funds, either for general purposes or for activities specified by the state or provincial government. The types of activities receiving such funding are usually such things as promotion and public relations, familiarization tours for tour wholesalers and travel writers, brochure preparation, tourism planning studies, and marketing research projects.

Room taxes are a common method of obtaining funding for local tourism organizations. This requires passage of a county or city ordinance after state or provincial enabling legislation has authorized counties or cities to establish such a tax. Room tax proposals are often resisted by local lodging groups as an unfair tax on only one segment of tourism. However, local residents are inclined to be supportive since these are taxes paid by the visitor, not the resident, i.e., they represent a ***user-pay*** approach. Counties and cities in some cases also receive an allocation from the general funds of the city, county, or state or province.

Another common method of financing local tourism organizations is through ***membership programs***. Dues are often set on a sliding scale based upon the member's volume of business or the number of employees. An ongoing task of a membership organization is to convince local businesses that it is worth their time and money to belong. Some communities obtain money through a variety of fundraisers including special dinners or events such as races and auctions. These events require a great deal of effort as well as the support of many local people and businesses. However, they provide a focal point for increasing community support for tourism.

Summary

Governments around the world have selected to take a leadership role in tourism planning and development because of the potential economic, social, cultural, and environmental impacts of tourism. The amount of involvement depends upon such factors as the political philosophy of the government and the maturity of the destination area. A tourism policy must be established to guide the tourism destiny of the country, region, state, or province. Without a policy and a mechanism for implementing it, tourism will increase or decline at the destination in a haphazard and potentially negative manner.

To bring a tourism policy into effect, there must be an organization responsible for its implementation. There are various levels of tourism policy and, therefore, a variety of policy-implementing agencies spread throughout the world.

Some cities derive support from a tax on gaming. Photo by Corel.

For example, the World Tourism Organization has a global responsibility for tourism, while there are several multi-country regional tourism organizations. Within an individual country, there is usually a national tourism organization (NTO), state, provincial, or territorial tourism organizations, regional tourism organizations, and local tourism organizations.

References

Bahamas Ministry of Tourism. (1997). Bahamas: Official Travel Guide. (http://www.interknowledge. com/bahamas/).

Baum, T. (1994a). The development and implementation of national tourism policies. *Tourism Management*, 15, 185–192.

Baum, T. (1994b). National tourism policies: Implementing the human resource dimension. *Tourism Management*, 15, 259–266.

Bramwell, B., & Rawding, L. (1994). Tourism marketing organizations in industrial cities: Organizations, objectives and urban governance. *Tourism Management*, 15, 425–434.

Braunlich, C.G., Morrison, A.M., & Feng, F. (1995). National tourist offices: Service quality expectations and performance. *Journal of Vacation Marketing*, 1, 323–336.

Choy, D.L. (1993). Alternative roles of national tourism organizations. *Tourism Management*, 14, 357–365.

Department of Environmental Affairs and Tourism. (1996). *White paper: The development and promotion of tourism in South Africa*. Pretoria: Government of South Africa.

Edgell, D.L., Sr. (1990a). *Model national tourism policy*. Washington, D.C.

Edgell, D.L., Sr. (1990b). *International tourism policy*. New York: Van Nostrand Reinhold.

Edgell, D.L., Sr. (1993). *World tourism at the millennium: An agenda for industry, government and education*. Washington, D.C.: U.S. Department of Commerce.

Fayos-Sola, E. (1996). Tourism policy: A midsummer night's dream? *Tourism Management*, 17, 405–412.

Gee, C.Y., Makens, J.C., & Choy, D.J.L. (1997). *The travel industry* (3rd ed.). New York: Van Nostrand Reinhold.

Greenwood, J. (1993). Business interest groups in tourism governance. *Tourism Management*, 14, 335–348.

Hall, C.M. (1994). *Tourism and politics: Policy, power and place*. Chichester, England: John Wiley & Sons, Inc.

Hall, C.M., & Jenkins, J.M. (1995). *Tourism and public policy*. London: Routledge.

Hawes, D.K., Taylor, D.T., & Hampe, G.D. (1991). Destination marketing by states. *Journal of Travel Research*, 30 (1), 11–17.

Johnson, P., & Thomas, B., eds. (1992). *Perspectives on tourism policy*. London: Mansell Publishing.

Judd, D.R. (1995). Promoting tourism in U.S. cities. *Tourism Management*, 16, 175–187.

Lavery, P. (1992). The financing and organization of national tourist offices. *EIU Travel & Tourism Analyst* (4), 84–101.

Lingard, R. (1990). Role of government and local authorities in U.K. tourism. In *Horwath Book of Tourism*, Quest, M., ed. London: The Macmillan Press.

Long, J. (1994). Local authority tourism strategies—a British perspective. *Journal of Tourism Studies*, 5 (2), 17–23.

Long, P.T., & Nuckolls, J.S. (1994). Organising resources for rural tourism development: The importance of leadership, planning and technical assistance. *Tourism Recreation Research*, 19 (2), 19–34.

McIntosh, R.W., Goeldner, C.R., & Ritchie, J.R.B. (1995). *Tourism: Principles, practices, philosophies* (7th ed.). New York: John Wiley & Sons, Inc.

Morrison, A.M., Braunlich, C.G., Kamaruddin, N., & Cai, L.A. (1995). National tourist offices in North America: An analysis. *Tourism Management*, 16, 605–618.

Owen, C. (1992). Building a relationship between government and tourism. *Tourism Management*, 13, 358–362.

Pearce, D. (1992). *Tourist organizations*. Harlow, Essex: Longman Group U.K.

Richter, L.K. (1993). Tourism policy-making in South-East Asia. In Hitchcock, M., V.T. King, & M.J.G. Parnwell (eds.), *Tourism in South-East Asia* (pp. 179–199). London: Routledge.

Trinidad & Tobago Tourism Development Authority. (1988). *Tourism policy*. Port of Spain: Trinidad & Tobago Tourism Development Authority.

U.S. Senate. (1977). *National tourism policy study: Ascertainment phase*. Washington, D.C.: Committee on Commerce, Science and Transportation.

World Tourism Organization. (1997). *Budgets of national tourism administrations*. Madrid: World Tourism Organization.

Surfing Solutions

http://www.atag/org/ (Air Transport Action Group)
http://www.apecsec.org.sg/ (Asia-Pacific Economic Cooperation)
http://www.caribtourism.com/ (Caribbean Tourism Organization)
http://www.visiteurope.com/ (European Travel Commission)
http://europa.eu.int/ (European Union)
http://www.bs.ac.cowan.edu.au/IOTO/ (Indian Ocean Tourism Organization)
http://www.iata.org/ (International Air Transport Association)
http://www.cam.org/~icao/ (International Civil Aviation Organization)
http://www.ilo.org/ (International Labour Organization)
http://www.oas.org/ (Organization of American States)
http://www.oecd.org/ (Organization for Economic Cooperation and Development)
http://www.dnai.com/~patanet/ (Pacific-Asia Travel Association)
http://www.tcsp.com/spt.htm (Tourism Council of the South Pacific)
http://www.un.org/ (United Nations)
http://www.world-tourism.org/ (World Tourism Organization)
http://www.wttc.org/ (World Travel & Tourism Council)

Acronyms

APEC (Asian Pacific Economic Cooperation)
ASEAN (Association of Southeast Asia Nations)
ATAG (Air Transport Action Group)
ATC (Australian Tourist Commission)
BTA (British Tourist Authority)
COTAL (Confederacion de Organizaciones Turisticas de America Latina)
CTC (Canadian Tourism Commission)
CTO (Caribbean Tourism Organization)
CVB (convention and visitors bureau)
EC (European Commission)
ECoNETT (European Community Network for Environmental Travel & Tourism)
ETC (European Travel Commission)
EU (European Union)
GATS (General Agreement on Trade in Services)
GATT (General Agreement on Tariffs and Trade)
IATA (International Air Transport Association)
ICAO (International Civil Aviation Organization)
ILO (International Labour Organization)
IOTO (Indian Ocean Tourism Organization)
ICOTTA (International Congress of Official Tourist Traffic Associations)
IUOTO (International Union of Official Travel Organizations)
NAFTA (North American Free Trade Agreement)
NTA (National Tourism Administration)
NTO (National Tourism Organization or National Tourist Office)
OAS (Organization of American States)
OECD (Organization for Economic Cooperation and Development)
NGO (non-government organization)
PATA (Pacific Asia Travel Association)
RTO (regional tourism organization)
SATOUR (South African Tourism Board)
TCSP (Tourism Council of the South Pacific)
UNCTAD (United Nations Conference on Trade and Development)
UNDP (United Nations Development Programme)
UNEP (United Nations Environment Programme)
USTTA (U.S. Travel and Tourism Administration)
WTO (World Tourism Organization)
WTTC (World Travel & Tourism Council)
WTTHRC (World Travel & Tourism Human Resource Center)
WTTTPC (WTTC Taxation Policy Centre)

> "Giving money and power to government is like giving whiskey and car keys to teenage boys."
>
> *O'Rourke, P.J. (1991),* Parliament of Whores

11

Tourism Regulation

···Controlling Tourism ·····

Purpose

Having learned the reasons for government legislation and regulations, students will be able to describe the types of legislation and regulations that are found in tourism.

Learning Objectives

Having read this chapter, you should be able to:

1. Explain why the government role in establishing tourism-related legislation and regulations is both essential and controversial.

2. Identify and explain the multilateral and bilateral agreements affecting tourism.

3. Explain the common reasons for introducing tourism-related laws and regulations in destination areas.

4. Identify the categories and types of tourism legislation and regulation found in destination areas.

5. Describe specific forms of destination area legislation and regulations.

6. Discuss the purposes and results of airline deregulation.

7. Explain the steps that private-sector businesses in tourism are taking to promote self-regulation.

Overview

The role of the government in regulating tourism is regarded by many as essential and by some as controversial. This chapter explores the many ways in which tourism is regulated by government.

At the multi-country level, there are a number of international agreements and treaties that affect tourism. The most significant of these involve air travel among countries. Multilateral and bilateral agreements affecting tourism are discussed in this chapter.

The categories and types of tourism legislation and regulations found in tourism destination areas are identified. Common reasons for introducing these measures are described. The chapter explains in more detail some of the major types of tourism-related legislation and regulations. The trend toward the deregulation of airlines is discussed. Attempts by tourism businesses at self-regulation are reviewed.

Government Role in Controlling Tourism

"The imposition of strict liability on the innkeeper found its origin in the conditions existing in England in the fourteenth and fifteenth centuries. Inadequate means of travel, the sparsely settled country, and the constant exposure to robbers left the traveler with the inn practically his only hope of protection. Innkeepers themselves, and their servants, were often as dishonest as the highwaymen roaming the countryside and were not beyond joining forces with the outlaws to relieve travelers and guests, by connivance or force, of their valuables and goods."

Goodwin, J.R., & Gaston, J.R. (1992), 4

One of the government roles in tourism identified in chapter 10 is setting and enforcing various forms of legislation and regulations. This role is both essential and controversial in most free-enterprise-system destination areas. It is essential because governments cannot totally rely upon the private sector to effectively control and regulate tourism; it is often controversial because the private sector feels that governments go too far in enforcing regulations.

Around the world, a multitude of government agencies have programs and regulations that directly or indirectly affect tourism. Countries with socialist or communist governments regulate tourism very comprehensively. The complexity of the tourism regulatory framework in most destination areas is a direct reflection of tourism itself; visitors cross international borders, are exposed to all of the cultural, historic, manmade, and natural resources of the destination area, and must be catered to in a safe, secure, and hygienic fashion. It is no surprise that a variety of government agencies have tourism-related regulations and not just one.

Governments are involved in tourism for political, environmental, and economic reasons. The roles of governments in tourism include coordination, policy-setting and planning, legislation and regulation, infrastructure development, operations, development stimulation and control, marketing and research, and training and education. The emphasis given to each of these eight roles varies from destination to destination, but it is usually related to the importance attached to tourism as an economic activity. The actions of those in government have to be supported by various bodies of law (legislation) and specific regulations to have legitimacy in democratic societies. It is with the actual enforce-

ment of the laws and with the structuring of regulations that the most controversy and conflict occurs between the private sector and government in the tourism system.

In introducing legislation and regulations, governments act in the general interests of their citizens and visitors. They do so to protect and conserve their destination area's natural, historical, and cultural resources, to ensure the health and safety of visitors, and to protect visitors from unscrupulous business practices. In these respects, the value of a government's role cannot be questioned.

However, government agencies are often accused of being too bureaucratic, of developing unnecessary "red tape," and of going too far in their policing efforts. This is especially true when the political pendulum and public sentiment swing more toward the free-enterprise approach, as they have in the airline industry worldwide. Governments have been sharply criticized for hindering the development of tourism destination areas because of their lengthy and complex project approval processes. Certainly, government agencies seldom appear to act or react with the speed with which the private sector requires.

The lack of coordination and cooperation between government agencies in their policies and programs is often quite prevalent in tourism. This is a reflection of the diversity of the tourism system itself and of the unavoidable conflicts between the goals of some agencies, such as natural resource conservation versus tourism promotion and development agencies. Any destination area with a vital interest in tourism should take steps to bring about the highest amount of coordination and cooperation among its government agencies.

Multilateral and Bilateral Agreements

"The air transport industry throughout the world is in a period of profound change. It is being transformed by pressures which will ensure that it is a totally different kind of business by the end of this decade than it was even 15 years ago. An industry which historically has been nationalistic and highly regulated is becoming a transnational and less economically regulated business."

Edgell, D.L., Sr. (1993), 32

In addition to the layers of national, state, provincial, territorial, regional, county, and municipal legislation and regulations, there are certain agreements that have been reached among foreign countries which have a direct impact upon tourism. These are called *multilateral agreements* meaning that several countries have signed and agreed to abide by the codes of conduct in the agreements. These agreements are increasingly leading to the liberalization of trade and travel among countries; a trend that will be beneficial to tourism in the future.

Multilateral Air Agreements

Perhaps the most significant multilateral agreements for tourism are those that relate to air travel. The embryonic period for these air travel agreements was during World War II. The *five freedoms* of international air travel were first discussed at an international civil aviation conference in Chicago in 1944 (the *Chicago Convention*) and were:

1. **Right of transit:** The freedom to fly over another country without stopping.

2. **Right of technical stop:** The right to stop at another country's airport for fuel and servicing.

3. **Right to discharge passengers:** The right to discharge passengers at another country's airport.

4. **Right to pick up passengers:** The right to pick up passengers from another country's airport and return them to their homes.

5. **Right to discharge and load passengers:** The right to discharge passengers at another country's airport and to then load passengers for countries farther on.

Although these freedoms had considerable support, especially from the U.S., they were never agreed to universally. This meant that there was a need to establish bilateral agreements between pairs of countries. The formation of the International Civil Aviation Organization (ICAO) in 1944 and the International Air Transport Association (IATA) in 1945 paved the way for the development of bilateral agreements. ICAO is an organization of national governments; IATA is a trade association that represents the airlines.

Chapter 10 indicates that approximately 183 countries including Australia, Canada, South Africa, the U.S., and the United Kingdom belong to ICAO. ICAOs aims and objectives are to develop the principles and techniques of international air navigation and to foster the planning and development of international air transport so as to (ICAO Website, 1997):

1. Ensure the safe and orderly growth of international civil aviation throughout the world.

2. Encourage the arts of aircraft design and operation for peaceful purposes.

3. Encourage the development of airways, airports, and air naviga-

tion facilities for international civil aviation.

4. Meet the needs of the peoples of the world for safe, regular, efficient, and economical air transport.

5. Prevent economic waste caused by unreasonable competition.

6. Ensure that the rights of Contracting States are fully respected and that every Contracting State has a fair opportunity to operate international airlines.

7. Avoid discrimination between Contracting States.

8. Promote safety of flight in international air navigation.

9. Promote generally the development of all aspects of international civil aeronautics.

At the end of 1996, 215 airline companies belonged to IATA, many of which were government-owned airlines. Any company offering a scheduled international air service may belong to IATA. IATA's mission is to represent and serve the airline industry. IATA's goals are (IATA Website, 1997):

- **Safety and security:** To promote safe, reliable, and secure air services.

- **Industry recognition:** To achieve recognition of the importance of a healthy air transport industry to worldwide social and economic development.

- **Financial viability:** To assist the industry to achieve adequate levels of profitability.

- **Products and services:** To provide high quality, value for money, and industry-required products and services that meet the needs of the customer.

- **Standards and procedures:** To develop cost-effective, environmentally friendly standards and procedures to facilitate the operation of international air transport.

- **Industry support:** To identify and articulate common industry positions and support the resolution of key industry issues.
- **Good employer:** To provide a working environment that attracts, retains, and develops committed employees.

In 1979, IATA was reorganized into a "two-tier" organization. First, IATA is a trade association that represents airlines. Second, IATA handles *tariff coordination* for passenger fares, cargo rates, and travel agent commissions for international air travel. Some 105 of IATA's members are Tariff Coordination Members including most of the major airlines in North America, Europe, and the Asia-Pacific region. IATA sets rates on international routes to which all member airlines agree. IATA operates a *Clearing House* for air-ticket coupons that allow passengers to fly internationally on several airlines while requiring only one flight coupon. When a passenger travels on two or more airlines on a trip this is called *interlining*. The IATA Clearing House is where debts between airlines, mainly resulting from interlining, are settled. In 1994, the total amount cleared was US$22.8 billion. Unlike the national regulatory agencies, IATA does not certify airlines, award routes, or act on market exit decisions. These powers remain with the national governments and their regulatory authorities.

IATA acts in an advisory capacity on mutual problems and issues, such as automation, fuel shortages, hijacking, navigation, and safety. IATA assisted in the development of international legal counter-measures on hijacking and sabotage at the Tokyo, Hague, and Montreal conventions. In addition, IATA is an important source of statistics on international air travel.

The *International Airlines Travel Agents Network* (IATAN),

a nonprofit subsidiary of IATA, appoints retail travel agencies in the U.S. to sell tickets on IATA-member airlines. For other travel agencies in the world, IATA operates a *Passenger Agency Programme*. Since 1971, IATA has operated a number of *Billing and Settlement Plans* (BSPs) that represent systems for reporting sales and settling the accounts between airlines and retail travel agencies for international air travel. In 1996, IATA had 59 BSPs that processed a total of US$102 billion and served more than 47,000 retail travel agencies.

Many multilateral agreements have been agreed to by countries on airlines' liabilities for passenger injuries and damage or loss of baggage. Three of the major agreements are the *Warsaw Convention*, the *Hague Protocol*, and the *Montreal Agreement*. The Warsaw Convention dates back to 1929 and constitutes the main body of international rules in this respect. The U.S. accepted the Warsaw Convention regulations in 1934; Canada and the United Kingdom are other adherents to it. Several Central American and South American countries are not members of the treaty. The Hague Protocol and the Montreal Agreement represent international agreements that have raised the dollar limit on an airline's liability to an individual passenger. In 1997, ICAO's Legal Committee drafted a new Convention to modernize the Warsaw Convention. If adopted by ICAO Contracting States, this would remove limits of liability of airlines in aircraft accidents where passengers are injured or killed.

Bilateral Air Agreements

A *bilateral agreement* is an agreement struck between two national governments. The U.K.-U.S. *Bermuda Agreement* of 1946 was the benchmark bilateral air travel

agreement. Bilateral air agreements mainly address the questions of which airlines can fly between two countries and to which airports they are allowed to fly. Since 1946, approximately 4,000 bilateral air agreements have been signed and registered with ICAO. These bilateral agreements are sometimes loose and often mask ongoing disputes between two countries over air services. The 1973 bilateral agreement between the U.S. and Canada was a good example. It was indicative of the inherent problems of a tourism system in which the market or political philosophies of nations are quite different. In 1978, the U.S. began the process of deregulating its domestic airline industry and has been a strong proponent of an open skies airline policy internationally. For some years, Canada maintained a policy of protecting its airline companies. Canada's refusal to completely open up the international air border between itself and the U.S. led in 1983 to a serious dispute over a proposed package of heavily discounted fares to be offered by Air Canada (the government-owned airline at the time) to several cities in the southern U.S. The U.S. Civil Aeronautics Board's obstinacy in not allowing these fare schedules caused many Canadians pre-booked on these flights to cancel their trips. The destination areas within the southern U.S. suffered because of the loss of potential income from the Canadian travelers.

In 1995, a new bilateral air agreement between Canada and the U.S., known as the Open Skies Agreement, was signed. This agreement allows full market access for the airlines of both countries between airports in the two countries. The U.S. and the Netherlands have also agreed to an open skies policy between the two countries. There are several conditions to an open skies policy and these are

(Vellas & Becherel, 1995) the following:

- Free access to all routes.
- No restriction on capacity and frequency on any route.
- No restriction on operation in all international markets.
- Flexibility in tariffs.
- Liberalization of charter rules and elimination of restrictions on charters.
- Liberalization of air cargo rules.
- No restrictions on the conversion of revenue to hard currency.
- Agreement on code-sharing.
- Airline companies are able to ensure their own ground services abroad.
- No regulation on commercial agreements concerning air transport operation.
- Non-discriminatory access and use of computer reservation systems.

Airlines are increasingly forming *strategic alliances* with for-eign airlines in an attempt to gain greater access to foreign countries (see figure below). This strategy allows the airlines to avoid the intergovernmental restrictions imposed by bilateral agreements. These alliances have been very popular in the U.S., where outbound international passenger volumes increased 47 percent between 1987 and 1993, compared with only a 6 percent increase in domestic passenger volumes (GAO, 1995). *Code-sharing* is one of the facets of these alliances. This arrangement allows one airline to use its own two-character code (e.g., NW for Northwest) to advertise a flight as its own in travel agent computer reservation systems, when the flight is actually being operated by its partner airline (e.g., KLM Royal Dutch Airlines).

Historically, one of the reasons for restrictions of airline operations was the protection of government-owned airlines. The need for these restrictions is becoming less as more countries are *privatizing national carriers*. The ICAO reported that in 1995 seven national carriers were privatized and nine were targeted for privatization. Twenty-five government-owned carriers were sold to private-sector operators in previous years. There has also been a trend in airports to allow these to be operated by companies and authorities that are autonomous of government (ICAO, 1996).

GATT and GATS

The General Agreement on Tariffs and Trade (GATT) is a treaty and represents the world's only multilateral agreement on the rules for international trade. The first agreement was signed in 1947. Generally, the purpose of GATT is to remove barriers to international trade. There have been several rounds of negotiations since 1947, with the latest known as the Uruguay Round between 1986–1994. The final stages of the Uruguay Round resulted in an agreement to create the World Trade Organization, which will become the world's regulator of trade (Kluwer Law International, 1996).

Air Canada, Lufthansa, SAS, Thai, and United begin their "Star Alliance." Reprinted by permission of United Airlines.

Another outcome of the Uruguay Round was the General Agreement on Trade in Services (GATS). GATS will liberalize trade in services and could have a major impact on tourism. GATS may result in free market access to suppliers of tourism services in foreign countries and equivalent treatment to domestic businesses. Barriers to market entry such as quotas and licenses may be removed.

Hotel Classification

Hotel classification on an international level also represents a tacit attempt by several nations to regulate standards within another important component of the tourism system. The World Tourism Organization (WTO) has taken the lead role in this regard. It was given this authority in 1963 when the United Nations Conference on International Travel and Tourism asked it to draft these standards. The main rationale for setting these was that "traveling problems can be eased to a considerable extent if hotels of a particular category in all countries were to present more or less the same characteristics of comfort and service" (World Tourism Organization, 1969).

Although many countries appear to agree in principle with the classification method and criteria that the WTO has developed, many have chosen to create their own classification and grading/rating systems since they have found the WTO guidelines to be too broad for their purposes. There are also a number of private-sector accommodation and restaurant rating schemes in operation around the world, and these have helped travelers to better determine quality standards in unfamiliar destinations. These include the systems operated by Michelin and the motoring organizations in several countries.

World Heritage List, UNESCO

UNESCO, the United Nations Educational, Scientific and Cultural Organization, is an agency of the United Nations concerned with education, science, and cultural and natural heritage. At its 1972 General Conference, an international agreement was signed titled the **Convention Concerning the Protection of the World Cultural and Natural Heritage**. The primary purpose of this agreement was to define and conserve the world's heritage by drawing up a list of sites whose outstanding values should be preserved for all humanity and to ensure their protection through a closer cooperation among nations (UNESCO World Heritage Centre Website, 1997). At the end of 1996, there were 506 sites around the world on the UNESCO **World Heritage List**. Some of the well-known tourism attractions on the list include the Great Barrier Reef, Kakadu National Park, Ayers Rock-The Olgas, and the Wet Tropics of Queensland (Australia); The Great Wall of China; the Canadian Rocky Mountain Parks; the Galapagos Islands

(Ecuador); the Pyramids of Egypt; the Cathedral of Notre Dame in Paris; the Acropolis in Athens; the Taj Mahal; Machu Picchu (Peru); the Kremlin and Red Square (Russia), Stonehenge and the Old and New Towns of Edinburgh (U.K.); Grand Canyon and Yellowstone National Parks and the Statue of Liberty (U.S.). The common characteristics of these sites according to UNESCO (1997) are:

"These cultural and natural sites constitute, together with many others, a common heritage, to be treasured as unique testimonies to an enduring past. Their disappearance would be an irreparable loss for each and every one of us. And yet, most are threatened, particularly in present times. The preservation of this common heritage concerns us all."

The World Heritage Committee was established under the Convention as a statutory body. The committee, consisting of 21 member countries, selects new sites for the World Heritage List and helps to protect the sites with assistance from the World Heritage Fund. The

The Buda Castle District in Budapest, Hungary is a World Heritage listed site. Photo from *Budapest in 101 Photos; Multimedia CD for the IBM PC* (Selester, Hungary, 1996). Printed with permission.

day-to-day management of the convention has been given to the UNESCO World Heritage Centre located in Paris. Evaluations of new sites are done with the assistance of the International Council on Monuments and Sites (ICOMOS) for cultural sites, and the World Conservation Union (UCN) for natural sites. Both of these organizations are located in Paris.

UNESCO maintains another list called the *List of World Heritage in Danger*. This list includes sites that are placed in danger because of civil disturbances or through environmental threats. For example, due to wars in the former Zaire and Yugoslavia, several sites in these areas were added to the list in the 1990s including the Old City of Dubrovnik in Croatia.

Free Trade Agreements

There are many other treaties and agreements governing trade and travel procedures among countries. These also play a key role in the tourism regulatory framework of destination areas. One of the major forces here in recent years has been the creation of *free trade areas* such as the European Economic Community (EEC) and the North American Free Trade Agreement (NAFTA). Australia and New Zealand are also working on a Trans-Tasman trade agreement.

Reasons for Destination Area Legislation and Regulations

"Food, to be merchantable, must be fit for human consumption, that is, it should not make you ill when you eat it. To pass muster, food does not have to be nutritional or taste great; it merely must be eatable."

Cournoyer, N.G., Marshall, A.G., & Morris, K.L. (1993), 413

Quick Trip 11.1
Criteria for World Heritage List Selection

UNESCO has developed an elaborate list of selection criteria for its World Heritage List. There are two sets of selection criteria: one for cultural properties, and the other for natural heritage. Three types of properties are considered in the cultural group:

- **Monuments:** Architectural works, works of monumental sculpture and painting, elements or structures of an archaeological nature, inscriptions, cave dwellings and combinations of features, which are of outstanding universal value from the point of view of history, art, or science.
- **Groups of buildings:** Groups of separate or connected buildings which, because of their architecture, their homogeneity or their place in the landscape, are of outstanding universal value from the point of view of history, art, or science.
- **Sites:** Human works or the combined works of nature and humans and areas including archaeological sites that are of outstanding universal value from the historical, aesthetic, ethnological, or anthropological points of view.

Natural heritage sites are also of three types:

- **Natural features:** Consist of physical and biological formations or groups of such formations, which are of outstanding universal value from the aesthetic or scientific point of view.
- **Geological and physiographical formations and precisely delineated areas:** Constitute the habitat of threatened species of animals and plants of outstanding universal value from the point of view of science or conservation.
- **Natural sites and precisely delineated areas:** Are of outstanding value from the point of view of science, conservation, or natural beauty.

Source: UNESCO. (1997).

Every country has a myriad of laws and regulations that affect tourism. These are established by various levels of governments from national to local. Laws and regulations allow governments to implement tourism policies and plans (chapter 12), to fulfill government roles in tourism (chapter 10), and to control the impacts of tourism (chapter 9).

There are several categories of laws that impact tourism. These vary from country to country. According to Goodwin & Gaston (1992), there are eight different classifications of laws that impact tourism in the U.S.:

- Judicial and administrative law
- Common and statutory law
- Common and civil law
- Public and private law
- Substantive and procedural law
- Contract and property law

- Tort and criminal law
- Law and equity

Many of the laws that directly affect tourism in most countries are in the statutory law category. These are laws created by acts of lawmaking bodies (governments). There are tort and criminal laws that impact tourism; most often when frauds are committed against travelers and people buying land for recreational purposes. Some of the most common reasons for introducing tourism-related laws and regulations are:

Controlling the entry of foreign visitors and goods: There is a need in every country to introduce laws and regulations regarding the entry of foreign nationals and goods from other countries. Protecting the national health interest is one of the reasons for immigration regulations and procedures.

Controlling the quality of the visitor experience: Laws and regulations may be introduced to ensure that visitors have a high quality experience in the destination area. For example, the use of some wilderness areas (e.g., scenic rivers) may be regulated so that the users experience of the wild is not spoiled by there being too many other visitors. Laws may be introduced to protect foreign visitors from being harassed or abused by local people who are begging or touting services and products.

Ensuring travel safety: Many laws and regulations are in force to ensure the safety of people traveling by air, rail, road, and sea. Regulatory agencies are created within each country to control and enforce safety standards. For example, many countries have a maritime regulatory agency that ensures the safety of all watercraft through

programs of licensing and regular inspections.

Establishing tourism organizations: Laws are often passed to establish new tourism organizations. For example, the Development of Tourism Act of 1969 established the British Tourist Authority, English Tourist Board, Scottish Tourist Board, and the Wales Tourist Board. The Australian Tourist Commission came into being as a result of the Australian Tourist Commission Act of 1987.

Gaming control: Laws are introduced at various levels of government to control the development of gaming operations including casinos and lotteries. Some countries and states strictly prohibit different forms of gaming due to social or religious reasons. Other governments allow only certain forms of gaming, e.g., casinos on riverboats.

Maintaining building standards: Building codes are introduced to ensure that building materials and specifications meet required standards.

Maintaining operating standards: Governments introduce

Quick Trip 11.2
The North American Free Trade Agreement

The North American Free Trade Agreement (NAFTA) became effective in 1994 and involves trade among Canada, Mexico, and the United States. NAFTA's objectives are to

- Eliminate barriers to trade in, and facilitate the cross-border movement of, goods and services between the territories of the Parties (Canada, Mexico, the United States).
- Promote conditions of fair competition in the free trade area.
- Increase substantially investment opportunities in the territories of the Parties.
- Provide adequate and effective protection and enforcement of the intellectual property rights in each Party's territory.
- Create effective procedures for further implementation and application of this Agreement, for its joint administration and for the resolution of disputes.
- Establish a framework for further trilateral, regional, and multilateral cooperation to expand and enhance the benefits of this Agreement.

It is expected that NAFTA will eventually benefit tourism by simplifying border entry procedures among the three countries. For business travel, simplified procedures will be introduced to expedite business travel including granting eligible business people with temporary entry without prior approval.

Source: Department of Foreign Affairs and International Trade, Canada and NAFTANET. (1997).

licensing and registration systems to maintain the operating standards in different parts of tourism. These may include regular inspection programs to ensure continued conformance to standards. Accommodation grading or rating systems are an example of this type of system.

Protecting the traveler: A variety of laws and regulations are introduced to protect visitors. These include fire safety laws for hotels, regulations on the safe handling of food, and laws to protect travelers from fraud and financial failures of travel trade companies. Other laws protect consumers from deceptive advertising practices. Regulations may also be in force to protect the safety of visitors when engaging in certain activities (e.g., adventure travel activities such as white water rafting and ballooning) and attending certain types of attractions (e.g., amusement parks with rides). Laws are also introduced to protect people when they are purchasing condominium resort offerings including timesharing.

Protecting the environment and culture: There are many laws and regulations dealing with environmental protection and conservation. These include laws creating national or state park systems, shoreline protection systems, regulations on sewage disposal systems, and other measures to protect physical environments. The Kingdom of Bhutan in the Himalaya Mountains allowed only 6,000 foreign visitors into the country in 1996 in order to control the impacts of tourism.

Raising funds for tourism: Some laws are introduced to institute taxes or other levies to provide for tourism marketing and development. In the U.S., uniform innkeepers' laws at the state level provide the mechanism for funding local convention and visitors bureaus.

Supporting physical planning guidelines: Laws and regulations are introduced to control land use. The zoning regulations and building permit systems in force in many municipalities are a good example.

Types of Destination Area Legislation and Regulations

> *"Today, more than ever before, the legal aspects of our actions are every bit as important as the financial and marketing implications. No longer can we routinely pursue our sales and service objectives without giving careful consideration to contracts, insurance, advertising, and the correct approach to the marketplace and competition."*
>
> Miller, J.R. (1987), vii

Before describing specific types of tourism legislation and regulations, it is useful to classify them into different groups. One method of classification is to group the tourism legislation and regulations into *functional areas*, such as those related to the protection of the environment, those related to economic development, and those related to frontier controls. Another means of classification is to group on a *sector basis* by identifying the legislation and regulations that relate to airlines, hotels, travel agents, and other tourism businesses. In this respect, *horizontal legislation or regulations* are those items that affect every sector, whether it be a tourism or non-tourism one, such as income tax and labor legislation. *Specific legislation or regulations* are those items that relate directly to a specific sector. An example of this is a grading system for hotels.

Figure 11.1 illustrates commonly found legislation and regulations classified on a sector-by-sector basis in tourism.

Forms of Destination Area Legislation and Regulations

> *"A debate still rages over whether deregulation has meant substantial improvements for the traveling public. But most travel industry people agree that, so long as air safety is preserved and essential air service is still available, it is better to let business people control their own fates."*
>
> Fredericks, A. (1985), 7

There are certain forms of legislation and regulation that are encountered in most destination areas. These include legislation and regulations governing the following:

- Accommodation standards
- Alcohol sales laws and regulations
- Civil aviation regulations
- Environmental protection and conservation regulations
- Health regulations
- Innkeeper liability laws
- Retail travel agency, tour wholesaler, and operator regulations
- Regulations on safety in activity participation
- Timesharing laws and regulations

Accommodation Standards

One of the aspects of tourism that receives much attention from governments around the world is the standards of accommodation facilities. Some countries have introduced mandatory *classification*

TOURISM SECTOR	TYPES OF LEGISLATION AND REGULATION
Accommodation and Food Services	• Alcohol sales and regulations • Building and zoning codes • Classification, grading, or rating of hotels and other establishment types • Fire safety regulations and codes • Health safety regulations and codes • Operating licenses and other regulations of the terms and conditions of operation • Liability laws with respect to guests and their belongings • Labor and taxation legislation
Travel Agents, Tour Wholesalers, Tour Operators	• Definition of responsibilities and limitations • Regulations and licensing of travel agents, tour wholesalers, and operators • Regulations of promotions • Labor and taxation legislation
Airlines, Railways, Buses, Ships, and Other Carriers	• Control of fares and tariffs • Control of route entry and exit • Labor and taxation legislation • Licensing of carriers • Limitation of weights and capacities • Negotiations of services • Regulation of safety procedures • Subsidization of routes
Attraction Operators, Adventure Travel Operators	• Regulation of safety procedures • Licensing or registration of operators • Inspection and licensing of equipment • Licensing or certification of guides

Figure 11.1   Types of Legislation and Regulation.

Accommodation properties must deal with many types of legislation and regulation. Photo courtesy of Brown County Convention & Visitors Bureau, Nashville, Indiana.

and grading systems for accommodation, while others operate similar programs on a voluntary basis. For example, Ireland operates a compulsory accommodation classification and grading system. This was created through national legislation in the Tourism Traffic Act of 1939 (CERT, 1993). This program is operated by the Irish Tourist Board. England and Scotland operate voluntary programs under the English and Scottish Tourist Boards.

Alcohol Sales Laws and Regulations

Regulations are required over the sale and consumption of alcohol. This is accomplished mainly through the licensing of establishments that are allowed to sell alcohol and where alcohol consumption is permitted. One of the main goals of licensing is to prevent inju-

ries that can result from the abuse of alcohol through car accidents, fights and other anti-social behavior. A second reason is to prevent the sale of alcohol to underage customers, to people who are already intoxicated, and to habitual drunkards (Cournoyer, Marshall, & Morris, 1993). Typically, licenses to sell alcohol are granted by state, provincial, or territorial governments.

Civil Aviation Regulations

Almost every country in the world has a government regulatory agency that controls air travel. In the U.S., this is the Federal Aviation Administration (FAA). Australia has the Civil Aviation Safety Authority (CASA) and the United Kingdom has the Civil Aviation Authority (CAA). One of the major roles of these regulatory agencies is to ensure the highest levels of safety when flying and when on the ground at airports.

One of the most talked about trends in civil aviation during the 1980s and 1990s was *airline deregulation*, meaning the relaxation of regulations governing the operation of commercial airlines. The deregulation of the domestic airlines in the U.S. is a benchmark case study for many other regions of the world. The U.S. established the Civil Aeronautics Board (CAB) in 1938 through the Civil Aeronautics Act. Its mandate was to protect the safety of the public and to maintain the viability of the U.S. airline industry. The CAB was given the authority to determine which airlines could operate in the U.S., which routes they could operate, and what fares they could charge. It was given powers over airline schedules, airline profit margins, and the types of working relationships permissible. Since its inception, the CAB was probably the most influential regulatory agency in the U.S. with respect to tourism.

The successful passage of the Airline Deregulation Act in Octo-

Scenic balloon flights fall under the Civil Air Regulations in some destinations. Photo from *Top Shots* CD Rom. Courtesy of Queensland Tourist and Travel Corporation.

Quick Trip 11.3
Accommodation Classification and Grading in Scotland

The Scottish Tourist Board has a Quality Assurance program for accommodation. Through inspections, an assessment is made of quality and service including the warmth of welcome, atmosphere, and efficiency of service, as well as the quality of furnishings, fixtures, and decor. Each property inspected is awarded one of four levels:

- **Deluxe:** An overall excellent quality standard.
- **Highly commended:** An overall very good standard.
- **Commended:** An overall good quality standard.
- **Approved:** An overall acceptable quality standard.

Supplementing these designations, a crown system is used to indicate the range of facilities and services provided in each property. One set of crowns is applied to hotels, guest homes, and bed and breakfasts, and another to self-catering accommodations. The five crown designations for hotels, guest houses, and bed and breakfasts signify the following:

- **One crown:** Your own bedroom key. Shared lounge area. Washbasins in bedrooms or in private bathrooms.
- **Two crowns:** Color TV. Early morning tea. Minimum of 20 percent of bedrooms with en suite/private bathrooms.
- **Three crowns:** Evening meal. Hairdryer. Shoe cleaning equipment. Ironing facilities and tea and coffee making facilities.
- **Four crowns:** Evening meal. Choice of dishes and selection of wine. Color TV, radio and television in bedroom. Laundry services, toiletries. Quiet seating area.
- **Five crowns:** All bedrooms with full en suite facilities. Restaurant serving breakfast, lunch, and dinner. Night porter and room service. 24-hour lounge service.

Source: Scottish Tourist Board. (1997).

---

ber 1978 was a very significant event for U.S. tourism. This act was historically unique since it was the first time that the U.S. government virtually abolished its role in the economic regulation of an industry. The decision to wind up the powerful CAB came after much public criticism of the agency and of its perceived over-regulation of the airline industry. The general concern was that the CAB had gone too far in trying to maintain the viability of the airline industry and was beginning to engage in activities that were not beneficial to the traveling public. Another major problem with the CAB was its tardiness in responding to proposals presented by individual airline companies. During the long lag time, airlines often changed their minds about their proposals or they lost the benefit of the marketing opportunity they were seeking. The Airline Deregulation Act of 1978 envisaged that the CAB would be completely phased out by January 1985. The CAB "sunset" time-table included the loss of its authority over route entry in 1982 and its jurisdiction over tariffs and pricing in 1983. The CAB ceased to be at the end of 1984.

According to the General Accounting Office Report on Airline Deregulation, the expected results of airline deregulation were (GAO, 1996):

- To lower fares at large-community airports, from which trips are long distance, and to increase fares at small- and medium-sized airports.

- To increase competition through new airlines referred to as "new entrant" airlines.

- To increase use of turboprop aircraft by airlines in place of jets in smaller markets that could not economically support jet service.

The U.S. air travel experiment, which was motivated by the desire to let the marketplace operate more freely to the ultimate benefit of travelers, has had its advantages and disadvantages. As the GAO report indicates, several new airlines were created and some of these introduced more discounted air fares for travelers. Several new airlines failed or were absorbed by the larger airline companies. Airline competition definitely increased. There were some consumer concerns with the quality of airline services and the safety of air travel. Airports and airplanes became more crowded, and overbooking was encountered more often.

Environmental Protection and Conservation Regulations

Governments at all levels have introduced laws and regulations aimed at promoting environmental protection and conservation. These measures help support the role of governments in sustainable tourism development. Among the most important laws are those that have initiated systems of national parks. Two of the landmark pieces of such legislation in the world are the Yellowstone National Park Act of 1872 in the U.S. and the Rocky Mountain Parks Act of 1887 in Canada, which established its first national park surrounding Banff, Alberta. The National Parks Act followed in Canada in 1930, and in 1953 the Historic Sites and Monuments Act was passed. The 1930 act stated that only such uses would be permitted within national parks that would "leave them unimpaired for the enjoyment of future generations" (Parks Canada, 1979). This clause has been quite controversial since some of Canada's national parks such as Banff, Lake Louise, and Jasper are among the nation's major tourist attractions and most favored destinations, particularly for foreign visitors.

In England, the government created the Countryside Commission

---

> ### Quick Trip 11.4
> # The U.S. Federal Aviation Administration (FAA)
>
> The Federal Aviation Administration (FAA) was established by the U.S. government through the Federal Aviation Act of 1958. There are seven business units within the FAA:
>
> - **Administration:** Provides the FAA organizations with the collective ability to acquire, account for, and maintain the resources necessary to meet the FAA mission requirements.
> - **Airports:** Provides leadership in planning and developing a safe and efficient national airports system.
> - **Air traffic services:** Ensures safety, efficient operation, and maintenance of the air transportation system
> - **Commercial space:** Regulates and promotes the commercial space and transportation industries.
> - **Regulation and certification:** Promotes the highest safety standards in the world and provides service to the public.
> - **Research and acquisitions:** Provides guidance related to acquisition policy, research, system prototyping, and information resource management.
> - **The Office of System safety:** Provides access to aviation safety-related databases, safety reports and publications, and information on the Global Analysis Information Network (GAIN) project.
>
> Air Traffic Services is one of the key FAA organizations concerned with passenger safety. Its mission is "to ensure the safe, efficient operation, maintenance and use of the air transportation system today, maximize utility of the airspace resources, and meet tomorrow's challenges to increase system safety, capacity, and productivity." The Regulation and Certification Group sets flight standards, certifies aircraft, and conducts investigations of aircraft accidents.
>
> Source: Federal Aviation Administration. (1997).

---

to provide advice on the conservation of the English countryside and how people can enjoy it. One of the Commission's tasks is to identify and designate special areas such as National Parks, Heritage Coasts, Areas of Outstanding Natural Beauty, and National Trails (Countryside Commission Website, 1997).

State, regional, county, and municipal governments usually have the authority to regulate land uses and to acquire land within their jurisdictions. Historically, these powers have been passed on to local governments at the city, town, and county levels. Cities, towns, and counties exercise these powers through the development of municipal plans, the enforcement of zoning regulations, and the operation of building permit systems.

Health Regulations

Governments introduce rules to protect visitors and residents from the risk of disease and illness resulting from exposure and food and water. Several countries insist that travelers from infected areas of other countries show proof of vaccination against certain diseases (e.g., yellow fever). The World Health Organization (WHO) and the World Tourism Organization identify great endemic and epidemic diseases (e.g., malaria), untreated water, accidents (e.g., animal bites), lack of services and equipment (e.g., ambulances and hospitals), unsanitary drinks, and food as the major health risks to visitors in many countries (World Tourism Organization, 1991). There is an obligation on the part of governments and tourism businesses to warn travelers of the risks of contracting certain diseases and precautions that are advisable to reduce such risks.

It is essential that governments protect people from food-borne illnesses when they eat in restaurants. This role is accomplished through regular inspections by health inspectors and rules regarding the storage, cooking, and handling of food and beverages. Often, this role is performed by local government agencies that have the right to close down establishments that do not meet standards.

Innkeeper Liability Laws

Most destinations have a variety of laws and regulations that indicate the extent of the liability of accommodation establishment operators for the personal injury of guests and the loss of guest possessions. These measures include fire safety laws that impose rules regarding the construction and operation of accommodation establishments. One of the major problems facing accommodation operators is how to protect guests' property when they are on the premises. Thefts from guest rooms and vehicles are quite common in tourism. In some countries, under common law, innkeepers have "absolute liability" for any loss of guest property. Other accommodation operators install elaborate security systems including guest room safes and electronic door card key systems.

Retail Travel Agency, Tour Wholesaler, and Operator Regulations

Travel trade intermediaries are another part of tourism that is frequently covered by tourism legislation and regulations. These measures are introduced to protect consumers from fraudulent practices and from the financial failure of tour wholesalers, tour operators, retail travel agencies, and other organizations that sell travel services. There has been a definite trend toward more regulation in this area as the number of travel-related frauds are increasing. Often these programs require travel companies to be licensed or register with a government agency before they are allowed to operate. They may also be required to post a bond or pay into a compensation fund.

An example of such a program is the Registration of Travel Wholesalers and Retailers Program operated by the Ontario government in Canada. This program was introduced through Ontario's Travel Industry Act and requires that all travel agencies and wholesalers register with the provincial government's Ministry of Consumer and Commercial Relations. Each company must pay a C$375 registration fee and make a C$2,300 payment into the Ontario Travel Industry Compensation Fund. This fund is operated by an independent board of trustees that reviews consumer claims when travel services are not provided and when travel agents refuse to refund money. The fund also assists in returning stranded travelers and with the immediate departure of travelers (Queens Printer of Ontario, 1997).

A number of U.S. states have introduced similar programs. Rhode Island, for example, passed a Travel Agency Act in 1977 giving the state the power to license retail travel agencies. The law was passed as a result of serious complaints from consumers about their experiences with certain agencies. Rhode Island was the first state in the U.S. to introduce such legislation, while Puerto Rico had done so earlier in 1974. Now known generically as *sellers of travel laws*, some of the states that have added them more recently are California, Florida, Oregon, and Washington. In California, anyone selling air or sea transportation must register with the state's Attorney General's Office and must use a state registration number on all advertising materials. They must also put 100 percent of their client's money into a trust account until the services have been provided. Florida's Sellers of Travel Law is administered by the state government's Department of Agriculture & Consumer Services. This law requires that any seller or promoter of travel related services register annually with the

Food must not only look good; it must be safe for consumption. Photo from *Top Shots* CD Rom. Courtesy of Queensland Tourist and Travel Corporation.

department and have a performance bond of US$25,000.

In the United Kingdom, the Civil Aviation Authority (CAA) grants licenses to companies that provide package vacations that include flights. These are called Air Travel Organisers Licences (ATOL). Every ATOL holder is examined each year to ensure that they are financially sound. Australia operates a national system of travel agent licensing and a Travel Compensation Fund to reimburse travelers if a licensed travel agency goes bankrupt or becomes insolvent.

Regulations on Safety in Activity Participation

There are many situations around the world in which travelers are exposed to danger within destination areas. These include situations when people are traveling by road, rail, and by water, and when visitors are engaging in certain activities that may result in injuries or death. Scenic boat trips, motor coach tours, scenic rail trips, and guided four-wheel drive trips are examples of tourism offerings where travelers are exposed to a certain level of physical danger. An element of danger is also present when riding on roller coasters and other equipment at theme and amusement parks. The trend toward the increasing popularity of adventure travel places more people each year in situations of personal risk.

The rapidly increasing popularity of adventure travel in many parts of the world has inevitably led to an increase in accidents involving travelers. These have occurred in activities including ballooning, kayaking, jet-boating, and white water rafting. Some destinations that are quite dependent on adventure travel are concerned about the negative publicity these incidents create for tourism. New Zealand is one of these countries and it is well known for its adven-

ture activities. As a result of a number of fatalities in 1995 involving foreign visitors, the Tourism Policy Group conducted an analysis of the safety of adventure tourism operators. The report stated that "the Ministry of Commerce's primary concern is whether there is a potential for long term damage to occur to tourism if New Zealand is perceived by overseas travelers as unsafe" (Tourism Policy Group, 1996). This shows that the government not only has a responsibility to protect the safety of visitors, but that failure to perform this role may have a negative effect on tourism marketing.

Timesharing Laws and Regulations

Another part of tourism that has received considerable attention has been the condominium real estate developments within resort areas, particularly **timesharing** projects. The early history of these projects in many countries involved several cases of fraud and misleading sales claims. Several governments

Adventure travel is a tourism growth market. Photo from *Top Shots* CD Rom. Courtesy of Queensland Tourist and Travel Corporation.

moved to protect customers from such abuses. For example, in the U.S., Nebraska was the first state to introduce a timesharing act to protect its citizens against any misleading claims of timesharing resort developers in Nebraska and elsewhere.

Self-Regulation in Tourism

> "Consumers may expect adventure activities to be safe, despite cost, and that differences in price (cost) between similar activities should indicate a difference only in those aspects of quality other than safety standards. This confidence may be based on their belief that the Government would not allow the continuation of tourism operations in which there is a significant risk of serious injury or death."
>
> Tourism Policy Group. (1996), 7

A government's main control over individual tourism business operators is through mandatory licensing or registration, which may or may not be supported by a system of regular inspections or reviews. Government licensing or registration systems operated by government protect travelers from tourism operators or operations that are either unsafe, incompetent, or financially unstable. An alternative to this type of government control is to have tourism businesses regulate themselves. This may be done through private-sector associations or specially created organizations. There has been a definite trend around the world toward more self-regulation in tourism. The types of programs that can be used to maintain professional and other standards in tourism include:

● **Accreditation:** Accreditation is a process by which an association or agency evaluates and recognizes a program of study or an institution as meeting certain predetermined standards or qualifications (American Society of Association Executives). The appointment of travel agents by organizations such as IATA is an example of this approach.

- **Certification:** Certification applies to individuals who work for tourism businesses. It is a process by which an individual is tested and evaluated to determine his or her mastery of a specific body of knowledge, or some portion of a body of knowledge (American Society of Association Executives). Certification usually follows after a course of study and after the individual has gained a prescribed number of years of experience. In the U.S., for example, the National Restaurant Association offers a certification program on food sanitation standards.

- **Codes of ethics or practice:** Trade associations may develop codes of ethics or codes of practice to which they require members to adhere. Chapter 16 indicates that several travel agency associations (including ASTA, AFTA, and ABTA) have developed codes of ethics for their members (see quick trip 16.3).

- **Consumer protection programs:** A trade association establishes a program to protect travelers in the event of the bankruptcy or insolvency of any of its members. All members are required to participate in this program. A self-imposed program may obviate the need for a government agency to introduce one. The consumer protection plan operated by the U.S. Tour Operators Association (USTOA) is a good example of this.

Self-regulation tends to be a more popular form of control among private businesses. For ex-

---

Quick Trip 11.5

The USTOA Million-Dollar Consumer Protection Plan

The U.S. Tour Operators Association, headquartered in New York, has approximately 40 active member tour operators. These include some of the largest tour operator companies in the world. Unlike other countries such as the United Kingdom and Australia, the U.S. does not have a national program of licensing or registration for tour operators. There is also no national-level travel compensation fund.

The USTOA voluntarily introduced a consumer protection plan several years ago and all active members must participate as a condition of membership. The plan requires that each member put up $1 million in the form of a bond, letter of credit, or certificate of deposit. This fund is used to protect travelers in the case of a bankruptcy or default by a member. The security is held by USTOA and may be used to reimburse travelers' deposits or payments to a member tour operator. Up to $1 million can be paid back to an individual traveler. According to Robert Whitley, president of USTOA, "It takes a financially stable company to demonstrate commitment to consumers by turning over $1 million that they cannot touch themselves. This kind of commitment assures consumers that our organization is made up of financially stable companies, and that, in an uncertain economy, travelers can continue to turn to USTOA as the standard for consumer protection in tours and vacation packages."

Source: U.S. Tour Operators Association. (1997).

---

ample, there has been a proliferation of professionalism certification programs in North America. These now cover association executives, corporate travel managers, hotel managers and sales executives, meeting planners, retail travel agents, and tour planners (Morrison, Hsieh, & Wang, 1992). The Certified Travel Counselor program offered for retail travel agents by the Institute of Certified Travel Agents (ICTA) is one of the oldest of these programs, having started in the mid 1960s. However, programs such as these are most effective if all members of the group participate in the program, and many of these programs in tourism are voluntary. Associations are often reluctant to enforce mandatory conditions of membership for fear that businesses will not join and mem-

bership revenues will be lost. In addition, it is essential that visitors understand the program objectives and the value of using businesses participating in the program.

Summary

Experience has shown that tourism development can have both positive and negative impacts on a destination area. Tourism also affects and is influenced by the national interests of a country including its natural and cultural resources and its immigration laws and policies. For these and other reasons, it is essential that governments play a role in developing legislation and in regulating specific parts of tourism.

All tourism destinations have many laws and regulations that affect tourism. Many of these are introduced to protect visitors and residents, as well as the environmental and cultural heritage of the destination.

There has been a strong global trend toward freer trade and travel among countries. This will have a positive influence on world tourism in the future. There has also been a definite trend toward deregulating parts of tourism and toward the privatization of previously government-operated organizations. The U.S. has been a leader in this regard having removed its regulation on airlines. Another trend that shows the increasing maturity and professionalism in tourism is the move toward greater self-regulation through accreditation, certification, and consumer protection programs. The development of programs such as these, along with more deregulation and privatization, may mean that the government influence on tourism will diminish in the future.

Tauck Tours advertises its tours to National Parks and its membership in the USTOA $1 million consumer protection plan. Reprinted by permission of Tauck Tours.

References

American Society of Association Executives. (n.d.). *Accreditation, certification, & standardization; Definitions & principles.* Washington, DC: ASAE

CERT. (1993). *Tourism and travel in Ireland.* Dublin: Gill & Macmillan.

Cournoyer, N.G., Marshall, A.G., & Morris, K.L. (1993). *Hotel, restaurant, and travel law: A preventive approach* (4th ed.). Albany, New York: Delmar Publishers.

Del Rosso, L. (1995). Travel sellers laws are a reality in more states than ever. *Travel Weekly,* 54 (98), 18–22.

Department of Foreign Affairs and International Trade. (1996). *Canada, the North American market and NAFTA.* Ottawa: DFAIT.

Dilts, J.C., & Prough, G.E. (1991). Travel agent perceptions and responses in a deregulated travel environment. *Journal of Travel Research,* 29 (3), 37–42.

Edgell, D.L., Sr. (1993). *World tourism at the millennium: An agenda for industry, government and education.* Washington: U.S. Department of Commerce.

Fredericks, A. (1985). The ripple effect. *Travel Weekly,* 44 (48), 6–7.

General Accounting Office. (1995). *International aviation: Airline alliances produce benefits, but affect on competition is uncertain.* Washington, DC: GAO.

General Accounting Office. (1996). *GAO report: Airline deregulation.* Washington, DC: GAO.

Goodwin, J.R., & Gaston, J.R. (1992). *Hotel and hospitality law: Principles and cases* (4th ed.). Scottsdale, AZ: Gorsuch Scarisbrick, Publishers.

Hiemstra, S.J., & Ismail, J.A. (1992). Analysis of room taxes levied on the lodging industry. *Journal of Travel Research,* 31 (1), 42–49.

Inskeep, E. (1991). *Tourism planning: An integrated and sustainable development approach.* New York: Van Nostrand Reinhold.

International Civil Aviation Organization. (1996). *The world of civil aviation 1995–98.* Montreal: ICAO.

Kluwer Law International. (1996). A history of GATT and the structure of WTO. *International Contract Adviser,* 2 (1).

Mihalic, B.J. (1992). Tourism impacts related to EC92: A look ahead. *Journal of Travel Research,* 31 (2), 27–33.

Miller, J.R. (1987). *Legal aspects of travel agency operation* (2nd ed.). Albany, New York: Delmar Publishers.

Morrison, A.M., Hsieh, S., and Wang, C.Y. (1992). Certification in the travel and tourism industry: The North American experience. *Journal of Tourism Studies,* 3 (2), 32–40.

Parks Canada. (1979). *Parks Canada policy.* Ottawa: Parks Canada, 1979.

Stanton, J., & Aislabie, C. (1992). Local government regulation and the economics of tourist resort development: An Australian case study. *Journal of Tourism Studies,* 3 (2), 20–31.

Tourism Policy Group. (1996). *Safety management in the adventure tourism industry: Voluntary and regulatory approaches.* Wellington, New Zealand: Ministry of Commerce.

Vellas, F., & Becherel, L. (1995). *International tourism.* New York: St. Martin's Press.

World Tourism Organization. (1969). *International hotel classification.* Madrid: World Tourism Organization.

World Tourism Organization. (1991). *Food safety in the tourism sector.* Madrid: World Tourism Organization.

Surfing Solutions

http://www.open.gov.uk/dot/ (Civil Aviation Authority, U.K.)
http://www.countryside.gov.uk/ (Countryside Commission, U.K.)
http://www.faa.gov/ (Federal Aviation Administration, U.S.)
http://www.iata.org/ (International Air Transport Association)

http://www.iatan.org/ (International Airlines Travel Agent Network)
http://www.cam.org/~icao/ (International Civil Aviation Organization)
http://www.nafta.net/ (NAFTANET)
http://www.holiday.scotland.net/ (Scottish Tourist Board)
http://www.moc.govt.nz/tpg/ (Tourism Policy Group, Ministry of Commerce, New Zealand)
http://www.unesco.org/ (UNESCO)
http://www.unesco.org/whc/index.html (UNESCO World Heritage Centre, Paris)
http://www. icun.org/ (World Conservation Union, Paris)

Acronyms

ABTA (Association of British Travel Agents)
AFTA (Australian Federation of Travel Agents)
ASTA (American Society of Travel Agents)
ATOL (Air Travel Organizers' License)
BSP (Billing and Settlement Plan)
CAA (Civil Aviation Authority, U.K.)
CAB (Civil Aeronautics Board, U.S.)
CASA (Civil Aviation Safety Authority, Australia)
EEC (European Economic Community)
FAA (Federal Aviation Administration, U.S.)
GAIN (Global Analysis Information Network)
GATS (General Agreement on Trade in Services)
GATT (General Agreement on Tariffs and Trade)
IATA (International Air Transport Association)
IATAN (Internation Airlines Travel Agent Network, IATA)
ICAO (International Civil Aviation Organization)
ICOMOS (International Council on Monuments and Sites)
ICTA (Institute of Certified Travel Agents)
IUCN (World Conservation Union)
OAS (Organization of American States)
NAFTA (North American Free Trade Agreement)
UNESCO (United Nations Educational Scientific and Cultural Organization)
USTOA (U.S. Tour Operators Association)
WHO (World Health Organization)
WTO (World Tourism Organization)

> "Achieving a nation's quality of life *through tourism* is a sobering challenge . . . It will come to pass only as an integral part of a regimented policy and planning process for the *development of tourism*, driven by a universal understanding of the global environment."
>
> *Edgell, D.L. (1993), 59*

12

Tourism Planning

···Selecting among Alternatives for ···················
the Future of Tourism

Purpose

Having learned about the reasons and purposes for tourism planning, students will be able to describe a process for planning tourism in a destination area.

Learning Objectives

Having read this chapter, you should be able to:

1. Describe the reasons for tourism planning and the consequences of unplanned development of tourism.

2. Explain the reasons for tourism planning.

3. Identify the barriers to tourism planning.

4. Explain the purposes of tourism planning.

5. Describe the steps in the tourism planning process.

6. Explain the major components of a destination area's market potential and the research techniques that can be used to assess market potential.

7. Describe and differentiate among tourism position statements, vision statements, goals, strategies, and objectives.

Overview

Because of the wide-ranging effects of tourism on a destination, it is vital that development be undertaken within the context of a plan. This chapter deals with the planning process as a method for selecting among future alternatives for a destination. Reasons are given why tourism planning should take place and the consequences of unplanned development are described. The purposes of planning are explained and barriers to planning examined in an attempt to understand why planning is sometimes neglected. The steps of a tourism planning process are described.

The Destination Area With and Without Tourism Planning

"Strategic planning of the tourism industry is of cardinal importance to maximize tourism's impact on socio-economic development and to avoid potential pitfalls. Poor tourism planning has left some countries at the mercy of seasonal variations. This resulted in boom periods which are followed by slumps leading to rapid human degradation and a sense of insecurity. Inadequate tourism planning has also led to environmental degradation in many countries."

Department of Environmental Affairs and Tourism, Government of South Africa. (1995). Tourism Green Paper.

Tourism planning does not guarantee success in tourism. A destination may have a tourism plan, yet fail to get the best out of tourism. However, tourism planning is an essential activity for every destination area, especially in today's rapidly changing business environ-

ments. Although it is true that some tourism destinations have flourished without any conscious planning, many have suffered serious consequences for not carefully considering future events and their impacts on the destination. Planning is a process of selection from among alternative courses of action. All planning involves an analysis of the future. Planning also entails selecting goals, strategies, and objectives for the destination area.

Reasons for Tourism Planning

There are many good reasons for tourism planning. Gunn (1994), in his authoritative book on tourism planning, suggests five basic reasons:

- Tourism development has both negative and positive impacts.
- Tourism is more competitive than ever before and there has been a proliferation in the promotion of tourism destinations.
- Tourism is a more complicated phenomenon than it was previously thought to be.
- Tourism has damaged many natural and cultural resources.
- Tourism affects everyone in a community and all people involved in tourism should participate in the tourism planning process.

The negative and positive impacts of tourism are well demonstrated through the ***destination life cycle*** concept (Butler and Waldbrook, 1991; Getz, 1992). This concept suggests that the evolution of all destination areas follows several predictable stages. In Butler's view, the destination life cycle has seven distinct stages (see figure 12.1):

1. **Exploration:** Small numbers of adventurous visitors are at-

tracted by the area's natural and cultural attractions. There is little or no infrastructure for tourism.

2. **Involvement:** Local investment in tourism and tourism advertising starts. Visitor numbers begin to increase and government agencies start to develop the infrastructure.

3. **Development:** There is a rapid growth in visitor numbers as the destination becomes heavily advertised. The type of visitors attracted changes to the less adventurous. Fabricated attractions replace natural and cultural ones. External investment replaces local.

4. **Consolidation:** Growth in visitor numbers begins to slow. Tourism becomes "mass market" and advertising is aimed at attracting new markets and correcting seasonality.

5. **Stagnation:** The destination area is no longer fashionable as peak visitor numbers are reached. There is a heavy reliance on repeat visitors. The carrying capacity limits on resources are reached. Occupancy rates are low and there are frequent changes in tourism business ownership.

6. **Decline:** The tourism infrastructure becomes run down as visitor numbers decrease. External investors begin to pull out.

7. **Rejuvenation:** New attractions are developed or new natural resources are used to reverse the negative trends in visitor arrivals.

Tourism researchers have used destination life cycle models to examine many destinations ranging from the Isle of Man in Britain to Wasaga Beach in Ontario (Getz, 1992). It should be easy to relate to destination areas around the world that fit into each of these categories. Antarctica and Bhutan could

Visitors are attracted to places of natural beauty, this one at the Lawn Hill Gorge National Park in the Queensland Outback. Photo from *Top Shots* CD Rom. Courtesy of Queensland Tourist and Travel Corporation.

be good candidates for the first two stages. Heavily developed destinations such as Acapulco in Mexico, Waikiki Beach in Hawaii, and Australia's Gold Coast perhaps belong in the third and fourth stages. Some of the traditional seaside beach areas of Australia, Britain, and the U.S. are in the decline stage. The gambling resort destinations of Atlantic City and Las Vegas could be good examples of rejuvenation, where new attractions have drawn different types of visitors than previously.

Another destination life cycle model that has been popular in tourism is the one developed by Plog (1973). Plog's hypothesis is that destination areas tend to rise and fall in popularity according to the whims of those in the predominant *psychographic groups* to which they appeal at different stages in their development histories. A new and exotic destination tends to appeal first to Plog's *allocentric* group; the innovators in travel markets who seek out uncrowded and unique destinations. As the destination area becomes more widely publicized and better known, it loses its appeal to the allocentrics and they are replaced by the *midcentrics,* who greatly outnumber the allocentrics in the

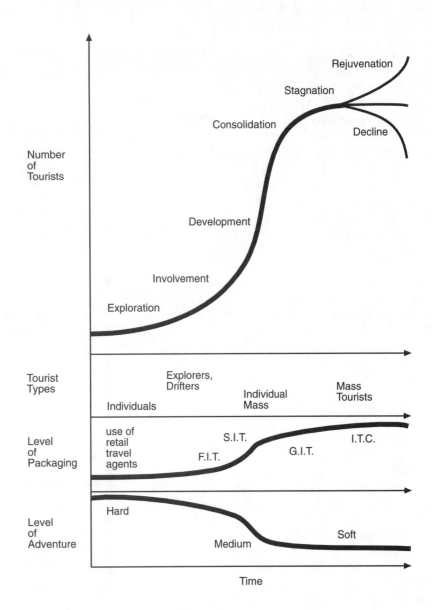

Figure 12.1   Butler's Tourism Destination Life Cycle Model.

population. Plog relates the midcentric appeal stage in the destination area's history to the maturity phase of the product life cycle where sales volumes are at their peak. Basically, the destination area can be said to have mass market appeal at this point. Eventually as time progresses, this destination area also loses its appeal to the midcentrics, and they are replaced by the **psychocentrics** who, like the allocentrics, represent a much smaller proportion of the population. According to Plog, the psychocentric stage is the final point in the destination area's life cycle; it has lost its appeal to both the market innovators and the mass market. One of the most important messages of the Plog hypothesis is that destination areas can "carry with them the potential seeds of their own destruction" if they allow themselves to become overcommercialized and to forsake the unique appeals that made them popular in the first place.

Although Plog's concept appears to suggest that all destination areas eventually face the same fate, the years of experience that have been gained since it was first publicized have shown that there have been several exceptions to this rule. This experience indicates that destination life cycles can be extended if change is anticipated, and if steps are taken to adapt to the change. One of the core functions of tourism planning is to provide the basic framework to allow the destination area to cope with change.

The most important lesson from studying destination life cycle models is not which destination fits where, but rather that the future of every tourism destination needs to be carefully charted. Tourism planning helps the destination make better choices for the future. It may help the destination avoid undesirable changes to natural environments and to the community's social and cultural values.

Consequences of Unplanned Development

What can happen if a destination area does not get involved in tourism planning? The examples are numerous and well-documented, especially as they relate to tourism's damaging impacts on many physical environments and local peoples. Some of the symptoms of a lack of tourism planning are shown in figure 12.2. The observers of tourism as an activity have done a good job of describing these negative impacts, particularly as they relate to environmental degradation and adverse cultural and social effects. In some cases, the lack of adequate tourism planning is as much to blame for these problems as tourism itself.

Barriers to Tourism Planning

> *"Many people feel that the idea of planning places too much power in a governmental bureaucracy. Because urban planning departments have become a legally sanctioned institution of many city governments, many people resent bureaucratic control over what they believe to be their freedoms, especially for land use and development."*
>
> Gunn, C. (1994).
> Tourism Planning, 19

Not every tourism destination in the world has a tourism plan. With

TYPES OF IMPACTS	SYMPTOMS OF LACK OF TOURISM PLANNING
Physical	• Damage or permanent alteration of the physical environment • Damage or permanent alteration of historical and cultural landmarks and resources • Overcrowding and congestion • Traffic problems
Human	• Less accessibility to services and visitor attractions for local residents resulting in local resentment of tourism activity • Dislike of visitors on the part of local residents • Loss of cultural identities • Lack of education of tourism employees in skills and hospitality • Lack of community awareness of the benefits of tourism
Marketing	• Failure to capitalize on new marketing opportunities • Erosion of market shares due to the actions of competitive destination areas • Lack of sufficient awareness in prime markets • Lack of a clear image of destination area in potential markets • Lack of cooperative advertising among tourism businesses • Inadequate capitalization on packaging opportunities
Organizational	• Fragmented approach to the marketing and development of tourism, often involving "competitive" splinter groups • Lack of cooperation among tourism businesses • Inadequate representation of tourism's interests • Lack of support from local government authorities • Failure to act upon important issues, problems, and opportunities of common interest to tourism
Other	• Inadequate interpretation and guiding services • Inadequate programs of directional signs • Lack of sufficient attractions and events • High seasonality and short lengths of stay • Poor or deteriorating quality of facilities and services • Poor or inadequate travel information services

Figure 12.2 Symptoms of a Lack of Tourism Planning.

so many good reasons for tourism planning, one might wonder why not. The simplest answer is that there are often many barriers to tourism planning and they include:

- The objections to the principle of tourism planning.
- The costs of conducting tourism planning processes can be high.
- The complexity of tourism and the large number of government agencies involved.
- The diversity of tourism businesses.
- The seasonality of tourism in many destinations.
- The high ownership turnover in tourism businesses.

The first barrier is that some people are against tourism planning in principle, particularly within the developed countries. This is especially true in parts of the Asia-Pacific region, Europe, and North America, where tourism has existed for many years without any formal tourism planning. Many business people view tourism planning as an encroachment into their domain of activity, and they are skeptical of its ultimate value to them. They point out that tourism has already succeeded without a formal tourism plan.

The high cost is a second barrier to tourism planning. Because effective tourism planning must be based upon detailed resource analysis and market research, it often becomes a very expensive process. Governments generally are required to fund tourism planning efforts on behalf of everyone involved. Private-sector businesses often object to this, believing that the money is better spent on more marketing or promotion of the destination.

A third barrier is the complexity of tourism and the large number of government departments whose activities affect tourism. Tourism planning is often made more difficult because the policies of these

departments are not coordinated and indeed are sometimes in direct conflict with one another. Additionally, tourism is not a readily identifiable industry; it is an activity that cuts across many other industries. Although the front-line recipients of visitors' expenditures, such as hotels, resorts, airlines, car rental agencies, campgrounds, commercial attractions, and restaurants are obvious, others including retail shops, banks, and municipal governments are not normally

seen as being part of tourism. Another complication is that some tourism businesses receive their income both from visitors and from local residents.

A fourth barrier to planning is that tourism is often characterized by having a few very large and a multitude of smaller businesses. There is also a tendency for individual operators to categorize themselves as being in particular business segments (e.g., the "hospitality industry" or the state park system)

Quick Trip 12.1
The Tourism Planning Vision for Hawaii

In 1995, the Department of Business, Economic Development, and Tourism in Hawaii, along with the Tourism Marketing Council, released a Strategic Tourism Plan. The following six vision statements for tourism were articulated for the upcoming five years:

1. Tourism should not be Hawaii's only industry. It is important that the state continue to make efforts to diversify Hawaii's economy as its long-term economic development strategy. Nonetheless, we foresee that the state's economy will continue to rely on tourism to provide its share of new jobs for our growing population.

2. As a mature destination, Hawaii cannot continue to host unlimited numbers of visitors in the future. Instead, we need to focus on "yield" rather than "volume." Thus, we aim to embrace a quality tourism development strategy. This means attracting high-spending visitors.

3. To minimize the environmental and cultural-social impact of tourism, Hawaii aims to encourage the development of low-impact tourism.

4. To take advantage of our unique qualities, we aim to make Hawaiian culture and our multi-cultural heritage a central theme in our tourism development strategy. Not only is this a good strategy, but it also promotes local pride and enhances our own cultural heritage and awareness.

5. Hawaii will continue to diversify the geographic source of our visitors. This means placing more emphasis in developing international tourism. Diversifying our tourism markets can provide greater economic stability in Hawaii and reduce volatility in employment and tax revenues.

6. The state shall continue to pursue a strategy of directing tourism's growth to the Neighbor Islands, particularly the Big Island, which has more capacity to accommodate tourism growth.

Source: State of Hawaii Strategic Tourism Plan. (1995–1999).

rather than acknowledging their broader role in tourism. Other problems encountered in planning tourism include the seasonality of business activity and the relatively high ownership turnover.

Despite these barriers to tourism planning, an increasing number of plans are produced each year around the world. Indications are that tourism planning will be given a higher priority in the future and that more destinations will become involved in planning. As they become involved, they will have at their disposal the prior planning experience of many other areas and thus a more refined "technology" of tourism planning.

Hawaii is making plans for the growth of tourism in the coming years. Photo by Corel.

Purposes of Tourism Planning

> "Belize, though, soon realized the ironies involved in using the slogan 'Undiscovered and Unspoiled' to lure tourists. How can you remain undiscovered and unspoiled when the purpose of every new visitor is to discover something, and the effect of every footfall in the jungle is to spoil something?"
>
> Krotz, L. (1996). Tourists: How our fastest growing industry is changing the world, 91

Tourism as an activity in a destination is created through the existence of unique attractions and events. These may include beaches, natural scenery, parks, historical buildings and landmarks, unique cultural characteristics, unique local events and festivals, and outdoor sports and recreation activities. If a destination area wants to maintain tourism as a long-term economic activity, it must use tourism planning to preserve and enhance these special factors that made it different from all other destinations in the first place. It must practice *sustainable tourism development*. Tourism planning has

the five basic purposes of identifying alternative approaches, adapting to the unexpected, maintaining uniqueness, creating the desirable, and avoiding the undesirable. Figure 12.3 shows the planning considerations and potential outcomes that accompany each of these five planning purposes.

One of the most important of these purposes of tourism planning is to avoid the negative physical, human, marketing, organizational, and other impacts that can occur when planning is not practiced. Tourism is definitely not the answer to every destination area's economic and social problems, and every community should not pursue tourism. Where the decision is made to develop tourism, it is much more likely to be successful if planning is done.

Roles and Responsibilities in Tourism Planning

> "We advise the New Zealand Government on the development of New Zealand tourism policy and represent the Government's tourism interests to other Governments, inter-governmental organizations and forums, and monitor overseas trends to assess their relevance to New Zealand. The Tourism Policy Group promotes the objective that long-term tourism development must be environmentally, socially and economically sustainable."
>
> Tourism Policy Group, Ministry of Commerce (http://www.moc. govt.nz/tpg/about_tpg.html)

Historically, tourism planning appears to have originated in Europe. France, Ireland, and the United Kingdom were among the pioneers of tourism planning, with all three nations being involved in some form of tourism planning in the early 1960s. Canada was also in the forefront of tourism planning, its efforts originating in the late 1960s and early 1970s. Following the lead of these developed countries, tourism planning quickly was adopted in several developing nations in Africa and Asia. Other countries such as Australia and South Africa have invested heavily in tourism

TOURISM PLANNING PURPOSES	PLANNING CONSIDERATIONS AND OUTCOMES
Identify alternative approaches	● Marketing ● Development ● Organization of tourism ● Community awareness of tourism ● Support services and activities
Adapting to the unexpected	● General economic conditions ● Energy supply and demand situation ● Values and lifestyles ● Performance of local industries ● Government legislation and regulations ● Technological advancements
Maintaining uniqueness	● Natural features and resources ● Local cultural and social fabric ● Local architecture and heritage ● Historical monuments and landmarks ● Local festivals, events, and activities ● Parks and outdoor sports areas
Creating the desirable	● Sustainable tourism development ● High level of community awareness of the benefits of tourism ● Clear and positive image of area as a tourism destination ● Effective organization of tourism ● High level of cooperation among tourism organizations and businesses ● Effective marketing, directional sign and travel information programs
Avoiding the undesirable	● Friction and unnecessary competition among tourism organizations and businesses ● Hostile and unfriendly attitudes of local residents toward visitors ● Damage or undesirable, permanent alteration of natural features and historical resources ● Loss of cultural identities ● Loss of market share ● Stoppage of unique local events and festivals ● Overcrowding, congestion, and traffic problems ● Pollution ● High seasonality

Figure 12.3 Purposes of Tourism Planning.

planning at the national, state, and regional levels. Interestingly, the U.S. has seen little organized tourism planning to date and certainly lags behind Canada and Mexico in this respect.

Tourism is important to governments around the world and is a mainstay of many private-sector businesses. It affects local communities and involves numerous nonprofit organizations. Tourism planning is most effective when it is highly participatory and has the input of the widest range of groups and citizens in a community. Past experience has shown that this

process produces the best results and that plans are more likely to be successfully implemented if communities and the private-sector tourism businesses are actively involved in the planning process. "Top-down" planning exercises by government agencies, or their hired consulting firms, have failed miserably in many parts of the world. These plans were developed in a vacuum, without adequate community and private-sector input. The participants in the tourism planning process and their potential roles are shown in figure 12.4.

Tourism planning needs to hap-

pen at many levels. Tourism plans have been developed for areas that include parts of several countries. An example would be the plan developed for the ASEAN nations in Southeast Asia. Planning takes place at the national level within a country and also at the state, provincial, or territorial levels. Tourism planning also occurs at the regional and local levels. Finally, planning can be done for specific resort areas or sites.

The starting point for the tourism planning process in a specific country is with the development of a *national tourism policy*. In chapter 10, a tourism policy model was described, and it was suggested that a national tourism policy is a combination of the principles upon which a nationwide course of action for tourism is based. The tourism policy represents the basic foundation upon which more specific goals, strategies, objectives, and plans are developed. All tourism planning efforts must be complementary to the national tourism policy. National tourism policies and tourism plans must have definite time spans and be evaluated and modified when these time periods expire. Change is inevitable and continuous, and tourism policy-making and planning have to be dynamic processes. Tourism policies tend to be more broad-scale than tourism plans, and they usually are valid for a greater number of years. The life span of a tourism plan is normally not more than three to five years.

Some classification of tourism planning terminology is necessary. First, it should be realized that the terms *tourism plan, master plan for tourism*, and *tourism strategy* are often used to refer to the same thing. In this book, the authors refer to the entire task as being tourism planning, irrespective of whether the eventual result is called a tourism strategy or a tourism plan. Under this definition, all tourism planning exercises pro-

Canada has long been at the forefront of tourism planning. The Parliament Buildings in Ottawa on Canada Day. Photo courtesy of the Canadian Tourism Commission, Photo Library, 235, rue Queen St., 400D, Ottawa, Ontario KIA 0H6.

3. Synthesis and visioning

4. Goal-setting, strategy selection, and objective-setting

5. Plan development

6. Plan implementation and monitoring

7. Plan evaluation

1. Background Analysis

Each of the seven steps in the tourism planning process involves a variety of steps, activities, participants, and outcomes, and these are illustrated for the Background Analysis step in figure 12.5.

The first step in the tourism planning process could be classified as being a *situation* or *SWOT analysis* that produces the basic direction for the succeeding steps. Because most destination areas have some level of existing tourism activity, as well as regulatory and policy frameworks for tourism, this is a logical starting point for most tourism plans.

duce alternative tourism strategies and a tourism plan. The tourism plan itself is a very specific course of action, and the tourism strategies are the alternative approaches available to achieve the tourism planning goals.

producing the plans follows a similar step-by-step pattern. There are seven steps in the tourism planning process:

1. Background analysis

2. Detailed research and analysis

Steps in the Tourism Planning Process

"Majorca was one of the first destinations for mass tourism in the Mediterranean, but visitor numbers began to fall at the end of the 1980s, suggesting that it was losing its appeal due to over-familiarity, falling standards relative to alternative Eastern Mediterranean or long-haul destinations, and adverse publicity in its main origin markets featuring the unruly behavior of some visitors."

Laws, E. (1995). Tourist destination management, 12

Tourism planning takes place at a variety of levels in a destination. However, the approaches used in

TOURISM PLANNING PARTICIPANTS	ROLES
Government tourism officials	● Coordinate the tourism planning process ● Fund tourism planning ● Provide liaison among all parties involved
Local community residents	● Identify community values ● Indicate satisfaction levels with tourism and acceptable future changes in tourism ● Provide opinions and suggestions
Nonprofit organization representatives	● Ensure consideration of programs of related nonprofit organizations ● Provide opinions and suggestions
Other government agency officials	● Ensure consideration of policies and programs of related government agencies
Tourism organization representatives	● Ensure consideration of programs of tourism organizations ● Provide opinions and suggestions
Tourism business operators	● Provide opinions and suggestions
Tourism consultants	● Conduct research and analysis ● Write tourism plan

Figure 12.4   Tourism Planning Participants and Roles.

STEPS	ACTIVITIES	PARTICIPANTS	OUTCOMES
1a. Review of government policies, goals, objectives and programs 1b. Inventory of existing destination mix elements and components 1c. Description of existing tourism demand 1d. Review of strengths, weaknesses, problems, and issues within tourism **1. BACKGROUND ANALYSIS**	• Resource inventory • Government policy and program review • Research of secondary sources of information • Polling of opinions and group workshops	• Government tourism officials • Selected tourism business operators • Selected tourism organization representatives • Officials from other key government agencies • Local residents • Representatives from nonprofit groups • Tourism consultants	• Catalog of government policies, goals, objectives, and programs • List of destination mix elements and components • Description of past visitor profiles • Description of major tourism strengths, weaknesses, problems, and issues

Figure 12.5   Tourism Planning Process: Background Analysis.

1a. Government Policies, Goals, Objectives, and Programs   In establishing a national tourism plan, the national tourism policy must be considered first. Also if a state, province, or territory has a tourism policy, then it must be carefully reviewed at the outset of the plan. Chapter 10 mentioned that tourism policy goals normally fall into six categories: economic, government operations, human resources development, market development, resource protection and conservation, and social and cultural. For example in South Korea, the Korea National Tourism Organization has set the following policy initiatives to improve the competitiveness of Korean tourism and to establish it as one of the top tourism nations (1995 Korean Tourism Annual Report):

● To develop Korean traditional culture into high-quality tourism products.

● To improve the international balance of trade by speeding up the development of more and better accommodation facilities for foreign visitors.

● To prepare to receive large numbers of foreign visitors as a result of the Asia Europe Meeting in 2000 and the 2002 World Cup.

● To develop the proper infrastructure and travel environment for domestic mass tourism.

Because other government agencies, apart from those directly involved in tourism, have policies, goals, and objectives that affect tourism, these must also be considered in the Background Analysis step. Existing tourism-related programs or activities of government and private-sector tourism associations and organizations are also identified.

1b. Existing Destination Mix Elements and Components   The Background Analysis produces an inventory of the area's destination mix elements. Figure 12.6 provides a description of these destination

DESTINATION MIX ELEMENTS	COMPONENTS OF DESTINATION MIX ELEMENTS
Attractions and Events	● Accessibility (proximity to markets) ● Climate (contrasts with market areas' climates) ● Culture (beliefs, attitudes, habits, traditions, customs, forms of behavior) ● Ethnicity (ethnic background of local people) ● Historical resources (government, habitation, religious, war) ● Natural resources (landscapes, scenery, beaches, lakes and rivers, flora and fauna, other unique natural features)
Facilities	● Lodging ● Food and beverage ● Support industries (souvenir and handicraft shops, duty-free shops, guides, festival areas, recreational facilities, laundries)
Infrastructure	● Telecommunication networks ● Health care facilities ● Power sources and systems ● Security systems ● Sewage disposal and drainage systems ● Water resources and systems
Transportation	● Transportation terminals ● Roads, streets, highways, and parking systems ● Railway systems, water transport systems, public transport systems
Hospitality Resources	● Community attitudes toward tourism ● Hospitality and service quality training programs ● Population and workforce ● Travel information centers

Figure 12.6   Destination Mix Elements and Components.

mix elements and their components. Some would say that these destination mix elements and components constitute the existing *tourism product* of the destination area.

1c. Existing Tourism Demand

Next, the Background Analysis step involves a description of existing tourism demand in the destination area using published **secondary sources** of information. This information provides a profile of the major characteristics of past visitors (see figure 12.7).

The quantity and quality of this information is determined by the priority that the destination area has given to tourism market research in the past. If gaps are found in the available information, these are usually identified in the Background Analysis step and an attempt is made to fill them in the Detailed Research and Analysis step.

1d. Tourism Strengths, Weaknesses, Problems, and Issues

The final step in the Background Analysis is a review of the major strengths, weaknesses, problems, and issues of tourism within the destination area. This is an important scene-setting step for the remainder of the tourism planning

process, and it is introspective, critical, and objective. It involves a variety of individuals, including government tourism officials, officials from other key government agencies, selected tourism business operators, selected tourism organization representatives, and local citizens. This exercise is likely to be most objective and productive if a broad variety of opinions and interests are sought. Private consulting organizations specializing in tourism are often used in the planning process. These consultants inject a degree of objectivity and broad tourism experience that may not be readily available in the destination area itself.

Another step that is taken in some tourism plans at this point is staging a series of *public meetings* with citizen groups in the destination area. These sessions are essential in determining community attitudes and awareness levels of tourism, and the types of future directions that citizens want for tourism.

2. Detailed Research and Analysis

A good tourism plan cannot be developed without research. Tourism plans that are prepared without research tend to reflect the subjec-

tive opinions of their authors and to perpetuate existing situations. Research is conducted in four areas: resources, activities, markets, and competition. The basic level of research during the Background Analysis step helps to pinpoint where the more detailed research needs to be focused (figure 12.8).

2a. Resource Analysis   Using the inventory of destination mix elements and components (figure 12.6) as a base, the first step involves the preparation of maps identifying the location of key resources. With the mapping completed, the *carrying capacities* of the resources are then measured. Although the capacities of some of the tourism resource components are easily measured (such as in guest rooms, restaurant seats, camp sites, and golf courses), the capacities of others (such as boating lakes/rivers, beaches, and historical landmarks) are not.

Another approach that can be used in resource analysis is the *Limits of Acceptable Change* (LAC). Gartner (1996) suggests a nine-step procedure for using LAC in tourism:

1. **Identify area issues and concerns:** Ask local residents and visitors to indicate the types of activities and acceptable levels of development.

2. **Define and describe tourist activity opportunity classes:** Determine acceptable and unacceptable developments for specific areas or zones.

3. **Select indicators of resource change:** Select indicators of change in biological, social, and other resource areas.

4. **Inventory existing conditions:** Find out the existing conditions using the indicators for each type of resource in specific areas or zones.

5. **Specify standards for resources and social conditions:**

PAST VISITORS PROFILE FACTORS	CHARACTERISTICS
Activity Participation and Facility Use	Activity participation, usage of facilities (such as accommodations, attractions, events, and recreation facilities)
Demographic	Age, gender, income, education, occupation
Geographic	Geographical origins, geographical destinations
Information Sources and Media Use	Sources of travel information used, media habits
Travel Planning and Arrangements	Length of trip planning period, types of travel arrangements preferred (e.g., group vs. independent travel)
Travel Trip	Expenditures, length of stay, number of previous visits, timing of visit, transportation used, trip purposes, travel party composition, travel party type (e.g., families with children, singles, tour groups, business groups, etc.)

Figure 12.7   Past Visitor Profile Factors and Characteristics.

STEPS	ACTIVITIES	PARTICIPANTS	OUTCOMES
2a. Resource analysis 2b. Activity analysis 2c. Market analysis 2d. Competitive analysis **2. DETAILED RESEARCH AND ANALYSIS**	• Resource mapping • Resource capacity measurement • Limits of acceptable change process • Resource classification • Primary market research • Activity identification and evaluation • Identification and evaluation of competition	• Government tourism officials • Physical planners • Market researchers or survey specialists • Tourism consultants	• Maps showing disposition of tourism resources • Capacity measurements for resources • LAC standards • Description of scope of appeal of resources • Research results on potential markets • Inventory of tourism and recreation activities • Competitive strengths and weaknesses

Figure 12.8 Tourism Planning Process: Detailed Research and Analysis.

Determine tolerable limits of change for each indicator and each resource.

6. **Identify alternative opportunity class allocations reflecting area issues and concerns and existing resource and social conditions:** Review and perhaps revise acceptable or unacceptable developments for specific areas or zones based on information collected for various indicators.

7. **Identify actions needed for each alternative:** Identify alternative actions for each area or zone to keep them within the LAC.

8. **Evaluate and select a preferred alternative:** Assess and pick a preferred set of actions for each area or zone by conferring with local residents and visitors.

9. **Implement the preferred alternative and monitor conditions:** Institute the preferred alternative and monitor to ensure that the LAC standards are not exceeded.

The final stage of the resource analysis is *resource classification*. This represents a ranking or grading of the scope of appeal of the tourism resources of the destination area. Thus, individual re-

sources or zones within the destination are normally defined as being of international, national, regional, or local significance, or as having international, national, regional, or local market appeal.

2b. Activity Analysis   The second step is the *activity analysis*. Activities include all of the things that the visitor can do in the destination area, ranging from outdoor recreational pursuits, such as alpine skiing, to more passive activities,

such as shopping and viewing scenery. Every destination area has a variety of existing activities and potential activities not yet being capitalized upon. As the activities available at the destination are often a prime motivating factor to travel, this exercise can be useful in identifying new demand generation opportunities. The activities are classified by range of appeal (local, regional, state, national, or international). It also is essential to identify the seasons and months of the

Shopping is a popular activity at many destinations. Cahill Avenue in the heart of Surfers Paradise has a lot of activity. Photo from *Top Shots* CD Rom. Courtesy of Queensland Tourist and Travel Corporation.

year in which the activities can be pursued. Because many destination areas suffer from seasonality of demand, this helps to pinpoint those activities that will generate demand outside of peak periods.

2c. Market Analysis   A good tourism plan incorporates some **primary research** on the existing and potential markets for the destination area. The market research carried out in the Background Analysis step was based upon already available information (secondary research). The primary research is done by conducting one or more surveys of existing and potential visitors. Surveys of existing visitors are normally done while the visitors are within the destination area. In addition to gathering visitor profile data as shown in figure 12.7, they are useful in producing the following information:

● Awareness of area attractions and other destination mix elements and components.

● Constraints or barriers to return visits.

● Expenditures within the destination area.

● Images of the destination area.

● Identification of attractions and other items that will increase the likelihood of return visits.

● Likelihood of return visits.

● Motivations for travel to the area.

● Ratings of attractions, facilities, services, and other destination mix elements.

● Satisfaction with trips.

● Sources of information used in planning trips and during trips.

Most often, the personal interview technique is used in these surveys of existing visitors, either at exit or entry points, or at key tourism facilities, attractions, and events.

The Background Analysis and Detailed Research and Analysis steps provide clues as to the sources of potential new market demand for the destination area. The eight main components of a destination area's market potential are shown in figure 12.9.

In addition to the potential markets shown in figure 12.9, the destination may concentrate on attracting current pleasure travelers as future pleasure travelers (i.e., encouraging repeat visits). Another potential market may be in attracting current business travelers as future pleasure travelers.

A variety of techniques are available to research potential visitor markets. These include personal interviews, focus groups, telephone interviews, mail and faxed questionnaires, and online World Wide Web surveys. Research can be directed toward the individual pleasure travelers in a specific geographic market (sometimes called **household surveys**) or be aimed at travel trade intermediaries (retail travel agents, tour wholesalers, tour operators, incentive travel planners, corporate travel departments, and convention and meeting planners) and other travel opinion leaders (club, association, and affinity group executives). This research helps to determine:

● Awareness of area attractions and other destination mix elements and components.

● Competitive destinations.

● Images of the destination area.

● Likelihood of future visits to the destination area.

● Steps needed to generate business from these potential visitors.

Research also provides an opportunity to "market test" new ideas for tourism attractions and events, tours or packages, hotel and resort developments, and new activity ideas that have been identified earlier in the planning process.

Another important aspect of the Detailed Market Analysis is an evaluation of the likely impact of **future travel trends** on the destination area. The information on these trends comes from a variety of available **futures** research studies and ongoing **tracking** research programs on travel trends. It is a fairly common practice at this point in the tourism planning process to

MARKET SEGMENTS	EXISTING GEOGRAPHIC MARKETS	NEW GEOGRAPHIC MARKETS
Pleasure travelers from existing market segments	Increase market penetration of existing pleasure travel markets within existing geographic markets (1.1)	Attract existing pleasure travel market segments from new geographic markets (1.2)
Pleasure travelers from new market segments	Develop new pleasure travel market segments within existing geographic markets (2.1)	Attract new pleasure travel market segments from new geographic markets (2.2)
Business travelers from existing market segments	Increase market penetration of existing business travel markets within existing geographic markets (3.1)	Attract existing business travel market segments from new geographic markets (3.2)
Business travelers from new market segments	Develop new business travel market segments within existing geographic markets (4.1)	Attract new business travel market segments from new geographic markets (4.2)

Figure 12.9   Components of a Destination Area's Market Potential.

forecast tourism demand volumes for the period of the tourism plan. For example, the Vietnam National Administration of Tourism in its Master Plan for Tourism Development: 1995–2010 has forecast 3.5 million international visitors in 2000 and 9 million by 2010.

When the forecasts are ready, a supply (capacities of resource components) and demand (forecast demand volumes) matching exercise is carried out. This step helps those in the destination area determine where there are likely to be shortfalls in different tourism resources and where there could be problems in preserving tourism resources due to excessive demand levels.

2d. Competitive Analysis No destination area is without competition and a tourism plan must consider the *competitive advantages* and future plans of competitors. It is most useful to define competitive markets in terms of their relative distance from prime geographic markets. Those destination areas closer to a prime market are often referred to as being *intervening opportunities*; the visitor must pass them to reach the subject destination area. For example, Hawaii is an intervening opportunity for tourism in Australia, while Canada's Yukon Territory and British Columbia are for tourism in

Alaska. The research described earlier assists in identifying the most competitive destinations, their strengths and weaknesses, and the steps that can be taken to make the subject destination area different from its competitors. In its Strategic Tourism Plan, Hawaii identified cruises, the Caribbean, Mexico, Nevada, Florida, Australia, California, Europe, Costa Rica, and South Pacific Islands as its major competitors. It then examined the strengths and weaknesses of each of these destinations.

Other types of research and analysis may be needed. This may include an evaluation of the tourism organizations, community tourism awareness levels, and the tourism marketing programs of the destination area. The Background Analysis step indicates the degree of emphasis to be given to these factors. For example, in some areas, organizational problems or conflicts may be so acute that they require detailed research and evaluation.

3. Synthesis and Visioning

The third step of the tourism planning process represents the point in which the major conclusions from all of the previous work are formulated (figure 12.10). Some tourism planning experts consider it to be one of the most important and creative steps in the process.

A comprehensive tourism plan produces recommendations on five topics:

- **Development:** Physical changes in the destination area including new attractions, facilities, infrastructure, travel information and interpretive centers, and transportation systems.
- **Marketing:** Changes to past marketing programs involving new marketing strategies, positioning approaches, packaging and tours, distribution, and promotional programs.
- **Tourism organization:** Changes to government and non-government organizations involved in tourism.
- **Community awareness of tourism:** Programs to increase community resident awareness of the benefits of tourism.
- **Support services and activities:** Changes in travel information center systems, directional sign programs, scenic tour systems, interpretive services, hospitality and service training programs.

3a. Position Statements The first step in the synthesis phase is the preparation of *position statements* for each of these five topics. The position statement describes the existing situation (*Where are we now?*)

STEPS	ACTIVITIES	PARTICIPANTS	OUTCOMES
3a. Preparation of preliminary position statements 3b. Preparation of vision statements **3. SYNTHESIS AND VISIONING**	• Information assembly • Writing of position statements • Writing of vision statements • Group workshops	• Government tourism officials • Selected tourism business operators • Selected tourism organization representatives • Officials from other key government agencies • Local residents • Tourism consultants	• Position statements on current conditions • Vision statements of desired future conditions • Critical success factors

Figure 12.10 Tourism Planning Process: Synthesis and Visioning.

Quick Trip 12.2
Critical Success Factors for Tourism in South Africa

Some tourism plans outline critical success factors or conditions that must be met if the vision for tourism is to be attained. For South Africa, the conditions were:

- Sustainable environmental management practices
- Involvement of local communities and previously neglected groups
- A safe and stable tourism environment
- Globally competitive practices, by offering quality services and value for money
- Innovative and responsive to customer needs
- Focus on product enhancement and emphasize diversity
- Effective tourism training, education, and awareness
- Creative and aggressive marketing and promotion
- Strong economic linkages with other sectors of the economy
- Appropriate institutional structures
- Appropriate supportive infrastructure

Source: Department of Environmental Affairs and Tourism. (1996). *White Paper: The Development and Promotion of Tourism in South Africa*, 14.

---

with respect to development, marketing, organization, community awareness, and other support services and activities. One of the participating groups is given the responsibility for preparing preliminary position statements, usually either the tourism consultants or government tourism officials. These are then reviewed and discussed by all participants, and a consensus is reached on the final wording of the statements. Position statements may be simply expressed in one sentence or be documented in several pages of text. A simple position statement on development could be "our destination area has historically been developed to appeal to a summer/warm weather market; facilities to attract tourism at other times of the year have not been constructed."

3b. Vision Statements The second step is known as *visioning* in which the desired future situation for tourism is determined (*Where would we like to be?*) The desired future states are expressed in terms of *vision statements* that reflect future tourism development, marketing, organization, community awareness, and support services and activities. In our simple example this could be "it is our desire to have year-round tourism facilities in our destination area." Tourism plans provide the "bridge" between the present situation and desired future situations in a destination area. They provide the means to the end. To accompany the vision statements, it is useful to identify *critical success factors* (CSFs) or conditions that must be met for the tourism vision to be realized.

4. Goal-Setting, Strategy Selection, and Objective-Setting

Now that the destination area has defined its future vision for tourism, goals, strategies, and objectives are defined (figure 12.11).

4a. Tourism Goals Tourism goals, strategies, and objectives must be complementary to tourism policy goals and objectives. The major policy goal for tourism may be to stimulate employment, income, and economic development through tourism; an economy-oriented policy approach to tourism. Another destination area suffering from overcrowding or an already too rapid pace of development may select a more conservation-oriented approach. Remember that a tourism plan has a relatively short life span, usually three to five years, and its goals should be achievable within that time period. A destination area with an economy-oriented policy approach may wish to obtain the maximum economic impact from tourism within the term of the plan. This area will probably adopt a goal that emphasizes the development and marketing of those regions or specific resource components likely to produce the greatest economic return within the planning period; it will concentrate on its major strengths. Yet another destination may have an economy-oriented approach but be more concerned with spreading the economic benefits of tourism more evenly throughout its regions. Its goal might be to concentrate on the development and marketing of those regions with the lowest levels of existing tourism activity.

4b. Tourism Strategies Once the planning goals are defined, a variety of strategies can be used to achieve them. Within a specific destination area, it should also be realized that different strategies may be used for the regions within it. Some regions may have econ-

STEPS	ACTIVITIES	PARTICIPANTS	OUTCOMES
4a. Definition of tourism goals 4b. Identification of alternative strategies and selection of desired strategies 4c. Definition of tourism objectives **4. GOAL-SETTING, STRATEGY SELECTION, AND OBJECTIVE-SETTING**	• Goal setting • Strategy mapping • Writing of goals, strategy statements, and objectives • Group workshops	• Government tourism officials • Selected tourism business operators • Selected tourism organization representatives • Officials from other key government agencies • Local residents • Tourism consultants	• Statements of tourism goals • Maps or other visual presentations of alternative strategies • Strategy statements • Rationale for selected strategies • Statement of tourism objectives

Figure 12.11 Tourism Planning Process: Goal-Setting, Strategy Selection, and Objective-Setting.

omy-oriented strategies and some may have conservation-oriented strategies.

A commonly found tourism development strategy involves dividing the destination into destination zones, touring corridors, and other areas. This can be applied to many geographic areas, including countries, states, provinces or territories, counties, and regions within counties. As well as being visually displayed through maps, a strategy is verbalized in a series of strategy statements. A comprehensive strategy incorporates in these statements the five elements of development, marketing, organization, community awareness of tourism, and support services and activities. Again, a strategy translates the existing conditions in these five elements into the desired future situations. For example, a destination area highly dependent on one specific geographic market for visitors may wish to adopt a strategy of diversifying its geographic markets, thereby reducing its dependence on one market. Those in a destination area with the planning goal of increasing the economic benefits of tourism to a specific region may select a strategy to increase visitation to that region.

4c. Tourism Objectives The tourism plan objectives flow logically from the selected strategy and support specific tourism goals. The objectives are more short-term than the goals and are more measurable.

5. Plan Development

The next step of the tourism planning process is the development of the plan itself. The plan details the programs and activities needed to achieve the goals, implement the strategy, and attain the objectives (figure 12.12).

5a. Programs, Activities, Roles, and Funding A comprehensive plan deals with the five topics of development, marketing, organization, community awareness, and support services and activities. The tourism plan takes the objectives and specifies the activities, programs, and other steps required to achieve them (see figure 12.13).

STEPS	ACTIVITIES	PARTICIPANTS	OUTCOMES
5a. Description of programs, activities, roles, and funding 5b. Writing of tourism plan reports **5. PLAN DEVELOPMENT**	• Plan detailing • Report writing • Report presentations • Report review and revisions	• Government tourism officials • Selected tourism business operators • Selected tourism organization representatives • Officials from other key government agencies • Local residents • Tourism consultants	• List of programs and activities • Description of government and private-sector roles and responsibilities • Funding requirements and sources • Description of specific development projects and marketing initiatives • Plan schedule and timetable • Tourism plan reports

Figure 12.12 Tourism Planning Process: Plan Development.

Quick Trip 12.3
Tourism Goals and Objectives for the Cairns Region of Australia

Tourism Goal:

To develop a diversified tourism product to support and sustain the economic development of the region; providing for the coordinated delivery of the infrastructure and services to support tourism; ensuring the sustainability of the region's natural and cultural assets through the establishment of appropriate organizational structures to manage and develop the tourism industry.

Objectives:

- To create a network of diverse and exciting destinations for visitors to the region.
- To maintain and enhance the region's position as a leading international nature tourism destination.
- To promote and share with visitors the distinctive history, heritage, lifestyle, and culture of the region.
- To maximize the advantage of the region's strategic location to attract business purpose visitors.
- To maintain a choice of accommodations for visitors to the region.
- To ensure the needs of the tourism industry are integrated into regional and local planning and decision-making processes.
- To provide transport facilities and services to support the tourism industry.
- To provide public infrastructure that supports the growth of the tourism industry.
- To promote tourism that will benefit the economic development of the region as a whole.
- To diversify the range of services to support tourism in the region.
- To maintain a skilled, professional, and motivated workforce to support the tourism industry.
- To encourage new investment in facilities, enterprises, and infrastructure to support tourism.
- To provide a regional tourism information system.
- To maintain community support for the tourism industry and to ensure visitor well-being while in the region.
- To conserve the region's natural assets while allowing for sustainable use by the tourism industry.
- To conserve the region's cultural values and assets.

Source: The Cairns Region Tourism Strategy.

5b. Tourism Plan Reports   Once it has been laid out in this detail, the tourism plan is then written up in formal reports, either by a private tourism consulting firm or by government tourism officials. The tourism plan reports are often presented in two parts. The first is a summary report containing the plan itself, and the second is a more detailed technical report providing all of the research, findings, and conclusions. The reports are usually prepared in draft and are reviewed and revised by government and tourism business representatives prior to being finalized for publication and for public presentations.

6. Plan Implementation and Monitoring

Many tourism plans have been written but never implemented. Why would so much good work and money be wasted? The answer is that plan implementation has been given inadequate attention. Responsibilities for the tourism objectives must be clearly allocated to specific organizations or people. The funds must be available to carry out the activities and programs in the plan (figure 12.14).

6a. Plan Implementation   The implementation of the plan occurs according to its schedule. The overall responsibility for coordinating its implementation is usually given to a governmental tourism agency. Proposed development projects and other proposals requiring physical changes are reviewed in feasibility studies and environmental impact assessments (EIAs). The process of development is discussed in full detail in chapter 13.

New marketing plans are written and implemented. These plans may involve creating a new positioning approach (image) for the destination, potential market development, the creation of new tours

TOURISM PLAN ELEMENTS	ROLES OF PLAN ELEMENTS
Outcomes and results	● The expected results and outcomes of the tourism plan
Activities and programs	● The programs and activities required to achieve each objective
Development projects	● The specific development projects needed to achieve certain objectives
Budget	● The money required to carry out specific programs and actions and the sources of these funds
Marketing initiatives	● The specific marketing initiatives needed to achieve certain objectives
Monitoring and evaluation procedures	● The monitoring and evaluation procedures for judging the success of the plan
Roles and responsibilities	● Roles and responsibilities of government, tourism businesses, tourism organizations, and others
Schedule and timetable	● The schedule and timetable for carrying out specific programs and activities

Figure 12.13   Tourism Plan Elements.

or packages, new distribution strategies, and promotional programs.

The tourism plan may also call for changes in existing tourism organizations or for the creation of new tourism organizations. New programs may be designed to increase community awareness of tourism and to improve the destination's hospitality resources.

6b. Plan Monitoring   While the plan is being implemented the coordinating agency continually checks

to ensure that progress is made as was originally planned. Monitoring is done for each tourism goal and for every objective that supports this goal. Modifications to the plan may be required if inadequate progress is made toward achieving certain goals and objectives.

7. Plan Evaluation

Plan evaluation occurs after the term of the tourism plan has expired. The basic purpose of plan

evaluation is to determine if the goals and objectives of the tourism plan were achieved. If they were not achieved, an analysis is conducted to determine the reasons for non-performance (figure 12.15).

7a. Performance on Goals and Objectives   The actual performance related to each individual goal and objective is measured. A variety of indicators may be used that involve evaluation research of different types. This might include surveys of visitors, local residents, and tourism business operators to determine their attitudes to the changes resulting from the plan's implementation. Specific measurement indicators such as visitor numbers and expenditures may also be used in the evaluation. Meetings are scheduled to discuss the findings of the tourism plan evaluation.

7b. Reasons for Non-Performance   It is highly likely that not all of the tourism goals and objectives will be achieved. The important thing here is to determine the reasons for non-performance on specific goals and objectives. Non-performance may result for many reasons such as unexpected changes in world events, the inabil-

STEPS	ACTIVITIES	PARTICIPANTS	OUTCOMES
6a. Plan implementation 6b. Plan monitoring **6. PLAN IMPLEMENTATION AND MONITORING**	• Feasibility studies • Environmental impact assessments • Marketing plan development • Implementation of development projects • Improvements to infrastructure and transportation • Improvements in hospitality resources and community awareness programs • Organizational changes	• Government tourism officials • Selected tourism business operators • Selected tourism organization representatives • Officials from other key government agencies • Developers • Tourism consultants	• Feasibility studies • Environmental impact assessments • Marketing plans • New organizational structures in place • New developments • New hospitality resource and community awareness programs • New support services and activities • Progress reports on plan implementation

Figure 12.14   Tourism Planning Process: Plan Implementation and Monitoring.

Quick Trip 12.4
Strategic Thrusts of Tourism in Singapore

1. **Redefining Tourism:** Repositioning Singapore not only as a tourist destination, but also as a tourism business center and a tourism hub.

2. **Reformulating the Product:** Reformulating the tourism product to ensure that our visitor's experiences are delightful and memorable.

3. **Developing Tourism as an Industry:** Putting in place a strategy to enable Singapore to become a tourism business center.

4. **Configuring New Tourism Space:** Attaining the status of a tourism hub, a springboard for visitors venturing into the region as well as a regional headquarters for tourism businesses.

5. **Partnering for Success:** Implementing the plans with a spirit of collaboration and partnership on a "win-win" basis.

6. **Championing Tourism:** Recognizing the importance of the tourism industry, ensuring that great ideas are championed, and overall coordination and leadership are provided.

Source: Singapore Tourist Promotion Board. (1996). *Tourism 21: Vision of a Tourism Capital*, 23.

ity to attract private development funding, or unanticipated competitive strategies and programs.

7c. Recommendations for Future Tourism Planning It is useful at this point to rewrite the position statements that were prepared earlier in the Synthesis and Visioning step. This allows the participants to evaluate if the vision statements were realized.

The final outcome of evaluation becomes a major input into the next round of tourism planning. Specific recommendations are made

based upon the lessons of this tourism planning process. The most important questions that need to be answered are: What goals were achieved? What goals were not achieved? Why were these goals not achieved? What should be done differently the next time tourism planning is done? The tourism planning process has come full cycle.

Summary

Every destination area interested in tourism must use the tourism planning process. Although tourism planning can be hard work, time consuming, costly, and difficult to sell, it is an essential activity in today's rapidly changing business environments. The absence of tourism planning in a destination can lead to irreversible economic, social and cultural, and environmental damage and to loss of market share. There are many barriers to tourism planning in every destination area, but the rewards resulting from an effective tourism planning process far outweigh the efforts needed to surmount these. Empirical evidence throughout the world clearly shows that the "model" destinations for successful tourism are those that have embraced the tourism planning concept.

STEPS	ACTIVITIES	PARTICIPANTS	OUTCOMES
7a. Measure performance against each goal and objective 7b. Analyze reasons for non-performance 7c. Prepare recommendations for future tourism planning processes **7. PLAN EVALUATION**	• Gathering of performance indicators • Surveys of local residents • Surveys of local tourism business operators • LAC measurements • Marketing plan evaluation	• Government tourism officials • Selected tourism business operators • Selected tourism organization representatives • Officials from other key government agencies • Local residents • Tourism consultants	• Performance indicators for each goal and objective • Local resident attitude surveys • Tourism business operator surveys • LAC results • Marketing plan evaluation results • Suggestions for future tourism planning processes

Figure 12.15 Tourism Planning Process: Plan Evaluation.

References

Alipour, H. (1996). Tourism development within planning paradigms: The case of Turkey. *Tourism Management*, 17 (5), 367–377.

Butler, R.W. (1980). The concept of a tourist area cycle of evolution: Implications for management of resources. *Canadian Geographer*, 24 (1), 5–12.

Butler, R.W., & Waldbrook, L.A. (1991). A new planning tool: The tourism opportunity spectrum. *Journal of Tourism Studies*, 2 (1), 2–14.

Department of Environmental Affairs and Tourism. (1996). *White paper: The development and promotion of tourism in South Africa*. Pretoria: Government of South Africa.

Ding, P., & Pigram, J. (1995). Environmental audits: An emerging concept in sustainable tourism development. *Journal of Tourism Studies*, 6 (2), 2–10.

Gartner, W.C. (1996). Tourism development: Principles, processes, and policies. New York: Van Nostrand Reinhold.

Getz, D. (1986). Models in tourism planning. *Tourism Management*, 7, 21–32.

Getz. D. (1992). Tourism planning and the destination life cycle. *Annals of Tourism Research*, 19, 752–770.

Gunn, C.A. (1994). *Tourism planning: Basics, concepts, cases* (3rd ed.). Washington, D.C.: Taylor & Francis.

Krotz, L. (1996). *Tourists: How our fastest growing industry is changing the world*. Boston: Faber and Faber.

Laws, E. (1995). Tourist destination management: Issues, analysis and policies. London: Routledge.

Long, P.T., & Nuckolls, J.S. (1994). Organising resources for rural tourism development: The importance of leadership, planning and technical assistance. *Tourism Recreation Research*, 19 (2), 19–34.

Manning, E.W., & Dougherty, T.D. (1995). Sustainable tourism: Preserving the golden goose. *Cornell Hotel and Restaurant Administration Quarterly*, 36 (2), 29–42.

Murphy, P.E. (1988). Community driven tourism planning. *Tourism Management*, 9, 96–104.

Pearce, D. (1992). *Tourist organizations*. Harlow, Essex: Longman Group UK.

Plog, S.G. (1973). Why destination areas rise and fall in popularity. *Cornell Hotel and Restaurant Administration Quarterly*, 14 (3), 13–16.

Ritchie, J.R.B. (1993). Crafting a destination image: Putting the concept of resident-responsive tourism into practice. *Tourism Management*, 14, 379–389.

Stynes, D.J., & O'Halloran, C. (1987). *Tourism planning*. East Lansing, Michigan: Tourism Information Series No. 2, Cooperative Extension Service, Michigan State University.

Tosun, C., & Jenkins, C.L. (1996). Regional planning approaches to tourism development: The case in Turkey. *Tourism Management*, 17, 519–531.

Turner, L., & Ash, J. (1975). *The golden hordes: International tourism and the pleasure periphery*. London: Constable.

Young, G. (1973). *Tourism: Blessing or blight*. Middlesex, England: Penguin Books.

Surfing Solutions

http://kumu.icsd.hawaii.gov/tourism/STP/stpindex.html (Hawaii Strategic Tourism Plan)

http://ourtown.sunrem.com/ourtown/brochure/ed&plan.html (Planning Tourism in Rural America Ourtown website)

http://www.msue.msu.edu/msue/imp/modtd/33000005.html (Tourism Planning article by Daniel J. Stynes and Cynthia O'Halloran)

http://www.batin.com.vn/dbotweb/tourinfo/phan4b.html (Master Plan of Vietnam Tourism Development)

Acronyms

CSF (critical success factor)
EIA (environmental impact assessment)
LAC (limits of acceptable change)
STD (sustainable tourism development)

"Planning for economic growth and development must go hand in hand with the protection of the environment, enhancement of cultural life, and maintenance of rich traditions which contribute so greatly to the quality of life and character of a nation."

Singh, G.Z. (1983). Speech before the General Assembly of the World Tourism Organization.

13

Tourism Development

···Building a Sustainable Future for Tourism ·········

Purpose

Having learned about the concept and principles of sustainable tourism development, students will be able to describe a process for evaluating individual tourism project development opportunities.

Learning Objectives

Having read this chapter, you should be able to:

1. Explain the concept and principles of sustainable tourism development.

2. Describe the main forms of tourism development.

3. Discuss government and private-sector roles in tourism development.

4. Describe the role and types of government incentives for tourism development and the criteria for government financial assistance.

5. Describe the objectives and steps in completing a pre-feasibility study and an economic feasibility study.

6. Identify the two main groups concerned with the results of economic feasibility studies and discuss the questions they typically want answered.

7. Explain the purposes of preparing an environmental impact assessment.

Overview

This chapter begins by describing the concept and principles of sustainable tourism development. The link between tourism development and tourism planning is emphasized. The tourism development roles of the private sector and government are outlined. Sources of financial assistance from government and the private sector are examined. A process for analyzing individual tourism development projects is described. Particular attention is paid to the analysis of the project from the economic feasibility and environmental impact viewpoints.

Building a Sustainable Future for Tourism

"There is no example of tourist use that is completely without impact. If the primary goal is one of protection and preservation of the environment in an untouched form then, in all truth, there cannot be tourism development at all."

Cater, E. (1993). Ecotourism in the Third World: Problems for sustainable tourism development. Tourism Management, 14, 89

Sustainable Tourism Development

Chapter 9 emphasizes the need to control the impacts of tourism through the application of the principles of *sustainable development*. According to Manning & Dougherty (1995), sustainable development "means the use of natural resources to support economic activity without compromising the environment's carrying capacity, which is its ability to continue producing those economic goods and services." The origination of the *sustainable development* concept is attributed to the 1980 World Conservation Strategy and the 1987 World Commission on Environment and Development (The Brundtland Commission).

The concept of *sustainable tourism development* (STD) is the application of the basic principles of sustainable development to tourism, which is highly dependent on the natural resources of destination areas. STD first started to be talked about in the early 1990s. Butler (1993) provides a good definition of STD as:

"Tourism which is developed and maintained in an area (community, environment) in such a manner and at such a scale that it remains viable over an indefinite period and does not degrade or alter the environment (human and physical) in which it exists to such a degree that it prohibits the successful development and well-being of other activities and processes."

It should be noticed that STD is not just concerned with natural and physical environments, but recognizes the need to maintain the cultures and lifestyles of local peoples. The World Tourism Organization (WTO) has prepared recommended STD guidelines in *Sustainable tourism development: Guide for local planners* (McIntyre, 1993). This WTO report recommends that tourism needs to be developed to satisfy three broad principles (Ding & Pigram, 1995):

- To improve the quality of life of the host community.
- To provide a high-quality experience for visitors.
- To maintain the quality of the environment on which both the host community and the visitors depend.

It is generally accepted that all tourism developments should respect the concept and principles of sustainable tourism development. However, there remains a practical problem of defining exactly what *sustainability* means. Gartner (1996) states the STD concept is hard to operationalize and that "there is yet no consensus on what it really means, let alone how to implement a sustainable tourism policy." It could be argued that the massive Walt Disney World development in Orlando, Florida,

ECOLOGICALLY SUSTAINABLE TOURISM

GOALS

- To improve material and non-material well being of communities.
- To preserve inter-generational and intra-generational equity.
- To protect biological diversity and maintain ecological systems.
- To ensure the cultural integrity and social cohesion of communities.

CHARACTERISTICS

- *Tourism* which is concerned with the quality of experiences.
- *Tourism* which has social equity and community involvement.
- *Tourism* which operates within the limits of the resource—this includes minimization of impacts and the use of effective waste management and recycling techniques.
- *Tourism* which maintains the full range of recreational, educational and cultural opportunities within and across generations.
- *Tourism* which is based upon activities which reflect the character of the region.
- *Tourism* which allows the guest to gain an understanding of the region visited and which encourages guests to be concerned about, and protective of, the host community and environment.
- *Tourism* which does not compromise the capacity of other industries or activities to be sustainable.
- *Tourism* which is integrated into local, regional and national plans.

Ecologically Sustainable Development Working Group. (1991). *Final report: Tourism.* Canberra: Australian Government Publishing Service.

Figure 13.1   Goals and Characteristics of Ecologically-Sustainable Tourism.

is not sustainable, yet it has already thrived for more than 25 years. Some have suggested that *ecotourism* or *alternative tourism* are the only types of developments to ensure sustainability. This has been hotly debated by others who state that some forms of ecotourism also harm the physical environment and local cultures (Ioannides, 1995). While this debate will continue for many years to come, the STD concept does, if nothing else, heighten the need for careful development planning that assesses all of the potential impacts of a tourism project development opportunity.

Forms and Impacts of Tourism Developments

There are many different forms of development that have occurred in tourism destinations around the world. According to Gartner (1996), all physical developments in tourism inevitably transform local environments. Some tourism experts refer to the scale of transformation as being from *low-impact* to *high-impact* developments. Low-impact or "soft" tourism developments are usually smaller scale and are designed to meet *ecologically sustainable tourism development* (ESTD) principles (Moscardo, Morrison, & Pearce, 1996). The goals and characteristics of ecologically sustainable tourism are shown in figure 13.1.

Some refer to low-impact or "soft" tourism developments as *alternative tourism* and compare this to the more high-impact *mass tourism* and *resort tourism* (Doggart and Doggart, 1996). Mass tourism is where thousands of visitors concentrate in particular areas and requires large-scale investment in accommodation, infrastructure, and services. Examples include parts of Florida (e.g., Orlando and Miami); Bali in Indonesia; Pattaya and Phuket in Thailand; the beach areas of France, Italy, and Spain; and the Surfers Paradise area of

Australia's Gold Coast. Resort tourism includes self-contained or integrated projects like the typical Club Med village.

The high-impact tourism development projects have the potential of causing major transformations in local environments and peoples. Mathieson & Wall (1982) identify four undesirable situations that

---

Quick Trip 13.1
Sustainable Tourism Development Statement of Western Samoa

In the past, we loved eating our bats and forest pigeons, our turtles and forest foods, but today we are having to conserve them. Our rainforests, our lagoons, our rivers and our mangroves are under threat. This modern way of life is forcing us to find instant cash, and all we have to 'cash in' are our forests and fish.

Fortunately, our tourism industry in Western Samoa is becoming very environmentally aware and we are now more conscious of the socio-economic benefits that can be derived from tourism. In fact, tourism has now become our major earner of foreign currency. All we have to do now is to make the tourist dollar work harder for the country, work harder to help protect our natural scenery and our culture. Ecotourism is just a small part of the solution, but an important part that you can directly participate in.

Listen, we know that you are coming here on holidays: You're here to relax and unwind and recuperate and enjoy yourselves. You're here to flex your muscles (sports-wise and adventure-wise). You're here to get a tan like ours (and good luck). You're not coming here to get involved in some idealistic, philosophical, altruistic developmental debate on whether your visit was or was not any benefit to our islands. Or are you?

We told you that we are still very much a developing nation and that we don't have all the mod-cons that you may have at home or expect while you're on holidays. In Samoa, it's the simple life, the back-to-nature and the culturally different way-of-life that takes the place of man-made entertainment. You're coming to see us, to see how we live and to have us share your holiday with you.

Oh, and let's get one thing straight. We only want a small number of travelers in Samoa. We are just not into "mass tourism." We've already explained that we want to keep these islands beautiful. Our ambition now, and hopefully your ambition, is to surreptitiously push our nation toward sustainable development, in this case via sustainable tourism. All that means is that our quality of life keeps rising while at the same time the quality of your visit keeps rising. It means that our natural resources, our culture and our economy are safeguarded for future generations.

Source: Western Samoa Visitors Bureau.

---

may result from high-impact developments which are poorly planned and developed:

1. **Architectural pollution:** The development of new architectural forms that are not compatible with local environments and cultural heritage. While spectacular, the new mega-resort de-

Surfers Paradise in Australia's Gold Coast is a mass-tourism destination. Photo from *Top Shots* CD Rom. Courtesy of Queensland Tourist and Travel Corporation.

velopments in Las Vegas are hardly compatible with the heritage of Nevada.

2. **Ribbon development and sprawl:** Strip development that follows along coastlines or on either sides of roads leading to important attractions. Sprawl is when development expands continuously from the site of the original attraction.

3. **Infrastructure overload:** The visitor use of infrastructure systems, including power and sewage disposal, is greater than the capacity of these systems.

4. **Traffic congestion:** Traffic volumes exceed the capacity of the local road and highway systems.

The problems caused by unplanned mass tourism are very real and have been witnessed around the world. Many alternatives to mass tourism have been suggested, especially for less developed countries (LDCs). One of the most talked about alternative in the past decade has been *ecotourism*. There are many definitions of ecotourism, with most emphasizing natural environments and a concern for local peoples. The Canadian Environmental Advisory Council definition of ecotourism is (Wight, 1993a):

"Ecotourism is an enlightening nature travel experience that contributes to the conservation of the ecosystem while respecting the integrity of host communities."

Another interpretation of ecotourism based on an analysis conducted in Germany is that it aims to (Kersten, 1997):

● Deter or minimize negative environmental and socio-cultural impacts.

● Take place within "relatively untouched" natural areas.

● Contribute to the conservation of areas.

● Improve the local economy of adjacent communities.

● Primarily address visitors who maintain a certain "non-consumerism," nature-loving, and ethical conscience toward tourism.

The increasing popularity of ecotourism has led to the development of a specialized form of accommodation known as *ecolodges* and to the creation of tour operators and tours that concentrate on nature and local cultures.

The Link Between Tourism Planning and Tourism Development

"When examining environmental damage related to tourism, a planner must distinguish between true causes. Whereas some erosion and pollution of resources is caused by great numbers of visitors, most environmental damage is caused by lack of plans, policies, and action to prepare for any economic growth."

Gunn, C.A. (1994).
Tourism Planning, 83

The tourism planning process in chapter 12 produces goals, strategies, and objectives for tourism development, marketing, organization, community awareness of tourism, and other support services and activities. The tourism development portion of the plan provides overall guidelines for development and outlines broad development concepts. These overall *tourism development guidelines* ensure that when development occurs it supports the area's economic, social and cultural, and environmental policies and goals. Specific guidelines describing the basic characteristics of the scale, quality, and types of development are written.

The tourism planning process also identifies individual *project development opportunities* worthy of in-depth research through feasibility studies and environmental impact analyses. The term *tourism product* is used for all categories of project development opportunities, both commercial and non-commercial. The economic feasibility and environmental impact of commercial (profit-making) project development opportunities is established with the techniques described in this chapter. The non-commercial development opportunities may include support facilities like travel information centers, infrastructure, transportation, and nonprofit attractions such as museums and other historic landmarks. The advisability of proceeding with these projects cannot be measured through an economic feasibility study since they may produce little or no revenue. These projects may be analyzed using a technique known as *cost/benefit analysis*, or are assessed for their contributions to the achievement of the tourism plan's goals and objectives.

Government and Private-Sector Participation in Tourism Development

> *"The relationship between politics and tourism is not primarily concerned with political parties and elections and their influence on tourism policy, although this is, of course, an aspect of the politics of tourism. The study of politics is inexorably the study of power."*
>
> Hall, C.M. (1994),
> Tourism and Politics, 2

Government and Private-Sector Roles

Both the government and the private sector have important roles to play in tourism development. The private sector's main role is to develop and operate tourism facilities and services for visitors while maximizing financial returns. In today's more enlightened times, companies accept that they have social and environmental responsibilities that they must uphold in achieving profit goals.

Quick Trip 13.2
Majorca: Sustainable Development in an Aging Resort Area

Majorca (Mallorca) is a Mediterranean island that belongs to Spain. One of the Balearic Islands, it has been a highly popular, mass tourism destination for Europeans since about the 1960s. The development of tourism in Majorca has suffered from over-building and environmental degradation. About one out of every three visitors to Majorca go to the town of Calvia. According to local planners, "The model of development has been based on short-term interests, unlimited building construction which is out of tune with local conditions, and an unsustainable exploitation of the exceptional natural resources."

The planners for Calvia produced a sustainable development plan known as *Calvia Local Agenda 21*. The plan's objectives include:

- Natural surroundings and tourist space of high environmental standard in an environmental framework that tends toward sustainability.
- A coastal tourist sector brought up-to-date, of adequate size and not sprawling or congested, with high-quality services and open to diversification.
- A local development plan that is based more on sustainable use of available resources and the transformation of the existing patrimony than on new growth.

Among the results of the plan to date, some coastline hotels were demolished that were considered to be obsolete and offensive to the environment. An environmental education program has been implemented, and 1,700 hectares of new development has been halted.

Bed and breakfasts may be a more sustainable form of accommodation. Photo courtesy of Brown County Convention & Visitors Bureau, Nashville, Indiana.

Not all tourism project development opportunities are identified in the tourism planning process. Many project ideas emerge from the private sector itself through sponsored research studies and assessments of supply and demand relationships. **Idea generation** is, therefore, a key role of the private sector.

The **entrepreneurial role** is the heart of the private sector's involvement in tourism development. This role embraces idea generation, development project implementation, financial risk-taking and investment, and the management of operations. The private sector also provides the **specialized technical skills** required in the development process through tourism consultants, market research firms, economists, environmental and social impact experts, architects, engineers, designers, lawyers, project managers, and builders. The private sector, through its financial institutions, other corporate lenders, and individual citizens, provides a large proportion of the **financing** for the investment in tourism development projects.

Nonprofit organizations (or the **volunteer sector**) play an important role in tourism development in most destinations. These organizations include convention and visitors bureaus, chambers of commerce, travel associations, foundations, historical and cultural societies, recreation and sports associations, service clubs, community associations, and religious groups. While their roles vary, nonprofits typically are involved in operating attractions (such as pioneer villages, historic buildings, museums, and art galleries), creating and running events and special meals, providing travel information services, and financing the development of community-oriented facilities (such as recreation and community halls, historical and cultural centers, and trail systems).

The most widely accepted function of government in tourism development is as a **stimulator** or catalyst for development. Governments complement the efforts of the private sector and nonprofit organizations. The World Tourism Organization (WTO) recommends as a general principle that governments should not try to do what the private sector is able and willing to do. Although this is a generally accepted principle in many countries, there are still many cases of overlapping activities and conflict between the government and the private sector. In some countries, the federal, state or provincial, and local governments are involved in the operation of parks, most of which include camping facilities. Many private campground operators feel that the government-operated facilities offer unfair competition and that the government should not be in the campground business. Another area of contention often found is in the provision of boat-docking facilities where both the private sector and government agencies operate competitive facilities. A further area of direct competition is that of government-owned airlines versus private air carriers.

There are several valid reasons behind the reversal in the government and private-sector roles in

tourism development. The most important is that it is not always reasonable to expect tourism to develop in the manner and at the speed contemplated in the tourism plan if left entirely to the private sector. Government agencies often find themselves with a more direct role in tourism development for the reasons shown in figure 13.2.

Due to profitability concerns, several provinces within Canada and states in the U.S. are directly involved in the resort business. These include the states of Indiana and Kentucky, where inns have been developed within certain state parks. In these parks, the inns are owned by the state government and are either operated by the state government or by the private sector through a management contract or lease arrangement.

The **social tourism** function of governments is a widely accepted phenomenon in several countries in Europe and elsewhere. For example, France has established a network of "village de vacances" (family-oriented resorts) and "gites familiaux" (family homes in resort settings) for its disadvantaged citizens.

Another major role of governments is as a **regulator** of tourism developments. Governments must ensure that developers follow all the laws, procedures, and codes in planning and constructing proj-

REASONS	SITUATIONS
Bankruptcy	Existing tourism facility becomes bankrupt and cannot be sold on the market; the government is obliged to acquire the facility.
Pilots or demonstration projects	Government wants to encourage private sector development by pioneering new types of developments through "demonstration" or "pilot" projects.
Profitability concerns	Private sector is unwilling to finance a project because of limited profit potential; the government has given this project a high priority due to its regional economic contributions or its pivotal role in stimulating tourism.
Social tourism	Government wants to provide low-cost vacation opportunities for disadvantaged groups within the population, such as the poor, the sick, and the aged.

Figure 13.2 Reasons for Government Involvement in Tourism Operations.

ects. This may mean that developers are required to conduct environmental impact analyses and to involve local residents in a process of consultation.

Role of Government Financial Incentives in Tourism Development

One of the major hurdles that all tourism projects face is securing the financing needed for their development. Many tourism projects have been economically feasible but have not been developed because the developers were not able to attract the right amount or types of financing. The number of government agencies providing specific financial incentives for tourism projects has greatly increased on a worldwide basis. This is part of governments' role as *stimulators* of tourism development.

Government financial incentives for tourism projects can be classified into two broad categories. *Fiscal incentives* are special allowances for income tax or other tax purposes. *Direct and indirect incentives* constitute the second main category, and include a wide variety of programs aimed at easing the financing requirements of projects. The basic objective of most of these incentive programs is to help businesses implement tourism development projects that, without assistance, may be abandoned or seriously delayed. On a global basis, all levels of government are involved in providing these types of incentive programs. Figure 13.3 provides a description of the types of financial incentive programs provided by government agencies to tourism development projects.

Because most government departments providing these financial incentives receive more applications for assistance than their budgets can handle, it is inevitable that not all projects that request monetary help receive it. In cer-

tain cases, this results in these projects not proceeding any further. A government agency involved in providing financial incentives, technical, or other assistance to individual tourism projects establishes a set of *project selection criteria*. These criteria assist the agency in identifying those projects that merit assistance and screening out other projects that are not as desirable. Typically, criteria fall into the categories shown in figure 13.4.

Quick Trip 13.3

Government Incentives in the Bahamas

The Bahamas is an island country that is highly dependent on tourism. Consisting of 700 different islands, about 80 percent of its visitors are from North America. It also receives significant numbers of visitors from Europe, South America, Japan, and South Africa. In 1992, the Bahamian government adopted a "market-friendly" economic policy to increase the benefits derived from tourism. This included selling off a number of government-owned hotels to the private sector. These companies, in turn, refurbished and redeveloped these hotels. This included a US$250 million dollar redevelopment project of the former Atlantis Resort on Paradise Island into the Sun International, a family resort, ecological/aquatic park, and gaming facility.

The government, through the Bahamas Investment Authority, provides several lucrative financial incentives for developers. These include:

- **Freedom from taxation:** The Bahamas is a "tax haven" where companies pay no taxes on personal or corporate income, capital gains, interest, royalties, sales, estate, inheritances, or payroll. This is a fiscal incentive.

- **Hotels Encouragement Act:** This allows for the duty-free entry of approved construction materials, furniture, and fixtures for hotels. Between 1993 and 1997, projects totaling US$200 million were approved under the Act. This is another type of fiscal incentive.

- **Ecotourism program in the Family Islands:** The government is providing infrastructure on certain islands for small ecotourism resort developments. The Hotel Corporation of The Bahamas has prepared conceptual plans for these projects. The Inter-American Development Bank (IADB) is providing funding for environmentally sensitive hotel and resort projects in the Bahamas.

Source: The Bahamas Ministry of Tourism. (1997).

Private Sector Financing for Tourism Development

Although governments are playing a greater role in providing financing to tourism projects, it is the private sector that supplies the majority of the financing. These private sources range from individual citizens to major institutional lenders such as banks, trust companies, credit unions, insurance companies, and other commercial finance companies. Typically, a private financing source requires that the

CATEGORIES OF INCENTIVES	TYPES OF INCENTIVES
Fiscal Incentives	● **Tax holidays or deferrals**. Government agency defers the payment of income taxes or other taxes for a predetermined time period. ● **Remission of tariffs**. Government agency relaxes or removes import duties on goods and services required by the project. ● **Tax reductions**. Government agency lowers the normal tax rates that would be paid by the project.
Direct and Indirect Incentives	● **Nonrefundable grants**. Reduces a project's capital budget. ● **Low-interest loans**. Reduces the amount of interest that the project must pay during its operating life. ● **Interest rebates**. Government agency rebates a portion of the project's interest costs during its operating life. ● **Forgivable loans**. Government agency loans funds to the project and then "forgives" all or part of these over an agreed-upon time period; this acts like a phased nonrefundable grant. ● **Loan guarantees**. Government agency guarantees a loan given to a project by a private financial institution. ● **Working capital loans**. Government agency loans funds to meet the working capital needs of a project. ● **Equity participation**. Government agency purchases some of the available shares in the project, and becomes an equity investor. ● **Training grants**. Government agency provides a nonrefundable grant to the project for staff training purposes. ● **Infrastructure assistance**. Government agency assumes the costs of some or all of the infrastructure required for the project. ● **Leasebacks**. Government agency purchases land, buildings, or equipment and then leases them to the project. ● **Land donations**. Government agency donates land free of charge to the project.

Figure 13.3   Categories and Types of Government Incentives.

following five criteria be met before lending money to tourism developers:

● Previous management experience in tourism and an established credit record within the management development team.

● Proof of economic feasibility via an independent economic feasibility study.

● Adequate collateral or security for the funds to be borrowed.

● Adequate equity invested by the owners of the project.

● Proof of stability in the tourism destination in which the project will operate.

Tourism development projects require **equity** from owners and investors as well as borrowed capital (**debt**). These individuals are the true "risk takers" in the development, and they are rewarded with profits for a return on their investments. Not all projects are able to secure the types and amounts of private financing that they require, although they may have successfully survived all of the earlier screening mechanisms.

Analysis of Individual Project Development Opportunities

"By the early 1990s, after the hotel industry ambled down the yellow brick road of the 1980s, it found it wasn't in the same business anymore. The real estate market had collapsed. The overall economy softened, the stock market fell, and companies laid off employees. There was a glut of hotel rooms in the marketplace. Travel had declined. Occupancy rates had dropped."

Lane, H.E., & Dupré, D. (1997). Hospitality world: An introduction, 355

Individual project development opportunities in tourism are either generated through the tourism planning process or by the private sector independent of this process. In destinations without tourism plans, governments may also be involved in identifying development

Some tourism projects, such as snorkeling lessons, require only human resources and equipment. Photo from *Top Shots* CD Rom. Courtesy of Queensland Tourist and Travel Corporation.

CRITERIA	CONDITIONS
Competitive Impact	● Project complements, rather than competes with, existing tourism businesses, and does not seriously jeopardize the financial viability of any individual business.
Compliance with Policies and Plans	● Project complies with the destination's tourism policies and plans.
Developer and Operator Capabilities	● Project developers and operators are capable of developing and operating the business successfully.
Economic Contributions	● Project creates significant levels of income and employment benefits.
Environmental Impact	● Project is developed in compliance with existing legislation and regulations governing the conservation and protection of the environment (sustainability guidelines).
Equity Contributions	● Where the project is profit-making, the investors have sufficient equity to inject into the venture.
Feasibility	● Where the project is profit-making, it is economically feasible.
Social-Cultural Impact	● Project does not jeopardize the social well-being of local citizens.
Tourism Impact	● Project adds to the destination's tourism potential by creating an attraction, by improving the area's capacity to receive and cater to visitors, or by being beneficial to tourism in some other way.

Figure 13.4   Criteria for Government Financial Assistance.

Explore Sydney on $20 a day

Sydney Discovery Tours
Infoline phone 131 500

The Sydney Explorer bus service is an important tourism development.

opportunities for private-sector investment. Although these development opportunities can have the potential of satisfying tourism planning goals and considerable initial appeal to those in the private sector, they may be undesirable due to financial, environmental, social, cultural, or other reasons. All individual tourism project development opportunities must be carefully analyzed before proceeding with construction.

There are many types of tourism project development opportunities. Projects differ in their ability to generate financial profits. Projects such as hotels and commercial attractions are inherent profit-generators. Profit-generating projects are analyzed in economic feasibility studies. Other projects, such as travel information centers and infrastructure, generate no direct financial returns. However, these projects are essential to an area's destination mix. Other projects are the subject of cost/benefit analyses or other types of *contribution analysis* studies. Some tourism projects involve building construction (*superstructure*) or the development of transportation and essential public services (*infrastructure*); others require only human resources and equipment (such as guided canoe or ecotourism trips).

Despite differences in the tourism project ingredients, individual project opportunities can be analyzed by using similar techniques. Figure 13.5 shows a tourism project evaluation system. There are several decision points in project analysis in which further consideration of a tourism development project may be terminated. These include:

● A pre-feasibility study produces negative results.

● The site for the project is not suitable, and no alternative site is available.

● The market analysis indicates that the market is not large enough to support the project.

● The project is not economically feasible.

● The environmental, social or cultural impacts are unacceptable.

● The results of a cost/benefit analysis are negative.

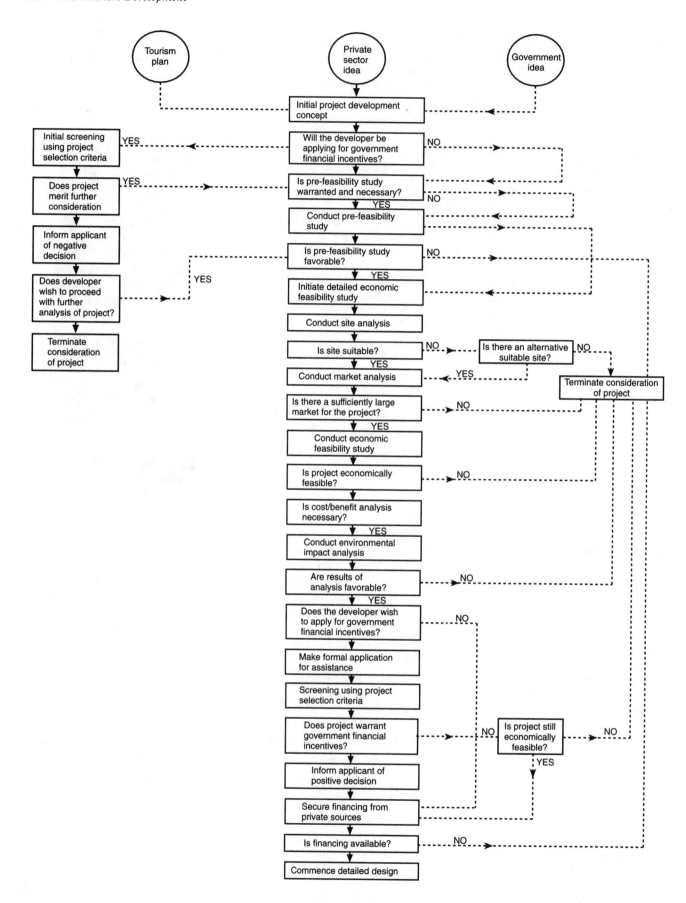

Figure 13.5 Conceptual Model of a Tourism Project Evaluation System.

Quick Trip 13.4
Tourism Development in Ireland

The two main organizations involved in Irish tourism are the Department of Tourism and Trade and the Irish Tourist Board (Bord Failte). The Department of Tourism and Trade has embarked on a major tourism development program with financing from the European Union (EU). Known as the *Operational Programme for Tourism (1994–1999)*, there are five main goals:

- Increase foreign exchange earnings to 2,250 million pounds by the end of 1999.
- Create 35,000 new jobs.
- Improve the seasonality factor (75% of visitors to come outside the peak as compared with 70% at present).
- Improve product range and quality.
- Improve service standards and value for money.

The plan calls for 652 million pounds to be invested between 1994 and 1999; the largest ever investment in tourism in Ireland. The EU will contribute 369 million and the Irish government will invest 84 million. There are five activities within the program: 1) national cultural tourism; 2) product development; 3) marketing; 4) training; and 5) technical assistance. The first activity provides capital grants for the arts, focusing on art centers, theaters, and galleries. The product development activity provides capital for five types of tourism developments:

- **Large tourism projects** (large tourism projects at the national level and weather-independent projects at the regional level).
- **Tourism information and heritage projects** (projects that provide more tourist information facilities, heritage products, interpretive centers, guest houses, etc.).
- **Fisheries and angling projects** (projects that support the fisheries sector that provides the basis for fishing as an activity).
- **Activity-based and special-interest projects** (projects that provide visitors with special-interest opportunities such as adventure holidays, themed cycling, equestrian, great gardens, language learning, angling, etc.).
- **Accommodation-related conference and leisure facility projects** (projects that create accommodation-related conference and leisure facilities, and also certain forms of specialist accommodation).

Source: Department of Tourism and Trade, Government of Ireland.

---

time-consuming, pre-feasibility studies can be extremely valuable to developers. The objectives of a pre-feasibility study are to determine whether:

1. The information available is adequate to show the project will not be viable or will not be attractive to investors or lenders.
2. The information available indicates that the project is so promising that an investment decision can be made on the basis of the pre-feasibility study itself; that is, a detailed study is not needed.
3. A preliminary assessment of potential environmental, social or cultural impacts shows that these potential impacts are significant and unacceptable to the local community.
4. Aspects of the project are so critical to its viability that they must be analyzed as part of the detailed economic feasibility study.
5. The availability of factors critical to the viability of the project (such as the availability of a specific site) must be confirmed prior to doing a detailed economic feasibility study.

Pre-feasibility studies can be completed by private developers, by government agencies considering financing projects, or by private consulting organizations on behalf of the developers or government agencies. In some cases, the tourism development component of the tourism planning process produces pre-feasibility analyses of key tourism project development opportunities.

- The government decides the project does not qualify for financial assistance and it is not feasible without these incentives.
- Sufficient financing from the private sector cannot be secured.

Pre-feasibility Study

A pre-feasibility study determines whether a detailed economic feasibility study is justified and which topics this detailed study should address. Because detailed economic feasibility studies are costly and

Detailed Economic Feasibility Study

If a project survives the pre-feasibility screening, it is then analyzed through a detailed economic feasibility study. The majority of tourism development project economic feasibility studies are carried out by private consulting organizations on behalf of private developers, investors, or government agencies, or a combination of these parties.

Although many successful tourism development projects have been developed without detailed economic feasibility studies, as have many that have not proven successful, these analyses are vital to many people involved in the development process including the developers, investors, potential lenders, and government agencies. Other players involved in the process may include **management companies** interested in operating the projects on behalf of the developers and investors under management contracts or leases. The potential lenders may fall into two groups: those providing the construction (**interim**) financing, and those providing the long-term (**permanent**) financing.

An **economic feasibility study** is a study to determine the economic feasibility of a tourism development project opportunity. A project is **economically feasible** if it provides a rate of return acceptable to the investors in the project. A **market study** is one component of an economic feasibility study which analyzes the project's market potential. Because of the need to acquire an unbiased opinion on a project's viability, economic feasibility studies are prepared by an independent third party and not by the developers, investors, or the potential lenders. Many lenders, including both private financial institutions and government agencies providing financial assistance programs, require that these independent studies be completed before they will seriously consider projects.

An economic feasibility study is designed to answer the questions, shown in figure 13.6, that are of concern to the participants in the development process.

PARTIES	QUESTIONS
Developers and Investors	● Which of several alternative site locations is the most appropriate?
	● Is a specific site appropriate for the development?
	● If not, is there another site available that would be suitable?
	● Is market demand large enough to support the project?
	● What are the optimum scale and components of the project?
	● What style of operation and quality levels should be provided?
	● What revenues and expenses will the project experience?
	● What will the capital costs be?
	● Will the project produce a satisfactory return on investment?
	● Should the developers and investors proceed with further analysis?
Lenders	All of the above questions should be of concern to the lenders, and:
	● How much money will be loaned to the developers and investors?
	● Do the developers and investors have sufficient equity to invest in the project, given the financing required?
	● Will the project produce sufficient operating profits and cash flow to cover the interest and principal payments when they become due?

Figure 13.6   Questions Addressed by a Feasibility Study.

The economic feasibility study has another important use for developers. It produces recommendations on the scale, sizes, facility types, and quality levels of operation. These recommendations are based upon the size and expectations of the market from the market study. At a later date in the development process, these findings will be used as the basis for the architect's preliminary drawings.

Site Analysis   Although not all tourism development project opportunities require physical site locations, a very large proportion do. An economic feasibility study can either specify a site (site specific), if a specific site location has been chosen for the project, or determine if an appropriate site exists within a given geographic area.

A tourism project site usually requires specific characteristics to be successful. This is not true of all sectors of an economy, as there are many "footloose" enterprises that are not location-dependent. In tourism, location has an extremely important bearing upon financial viability.

The characteristics or criteria for site selection and evaluation vary with the type of tourism project under consideration. For example, a

A proposed ski area is dependent upon the snow and slope conditions in a given location. Pictured here is South Lake Tahoe, Heavenly Valley, California. Photo courtesy of California Division of Tourism: Robert Holmes.

proposed new alpine ski area is dependent on the snow conditions and slope characteristics in a given location, while an urban hotel requires proximity to a concentration of industry and commerce. Similarly, a motor hotel requires ease of access and proximity to highways, while the placement of tennis courts is dictated by the wind and sun conditions at the site. The first step in the site analysis is to identify the criteria that are crucial to the project. Tourism development project site criteria or characteristics can be divided into three categories:

- Market-related criteria
- Physical characteristics
- Other criteria

Figure 13.7 provides a master list of individual criteria within each of these categories.

The identification of the most important site characteristics for a project is crucial. This requires a familiarity and experience with the particular project type, and a broad knowledge of construction and site engineering. Ideally, a multi-disciplinary team consisting of a specialized tourism consultant, engineer, environmental and social impact experts, landscape architect, and architect should be used.

When a specific site has not been selected, a "long list" of potentially suitable sites is identified and these sites are ranked on their compatibility with the project. This ranking can be done by attaching a weighting factor to each site selection characteristic and giving each site a numerical score for that characteristic. The weighting factor reflects the relative importance of each site characteristic, and the numerical score (say on a 0 to 10 basis) indicates the quality or quantity of that characteristic for the site. The multiplication of the weighting factor and the numerical score provides a final score for each characteristic at each alter-

CRITERIA	SITE CHARACTERISTICS	SITE CHARACTERISTICS
Market-related Criteria	**Proximity and Accessibility to:** ● Attractions and events ● Competitors ● Facilities (accommodations, restaurants, shopping) ● Potential visitor markets ● Transportation facilities	**Visibility:** ● If required, is site visible to potential visitors? ● If required, is site sufficiently private?

Physical Characteristics	**Aesthetics:**
	● Adjoining lands and land uses
	● Focal points
	● Noise
	● Scale
	● Variety (features, forms, colors)
	● Views
	
	Geology and Geomorphology:
	● Bedrock type
	● Geologic history
	● Water-table level and quality
	● Infrastructure Availability:
	  ● Energy sources
	  ● Sewage disposal system
	  ● Transportation facilities and systems
	  ● Water supply (drainage and flooding problems, lakes and seas, natural springs, rivers and streams, waterfalls and cascades)
	
	Natural Conditions:
	● Ability to support specific types of recreational activities
	● Climate and micro-climate (humidity, precipitation, purity of air, seasons, sunshine and clouds, temperatures, winds)
		Soils and Topography:
		● Depths
		● Slopes
		● Soil types
		● Vegetation:
		  ● Clearing problems
		  ● Ground cover type
		  ● Tree types
		  ● Visual and physical condition
		
		Wildlife and Fish:
		● Effects of development on these
		● Species and types
		
		Other Site Characteristics:
		● Dimensions and shape
		● Geographical orientation
		● Height above sea level
		● Length of shoreline
		● Rights of way and easements

Other Criteria	● Availability of a suitable quality of land for project ● Availability of staff accommodation ● Cost of land ● Labor laws and labor relations history ● Manpower availability	● Social and economic characteristics of host area ● Sources and types of financial assistance in host area ● Zoning laws and other government regulations

Figure 13.7 Master List of Site Selection Criteria.

native site. The final scores for all characteristics are added to give a total score for each alternative site. The most appropriate site for the project is the one earning the highest total score.

The evaluation of sites for certain tourism projects requires a

high degree of specific technical expertise. Generally, these projects are highly dependent on the characteristics of the natural resource base and have high construction costs, such as alpine skiing areas and large full-service marina projects. Private organizations specializing in site evaluations for projects are normally contracted to perform these analyses.

An economic feasibility study may be terminated after the site analysis if an essential site characteristic is missing or if some insurmountable legal or zoning restriction or other barrier to development is found. The study moves on to the market analysis if this is not the case.

Market Analysis   The market analysis portion of an economic feasibility study is often the most costly and time-consuming element. The costs and time required are dependent on the mix of primary and secondary research conducted. **Secondary research** is the analysis of available, published sources of information and is far less expensive than primary research. Market surveys aimed at producing new information and conclusions for the project are classified as **primary research**. Although pre-feasibility studies are often based only on secondary research, detailed economic feasibility studies must contain a mixture of both secondary and primary research.

The market analysis starts with the collection and review of secondary sources of information since this provides a clearer focus on the type and scope of primary market research needed. With the growing attention being given to tourism on a worldwide basis, the amount of available tourism research is enormous. An analysis of secondary sources in tourism can be time-consuming and exhausting, unless the researcher knows about the major tourism journals, reference centers, libraries, and online sources of information.

When the review of secondary sources of information is complete, a primary research plan is drawn up and implemented. This may involve conducting a variety of surveys. It requires that the research-

ers have a thorough understanding of marketing research techniques. The survey methods include:

- Questionnaires (personal interview, telephone, mail, fax, World Wide Web, self-administered)
- Focus group
- Delphi method

Questionnaires are the most frequently used instruments in tourism project feasibility studies. Researchers direct their questions to potential visitors or to the managers of competitive or similar operations. In the latter case, the questions are aimed at gathering information on the facilities and services offered, and on the existing market volumes and characteristics through such competitive performance statistics as room occupancy rates or attendance figures. The common factor in all questionnaires is that they require responses (written or oral) to questions (written or oral). The three major advantages of questionnaires are versatility, speed, and cost. Questionnaires are versatile because almost every research problem can be addressed, including the respondent's knowledge, opinions, motivations, and intentions. The use of questionnaires is usually faster and cheaper than the **observational method** of research. The observational method is a process of observing and studying the behavior of people, objects, and occurrences rather than of questioning people to get the same information.

The questionnaire method has recognized limitations. Respondents may be unwilling to provide the information. They may not agree to be interviewed or refuse to answer specific questions. Mail surveys typically have low response rates with sometimes as many as 90 percent of the questionnaires not being returned. Skilled and experienced researchers can bring the response rates up to 50 percent or

more. Personal and telephone surveys have higher response rates. A second disadvantage of questionnaires is that the respondent may be willing to cooperate but is unable to provide accurate answers to some questions. For example, the respondents may not have thought through their motivations for particular purchases or activities. A third limitation of questionnaires is that the respondent may intentionally supply incorrect or inaccurate information. Some respondents may give the types of answers that they think the researchers are looking for, or they may deliberately give misleading information. Others may answer in a particular way so as not to be embarrassed or to have their egos damaged. Respondents may also wrongly interpret the meanings of particular questions and may give less than satisfactory answers because of this.

Broad-scale questionnaire surveys, although relatively inexpensive when compared to other market research techniques, can be very expensive if they are conducted at the individual household level. This is particularly true if the potential users reside in countries distant from the destination area. Unlike consumer product research, market research using broad-scale questionnaires may encounter difficulties in determining the exact geographical origins of potential users of a tourism project and their relative proportions. Because there are these problems in defining the statistical universe, it is also extremely difficult to accurately state what the size and structure of a sample should be.

Due to the unique challenges in conducting surveys of potential users of proposed tourism projects, it is common to survey people in the channels of distribution (retail travel agents, tour wholesalers, and tour operators) and other travel decision-makers (such as convention-meeting planners, corporate travel managers, and association executives) or to utilize the focus groups or the Delphi method as a supplement to questionnaire surveys.

The *focus-group method* involves bringing together a small group of people (ideally eight to twelve) in one place and asking them to focus upon the research topic. The research team supplies an experienced focus group moderator. The objectives of these sessions are to get the group to reach consensus on questions posed by the moderator. The focus group can be drawn from householders in general, or each participant may have common characteristics, such as being convention-meeting planners, retail travel agents, tour operators, tour wholesalers, or club executives. Because focus group participants tend to interact with one another and because there is a greater opportunity to explore individual preferences and attitudes, this method overcomes some of the drawbacks of questionnaires. Focus-group participants are often prescreened before being invited to the meetings.

The *Delphi method* is often used for forecasting and futures exercises in tourism, but it can also be applied to a tourism development project. It can also be called the "knowledgeable panel" method since it involves recruiting a team of experts on a particular topic. The team acts as a sounding board on alternative approaches, ideas, or concepts. The Delphi group participants do not have to meet in person, but each one is required to give responses to a variety of written propositions prepared by the researchers, such as "What probability do you attach to this resort succeeding at this location?" (Provide a probability percentage between 0 percent and 100 percent.)

Another type of research that has been used for some tourism projects is *analogy research*. This does not involve any surveying of potential visitors; it means doing detailed research on the perfor-mance of comparable (or analo-gous) operations. By studying the success of comparable projects, conclusions are drawn on the likely success of the proposed project. Because many factors contribute to a tourism business' success, analogy research must be applied with great caution.

In economic feasibility studies, it is often necessary to forecast demand for either the project itself or for the destination area in general, or for both. There are many *forecasting* techniques available to the researcher. Forecasts are divided into time spans that are considered to be accurate. There is general agreement that there are four basic forecasting horizons; short-term (one day to two years), medium-term (between two and five years), long-term (between five and fifteen years), and futurism (over fifteen years). For example, the *extrapolation method* is thought only to be useful for short-term forecasts, while *correlation techniques* are considered to be good for short-, medium-, and long-term forecasting.

The forecasting of potential market demand for a project usually covers the medium-term to long-term forecasts, that is, the initial five to fifteen years of operation. This seems appropriate since the critical financial years of a purely commercial project are its first one to ten years. Most commercial tourism projects are expected to reach their full financial and operating potential within their first five years of operation and to pay back their investor's equity within ten years. Also the *present value concept* dictates that the earlier the financial returns are received from a project the greater is their contribution to economic feasibility.

The actual forecasting of potential demand levels for a tourism development project can be approached through several different methods (figure 13.8). It is ad-visable to use two or more of the methods shown in figure 13.8 and then to cross-check their results. Once a technically acceptable potential market demand forecast has been developed, an initial judgment can be made as to whether the market is of sufficient size with the appropriate characteristics to support the project. This requires considerable experience with the business type being considered. It has to be very clear that the potential demand levels are large enough to make the project viable. For example, if a hotel requires an annual occupancy percentage of 70 percent to be viable, and the potential demand generates an occupancy of only 30 percent in the project's fifth year, the proposed hotel will not be viable. In most cases, this judgment is not so obvious, and more analysis needs to be done to determine if the demand levels justify the investment.

Economic Feasibility Analysis

The economic feasibility analysis determines if a tourism development project can produce a satisfactory financial return for investors. It is composed of the following seven steps:

- **Project description:** The components, scale and sizes, and quality levels required to capture the potential market demand.
- **Pricing:** The unit prices and rates to be charged.
- **Revenues:** The market demand levels multiplied by unit prices and rates.
- **Expenses and profits:** The operating expenses and profits.
- **Capital costs:** The capital budget for the project.
- **Cash flow:** The capital expenses, net income, and cash flow.
- **ROI:** The rate of return on investment.

METHODS	APPROACHES
Alternative Scenario	● Uses either the calculation, market share/penetration, or survey/potential demand quantification methods and produces optimistic, realistic, and pessimistic scenarios of potential demand levels.
Analogy	● Assumes that the project will achieve certain demand levels based upon the known performances and penetration levels of similar projects elsewhere.
Calculation	● Projects potential demand by using "rules-of-thumb" or consumer expenditure and behavior patterns.
Market Share or Market Penetration	● Calculates total market demand and the project's share of total demand by using information from competitive facilities, historic demand growth rates, and anticipated future occurrences, or other forecasting techniques.
Survey and Potential Demand	● Quantifies total potential demand by using the results from questionnaire and other survey methods, by "grossing up" from the sample size taken.

Figure 13.8   Forecasting Methods and Approaches.

The forecasts of potential market demand and the desires and expectations of people interviewed provide the key inputs for detailing the *project concept*. The project concept describes the components, scale, sizes, and quality levels of facilities and services needed to satisfy the potential demand. Unit prices and rates are then prepared.

The next two steps are referred to as the production of forecast or *pro forma income statements* indicating the estimated revenues, operating expenses, and operating profits for the project. When estimating revenues, the total potential demand is broken down into segments, and the applicable unit prices and rates are multiplied by the resulting volumes in each segment. The operating expenses include the costs of operating the project, such as the cost of food and other merchandise for resale, labor, marketing, energy, and repairs and maintenance. Publications containing average business performance statistics can be helpful in estimating these operating costs. Greater individual accuracy occurs when the forecaster is familiar with the type of business under consideration, and when detailed staffing schedules and other operating standards are developed for the project.

There are other ongoing expenses that the project will encounter, and these all relate to the *capital investment* in the development. To estimate the expenses requires that a *capital budget* be prepared first. A capital budget is a detailed, itemized forecast of the capital investment required by the project. For a tourism development project, these costs include building construction, professional fees, infrastructure, recreational facilities, furniture, fixtures and equipment, interim financing, contingencies, and miscellaneous other items. The most realistic capital budgets are produced by a multi-disciplinary team consisting of specialized tourism consultants, civil engineers, quantity surveyors, interior designers, architects, and landscape architects. The capital budget is prepared by identifying all of the capital costs that will be encountered, and then pricing each item. A contingency factor, normally between 10 and 20 percent, is added to cover unforeseen cost overruns or overlooked items. Once the capital budget is complete, the capital-related expenses for the project are calculated. These expenses include financing charges on long-term debt, depreciation, municipal taxes, and insurance premiums on fixed assets. The capital-related expenses are deducted from the operating profits to give net income figures (after tax profit) and cash flow forecasts. The net income and cash flow projections cover the useful life of the project.

One or more financial analysis techniques are used to measure the rate of return produced by these forecast net income and cash flow levels. Most experts in the field favor *present value yardsticks* that use the *discounted cash flow* (DCF) method, especially the net present value (NPV) and internal rate of return (IRR) techniques. The present value concept implies that money has a time value. Thus, a dollar received today is worth more than a dollar received a year from now, since the dollar received today can be reinvested to produce a higher overall return. With present value methods, the dollars received in profits in the earlier years are more valuable than those earned in later years. Both the NPV and IRR techniques use cash flow figures as a basis for projections and discount the value of future cash flows at certain assumed rates of return. Based upon the rates of return predicted, a decision is made as to whether the tourism development project is economically feasible. If the rate is less than what the investors require, the project is not economically feasible.

The positive impact of government financial incentives upon a project's economic feasibility has not been discussed. Many tourism projects that are not economically feasible with only private-sector financing are developed because of the injection of government financial assistance. These incentives increase the rates of return for investors by reducing the interest burden on projects or reducing financing costs in some other way. In many cases, the increases are great enough to change a project into a feasible venture. However, if a project is not feasible and there is no possibility of receiving government financial assistance, it will probably be terminated at this point.

Cost/Benefit Analysis

Profit-making projects that are found to be economically feasible may or may not have to be further analyzed using cost/benefit analysis. Cost/benefit analyses are useful for evaluating non-commercial tourism projects that generate no direct revenues or that have, at best, operating revenues equaling operating expenses. Cost/benefit analyses are done by or on behalf of government agencies. They help these agencies measure and weigh all of the costs and benefits of alternative projects. The agencies are then able to determine which project will produce the largest net economic benefits and for society as a whole.

Economic feasibility analyses are just one aspect of cost/benefit analysis. There are several financial analyses or *capital budgeting* techniques available that permit comparisons between alternative projects. In purely financial terms, the project that creates the highest rate of return for its investors is the best alternative. However, from a government viewpoint, the size of the return on private investors' capital cannot be the only criterion for support. A government agency has broad-scale economic, environmental, social, and cultural responsibilities that have to be considered before giving financial assistance or other support to a project. For example, a proposed casino may generate spectacular returns for investors, but a government agency may feel that such a project will undermine the social well-being of the destination area.

A cost/benefit analysis attempts to weigh the quantifiable and non-quantifiable costs and benefits of a tourism project against each other. Some subjectivity and judgment has to enter into this because there can be no single measurement or set of measurements of a project's overall worth to a destination area. Assuming that the cost/benefit analysis results are positive, the project can progress to the next level of evaluation. Some project developers may wish to apply for government financial assistance, while others may go ahead without such assistance.

Environmental Impact Analysis

The purpose of an *environmental impact assessment (EIA)* is to identify in advance factors that may affect the ability to build a proposed tourism development and the environmental attributes that will be affected by the development (Manning & Dougherty, 1995). Three objectives of an EIA are (Ecologically Sustainable Development Working Group, 1991):

- To identify risks, minimize adverse impacts, and determine environmental acceptability.
- To achieve environmentally-sound proposals through research, management, and monitoring.
- To manage conflict through the provision of a means for effective public participation.

Many countries require that EIAs be conducted before final government approval is given. These analyses are usually paid for by the developers and conducted by expert consultants. The consultants attempt to predict and evaluate the impact of the tourism development project on various environmental attributes (e.g., beaches and coastlines, wetlands, flora and

Railroad cars provide a unique style of accommodation at the Undara Experience in Far North Queensland, Australia. Photo from *Top Shots* CD Rom. Courtesy of Queensland Tourist and Travel Corporation.

Sustainable tourism development implies maintaining important historic, as well as ecological resources: The Equestrian Statue of Prince Eugene of Savoy, Buda Castle Hill, Hungary. Photo from *Budapest in 101 Photos; Multimedia CD for the IBM PC.* (Selester, Hungary, 1996.) Printed with permission.

fauna). They also recommend environmental safeguards that must be taken to ensure that the development does not cause the adverse impacts that have been predicted. Governments often require that the developer and their consultants establish a process of public input into the EIA.

There is growing public concern for the impact of developments on the environment. Around the world, several proposed tourism projects have been vigorously opposed by conservation and other interest groups. So great has been the protests that, in some cases, the developers have given up on the projects. There can be no doubt that these types of public opposition on environmental grounds will continue in the future as society becomes more environmentally sensitive. This will place an even greater premium on careful planning by developers and the adoption of "best environmental practices."

Detailed Design and Construction

In the final stages of realizing a tourism development project, various levels of architectural designs and drawings are prepared. Normally, this procedure includes:

1. Preparation of preliminary architectural concepts.
2. Preparation of a preliminary architectural design.
3. Preparation of a final architectural design.
4. Construction.

At each of the first three stages, the drawings become increasingly more detailed and exact. When the final drawings have been approved, the project moves into construction.

Summary

The tourism plan for a destination area provides overall guidelines for development, and identifies project development opportunities worthy of more in-depth analysis through economic feasibility studies, cost/benefit analyses, and environmental impact assessments. Governments play a key role in ensuring that developers abide by the overall guidelines and the broad development concepts are realized. Government agencies are also playing an ever-increasing role in stimulating the development of tourism project development opportunities through many types of financial incentive programs.

Only a small proportion of tourism project development opportunities actually reach the construction stage, as most are unable to meet certain criteria or to secure the necessary financing. Many are screened out because they are not economically feasible or due to environmental impacts that are expected to be adverse and unacceptable.

References

Bramwell, B. (1991). Sustainability and rural tourism policy in Britain. *Tourism Recreation Research*, 16 (2), 49–51.

Butler, R.W. (1993). *Pre- and post-impact assessment of tourism development.* Tourism research: Critiques and challenges, 135–155. New York: Routledge.

Cater, E. (1993). Ecotourism in the Third World: Problems for sustainable tourism development. *Tourism Management*, 14, 85–90.

Ding, P., & Pigram, J. (1995). Environmental audits: An emerging concept in sustainable tourism development. *Journal of Tourism Studies*, 6 (2), 2–10.

Doggart, C., & Doggart, N. (1996). Environmental impacts of tourism in developing countries. *Travel & Tourism Analyst* (2), 71–86.

Ecologically Sustainable Development Working Group. (1991). *Final report: Tourism*. Canberra: Australian Government Publishing Service.

Gartner, W.C. (1996). *Tourism development: Principles, processes, and policies*. New York: Van Nostrand Reinhold.

Glasson, J., Godfrey, K., & Goodey, B. (1995). *Towards visitor impact management*. Aldershot, England: Avebury.

Gunn, C.A. (1994). *Tourism planning: Basics, concepts, cases* (3rd ed.). Washington, D.C.: Taylor & Francis.

Hall, C.M. (1994). *Tourism and politics: Policy, power and place*. Chichester, England: John Wiley & Sons, Inc.

Harrison, D. (ed.). (1992). *Tourism & the less developed countries*. London: Bellhaven Press.

Inskeep, E., & Kallenberger, M. (1992). *An integrated approach to resort development: Six case studies*. Madrid: World Tourism Organization.

Ioannides, D. (1995). The flawed implementation of sustainable tourism: The experience of Akamas, Cyprus. *Tourism Management*, 8, 583–592.

Kersten, A. (1997). *Community based ecotourism and community building: The case of the Lacandones (Chiapas)*. http://txinfinet.com/mader/planeta/0597/0597lacandon.html.

Lane, H.E., & Dupré, D. (1997). *Hospitality world: An introduction*. New York: Van Nostrand Reinhold.

Laws, E. (1995). *Tourist destination management: Issues, analysis and policies*. London: Routledge.

Lindberg, K., & Hawkins, D.E. (eds.). (1993). *Ecotourism: A guide for planners & managers*. North Bennington, Vermont: The Ecotourism Society.

Lundberg, D.E., Stavenga, M.H., & Krishnamoorthy, M. (1995). *Tourism economics*. New York: John Wiley & Sons, Inc.

Manning, E.W., & Dougherty, T.D. (1995). Sustainable tourism: Preserving the golden goose. *Cornell Hotel and Restaurant Administration Quarterly*, 36 (2), 29–42.

Mathieson, A., & Wall, G. (1982). *Tourism: Economic, physical, and social impacts*. New York: Longman Scientific & Technical.

McIntyre, G. (1993). *Sustainable tourism development: Guide for local planners*. Madrid: World Tourism Organization.

Moscardo, G.M., Morrison, A.M., & Pearce, P.L. (1996). Specialist accommodation and ecologically-sustainable tourism. *Journal of Sustainable Tourism*, 4 (1), 29–52.

Pearce, D. (1992). *Tourist organizations*. Essex, England: Longman Group U.K.

Smith, V.L., & Eadington, W.R. (eds.). (1992). *Tourism alternatives: Potentials and problems in the development of tourism*. Philadelphia: University of Pennsylvania Press.

Swarbrooke, J. (1995). *The development & management of visitor attractions*. Oxford: Butterworth-Heinemann.

Vellas, F., & Becherel, L. (1995). *International tourism*. New York: St. Martin's Press.

Weiler, B., & Hall, C.M. (eds.). (1992). *Special interest tourism*. London: Bellhaven Press.

Whelan, T. (ed.). (1991). *Nature tourism: Managing the environment*. Washington, D.C.: Island Press.

Wight, P.A. (1993a). Sustainable ecotourism: Balancing economic, environmental and social goals within an ethical framework. *Journal of Tourism Studies*, 4 (2), 54–65.

Wight, P.A. (1993b). Ecotourism: Ethics or eco-sell? *Journal of Travel Research*, 31 (3), 3–9.

Surfing Solutions

http://www.irlgov.ie/dtt/default.htm (Department of Tourism and Trade, Ireland)

http://www.earthpledge.org/about/stoulinks.html (Earth Pledge sustainable tourism links)

http://Lorenz.mur.csu.edu.au/ecotour/EcoTrHme.html (Ecotourism Information Centre at Charles Sturt University, Australia)

http://www.ecotourism.org/ (The Ecotourism Society, U.S.)

http://public-www.pi.se/~orbit/samoa/19sust.html (Western Samoa Visitors Bureau)

http://www.wttc.org/ (World Travel & Tourism Council and links to Green Globe and ECoNETT)

Acronyms

EIA (environmental impact assessment)
EU (European Union)
ESTD (ecologically sustainable tourism development)
IRR (internal rate of return)
LDC (less-developed country)
NPV (net present value)
ROI (return on investment)
STD (sustainable tourism development)
WTO (World Tourism Organization)

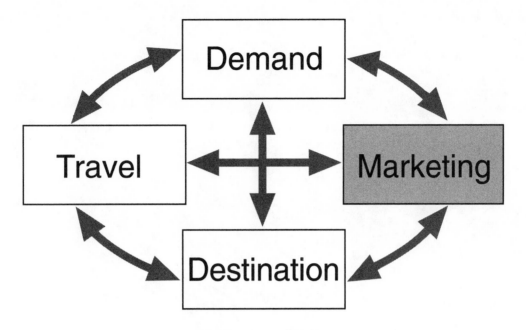

Part IV

Marketing

Strategy, Planning, Promotion, and Distribution

The destination mix of an area becomes its tourism product, shaped by market demand as well as its tourism policy, plan, legislation and regulations, and tourism development. Part 4 of *The Tourism System* examines the strategies, procedures, and techniques that a destination area can use to market its tourism product in such a way as to have an effective influence on demand.

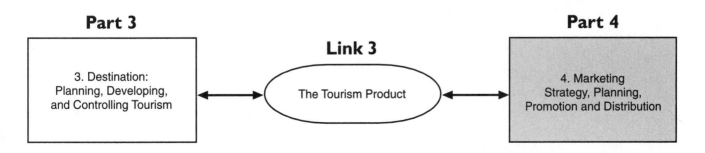

Part 3

3. Destination: Planning, Developing, and Controlling Tourism

Link 3

The Tourism Product

Part 4

4. Marketing Strategy, Planning, Promotion and Distribution

"With the increasing number of travelers during the last decade, tourism marketing is sometimes viewed as an easy task. After all, there should be enough visitors for everyone, and if increases in tourism are any indication, tourism marketing has been very successful. That is not necessarily the case. While success can be measured in terms of increased visitors, revenues, employment, number of businesses, or in many other ways, growth does not always imply success. Growth must be directed and planned if it is to proceed without major surprises."

Gartner (1996), 404

14

Tourism Marketing

···Bringing All of the Parts of Tourism Together ·····

Purpose

Having learned about the basic principles and concepts of marketing as applied to tourism, students will be able to describe the procedures that should be used in marketing tourism destinations and organizations.

Learning Objectives

Having read this chapter, you should be able to:

1. Describe the differences between the marketing of tourism services and traditional product marketing.

2. Compare and contrast the different approaches to marketing associated with production, selling, marketing, and societal marketing orientations.

3. Explain the concept of market segmentation and how target markets are selected.

4. Define positioning and explain how it is used in tourism.

5. Explain the product life cycle concept and how it applies to tourism.

6. Describe each of the steps of the marketing planning process in tourism.

7. List and describe the elements of the marketing mix.

Overview

The marketing of tourism services is unique. This chapter begins by reviewing the factors that make tourism marketing different from the marketing of other products and services. Several definitions of tourism marketing are provided that emphasize the need for a marketing orientation and market segmentation. A five-step procedural model for marketing planning is described. Through the process of market segmentation, target markets are selected, and an appropriate marketing mix for each target market is selected. The elements of the marketing mix are described.

Tourism Marketing Is Unique

"When we say certain rooms have kings and queens in them we may not necessarily be referring to the size of the beds. The Luxury Collection. (ITT Sheraton). Forty-eight of the world's finest hotels. Each one from The Hotel Danieli in Venice to The Phoenician in Scottsdale, in its own unique way makes their guests feel like Royalty. Not surprisingly, some actually are."

The Luxury Collection, ITT Sheraton advertisement, (1997)

The challenges in tourism marketing are unique and different from those of traditional product marketing. These differences are the result of the characteristics of tourism supply and demand. Tourism is a combination of personal services and certain physical facilities and products. An *intangible experience* is offered, not a physical good that can be inspected before it is bought. Because tourism is a service business, production and consumption take place at the same time. In manufacturing, goods are produced, stored, and sold. The inventory process for products serves as a way of linking these stages of production and consumption. Tourism supply cannot be stored. Unlike a can of food which, if it is not sold one day can be sold the next, airline seats, hotel rooms, cruise ship berths, places on an escorted tour, and restaurant seats not sold today are lost forever. Tourism is a highly *perishable* commodity. While the "tourism inventory" cannot be stored and adjusted to changes in demand, the capacity to produce tourism services must be developed ahead of time. This puts great pressure on tourism developers to effectively plan the proper amounts of facilities and to keep them as fully used as possible. This creates another kind of challenge: Tourism supply is relatively fixed. The resources and infrastructure of a destination cannot change as quickly as can visitor demand.

A second factor that makes tourism unique is that the service provided is a *mixture of several services and some facilities and products*. For example, most travel trips have information, transportation, lodging, food and beverage, attraction, and activity components (the destination mix concept discussed in chapter 8). These components are offered by different organizations and may be marketed directly to the visitor by each organization or combined into a package where the services are supplied by a group of organizations. This lack of one single organization's control over the entire travel trip experience means that a great deal of *interdependence* exists among tourism organizations. For the visitor to leave having had a satisfactory experience, every tourism organization must have performed to the same standard. One bad service experience can spoil an otherwise perfect vacation or business trip. Therefore, the marketing success of each organization in the tourism service chain is dependent on the efforts of the other organizations providing all the other trip components.

A third unique feature of tour-

Tourism is a perishable commodity—any cruise berths not sold on this ship when it leaves the dock are lost forever. Ship docked at Canada Place, Vancouver, British Columbia. Photo courtesy of the Canadian Tourism Commission, Photo Library, 235, rue Queen St., 400D, Ottawa, Ontario KIA 0H6.

ism is that the organizations that market tourism destinations usually have **little control over the quality and quantity of services provided**. Destination marketing organizations (DMOs) such as convention and visitors bureaus and state and national tourism organizations are seldom directly involved with the operation of tourism businesses providing visitor services. While these organizations are held accountable for the successful marketing of all the destination's tourism offerings, they must rely on the other tourism organizations to provide satisfactory experiences for visitors.

Fourth, the guest's satisfaction is a **function of the staff providing the service**. Tourism is a people business; people providing personal services to other people. Because of the great amount of variation in human personalities, it is very difficult to always provide a consistent quality of service. It is impossible to fully standardize tourism services. As one person has said, although we may want to, "You can't paint a smile on a human being's face." The tourism organizations that invest most heavily in hospitality skills and other types of service training are the ones most likely to enjoy the greatest success.

A fifth factor that makes tourism different from other industries is the role of **travel trade intermediaries.** Because visitor services are located at a distance from potential customers, specialized intermediaries—organizations that operate between the producer and the visitor—are required to bridge the gap. Additionally, since many tourism organizations are small, they cannot afford to set up their own retail outlets in every visitor's hometown. In most industries, the producer exerts great control over every stage in the development and delivery of the product. There is **no physical distribution process** in tourism. In the place of physical distribution is

a network of professional travel trade intermediaries. These skilled, knowledgeable travel trade intermediaries can influence, if not determine, which services are offered, to whom, when, and at what price.

The sixth factor that makes tourism different from other industries relates to demand. Tourism demand is **highly elastic, seasonal** in nature, and is influenced by **subjective factors** such as taste and fashion as well as more objective factors such as price and the physical attractions at the destination. In many cases, the services and experiences sought can be provided by any number of destinations or organizations. For example, many destinations around the world offer unique natural environments together with interesting flora and fauna. However, during the late 1980s and early 1990s, the Central American countries of Costa Rica and Belize became very popular and somewhat "fashionable" nature-based tourism destinations (see figure 14.3).

Finally, the **intangible** nature of tourism services means that the visitor's travel experiences exist only in memory after the trip is over. Many products can be reused several times after they are bought. Many products have guarantees or warranties; tourism services do not. While vacation photographs, videos, and souvenirs help visitors remember their trips, a re-purchase is necessary to enjoy a similar trip experience again. This places a greater onus on tourism organizations to deliver satisfactory experiences to their customers.

Tourism Marketing Defined

"Our job is to get them (potential travelers) into the store, and use brand names to hook them, and then get them to buy. One of the reasons we decided on humor and

wit was that our state was not perceived as fun. It always has been perceived as a quality destination, with beautiful places, but not very fun."

Margaret Lesniak, Virginia Division of Tourism, The Richmond News Leader. (January 30, 1989) B-16

There are many definitions of marketing but few specifically address the unique characteristics of marketing tourism services. One of the definitions designed to fit tourism is that "marketing is a management philosophy which, in light of tourist demand, makes it possible through research, forecasting and selection to place tourism products on the market most in line with the organization's purpose for the greatest benefit" (World Tourism Organization, 1975). This definition suggests several things. First, it indicates that marketing is a way of thinking about a situation that balances the needs of the visitor with the needs of the organization and the destination. A marketing orientation is needed to meet this requirement. Second, the definition stresses tourism research and forecasting that culminate in the selection of target markets (market segmentation). Third, the concepts of positioning and the product life cycle ensure the proper placement of tourism services on the market and suggest the appropriate marketing strategies and plans.

Other definitions of marketing emphasize the need for a **systems approach** and recommend a step-by-step process for marketing tourism services. "Marketing is a continuous, sequential process through which management in tourism plans, researches, implements, controls, and evaluates activities designed to satisfy both customers' needs and wants and their own organization's objectives. To be effective, marketing requires the efforts of everyone in an organization and can be made more or less effective by the actions of complementary organizations" (Morrison, 1996). This second definition indicates that marketing should be an ongoing concern in a tourism organization, not just a one-time effort each year. It also suggests that marketing should involve everyone in the organization, not just the marketing department. Five key functions of marketing are identified as *planning*, *research*, *implementation*, *control*, and *evaluation*. The interdependency of tourism organizations in providing satisfying visitor experiences is also highlighted in this definition.

Another important characteristic of marketing is identified in a third definition: "Communicating to and giving the target market customers what they want, when they want it, where they want it, at a price they are willing to pay. Any business that does this will fulfill its twofold purpose of creating and keeping customers and, in turn, will produce revenue" (Lewis, Chambers, and Chacko, 1995). This definition emphasizes that it is not enough to attract first-time visitors. Bringing people back for repeat visits is at least equally important to a tourism organization.

Marketing Orientation

"The standard textbooks on travel marketing are being rewritten. The emphasis is increasingly on relating to individual customers by developing the product they need, delivering that product with skilled staff and having the systems to tie it all together. This has led to new marketing requirements for reaching individual customers and responding to their needs. These changes are made possible by the technology that facilitates direct supplier/customer contact and delivery."

Jones (1996)

As an essential first step in marketing, an overall marketing orientation must be developed to guide marketing efforts. This philosophy sets the tone for every subsequent decision. Although several different orientations are possible, experience has shown that they are not all equally effective.

Some organizations' marketing efforts are guided by a **production orientation.** With a production orientation, the greatest emphasis is placed on the services or products provided to the visitor. For example, a destination area may have many physical, historical, and cultural resources. The extent to which the destination's resources are better than those of its competitors determines, in part, how many people visit the destination. This orientation was used at one time by the local authorities in a town on the south coast of England. They decided in the late 1960s to print brochures only in English. It was pointed out that a major potential market was the French residents across the English Channel. The reply was given that if the French wanted to visit, then they should be interested enough to learn to read English in order to understand what was available. Although it cannot be denied that resources are important, a total emphasis on tourism supply fails to recognize the visitor's needs and expectations. A production orientation is only successful if there is a surplus of demand over supply (which rarely happens in the modern, highly competitive tourism environment). In this case, the destination or company that offers the best product will get the visitor. An old adage says "Build a better mousetrap, and the world will beat a path to your door." Often referred to as the "better-mousetrap fallacy," this form of competitive advantage is normally short-lived in today's business climate.

When supply exceeds demand, the problem becomes "How can I sell all these mousetraps?" The number of destinations actively seeking tourism has increased as has the number of travel destinations throughout the world with easy accessibility. The emergence of more professional destination marketing organizations, tour operators, and travel agencies has increased the intensity of competition for the visitor dollar. It has meant that destination areas can no longer sit back and wait for visitors to come to them. Visitors must be convinced of the benefits of traveling to a particular destination. This has caused a shift in orientation from emphasizing the product to intensified selling. The emphasis in this orientation is on promoting what is available for sale. Yet, this *sales orientation* still focuses on the needs of the seller—How can we sell more product?—rather than on the visitor's needs and wants— What will satisfy the visitor? The first priority here is to convince potential visitors that what is available for sale will please them.

A newer development is an orientation in which the needs and wants of the visitors are the first priority for the marketer. This is called a *marketing orientation*. A tourism organization begins with the needs and wants of the visitor and attempts to provide the services to satisfy them. It involves being open when the visitor wants it to be open; serving breakfast when the visitor wants it rather than when it is convenient for management; providing the kind of experiences that visitors want rather than what we feel they should have. It is realizing that, using the earlier metaphor, an individual does not want to buy a mousetrap; rather she wants to kill mice. Some say this is an exercise in "putting yourself in the visitor's shoes"; always trying to see things from the visitor's viewpoint. If and when a better way is developed of satisfying a need, people are likely to try it. This marketing orientation was mentioned at the beginning of this book when an emphasis was placed on the satisfaction of needs and wants.

Many tourism organizations have come to realize that they have a responsibility to society and local communities as well as to their visitors. Strictly concentrating on their visitors' needs and wants may cause long-term damage to the environment, society, and local communities. For example, fast-food companies are beginning to shoulder some *social responsibility* by improving (or at least providing more information on) the nutritional content of menu items and using recyclable materials in their packaging. Beer companies and distilleries have joined the movement against drunk driving by developing advertisements that emphasize the consequences of drinking and driving.

Having a sense of social and community responsibility is especially important in tourism. A marketing orientation that concentrates solely on visitors' needs is not the ideal philosophy, even for the visitors themselves. A tourism destination relies on the resources of its community, which both visitors and residents share. To become totally marketing oriented, all aspects of the community would have to be oriented toward satisfying visitors' needs and wants. The risk for the community is that by orienting totally for visitors' needs, the needs, integrity, and long-term interests of the community and local residents may be harmed. Consider the situations explored in earlier chapters of destination areas that have adapted to the needs of the visitor and, in the process, have lost their uniqueness, heritage, and natural resources while receiving a relatively poor economic return on investment. Destination areas that adapt their resources to satisfy visitors' needs may lose the very thing that makes them attractive and unique in the first place. The

---

Quick Trip 14.1
Hawaii: Environmental Concerns—Preserving a Path to the Future

"Sustainable development of tourism has a direct impact on the quality of life for residents, the economic well-being of businesses and the experiences of our visitors. If a destination is planned and managed so that its physical, social and cultural bases are conserved, the destination will attract visitors and be able to maintain the resulting jobs, income and revenue."

"The natural and cultural environment of Hawaii is one of the travel and tourism industry's major assets. Without proper preservation of these assets, travel may decrease. As demand to visit these locations increases, the industry must preserve and ensure the appropriate use of these assets. This includes tourism development and activities that sustain or improve the natural, social and cultural foundations."

"Environmental concerns are addressed through any activity that works to ensure tourism activities are carried out in such a manner as to sustain or improve the natural, social and cultural environmental foundations of a destination."

Source: State of Hawaii Strategic Tourism Plan, 1995–1999.

---

visitor is the ultimate loser, as more and more destinations take on an increasingly similar and familiar appearance.

The erosion of natural, historic, and cultural resources is not the only potential pitfall of tourism development. In the late 1980s, the Caribbean, long a favorite destination of North American and European visitors, began to realize that tourism contributed to social problems such as increased prostitution, drug trafficking, and the spread of AIDS. The Barbados Board of Tourism acted on this problem by airing television commercials that warned against harassing visitors on beach fronts to buy drugs (Hart, 1989).

The best solution to these potential problems with tourism is to develop a marketing approach that focuses on the satisfaction of visitor needs and wants while respecting the long-term interests of the community. This approach is referred to as a *societal marketing orientation*. This orientation provides for planning, development, and marketing activities that focus on the needs of the visitor, but that also consider the effects of these activities on the long-term interests of the community before any action is taken. It is also known as encouraging *sustainable tourism development* (as discussed in chapter 9).

All marketing activities are influenced by the orientations of those people directly responsible for marketing. It is essential that these individuals' decisions reflect a predetermined philosophy or corporate culture that provides an overall guide for the development and marketing efforts of the destination or organization.

Market Segmentation

> "Overseas Adventure Travel is committed to being the world leader in international adventures for active, mature travelers— all at unsurpassed value. We offer walking, cultural and wildlife explorations on the road less traveled that are conducted in small groups, with unique lodgings, unconventional modes of transportation, opportunities for varied levels of physical activity, and expert trip leadership."
>
> Overseas Adventure Travel, Joy of Discovery 1997–1998 brochure, 3

Another important marketing decision is the selection of groups of potential visitors with whom we wish to do business. **Market segmentation** is a recognized and universally accepted way of analyzing tourism markets and selecting from among them. Market segmentation is a process through which people with similar needs, wants, and characteristics are grouped together so that a tourism organization can use greater precision in serving and communicating with these people. Market segmentation is a two-step process: (1) deciding how to group all potential visitors (the **market segments**), and (2) selecting specific groups from among these (the **target markets**) to pursue.

Market segmentation is based on four assumptions. First, the market for a service is made up of several segments whose members have distinctive needs and preferences. In other words, not all visitors are alike. Second, potential visitors can be grouped into segments whose members have similar and identifiable characteristics. Third, a single travel trip offering, such as a Caribbean cruise, appeals to some segments of the market more than others. Fourth, destinations and organizations can make their marketing more effective by

developing specific travel trip offerings for specific segments of the market. A cruise package may suit one group of potential visitors, while a white water rafting trip may appeal more strongly to another group.

The process of segmenting the tourism market should be the basis for **strategic** (long-term) marketing decisions. Market segmentation is more than a process for analyzing demand. It is a management tool that leads to specific marketing decisions. The development of a marketing strategy begins with the identification of market segments and their characteristics. A tourism organization or destination may decide to develop unique offerings for every potential visitor market segment. However, limitations of time and money usually prevent this. Time and money can be saved by offering one basic option to everyone, such as Club Med used to do in the 1950s, 1960s, and 1970s. Although this one option undoubtedly appeals to some potential visitors, it will not to others. The compromise is to separate visitors into segments with similar characteristics and produce offerings geared to the needs of certain selected segments.

Select Market Segmentation Method

Two overall types of methods used to segment tourism markets are: (1) **forward segmentation** (a priori methods) and (2) **backward segmentation** (a posteriori methods) (Smith, 1989; Pearce, 1989). Forward segmentation methods have traditionally been the most frequently used in tourism primarily because they are the easier of the two to use. Here, the marketer predetermines the segmentation base or bases to be used for market segmentation, for example purpose-of-trip and/or geographic origin. Usually the marketer acts on information such as previous research

studies by others that suggest an **a priori** segmentation base is a key factor in determining visitor behavior. For example, it is a common practice in international tourism to treat the residents of each tourism-generating country as unique target markets. In addition, most practitioners make the a priori decision to address business and pleasure travelers as two separate and distinct target markets.

Backward segmentation methods, including using factor-cluster analysis, result in segments derived from the application of specific statistical analysis techniques. The marketer does not predetermine the segments; the statistical analysis suggests them. In an analysis of Hong Kong residents, five distinct travel segments were identified on the basis of preferred sets of vacation activities: (1) visiting friends and relatives, (2) outdoor sports activity, (3) sightseeing, (4) entertainment, and (5) full-house activity. The study used the cluster analysis technique to maximize the heterogeneity between the clusters and maximize the homogeneity within each individual cluster (Hsieh, O'Leary, & Morrison, 1992).

Identify Market Segmentation Bases and Segments

A viable visitor market segment must meet the following criteria by being:

Measurable. Can the number of potential visitors within the segment be estimated with a reasonable degree of accuracy?

Accessible. Can these visitors be reached with specific promotional techniques or media? Can they be reached and influenced by existing or potential travel trade distribution channels?

Substantial. Are there sufficient numbers of visitors in this visitor market segment to justify a tailor-made marketing effort?

Defensible. Are the visitor market segment's characteristics different enough to justify separate marketing activities and expenditures just for them, or can they be grouped with one or more other target markets? If competitors decide to use more of a mass marketing approach, will this have an adverse effect on us?

Durable. As the market develops, will this visitor market segment maintain its uniqueness, or will these differences disappear with time?

Competitive. Do we have a relative advantage over the competition in serving this visitor market segment?

Homogeneous. Are the people within the visitor market segment similar enough?

Compatible. Is the visitor market segment compatible with the other visitor market segments that the organization or destination attracts?

Many bases or characteristics are used to segment the tourism market. Seven general categories are: (1) demographic and socioeconomic, (2) geographic, (3) purpose of trip, (4) behavioral, (5) psychographic, (6) product related, and (7) channel of distribution (see figure 14.1).

1. Demographic and Socioeconomic Segmentation

Many early segmentation studies in tourism used demographic and socioeconomic statistics as the basis for forming market segments. These remain the most commonly used today due to the relative ease of acquiring the statistical data, the comparability of the information through census as well as media-generated data, and the fact that the data are easy to understand and apply. For example, age and income have been very successful predic-

SEGMENTATION	CHARACTERISTICS
Demographic and socioeconomic	Age, education, gender, income, family size and composition, family life cycle stage, social class, type of residence/home ownership status, second home ownership, race or ethnic group, occupation
Geographic	Country, region, market area, urban/suburban/rural, city size, population density, zip or postal code, neighborhood
Purpose of trip	Regular business travel; business travel related to meetings, conventions, and congresses; incentive travel; visiting friends and relatives; close-to-home leisure trips; touring vacation; city trip; outdoors vacation; resort vacation; cruise trip; visit to theme park; exhibition or event
Behavioral	Volume of use, frequency of use, usage status, use occasions, brand loyalty, benefits sought, lengths of stay, transportation modes used, expenditure levels, experience preferences, activity participation patterns
Psychographic	Lifestyle, attitudes/interests/opinions, values
Product related	Recreation activity, equipment type, price level, type of hotel/resort property
Channel of distribution	Principal function, area of specialization, size and structure, geographic location

Figure 14.1   Tourism Market Segmentation Bases and Characteristics.

tors of recreation participation. However, the use of only demographic data to segment markets has come under attack. The rapidly changing nature of society makes it impossible to rely solely on this data as a means of developing a marketing strategy. Just because a segment of people are within a particular age or income group does not necessarily mean they have similar travel preferences. Also, socioeconomic information does not give the marketer sufficient information about likes and dislikes to properly position the tourism destination or organization in the marketplace.

Greater success has been found in using demographic criteria that are *multivariate* (using two or more demographic variables). Status, for example, includes dimensions of income, education, and occupation. Family life cycle is a composite of marital status, age, and the numbers and ages of children at home. Life cycle segmentation has proven to be an effective way of segmenting in a number of tourism and recreation cases.

It is unlikely that segmentation on the basis of demographics will ever be abandoned. Although other segmentation bases provide information useful for strategic decisions on what to offer in the way of tourism services, it is still necessary to communicate with an individual market segment. For all its shortcomings, demographic segmentation offers the best way to access a specific segment of the market.

2. Geographic Segmentation

Geographic considerations are very important to tourism. Much of the attractiveness of a visitor destination is based on contrasting cultures, climates, or scenery. This implies there being a certain distance between origin and destination. This book has already discussed the crucial role in tourism the accessibility of a destination plays. To date, destinations have used geographically based studies solely to identify primary, secondary, and in some cases, tertiary markets. National and state tourist organizations tend to use geographic segmentation for the purposes of guiding promotional efforts. National tourism statistics have traditionally been collected by country of origin and marketing priorities are set according to the contributions of each country to total arrivals.

Another important aspect of geographical segmentation along with demographics is that both provide the means of access to target markets. In marketing, it is essential to know where potential customers live or work in order to communicate with them (see figure 14.2).

3. Purpose-of-Trip Segmentation

The established tradition in tourism is to divide the market into two broad purpose-of-trip segments: (1) business and (2) pleasure/personal travel markets. A modified version of this approach was used in a segmentation study of a hotel located in Singapore. Two broad segments were first defined: (1) the group segment and (2) the individual segment. The group segment was then further subdivided into group tours, conventions, corporate meetings, and airline crews. The individual segment consisted of corporate, full-rate and miscellaneous, frequent travelers, and group inclusive tours (GITs). The research for this study showed that purpose of trip was a better way of differentiating segments than nationality or income (Mehta & Vera, 1990).

4. Behavioral Segmentation

Behavioral segmentation divides customers by their usage rates, benefits sought, use occasions, usage status and potential, and brand loyalty (Kotler, Bowen, & Makens, 1996). Usage rate was increasingly used by the tourism industry in the 1980s and 1990s, especially as greater attention became focused on frequent travelers.

Heavy-half segmentation is an example of usage-rate or use frequency segmentation. Some at-

Checkpoint Charlie beckons American veterans back to Europe: using geographic and demographic segmentation. Reprinted by permission of the German National Tourist Office.

tempts have been made in recreation and tourism to use this segmentation base. Heavy-half segmentation refers to the idea of segmenting a market on the basis of quantity purchased or consumed. As with other types of products, however, heavy-half segmentation has been found lacking. A major problem is that the characteristics of the heavy half (the major purchasers) have been found to be similar to those of the light half. Similar difficulties have been found with segmentation on the basis of brand loyalty.

Benefit or attribute segmentation is becoming a very popular segmentation base in tourism. It involves segmenting a market according to the relative importance assigned to benefits that visitors expect to realize after purchasing the product. The relative impor-

A growing number of destinations are pursuing the honeymooner market. Photo from *Top Shots* CD Rom. Courtesy of Queensland Tourist and Travel Corporation.

tance of specific product benefits to prospective visitors is determined. Clusters of people are formed who attach similar degrees of importance to the same product benefits. The results can have important ramifications for developing new products and advertising messages. However, it is necessary to develop demographic profiles of the benefit clusters to reach them.

Use-occasion segmentation is enjoying greater popularity in tourism. Perhaps the best example of this is the growing number of resorts and destinations pursuing the honeymooner market. Here, the use-occasion is a honeymoon. The Japanese honeymooner market has drawn special attention among destinations in the Asia Pacific region. Destinations such as Australia, Hawaii, Hong Kong, and Singapore have been particularly successful in appealing to Japanese honeymooners.

5. Psychographic Segmentation

Although expensive to use and difficult to carry out, this newer technique of market segmentation can be very helpful in describing visitors. It is especially useful in highly specialized and extensively developed markets where psychographic profiles supplement the information gained from simpler analyses. Demographic data may be likened to the bones of a skeleton; psychographic data represents the flesh. The bones form the basis of the structure, but it is only by covering the form with flesh that the features become recognizable. Information about an individual's attitudes, interests, and opinions gives a much clearer picture of the people in a market segment.

In chapter 1, the VALS 2 (Values and Life Styles) program was described as the most widely recognized application of psychographic segmentation in the U.S. There are other psychographic or lifestyle segmentation methods available including the Prizm Cluster System. The Prizm system identifies forty lifestyle clusters. One of these, the Gray Power cluster is said to favor cruise ship vacations, while the Blue Blood Estates do not like travel by recreation vehicles.

6. Product-Related Segmentation

A major advantage of segmenting by means of product-related variables is that the information gained is directly related to the particular tourism service under consideration. Indeed, a major flaw in some studies is that information is sought from the potential visitor that deals with general benefits sought or, in the case of psychographic segmentation, general attitudes about types of products and services rather than about specific products and services.

7. Channel-of-Distribution Segmentation

This chapter has already indicated that tourism's distribution channels are unique and play a more powerful role than the intermediaries in other industries. Chapter 16 provides a detailed description of these distribution channels. It is important to recognize that these intermediaries should be segmented by the other tourism organizations that depend upon them for business. Intermediaries vary according

---

Quick Trip 14.2
Luring Frequent Air Travelers with Airport Club Lounges

"In essence, an airline club lounge is a pseudo-living room where you can escape the hordes, sprawl in a comfortable chair, grab a drink at the bar, munch on cold snacks, watch TV, and raid the magazine rack. For extravagance, though, it's hard to beat Virgin Atlantic's Clubhouse departure lounge at Heathrow (Airport)—a duplex with a four-hole putting green, a virtual ski machine and other interactive sports games, a music room with a selection of CDs, a 5,000-volume library, a hydrotherapy bath, and a salon offering free massages, manicures, and hairstyling. Virgin club members at the separate arrivals lounge need not feel jealous: They get to golf on a nine-hole indoor course."

Source: Perrin, (1997).

to their principal function (e.g., retailing versus wholesaling travel services), area of specialization by travel service, market segment, or destination (e.g., cruise-only travel agents, corporate and ethnic travel agencies), size and structure (e.g., large franchised travel agency chains versus the small independent retailer), and, of course, geographic location.

While segmentation schemes for distribution channels have received little attention from tourism researchers, the importance of intermediaries in tourism is increasing. Most organizations who target travel intermediaries in their marketing use a two-step process: (1) identify the target market of travelers; and then (2) select the intermediaries who serve these target markets.

Select Target Markets

Once market segments have been identified and profiled, the tourism destination or organization must select the target market or markets that it wants to attract and serve. This decision is based upon an analysis to determine which segments will produce the greatest benefits and which the destination or organization can serve best. The analysis involves four concerns:

1. **Income potential and yield**—What is the current and future potential for income from this segment? Income is a combination of the number of current and potential visitors and their current and potential per-person spending.

2. **Competition**—To what extent does competition exist for the segment in question? How strong is our advantage compared to competitors?

3. **Cost**—How much investment is required to develop services to attract this segment and to communicate with its members?

4. **Ability to serve**—Are the financial and managerial capabilities in place to design, promote, and distribute the appropriate services and satisfactorily serve this market segment?

The segments chosen become the destination's or organization's target markets. Developing marketing programs to meet the needs of these target markets should begin with a technique known as *positioning*.

Positioning

> "We've always defined 'positioning' not as what you do to the product, but what you do to the mind. The ultimate marketing battleground is the mind, and the better you understand how the mind works, the better you'll understand how positioning works."
>
> Trout, J. (1996)

Positioning is a relatively new concept in marketing. Most experts agree that its origins date back to around 1972 and a series of articles written by advertising executives Al Reis and Jack Trout. These articles were later expanded into a book titled, *Positioning: The Battle for Your Mind*. In these authors' own words, "Positioning is what you do to the mind of the prospect" (Ries & Trout, 1981). Other authors have elaborated on this original definition including Lewis, Chambers, and Chacko (1995) who say that positioning is "the consumer's mental perception of a product, which may or may not differ from the actual characteristics of a product or brand." Most experts agree that the purpose of positioning is to create a perception or *image*—to establish a position—in the targeted visitor's mind. Since the objective is to influence the individual visitor's perception of the

destination or organization, there is a clear link to the psychological dimensions of perception discussed in chapter 3. Effective positioning is expected to grow in importance as the number of tourism destinations and organizations competing for visitors continues to increase.

In using positioning, the logical place to start is with the questions "Do we have a position in our potential visitors' minds?" and, if so, "What is that position?" Answering these questions must involve some marketing research. Focus group research done in Los Angeles for the Tahiti Visitor Board showed that a variety of misperceptions were hindering further tourism growth from the Southern California market. These were that Tahiti was 14–16 hours from Los Angeles (rather than just 8); it was an isolated, single-island nation (it actually has 130 islands); it has limited accommodations; and it is difficult to get there (Covey, 1988). Another study about India as a travel destination highlighted two significant misperceptions: not many people in India speak English and there are few first-class hotels there (Kale & Weir, 1986). The message from these two examples should be clear; the flow of information to visitors is imperfect and it is a major error to assume that they have an accurate image or perception of the destination or organization.

The next step in positioning is to determine whether the visitor's perception or image needs to be established, changed, or reinforced. Here, two forms of positioning can be used: objective positioning and subjective positioning. With *objective positioning*, the destination or organization attempts to tailor-make its services and products to match the needs and wants of a selected target market or markets. Some refer to this as "product-market matching." The emphasis is placed on adding or modifying one or more objective characteristics of the services or facilities being offered. For example, a destination that decides to pursue the scuba diving market will need to add dive shops, dive boats, dive maps, diving guides/instructors, and other services required by this specialized target market. Once the objective attributes have been altered to suit the target market, these changes must be communicated to potential visitors through various types of consumer and travel intermediary promotions. The following are some examples of objective positioning statements in tourism:

Arizona: "Grand Canyon State."
Courtyard by Marriott: "The hotel designed by business travelers."
Czech Tourist Authority: "The Country of History."
Qantas: "Qantas: The Australian Airline."
Scandinavian Airlines: "Scandinavian by design."
SuperClubs: "The Caribbean's Only Super-Inclusive Resorts."

Subjective positioning is an attempt to form, reinforce, or change the potential visitor's image without altering the physical characteristics of the services and products offered. Subjective positioning normally follows objective positioning. It is often used when research shows that there are misperceptions about a destination or organization, or when a negative image has developed through adverse publicity or for other reasons. This is usually called "*repositioning*." When Tahiti discovered its distance misperception, an advertising campaign was launched stating that it was just *Two and a half hours beyond Hawaii and fifty years behind it.*" Another major application of subjective positioning is to communicate emotional appeals and messages, rather than rational (objective). The following are some examples of subjective positioning statements in tourism:

Quick Trip 14.3
Positioning Singapore for the Twenty-First Century

In 1995, the Singapore Tourist Promotion Board completed a long-range planning exercise for tourism. This process resulted in the publication of a strategic plan for tourism under the title of "Tourism 21: Vision of a Tourism Capital." One part of this plan was devoted to a new positioning approach for tourism in Singapore as "New Asia." The following excerpts from the plan summarize this new positioning:

"Singapore is a vibrant, multi-cultural and progressive Asian city, located in the heart of one of the world's most exciting and fastest-growing tourism and economic regions. As a *Tourist Destination,* it offers memorable, world-class experiences—the ultimate in entertainment, fun and relaxation. As a *Business Centre,* it offers all the critical support for a thriving, hassle-free business operation: superior infrastructure—seamless, efficient, state-of-the-art; a skilled and knowledgeable workforce; favorable operating environment; supportive government regulations; ready source of capital; critical mass and a strong healthy market base. As a *Tourism Hub,* it offers excellent inter-connectivity to the region's plethora of fun and seemingly, limitless business opportunities. In other words, it embodies the essence of 'New Asia.'

"After all, Singapore with its progressiveness, sophistication and unique multi-cultural Asian identity, can be said to be an expression of modern Asia dynamism that marks the entire region—the island is a place where tradition and modernity, East and West meet and intermingle comfortably.

"New Asia-Singapore, is thus a possible destination positioning, which suggests a Singapore that has managed to preserve and nurture its Asian heritage, even as it embraces and harnesses the marvels of high technology. It successfully conveys the innovative, enterprising and confident city-state that is the Singapore of today, as well as of the coming millennium. The positioning also reflects the *Un*limited approach to tourism development which Singapore proposes to adopt under the Tourism 21 initiative."

Source: "Tourism 21: Vision of a Tourism Capital," Singapore Tourist Promotion Board, (1996).

Aruba: "Where happiness lives."
Hyatt: "Feel the Hyatt touch."
Ireland: "Awaken to a different world."
Jamaica: "Come to Jamaica and feel all right."
Norwegian Cruise Line: "It's different out here."
Singapore: "New Asia-Singapore: So easy to enjoy, so hard to forget."
Zambia: "Zambia. The Very Soul of Africa."

Once the decision is made to use either or both objective and subjective positioning, the next step is to determine how this will be communicated to potential travelers and travel trade intermediaries. There are at six broad positioning approaches: (1) positioning on specific product features; (2) positioning on benefits, problem solution, or needs; (3) positioning for specific usage occasions; (4) positioning for user category; (5) positioning against another product; and

(6) positioning by product class dissociation (Kotler, 1984). The following are examples of each of these positioning approaches:

- **Positioning on specific product features:** "No artificial ingredients" (Costa Rica Tourist Board, see figure 14.3).

- **Positioning on benefits, problem solution, or needs:** "Icelandair: Your best value to Europe. Always" (Icelandair).

- **Positioning for specific usage occasions:** "The ever radiant memories of Martinique honeymoon packages" (Martinique Promotion Bureau).

- **Positioning for user category:** "No. 1 in travel for 18–35s" (Contiki Holidays).

- **Positioning against another product:** "If you're going to _____, you better take your VISA card. They don't accept American Express" (VISA).

- **Positioning by product class dissociation:** "The Uncommon Route" (World Explorer Cruises).

Product Life Cycle

"Belize is a tiny country the size of Vermont on Central America's Caribbean coast. In 1993, when I went there, it was that season's tourist world hot spot. This bizarre, flavor-of-the-month phenomenon happens regularly in tourism; countries, like restaurants in your home town, are 'hot' or they're not. They are 'in,' or they're out. As you might expect, however, almost by definition, the phenomenon of their being hot doesn't last. They get chewed up quickly, and then, when that word gets out, the tourist droves move on and the country is discarded, passé."

Krotz (1996)

Costa Rica has been very successful in positioning its natural features. Reprinted by permission of the Instituto Costarricense de Turismo, San José.

The concept of the product life cycle (PLC) is useful in choosing, attracting, and serving target markets. The PLC concept suggests that a destination, service, or product moves through four distinct stages: **Introduction, growth, maturity,** and **decline**. In chapter 12, the various stages were described from a planning perspective. It is important that the destination or organization examines the PLC concept at two different levels. First, at what stage in the PLC is our part of tourism? Second, at what stage in the PLC is our own destination, service, or product? Since the spectacular growth of international tourism in the 1970s and before, year-to-year increases have been much more modest, suggesting a maturing of the industry. In the developed countries, some parts of the industry such as domestic airlines and hotels are also in the maturity stage.

It is important to identify the PLC stage situation because the effectiveness of different marketing strategies vary by stage. For example, in the maturity stage, more emphasis must be placed on drawing business away from competitors, or on finding new target markets or uses.

Butler and Waldbrook (1991) describe a cycle of development apparent in tourist destinations that is based on the traditional product life cycle. The seven stages of development are: exploration, involvement, development, consolidation and stagnation, followed by either decline or rejuvenation (see figure 12.1). There is a link between the type of visitors attracted to a destination and its development as it changes to attract greater numbers of tourists (Butler & Waldbrook, 1991).

Marketing Planning Process

"Failing to plan is planning to fail."

(Famous business saying, source unknown)

A tourism destination or organization must segment the market using the most appropriate methods and bases, select target markets and, taking into account the PLC stages of the industry and its own offerings, position these effectively within the minds of the targeted potential visitors. Having made these decisions, specific marketing programs using pricing, services and products, promotions, and distribution channels (marketing mixes) are designed. The process used to develop marketing mixes should be systematic; it should follow a step-by-step procedure known as the *marketing planning process*.

Marketing planning implies a future orientation. It involves identifying suitable marketing goals and objectives as well as determining the most appropriate marketing strategies to achieve these goals and objectives. Marketing planning takes place at two levels: *strategic marketing planning* for three to five years or more in the future, and *tactical marketing planning* for the next year. Both levels of planning must be closely integrated with the other.

A model of the marketing planning process containing five basic questions has been suggested by Morrison (1996) (see figures 14.2 and 14.3). The five questions are: (1) Where are we now? (2) Where would we like to be? (3) How do we get there? (4) How do we make sure we get there? (5) How do we know if we got there?

I. Where are we now?

The planning of marketing must begin by addressing the question "Where are we now?" This involves a thorough analysis of the existing situation. Marketing goals, strategies, and objectives should not be defined until this analysis has been completed. Many marketing experts refer to this step as a *situation analysis* or *SWOT* (strengths, weaknesses, opportunities, threats) analysis. The factors that should be analyzed include the marketing environment, development goals and strategies, services, products and destination, market profile, and competition.

Scan the Marketing Environment

Planning must be accomplished within the framework of the external environment that is constantly changing, but over which the marketing manager has little or no control. The technique of identifying and analyzing the impact of external environmental forces is known as *environmental scanning.* The basic reason for doing an environmental scan is that it is better to anticipate change before it happens than to react to change after it has happened. This can be accomplished by answering these key questions: What are the major trends? Will they affect us and how will they affect us? How much will they affect us? How will they affect our closest competitors? What should we do differently in the future to adapt to these trends and their likely impacts?

MARKETING PLANNING PROCESS STEPS	TECHNIQUES AND CONCEPTS	OUTCOMES AND RESULTS
I. Where are we now?	Environmental scan Situation analysis	Strengths and weaknesses Challenges, opportunities, threats Visitor market profile Competitive analysis
2. Where would we like to be?	Visioning Market segmentation Positioning	Vision, goals, and objectives Marketing strategy Target markets Positioning approach
3. How do we get there?	Marketing mix	Marketing plan (eight Ps)
4. How do we make sure we get there?	Control	Progress reports Marketing plan modifications
5. How do we know if we got there?	Evaluation	Marketing effectiveness or accountability

Figure 14.2 Tourism Marketing Planning Process Model.

The environmental forces to be scanned should include legislation and regulation; political situations; social and cultural characteristics; economic conditions; technology; transportation; and competition at a macro level. For a tourism organization or destination that attracts visitors from several countries, an environmental scan is needed for each individual visitor-generating country.

The first of the forces to be considered is the **legal and regulatory environment**. Certain countries, including South Korea, have in the past placed legal restrictions on their residents that have hampered the flow of outbound tourism. Residents may be restricted from traveling, or they may be unable to take more than a certain sum of money out of the country. Political factors must also be considered. Tensions or hostilities between the country of origin and the country of destination will affect marketing success. A good example of this is the uneasy relationship between Cuba and the U.S. It is important to consider the social and cultural characteristics of the host destination's residents including educational backgrounds, traditions, religions, and the overall way of life. Most international travel is generated from countries with higher educational standards, from societies regarded as more cultured, and from countries having a higher degree of industrialization.

The pace of **technological change** within tourism and society in general is accelerating. Profound changes are resulting from the direct and indirect impacts of new technologies, including the use of the Internet and particularly the World Wide Web. Tourism is rapidly transforming from dependence on paper-based information to dependence on electronic information. Other technologies that are having a significant impact are global distribution systems (GDS), computerized reservation systems

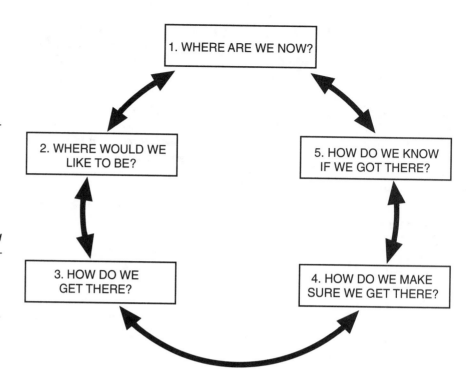

Figure 14.3   A Systems Approach to Tourism Marketing. Adapted from Morrison, (1996).

(CRS), and video- and teleconferencing using satellite and other technologies.

Another important factor is **transportation** and other aspects of **accessibility** such as documentation requirements. The destination must be accessible to visitors from generating countries or regions. The current and projected **economic conditions** in generating countries is a factor of great importance in tourism. It is essential that there is a sufficient number of people in the country who can afford to travel. Japan's increasing affluence, for example, has attracted much greater attention from destinations in the Asia Pacific region and elsewhere. The **exchange rate** between the host country and generating countries is another key economic concern. Past history has shown that major exchange rate shifts have a direct impact on travel volumes between specific pairs of countries.

Although commonly overlooked, the destination or organization's **macro-competition** should be analyzed. These are not head-to-head competitors, but represent the other products and services competing for the same disposable income. For example, the purchase of an expensive home entertainment system may take the place of a foreign vacation trip. A new car purchase may result in less frequent and shorter vacations being taken. There are potential substitutes for travel and they should be taken into consideration in marketing planning.

Consider the Development Goals and Strategies   The marketing plan should be just one part of the overall **strategic plan** for the destination or organization, and just one element in the comprehensive tourism plan for a destination area. Tourism is one, and only one, strategy for development. As noted in chapter 9, tourism can be used as a political, social, and economic force. Yet, other alternatives are available. A comprehensive plan for tourism must be consistent with the overall planning and development goals and strategies for the destination area.

Evaluate Services, Products, and the Destination Mix One of the principal outcomes of a situation analysis is the determination of the destination's or organization's strengths and weaknesses, especially when compared to its closest competition. Competition is defined as anyone who serves the same target market or markets. The situation analysis reviews the destination's or organization's services and products, target markets, and competition. A tourism destination should compare the five components of its ***destination mix*** against those of its closest competitors:

a. Attractions (natural resources, climate, cultural and historical resources, ethnic attractions, accessibility, manmade attractions).

b. Facilities (lodging, food and beverage, support industries).

c. Infrastructure (fresh water supply, sewage disposal systems, communications systems, road systems, health care facilities, energy systems, security systems).

d. Transportation (airports, railway systems, cruise ship terminals, bus transportation).

e. Hospitality (hospitality training programs, friendliness of local residents, overall service levels).

Prepare a Visitor Market Profile The crucial task is to develop a profile of the visitor and then to project that profile into the future by considering trends in the country or region of origin. The profiling task should address the questions and provide the visitor characteristics shown in figure 14.4.

When the existing target markets have been profiled, consideration is then given to new visitor target markets. Jones (1996) suggests that four categories of potential new visitors should be analyzed:

- ***Existing market segments:*** Other people from existing target markets who have not yet visited the destination or used the service. For example, if most people in the existing market come from within a 500-mile radius, potential markets may be discovered from areas within 500 miles from which visitors do not yet come (e.g., specific cities or communities).

- ***Proximate potential market segments:*** Past visitors to nearby destinations who have similar characteristics to existing target markets. These people have used a region and have demonstrated an interest in what it has to offer.

- ***Expanded potential market segments:*** Travelers who want similar products and services to that offered by the destination, but who have not yet visited the region. These might include special-interest markets such as adventure travel, golf, and scuba diving.

- ***Potential market segments for additional/enhanced products:*** New visitors that would be attracted if new attractions or facilities were added. Examples might include a casino operation, convention center, golf courses, or guided nature tours.

Analyze Competition It is very important to analyze the marketing programs, positioning, and overall management of competing destinations or organizations, and to compare this with those of the subject destination or organization. What image do competitors have in the

TOPICS	QUESTIONS	CHARACTERISTICS
WHO?	Who are they? Who makes the travel decision? Who helps them with travel decisions?	Behavioral characteristics Demographic/socioeconomic Influence of travel trade intermediaries Psychographic
WHERE?	Where do they live? Where do they travel within the destination? What other destinations do they visit?	Geographic characteristics Travel routes and patterns
WHAT?	What do they buy?	Services, products, facilities Usage of packages or tours
WHY?	Why do they travel? What do they like to do?	Activity preferences Motivations
WHEN?	When do they travel? When is the travel decision made? How long do they stay?	Length of stay Planning or "lead" time Seasonality of demand
HOW MANY?	How many of them are there? What are the sizes and composition of travel parties?	Market size Trip party size
HOW?	How do they make travel plans?	Booking preferences Use of travel trade

Figure 14.4 Components of a Visitor Market Profile.

minds of potential customers? How successful were their past marketing programs? What have been their most successful marketing efforts? Do they have a cohesive, experienced, and marketing-oriented management team?

Determine Strengths and Weaknesses
The culmination of this analysis is the identification of competitive strengths and weaknesses (What is there that is better than competitors?) The typical broad approach in marketing is to build upon and enhance competitive strengths and to take steps to address and improve upon weaknesses.

2. Where would we like to be?

The second step in marketing planning is to define what the tourism destination or organization wants to achieve in the future. This is accomplished by considering alternative approaches to marketing for the next three to five years. The process involves defining a vision, establishing marketing goals, selecting target markets, creating a positioning approach, and setting marketing objectives.

Define a Vision and Vision Statement
When the situation analysis is completed, the tourism organization or destination now must describe where it wants to be in the future. The first step in sketching the desired future situation should be the determination of a **vision** and **vision statement** for the destination or organization. According to Ritchie (1993), the visioning process consists of three distinct stages: (1) envisioning of an image of a desired future organizational state which when, (2) effectively communicated to followers, (3) serves to empower those followers so they can enact the vision. In some ways, a vision is like a **super long-term goal** that becomes the foundation for defining the whole program of marketing action.

While there are few specific guidelines as to what a vision statement should include, it should at a minimum be measurable. The following are examples of vision statements for tourism destinations:

- **Calgary, Alberta, Canada:** "To establish the city as a major host, consultant and educator to the world" (Ritchie, 1993).

- **Durban, South Africa:** "To position metropolitan Durban as the international gateway to the region and a unique tourism destination, providing a true African experience supported by world-class facilities and infrastructure" (Tourism Durban).

- **Singapore:** "'Tourism 21: Vision of a Tourism Capital' envisages Singapore becoming a Tourism Capital of the twenty-first century, assuming three roles: a dream destination offering visitors memorable experiences, a premier tourism business centre, and a leading tourism hub in Asia Pacific" (Singapore Tourist Promotion Board, 1996).

- **Western Australia:** "To work in partnership with the private sector and government to make tourism the premier industry in Western Australia" (Western Australia Tourism Commission Annual Report 1995).

Establish Tourism Marketing Goals
A set of **marketing goals** are now required to translate the vision into a program of marketing action for the next three to five years. Marketing goals describe the overall purposes and desired outcomes of future marketing programs. Marketing goals may be statements about the types of target markets to be attracted, images and perceptions to be communicated, marketing partnerships to be created, and forms of tourism development desired. They may set targets for visitor arrivals, expenditures, and foreign exchange earnings. Marketing goals provide the framework for the selection of target markets and the identification of more specific marketing objectives.

Select Target Markets
For marketing goals to be realized, there must be a clear strategy about which segments of the tourism market will be targeted in the next three to five years. This involves the use of the **market segmentation analysis**. First, market segments are defined using one or more of the seven segmentation bases discussed earlier: demographic and socioeconomic, product-related, psychographic, geographic, purpose of trip, behavioral, or channel of distribution. The segments selected as target markets must meet the criteria of being measurable, accessible, substantial, defensible, durable, homogeneous, and compatible. The size (substantiality) of the market can be measured in terms of the number of visitors, the number of visitor nights, or the amount of visitor expenditures. Market segments that are large offer less risk than ones that are relatively small. Other factors that should be considered are the income potential, competition, cost, and the ability to serve potential target markets. The destination or organization should also have some advantage over one or more competitors in serving the target market.

American Hawaii Cruises provides a good example of targeting a specific market segment. Along with several other cruise lines, American Hawaii is targeting older travelers who have grandchildren under the age of 18. In their 1997 "Grand-Kids Cruise Free!" program, grandchildren cruised for free if they shared a cabin with their two full-fare paying grandparents during the period of June 14 to September 6. Special programs and meals were provided for the children while on board. American Hawaii's segmentation strategy was a combination of demographic (grandparents and grandchildren under 18) and behavioral (use-occasion of traveling with grandchildren) segmentation. Another excellent example of a highly targeted marketing strategy is that used by Contiki Holidays. This tour operator provided escorted tours to various parts of the world for people between ages 18 and 35.

Create a Positioning Approach

Next, the positioning of the destination or organization for each selected target market must be developed. Positioning should involve answering the following questions: Is there an existing image or perception in potential visitors' minds? What is this image or perception? Is there a need to create, change, or reinforce this image or perception? How should objective or subjective

Destinations may offer special discounts for children to entice parents to visit with the family. Photo from *Top Shots* CD Rom. Courtesy of Queensland Tourist and Travel Corporation.

positioning be used to create the desired future positioning? and Which positioning approach should be used?

The Australian Tourist Commission (ATC) is considered to be one of the best national tourist offices in the world and is certainly one of the best funded. During 1997, ATC introduced a new promotional campaign in the Americas based upon an established image that Australians are a very friendly people. The 30- and 60-second spots featured Australian people. A surf guard tells viewers "You Americans work too hard" and a farmer says "If you ask me, you could use a holiday in a place made for it" (*Travel Weekly*, 1997).

Set Marketing Objectives *Objectives* are established for the next year and should meet four tests. First, they must be capable of being measured. Second, they must address a specific target market. Third, they must be stated in terms of a desired result or outcome that relate directly to either the environmental scan, situation analysis, or development goals and strategies. Finally, a specific deadline for achievement must be stated. The accountability for marketing should be measured against the degree to which objectives are achieved (see "5. How do we know if we got there?").

Quick Trip 14.4

Marketing Goals for Luton, England

The Luton Borough Council has established a number of marketing goals for the next three to five years. These marketing goals include the following:

● Promote Luton as a destination for conferences and investigate the use of facilities for exhibitions, conferences, and promotions.

● Develop a conference bureau and conference consortium in partnership venues in the town.

● Continue to work in partnership with other local authorities, the East Anglia Tourist Board and tourism operators.

● Carry out research to establish the present level of tourism, identify programs to develop tourism in Luton and investigate opportunities for grant assistance.

● Continue to support existing events and work with other organizations to develop and attract new events.

● Support the Luton Tourism Marketing Group and publish a tourism newsletter.

Source: Luton Borough Council, 1996 (http://www.luton.gov.uk/tourmg.htm)

ON SOME CRUISE LINES, PEOPLE WHO DON'T PAY ARE CALLED STOWAWAYS. WE CALL THEM KIDS.

Kids Cruise Free An American Hawaii cruise offers so much more than other cruises. In 1996, kids 18 and under cruise free when sharing a cabin with two full-fare adults. It's a voyage of discovery aboard a classic steamship. Four islands, five ports and seven days your family will remember for a lifetime. Over 50 exciting excursions. And we've brought the history, culture and spirit of the islands right on board with special Hawaiian arts and crafts and language lessons. For more information call your Cruiselink Plus travel agent.

AMERICAN HAWAII CRUISES
The way Hawaii was meant to be seen.

2 North Riverside Plaza, Chicago, IL 60606   American owned and operated. ©1996 American Hawaii Cruises.

Target marketing by American Hawaii Cruises. Courtesy of American Hawaii Cruises.

3. How do we get there?

The third step is to prepare an action plan to achieve the marketing goals and objectives. Using the marketing objectives for each selected target market as a basis, marketing mixes are designed and detailed in a written **marketing plan**. Traditional approaches to marketing suggest that a **marketing mix** is comprised of four components: product, price, promotion, and place (distribution). These are called **the**

four Ps of marketing (Perreault & McCarthy, 1996). Some authors have suggested that there are additional components to the tourism marketing mix. Because of the uniqueness of tourism marketing, it is recommended that packaging, programming, people, and partnership be considered as four additional marketing mix components (Morrison, 1996). The traditional four Ps, then expands to eight Ps (product, price, promotion, place, packaging, programming, people,

and partnership). It is essential that each address the needs and characteristics of people in the selected target markets.

Product   Travel experiences consist of several different services and products ranging from transportation and lodging to sightseeing and souvenirs. These services and products are usually offered by a variety of tourism organizations. Each organization is dependent on the others to offer an attractive and satisfying overall travel experience. A marketing orientation suggests that services and products be designed to match the needs and wants of the targeted visitors. In addition, the market segmentation concept is based on the assumption that no single tourism destination or organization can provide services and products that will satisfy everyone. An organization must select a target market, and provide a variety of services and products to satisfy the targeted customers' needs. Striking the right balance between providing customized services to appeal to a particular target market, while having enough variety to be attractive to more than one target market, is a difficult decision for tourism marketing managers. The relatively fixed supply of tourism facilities and services, coupled with seasonal fluctuations in demand levels and customer types, make this task more complex.

Crissy, Boewadt, and Laudadio (1975) suggested several important criteria that should be met when deciding to provide a service or product. First, there should be a relatively heavy demand for the service or product from at least one important market segment, with the possibility of additional business from other segments of the market. It may be that the product can expect to break even on the basis of business from the major market segment and produce profit from business from the rest of the market. There may, of course, be a period of time before sales for a new attraction or service reach the break-even point.

Second, new products and services should fit in with the positioning or image of the tourism destination area or organization. It should also complement existing offerings. This does not mean that a destination area must appeal only to one segment of the market and that all its services and products must meet the needs of that market segment. A great deal obviously depends upon the size of the destination area. One part of a destination area may appeal to the younger singles and couples, while another part may be more attractive to senior citizens. It is important, however, that each individual part of the destination area develop the services, products, and positioning to fit one or more selected target markets.

Third, new services and products must be in accordance with the available supply of personnel, capital, management expertise, and natural resources. Although new services and products should be based on an identified competitive advantage, they may not be feasible due to a lack of the right quality of human or financial resources. For example, a destination area may have magnificent mountain terrain suitable for skiing but may lack management knowledge in ski-area operations. Experienced management may have to be hired on a permanent or temporary basis before a ski area can be proposed. It is also possible in tourism that certain new services or products may be undesirable for social, cultural, or environmental reasons.

Finally, it is necessary that any new services or products contribute to the profit and/or growth of the entire tourism destination or organization. In some cases the new offering may bring in no profit itself, but its provision may contribute to growth. The hotel pool,

---

Quick Trip 14.5
Marketing Objectives for Durban, South Africa

Tourism Durban is the official tourism marketing agency for the metropolitan Durban in South Africa. The organization's 1996–97 plan included the following objectives:

- To secure conference and convention business for the metropolitan Durban region with a positive annual economic impact of at least R150 million.

- To secure and promote sports and other events for the metropolitan Durban region which will attract visitors to the region, and generate an annual economic impact of at least R75 million.

- With a 25% market share of domestic tourism with an economic impact to the City of about R3.3 billion, our aim is to increase our market share to 28% representing some 3.6 million visitors by December 1997.

- To maintain Durban's leading position as the country's most popular domestic holiday destination and increase the 3.4 million annual visitors to the City, and the R3.3 billion cash inflow from tourism by at least 5%.

- To maintain the present level of international holiday visitors from our traditional markets, and to also aggressively explore the holiday tourism potential in the Indian Ocean rim countries. To provide a level of visitor information and reservation services that is comparable with the best in the world.

Source: Tourism Durban World Wide Web site, http://www.durban.org.za/bpobjectives.html

---

for example, may cost the operation money while bringing in no direct revenue. However, its availability may bring in additional room business. On the other hand, if the pool is eliminated, this may cause guests to use another hotel or resort. Similarly, a destination may introduce its own airline, not as a revenue-producing venture but as part of a strategy to attract more visitors.

Price In pure economic terms, price is a result of supply and demand. When supply exceeds demand, price will tend to decrease. The reverse is also true. Of greater importance is the extent to which demand changes (as measured by

the amount purchased) as price changes—the elasticity of demand. A 5 percent reduction in price may result in a corresponding 10 percent increase in the number of buyers and a subsequent increase in total sales revenue. Demand in this case is elastic. Generally, products aimed at the luxury end of the customer scale are less susceptible to changes in price and tend to be price inelastic. For businesses that are open only part of the year, supply is limited and prices have to be higher (everything else begins equal) than businesses open year round. Because demand is not often uniform throughout the year, it is common to charge higher prices during the peak season and lower prices when demand slackens.

The expected length of the product life cycle and the destination's or organization's position on it also affect pricing decisions. A fad item with an expected short life cycle will have to charge high prices to recoup the investment in a relatively short period of time. A product that expects a longer life can be priced lower.

The price charged is influenced by competition. If a destination's facilities and services are very similar to competitors, its prices must be similar to theirs. The extent to which the destination area or other tourism service is unique influences whether it can charge more than the competition. Related to the influence of competition is the management policy regarding market share. If the decision is made to increase market share, prices will probably be lower than if we decide to "skim" a small number of visitors from several market segments.

Pricing policy is also influenced by the needs of the selected target market. If a tourism destination or organization serves the needs and wants of the market and if those needs and wants are perceived as being important to the members of the market segment, those people will be willing to pay a higher price. The price charged must also be perceived by the market as less than or at least equal to the value received. In some situations the influence of the market seems to go against economic principles. With certain luxury items, demand may increase as price increases. This phenomenon reflects a degree of snobbishness on the part of the market. The feeling may be that the higher the price the greater the perceived value and the greater the demand. But the actual value in the minds of the buyers must still equal or exceed the price paid.

Promotion The topic of promotion is covered in detail in chapter

15. Promotion is the most visible part of the marketing mix, apart from the services or products themselves. Many people fall into the trap of confusing marketing and promotion, thinking of them as being exactly the same. However, there is much more to marketing than just promotion. The ***promotional mix*** consists of several elements including advertising, sales promotion, merchandising, personal selling and sales, and public relations and publicity. All promotions involve some form of communications with potential customers.

Place (Distribution) Tourism distribution is unique. In the absence of a physical distribution system, tourism has developed a unique set of ***distribution channels*** and travel trade intermediaries. These intermediaries influence visitor's choices of tourism destinations and businesses, and require separate attention by the tourism marketer. The choice of specific channels of distribution and intermediaries is influenced by several factors including the target market, type of tourism service or destination, and the location of the services relative to the customers' residences. Chapter 16 provides detailed information on tourism distribution and individual categories of travel trade intermediaries.

Packaging Packages in tourism are unique. They are especially important because they can be used to help cope with the problems of the immediate perishability of services, and the difficulties of matching demand volumes with supply capacities. Packaging also provides a way to match tourism services and products with visitors' needs. For example, tourism businesses now offer many packages for special-interest groups ranging from anthropologists to zoologists.

Packaging is significant because it brings together many of the elements of the destination mix. Packages combine the services and products of several tourism organizations. The package is more convenient for visitors since it includes several services and products at an all-inclusive price. Other advantages of packages are listed in figure 14.5.

Programming Programming involves special activities, events, or other types of programs to increase customer spending or to give added appeal to a package or other tour-

GROUP	REASONS
VISITORS	1. Greater convenience (saves time) 2. Greater economy (saves money) 3. Ability to budget for trips (makes planning easier) 4. Implicit assurance of consistent quality (less risk) 5. Satisfaction of specialized interests 6. Added dimension to traveling
PARTICIPATING BUSINESSES	1. Increased business in off-peak periods 2. Enhanced appeal to specific target markets 3. Attraction of new target markets 4. Easier business forecasting and improved efficiency 5. Use of complementary facilities, attractions, and events 6. Flexibility to capitalize on new market trends 7. Stimulation of repeat and more frequent usage 8. Increased per capita spending and lengths of stay 9. Public relations and publicity value of unique packages 10. Increased customer satisfaction

Figure 14.5 Reasons for the Popularity of Vacation/Holiday Packages.

Adapted from Morrison, 1996.

Tourism is a people business! Photo from *Top Shots* CD Rom. Courtesy of Queensland Tourist and Travel Corporation.

ism service. Many vacation packages include some form of programming such as escorted ground tours, sports instruction, and entertainment events. A popular approach among travel destinations is to designate particular years for special celebrations and to focus attention on programs that support specific themes. For example, the Tourism Authority of Thailand launched the tourism promotion project "Visit Thailand Year" to coincide with the sixtieth anniversary of the reign of their king. China organized theme years in 1993 (China Landscape '93), 1994 (China Heritage '94), 1995 (China Folklore '95), and 1997 (Visit China '97).

People (Human Resources)

Tourism is a people business. No amount or quality of facilities can make up for poor service. A tourism marketer must ensure that staff are adequately trained in their specific function, and that tourism employees and local residents have hospitable attitudes toward visitors.

Partnership

Partnership means **cooperative marketing** programs involving two or more tourism destinations or individual organizations. In an increasingly competitive tourism industry, the pooling of resources with other organizations may provide the added edge necessary for success. Packaging, when it involves two or more organizations, represents one important application of the partnership concept. Cooperative advertising is a second application. For example, the Caribbean islands of St. Thomas, St. Croix, St. Martin, St. Barth, Antigua, Aruba, Curacao, and the Bahamas have joined forces to advertise the "Little Switzerland" concept. This joint advertising campaign promotes the availability of duty-free jewelry, watches, crystal, and perfume in each of these island destinations. Another example of a regional partnership is the joint promotion by the countries of Europe that share the Alps (Austria, Germany, Italy, Slovenia, and Switzerland).

Strategic alliances are another form of cooperation in tourism. These are long-term agreements between companies or countries to invest in joint marketing programs. Strategic alliances have been especially popular among airline companies. Alliances are also being formed among hotels, airlines, and car rental companies to gain competitive advantages through reciprocal frequent traveler award programs, and to provide travelers with greater speed and flexibility (Dev, Klein, & Fisher, 1996). Good examples of strategic alliances are that of Northwest Airlines and KLM, and the cooperation between the Scandinavian countries in tourism promotion (Denmark, Finland, Iceland, Norway, and Sweden).

There are eight criteria for successful inter-organizational partnerships (Kanter, 1994):

Individual excellence: All the partners are strong organizations and want something positive from the partnership.

Importance: The partnership fits with each partner's long-term strategy.

Interdependence: The partners need each other because they have complementary skills and assets.

Investment: The partners invest in each other.

Information: Communication is open among the partners.

Integration: Partners develop links and shared methods of operation.

Institutionalization: The partnership is given a formal status.

Integrity: The partners behave honorably toward each other.

4. How do we make sure we get there?

Marketing does not stop after the marketing plan has been written. Steps must be taken to ensure that the plan is successful in achieving its objectives. Progress toward the achievement of objectives must be made as the plan is being implemented. This is done by checking

Let them discover the joys of Europe's oldest kingdom, starting with the rich pageantry of its capital, Copenhagen.

A cosmopolitan hub for Scandinavia, the vibrant culture and nightlife combined with a reputation for safety and efficiency have made Copenhagen highly appealing for business and pleasure travelers.

Your clients can choose from selected packages, including luxury weekends, 5-night mini-weeks and fly/drive packages.

Want help in selling your clients a spring vacation in Scandinavia? Send for our spring travel kit, including free copies of our colorful, information-packed brochure.

Call 1-888-GET-SPOILED. Or fax: 212-885-9710. Or e-mail: info@goscandinavia.com

FINNAIR   SAS   ICELANDAIR

The Scandinavian countries' marketing of tourism is a long-term, team effort. Reprinted by permission of Scandinavian Tourism Inc.

progress at predetermined times to see if things are going as planned. If significant deviations from the expected results are found, it may be necessary to modify the marketing plan. This process is often referred to as *marketing control*.

5. How do we know if we got there?

The last step in the marketing planning process is to determine *marketing effectiveness*. Results and outcomes are evaluated to deter-mine if the marketing goals and objectives have been attained. It has become popular to refer to this as a procedure to ensure the *accountability* of those responsible for tourism marketing. Marketing effectiveness is measured by accountability or evaluation research.

Summary

The marketing of services is different from the marketing of products. Since tourism is a service business and since it is a unique form of service, tourism requires different types of marketing programs and activities. Tourism marketing has evolved through a series of stages or eras. The current societal marketing era is most appropriate for destination tourism marketing since it goes beyond pure economic considerations and is consistent with the sustainable tourism development concept.

Tourism marketing must follow a systematic marketing planning process. It is important to consider the external marketing environment as well as those factors that the organization or destination can control. Careful attention must be given to market segmentation and the selection of target markets. Every tourism organization needs to choose a unique blend or marketing mix of these factors to meet the needs of its target markets. In tourism, the marketing mix consists of eight elements: products and services, price, place (distribution), promotion, packaging, programming, people, and partnership. Marketing plans must be controlled and evaluated to ensure that they are effective.

References

Butler, R.W., & Waldbrook, L.A. (1991). A new planning tool: The tourism opportunity spectrum. *The Journal of Tourism Studies*, 2 (1), 2–14.

Covey, C. (1988). Tahiti sets out to dispel myths that deter tourists. *Travel Agent Magazine* (March 31), 8–9.

Crissy, W.J.E., Boewadt, R.J., & Laudadio, D.M. (1975). *Marketing of hospitality services: food, lodging, travel*. East Lansing, MI: Educational Institute of the American Hotel and Motel Association.

Dev, C.S., Klein, S., & Fisher, R.A. (1996). A market-based approach to partner selection in marketing alliances. *Journal of Travel Research*, 35 (1), 11–17.

Gartner, W.C. (1996). *Tourism development: Principles, processes, policies*. New York: Van Nostrand Reinhold.

Hart, C. (1989). The Caribbean—caught in a tourist trap. *World Development*, November, 7–9.

Hsieh, S., O'Leary, J.T., & and Morrison, A.M. (1992). Segmentation of the Hong Kong travel market by activity participation. *Tourism Management*, 13, 209–223.

Jones, C.B. (1996). Destination databases as keys to effective marketing. San Francisco: Economics Research Associates (http://www.erasf.com/dest_dbase.html).

Kale, S.H., & Weir, K.M. (1986). Marketing third world countries to the Western traveler: The case of India. *Journal of Travel Research*, 25 (2), 2–7.

Kanter, R.M. (1994). Collaborative advantage. *Harvard Business Review*, 72 (4), 96–108.

Kotler, P. (1984). *Marketing management: Analysis, planning, implementation, and control* (5th ed.). Englewood Cliffs, NJ: Prentice-Hall, Inc.

Kotler, P., Bowen, J., & Makens, J. (1996). *Marketing for hospitality & tourism*. Upper Saddle River, NJ: Prentice-Hall, Inc.

Krotz, L. (1996). *Tourists: How our fastest growing industry is changing the world*. Boston: Faber and Faber.

Lewis, R.C., Chambers, R.E., & Chacko, H.E. (1995). *Marketing leadership in hospitality* (2nd ed.). New York: Van Nostrand Reinhold.

Mehta, S.C., & Vera, A. (1990). Segmentation in Singapore. *The Cornell HRA Quarterly*, 31 (1), 80–87.

Morrison, A.M. (1996). *Hospitality and travel marketing* (2nd ed.). Albany, NY: Delmar Publishers.

Pearce, D. (1989). *Tourist Development* (2nd ed.). Essex, England: Longman Scientific & Technical.

Perreault, W.D., Jr., & McCarthy, E.J. (1996). *Basic marketing: A global-managerial approach* (12th ed.). Homewood, IL: Irwin.

Ries, A., & Trout, J. (1981). *Positioning: The battle for your mind*. New York: Warner Books, Inc.

Ritchie, J.R.B. (1993). Crafting a destination vision: Putting the concept of resident-responsive tourism into practice. *Tourism Management*, 14, 379–389.

Smith, S.L.J. (1989). *Tourism analysis: A handbook*. Essex, England: Longman Scientific & Technical.

Travel Weekly. (1997). Australia showing personality in latest ad campaign. *Travel Weekly*, 56 (14), 26.

Trout, J. (1996). *The new positioning: The latest on the world's #1 business strategy*. New York: McGraw-Hill, Inc.

World Tourism Organization. (1975). *Testing the effectiveness of promotional campaigns in international travel marketing*. Ottawa: WTO Seminar.

Surfing Solutions

http://adage.com (*Advertising Age* magazine)
http://www.cruisehawaii.com (American Hawaii Cruises)
http://www.ama.org/ (American Marketing Association)
http://www.germany-tourism.de/ (German National Tourist Office)
http://www.goscandinavia.com/tourism/tourism.html (Scandinavian Tourism Inc., New York)
http://www.travelcom.sg/sog/stpb.html (Singapore Tourist Promotion Board)
http://www.durban.org.za/ (Tourism Durban, South Africa)

Acronyms

ATC (Australian Tourist Commission)
CRS (computerized reservation system)
DMO (destination marketing organization)
GDS (global distribution system)
PLC (product life cycle)
SWOT (strengths, weaknesses, opportunities, threats)

"More and more, marketers are turning to tailored and targeted marketing to individuals. This trend is particularly appropriate for tourism marketing since there is a world of paradoxes in leisure behavior. Sameness and diversity and security and risk seem side by side. Some accountants sky dive; people eat at McDonald's for lunch and a four-star restaurant for dinner; take luxury BMWs to the self-service petrol pump; trade a large investment portfolio through a discount broker; visit Hawaii and never go in the ocean. Leisure lifestyles, in particular, are inconsistent, contradictory, and individual. This multi-profile customer is difficult to motivate by traditional institutional means. The 1990s and beyond belong to the individual. Destination marketing and leisure product development must adjust to this new environment."

Jones (1996), 1

15

Tourism Promotion

···Communicating with Target Markets ···············

Purpose

Having learned about the general principles of communications and promotion, students will be able to describe a program for implementing a promotion in a tourism destination or organization. They will also be able to explain the roles of destination marketing organizations at all levels.

Learning Objectives

Having read this chapter, you should be able to:

1. Identify and describe which promotional methods are most effective during the various stages of the visitor's buying process.

2. Distinguish between informative promotion, persuasive promotion, and reminder messages, and identify when the use of these techniques is most appropriate.

3. List and describe the main elements in the communication process.

4. List and describe the elements of the promotional mix.

5. Identify and explain the procedures involved in implementing a promotional program.

6. Describe the roles and activities of national tourist offices related to promotion.

7. Describe the promotional programs operated by agencies at the state, provincial, territorial, regional, and local levels.

Overview

The process of promotion is a process of communication; communication between seller and buyer. This chapter discusses the promotional mix concept. A link is established between the goals of promotion and the customer's buying process stages described in chapter 4. Appropriate types of promotion are suggested for each of the traveler's buying process stage.

The process of communication is explained. An eight-step program for implementing promotions is described. A target market and promotional objectives need to be established. Once a promotional budget has been set, the message idea and format for the promotion can be designed. A promotional mix and the appropriate media are selected. At each step of the program, controls are used to ensure that promotional campaigns progress as planned and achieve the objectives. It is important to evaluate promotions after they have been implemented to measure their effectiveness and to ensure accountability.

The promotional roles and programs of destination marketing organizations at the national, state, regional, and local levels are described.

Promotion = Communication

> "Germans are key targets in all the major promotional campaigns that the British Tourist Authority (BTA) is undertaking in 1997, especially Germans aged between 25–40 and working couples with no children, most likely to be receptive to the new image of Britain as a stylish, contemporary, 'in' destination."
>
> Messe Berlin, (March 9, 1997)

Developing the promotional mix is an exercise in communication. Destination marketing organizations, suppliers of tourism services, and travel trade intermediaries have to communicate messages to potential visitors. Through *explicit communications*, language and images are used in advertisements and other promotions to create a common understanding between the organization (sender) and the visitor (receiver). Messages can also be transmitted through *implicit communications* in nonverbal means such as gestures and facial expressions, and by non-explicitly communicated items such as prices and the physical characteristics of the facilities provided.

Goals and Types of Promotions

Tourism promotions may have several goals. The ultimate goal of promotion is *behavior modification*. The first behavioral goal may be to create a booking or sale by convincing the visitor to purchase for the first time. Second, the goal may be to modify the repeat visitor's purchase behavior by having them switch to another destination, package, or service. Third, the goal may be to reinforce existing behavior by having the repeat visitor continue to purchase the same destination, package, or other service. Promotion accomplishes this by informing, persuading, or reminding the visitor about the promoter's services.

The effectiveness of different types of promotions varies with product life cycle (PLC) stage. For example, *informative promotions* are more important during the first stage of the PLC (introduction) when a new destination or business is entering a market. Potential visitors must be given enough information and knowledge before they will buy. *Persuasive promotions* try to get a visitor to buy and

become the objective during the growth stage of the PLC. In the maturity stage, reminder promotions become important. Visitors have already used the tourism services or been to the destination before. *Reminder promotions* jog visitors' memories and help keep the tourism destination or organization in the public eye.

Promotion and the Visitor's Buying Process

The goals of behavior modification are more effectively achieved by matching the three types of promotion with the stages of the visitor's buying process (as discussed in chapter 4). For example, informative promotions are most effective at the earlier buying process stages of attention and comprehension (figure 15.1). Promotional messages must grab the visitor's attention, while providing enough information and convincing arguments to assist with comprehension. A 1997 advertisement by the Canadian Tourism Commission provided a good example of this approach. With the attention-getting headline of "When cars dream," the copy of the advertisement provided several convincing arguments for Americans to visit Canada and a means for requesting more detailed travel information on Canada's regions:

> "They dream of touring Canada. When you can weave through majestic mountains. Dance on polished city streets. Glimpse wildlife around every bend. And feel your spirit soar. Discover Canada's five unique regions (The West, Heartland, Ontario, Quebec, Atlantic Coast) with free Canadian Explorer Touring Guides. Remember that with a 32% exchange rate, you get more mileage for your dollar."
>
> (Advertisement in Condé Nast Traveler, April 1997, 22–23)

The beauty of Banff National Park draws many visitors to Canada. Photo courtesy of the Canadian Tourism Commission, Photo Library, 235, rue Queen St., 400D, Ottawa, Ontario KIA 0H6.

The Communications Process

The communications process is shown in figure 15.2. The sender (tourism destination or organization) sets marketing objectives for the target market (receivers). A budget is established for communications. The *message strategy* (message idea and format) for the promotion are developed. Based upon the chosen message idea and format, an appropriate promotional mix and medium are selected. Steps are taken to generate responses from the receivers (potential visitors). The responses are compared to the marketing objectives to determine the overall effectiveness of the promotional campaign.

Many destination marketing organizations use *direct-response advertising*. This advertising generates requests for *printed collateral materials* including visitor guides, calendars of festivals and events, and maps. The process of sending collateral materials to people who request them is known as *fulfillment*. Destination marketing organizations measure the effectiveness of direct-response advertisements by keeping records of the telephone, mail, fax, and electronic (e-mail and World Wide Web) inquiries after the advertising has been run. Some agencies go further and determine, through techniques like *conversion studies*, how many inquirers actually visit the destination or use the service after being sent the requested collateral materials.

This analysis only goes part of the way in determining promotional effectiveness. If the response rates do not match objectives, time and money have been wasted. The analysis does not indicate where the problems were; it shows the effects rather than the causes of the problems. Were the objectives set too high? Were the message idea and format appropriate but communicated to the wrong target market? Were the right media used to communicate the message? Were

Persuasive promotions work better at intermediate buying process stages (attitudes, intention, and purchase). They can be used to change attitudes, develop intentions to buy, and to initiate purchases. A promotional approach used by Bermuda shows how this can be done effectively. A group of hotels and resorts in Bermuda offers a "temperature guarantee." The advertising copy supporting this guarantee is as follows:

> *"Although we guarantee it will be 68°F, our winter visitors always find it much warmer than that. If it fails to reach 68°F on any day during January, February, and March, your clients will receive 10% off that night's room rate at the resorts below, as well as discounts at participating shops the following day. So even on the off chance that it's not the perfect climate, we'll still create one. Come bask in a different kind of warmth."*

(Advertisement in Travel Weekly, *February 13, 1997, 34)*

Reminder promotions are more effective after the first visit to the destination or first use of the organization's services. Reminder promotions help stimulate repeat visits or purchases. A process known as *database marketing* is increasingly being used in tourism to encourage repeat usage. Computer technology that allows the manipulation of *relational databases* on past and potential visitors is facilitating this process. Cruise line companies and casino operators have been especially successful in building databases and using reminder promotions. There are four major objectives of database marketing (Jones, 1996):

- To know more about what existing and potential visitors want.
- To reach these visitors and tell them what the destination/organization has to offer.
- To satisfy customers so that they come back and spread the good word (word of mouth).
- To operate profitably.

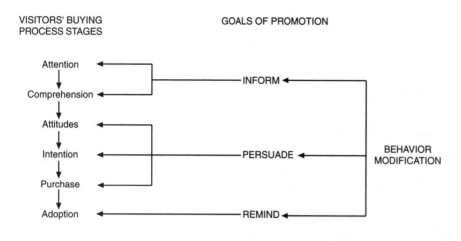

VISITORS' BUYING
PROCESS STAGES

GOALS OF PROMOTION

Figure 15.1   Goals of Promotion and the Visitor's Buying Process.

the wrong information or images communicated? To avoid these kinds of problems, the communications process must be controlled during every step in the promotional program (see figure 15.2).

Implementing a Promotional Program

> "Now, electronic innovations such as computers and the Internet are again transforming the potentials and capabilities of direct marketing. They are destined to profoundly impact the travel industry and the travel agency network, the traditional channel of distribution within the industry."
>
> *Walle, (1996)*

Select the Target Market

The process of target market selection was explained in chapter 14. This should include an analysis of published (**secondary research**) market data and **primary research** results from such techniques as surveys or **focus groups**. A target market must be accessible through one or more promotional mix elements, or through a specific type of media.

Certain basic information must be available on a target market's demographics and geographic origins (place of residence or business). A target market may be more finely pinpointed by overlaying demographic and geographic characteristics with one or more of five other segmentation bases (psychographics or lifestyles, purpose of trip, product related, behavioral, or channel of distribution). The target market

must include people with similar characteristics who are the best prospects for future business. This first element of the tourism communication process can only be effective if a complete market segmentation analysis has been done.

Develop Promotional Objectives

The next step is to establish the objectives for the promotional campaign. To be effective, objectives must be target-market specific, stated as a desired result or outcome, measurable, realistically attainable, and have a deadline for achievement.

When setting promotional objectives, it is important to consider the targeted visitors' buying process stage, as well as the destination or organization's product life-cycle stage. The current level of awareness of the tourism destination or service must be established. If people in the target market are at the intention stage of the buying process, then informative messages are a poor use of time and money. Similarly, the promotion of a new

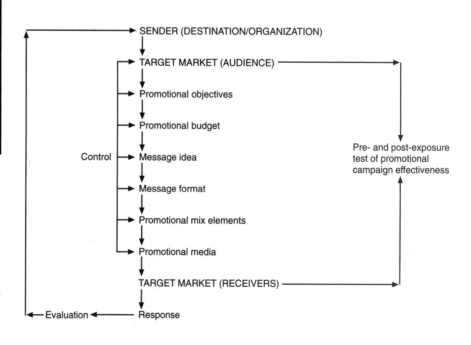

Figure 15.2   The Communication Process in Tourism.

package will not be effective if the intention to buy already exists. By conducting an awareness study, either through a survey or focus groups, the buying process stage of the targeted visitors can be determined. At the attention or awareness stages, the objective may be to expose the message to a specified number of target market members within a specific time period. At the intention stage, the objective may be oriented toward increasing purchases. Controlling this second element in the tourism communication process involves two steps: (1) ensuring through research that the buying process stage of the target market has been correctly identified, and (2) ensuring that promotional objectives are target-market specific, results-oriented, measurable, reasonably attainable, and time-specific.

Establish the Promotional Budget

The promotional objectives must provide the basic foundation for establishing the promotional budget. This is called the *objective-and-task budgeting method*, which uses a "bottom-up" or *zero-based budgeting* approach. Only by planning what is required (the tasks or activities) to achieve objectives, can an accurate estimate be made of how much to spend on promotions. Often objectives are based upon how much money the destination or organization has to spend; the "top-down" budgeting or *affordable budgeting method*. Tourism destinations and organizations do not have unlimited funds for marketing and many operate with very small promotional budgets. Despite this, setting marketing objectives after, rather than before, the budget is established can produce objectives that will never be achieved. When a tentative budget amount has been estimated based upon the objectives and tasks (promotional activities), other factors need to be considered. These include the promotional budgets of competitors and the funds available to the tourism destination or organization. All marketing plans and budgets must be flexible enough to allow for changing market conditions and competitive activities; therefore, a contingency amount needs to be attached to the promotional budget.

When preparing the budget, consideration is given to *cooperative promotions* with other organizations. Many destination marketing organizations have extensive cooperative marketing programs, especially with efforts to attract international visitors. The Partnership Australia program operated by the Australian Tourist Commission is an excellent example of cooperation between a national tourist office, state tourist offices, and private-sector tourism organizations. The pooling of promotional dollars creates great synergy for all parties involved; in effect, it increases everyone's promotional budget.

Determine the Message Idea

Primary research techniques such as focus groups, one-to-one interviews, and surveys can be used to pinpoint the target market's perceptions (images), needs, wants, motives, and expectations. The findings may be used to determine what to communicate in the message (the *message idea*). Alternative message ideas can be developed and discussed with a sample of people from the target market, perhaps in a small-group setting like a focus group. Based on people's ratings of the alternative approaches, the most effective message idea is chosen. Message ideas must support the *positioning approach* selected by the tourism destination or organization. Control is achieved through this process of pre-testing alternative message ideas; by choosing a message idea that communicates best to representatives of the targeted visitors.

Select the Message Format

Message ideas can be communicated in many different ways. How a message is communicated to the target market is called the *message format* or *creative format*. The objective is to choose a format that effectively communicates the message idea in a way that is understandable, distinctive, and believable for the target market. *Advertising agencies* are often used to assist with this creative task. The alternative formats that can be used are (Morrison, 1996):

Analogy, association, symbolism: The format here is to link the tourism destination or service with an object or concept that supports the message idea. Thai Airways International uses the slogan "Smooth as silk" to emphasize the quality (smoothness) of its in-flight service. Ghana "proudly welcomes you to the land of gold," emphasizing not only the country's association with gold, but also its sunny climate and warm hospitality.

Comparisons: The tourism destination or service is compared with a specific competitor or against all competition to communicate an important difference. For example, The Palace of the Lost City at Sun City, South Africa, claims to be "The Most Extraordinary Hotel in the World." Avis' "We try harder" campaign has for many years compared the car rental company with industry leader Hertz.

Fear: The approach here is to warn potential visitors about doing or not doing something. One classic example of this format is in the credit card business with American Express' "Don't leave home without it" campaigns.

Honest-twist: This format starts with a statement of fact and then "twists" this fact to the benefit of the advertiser. A classic example is the approach used by Avis. They launched a campaign saying that they were the number two car rental company (behind Hertz); the "honest." Then they said that, because of this, "they try harder" (the "twist").

Slice of life: These promotions show typical or realistic scenes from everyday life. A popular approach in tourism is to show people in their highly stressed jobs or suffering through very bad weather in their home locations, and then to show them in a very relaxing, warm-weather situation.

Testimonials: Testimonials are endorsements of the tourism destination or service by celebrities, noted experts, past visitors, or travel trade intermediaries. The Cayman Islands used the visit of Michel Cousteau, son of Jacques Cousteau, to promote its scuba diving opportunities.

Trick photography or exaggerated situations: Here photographic tricks, graphics, and special effects are used to emphasize the message idea. A 1991 Qantas advertisement demonstrates this approach. With the heading "We'll move heaven and earth," a map is shown where Australia is much closer to the U.S. The message idea seems to be that if you fly transpacific with Qantas, they will make the trip seem much shorter.

Once the message format has been chosen, several alternative approaches to using it may be developed and pre-tested by showing them to groups of people from the target market. Based upon their reactions, the alternative approaches are compared and one of them is selected. To test the promotional effectiveness of the selected approach, surveys of the target market may be conducted after people have been exposed to the message. These surveys can be used to determine what images were conveyed or what was remembered from the message. They may also find out if visitor attitudes toward the tourism destination or organization have changed as a result of being exposed to the promotion.

Select Promotional Mix Elements

Many promotional tools exist to communicate messages to people in the target market. There are five major elements of the promotional mix that can be used separately or together (Morrison, 1996):

Advertising: Any paid form of nonpersonal presentation and ideas, goods, or services by an identified sponsor.

Personal selling: Oral conversations, either by telephone or face to face, between salespeople and prospective customers.

Sales promotion: Approaches other than personal selling, advertising, and public relations and publicity where customers are given a short-term inducement to make an immediate purchase or booking, or to communicate with potential visitors or travel trade intermediaries.

Merchandising: Materials used in-house to stimulate sales including brochures in display racks, signs, posters, photographs, displays, tent cards, and other *point-of-sale* promotional items.

Public relations and publicity: All the activities that maintain or improve relationships with other organizations and individuals. Publicity is one public relations technique that involves

A destination can be marketed to show a slice of life:

This is what it's like where you are now.

Photos by Corel.

This is what it's like where you can easily go!

nonpaid communication of information about a destination's or organization's services.

The selection of promotional mix elements varies with the characteristics of the target market, the type of destination or tourism service, and the promotional funds available. The more expensive and complex the service or destination being promoted, the greater the need for some form of personal selling. While an advertisement may induce a couple to spend a weekend at a resort, a meeting planner choosing a site location for a convention of more than a thousand delegates will require more detailed information and some personal selling. Likewise, a couple planning to take a cruise or an extensive foreign tour will need the advice of an experienced travel agent.

Tourism destinations and organizations usually have four different groups at which they need to direct promotional messages: visitors, travel trade intermediaries, the media, and the local community (see figure 15.3). Two of these branches of promotion are called **consumer promotions** (visitors) and **trade promotions** (travel trade intermediaries). Consumer promotions can be further categorized into potential visitors, past visitors, and present visitors. Messages also need to be directed at the **media** (newspapers, magazines, television, and radio stations) and the **local community** (residents, elected officials, government agencies).

The effectiveness of specific promotional tools varies according to which of the four groups are being targeted (figure 15.3). For example, sales promotions and educational workshops or seminars can be very effective when promoting to travel agents. Advertising on television or in a consumer travel magazine may be more effective in communicating with potential visitors. The emergence of the World Wide Web in the mid 1990s provided a vehicle for reaching all four groups.

Most promotional budgets in tourism include amounts for each of the five promotional mix elements. However, the relative proportions of each mix element will vary according to the absolute size of the budget. For example, maintaining a large sales force and placing national-level advertising require a large minimum investment. Many forms of advertising are relatively expensive and advertising typically represents a large share of all promotion spending. For example, a four-color advertisement in a national consumer travel magazine may cost several thousand dollars.

Select Promotional Media

The appropriate media to communicate the message idea are then selected. The media used in tourism include newspapers, magazines, television (network and cable), radio, the World Wide Web, outdoor, and direct mail. Each medium has distinctive advantages and disadvantages. The crucial part of media selection is choosing those that will be seen, read, or heard by the intended target market. Most media companies provided market research statistics on the profiles of their readers, viewers, or listeners. In addition, there are general criteria against which media can be compared to determine which is the most appropriate:

Cost per contact: The cost of reaching one person in the target market.

VISITORS	TRAVEL TRADE/MEDIA/LOCAL COMMUNITY
POTENTIAL VISITORS	**TRAVEL TRADE INTERMEDIARIES**
Consumer travel, sports, recreation shows	Collateral materials (visitor guides, calendars of events, maps, etc.)
Direct mail and direct fax advertising	Contests and games
Help desks	Direct mail and direct fax advertising
Inquiry handling and fulfillment	Display materials (maps, posters, brochures)
Media advertising	Destination "expert" programs
Telemarketing	Familiarization trips
Travel videos and films	Inquiry handling and fulfillment
World Wide Web site	Newsletters
	Preferred supplier programs
	Press releases
	Recognition and award programs
	Trade journal advertising
	Travel trade fairs, shows, exhibitions
	Workshops and seminars
	World Wide Web site
PAST VISITORS	**THE MEDIA**
Direct mail and direct fax advertising	Editorials/feature stories
Frequent traveler clubs	Familiarization trips for travel writers
Newsletters	Newsletters
Telemarketing	Photo galleries
World Wide Web site	Press conferences and releases
	World Wide Web site
PRESENT VISITORS	**LOCAL COMMUNITY**
Hospitality and service training programs	Community tourism awareness programs
Reception and welcoming services	Newsletters
Travel maps and literature	Hospitality/service quality award programs
Travel information centers	World Wide Web site

Figure 15.3 Promotional Activities and Communications Channels.

Cost per inquiry (CPI): The cost of an advertisement divided by the total number of inquiries it generates.

Cost per thousand (CPM): The cost of reaching 1,000 people in the target market.

Geographic selectivity: The ability to target specific geographic areas.

Life span: The length of time that the target market will be exposed to the message.

Market selectivity: The ability to communicate with specific target markets.

Noise level: The amount of competitive advertising in the medium.

Pass-along rate: The rate at which people pass along materials (e.g., magazines) to other people.

Reach: The total number of people that are exposed to the message.

Source credibility: The credibility or reputation of the medium for accuracy and lack of bias.

Timing flexibility: The amount of lead time required to place the message; shorter lead times give greater flexibility.

Total Cost: The total cost of developing and communicating the message.

Visual quality: The level of quality of the visual presentation, especially when in color.

Although the cost per contact is low for television advertising, the total cost is very high. Television allows the tourism advertiser to be geographically selective and select the target market by the specific type of shows or programs. The visual quality of television advertisements can be extremely high. Television suffers from a rather low level of credibility and trust among viewers, however. Because of the tendency to watch television with other people, the noise level tends to be higher than average. Since advertising schedules often have to be decided far in advance, the timing flexibility for television is below average.

Radio offers a medium that is low in total cost and cost per contact. Like television, radio is selective for broad market groups and has high geographic selectivity. The credibility and noise level are similar to those for television. However, the timing flexibility is far greater; radio advertisements can be placed on very short notice.

Newspapers also offer a low total cost and cost per contact. Market selectivity is low, but geographic selectivity is good since it is possible to target specific cities and towns. Certain nationally distributed newspapers allow tourism marketers to pinpoint business travelers, such as *The Wall Street Journal, Globe & Mail, The Australian, London Times,* and the *Daily Telegraph*. The trust factor for newspapers seems to be low, and the visual quality is less than average. To compensate for a high noise level, short life span, and low pass-along rate, newspapers offer a great deal of flexibility in the timing of advertisements.

Magazines have a much higher cost per contact and total cost than newspapers. However, the specialized nature of magazines, the market selectivity, can be very high. The regional editions available for certain magazines offer some geographic selectivity. The visual quality of magazines is much higher than for newspapers, and the noise level is usually much lower. Both the life span and pass-along rate are above-average. The timing flexibility is low with magazines as they have relatively long lead times for placing advertisements.

Although the total cost of a direct-mail campaign tends to be rather high, the cost per contact varies widely depending upon the quality of the materials to be sent. Market selectivity and geographic selectivity are the highest of all media; direct mailings can be highly personalized. The source credibility is below average due to the ever-increasing volume of junk mail that most people receive. The life span of a direct mail piece tends to be short, especially if the mailing is not highly personalized. The visual quality can be very high and the noise level is low, but increasing. A direct-mail piece can have a strong impact on a purchase decision, again if the message is highly personalized. Timing flexibility can be good with direct mail but is dependent on the type of items to be included in the mailing and their production times.

All of these media, except direct mail, suffer from a lack of personalization; they are mass media. With the emergence of the concept of **relationship marketing** (building and enhancing long-term relationships with individual visitors and other organizations), a greater emphasis is now being placed on one-to-one communications (Jones, 1996; Peppers and Rogers, 1993) (see figure 15.4). Media that provide for individualized messages are fast growing in popularity in tourism. These include all forms of **direct marketing** including direct mail and **telemarketing** (telephone selling). Additionally, the interactive potential of using the **World Wide Web (WWW)** has attracted great attention from tourism marketers in recent years. The perceived major advantages of "electronic brochures" on the World Wide Web over traditional tourism brochures are (adapted from Lennon, 1995):

- WWW pages reach far more people than brochures.
- No physical distribution is required with WWW pages.

Turning away from:	And turning toward:
MASS MARKETING	**DIRECT CUSTOMER COMMUNICATIONS**
Socioeconomic	Customer databases
Media placement	Telemarketing/targeted messages
One-way communication	Building customer relationships

Source: Jones, 1996

Figure 15.4   Changing Approaches to Tourism Marketing and Communications.

- The cost per access with WWW pages is much lower than the cost of printing a brochure.
- Errors on WWW pages can be corrected more easily and more quickly.
- WWW pages can be updated constantly; brochures need to be reprinted.
- WWW page development costs less than designing a brochure.
- WWW pages can offer interactivity; traditional brochures do not.

The print media (newspapers and magazines) are the most popular with travel, hotel and resort organizations (see figure 15.5). For example, two-thirds of the total amount in measured advertising media by U.S. companies in 1995 was spent in the print media. Some 26.4 percent was spent in the electronic media (television and radio) and 7.2 percent on outdoor advertising. Although newspapers are expected to continue to be the most used advertising medium for tourism, their effectiveness is eroding. The travel sections of newspapers tend to be read only after the decision to travel has been made. People who read the travel sections are highly motivated to travel. In order to expand the travel market, other media such as television, radio, direct mail, and the World Wide Web will get greater use in the future.

Restaurant companies (especially fast-food chains), hotel chains, and airlines tend to spend the largest amounts on media advertising. Restaurant companies spend the largest proportion of their media advertising budgets on the electronic media, especially on television. For example, McDonald's spent 94 percent of their measured media advertising budget on television and radio, while Darden Restaurants (Red Lobster and The Olive Garden) spent 99 percent on the electronic media (*Advertising Age*, 1996). Hotels and airlines make more balanced use of the media, but tend to favor the print media (newspapers and magazines). For example, Marriott International spent 70 percent of its measured media budget on the print media in 1995. Destination marketing organizations appear to make the greatest use of magazines and television for their advertising.

Measure and Evaluate Promotional Effectiveness

The response to a promotion can be measured in terms of changes in the awareness levels of the tourism destination or organization, the way the message is perceived by visitors (see chapter 2), the number of responses, and, if appropriate, the conversion rates. Potential problems are minimized if campaigns are controlled and effectiveness tested at each step in the promotional program. However, the measurement of promotional effectiveness appears to be something that needs to be improved among tourism organizations. There is a belief among industry experts that many tourism organizations are not doing enough to measure the effectiveness of their promotional campaigns and to be accountable for the funds they are using (Davidson & Wiethaupt, 1989).

There are several specific techniques that can be used to measure promotional efficiency and effectiveness. These include (Davidson, 1994; Koth, 1988; Perdue & Pitegoff, 1994; Pizam,

TRAVEL, HOTELS & RESORTS	1995 (USD MILL.)	PERCENTAGE
Consumer magazine	$ 460.5	19.5%
Sunday magazine	31.7	1.3
Local newspaper	975.5	41.3
National newspaper	100.9	4.3
Outdoor	170.5	7.2
Network television	311.9	13.2
Spot television	6.1	0.3
Syndicated television	101.8	4.3
Cable television networks	29.4	1.2
Network radio	58.6	2.5
National spot radio	116.6	4.9
Total U.S. advertising spending	**$2,363.6**	100.0%

Note: These figures are for measured media only. Spending on items such as direct mail and the World Wide Web are not included.

Source: Advertising Age. (1996). 100 leading national advertisers, *Advertising Age, 67*, (40), 54.

Figure 15.5   Total U.S. Advertising Spending By Travel, Hotels and Resorts, 1995.

1994; Siegel & Ziff-Levine, 1994; Woodside & Ronkainen, 1994):

Advertising tracking studies: These studies track the awareness levels and images of the tourism destination or organization before and after the placement of the advertising.

Cost-comparison method: This method calculates ratios such as cost per inquiry, cost per visitor, and return on investment. These ratios may be produced in a conversion study.

Concept testing: Small-scale, qualitative studies of rough drawings of message ideas or campaigns.

Conversion studies: These studies determine how many inquirers from tourism advertising convert to visitors and what are the converted visitors' demographic and travel-behavior characteristics, including length of stay, travel-party size, destination activities, and expenditures.

Inquiry and lead tracking: These are measures of promotional efficiency in which records are kept of direct-response advertising inquiries or sales leads (from sales calls or travel and trade shows).

Pre-testing: Studies that expose samples of the target market to preliminary or finished versions of the proposed promotions.

Post-testing: Studies done after the promotional campaign has ended to determine changes in images, awareness, attitudes, and recall.

Travel or trade show audits: Studies on the past attendance and characteristics of the people who attend consumer travel and travel trade shows.

Broader analyses of marketing effectiveness may measure market share changes, public relations yield ratio, and the ratio of industry and cooperative promotion funding to total funding (Lavery, 1992).

Uses of Promotion by National Tourist Offices

"The WTO study Budgets of National Tourism Administrations shows that global spending on tourism promotion by national governments reached US$1.2 billion in 1995, an increase of seven percent over the previous year. However, the total amount is ridiculously small. For most countries, it is not nearly enough to cope with the fierce competition that destinations are facing."

Enzo Paci, World Tourism Organization, (1997)

A national tourist office (NTO) is the organization officially responsible for the marketing and development of tourism for a country. When there are two national-level tourism organizations, the agency responsible for marketing is usually designated the NTO. The development function is given to a national tourism administration (NTA). According to the World Tourism Organization, a total of U.S. $1.2 billion was spent on tourism promotion in 1995 by NTOs (World Tourism Organization, http://www.world-tourism.org/pressrel/10-02-97.htm). The five NTOs with the largest promotional budgets were Australia, United Kingdom, Spain, France, and Singapore (see figure 15.6).

There is great variation among NTOs in the amounts of promotional spending and in the allocation of funds to promotional mix elements. The World Tourism Organization estimated that 56 percent of NTO budgets in 1995 was spent on tourism promotion. The world-leading Australian Tourist Commission devoted 42.3 percent of its 1994–1995 total operating expenses to advertising; 12.1 percent to promotions and publicity; and 11.7 percent to films, publications, and distribution (Australian Tourist Commission Annual Review, 1995). The Singapore Tourist Promotion Board allocated 52.8 percent of its total expenditures to overseas and local publicity and promotion (SPTB Annual Report, 1994–1995).

Most NTOs maintain head offices in their own countries and operate a network of offices in other countries. The majority of most NTO budgets is spent abroad for the operation of these offices and in promotional programs. NTOs locate in countries that generate most of their international visitor arrivals. The number of offices in a country depends upon the importance of the market and the size of the country. For example, most of the major NTOs have more than one office in the United States, and several have two or more offices in Japan.

There are now several hundred NTO offices abroad. A relatively small country, New Zealand, operates sixteen overseas offices in seven regions (Australia, United Kingdom and Nordic, Central Europe, North Asia, South Asia, Japan, and North America). It is certainly possible to operate overseas marketing campaigns from a head office. Smaller countries with low NTO budgets are forced to do this. Some NTOs contract with **sales representative firms** or **public relations consultants** to handle their promotional efforts. Others work through the offices of their national airlines. Some use their embassies or consulates to represent the NTO, but this tends not to be an effective solution. One explanation is that embassies located in the country's capital, are often not in the best places for promoting to potential visitors and travel trade intermediaries (e.g., Canberra in Australia, Ottawa in Canada, and Washington

COUNTRY	PROMOTIONAL SPENDING IN 1995 (U.S. $)	PROMOTIONAL SPENDING PER TOURIST ARRIVAL (U.S. $)	PROMOTIONAL SPENDING PER U.S. $1,000 IN TOURISM REVENUES	REVENUES PER U.S. $1 SPENT ON TOURISM PROMOTION
1. Australia	$87,949,000	$23.32	$12.80	$ 78
2. United Kingdom	78,710,000	3.47	4.50	222
3. Spain (G)	78,647,000	1.74	3.10	319
4. France	72,928,000	1.20	2.70	375
5. Singapore (G)	53,595,000	8.35	7.10	1.41
6. Thailand (G)	51,198,000	7.42	6.80	148
7. Netherlands*	49,700,000	7.88	8.20	122
8. Austria	47,254,000	n/a	n/a	n/a
9. Ireland	37,811,000	8.60	21.00	121
10. Portugal	37,271,000	3.92	8.30	77

Note: (G) Wholly funded by National Government.

* National government provides less than half of the promotional funding; all others receive more than half of their promotional funds from the national government.

n/a = not available

Source: World Tourism Organization. (1997). More money needed for tourism promotion. Madrid: WTO press release.

Figure 15.6   Top Ten NTO Spenders on Promotion.

in the U.S.). It is much more effective to locate NTO offices in the country's largest cities (e.g., Sydney, Melbourne, Toronto, Montreal, Vancouver, New York, and Los Angeles).

The first NTO was established in 1901 by the New Zealand Department of Tourism. In their nearly 100 years of operation, and particularly since the 1960s, the roles of NTO offices have evolved and changed (Morrison, Braunlich, Kamaruddin, & Cai, 1995). In their earlier days, the principal function of an NTO office was to distribute printed literature to potential visitors. They played a rather passive role as an "order taker" rather than an "order maker." Increased competition from other foreign destinations and travel options (cruises, gambling, and theme parks) forced NTOs to become more aggressive marketers of their countries. The growth in the popularity of tours and packaged vacations also shifted more of the emphasis away from the individual visitor toward travel trade intermediaries. The new electronic media distribution systems, including the World Wide Web, also may have a profound effect on the roles of NTOs, as the emphasis on print materials lessens and more people are able to access instant

travel information in an electronic form.

NTOs staff their foreign offices mainly with their own citizens. A study of NTO offices in the U.S. found that 70 percent of staff were the destination country's citizens and the remainder were locals of the origin country (Morrison, Braunlich, Kamaruddin, & Cai, 1995).

NTO offices abroad play the following seven major roles:

1. *Image creation and enhancement role:* To promote a favorable image of the country as a tourism destination, and to maintain or enhance this image.

2. *Literature distribution and fulfillment role:* To increase

---

Quick Trip 15.1
The British Tourist Authority

The British Tourist Authority (BTA) was established by an Act of Parliament in 1969 (The Development of Tourism Act). The Act also established the English Tourist Board, the Scottish Tourist Board, and the Wales Tourist Board. BTA's principal role is to promote tourism to Britain from overseas. BTA's main functions are:

● To increase tourism spent in Britain from overseas.

● To advise the government and public bodies on tourism matters that affect Britain as a whole.

● To encourage the provision and improvement of tourist facilities and amenities in Britain.

BTA receives funding from the government, via the Department of National Heritage, and boosts the monies raised from commercial activities and other private and public sector partnership initiatives.

Source: British Tourist Authority Web site, http://www.bta.org.uk, (1997).

One NTO goal is to show a country in its most positive way, such as emphasizing beautiful scenery. Photo from *Top Shots* CD Rom. Courtesy of Queensland Tourist and Travel Corporation.

Quick Trip 15.2
Most Important Activities of an NTO Office Abroad

A study of foreign NTO offices located in the United States was conducted by researchers at Purdue University (Morrison, Braunlich, Kamaruddin, & Cai, 1995). The respondents in this study gave the following rankings to specific NTO office activities (scores are out of 10, with 10 being most important):

1. Distributing promotional literature to travel trade intermediaries (9.03).
2. Distributing promotional literature to consumers (8.78).
3. Organizing educational/training seminars/workshops for the travel trade (8.69).
4. Developing new packages with the travel trade (8.55).
5. Arranging familiarization trips for travel writers (8.03).
6. Advertising in consumer travel magazines/newspapers (7.94).
7. Arranging familiarization trips for travel trade intermediaries (7.54).
8. Making sales calls on travel trade intermediaries (7.51).
9. Maintaining a computerized database of inquiries (7.45).
10. Exhibiting at travel trade shows (7.40).
11. Advertising in travel trade magazines/newspapers (7.17).
12. Exhibiting at consumer travel shows (5.48).
13. Making sales calls on consumers (e.g., groups) (5.24).

and make more effective the supply of information on the tourism services and products of the destination.

3. **Marketing research and database development role:** To collect information and create databases that help to increase the effectiveness of marketing decisions.

4. **Package and tour development role:** To increase the availability of the tourist products of the destination by increasing the number of new tour programs and packaged vacations and the capacity of existing ones, or to maintain at targeted levels the number and capacity of such programs.

5. **Partnership development role:** To play a leadership role in the development of marketing and promotional partnerships between transportation carriers, suppliers, travel trade intermediaries, and other businesses in the host country and the originating countries.

6. **Consumer marketing and promotional role:** To secure maximum promotional exposure for the destination mix of the country.

7. **Travel trade marketing and promotional role:** To familiarize travel trade distribution channels with the destination's services and products and stimulate them to increase sales.

1. Image Creation and Enhancement

Through its promotional programs, an NTO must communicate a distinctive and favorable image (positioning) of the country as a destination. It must seek to maintain and enhance this image, even in the face of adverse publicity.

2. Literature Distribution and Fulfillment

Literature distribution has been a traditional role of all NTOs, and they print large quantities of printed collateral materials to support promotional programs. In recent years, the concept of literature has expanded to *information distribution* through print, video/film, CD-ROM, and the World Wide Web. In an analysis of NTO informational materials distributed in the United States, the following five categories of informational materials were identified (Braunlich, Morrison, & Feng, 1995):

- Maps
- Travel planners (also known as travel or visitor guides)
- Accommodation guides
- Special event calendars
- Guides to tour packages

3. Marketing Research and Database Development

NTO offices abroad are increasingly being used to gather marketing research information and to build databases of travel trade intermediaries, groups, and other types of visitors. The generation of inquiries as a result of direct-response advertising is one good source of databases. Databases may also be bought from mailing list brokers when special-interest markets are to be targeted.

4. Package and Tour Development

One way to increase the flow of visitors to a country is to increase the number of tour programs and packaged vacations to that destination. A good example of this is the Tourism Marketing Joint Venture Fund operated by the New Zealand Tourism Board. This fifty-fifty cost-sharing program encourages tour operators in other countries to de-

velop new tours featuring New Zealand.

5. Partnership Development

Many NTOs actively try to create marketing and promotional partnerships between themselves and other tourism and nontourism organizations. The Partnership Australia (Australian Tourist Commission) and the Tourism Marketing Joint Venture (New Zealand Tourism Board) are two excellent examples that have already been mentioned. The English Tourist Board has been instrumental in creating marketing alliances known as TDAPs (Tourism Development Action Programs) (Palmer & Bejou, 1995). These TDAPs bring the public and private sectors of tour-

ism together, and are given the responsibility of developing a comprehensive and integrated approach to the development and marketing of tourism in a local area.

NTOs may work with the manufacturers of food and beverage products in promoting their countries. The Canadian Tourism Commission in 1997 placed a special advertising section in a consumer travel magazine in partnership with Silversea Cruises and Dove Dark Chocolate Promises.

6. Consumer Marketing and Promotion

A full range of promotional activities was shown in figure 15.3. Recent surveys suggest that NTOs place more emphasis on travel trade

---

Quick Trip 15.3
The South African Tourism Board

The South African Tourism Board (SATOUR) is a statutory board created by the Tourism Act. It is responsible for the international marketing of South Africa as a tourist destination. SATOUR's programs are built around a vision:

- To promote South Africa as a tourist destination into the twenty-first century and beyond.
- To make tourism the leading industry in South Africa.
- To use tourism to improve the quality of life of all South Africans, through job creation and instilling a sense of pride in themselves, the environment, and their country.

The underlying values of this vision are:

- A quality experience for all visitors.
- Optimum social and economic benefits for all South Africans.
- Cooperation with all stakeholders in the industry, both locally and overseas.
- The preservation of South Africa's unique natural and sociocultural environment.

Source: SATOUR Web site (http://www.africa.com/satour/main/satour.htm)

Quick Trip 15.4
ITB Berlin and the World Travel Market

The two largest travel trade exhibitions in the world are held annually in Berlin and London. ITB Berlin (International Tourism Exchange Travel and Tourism World Trade Fair) is held at the Berlin exhibition grounds. At the 1996 exhibition, more than 6,000 exhibitors represented 176 countries. Some 4,851 of the 6,125 exhibitors were from countries other than Germany. The total attendance was almost 120,000 and 52,000 of these were members of the travel trade. The exhibition occupied an overall area of 103,000 meters and a net area of 64,893 meters. The 1997 ITB experienced a 7 percent increase in exhibitors, 75 percent of whom were from foreign countries.

The World Travel Market is held in November each year at Earls Court in London. At the 1995 World Travel Market, there were 4,249 exhibitors and an attendance of 45,130. The exhibitors are drawn from over 150 countries. Unlike ITB, the World Travel Market is open for travel trade visitors only. The net area of the exhibition is 32,183 meters.

Source: Messe Berlin and World Travel Market Web sites. (1997).

---

than on consumer promotions. Advertising to potential visitors is very important in creating awareness of the country and generating enough interest so that visitors want more information. However, consumer advertising tends to be relatively expensive. The NTOs with larger budgets are able to mount substantial consumer campaigns in certain markets using mainly magazine and television advertising. Smaller-budget NTOs are forced to concentrate on travel trade marketing and use public relations and publicity to promote to the consumer.

7. Travel Trade Marketing and Promotion

An important NTO role is to inform travel trade intermediaries about the country and to familiarize them with its tourism attractions, events, and other resources. One effective way of doing this is through *familiarization tours*. NTOs organize these educational tours for selected tour wholesalers and retail travel agents. Having experienced the country firsthand, the intermediaries are in a much better position to sell it as a tourism destination. During familiarization tours, the foreign travel trade intermediaries inspect facilities, visit tourism attractions, and make contacts with the local travel trade, who may act as their partners in channeling visitors to the country. Such tours may be conducted in small groups or on an individual basis. Familiarization tours are also often organized for travel writers.

Another major activity of NTOs is exhibiting at *travel trade exhibitions* or shows. Two of the largest shows in the world are ITB Berlin (held in March each year in Germany) and the World Travel Market (held in November each year in London, England).

Educational workshops and seminars are organized and staged in overseas countries. They bring together all the main components of tourism, such as hotels, travel agents, airlines, and providers of tourist services, from both the generating and the destination country. The main objective of these workshops and seminars is to promote the destination mix of the country to the travel trade and other principals of the generating country. They motivate travel trade intermediaries to increase sales of group tours and FIT (foreign independent tour) travel. They familiarize travel trade intermediaries with the country's facilities and services and the latest developments in tourism. They provide an opportunity for the *travel principals* of the destination and generating countries to establish working relationships.

Several NTOs have gone further with their trade education efforts to set up training programs that lead to travel agent *accreditations*. These include the "Aussie Specialist" program operated by the Australian Tourist Commission and the SCOTS (Specialist Counsellors on Travel to Scotland) program run by the Scottish Tourist Board.

Sales calls are made by NTO staff to retail travel agents and tour wholesalers. The aim of these calls is to assist the travel trade in selling the country by providing them with information, advice, and promotional *collateral materials*. To keep the travel trade well-stocked with promotional materials on the country, NTOs have regular direct mailings of brochures and other collateral materials. With this information, the travel trade is in a better position to effectively service client inquiries and promote the country.

Many NTOs establish a permanent channel of communications with the travel trade through the regular distribution of *newsletters*. The newsletters inform the travel trade about upcoming events, developments in the destination's facilities and services, and other interesting facets of its tourism. As well as maintaining an ongoing relation-

Irish Tourist Board travel seminars. Reprinted by permission of the Irish Tourist Board.

ship, these newsletters also attempt to promote sales by the travel trade to the country.

Some NTOs provide incentives or bonuses in the form of free vacations or gifts. These incentives are often linked with promotional *contests* or *games*. These sales promotions are often done in partnership with the main tourism principals of the country (hotel and airline companies).

Promotional evenings may be organized exclusively for members of the travel trade and are basically public relations' exercises. They are often staged in hotels or resorts. Food, beverages, and entertainment, often imported from the NTO's country, are provided.

More recently, the operation of sites on the World Wide Web has provided instant access to the NTO's information and services. Almost every major NTO has an official Web site.

State, Provincial and Territorial Tourist Offices

Around the world, wherever there are systems of state, provincial, or territorial governments, tourist offices (STOs) have been created with roughly similar roles to NTOs. These include the provinces and territories of Canada, the states and territory of Australia, and the states and territories of the U.S. The major difference between the promotional activities of these agencies

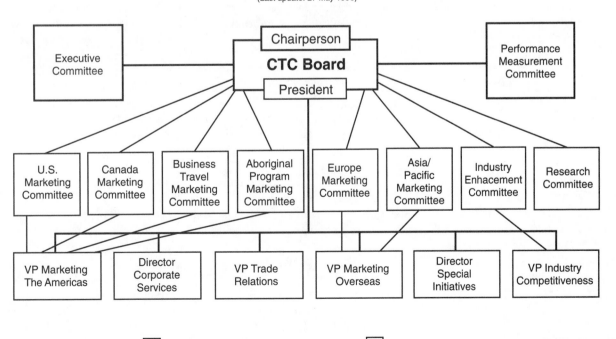

Organizational Structure of the Canadian Tourism Commission
(Last update: 27 May 1996)

Quick Trip 15.5
The Canadian Tourism Commission

In contrast with its neighbor to the south, Canada's national tourism office has traditionally enjoyed much greater federal government financial support and an enhanced stature within the political system. The Canadian Tourism Commission (CTC) replaced the federal government's Tourism Canada in the mid-1990s. The CTC is a working partnership between tourism industry businesses and associations, provincial and territorial governments, and the government of Canada.

The CTC has authority to plan, direct, manage, and implement programs to generate and promote tourism in Canada. It is made up of industry representatives from across Canada, acting to ensure that the tourism industry remains a vibrant and profitable part of the Canadian economy. The main thrusts of the Commission are to position Canada as a desirable destination to both international and domestic travelers, and to provide timely and accurate information to the tourism industry to assist in decision making.

The commission coordinates the efforts of the many players in the tourism sector, among them hoteliers, attractions, tour operators, airlines, local and provincial associations, and government agencies. This partnership arrangement provides a unique opportunity to develop coordinated programs that will benefit the industry, governments, and the country as a whole. For the federal government, establishing the commission represents an increased commitment to tourism in Canada.

Both private and public sectors join forces with the CTC in designing and implementing effective marketing strategies and programs that will increase tourism revenues to Canada. Some of these activities include: gathering and maintaining data on potential markets; analyzing international and domestic marketplace opportunities and issues; performing market research and analysis; advertising; ongoing public relations; updating promotional projects; and creating travel trade activities.

Source: Canadian Tourism Commission, 1996 (http://info.ic.gc.ca/tourisme/ctc.html).

---

gets are greater than many NTO budgets. For example, the STO in Illinois had a budget of US $31.5 million in 1995–1996 (U.S. Travel Data Center, 1996), while the Queensland Tourist & Travel Corporation (QTTC) in Australia had an even larger budget at AU$ 65.7 million in 1994–95 (Queensland Tourist and Travel Corporation Annual Report, 1995). Some of the Australian STOs are unique in their operation of travel information centers (which generate retail sales) in other states and, in QTTC's case, the operation of a tour wholesaling operation that develops and sells vacation packages.

Regional and Local Tourism Organizations

Another level of tourism promotion agencies is at the regional level (within states, provinces, or territories) and at the local community level. The format of these agencies varies by country, mainly due to the organizational structure of government and the physical size of the country, state, province, or territory. In smaller countries such as England and Ireland there tends to be a structure of regional tourism agencies under the NTO. For example, in England there are eleven regional tourist boards under the English Tourist Board (ETB). These receive funding from ETB, local authorities, and private-sector businesses. One of these boards is the Northumbria Tourist Board (NTB), which covers the counties of Durham, Northumberland, and Tyne and Wear and the Tees Valley area. The NTB's main areas of work are regional tourism marketing and public relations campaigns, planning and development advice and training initiatives, specialist tourism business advice and training initiatives, business and marketing campaign research, promotion of quality awareness programs,

---

and those of NTOs is that they tend to focus more on domestic travelers than on international. Their primary promotional role is to draw visitors from other states, provinces, or territories within the country. Having said this, it must be realized that several individual states have significant numbers of international visitors and mount extensive international promotion programs. Some states and provinces even operate full-time offices abroad, including the Australian

states of Queensland and Victoria. The greater focus on domestic markets means that STOs tend to place less emphasis on travel trade marketing than on consumer marketing. Otherwise, the roles of STOs are similar to those outlined earlier for NTOs.

While these organizations usually have budgets less than their respective NTOs, they have been receiving increased funding in recent years (see figure 15.7 for U.S. state tourist offices). Some STO's bud-

YEAR	TOTAL BUDGETS	AVERAGE TOTAL BUDGET	AVERAGE AMOUNT ALLOCATED TO ADVERTISING
1991–1992	$330,793,042	$6,615,861 (50)	$2,212,377 (48)
1992–1993	$330,805,530	$6,891,782 (48)	$2,253,861 (45)
1993–1994	$372,181,748	$7,595,546 (49)	$2,508,601 (46)
1994–1995	$403,900,746	$8,242,872 (49)	$2,383,009 (47)
1995–1996*	$413,931,540	$8,447,582 (49)	$2,509,768 (44)

Note: Figures in parentheses are number of states reporting.

* Projected budgets for 1995–1996.

Source: U.S. Travel Data Center.

Figure 15.7   Budgets of U.S. State Tourist Offices in U.S.A.

monitoring of accommodation standards, and support of visitor information services. In Ireland, under the Department of Tourism and Trade and the Irish Tourist Board (Bord Failte Eireann), there are seven regional tourism organizations. In larger countries and states/provinces, the regional tourism organizations operate under the level of the state, provincial, or territorial tourism offices. This is the case in both Australia and Canada.

Another interpretation of the term "region" in tourism is that this represents an area encompassing several different countries and NTOs. For example, the NTOs in the Scandinavian region in Northern Europe operate their international travel promotions in a regional partnership, the Scandinavian Tourist Boards. Other regional partnerships in tourism include El Mundo Maya (the Mayan World) involving the countries of Belize, El Salvador, Guatemala, Honduras, and Mexico in Central America and the Greater Mekong region (Cambodia, China, Laos, Myanmar, Thailand, and Vietnam). The Caribbean Tourism Organization, European Travel Commission, Indian Ocean Tourism Organization, and the Pacific Asia Travel Association are examples of permanent organizations that have been created to encourage the development and promotion of tourism in their multi-country regions.

Some countries, including the United States, have strong local tourism organizations and do not have a formal system of regional tourism organizations. In the United States, the introduction of room taxes by city and county governments has helped to finance an extensive network of local *convention and visitors' bureaus (CVBs)*. The first CVB was opened more than 100 years ago in Detroit, Michigan. Most of the larger CVBs in the world are members of the International Association of Convention and Visitor Bureaus located in Washington, D.C. A traditional role of CVBs, as their name suggests, has been to attract business from the *MICE markets* (meetings, incentives, conventions, and exhibitions). Recently, CVBs have been placing more emphasis on attracting group and individual pleasure travelers.

Summary

Promotion provides the means with which the tourism destination or organization communicates with past and potential travelers. In so doing, the five promotional mix elements of advertising, personal selling, sales promotion, merchandising, and public relations and publicity are used to achieve predetermined objectives. These objectives range from very broad image campaigns to promotions geared to immediately increase revenues. Each of the five promotional mix elements and the available communications media has distinct advantages and disadvantages, and it is important to carefully weigh these against a set of evaluation criteria.

National tourist offices (NTOs) play a pivotal role in promoting their county's tourism attractions, facilities, and services in foreign countries. The role and amount of financial support given to NTOs by their respective governments varies greatly.

Quick Trip 15.6

The U.S. National Tourism Organization

The U.S. National Tourism Organization (USNTO) was signed into existence in October 1996 by President Bill Clinton. The former U.S. Travel and Tourism Administration (USTTA) was closed down. The amount of government funding provided to the USTTA was a constant problem and source of friction within U.S. tourism. Most experts and industry participants believe that the agency has been inadequately funded, reflecting a lack of sufficient political commitment to tourism in the United States (Ahmed & Krohn, 1990; Morrison, 1987; Ronkainen & Farano, 1987). For most of the 1980s and 1990s, the USTTA's total budget was in the range of $10 to $20 million.

References

Ahmed, Z.U., & and Krohn, F.B. (1990). Reversing the United States' declining competitiveness in the marketing of international tourism: A perspective on future policy. *Journal of Travel Research*, 29 (2), 23–29.

Braunlich, C.G., Morrison, A.M., & Feng, F. (1995). National tourist offices: Service quality expectations and performance. *Journal of Vacation Marketing*, 1, 323–336.

Davidson, T.L. (1994). Assessing the effectiveness of persuasive communications in tourism. In Ritchie, J.R.B., & Goeldner, C.R. (eds.), *Travel, tourism, and hospitality research: A handbook for managers and researchers* (2nd ed., 537–543). New York: John Wiley & Sons, Inc.

Davidson, T.L., & Wiethaupt, W.B. (1989). Accountability marketing research: An increasingly vital tool for travel marketers. *Journal of Travel Research*, 26 (4), 42–45.

Dommermuth, W.P. (1989). *Promotion: Analysis, creativity, and strategy* (2nd ed.). Boston: PWS-Kent Publishing Company.

Economist Intelligence Unit. (1996). The role and functions of a national tourist office abroad. *International Tourism Quarterly*, 3, 39–58.

Hawes, D.K., Taylor, D.T., & Hampe, G.D. (1991). Destination marketing by states. *Journal of Travel Research*, 30 (1), 11–17.

Jones, C. (1996). *Database marketing in the tourism industry.* San Francisco: Economics Research Associates (http://www.erasf.com/erasf/dbase_mktg.html).

Koth, B.A. (1988). *Evaluating tourism advertising with cost-comparison methods.* St. Paul, MN: Minnesota Extension Service, University of Minnesota.

Lavery, P. (1992). The financing and organisation of national tourist offices. *EIU Travel & Tourism Analyst*, 4, 84–101.

Lennon, M. (1995). *Tourism promotion using the World Wide Web.* (http://info.isoc.org/HMP/PAPER/html/paper.html).

Morrison, A.M. (1987). Selling the USA: Part 1: International promotion. *Travel & Tourism Analyst*, 2, 3–12.

Morrison, A. M. (1996). *Hospitality and travel marketing* (2nd ed.). Albany, NY: Delmar Publishers, Inc.

Morrison, A.M., Braunlich, C.G., Kamaruddin, N., & Cai, L.A. (1995). National tourist offices in North America: An analysis. *Tourism Management*, 16, 605–618.

Palmer, A., & Bejou, D. (1995). Tourism destination marketing alliances. *Annals of Tourism Research*, 22, 616–629.

Peppers, D., & Rogers, M. (1993). *The one to one future: Building relationships one customer at a time.* New York: Currency Doubleday.

Perdue, R.R., & Pitegoff, B.E. (1994). Methods of accountability research for destination marketing. In Ritchie, J.R.B., & Goeldner, C.R. (eds.), *Travel, tourism, and hospitality research: A handbook for managers and researchers* (2nd ed., 565–571). New York: John Wiley & Sons, Inc.

Petrison, L.A., Blattberg, R.C., & Wang, P. (1993). Database marketing: Past, present, and future. *Journal of Direct Marketing*, 7, (3), 27–43.

Pizam, A. (1994). Methods of accountability research for destination marketing. In Ritchie, J.R.B., & Goeldner, C.R. (eds.), *Travel, tourism, and hospitality research: A handbook for managers and researchers* (2nd ed., 573–581). New York: John Wiley & Sons, Inc.

Ronkainen, I.A., & Farano, R.J. (1987). United States' travel and tourism policy. *Journal of Travel Research*, 25 (4), 2–8.

Siegel, W., & Ziff-Levine, W. (1994). Methods of accountability research for destination marketing. In Ritchie, J.R.B., & Goeldner, C.R. (eds.), *Travel, tourism, and hospitality research: A handbook for managers and researchers* (2nd ed., 559–564). New York: John Wiley & Sons, Inc.

U.S. Travel Data Center. (1997). *Survey of state travel offices: 1996–97.* Washington, DC: Travel Industry Association of America.

Walle, A.H. (1996). Tourism and the Internet: Opportunities for direct marketing. *Journal of Travel Research*, 35 (1), 72–77.

Woodside, A.G., & Ronkainen, I.A. (1994). Methods of accountability research for destination marketing. In Ritchie, J.R.B., & Goeldner, C.R. (eds.), *Travel, tourism, and hospitality research: A handbook for managers and researchers* (2nd ed., 545–557). New York: John Wiley & Sons, Inc.

Surfing Solutions

http://www.aussie.net.au/ (Australian Tourist Commission)

http://www.bta.org.uk/ (British Tourist Authority)

http://info.ic.gc.ca/tourisme/ctc.html (Canadian Tourism Commission)

http://www.erassf.com/erasf/dbase_mktg.html ("Database marketing in the tourism industry" by Clive B. Jones)

http://www.erassf.com/erasf/dest_dbase.html ("Destination databases as keys to effective marketing" by Clive B. Jones)

http://www.Ireland.travel.ie/ (Irish Tourist Board)

http://www.messe-berlin.de (ITB Berlin International Tourism Exchange)

http://www.nztb.govt.nz/index.html (New Zealand Tourism Board)

http://www.africa.com/satour/ (South African Tourism Board)

http://www.world-tourism.org/ (World Tourism Organization)

http://www.world-travel-net.co.uk/reedtravel/wtm.htm (World Travel Market exhibition)

http://info.isoc.org/HMP/PAPER/html/paper.html ("Tourism promotion using the World Wide Web" by M. Lennon)

Acronyms

ATC (Australian Tourist Commission)

BTA (British Tourist Authority)

CTC (Canadian Tourism Commission)

CVB (Convention and visitors bureau)

DMO (Destination marketing organization)

ETB (English Tourist Board)

IACVB (International Association of Convention and Visitor Bureaus)

ITB (International Tourism Exchange, Berlin)

MICE (Meetings, incentives, conventions, and exhibitions)

NTO (National tourist office or organization)

NZTB (New Zealand Tourism Board)

PLC (Product life cycle)

QTTC (Queensland Tourist & Travel Corporation)

SATOUR (South African Tourism Board)

STO (State tourist office)

TDAP (Tourism Development Action Programs)

USNTO (U.S. National Tourism Organization)

USTTA (U.S. Travel and Tourism Administration)

WWW (World Wide Web)

> "How can you travel abroad and learn nothing from the experience?
>
> Take a package tour."
>
> *Jacobs, K. (1995). "Six Countries: Seven Days."*
> Colors: Travel Special

16

The Distribution Mix in Tourism

···Getting Messages and Services to the Market ····

Purpose

Having learned about the tourism distribution system, students will be able to explain direct and indirect distribution, and describe the functions of the main travel trade intermediaries.

Learning Objectives

Having read this chapter, you should be able to:

1. Describe the tourism distribution system using a diagram to illustrate the relationship of the various tourism organizations involved.

2. Define direct and indirect distribution, and explain the difference between these two concepts.

3. Identify and describe the major types of travel intermediaries.

4. Explain the functions of tour wholesalers and operators, and the economics of the tour business.

5. Explain the functions of retail travel agencies.

6. Describe the reasons for creating corporate travel departments and the functions of these departments.

7. Explain the functions of incentive travel and convention-meeting planners.

Overview

The final link in the tourism system involves getting messages and services to the market. This is accomplished through the tourism distribution system. The purpose of the tourism distribution channel is twofold: To get sufficient information to the right people at the right time and in the right place to allow a purchase decision to be made, and to provide a mechanism whereby travelers can make and pay for their purchases. The distribution mix is an important component of the overall marketing mix in tourism.

The concept of vertical integration within tourism distribution channels is discussed. The histories and functions of tour wholesalers and operators, retail travel agencies, corporate travel departments, incentive travel and convention-meeting planners are explained. The implications of changes in electronic distribution systems are reviewed.

Tourism Distribution Is Unique

"And travel agents were equally slow in accepting the plane as a reliable mode of transport, sharing the conviction of clients that a journey on land and sea was considerably less risky, and leaving the ground was for barnstormers, wing-walkers and other associated daredevils."

Eric Friedheim. (1992). Travel agents: From Caravans and Clippers to the Concorde. Universal Media, 160

The purpose of distribution is to establish a link between supply and demand; between tourism destinations and organizations, and visitors. The distribution system makes tourism services and products available to visitors. Tourism distribution is different than the distribution in other industries. There is no physical distribution since tourism services are *intangible*. Tourism services cannot be physically packaged and shipped to visitors and they cannot be stored in inventory.

While the complexities of transportation and warehousing are eliminated, there are other unique challenges in tourism distribution. Tourism services are *perishable*. The hotel room, airline seat, or cruise berth must be sold each and every day, flight, or sailing. A tourism sale lost today is lost forever. *Travel trade intermediaries* (organizations that operate between the providers of tourism services and visitors) have a strong influence on visitors' purchase decisions. A major role of travel trade intermediaries is the *packaging* of complementary tourism services and products to provide a more satisfying travel experience for the visitor. Retail travel agents book airline seats, hotel rooms, cruises, tours and packages, and rental cars and provide individualized packaged vacations in the form of foreign independent tours (FITs). Tour operators assemble these components into packaged vacations or tours and offer these for sale through retail travel agents. The tourism distribution system is different because it includes these and other unique intermediaries that each perform specialized roles. This system communicates promotional messages to potential visitors, along with the necessary factual information, and makes booking easier for the visitor.

Distribution's Role in the Marketing Mix

"The tourism distribution system is both complex and unique. It is unique because of the influence that travel trade intermediaries have on customers' choices. It is complex because of the diversity of organizations involved and their relationships with each other."

Morrison, A.M. (1996). Hospitality and Travel Marketing, 2nd ed., 313

Cruise ships rely heavily on retail travel agencies for bookings. The Canadian Empress in the 1000 Islands, Ontario, Canada. Photo courtesy of the Canadian Tourism Commission, Photo Library, 235, rue Queen St., 400D, Ottawa, Ontario KIA 0H6.

The tourism distribution system or ***distribution mix*** is a component of the marketing mix. Distribution mix decisions must be consistent with the overall marketing mix. The goal of the marketing mix is to reach target markets and achieve the objectives for these markets. The distribution mix affects other marketing mix components and is itself affected by these other components. For example, cruise lines rely almost completely on retail travel agents for their bookings. Therefore, the cruise lines' pricing structures must be such as to allow for attractive commission rates for agents.

Promotional approaches need to be adapted to suit the choice of travel trade intermediaries. Because retail travel agents have no inventory, there is no incentive for them to promote specific destinations. The promotional burden rests with destination marketing organizations, transportation companies, and the suppliers of tourism services. In contrast, tour operators carry an inventory of airline seats, hotel rooms, and other tourism services. They have a prior investment (in terms of ***blocked space***) with airlines and suppliers in the tour destination areas and are often willing to share the costs of promoting the destination to sell their tours. For the airlines and suppliers of services, the promotional burden is shared through partnerships with tour operators. These partnerships may include joint advertising, joint sponsorship of agent familiarization trips, and other sales promotion activities.

The pricing approaches of tourism suppliers and carriers are influenced by the decision either to distribute directly to the traveler or indirectly through a travel intermediary. When tour operators buy in bulk—such as blocking 100 rooms per night for three months—they expect and receive lower room rates.

The Tourism Distribution System

> *"Travel is heaven and hell, a chaotic marriage of the sublime and the iniquitous. To shift the balance in favor of pleasure, the modern traveler needs to understand and master the process of travel; the boring stuff about airline schedules, special fares, hotel prices, crime, tax breaks, and so forth."*
>
> Paula Szuchman. (1997). *How travel has changed.* Condé Nast Traveler. *May,* 59

Direct and Indirect Distribution Channels

Tourism distribution is either direct or indirect. ***Direct distribution*** occurs when a carrier, supplier, or destination marketing organization sells directly to the traveler; ***indirect distribution*** is when the sale is made through one or more travel trade intermediaries. This results in a rather complex distribution system (see figure 16.1).

Carriers (airlines, railroad companies, and other transportation providers), ***suppliers*** (attractions, lodging, cruise line, food service, rental car companies, and gaming facilities), and ***destination marketing organizations*** face a two-step decision process when selecting their distribution mixes. First, they must make a choice of ***distribution channel***. Second, if indirect channels are chosen, they must select specific travel trade intermediaries. McIntosh, Goeldner, & Ritchie (1995) define a tourism channel of distribution as "an operating structure, system or linkages of various combinations of travel organizations through which a producer of travel products describes, sells, and confirms travel arrangements to the buyer." A tourism distribution channel has a twofold purpose: (1) ensuring that travelers obtain the information they need to make trip arrangements and, (2) accepting the bookings and processing the necessary reservations for travelers.

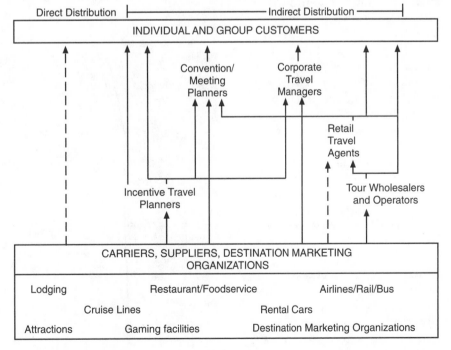

Figure 16.1 The Tourism Distribution System.

Source: Morrison, A.M. (1996). *Hospitality and Travel Marketing* 2nd ed., 315.

Travel Trade Intermediaries

Tour Wholesalers and Operators

Tour operators are "commercial tourism firms that specialize in the manufacture of travel packages" (Vellas & Becherel, 1995). Another definition of a tour operator is "the company that puts together the components of a tour for sale to the public and operates the tour" (Starr, 1997). The terms **tour wholesaler** and **tour operator** are often used interchangeably. The **wholesaling** function means assembling the tour. It involves tour planning, preparation, marketing, and reservations. By definition, a wholesaler does not sell directly to the public but receives reservations through other travel intermediaries such as retail travel agents or airline sales offices. The **operating** part of the tour means managing the tour by providing tour escorts, sightseeing services, or transportation. Many tour operators perform both the wholesaling and operating functions.

A distinction needs to be made between **outbound tour operators** and **inbound tour operators**. Outbound tour operators are companies that arrange tours for people leaving their home town, state, or country (Poynter, 1993). Inbound tour operators are tour operators who function in the visitors' tour destinations. They are also called reception or **receptive tour operators** or **receptive services operator** (De Souto, 1993), or **destination management companies** or **specialists**. Inbound tour operators (ITOs) normally provide ground transportation, guiding, and welcoming services at the tour destinations.

Retail Travel Agencies   Travel

agents handle the sale and reservations of tours, vacation packages, airline tickets, hotel rooms, car rentals, cruises, travel insurance, and other related services. The **retail travel agent** is compensated

through **commissions** from suppliers, carriers, and other intermediaries such as tour operators; the traveler usually pays nothing for the travel agent's services. Although some travel agencies have begun to charge fees to the traveler, it will be many years, if ever, before this practice becomes widespread. The principal value of retail travel agents to travelers is the agents' independence and impartiality, coupled with their knowledge of tourism services and access to

the inventory of other tourism organizations. Travelers expect that agents can recommend the best services to fit their travel needs. For suppliers, carriers, destination marketing organizations, and other intermediaries, retail travel agencies represent additional sales outlets for their services and products. For most of them, it would be prohibitively expensive, if not impossible, to establish their own in-house system of nationwide distribution.

DER Travel Services: A major German tour operator. Reprinted by permission of DER Travel Services.

Gift shops provide services and souvenirs—for travelers in the area. Photo by Corel.

A *travel consolidator* is a special form of travel agent. These are private firms that buy unsold airline seats in bulk and sell these at a discount to travelers (Gee, Makens, & Choy, 1997). They also work with retail travel agencies to help agencies receive discounted tickets for individual or group travelers.

Corporate Travel Departments

While traditionally considered as just one aspect of the retail travel agent's business, the growth in business travel has led to the emergence of a new breed of specialized travel agency servicing the corporate traveler; the *corporate travel agency*. At the same time, an increasing number of companies have established in-house *corporate travel departments* to establish company-wide travel policies and to negotiate the best prices on travel. These corporate travel departments are administered by *corporate travel managers*.

Incentive Travel Planners

Another recent newcomer to the tourism industry has been the *incentive travel planning company*, a specialized tour wholesaler who primarily serves corporate clients. The trips they arrange are given to certain of their client's employees or dealers as a reward for outstanding sales or work performance. Incentive travel is increasing in popularity as a work-related motivational and marketing tool. Corporations pay for the incentive travel planner's services either through a mark-up on the incentive package or on a fixed-fee basis.

Convention-Meeting Planners

These are employees of corporations, associations, government agencies, and other nonprofit groups who plan and coordinate meetings, conventions, conferences, exhibitions or trade shows. *Convention-meeting planning consultants* are specialized firms that assist planners with on-site negotiations and arrangements.

Other Intermediaries and Electronic Distribution

Two other intermediaries are travel clubs and sales representatives. **Travel clubs** are groups of individual travelers who use their collective buying power to bargain for discounted prices on tourism services. These include the increasingly popular "last-minute" travel clubs. *Sales representatives* are marketing or public relations specialists who represent hotels, resorts, destination areas, and other tourism organizations in foreign countries. These representative firms provide a more economical alternative to having a fully staffed office in each country.

The number of ways of distributing travel services have increased in recent years and will continue to in the future. Some of these distribution methods will involve new organizations entering the tourism industry (e.g., banks and insurance companies) or the creation of new types of service businesses, while others will rely primarily on *electronic distribution* using advances in computer and telecommunications technology.

During the 1980s and 1990s, technological advances have had the greatest impact on tourism distribution and the future promises even greater potential for the electronic distribution of tourism information and services. Most retail travel agencies are hooked into airline *computerized reservation systems* (CRS) or *global distribution systems* (GDS), giving them instant access to the inventory of the airlines and other tourism suppliers. Computer software programs and *World Wide Web* sites linked to online database/reservations services are now available to allow travelers to make travel reservations in their own homes or offices via personal computers and telephone lines. For example, there are now several large *online travel agencies* who make travel reservations for people using the World Wide Web, including Travelocity, Preview Travel, and Expedia (see figure 16.3).

Integration and Classification of Channels

"By acquiring a minority interest in Edelweiss Air, a charter company founded in the autumn of the year under review, we wish to secure for our own use the entire flight capacity of the company and to obtain the right to have a say in the marketing area. This way we are in a position to offer an original, first rate and low-cost product which meets Swiss quality standards in every respect."

Kuoni Annual Report (1995), Switzerland

Welcome to Travelocity

http://www.Travelocity.com/

Travelocity: an online travel reservation service. Travelocity is a service mark of an affiliate of the SABRE Group. © 1997 the SABRE Group, Inc.

Vertical Integration

Every transportation carrier, supplier, destination marketing organization, and travel intermediary within the tourism distribution system wants potential travelers to have the maximum amounts of exposure and access to their information to encourage inquiries, bookings, reservations, and payments.

The more direct control an organization has over the distribution of its services (through vertical integration), the greater is the assurance that information will be available and that reservations and payments can be made easily and conveniently. *Vertical integration* refers to the ownership by one organization of all or part of a tourism distribution channel.

Horizontal Integration

Tourism companies may also expand their power in a distribution channel through horizontal integration. *Horizontal integration* refers to the ownership of similar businesses by one organization in the tourism distribution channel. This happens often in tourism and usually involves a larger company taking over a smaller organization in the same business. Examples of this in the retail travel agency field include American Express' acquisition of Thomas Cook's operations in the United States, and Carlson's acquisition of A.T. Mays in the United Kingdom and Travel Agents International.

Classification of Channels

Distribution channels can be classified in terms of degree of control into three types: (1) consensus channels; (2) vertically integrated channels commanded by suppliers, carriers, tour operators, retail travel agents, or other intermediaries; and (3) vertically coordinated channels led by suppliers, carriers, tour operators, retail travel agents, or other intermediaries.

1. *Consensus Channels*   In a consensus channel, no single type of tourism organization exercises control over the entire distribution system. The many participants work together because they see it in their mutual interest to do so. Distribution channels in North America, the United Kingdom, and Australia tend to be of the consensus type.

2. *Vertically Integrated Channels* Vertically integrated channels are those in which the supplier and retail distribution functions are owned or controlled by a single organization. Because tour operators have historically emerged from the retail travel agency field, vertically integrated channels controlled by retail travel agents are commonly

found in the United Kingdom (Thomson Travel Group), Germany (Deutsches Reiseburo), and North America (American Express and Carlson). In Australia, the Queensland Tourist & Travel Corporation not only acts as the state's official destination marketing organization, but also operates a series of domestic retail travel agencies (Queensland Government Travel Centres) and a wholesaling division (Sunlover).

A tour operator may exert control over the entire channel activity through retail travel agency ownership and the organization of the channel. This system is found in Germany where tour operators control not only their own chain of retail travel agency outlets, which deal exclusively with the products of one operator, but also their own system of general retail and direct mail distribution. TUI (Touristik Union International), one of the largest German tour operators, controls a network of travel agencies and a large number of resorts and hotels (Club Robinson and Iberhotel).

3. **Vertically Coordinated Channels**   A vertically coordinated channel led by tour operators is one in which the tour operator's power of control over the channel come from contractual or financial commitments with retail travel agents. **Franchising** is an obvious example of such a system. In Germany, franchising is a large part of travel distribution. Retail travel agency franchising is also rapidly increasing in popularity in Australia, the United Kingdom, the U.S., and Canada. The franchisor of a particular company agrees to retail only through certain retail outlets (its franchisees) and to promote no other methods of distribution. The retail franchisee benefits from the much larger pool of marketing resources of the franchiser and the "name recognition" it shares

---

Quick Trip 16.1
Integration by the Carlson Companies and the Thomson Corporation

The Carlson Companies, Inc. based in Minneapolis, Minnesota, provides a good example of vertical and horizontal integration in tourism. Carlson's three main business divisions are the Carlson Marketing Group, Carlson Travel Group, and Carlson Hospitality Worldwide. The company's operations encompass the roles of a tourism supplier (hotels and resorts, restaurants, and cruise ships) and travel trade intermediary (retail travel agencies and incentive travel planning). The specific operations included under the Carlson umbrella include:

- Hotels and resorts: Radisson Hotels Worldwide; Country Inns & Suites By Carlson.
- Restaurants: Friday's Hospitality Worldwide Inc.; Country Kitchen restaurants.
- Cruise: Radisson Seven Seas Cruises; SSC Radisson Diamond.
- Travel agencies: Carlson Wagonlit Travel; A.T. Mays; Neiman Marcus Travel; Travel Agents International.
- Incentive travel: Carlson Marketing Group.

Carlson began its operations in the incentives business and when it began operating Radisson Hotels, it was practicing vertical integration (moving into the supply side of the tourism distribution channel). The decision to enter the cruise business with the SSC Radisson Diamond was another example of the company becoming more vertically integrated. However, when Carlson acquired the Scottish-headquartered travel agency chain, A.T. Mays, and the Travel Agents International franchise travel agency group, this was horizontal integration (Carlson was already in the travel agency business).

The Thomson Corporation is a marketing and communications company with its headquarters in Canada. It publishes six daily newspapers including *The Globe and Mail*. In the 1960s, Thomson purchased the independent British tour operator, Skytours. Later, Thomson acquired the British travel agency group Lunn Poly, the charter airline Britannia Airways, and another independent tour operator, Horizon Holidays. Thomson also owns another tour company called Portland Holidays whose tours are sold directly to the public. Finally, Thomson operates Holiday Cottages Group, the largest rental agency for holiday cottages in the United Kingdom. Now the Thomson Travel Group is probably the largest leisure travel company operating in Britain with total sales of U.S. $7,225 million in 1995. Its Thomson Tour Operations group is the United Kingdom's largest inclusive tour operator with 4.1 million tour patrons in 1995 (24% of the market).

Source: Web sites of The Carlson Companies, Inc. and The Thomson Corporation.

with the many other franchised agencies under the same umbrella. Travel Agents International is a good example of this in North America, while Traveland is a major franchised travel agency in Australia.

Distribution Mix Strategies

"Online services for the travel industry have proliferated recently, and the trend shows no signs of abating. Consumers are now gathering information via the Internet, and also using digital means to book their hotel rooms, plane tickets, cruises, and even entire vacation packages."

Jupiter Communications. (1997) (http://www.jup.com/research/ reports/travel.shtml)

Intensive, Exclusive, and Selective Distribution

Each tourism organization must decide on its *distribution mix strategy* or how it will make its services available to potential travelers. The rapidly expanding number of retail travel agencies and tour operators in many countries is making these decisions more complex and difficult. The costs of distribution and the need to have the maximum exposure to potential travelers (*market coverage*) suggest using the largest possible number of travel trade intermediaries. However, the image of the services or destination and the motivations of individual travel trade intermediaries favor vertically integrated or vertically coordinated strategies or direct distribution. These strategies provide suppliers, carriers, destination marketing organizations, and travel trade intermediaries with the maximum control over sales and reservations.

The three broad strategy options

available are intensive, exclusive, or selective distribution. An *intensive distribution* strategy means maximizing the exposure of travel services by distributing through all available travel trade intermediaries (high market coverage). *Exclusive distribution* occurs when a carrier, supplier, tour wholesaler or operator, or destination marketing organization restricts the number of retail outlets for its services and attempts to have travel agents sell only its services, not those of competitors. This may be accomplished through franchising or ownership of retail outlets, i.e., through a vertically integrated or vertically coordinated approach. *Selective distribution* is a strategy somewhere between intensive and exclusive distribution. More than one but less than all available outlets are used.

Factors Affecting Distribution Mix Strategy Decisions

For the tourism marketer, the task is to select and design a distribution mix strategy that not only is the most effective in communicating with potential travelers and in accepting reservations, but that is also affordable. The following six factors are evaluated in making distribution mix strategy decisions.

1. *Market Coverage*   If a tour operator, supplier, carrier, or destination marketing organization decides not to use the retail travel agency network, an alternative distribution network has to be developed. In travel trade terms, this is called *bypassing* the retail travel agency network. This may be a lucrative strategy because the costs of travel agency commissions are eliminated. The use of electronic distribution through the World Wide Web and electronic mail is facilitating this strategy of dealing directly with travelers. However, in most countries, retail travel agencies offer widespread and growing market

coverage that is difficult for one single organization to duplicate.

2. *Costs*   The costs of establishing a retail or other direct distribution channel (e.g., a reservations service) are mainly fixed or overhead expenses. Salaries must be paid and offices maintained irrespective of the sales volume generated. Although a part of the compensation of sales representatives may be in the form of commissions, not many people are willing to work on a commission-only basis. In contrast, when working through travel trade intermediaries only variable costs are incurred. In fact, many travel agency commission payments are made after sales have been made. Fixed costs are reduced to a minimum.

3. *Positioning and Image*   The choice of distribution channel must be consistent with the positioning and image of the supplier, carrier, destination marketing organization, or tour wholesaler or operator. An expensive, high-quality tour, destination, or service should be marketed to an upscale demographic market segment through quality intermediaries who cater to upscale travelers.

4. *Motivation of Travel Trade Intermediaries*   Each organization within the tourism distribution system has a unique set of objectives and needs. These objectives and needs are not always compatible and create conflicts and stresses in the tourism distribution system. Travelers want a variety of services and products from which they can select the most satisfying travel experiences. Retail travel agents want to offer travelers a large inventory of destinations and travel services, but need to sell a mix of travel services that produce the maximum commissions. Tour wholesalers and operators want high volume and high profit margins but are concerned about

A high-quality destination such as Lake Geneva, Switzerland should be marketed to upscale travelers. Photo by Corel.

developing tours that motivate retail travel agents to sell them, while representing a minimum level of risk. Suppliers, carriers, and destination marketing organizations want to minimize distribution costs while getting the maximum exposure for their services. They want to generate high traffic volumes and encourage repeat business. The more integration within the channel, the more customer-contact employees are motivated to sell particular services or destinations at the expense of others.

When direct ownership is not feasible or legally permitted, suppliers, carriers, tour wholesalers and operators, and destination marketing organizations use a variety of motivation tactics with retail travel agencies. They offer higher commission rates (*overrides*) for higher volumes of booking. These higher rates of commission may be provided through *preferred supplier* or *vendor* relationships between the two parties. Familiarization trips or training seminars are arranged to increase product knowledge. A variety of sales support services may be provided to travel agents including toll-free telephone

"help desks," World Wide Web sites, and in-store merchandising displays.

5. *Characteristics of the Tourism Destination or Service* Not all tourism destinations and services are the same. Some tourism services, including domestic airline tickets, are purchased frequently and are often subject to discounting. They may be distributed through large numbers of retail outlets and in a variety of different ways. Other tourism services and destinations, such as long-haul tours and cruises, can be highly priced, are purchased infrequently, and are usually not subject to any discounting. Travelers perceive these services to be distinctive, complex, and expensive. The expertise of the travel agent and personal selling by the agent is required to secure bookings. In this case, the tourism destination or organization should be more selective in its choice of retail travel agency outlets.

6. *Economic Concentration* The amount of channel power depends upon the degree of economic con-

centration among a particular category of tourism organizations. The fewer tour wholesalers or operators serving a particular destination, the greater is the power of these companies in dealing with the destination's suppliers and carriers. This is especially true of smaller, long-haul tourism destinations that do not provide the volumes of visitors to be attractive to many tour companies. Examples of these destinations include Sri Lanka and Bhutan; two countries that are highly dependent on relatively few tour operators.

Germany is a country in which travel is exclusively distributed through vertically integrated channels; there is high economic concentration in the travel trade. Two tour operators (TUI and Neckermann und Reisen - NUR) account for over 50 percent of tour sales (Vellas & Becherel, 1995). These companies exert considerable power over destinations that are highly dependent on German visitors. Japan is another country in which there is a concentration of power among relatively few tour operators.

With the growth in the retail travel agency field in the United Kingdom and North America, there has been a movement away from distributing through as many retail travel agencies as possible (intensive distribution) to being more selective in choosing retailers (selective distribution). Carriers, suppliers, and destination marketing organizations want the maximum sales volumes. For tour wholesalers and operators, volume is even more critical to profitability. This suggests a strategy of using a maximum number of retail travel agencies. However, many tourism destinations and organizations have found that, while it is more risky to deal with a smaller number of travel agencies, the costs of servicing all agencies are prohibitive. Additionally, a small percentage of travel agencies often produces the majority of the business. Concentrating on those agencies that produce most sales results in a more efficient distribution system.

Tour Wholesalers and Operators

> "The choice of tour operators represents an essential part of any travel agency's business equation. Using reliable tour operators who deliver a quality product helps ensure customer satisfaction, a crucial ingredient to building repeat business and referrals."
>
> USTOA World Tour Guide (1994), 12

History

Although tour wholesaling began in the mid-nineteenth century, it was not until the 1960s and 1970s that the packaging of tours increased dramatically. The increase resulted from the development of larger aircraft capable of flying greater distances (the first Boeing 747 flew in 1970). Increased capacity led to lower airfares that stimulated demand for low-cost vacations. Although it is true that demand stimulates supply, supply can also create demand. To meet this demand, tour companies were established to assemble low-cost vacation packages.

Categories of Tours and Packages

Four main categories of tours and packages are offered by tour wholesalers, tour operators, travel agencies, airlines, and some suppliers:

1. **Escorted tours:** A type of organized tour that includes the services of a tour director who accompanies an individual or group throughout the tour.

2. **Hosted tours:** A type of organized tour that includes the services of a tour host who meets an individual or group at each destination to make local arrangements, but does not accompany the group through the entire tour.

3. **Package tours:** A type of organized, individual or group tour, that includes airfare and some ground transportation arrangements, but does not necessarily include the services of anyone meeting the individual or group at the destination.

4. **Independent tours:** An individualized tour assembled by a travel agent, airline, or tour wholesaler to a specific destination in which the tour patron travels independently with selected family members or friends, but not with groups of strangers.

The term *all-inclusive package* is also used a great deal in tourism. This refers to the complete range of tourism services included in the price of the package. The packages offered by all-inclusive resort chains such as Club Med and Sandals fit into this category, as do the vacations provided by cruise lines. These are often American Plan or "full-board" packages including three main meals per day (Vellas & Becherel, 1995).

Economics of Tour Wholesaling and Operations

As mentioned earlier, the independent tour wholesaling and operations business is very concentrated in several countries, with a small number of companies accounting for a large percentage of the total revenue generated. The tour business is also characterized by relative ease of entry, high velocity of cash flow, low return on sales, and the potential for a high return on equity investment.

Ease of Entry   Some countries, states, or provinces force tour companies to be licensed by a government agency. This is due to a history of tour operator business failures and also to unscrupulous practices of some past operators (e.g., taking deposits from travelers and then disappearing). Several countries require tour operators to have a proven track record of several years of operation and to post bonds to protect their tour patrons in the event of a bankruptcy.

Other countries, including the U.S., do not require tour operator licensing by government agencies. Instead, governments constrain tour companies by various regulations or tour operators themselves are self-policing. For example, in the U.S. the U.S. Tour Operators Association (USTOA) requires its active members to post a bond of $1 million in trust to protect customers' deposits and payments in the event of the company's closure or bankruptcy. Often members of travel trade associations adopt a *code of ethics* or *conduct* that shows their commitment to ethical business practices that protect travelers. Despite the existence of these measures, in many countries it is relatively easy to become a tour wholesaler or operator. This is a result of the low initial investment required to get started in tour wholesaling.

Cash Flow   The flow of cash is crucial to a tour wholesaler. The wholesaler signs contracts for bulk quantities of transportation and *ground services* (airport transfers, lodging, meals, entertainment, sightseeing, ground transportation by coach or other means). By contracting in bulk for ground services, the wholesaler receives discounts on regular rates and prices. For example, a wholesaler may contract for 200 rooms in a hotel every night for three months. The ground or *land tour* portion is then marked up by about 10 to 15 percent by the tour wholesaler to provide their profit (Poynter, 1993). The tour wholesaler must also allow for a *travel agent commission*, which may be in the range of 10 to 15 percent of the ground services costs. If air fares are to be included in the tour price, they are then added to the marked-up ground services portion of the tour to arrive at a final tour selling price. The air fares usually cannot be marked up because the commissions go directly to the retail travel agents who are the only ones accredited by the appropriate regulating bodies to sell airline tickets.

The tour wholesaler must make *advance deposits* for ground services to secure them. To offset these advance payments to suppliers (or *vendors*), cash flow or *float* is generated when customers' deposits and final payments are received prior to the tour departure date. Tour wholesalers usually do not pay the outstanding balances for ground service (less the advance deposits) until after the tour. The cash flow (excess of customer deposits and final payments over advance deposits to suppliers) is used to pay the tour wholesalers' operating expenses. Problems arise when the cash flow from one tour has to be used to finance the preparation of another. If demand slows, tour wholesalers with few liquid assets to protect them against cash deficits may become insolvent or bankrupt.

Return on Sales The average return on sales for an independent tour wholesaler is low and sales volume is the key to profitability. Where airfares are included in the tour price, a significant proportion of tour sales comes from the transportation component, of which 85 percent or more goes to airlines. The tour wholesaler does not receive any of the air ticket revenue. The remaining share of the tour sales price covers the ground services, travel agent commission, and tour wholesaler's profit. Assuming that these represent about 50 to 60 percent of the tour sales price, and that travel agents get a 10 to 15 percent commission on the ground services portion, then the tour wholesaler makes a 10 to 15 percent profit on about 40 to 55 percent of the tour sales price. This means that the tour wholesaler's return on sales is low, at about 4 to 8 percent.

In costing a tour, the tour wholesaler must allow for *variable costs* and *fixed costs*. Variable costs fluctuate directly with the number of people on the tour. They include the amounts paid to airlines, ground suppliers, and retail travel agents (in agent commissions). Travel agents receive commissions from the airline (transportation component) and the tour wholesaler (ground services or land tour component). Fixed costs do not vary at all with the number of people on the tour. They include the tour wholesaler's employee wages and benefits for such items as tour preparation, reservations, record keeping, and accounting. The fixed costs also include promotion expenses, which may encompass brochure printing and distribution costs. Finally, some of the land tour costs are fixed including the cost of the tour director or manager (if the tour is escorted) and the cost of any chartered vehicles (e.g., motor coaches).

Return on Equity Because the capital required to become a tour wholesaler is low, a large return on equity can be made. This potentially high return on equity (tour profits divided by the wholesaler's equity investment) results from the

---

Quick Trip 16.2
What Travel Agents Look For in a Tour Operator

In 1995, the Institute of Certified Travel Agents (ICTA) conducted a survey of 500 travel agents related to tour operators and destinations. One of the questions included in this survey was "How important are the following attributes when choosing a tour operator?" The agents were asked to rank the attributes on a 10-point scale with a score of 10 being the highest level of importance. The results were as follows:

- Reputation of the tour operator (9.5)
- Previous client satisfaction (9.4)
- Package quality and diversity (9.1)
- Price (8.7)
- Commission incentives (8.3)
- Cancellation policies (8.0)
- Override or compensation plan (7.9)
- Payment policies (7.1)
- Deposit policies (6.7)

Source: 1995 ICTA Travel Agency Survey: Tours & Destinations. *Travel Weekly*, (January 22, 1996), 4.

low equity investment and not from the net profit on tour sales (which is relatively low).

Functions of Tour Wholesalers and Operators

The main function of a tour wholesaler is to combine both transportation and ground services into tours to be sold through retail travel agencies to individual or group travelers. This role is performed by independent tour wholesaling companies. The term wholesaling implies that these companies do not sell directly to the public.

Many tour wholesalers tailor their tour offerings by target market, destination, mode of transportation, or type of activity or special interest. Some wholesalers cater to specific segments of the market (such as national or ethnic groups), while others "mass market" by promoting popular "sun and sand" destinations. Still other wholesalers specialize in developing tours to specific destinations or regions of the world (e.g., AAT Kings Australian Tours, African Travel, Australian Pacific Tours, CIE Tours International/Ireland, and Pacific Delight Tours). Some wholesalers specialize in one type of transportation. The majority of tours marketed by independent tour wholesalers involve air travel.

Tour and package development is also done by other types of organizations. Retail travel agents prepare individual (*foreign independent tours* or *FITs*) and group tours (*group inclusive tours* or *GITs*) that they sell to travelers. Airlines and railway companies have wholesaling divisions that put together tours. Companies specializing in incentive travel, cruise lines, travel clubs, educational institutions, and nonprofit organizations (unions, religious groups, associations, government and quasi-government agencies) also assemble tours and packages.

A single tour program consists of four parts: (1) Tour planning and preparation; (2) tour marketing; (3) tour administration; and (4) tour evaluation.

1. *Tour Planning and Preparation*

The planning of a tour must begin with some market research. The purpose of this research should be to indicate to the wholesaler which tours will sell and which tour ingredients are essential to attract tour patrons. Both secondary (previously published information) and primary (information collected for the first time) research should be used. The secondary research sources might include the reports of tour operator associations and research organizations, published statistics on arrivals to tourist destinations, directories of tour programs, competitors' brochures, and the wholesaler's own past operating results that show which tours have sold well and been profitable. The primary research steps might include surveying retail travel agents and past and potential tour patrons.

When planning and developing tours for new destinations, tour wholesalers may participate in *familiarization trips* (or FAMs) sponsored by destination marketing organizations, carriers, or suppliers. These trips help the tour wholesaler to determine tour potential, evaluate ground services, and solicit potential government and private-sector partnerships for promoting the tour program. At this point, detailed tour specifications are prepared such as departure dates, tour length, and modes of transportation and ground services to be used. These activities often take place a year to eighteen months before the first tour departure date.

The actual *tour program* is usually confirmed from twelve to fourteen months prior to the first tour departure. Ground services are

negotiated and supplier agreements signed. Transportation commitments are made. When these steps are completed, the tour program can be finalized. The tour price is calculated by taking the negotiated costs for ground services and adding a mark-up that, when the expected number of tour patrons is considered, is sufficient to cover fixed costs and the tour wholesaler's profit. A checklist for pricing a tour is illustrated in figure 16.2.

The three columns in part D of figure 16.2 show the cost computations for three different group sizes. The first is the minimum size of group necessary. This would be based upon a specified minimum number of people that the airline or ground service suppliers require to guarantee prices to the tour wholesaler. In some cases, the type of airfare used may necessitate that the wholesaler guarantee a certain minimum number of passengers. The third column shows costs based upon the maximum number of travelers possible on the tour. The costs in the middle column are based on the tour wholesaler's best estimate of the most likely number of tour patrons.

The tour wholesaler's mark-up is expressed as either a percentage of ground service costs or as a dollar figure. The mark-up has to be realistic yet also reflect the time and effort involved in organizing the tour. Airfare is added to total ground services costs and mark-up to arrive at the selling price for the retail travel agent. The final selling price is calculated by adding a retail travel agent commission.

The mechanics of handling reservations and payment are made and brochure production begun. Brochure production is very expensive and part of the production costs may be paid by the airline involved in the tour or one or more of the ground service suppliers. Appropriate commission rates and vol-

Tour _____   Tour Dates _____

Compiled _____   Cancellation Date _____

Revised _____   Gateway _____

A. Variable Costs (per person)
1. Airfare Basis .... _____
2. Surcharges .... _____
3. Airport Taxes .... _____
4. Transfers .... _____
5. Baggage Tips .... _____
6. Hotel Rooms .... _____

Single Room Supplement ...... _____

7. State/VAT taxes .... _____
8. Service Charges .... _____
9. Meals .... _____
10. Meal Taxes & Tips .... _____
11. Sightseeing .... _____
12. Admissions .... _____

13. Package .... _____
    based on ( )
14. Insurance .... _____
15. Publications/   _____
    Postage ....
16. Miscellaneous................. _____

Total .... _____

B. Fixed Costs (Tour Director)
1. Transportation................ _____
   (home/gateway/home)
2. Transportation................ _____
   (on tour)
3. Airport Taxes .... _____
4. Hotel Rooms .... _____
5. Meals, Taxes, Tips .... _____
6. Transfers .... _____

Include only costs not complemented

7. Sightseeing/ .... _____
   Admissions
8. Baggage Tips .... _____
9. Insurance .... _____
10. Meals/Hotels .... _____
    (Day before/
    Day after tour)
11. Travelers Checks .... _____

12. Passports/Visas .... _____
13. Vaccinations .... _____
14. Currency Conversion ..... _____
15. Miscellaneous................ _____
16. Salary .... _____
    (days@   )

Total .... _____

C. Fixed Costs (Group)
1. Chartered Vehicles .... _____
2. Tolls/Ferries .... _____
3. Sightseeing .... _____
4. Admissions .... _____
5. Local Guides .... _____
6. Transfers .... _____

7. Programs .... _____
8. Speaker Fee .... _____
9. Driver Tips.................. _____
10. Brochures .... _____
11. Promotion .... _____
12. Communications .... _____

13. Administrative .... _____
14. Miscellaneous................. _____
15. Orientation .... _____
16. Fund Raising .... _____

Total .... _____

Grand Total of all Fixed Costs

D. Computations Group Size .... _____ _____ _____

Land Costs

A. Total Variable Costs .... _____ _____ _____

B. Grand Total of Fixed Costs
   (Divided by Size of Group) .... _____ _____ _____

C. Sum of A and B .... _____ _____ _____

D. Dollar Markup (%) .... _____ _____ _____

E. Airfare .... _____ _____ _____

F. Sum of C, D, and E .... _____ _____ _____

Selling Price .... _____ _____ _____

E.
Minimum number of paying passengers. _____   Mark-up on Land (D)_____
_____   Air Commission_____
Maximum number of paying passengers._____   Gross Net _____
_____   (Per Person)

Source: Howe, R.M. Analyzing the trip: Checklist of steps. The 1980 Travel Agency Guide to Business and Group Travel. *Travel Weekly*. (April 1980), 110.

Figure 16.2   Tour Price Structure Sheet.

ume incentives are also negotiated with retail travel agents. At this point, there are typically ten months left before the first tour departs.

2. *Tour Marketing*   The marketing of a tour is the aspect most crucial to its success. The characteristics of the tour marketing program depend upon the size of the wholesaler and the market segments being targeted. All marketing programs involve brochure distribution, advertising, personal selling, and other sales promotions (e.g., promotional evenings).

Brochures are often large and expensive to produce in high-quality color. While the brochures may be distributed to all travel agencies, it is more efficient to use a selective distribution process. Emphasis should be given to agencies who have provided tour patrons to the wholesaler in the past and especially those that have generated the greatest volumes of past tour patrons. Brochures may also be provided to agencies whose customers fit the profile of the target market for the tour program.

Travel trade advertising may be used to promote a specific tour program or to promote the tour wholesaler's overall services. Advertisements placed in travel trade journals, such as *Travel Weekly* are normally factual, describing the tours and giving travel agents booking information. Toll-free telephone numbers, electronic mail numbers, and World Wide Web addresses are included to encourage travel agents to request tour brochures and other sales materials. In addition, tour wholesalers and operators employ sales representatives who concentrate on selling tours to travel agents regarded as the best prospects.

Consumer advertising tends to be less factual and more emotional. Very colorful and eye-catching images are used to attract attention and create interest in the tours. Ads may be placed in consumer travel magazines and usually advise travelers to book through travel agents. Advertising is also done through direct mail using the tour wholesaler's list of past tour patrons and mailing lists of potential patrons. Again, consumer advertisements tend to be of the direct-response variety, urging potential travelers to request a brochure by a toll-free telephone number, fax number, or through electronic mail and the World Wide Web.

Marketing begins 9 to 12 months prior to departure and continues until a few days beforehand. Reservations, deposits, and payments are requested from one to two months in advance of the departure. If insufficient advance bookings are made, tours may be consolidated or promotion increased.

3. *Tour Administration*   The administration of a tour begins six months prior to departure. Detailed schedules or worksheets are prepared describing the tour program, and a reservation system sufficient to detail the documentation and payment status of each tour patron is set up. Liaison procedures are established between the reservation system and the ground service suppliers at each destination.

Reservations are usually received by telephone, fax, or via computer from retail travel agencies. They are confirmed, recorded, and filed. Deposits and payments are processed and documentation sent to the travel agency for distribution to travelers. Upon completion of the tour, the suppliers are paid. The tour operation part of the tour may be handled by the tour wholesaler or by ground service operators (e.g., inbound tour operators or motor coach companies) or other destination management companies based in the destinations.

4. *Tour Evaluation*   When the tour is over, the tour wholesaler may evaluate its success through a variety of means. First, it is most important to get each tour patron's opinions on the success of the tour and their satisfaction levels. The tour wholesaler might do this by having each tour patron complete a questionnaire or comment card at the end of the tour or soon after its completion. Second, the wholesaler might contact all the suppliers involved in the tour to get their reactions. Finally, the tour wholesaler needs to complete an internal evaluation to determine the return on investment for each tour.

Operating Cycle

The tour wholesaling and operations business tends to be seasonal. At any one time the wholesaler's staff may be preparing the following year's program while marketing

and operating the existing year's offering. To reduce seasonality, tour wholesalers may operate tour programs to several destinations that each have different seasonal patterns of demand (e.g., winter sports destinations in winter and sun-and-sand destinations in summer).

Retail Travel Agencies

"Why use an AFTA Travel Agent? Today the travel industry is highly specialised and the average traveler is presented with numerous alternatives to choose from —the type of transport, the standard and location of accommodation, the dollar value of packaged holidays and the quality of service provided by staff. A good agent is something of a personal counsellor, a psychologist and an expert in the art and science of travel!"

The Australian Federation of Travel Agents Limited. (1995)

History

Thomas Cook is credited with developing the concept of a travel agent in 1841 when he chartered a train to carry people from Leicester to Loughborough, a distance of 22 miles, to attend a temperance convention. Today, The Thomas Cook Group is a travel agency giant, owned by a German bank, with 1,800 offices in 100 countries.

In the early 1900s, rail travel was the primary mode of transportation for business travelers. Little pleasure travel existed. The travel agent of the day was the hotel porter, who would make reservations for business travelers staying at the hotel. The porter received a commission from the railroad and would add a delivery charge for going to the railroad station to purchase the ticket. The airlines, which first purchased planes with seats for passengers in the late 1920s, saw the railroads as their major competitor for the business market. (The pleasure market would not become significant for another ten years.) The airlines approached the hotel porters, equipped them with ticket stock, and offered a 5 percent commission for making the sale. Little expertise was required as most carriers had only one route and the tickets already contained information about fare origin and destination of the flight. The feeling of the carriers was that the porters were providing a ticketing service for business that was already there rather than creating new business. Thus, from the beginning hotel porters and then travel agents were seen as distributors of tickets and entitled to a small commission.

Airlines then began to open their own offices in hotels and this provided large enough traffic volumes to justify the expense. The porters were forced out of business. Airlines restricted the new breed of travel agent from opening offices since they would compete with the airlines' sales offices. After World War II, two trends assisted the growth of retail travel agencies: the expansion of vacation or holiday travel and increasing popularity of international travel. The airlines continued to exert considerable influence over the opening of travel agencies. For example, in the U.S. prior to 1959, when the so-called need clause was abolished by the Civil Aeronautics Board, a U.S. travel agency could be opened only if it was sponsored by an airline and its opening approved by two-thirds of the airlines represented. The sponsoring airline was responsible for checking that the agency had financial stability, an acceptable location, and staff with sufficient experience. Today, it is necessary for agencies to be appointed by their national and international airline agencies to sell tickets and receive commissions. For example,

to book tickets on international airlines, retail travel agents must be approved by IATA (International Air Transport Association).

Functions of Retail Travel Agents

In essence, retail travel agencies are the department stores of tourism. Around the world, they provide thousands of "travel shops" for suppliers, carriers, destination marketing organizations, and the other travel trade intermediaries. A customer can buy all types of travel services at an agency including tickets for planes and railways, hotels and resorts, packages and tours, car rentals, and travel insurance. The main functions of retail travel agencies are as follows:

Distribution and Sales Network
Travel agents bring together the sellers and buyers of travel; in this role they can be called "travel brokers." They act as the official "agents" of travel **principals**; the organizations that actually provide the travel services. Travel agents provide an enormous distribution network for suppliers, carriers, destination marketing organizations, and other travel intermediaries. According to the IATA, there were over 83,000 accredited travel agency locations in the world in 1996 (see figure 16.3).

The U.S. has the largest concentration of travel agencies, followed by Europe. According to

the Airlines Reporting Corporation (ARC), there were 33,715 full-service travel agencies and 13,571 satellite ticket printer locations in the U.S. at the end of 1996. The greatest growth in the number of travel agencies appears to be in the Asia-Pacific region.

In return for their services, suppliers, carriers, and other travel trade intermediaries pay travel agents **commissions**, which are normally based on a certain percentage of the total value of the reservation. In most countries, travel agency commission rates are in the 5 to 10 percent range. Special arrangements between individual carriers and suppliers, known as **preferred supplier** or **vendor relationships**, allow the travel agents to earn extra points of commission (**overrides**). During the 1990s, some agencies began charging their customers **service fees** in an effort to improve profitability in the face of shrinking airline commissions.

Reservations and Ticketing
The placement of reservations and the distribution of tickets (mainly for airlines) are traditional roles of retail travel agencies. Reservations and ticketing used to be very time-consuming and labor-intensive but advances in computer and telecommunications technology have speeded up these processes. **Computerized reservation systems** or CRSs, which were first introduced in the early 1970s, have provided

AREAS	APPROVED TRAVEL AGENCY LOCATIONS	PERCENTAGE GROWTH OVER 1995
Americas (excluding the United States and Canada)	6,574	1.3%
Asia-Pacific	7,460	11.4%
Canada	4,031	0.7%
Europe, Middle East, Africa	27,693	8.6%
U.S.A.	37,854	0.6%
Total	**83,612**	**4.1%**

Source: International Air Transport Association, Montreal, Quebec. Figures are at June 30, 1996.

Figure 16.3 Agency Locations Accredited by IATA, 1996.

Quick Trip 16.3
The ASTA Code of Ethics

The American Society of Travel Agents (ASTA) is one of the largest travel agency associations in the world. Although its headquarters are in the U.S., the 25,000 ASTA members are located in over 136 countries. The ASTA Code of Ethics is as follows:

1. **Accuracy**. ASTA members will be factual and accurate when providing information about the services of any firm they represent. They will not use deceptive practices.

2. **Disclosure**. ASTA members will provide in writing, upon written request, complete details about the cost, restrictions, and other terms and conditions, of any travel service sold, including cancellation and service fee policies. Full details of the time, place, duration, and nature of any sales or promotional presentation the consumer will be required to attend in connection with his/her travel arrangements will be disclosed in writing before any payment is accepted.

3. **Responsiveness**. ASTA members will promptly respond to their clients' complaints.

4. **Refunds**. ASTA members will remit any undisputed funds under their control within the specified time limit. Reasons for delay in providing funds will be given to the claimant promptly.

5. **Cooperation**. ASTA members will cooperate with any inquiry conducted by ASTA to resolve any dispute involving consumers or another member.

6. **Confidences**. ASTA members will not use improperly obtained client lists or other confidential information obtained from an employee's former employer.

7. **Confidentiality**. ASTA members will treat every client transaction confidentially and not disclose any information without permission of the client, unless required by law.

8. **Affiliation**. ASTA members will not falsely represent a person's affiliation with their firm.

9. **Conflict of interest**. ASTA members will not allow any preferred relationship with a supplier to interfere with the interests of their clients.

10. **Compliance**. ASTA members shall abide by all federal, state and local laws and regulations.

Source: ASTA Web site.

Amadeus, Galileo, Sabre, and Worldspan).

The electronic distribution of airline and other tickets began in the late 1980s. Today, **satellite ticket printers** are being used by many travel agencies and corporations to print out tickets through special machines at locations away from the main agency office. During the 1990s, the concept of **ticketless travel** by air arrived. Also known as **electronic ticketing**, this allows travelers to show up at airline check-ins without a paper ticket. Although many of these reservations are being made by travel agents, travelers are increasingly being able to use electronic ticket through their own personal computers.

Information Provision and Travel Counseling   The most traditional role of the retail travel agent is that of serving as a "travel expert." Travel agents are a major source of travel information for individual and group travelers. Travel agents are knowledgeable professionals whose advice and counseling is crucial to many travelers. Travelers expect agents to possess a wide knowledge of travel services and companies, along with an in-depth command of world geography.

Throughout the world, travel agency associations are working hard to increase the professionalism of travel agents. The Association of British Travel Agents (ABTA) offers a Travel Agents Certificate course (ABTAC) that can be taken through a self-study, distance education format. The Institute of Certified Travel Agents (ICTA) in the U.S. has offered the Certified Travel Counselor program since the early 1970s. The Canadian Institute of Travel Counsellors (CITC) is ICTA's equivalent in Canada and offers the Canadian Travel Counsellor designation. The Australian Federation of Travel Agents (AFTA) established the

---

travel agents with instant access to an ever-expanding inventory of the services of the airlines, suppliers, and other travel trade intermediaries. Almost all travel agencies today are equipped with CRS systems.

While CRS systems began to develop within individual countries, they soon became global in their coverage. During the 1980s, five major **global distribution systems** or GDSs emerged (Abacus,

Australian Travel Agents Qualifications program in 1992 to increase agent professionalism through education and training.

Design of Individualized Tour Itineraries   Another traditional role of the retail travel agent has been the design of individualized tour itineraries for their customers. The preparation of ***foreign independent tours*** used to be a mainstay source of business for many travel agencies before the issuing of airline tickets and the booking of pre-packaged group tours became more predominant. In this role, the travel agent arranges all the air travel and land arrangements for an individual customer in the traveler's destination of choice.

Corporate Travel Departments

"Travel managers have existed in larger corporations since approximately 1968. However, in many small and medium-sized companies, the traveler controlled the purchase decision and travel was not necessarily viewed as a separate and controllable cost item. A company would use multiple travel agencies. There was limited travel data, and the corporation received almost no financial benefits because of its lack of control and knowledge."

> Jenkins, D. (1993).
> Managing Business Travel.
> Business One Irwin, 3

History

Corporate travel departments are a relatively new phenomenon in tourism. Historically, business travel arrangements within a company were made on a decentralized basis. Each department, division, or unit made its own reservations. In most cases, this meant that many carriers, suppliers, and travel agencies were used by one company. The most important factor in making travel arrangements was the individual traveler's own preferences.

Since about the 1970s, many corporations, government agencies, and nonprofits have created their own in-house corporate travel departments. These departments are often administered by full-time ***corporate travel managers*** who are professionals in the arrangement, negotiation, and control of business travel. The traditional ways of organizing travel were increasingly found to be inefficient as cost control became more critical in worsening general economic conditions. Corporate travel departments were created for three main reasons: (1) to cut business travel expenses; (2) to provide better service to travelers, and (3) to increase corporate purchasing power in travel (Morrison, Ladig, & Hsieh, 1994).

Functions of Corporate Travel Departments

The major function of a corporate travel department is to coordinate and control all of the travel by employees and associates of the organization. The typical roles of the corporate travel department include the following:

Quick Trip 16.4
The U.S. Travel Agency Business

Every two years beginning in 1970 *Travel Weekly* magazine has conducted the U.S. *"Travel Agency Survey"* with the help of the research company Louis Harris and Associates. The *"1996 U.S. Travel Agency Survey"* released in August 1996 showed that there were 33,593 travel agencies at the end of 1995 compared with just 6,686 in 1970. The total revenues of U.S. travel agencies in 1995 was $101 billion and the average travel agency grossed $3 million. Some of the highlights of the 1996 survey were:

- **Organization:** Single-location agencies (69%), branch offices (19%), head offices (12%).
- **Sources of revenues:** Airlines (61%), cruise lines (14%), hotels (10%), miscellaneous (8%), car rentals (7%).
- **Trip purpose segments:** Leisure/pleasure travel represented 49% of total revenues; business travel was 42% and combined leisure/business travel was 9%.
- **Domestic versus international revenues:** Domestic bookings (69%); international bookings (31%).
- **Staffing:** Average of 5.9 full-time employees per travel agency.
- **Automation:** 95% of agencies use CRS systems; 21% use the Internet.
- **Retail and wholesale operations:** 24% of retail travel agencies also have wholesale operations; 76% were retail only.

Source: 1996 U.S. Travel Agency Survey. *Travel Weekly*, 55, (69), Section 2, August 29, 1996.

Negotiation with Carriers and Suppliers

A primary role of the corporate travel department is to negotiate for the most competitive prices with airlines, hotels and car rental companies. The central coordination of travel has given many corporations great purchasing and negotiating power when dealing with the carriers and suppliers. From a fiscal standpoint, it is in the corporation's best interest that the corporate travel department negotiate the lowest possible travel prices.

Development of Corporate Travel Policy

Another important role is the creation of a corporate travel policy outlining the conditions, practices, and processes that must be followed when employees are traveling out of town.

Travel policies should be written and communicated to all employees. The written guidelines cover reservation and ticketing procedures, preferred airlines and travel suppliers, per diems (maximum expenses reimbursed per day), allowable travel expenses, and expense reporting procedures.

Monitoring of Travel Expenses and Travel Policy Compliance

The corporate travel department is usually responsible for setting an annual budget for travel for the company. The control of this budget during the year is exercised by monitoring employee expense reporting and, in particular, ensuring *compliance* with the written corporate travel policies. Since the early 1980s, these departments have helped their organizations gain more control over the use of the growing number of frequent travel reward programs provided by airline, hotel, and car rental firms.

Reservations and Ticketing

Some corporate travel departments act as in-house travel agents and take care of the reservations and ticketing for employees. It is more common, however, for the reservations and ticketing function to be *outsourced* to retail travel agencies. In many countries, the importance of corporate travel accounts to retail travel agents has greatly increased in the past 30 years. The streamlining of corporate travel has brought the independent agent more business and has also provided the basis for the establishment of large *corporate travel agencies* exclusively serving corporations (often called *outplants*). There has also been growth in *inplants*; travel agent offices located within the physical premises of corporate clients. Another route followed by some corporations is to themselves become travel agents, operating their own in-house, fully accredited agencies.

Meeting and Incentive Planning

Some corporate travel departments are involved in the organization of corporate meetings and incentive travel trips. In most cases, these tasks are outsourced to other companies that specialize in the organization of meetings and incentive travel. It is also possible that the corporation may employ a full- or part-time meeting planner who may work in a unit outside of the corporate travel department.

Monitoring Travel Agency Performance

Most corporations work with one or more retail travel agencies. The corporate travel department monitors the performance of these travel agencies both in financial terms and in employee satisfaction with agency service levels.

As with travel agents, efforts are growing to increase the professionalism and professional recognition of corporate travel managers. Associations of corporate travel executives have been created. In North America, the two major associations representing corporate travel managers are the National Business Travel Association (NBTA) and the Association of Corporate Travel Executives (ACTE). The NBTA is perhaps the biggest organization of its type in the world and has 1,200 professional travel manager members. It also operates the Certified Corporate Travel Executive (CCTE) program.

Incentive Travel Planners

> "A new study being released this month supports the proposition that incentive travel programs result in increased sales—and shows that at one company, those increases amounted to 250 percent."
>
> Rosen, C. (1996). SITE releases case study. Business Travel News, (337), A6

History

The first incentive travel trip was offered by the National Cash Register Company of Dayton, Ohio in 1906. The winners of this award at NCR received a trip to company headquarters (Ricci & Holland, 1992). Since then incentive travel has enjoyed significant growth—especially since the 1970s. It is used by large- and medium-sized corporations to reward company employees, distributors, and sometimes potential customers, typically for outstanding work-related performance. Free travel as a motivational tool is becoming increasingly potent in the developed countries.

Historically, incentive travel trips have been used to recognize outstanding sales performance by company employees as well as dealers and distributors. The number of motivational applications of incentive travel has grown and it is now being used for increasing plant production, encouraging better customer service, improving plant safety, introducing new products, selling new accounts, and enhancing morale and good will. The variety of incentive travel offerings has also expanded and now includes more modest weekend vacations as well as the more traditional, once-in-a-lifetime trips to exotic destinations.

Functions of Incentive Travel Planners

The lucrative nature of incentive travel has attracted great interest among all types of tourism organizations including travel trade intermediaries, suppliers, carriers, and destination marketing organizations. The growth of incentive travel has been beneficial for retail travel agents, airlines, hotels, resorts, and other suppliers. It also represents an area of new market potential for national, state, regional, and city tourism marketing agencies. Many airlines, hotel companies, NTOs, and convention and visitors bureaus have established special divisions or departments to serve the growing incentive travel market.

The outcome of the rapidly growing popularity of incentive travel has been the emergence of a rather complex distribution system. The key players are a small number of full-service *incentive houses* and a growing number of smaller, more specialized *incentive travel planning companies*. The full-service incentive houses provide the full range of incentives, including both merchandise and travel. They include two incentive industry giants based in the U.S., the Carlson Marketing Group, Minneapolis, and Maritz, Inc., Fenton, Missouri. The functions of incentive travel planners vary by the type of company but they include the following:

Design and Implementation of Motivational Program

When a company decides to use incentive travel, this is usually done to motivate people to achieve higher levels of work performance. Incentive travel planning companies are en-

---

> ### Quick Trip 16.5
> ## Objectives of Incentive Travel Programs
>
> *Incentive* magazine prepares the FACTS Survey of Incentive Travel. The 1995 FACTS Survey indicated the following objectives for incentive travel programs:
>
> - Increase overall volume (78%)
> - Sell new accounts (55%)
> - Improve morale/good will (50%)
> - Introduce new products (41%)
> - Move full line/slow items (34%)
> - Support consumer promotions (29%)
> - Offset competition (27%)
> - Prepare for stronger season (22%)
> - Build dealer traffic (22%)
> - Bolster slow season (17%)
>
> Witt, Gammon, & White (1992) suggest that there are five broader objectives for a company to engage in incentive travel:
>
> - To attain business objectives through individual and/or group targets.
> - To facilitate communications and "networking" opportunities, particularly with company executives.
> - To foster corporate culture and social interaction.
> - To generate enthusiasm for the following business period.
> - To foster loyalty to the company.
>
> Source: 1996 FACTS Survey, *Incentive* magazine; Witt, S.F., Gammon, S., & White, J. (1992). Incentive travel: Overview and case study of Canada as a destination for the UK market. *Tourism Management, 13,* 275–287.

---

gaged to design and implement the incentive travel programs. The first function of the incentive travel planner is usually to design the motivational program. The objective is to excite potential trip winners about the prospect of winning so that they will increase their performance levels. The motivational program may include color brochures, slide shows, videotapes, or special meetings with presentations on the trip.

Design of Tour Program Incentive travel planners function as a specialized tour wholesaler. They design incentive tour programs according to their clients' specifications and budgets. Negotiations are made with carriers and suppliers for the trip components. Both domestic and international trips are developed.

Tour Operation The incentive travel planning company may also operate the incentive travel program including providing tour escorts to accompany the group. More often, however, *destination management companies* or *inbound tour operators* are subcontracted to provide the on-site services to the incentive trip recipients. Often these on-site arrangements include the staging of special activities and events, tours, and elaborately themed meals.

Reservations and Ticketing   The incentive travel company may itself do the reservations and ticketing, if it is accredited by the appropriate airline and supplier agencies. In other cases, these tasks may be given to retail travel agencies. Some retail travel agencies have themselves become involved in planning incentive trips, others simply play the travel fulfillment role by making air and hotel reservations for the incentive travel planning companies.

Program Evaluation   Because incentive travel is being used as a marketing tool, it is especially crucial to evaluate the effectiveness of each incentive travel program. The incentive travel planner may assist with program evaluation by comparing program costs to benefits, especially increased sales. For the company sponsoring the trips, it is important to calculate the return on investment. The incentive travel winners may also be surveyed to determine their satisfaction with trips.

Many incentive travel planners, carriers, and suppliers belong to the Society of Incentive and Travel Executives (SITE). SITE's mission is to be "a worldwide organization of business professionals dedicated to the recognition and development of motivational and performance improvement strategies of which travel is a key component." SITE offers a variety of educational services, which include its "University of Incentive Travel" programs in North America and Europe.

Convention-Meeting Planners

> "Conventions represent a special kind of tourism. People leave their home community as individuals or in small groups to join hundreds or thousands of others at a destination for a common purpose. In many ways, the destination is less important than the purpose for the group gathering, and the 'tourism product' is the facilities to host the event at the destination."
>
> Hiller, H. (1995). Conventions as mega-events. Tourism Management, 16, 375

History

Another part of tourism that has enjoyed great growth since the 1970s has been the staging of conventions, corporate meetings, congresses, exhibitions and trade shows, and other similar events. This component of business travel is often referred to as the **MICE** business, an acronym for meetings, incentives, conventions, and exhibitions. The increased popularity of these events has benefited all parts of tourism and many destinations throughout the world. As with incentive travel, it has provided the foundation for new types of specialists, called convention-meeting planners, and has created new linkages in the tourism distribution system.

Functions of Convention-Meeting Planners

The major functions of convention-meeting planners are to develop, coordinate, implement, and evaluate conventions and meetings of various sizes and types. There are three distinct stages to this function.

1. *Convention-Meeting Planning*   Convention-meeting planners prepare and administer budgets for each event. They coordinate the selection of sites, hotels, meeting and exhibit space, and other suppliers. This development of bid packages or *request for proposals* (RFPs) and conduct *site inspections*. They negotiate with hotels, airlines, audiovisual suppliers, meeting facility managers and other suppliers to get the best deals for their groups. Planners may set up committees to help with the design of speaker, sponsorship, entertainment and guest programs. Convention-meeting planners design promotions and communicate this information to company employees or association members. For conventions, exhibitions, and conferences, this role involves promotions to build attendance to acceptable levels.

2. *On-site Coordination*   The convention-meeting planner plays a crucial role during the staging of each event as the liaison between the sponsoring association or company and the service providers at the destination. This person is the key to ensuring that the event runs as it was planned and that unexpected problems are corrected.

3. *Convention-Meeting Evaluation*   As with incentive travel, the convention-meeting planner must carefully evaluate the success of each event after its completion. A cost-benefit analysis is prepared that may include a comparison of costs with the revenues created through registration and other participant services.

There are several associations of professional convention-meeting planners around the world. Two of the largest are ICCA (International Congress and Convention Association) and MPI (Meeting Professionals International). MPI operates the Certified Meeting Professional (CMP) designation program.

Electronic Distribution Systems and the Future

> *"Almost 37% of respondents claim that they use the Web instead of watching TV on a daily basis. An additional 29.03% say the Web replaces TV on a weekly basis, usually more than once a week. These numbers, when used in conjunction with the use of e-mail as being on equal par with the phone, paint a tremendously strong picture of the rapid integration of the Internet and the World Wide Web into the fabric of the lives of those who currently use it. This is truly an amazing time."*
>
> *GVU's sixth WWW User Survey, (http://www.cc.gatech. edu/gvu/user_surveys/ survey-10-1996/#exec/)*

Technological advances will completely reshape the tourism distribution system of the future, as they have had in the past 30 years. The electronic distribution of travel services is now a major trend around the globe. One aspect of this has already been mentioned in the form of increased use of computerized reservation systems (CRS) and global distribution systems by travel trade intermediaries, carriers, and suppliers.

In the early 1990s, the concept of the "information superhighway" began to exert a great influence on travel information dissemination and distribution. This was the decade of the *Internet*, which with the click of a mouse button brought the whole world of travel into the homes and offices of millions of people. The hypertext-based *World Wide Web* gave travelers instant access to information on the services of thousands of travel destinations and organizations around the world. The Web also presented carriers, suppliers, travel trade intermediaries, and destination marketing organizations with the ability to communicate their messages directly to individual customers who were now able to make their own travel reservations and payments through homes or office personal computers. Internet communications through *electronic mail* also became commonplace.

Some retail travel agents fear that advances in electronic distribution and communications systems will cause suppliers, carriers, destination marketing organizations, other travel trade intermediaries, and travelers to bypass them altogether. As the twentieth century closed, all of the major tourism organizations and destinations in the world had established a presence on the Internet and the World Wide Web. More people than ever before chose to flip through "electronic brochures" on their PCs than to visit their local travel agencies to get the traditional printed copies. New types of *online travel agencies* were established hundreds of miles away from their clients, but linked to them by the Internet.

While some believe that the Internet will cause the eventual demise of the travel agency system, others feel that it is unlikely that systems such as the World Wide Web will ever completely displace retail travel agencies. The expertise and personal touch of the knowledgeable travel agent may even become of greater value to travelers overwhelmed by the volume of information on the Internet. It is difficult to say exactly who will eventually be right, but what seems certain is that technology will change the roles of everyone in the tourism distribution system.

References

Cockerell, N. (1991). The European incentive travel market. *EIU Travel & Tourism Analyst* (4), 76–89.

De Souto, M.S. (1993). *Group travel* (2nd ed.). Albany, NY: Delmar Publishers Inc.

Friedheim, E. (1992). *Travel agents: From caravans and clippers to the Concorde*. New York: Universal Media.

Gee, C.Y., Makens, J.C., & Choy, D.J.L. (1997). *The travel industry* (3rd ed.). New York: Van Nostrand Reinhold.

Hiller, H.H. (1995). Conventions as mega-events: A new model for convention-host city relationships. *Tourism Management*, 16, 375–379.

Jenkins, D. (1993). *Managing business travel*. Homewood, IL: Business One Irwin.

Lang, J. (1994). *The American Express guide to corporate travel management*. New York: American Management Association.

McIntosh, R.W., Goeldner, C.R., & Ritchie, J.R.B. (1995). *Tourism: Principles, practices, philosophies* (7th ed.). New York: John Wiley & Sons, Inc.

Mehta, S.C., Loh, J.C.M., & Mehta, S.S. (1991). Incentive-travel marketing: The Singapore approach. *The Cornell H.R.A. Quarterly*, 32 (3), 67–74.

Morrison, A.M., Ladig, K.A., & Hsieh, S. (1994). Corporate travel in the USA: Characteristics of managers and departments. *Tourism Management*, 15, 177–184.

Poynter, J.M. (1990). *Corporate travel management*. Englewood Cliffs, NJ: Prentice-Hall, Inc.

Poynter, J.M. (1993). *Tour design, marketing, & management*. Englewood Cliffs, NJ: Regents/Prentice-Hall, Inc.

Reiff, A. (1995). *Introduction to corporate travel*. Cincinnati, OH: South-Western Publishing Co.

Ricci, P.R., & Holland, S.M. (1992). Incentive travel: Recreation as a motivational medium. *Tourism Management*, 13, 288–296.

Rosen, C. (1996). STTE releases case study. *Business Travel News*, (337, January 29), A6.

Shinew, K.J., & Backman, S.J. (1995). Incentive travel: An attractive option. *Tourism Management*, 16, 285–293.

SITE. (1996). *Incentive travel factbook*. New York: Society of Incentive and Travel Executives.

Schmid, B. (1997). Electronic markets in tourism. University of St. Gallen, Switzerland. (http://www-iwi.ch/iwi4/cc/genpubs/enter/)

Starr, N. (1997). *Viewpoint: An introduction to travel, tourism, and hospitality* (2nd ed.). Upper Saddle River, NJ: Prentice-Hall, Inc.

Vellas, F., & Becherel, L. (1995). *International tourism*. New York: St. Martin's Press.

Witt, S.F., Gammon, S., & White, J. (1992). Incentive travel: Overview and case study of Canada as a destination for the UK market. *Tourism Management*, 13, 275–287.

Surfing Solutions

http://www.abacus.com.sg/ (Abacus global distribution system)

http://www.abtanet.com (Association of British Travel Agents)

http://www.amadeus.net (Amadeus global distribution system)

http://astasrvr.astanet.com/ (American Society of Travel Agents)

http://www.waveconcepts.com/ARTA/ (Association of Retail Travel Agents)

http://www.afta.com.au (Australian Federation of Travel Agents)

http://www.carlson.com/ (Carlson Companies, Inc.)

http://www.iata.org/ (International Air Transport Association, IATA)

http://www.kuoni.ch (The Kuoni Group, Switzerland)

http://www.maritz.com/ (Maritz, Inc.)

http://www.nbta.org/ (National Business Travel Association, U.S.)

http://www.thomson-holidays.com/ (Thomson Travel Group, UK)

http://www.travelleader.com/tlpr/ustoa/ustoatoc.htm (U.S. Tour Operator Association)

Acronyms

ABTA (Association of British Travel Agents)
ACTA (Alliance of Canadian Travel Associations)
ACTE (Association of Corporate Travel Executives, U.S.)
AFTA (Australian Federation of Travel Agents)
ARC (Airlines Reporting Corporation, U.S.)
ARTA (Association of Retail Travel Agents)
ASTA (American Society of Travel Agents)
CCTE (Certified Corporate Travel Executive, NBTA)
CITC (Canadian Institute of Travel Counsellors)
CLIA (Cruise Lines International Association)
CRS (computerized reservation system)
CMP (Certified Meeting Professional)
CTC (Certified Travel Counselor)
DMC (destination management company)
FAM (familiarization trip)
FIT (foreign independent tour)
GDS (global distribution systems)
GIT (group inclusive tour)
IATA (International Air Transport Association
ICCA (International Congress and Convention Association)
ICTA (Institute of Certified Travel Agents, U.S.)
ITO (inbound tour operator)
MICE (meetings, incentives, conventions, exhibitions)
MPI (Meeting Professionals International)
NBTA (National Business Travel Association, U.S.)
NTA (National Tour Association, U.S.)
PCO (professional congress organizer)
RFP (request for proposals)
SITE (Society of Incentive and Travel Executives)
STP (satellite ticket printer)
SMERF (social, military, educational, religious, fraternal)
UFTAA (Universal Federation of Travel Agents' Associations)
USTOA (U.S. Tour Operators Association)
WATA (World Association of Travel Agencies)

Additional Sources

WWW Data Sources

CAB International: http://www.cabi.org/
Canadian Tourism Commission Tourism Reference and Documentation Centre: http://xinfo.ic.gc.ca/ic-data/industry/tourism/
Hospitality Net: http://www.hospitalitynet.nl/
Pacific Asia Travel Association: http://www.dnai.com/~patanet/
Tourism Resources: http://www.vir.com/~chamonix/tourism.htm
Travel & Tourism Research Association: http://www.ttra.com/
World Tourism Organization: http://www.world-tourism.org/
World Travel & Tourism Council: http://www.wttc.org/

Tourism Books

Ashworth, G., & Dietvorst, A. (1995). *Tourism and spatial transformations: Implications for policy and planning*. Wallingford, England: CAB.

Boissevain, J. (1996). *Coping with tourists: European reaction to mass tourism*. Oxford, England: Berghahn Books.

Bull, A. (1994). The *economics of travel and tourism*. London: Pitman.

Butler, R., & Hinch, T. (1996). *Tourism and indigenous peoples*. London: International Thomson Business Press.

Coccosis, H., & Nijkamp, P. (1995). *Sustainable tourism development*. London: Avebury-Gower.

Cooper, C., Fletcher, J., Gilbert, D., & Wanhill, S. (1993). *Tourism: Principles and practice*. London: Pitman.

Dann, G.M.S. (1996). *The language of tourism: A socio-linguistic perspective*. Wallingford, England: CAB International.

Edgell, D. (1990). *International tourism policy*. New York: Van Nostrand Reinhold.

Fridgen, J.D. (1991). *Dimensions of tourism*. East Lansing, Michigan: Educational Institute of the American Hotel & Motel Association.

Gartner, W.C. (1996). *Tourism development: Principles, processes, policies*. New York: Van Nostrand Reinhold.

Gee, C.Y., Makens, J.C., & Choy, D.J.L. (1997). *The travel industry* (3rd ed.). New York: Van Nostrand Reinhold.

Gunn, C.A. (1994). *Tourism planning: Basics, concepts, cases* (3rd ed.). Washington, DC: Taylor & Francis.

Hall, C.M. (1994). *Tourism and politics: Policy, power and place*. Chichester, England: John Wiley & Sons Ltd.

Hall, C.M., and Jenkins, J.M. (1995). *Tourism and public policy*. London: Routledge.

Heath, E, & Wall, G. (1992). *Marketing tourism destinations: A strategic planning approach*. New York: John Wiley & Sons, Inc.

Holloway, C. (1994). *The business of tourism*. Plymouth, England: Pitman.

Holloway, C., & Robinson, C. (1995). *Marketing for tourism* (3rd ed.). London: Longman.

Inskeep, E. (1991). *Tourism planning: An integrated and sustainable development approach*. New York: Van Nostrand Reinhold.

Kotler, P., Bowen, J., & Makens, J. (1996). *Marketing for hospitality & tourism*. Upper Saddle River, NJ: Prentice-Hall, Inc.

Law, C. (1993). *Urban tourism: Attracting visitors to large cities*. London: Mansell.

Laws, E. (1995). *Tourist destination management: Issues, analysis and policies*. London: Routledge.

McIntosh, R.W., Goeldner, C.R., & Ritchie, J.R.B. (1995). *Tourism: Principles, practices, philosophies* (7th ed.). New York: John Wiley & Sons, Inc.

McIntyre, G. (1993). *Sustainable tourism development: Guide for local planners*. Madrid: World Tourism Organization.

Mathieson, A., & Wall, G. (1982). *Tourism: Economic, physical, and social impacts*. New York: Longman Scientific & Technical.

Medlik, S. (1993). *Dictionary of travel, tourism, and hospitality*. Oxford, England: Butterworth-Heinemann.

Medlik, S. (1995). *Managing tourism*. London: Butterworth-Heinemann.

Morrison, A. M. (1996). *Hospitality and travel marketing* (2nd ed.). Albany, NY: Delmar Publishers, Inc.

Nash, D. (1996). *Anthropology of tourism*. Oxford: Pergamon.

Page, S. (1994). *Urban tourism*. London: Routledge.

Pearce, D. (1989). *Tourist development* (2nd ed.). Essex, England: Longman Scientific & Technical.

Pearce, D. (1992). *Tourist organizations*. Essex, England: Longman Group UK Ltd.

Pearce, D., & Butler, R. (eds.). (1993). *Tourism research: Critiques and challenges*. London: Routledge.

Pearce, P.L., Moscardo, G., & Ross, G.F. (1996). *Tourism community relationships*. Trowbridge, England: Pergamon.

Quest, M. (ed.) (1990). *Horwath book of tourism*. London: The MacMillan Press Ltd.

Ritchie, J.R.B., & Goeldner, C.R. (eds.) (1994). *Travel, tourism, and hospitality research: A handbook for managers and researchers* (2nd ed.). New York: John Wiley & Sons, Inc.

Ross, G.F. (1994). *The psychology of tourism*. Melbourne: Hospitality Press.

Ryan, C. (1992). *Recreational tourism*. London: Routledge.

Ryan, C. (1995). *Researching tourist satisfaction*. London: Routledge.

Seaton, A., & Bennett, M. (1996). *Marketing tourism products: Concepts, issues and cases*. London: Thomson Business Press.

Smith, S.L.J. (1994). *Tourism analysis: A handbook*. Essex, England: Longman Scientific & Technical.

Smith, V.L. (1976). (ed.). *Hosts and guests: The anthropology of tourism*. Philadelphia: The University of Pennsylvania Press, Inc.

Smith, V.L., & Eadington, W.R. (eds.). (1992). *Tourism alternatives: Potentials and problems in the development of tourism*. Philadelphia: University of Pennsylvania Press.

Starr, N. (1997). *Viewpoint: An introduction to travel, tourism, and hospitality* (2nd ed.). Upper Saddle River, NJ: Prentice-Hall, Inc.

Theobald, W. (ed.). (1994). *Global tourism: The next decade*. Oxford: Butterworth-Heinemann.

Urry, J. (1990). *The tourist gaze: Leisure and travel in contemporary societies*. London: Sage Publications.

Vellas, F., & Becherel, L. (1995). *International tourism*. New York: St. Martin's Press.

Weiler, B., & Hall, C.M. (eds.). (1992). *Special interest tourism*. London: Bellhaven Press.

Witt, S., & Moutinho, L. (eds.). (1994). *Tourism marketing and management handbook* (2nd ed.). Hemel Hempstead, England: Prentice-Hall, Inc.

World Tourism Organization. (1996). *Agenda 21 for the travel and tourism industry: Towards sustainable development*. Madrid: World Tourism Organization.

Zieger, J.B., & Cameday, L.M. (eds). (1991). *Tourism and leisure: Dynamics and diversity*. Arlington, VA: National Recreation and Park Association.

Annual Publications on Tourism

Fairchild's Travel Industry Personnel Directory. Fairchild Publications, 7 West 34th Street, New York, NY 10001.

Outlook for Travel and Tourism. U.S. Travel Data Center, Two Lafayette Centre, 1133 21st Street, Washington, DC 20036.

Tourism Policy and International Tourism in OECD Member Countries. OECD, 2, rue Andres-Pascal, 75775 Paris Cedex 16, France.

Travel & Tourism: The World's Largest Industry. World Travel and Tourism Council, 20 Grosvenor Place, London SW1X 7TT, U.K.

Academic Journals

ACTA Turistica (Croatia) c/o Dr. Boris Vukonic, Editor-in-Chief, Ekonomski Fakultet-Zagreb, Croatia 41000. Tel: 041-231-111 Fax: 041-235-633

ANATOLIA: An International Journal of Tourism and Hospitality c/o Metin Kozak, Sheffield Hallam University, Leisure Industries Research Centre, Sheffield Science Park Unit 1, City Campus, Sheffield S11WB U.K. Editor-in-Chief: Metin Kozak, M.Kozak@shu.ac.uk

Annals of Tourism Research. Elsevier Science Ltd. Pergamon, P.O. Box 800, Kidlington, Oxford OX5 1DX England. Tel: 44-1865-843000 Fax: 44-1865-843010. Editor-in-Chief: Jafar Jafari
e-mail: jafari@uwstout.edu
http://www.elsevier.nl:80/inca/publications/store/6/8/9/689.pub.istaut.shtml
http://www.elsevier.nl:80/inca/publications/store/6/8/9/

Asia Pacific Journal of Tourism Research (USA & Korea). Department of Tourism, Dong-A-University, 840, Hadan-Dong, Saha-gu, Pusan 604-714 Korea. Tel: 82-51-200-7427, Fax: 82-51-205-7767, Editor-in-Chief: Kaye Chon, Kchon@uh.edu

Cornell Hotel and Restaurant Administration Quarterly. Elsevier Science Inc., Box 945, NY. Tel: 212-633-3730 Fax: 212-633-3680. Editor-in-Chief: Glenn Withiam.
http://www.elsevier.nl:80/inca/publications/store/5/2/3/0/4/0/

Festival Management & Event Tourism. Cognizant Communication Corporation, 3 Hartsdale Road, Elmsford, NY 10523. Tel: 914-592-7720 Fax: 914-592-8981. Editors-in-Chief: Donald Getz and Bruce Wicks.
http://www.als.uiuc.edu/leist/fmet/home.html

FIU Hospitality Review. Florida International University, North Miami Campus, 151 1st St. and Biscayne Blvd., N. Miami, FL 33181. Tel: 305-948-4500 Fax: 305-048-4555

Hospitality Research Journal. Council on Hotel, Restaurant and Institutional Education, 12001 7th St., Washington, DC 20036. Tel: 202-331-5990 Fax: 202-785-2511 Editor-in-Chief: Kaye Chon.
http://www.access.digex.net:80/~alliance/pubresea.html

Hospitality and Tourism Educator. Council on Hotel, Restaurant and Institutional Education, 12001 7th St., Washington, DC 20036. Tel: 202-331-5990 Fax: 202-785-2511.
http://www.access.digex.net:80/~alliance/pubeduca.html

International Journal of Contemporary Hospitality Management. (U.K.) MCB University Press Limited, 60/62 Toller Lane, Bradford, West Yorkshire, England, BD8 9BY. Tel: 44 (0) 1274 777700 Fax: 44 (0) 1274 785200. Editor-in-Chief: Richard Teare.
http://www.mcb.co.uk/liblink/ijchm/jourhome.htm

International Journal of Hospitality Management. (U.K.). Butterworth-Heinemann, Reed Elsevier Group, Linacre House, Jordan Hill, Oxford OX2 8DP England. Tel: 44-1865-310366 Fax: 44-1865-310898. Editor-in-Chief: John O'Connor.

Journal of Applied Recreation Research. (Canada) Wilfrid Laurier University Press, Waterloo, Ontario, Canada N2L 3C5. Tel: (519) 884-1970, ext. 6124 Fax: (519) 725-1399.
http://info.wlu.ca/~wwwpress/jrls/jarr.html

Journal of Convention & Exhibition Management. Haworth Press Inc., 10 Alice St., Binghamton, NY 13904. Tel: 607-722-5857 Fax: 607 772-1424 Editor-in-Chief: Je'Anna Lanza Abbott.

Journal of Hospitality & Leisure Marketing. Haworth Press Inc., Food Products Press, 10 Alice St., Binghamton, NY 13904. Tel: 607-722-5857 Fax: 607-722-1424 Editor-in-Chief: Bonnie Knutson.

Journal of International Hospitality, Leisure, & Tourism Management. Haworth Press Inc., 10 Alice St., Binghamton, NY 13904. Tel: 800-895-0582 Fax: 607-772-6362. Editor-in-Chief: Mahmood Khan.

Journal of Leisure Research. National Recreation and Parks Association, 2775 S. Quincy St., No. 300, Arlington, VA 22206. Tel: 703-820-4940 Fax: 703-671-6772.

Journal of Park and Recreation Administration. Sagamore Publishing, P.O. Box 647, Champaign, IL 61824-0647. Tel: 217-359-5940. Editor: John Hultsman, atjth@asuvm.inre.asu.edu
http://http.tamu.edu:8000/~wwwrpts/journal.html

Journal of Restaurant & Foodservice Marketing. Haworth Press Inc., Food Products Press, 10 Alice St., Binghamton, NY 13904. Tel: 607-722-5857 Fax: 607-722-1424.

Journal of Sports Tourism. Sports Tourism International Council, International Headquarters, P.O. Box 5580-Station F, Ottawa, Canada K2C 3M1. Fax & Phone: 1-613-226-9447. Editor: Joseph Kurtzman.
http://www.free-press.com/journals/jst/

Journal of Sustainable Tourism. (U.K.). Channel View Books/Multilingual Matters Ltd., Frankfort Lodge, Clevedon Hall, Victoria Road, Clevedon BS21 7SJ, U.K. Editors-in-Chief: Bill Bramwell and Bernard Lane.
http://www.monash.edu.au/journals/view.html

Journal of Tourism Studies. (Australia). Department of Tourism, James Cook University, Townsville Qld, Australia 4811. Tel: 61-77-815133 Fax: 61-77-25116. Editor-in-Chief: Phillip Pearce.
http://www.jcu.edu.au/dept/Tourism/JTS/jts.htm

Journal of Travel Research. Business Research Division, Campus Box 420, University of Colorado at Boulder, Boulder, Colorado 80309-0420. Tel: 303-492-8227 Fax: 303-492-3620. Editor-in-Chief: Chuck Goeldner.
http://bus.colorado.edu/BRD/JTR.htm

Journal of Travel & Tourism Marketing. Haworth Press Inc., 10 Alice St., Binghamton, NY 13904. Tel: 607-722-5857 Fax: 607-772-1424. Editor-in-Chief: Kaye Chon, Interim Co-editor: Martin Oppermann. e-mail: oppermann@bmt.waiariki.ac.nz
http://www.waiariki.ac.nz/~oppermann/jttm.html

Journal of Vacation Marketing. (U.K.). Henry Stewart Publications, Russell House, 28-30 Little Russell St., London WC1A 2HN, England. Tel: 44-171-404-3040 Fax: 44-171-404-2081. Director: Daryn Moody. e-mail: darynm@henrystewart.demon.co.uk

Leisure Sciences. (U.K.). Taylor and Francis Ltd., Pankine Rd, Basingstoke, Hants RG2 48PR, England. Tel: 44-1256-840366 Fax: 44-1256-479438.

Leisure Studies. (U.K.). Chapman & Hall Journals, Dept 2-6, Boundary Row, London, SE1 8HN. Tel: 171-8650066 Fax: 171-5229623. Editor: Celia Brackenridge.
http://www.chapmanhall.com/ls/default.html

Managing Leisure. (U.K.). Chapman & Hall Subscriptions, ITPS Ltd., Cheriton House, North Way, Andover, SP10 5BE, United Kingdom. Tel: (+44) 1264 342 713 Fax: (+44) 1264 342 807. Editor-in-Chief: Peter Taylor.
http://www.chapmanhall.com/ml/default.html

Pacific Tourism Review. (New Zealand). Cognizant Communication Corporation, 3 Hartsdale Road, Elmsford, NY 10523-3701. Tel: 914-592 7720 Fax: 914-592 8981. Editor-in-Chief: Martin Oppermann. oppermann@bmt.waiariki.ac.nz
http://www.waiariki.ac.nz/~oppermann/ptr.html

Progress in Tourism and Hospitality Research. (U.K.). John Wiley and Sons Ltd. Baffins Lane, Chinchester, West Sussex, PO19 1UD, England. Editor-in-Chief: Dimitrios Buhalis.
http://www.wiley.com/journals.pthWiley

The Tourist Review. (AIEST/Switzerland). AIEST, Varnbuelstrasse 19, CH-9000, St. Gallen, Switzerland. Tel: 41-71 30 25 30 Fax: 41-71-30 25 36. Editor-in-Chief: Peter Keller.

Tourism Analysis. Cognizant Communication Corporation, 3 Hartsdale Road, Elmsford, NY 10523. Tel: 914-592-7720 Fax: 914-592-8981. Editors-in-Chief: Muzaffer Uysal and Daniel Fesenmaier.

Tourism, Culture & Communication. (Australia). Victoria University of Technology, Department of Hospitality and Tourism Management, P.O. Box 14428, MCMC, Melbourne, Victoria 8001, Australia. Editors-in-Chief: Brian King and Lindsey Turner. e-mail: Brian=king%Hosp2_admin%VUT@crock.vut.edu.au

Tourism Economics. (U.K.). In Print Publishing Ltd., 9 Beaufort Terr., Brighton, BN2 2SU England. Tel: 44-1273-682836 Fax: 44-1273-620958. Editor-in-Chief: Stephen Wahnill.

Tourism Management. (U.K.). Butterworth-Heinemann, Linacre House, Jordan Hill, Oxford OX2 8DP, England. Tel: 44-1865-310366 Fax: 44-1865-310898. Editor-in-Chief: Chris Ryan. e-mail: christopher.ryan@ntu.edu.au

Tourism Recreation Review. (India). Centre for Tourism Research and Development, A-965/6 Indira Nagar, Lucknow 226016 India. Tel: 91-522 381586 Fax: 91-522 234023. Editor-in-Chief: Tej Vir Singh.

Travel & Tourism Analyst. (U.K.). The Economist Intelligence Unit Ltd., 40 Duke Street, London, W1A 1DW, U.K.

Visions in Leisure and Business. Appalachian Associates, 615 Pasteur Avenue, Bowling Green, OH 43402.

Glossary

- **Accreditation (Chapter 11):** Accreditation is a process by which an association or agency evaluates and recognizes a program of study or an institution as meeting certain predetermined standards or qualifications (American Society of Association Executives).

- **All-inclusive package (Chapter 16):** This is a vacation package that includes a complete range of tourism services included in the price. Items normally included are air fares, ground transfers and baggage handling, accommodation, meals, local sightseeing, recreational activities and entertainment.

- **Alternative tourism (Chapter 13):** This term refers to various forms of low-impact or "soft" tourism. These forms of tourism provide an alternative to mass and resort tourism which may have a high impact on the environment and local peoples.

- **Balance of payments (Chapter 9):** A type of economic accounting system, this is the difference between what a country exports (sells) to other countries and what it imports (buys) from other countries. When a country exports more than it imports, it has a positive balance of payments or trade. A negative balance of payments is where a country imports more than it exports.

- **Benefit segmentation (Chapter 3):** A process used to divide travelers into groups of people who are seeking similar benefits from their trips.

- **Bilateral agreement (Chapter 11):** An agreement between two countries, often in trade or transportation. Bilateral air agreements are an example; these agreements mainly address the questions of which airlines can fly between the two countries and to which airports they are allowed to fly.

- **Brands, regional destination:** A marketing concept in which tourism destination areas join together in multi-destination partnerships and promote a region under a single brand name. Examples include El Mundo Maya in Central America and Jewels of the Mekong in Southeast Asia.

- **Business travel market (Chapter 5):** Travel where the primary motivation is to conduct business. This includes regular business or corporate travel, incentive travel, and travel related to meetings, conventions, congresses, trade shows and exhibitions.

- **Carriers (Chapter 16):** These are companies that provide transportation for visitors and include airlines, railroad companies, bus operators, ferry services, and other transportation providers.

- **Carrying capacity (Chapter 9):** A measurement that indicates the ability of an environment or natural resource to accommodate a certain type of use. There is also the concept of social carrying capacity, which refers to a society's capacity to cope with a certain type of activity.

- **Certification (Chapter 11):** Certification is a process by which an individual is tested and evaluated to determine his or her mastery of a specific body of knowledge, or some portion of a body of knowledge (American Society of Association Executives).

- **Code sharing (Chapter 11):** One common feature of a strategic alliance between two airline companies. This arrangement allows one airline to use its own two-character code (e.g., NW for Northwest) to advertise a flight as its own, when the flight is actually being operated by its partner airline (e.g., KLM Royal Dutch Airlines).

- **Cognitive dissonance (Chapter 4):** A feeling of anxiety or doubt that people experience after they have made purchases. This anxiety revolves around whether they have selected the best tourism destination area or other travel service.

- **Collateral, printed (Chapter 15):** Printed materials produced by tourism organizations including visitor guides, calendars of festivals and events, and maps.

- **Commission (Chapter 16):** An amount of money, normally expressed as a percentage of the fare, rate or price, paid to a retail travel agency by suppliers, carriers, and other intermediaries such as tour operators.

- **Computer reservation systems (CRS) (Chapter 16):** A computer system operated by an airline, hotel chain, rental car, or other travel company which allows retail travel agencies to check the availability and prices, and make reservations for their clients. Some systems also provide access for individual travelers.

- **Consolidator, travel (Chapter 16):** A special form of travel agent. These are private firms that buy unsold airline seats, cruise berths, and other types of travel options in bulk and sell these at a discount to retail travel agencies and individual travelers. The "consolidator" term comes from the combination of these firms' bookings to qualify for group or discounted prices.

- **Convention-meeting planners (Chapter 16):** Employees of corporations, associations, government agencies, and other nonprofit groups who plan and coordinate meetings, conventions, conferences, exhibitions or trade shows.

- **Conversion study (Chapter 15):** A research technique used to determine the percentage of people who request travel information materials that actually visit the destination or use the service after being sent the materials.

- **Corporate travel department (Chapter 16):** Special departments created by corporations, government agencies, and nonprofit organizations to coordinate and control all of the travel by employees and associates of the organization. These departments establish organization-wide travel policies and negotiate the best prices on travel.

- **Cost-benefit analysis (Chapter 9):** An economic analysis technique used to determine which economic sector produces the most benefit in terms of foreign exchange, employment, taxes, or income generated relative to the costs of development.

- **Culture (Chapter 1):** A set of beliefs, values, attitudes, habits, and forms of behavior shared by a society and passed from generation to generation (Bennett & Kassasjian).

- **Database marketing (Chapter 15):** A process increasingly being used in tourism to encourage repeat usage. Computer technology allows the manipulation of relational databases on past and potential visitors, and is facilitating this process.

- **Decoy effect (Chapter 4):** The introduction of an offer into a set of alternative choices that results in a segment of consumers shifting their choice to a higher priced targeted item (Josiam & Hobson).

- **Demonstration effect (Chapter 9):** An economic phenomenon that occurs when local residents, exposed to goods imported for visitor use, begin to demand those goods for themselves. This automatically increases the demand for imports.

- **Destination area:** A geographic area, ranging in size from an individual community to a group of several countries, where there is a concerted effort to develop and market tourism.

- **Destination management company (DMC) (Chapter 16):** Also known as inbound tour operators, receptive tour operators or receptive services operator. These are companies who provide sightseeing, guiding, and transportation services within specific destination areas. Other types of DMCs specialize in catering to meeting and incentive travel groups.

- **Destination marketing organization (DMO) (Chapter 15):** Government and non-governmental organizations with the responsibility of marketing specific tourism destinations to the travel trade and individual travelers. These organizations operate at all geographic levels from multi-country regions (e.g., European Travel Commission) to individual communities (e.g., convention and visitors bureaus).

- **Destination mix (Chapter 8):** The combination of attractions, events, and services that a destination provides for visitors. The destination mix includes attractions and events, facilities, infrastructure, transportation, and hospitality resources.

- **Distribution mix (Chapter 16):** The combination of direct and indirect (through travel trade intermediaries) distribution that a tourism organization selects to use to market its services or destination area.

- **Domestic tourism:** The combination of internal tourism (visits by residents of a country within their own country) and inbound international tourism (visits to a country by nonresidents of that country) (World Tourism Organization).

- **Economic feasibility study (Chapter 13):** A study to determine the economic feasibility of a tourism development project opportunity. A project is economically feasible if it provides a rate of return acceptable to the investors in the project.

- **Ecotourism (Chapter 13):** Nature-based tourism that involves education and interpretation of the natural and cultural environment, and that is managed to be ecologically and culturally sustainable (adapted from Australian National Ecotourism Strategy).

- **Environmental impact analysis (Chapter 13):** An analysis which identifies in advance factors that may affect the ability to build a proposed tourism development and the environmental attributes that will be affected by the development (Manning & Dougherty).

- **Environmental scanning (Chapter 14):** A technique used to identify and analyze the impact of external environmental forces on a tourism organization's marketing. These external forces include legislation and regulation, political situations, social and cultural characteristics, economic conditions, technology, transportation, and competition.

- **Escorted tour (Chapter 16):** A type of organized tour that includes the services of a tour director or manager who accompanies an individual or group throughout the tour.

- **Facilities (Chapter 8):** Part of the destination mix, facilities include the physical facilities and services provided in lodging, food and beverage, and support businesses (e.g., souvenir and duty-free shops).

- **Familiarization tour or trip (Chapter 15):** Also known as a "fam," these trips are organized for selected tour operators or wholesalers, retail travel agents, or travel writers. Having experienced the destination or travel service first hand, the intermediaries are in a much better position to sell it. Familiarization tours may involve the inspection of facilities, visits to tourism attractions, and contacts with the local travel trade (e.g., inbound tour operators). Fams may be conducted in small groups or on an individual basis.

- **Family life cycle (Chapter 1):** Distinctive stages through which families progress over time. These stages are given certain titles or labels, and range from the "bachelor" to "solitary survivor" stages.

- **Focus group (Chapter 15):** A marketing research technique involving a small group of people, typically 8–12 persons. A moderator is used to lead the group to reach a consensus on one or more questions or issues.

- **Foreign independent tour (FIT) (Chapter 16):** A service provided by retail travel agencies and some tour operators in which all the air travel and land arrangements are made for an individual customer in the traveler's destination of choice.

- **Frequent flyer program (FFP) (Chapter 14):** Recognition programs that were first introduced in the early 1980s to reward frequent travelers and to build loyalty among these travelers with the airline. Frequent flyer miles are the "currency" of these programs.

- **Frequent guest program (FGP) (Chapter 14):** Guest recognition programs that were first introduced in the early 1980s to reward frequent travelers and to build loyalty among these travelers with the hotel chain. These programs reward guests with room upgrades, free stays, merchandise, or frequent flyer miles.

- **Fulfillment (Chapter 15):** The process used by tourism organizations to send printed collateral materials to people who request them.

- **Group inclusive tour (GIT) (Chapter 16):** An all-inclusive package with a specified minimum size (number of travelers) involving one or more groups traveling on scheduled or chartered air service (Morrison).

- **Global distribution systems (GDS) (Chapter 16):** Computerized reservation systems that are global in their coverage. Five of the major systems are Abacus, Amadeus, Galileo, Sabre, and Worldspan.

- **Ground or land tour arrangements (Chapter 16):** Travel arrangements made for group or individual travelers at a destination. These include items such as airport transfers, lodging, meals, entertainment, sightseeing, ground transportation by coach or other means.

- **Hierarchy of needs, Maslow's (Chapter 2):** A theory of motivation suggested by Maslow in which needs are arranged in a hierarchy ranging from physiological to psychological needs.

- **Horizontal integration (Chapter 16):** The acquisition and ownership of similar businesses by one organization in the tourism distribution channel.

- **Hospitality resources (Chapter 8):** Refers to the general feeling of welcome that people receive while visiting a destination area. It is the way that tourism services are delivered by the service providers, as well as the general feeling of warmth from the local resident population.

- **Import substitution (Chapter 9):** An economic strategy aimed at minimizing the leakage from a destination area's economy caused by imported goods and services.

- **Inbound tour operator (Chapter 16):** Tour operators who provide the ground or land tour arrangements within specific destinations for group and individual travelers. They are also called receptive tour or receptive services operators.

- **Incentive travel planning company (Chapter 16):** A specialized tour wholesaler who primarily serves corporate clients and arranges trips that are given to certain of their client's employees or dealers as a reward for outstanding sales or work performance.

- **Input-output analysis (Chapter 9):** An economic analysis technique which examines the interactions among different economic sectors. It is used to determine the impacts of tourism on the other economic sectors of a destination area.

- **Interlining (Chapter 11):** Travel by an air passenger on two or more airlines on a trip. More broadly, interlining refers to cooperative agreements between two or more airlines.

- **Internal tourism:** Visits by residents of a country within their own country (World Tourism Organization).

- **Internet (Chapter 15):** A worldwide network of connected computer networks. Also known as "cyberspace" or the "information superhighway," one of the most popular Internet functions is the World Wide Web.

- **Invisible export (Chapter 9):** Because of the intangible nature of tourism services, it is said to be an invisible export when foreigners visit another country and spend money there. Tourism is not a physical good that must be shipped out to other countries.

- **Leakage (Chapter 9):** An economic term that refers to the monetary value of goods and services that must be imported to service the needs of tourism.

- **Marketing mix (Chapter 14):** The combination of factors that tourism marketing managers use to attract visitors. These factors include product, price, place, promotion, packaging, programming, partnership, and people.

- **Marketing plan (Chapter 14):** A written document that describes the actions that a tourism organization will undertake to achieve its marketing goals and objectives.

- **Market segmentation (Chapter 14):** The division of the tourism market into groups which share common characteristics.

- **MICE markets (Chapter 16):** An acronym for the meetings, incentives, conventions, and exhibition markets.

- **Motivation (Chapter 2):** A physiological or psychological drive in a person to take action to satisfy a need.

- **Motives (Chapter 2):** People's personal desires or drives to satisfy their wants (Morrison).

- **Multiplier effect (Chapter 9):** An economic term that describes the indirect and induced effects of income and employment generated by tourism. Income multipliers measure the amount of local income generated per unit of visitor expenditure (Wanhill, 1994).

- **Multilateral agreement (Chapter 11):** An agreement between several countries, often in trade or transportation. The General Agreement on Tariffs and Trade (GATT) is one example.

- **National tourism:** The combination of internal tourism (visits by residents of the country within their own country) and outbound international tourism (visits by the residents of the country to other countries) (World Tourism Organization).

- **Needs (Chapter 2):** Gaps between what people have and what they would like to have (Morrison).

- **Online travel agencies (Chapter 16):** Online databases and reservations services that allow travelers to make travel reservations in their own homes or offices via computer modems and the World Wide Web. Examples include Travelocity, Preview Travel, and Expedia.

- **Packaging (Chapter 14):** The assembly of travel packages that combine the services and products of several tourism organizations into a single-price offering.

- **Perception (Chapter 3):** The mental process in which people employ their five senses (sight, hearing, taste, touch, and smell) to develop images of tourism destinations and services.

- **Pleasure and personal travel market (Chapter 5):** Travel where the primary motivation is to take a vacation or holiday, or to travel for some other personal (non-business) reason.

- **Positioning (Chapter 14):** A marketing process used by tourism organizations to create a perception or image in the targeted visitor's mind.

- **Primary research (Chapter 15):** Also known as original research, this is information collected for the first time by an organization or individual.

- **Principals, travel (Chapter 15):** A term in travel used to refer to suppliers and carriers who use retail travel companies as their agents.

- **Receptive tour operator (Chapter 16):** Tour operators who provide the ground or land tour arrangements within specific destinations for group and individual travelers. They are also called inbound tour operators.

- **Relationship marketing (Chapter 15):** Marketing activities in which a tourism organization engages to build and enhance long-term relationships with individual visitors and other organizations.

- **Representative firms (Chapter 15):** Companies that represent a tourism destination area or tourism organization in a foreign country, and which provide public relations and other promotional services.

- **Retail travel agency (Chapter 16):** In essence, they are the department stores of tourism. They provide thousands of "travel shops" for suppliers, carriers, destination marketing organizations, and the other travel trade intermediaries, and receive commissions for their services. A customer can buy all types of travel services at an agency including tickets for planes and railways, hotels and resorts, packages and tours, car rentals, and travel insurance.

- **Satellite tourism accounting (Chapter 9):** An economic accounting system for complex service sectors such as tourism. For tourism, this means adding up the impacts of tourism that have traditionally been allocated to other economic sectors.

- **Situation or SWOT analysis (Chapter 14):** A marketing technique used to analyze the strengths, weaknesses, opportunities, and threats of a tourism destination area or tourism organization.

- **SMERF markets (Chapter 16):** An acronym commonly used in tourism for meetings and other events held by social, military, educational, religious, or fraternal groups.

- **Strategic alliances (Chapter 14):** These are long-term agreements between companies or countries to invest in joint marketing programs. Strategic alliances have been especially popular among airline companies.

- **Strategic planning (Chapter 12):** A long-range planning process used in overall tourism planning where the time frame is three or more years into the future.

- **Superstructure (Chapter 13):** Generally considered to imply building construction for tourism development.

- **Suppliers (Chapter 16):** Tourism organizations that provide facilities and services within and between tourism destinations. These include hotels, restaurants, attractions, car rental firms, casinos and other gaming operations, and cruise lines.

- **Sustainable tourism development (Chapter 13):** Using the natural and cultural resources of a destination area to support tourism without compromising their carrying capacities, which is their ability to continue to contribute towards tourism activity.

- **System:** A set of interrelated elements and components that work together toward common goals or objectives. Von Bertalanffy defines a system as "a set of elements standing in interrelation among themselves and with the environments."

- **Testimonial (Chapter 4):** A format used in advertising in which a celebrity, satisfied customer, or other person "endorses" or recommends a specific product, service, or destination area.

- **Timesharing (Chapter 11):** Also known as interval ownership, this is a procedure where the ownership of a hotel or resort is split among multiple owners according to time intervals such as weeks.

- **Tourism:** The activities of a person outside his or her usual environment for less than a specified period of time and whose main purpose of travel is other than the exercise of an activity remunerated from the place visited (Chadwick, 1994).

- **Tourism product (Chapter 13):** A term that is roughly synonymous with the destination mix, meaning all the facilities and services offered for the visitors to a destination area.

- **Tourism system:** A systematic approach to the study of tourism consisting of four main elements (demand, travel, destination, and marketing) and four major links (the travel purchase, the shape of travel, the tourism product, and the promotion of travel). The tourism system approach emphasizes the interdependency in tourism; that it consists of several interrelated elements working together to achieve common purposes.

- **Tour operator (Chapter 16):** Tour operators assemble the numerous components of travel into packaged vacations or tours and offer these for sale through retail travel agents. Tour operators are tour wholesalers, but also operate all or part of their tours by providing tour escorts or managers, and ground/land tour arrangements.

- **Tour wholesaler (Chapter 16):** Tour wholesalers assemble the numerous components of travel into packaged vacations or tours and offer these for sale through retail travel agents. They do not provide tour operating services.

- **Travel career ladder (Chapter 4):** A concept developed by Philip Pearce which suggests that people's needs, travel decisions and decision-making processes are not static; they change over a person's lifetime based upon their actual travel experiences.

- **Travel trade intermediaries (Chapter 16):** A term used to collectively refer to all the travel distribution channels including retail travel agencies, tour wholesalers and operators, corporate travel departments, incentive travel planning companies, and convention/meeting planners.

- **Vertical integration (Chapter 16):** The acquisition and ownership by one organization of all or part of a tourism distribution channel.

- **Visioning (Chapter 12):** A process used in long-term or strategic planning in which the desired future situation for the destination area or tourism organization is determined.

- **VFR (Chapter 5):** An acronym used for people who are visiting their friends or relatives in a destination area.

- **Wants (Chapter 2):** People's desires for specific satisfiers of their needs, e.g., specific tourism facilities, services, or destination areas (Kotler).

- **Word of mouth (Chapter 15):** Recommendations given about tourism destinations or services by people to their friends, relatives, or business colleagues.

- **World Heritage List (Chapter 11):** A list of natural and cultural sites (maintained by UNESCO) whose outstanding values should be preserved for all humanity and to ensure their protection through a closer cooperation among nations (UNESCO World Heritage Centre).

- **World Wide Web (WWW) (Chapter 15):** An Internet function which provides a worldwide collection of sites containing text, graphics, sound, and video that are created in hypertext and can be accessed through the use of Universal Resource Locators (URLs).

Index

THE

TOURISM SYSTEM

THIRD EDITION

AN INTRODUCTORY TEXT

ROBERT CHRISTIE MILL, Ph.D., CHA, CHE

Robert Christie Mill is a Professor in the School of Hotel, Restaurant and Tourism Management at the University of Denver where he is also Director of Undergraduate Programs in the Daniels College of Business. His teaching career began in 1972 at Niagara University. He subsequently served on the faculties of Lansing Community College and Michigan State University. Dr. Mill holds a Ph.D. and MBA from Michigan State University and a BA from the University of Strathclyde's Scottish Hotel School. He is also a Certified Hotel Administrator and a Certified Hospitality Educator.

His industry experience includes positions with Trust House Forte in Europe, on board ship as a cook with Canadian Pacific, and as assistant to the vice president of Manpower Development with the Inter-Continental Hotel Corporation in New York City. A two-time Fulbright lecturer to India and Hungary, Dr. Mill has conducted over 100 workshops in 16 states and 13 countries for the management and employees of various companies, industry groups and government organizations including the World Tourism Organization, the American Hotel and Motel Association, and the National Restaurant Association. In addition, he has worked as a member of tourism development project teams for Kintyre in Scotland, Northern Ireland, Algeria, and Tunisia.

Dr. Mill is the author of three books, co-author of a fourth, and chapter contributor to an additional five in the areas of tourism and hospitality operations. Titles include *The Tourism System: An Introductory Text*; *Tourism: The International Business*; *Managing for Productivity in the Hospitality Industry*; and *Restaurant Management: Customers, Operations, Employees*. In addition, he is the author of scores of refereed articles in academic journals in addition to being an extensive contributor to the trade press.

ALASTAIR M. MORRISON, Ph.D., CTME

Alastair M. Morrison is a Professor in the Restaurant, Hotel, Institutional, and Tourism Management Department at Purdue University where he is also the Director of the Purdue Tourism & Hospitality Research Center. Prior to beginning his academic career at Purdue in 1985, he spent 11 years in Canada as a management consultant specializing in tourism and hospitality marketing, planning and project development with Pannell Kerr Forster and most recently as President of The Economic Planning Group of Canada. He has won numerous teaching awards at Purdue University including the Charles B. Murphy Award for Outstanding Undergraduate Teaching, Purdue's most prestigious award for undergraduate teaching. Dr. Morrison holds a Ph.D. from Purdue University, and MBA from Michigan State University and a BA from the University of Strathclyde's Scottish Hotel School in Glasgow, Scotland. He is also a Certified Travel Marketing Executive.

Dr. Morrison has had a wide variety of experience in the global tourism industry. He has conducted training programs and provided tourism marketing and development advice in Australia, Bahrain, Canada, Ghana, Trinidad & Tobago, Jamaica, India, New Zealand, Singapore, Sri Lanka, Thailand, Slovenia, Vietnam, and the U.S. During 1992, Professor Morrison was the Queensland Tourist & Travel Corporation Visiting Lecturer at James Cook University in Queensland, Australia.

Dr. Morrison is the author of one textbook, and co-author of two others in the areas of tourism and hospitality and travel marketing. The titles include *The Tourism System: An Introductory Text*; *Hospitality and Travel Marketing*; and *Tourism: Bridges Across Continents*. He has authored many articles related to tourism in academic and trade journals. In addition, he has written and developed correspondence courses in tourism and tourism marketing for the World Tourism Organization and co-authored several publications on behalf of the national tourism agency in Canada and the Queensland Tourist & Travel Corporation. He is a member of the International Academy of Scholars in Tourism (IAST) and an Editorial Board Member of several major hospitality and tourism academic research journals.

ISBN 0-7872-3327-7

KENDALL/HUNT PUBLISHING COMPANY
Dubuque, Iowa

90000

9 780787 233273